Comprehensive Computer Learning

Desktop Publishing (DTP)

AF539104

by

Bittu Kumar

V&S PUBLISHERS

Published by:

F-2/16, Ansari Road, Daryaganj, New Delhi-110002
☎ 011-23240026, 011-23240027 • *Fax:* 011-23240028
Email: info@vspublishers.com • *Website:* www.vspublishers.com

Branch : Hyderabad
5-1-707/1, Brij Bhawan (Beside Central Bank of India Lane)
Bank Street, Koti, Hyderabad - 500 095
☎ 040-24737290
E-mail: vspublishershyd@gmail.com

Follow us on:   

For any assistance sms **VSPUB** to **56161**

All books available at **www.vspublishers.com**

© **Copyright:** V&S PUBLISHERS

ISBN 978-93-505701-3-5

Edition 2013

The Copyright of this book, as well as all matter contained herein (including illustrations) rests with the Publishers. No person shall copy the name of the book, its title design, matter and illustrations in any form and in any language, totally or partially or in any distorted form. Anybody doing so shall face legal action and will be responsible for damages.

Printed at : Param Offsetters, Okhla, New Delhi-110020

Publisher's Note

After successfully publishing youth-oriented books and getting commendable appreciation from students, teachers and parents alike, V&S Publishers is venturing into the arena of student and job-oriented books with a series of computer books on various important subjects for readers of all ages. Written and presented in lucid language and simple terms, without any computer jargon, these books are an easy-to-follow manual for readers. For the convenience of readers the information is set out in an easy to understand, step-by-step format, with clear illustrations and detailed explanations to accompany each action. Besides, every book is accompanied by an interactive CD/DVD for better understanding of the readers.

Today we live in a world of computers. The present scenario is that computers are used in every field be it education, business, trade and commerce, home and hobby, or even our ordinary day-to-day life. The importance of computers is an undeniable fact in today's world. In fact, we can't think of a world without computers.

Realising this indisputable fact, we are coming up with the series of **"Comprehensive Computer Learning (CCL)"** books. The series currently includes –

1. Comprehensive Computer Learning (CCL)
2. Comprehensive Computer Learning – A Youngsters' Guide
3. Comprehensive Computer Learning – Microsoft Office 2010
4. Comprehensive Computer Learning – Desktop Publishing (DTP)
5. Comprehensive Computer Learning – Adobe Photoshop

Key features of these books:

- Written in simple and lucid language
- Presented in step-by-step, easy-to-understand format with detailed explanations with appropriate images & screenshots, charts & tables
- Useful tips and notes given in every chapter as additional information
- Accompanied by interactive CD/DVD for better understanding

This book **"Comprehensive Computer Learning – Desktop Publishing"** has been explicitly written keeping in mind those young excutives who wish to pursue DTP as their career. The book incorporates all the essential softwares, viz., InDesign, Illustrator, Corel Draw, Photoshop, QurakXpress, Flash, Math Type, etc.

While every effort has been made to minimise printing and other errors, it may be possible that a few might have managed to escape the wakeful eyes. We would like to request the readers to bring these errors to our notice so that we can rectify the same in subsequent editions.

Contents

Introduction

What is DTP?

Desktop Publishing is an integration of computer and publishing technologies that lets you produce high quality documents quickly and easily at a fraction of the cost normally charged by most commercial services.

This definition can be expanded upon greatly, but it simply states the case. Desktop publishing encompasses most types of hardware and software. It's not, as some individuals seem to think, simply a page-layout program used to design and print pages. DTP systems use a variety of software including word processors, draw-and-paint programs, CAD packages and page-layout programs. It combines computer hardware to increase its power and versatility, including scanners, high-resolution monitors, hard disks, laser printers and more.

Why Desktop Publishing?

There are many reasons that DTP systems have flourished in the last five years. Some of the primary reasons for growing uses of DTP are:

Cost Effectiveness

When you break down the per-page cost you'll find that DTP is extremely inexpensive when compared with other options. Many commercial publications use DTP systems to produce preview copies of documents for examination by writers and editors. One person can produce quality documents without the assistance of layout specialists and other technical staff, thereby saving money on salaries, office space, etc.

Faster Production and Timeliness

Creating documents by you can dramatically decrease production time. Instead of waiting hours for a backlogged printing house to produce a report or sales presentation, you can print it yourself. When you can create page layouts yourself, you spend less time telling a printer what you want; it reduces foot work and lets you make last-minute changes without returning to the print shop.

A DTP system will help businesses produce documents that meet the needs of clients in a more relevant manner. Instead of pencilling in data on a brochure because the old copy is outdated, you can quickly print a new version with your changes. When a customer wants revisions in a layout, a few minutes of work will let them see an actual copy of what will be printed.

Quality

Documents you produce with a word processor generally rely on a printer's built-in font set or a limited range of fonts included with the software. Page-layout programs include a wider range of fonts in a variety of sizes and styles that word processors can't access. Graphics can be imported, lines and boxes can be added and each component can be precisely placed without the telltale signs of cut and paste. DTP systems produce camera-ready copy that is identical to the final version which means, no more mock-ups to approximate the finished product.

Control

When a document is finished it looks exactly the way you want it to, not the way a layout artist or editor thought you wanted it. From the size of the headline to the font style and line width used, DTP lets you display your message in exactly the format you want. If the printout is inadequate, you can make some quick changes and print it again.

Satisfaction

Doing it yourself can be enjoyable. It is a creative form of self-expression that can be used for virtually any type of document. DTP requires a little patience but the results are quite pleasing.

Who Uses Desktop Publishing?

Small businesses have embraced the technology more firmly than any other group. Many businesses that can't afford to patronize a print shop can still add DTP capabilities to their existing computer system at a reasonable price.

Educators are avid fans of DTP as the quality documents they produce can be directed to a specific group of students and help improve grades and increase comprehension.

Home computer users desire DTP systems to produce documents such as garage sale flyers, school reports and church bulletins. Documents are more likely to be read when they are carefully prepared with a variety of fonts and graphics.

Look Beyond Desktop Publishing

It's easy to forget that desktop publishing software is only a tool for implementing your designs. All too often, desktop publishers will un-consciously bend their designs to fit the built-in features of their favourite software. Don't fall into this trap. Keep the creative process separate. There's always a way to implement a great idea.

To focus on design without the technological trappings, skim professional design publications that showcase elegant design examples.

Try joining a local advertising group, art directors club, or communications forum. It doesn't matter if you're not involved in the advertising or public relations fields. Desktop publishers share a common goal of informing, motivating, and persuading others. You're likely to return from these meetings with a fresh perspective on your communication and design efforts.

Softwares Used in DTP

Now a days, many softwares are used in DTP. In this book, we will learn to use the following:

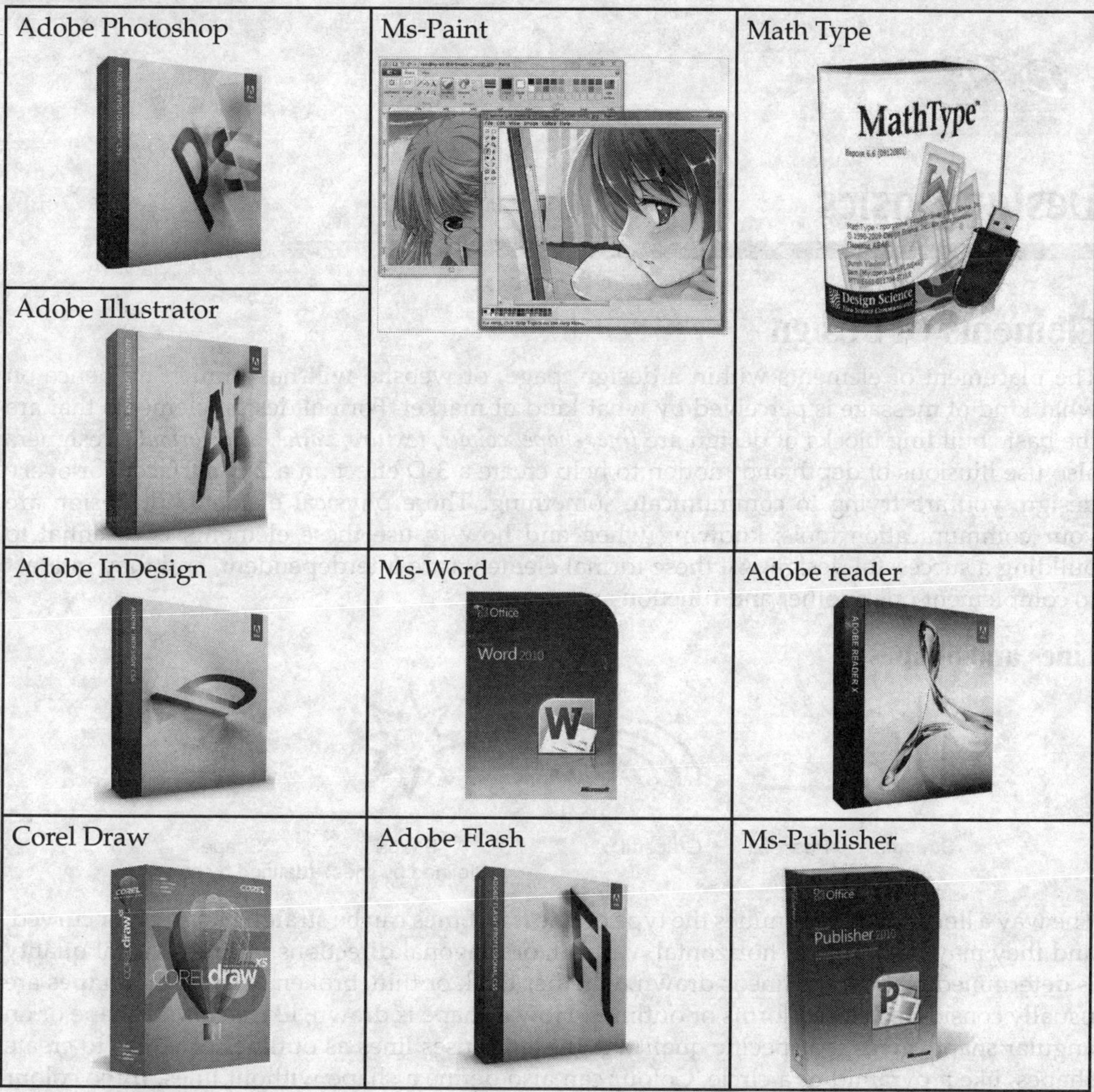

Conclusion

DTP Softwares are valuable Tools in designing industry. Ranging from small buisiness to large business everyone uses DTP Software for a variety of work. There is a huge demand of DTP Operators worldwide. Learn these softwares, and increase your hiring potential in the marketplace.

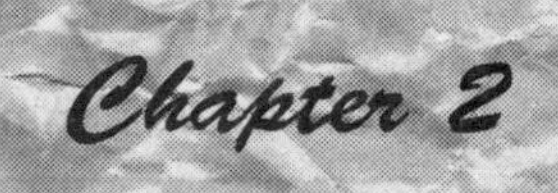

Design Basics

Elements Of Design

The placement of elements within a design, page, or website will have much influence on what kind of message is perceived by what kind of market. Formal design elements that are the basic building blocks of design are *line, shape, colour, texture, value,* and *format.* Designers also use illusions of depth and motion to help create a 3-D effect on a 2-D surface. For every design, you are trying to communicate something. These physical elements of design are your communication tools; knowing when and how to use these elements is essential to building a successful design. All these formal elements are interdependent, and they interact to complement one another and function as a team.

Lines and Shapes

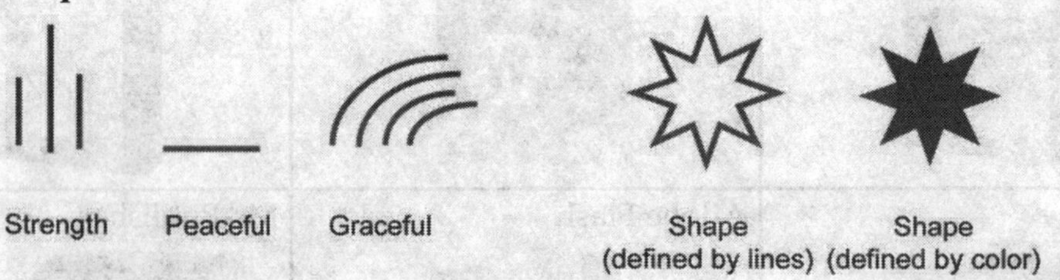

The way a line moves determines the type of line it is. **Lines** can be straight, angular, or curved, and they may be drawn in horizontal, vertical, or diagonal directions. A line's visual quality is determined by how the line is drawn, whether thick or thin, broken or smooth. **Shapes** are usually considered closed forms or outlines. How a shape is drawn, like a curved shape or an angular shape, gives it a specific quality. A designer uses lines as outlines or edges to create shapes, like a pyramid or a circle. Colour can also define a shape without lines. If the colour creates an edge, it also defines the shape.

Texture

Texture describes surface quality, like rust, velvet, or sandpaper. The two categories of texture in the artistic sense are *tactile* and *visual.* **Tactile texture** involves the actual feeling of a surface texture like a sculpture. Designers and artists use **visual texture** to create the illusion of texture in artwork, using varying line qualities, patterns, or adjusting the value and colours of an element. Computers can create digital textures through various filters and effects within software programs.

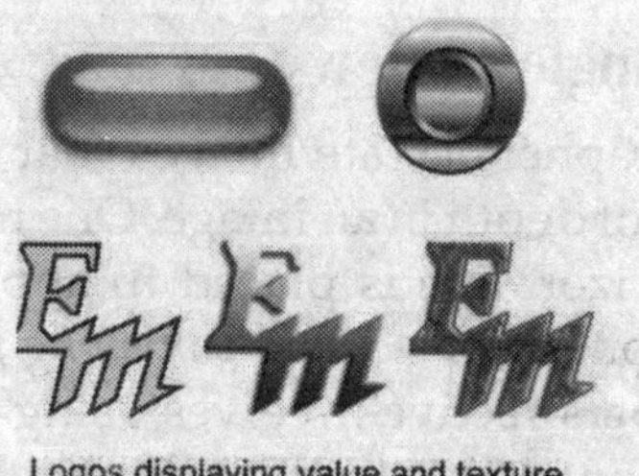

Logos displaying value and texture

High contrast images evoke a different response than low contrast images

Value

Value determines depth and dimension by the range of lightness or darkness of an element. Value is the shading, tonality, and tint of a colour (light blue and dark blue). The use of shading can help provide a three-dimensional value to an image. Value creates a focal point or centre of attention. **Value contrast** is the relationship between black and white or lightness and darkness of an image, and it is a result of the relationship between different elements; it produces both visual and emotional effects. As the viewer observes an image and interprets its value, the eye is drawn to light areas first, which the designer or artist can use to provide contrast and balance in an image.

Values in colour and contrast can provoke a variety of emotional responses. Low contrast or closely related values can evoke a sense of calmness or tranquility, while high-contrast images or sharp value images can create a sense of excitement, drama, or conflict between elements. An overall darker image can promote a sense of mystery or even sadness, while an overall lighter image invites the viewer with an uplifting tone or feeling of relaxation.

Depth Perception

In the two-dimensional world of drawings, photographs, paintings, and prints, designers often need to convey a feeling of space or depth perception. Some of the elements that convey these characteristics are the sizes of objects and their relationship to one another, the overall blending of colours and shapes by adjusting tonal values, and the point of view or depth perspective. By varying the size of similar shapes—for example, rectangles—the illusion is more pronounced than with differing shapes. Spatial depth is more pronounced if shapes become smaller as they overlap, creating the illusion of objects receding. This is a form of **spatial recession**. By combining elements and blending the tonal values to match the background, the illusion of receding into the background creates an even more pronounced sense of depth. **Tonal value** involves the lightness and darkness of an image by varying its tone or value to the surrounding background. In landscape, objects are placed in the foreground to give a feeling of depth; or **framing techniques** are employed in which another subject surrounds the main subject for emphasis. Using tree branches in the foreground, for instance, provides emphasis to a distant subject.

Depth Perception

Perspective and Angle of View

Artists and photographers create images that show a higher or lower point of view that can enhance the feeling of depth in an image. One technique involves the use of **linear perspective**. This is where a horizon line is placed to approximate the eye level of the artist. From this line, invisible lines or edges—called *vanishing points*— are directed to lead the viewer into the image. **One-point perspective** involves using converging lines to lead the eye to a subject or point along a horizontal line to provide depth in perspective within the image. **Two-point perspective** involves a more natural approach, similar to how we view the world around us, at an angle with two edge points along the horizon line. In this view, vanishing points recede at either end of a horizontal line. Vertical lines would be parallel to the edges of the picture. An example would be if the viewer were standing on a city street corner, taking a photo of the buildings; there would be little or no vertical convergence, but rather parallel alignment of the sides of the buildings. It is not as dramatic an approach as using converging lines, and it permits the viewer to scan an image from one edge to the other.

Artists can also use fences, roads, stairways, and other techniques in compositions involving **leading lines** to create the effect of depth perception. **Aerial perspective** uses the lighter background contrast of the atmosphere with darker subjects that are closer to the viewer in landscapes to show a sense of depth. The background recedes to the lighter contrast from the darker foreground subject. To add drama to an image, artists and photographers constantly create images from lower and higher angles than a viewer's normal eye level.

Perspective and angle of view

Using Motion

Creating the illusion of motion can suggest an anticipation of movement either in slow motion or in what is termed as **stop action**. Artists use these techniques to trigger memories or record events, or with special effects like blurring water to give an image an ethereal quality. The feeling of movement can also be heightened by contrast, showing activity. Repeating figures or multi-exposed images have also been used to create the illusion of motion

Creating the illusion of motion

Colour

Colour is one of the most powerful design elements. A designer needs to understand which colours are appropriate to complement the message. Colour is based on wavelengths of light and contains a wide range of visual differences and contrasts. Colour is divided into three categories: *hue, value,* and *saturation.* **Hue** is the name of the colour (red, green, and blue). **Value** is the shading, tonality, or tint of a colour (light and dark blue). **Saturation** is the intensity of colour (bright red or dull red).

In design, a colour wheel that displays basic colours and their **complementary colours**, or opposite colours, is used as a guideline. Most colour wheels use 12 colour hues as the basis for all colour mixtures. With pigment colours that are used for painting or traditional artwork, the **traditional primary colours** are *red, yellow,* and *blue.* These are the main colours that create all others. For instance, combining red and yellow creates orange. The **secondary colours** are *orange, green,* and *purple,* and they can be further mixed for many colour variations. The six **tertiary colours** are created by mixing one primary and one secondary colour. They consist of *yellow orange, red orange, red violet, blue violet, blue green,* and *yellow green.*

Colour intensity or saturation is the brightness of a colour. To lower a colour's intensity without changing its value, a designer can add gray or combine the colour with its complementary colour, which is the colour across from it on the colour wheel. When complementary colours are placed next to each other, their brightness is intensified. For example, the opposite of orange is blue; a designer might package oranges using blue lettering to highlight the fruit, thus making it look fresher. When various colours are coordinated together in the colour scheme of an image, warm colours like reds, yellows, and oranges generally seem to come forward, while cool colours like blues, greens, and purples appear to fade to the back. High-contrast colours appear to come forward visually, while low-contrast colours appear to recede. Low-intensity versions of a colour are generally considered the *tones* of a colour. Colours mixed with neutral grays can result in different **tones** of colour.

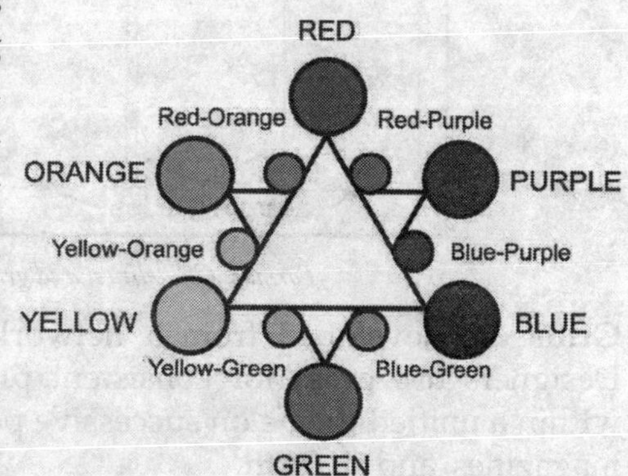

Colours created on the computer are made by adding the primary colours of light – *red, green,* and *blue* (*RGB*), which act differently than pigment but are fine for electronic document design such as web pages. The colours *cyan, magenta, yellow,* and *black* (*CMYK*) are used for commercial printing. Colour plates used in commercial printing use the colours *cyan, magenta,* and *yellow* (*CMY*) as the basis for creating all other colours for print. *Black* (*K*) is then added for purity and contrast.

Format, Guidelines, and Grids

Brochures, CD covers, business cards, and posters are some of the **formats** designers use for their clients. The project the client brings to you will determine the format. Your design should work well within the given format. Formats have advantages and limitations that need to be considered in creating a particular design. For instance, will the final layout be a vertical or

portrait orientation, or a horizontal display of elements, called a **landscape orientation**? What size paper and shape will it be? How will it be used, and where will it be seen? These are all considerations as you work with a particular format.

Most graphic computer applications have a set of rulers, or ruler guides, displayed along the top and left side of the document that a designer can use for measuring. A designer can click and drag from one of the ruler guides onto the document, creating what are called **guidelines**. These nonprintable guidelines are used for exact placement of specific sized text and graphics boxes on brochures, flyersweb pages, and so on. They also can be used to create **margin guides,** usually purple or blue in colour, for outer margins and for spacing between text and graphic boxes for folding procedures and alignment, web pages, and so on.

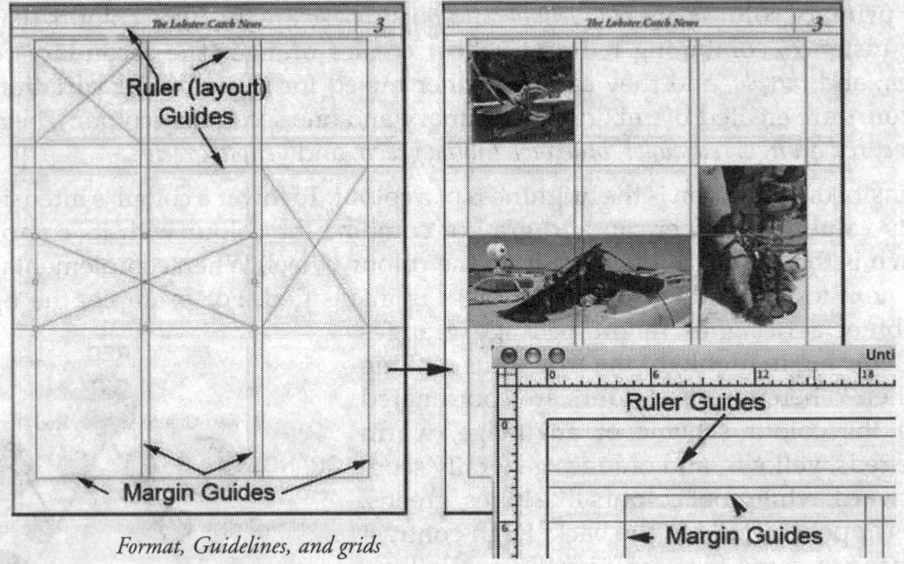

Format, Guidelines, and grids

Grids are developed from a network of intersecting horizontal and vertical guidelines. Designers use grids for consistent placement and spacing of text and graphic elements within a unified theme on successive pages to create catalogs, books, newsletters, pamphlets, magazines, and so forth.

Design Principles

A designer must be careful to understand the client's needs. By researching what the client wants to convey to the target market, the designer will be able to create the appropriate message. Principles in design are followed to combine individual elements into one harmonious piece. This involves taking various elements and providing proper balance, adding selective emphasis to create a focal point, using rhythm to set the mood, and establishing unity.

Balance

The concept of balance is to arrange elements within an area so that these elements promote a harmonious response. Visual balance is determined by the weight, position, and arrangement of elements. Balance can be formal, informal, or radial. **Formal balance**, also referred to as

symmetrical balance, places elements with equal distribution to convey trustworthiness and integrity, as used by financial institutions or insurance companies. **Informal balance**, also referred to as **asymmetrical balance**, uses elements that counterbalance one another instead to create a harmonious composition. This type of balance gives the appearance of being casual, energetic, or trendy. **Radial balance** arranges elements around a central point and is used to promote unity or teamwork.

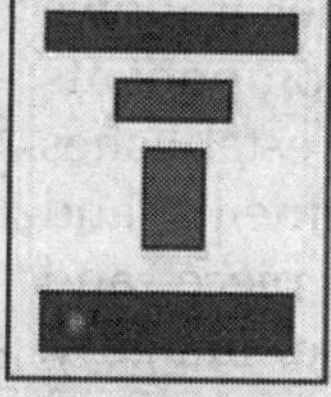

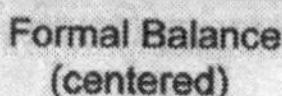

Formal Balance (centered)

Informal Balance (off-centered)

Radial Balance (equal value)

Use of Negative and Positive Space

Using empty or **negative space**, absent of visual elements, is a visual element in itself that actually does more to promote luxury or elegance, and sometimes a sense of mystery, than most other effects. This may utilise the "less is more" concept in design. **Positive space** uses content to fill up space to identify or explain something in a particular page. In an ad using empty space, a line of black type on a white background, or a line of white type on a black background, can change perception of the content of the page. Reversing colours sometimes makes an ad stand out in a crowd of ads. Care needs to be taken in the use of empty space over positive space, including type size in relation to the graphic.

Negative and positive space

Rhythm

Rhythm is a visual pattern of repeating elements that creates a sense of movement. It is constantly used in printed media as well as in architecture. Variation in rhythm can be adjusted by changing the shape, size, colour, spacing and position of elements in a design. This change in arrangement helps to promote the mood of the design. The viewer looks at certain elements before others. Those elements that are larger, darker, or have a more unusual shape than their surrounding counterparts are used to draw the viewer's eyes into the composition.

Visual pattern of rhythm

Unity

Unity is the organisation of elements in a design as though they belong together. It allows the designer to view individual components as one integrated whole. Unity establishes continuity with a variety of elements and promotes consistency within the piece, and it combines balance, rhythm, type, imagery, and tone to evoke a particular emotion from the viewer.

Unity in a design

Design Stages: From Concept to Completion

A design solution's "personality" is created when the formal elements of colour, line, shape, texture, format, and value are put together using the principles of graphic design in spacial relationships, balance, rythm, emphasis, and unity. These elements collaborate to elicit the kind of audience reaction the client desires.

Working with the Client

The whole idea behind designing is being able to solve problems visually that help the client best communicate his or her message. Before you start designing, talk to your client and listen; then keep your client involved in the process

- ❑ Listen to the client to understand the design challenge. Make the client feel involved. Try to assist gently when suggesting changes you feel would create a better product, but do not make the client feel incompetent. You need to fully understand the client's project in order to help.
- ❑ You need to know the market the design is intended for and what the client's design specifications are. Is this design going to be used for print and electronic media?

If so, then understanding different ways images and text are going to be presented for each medium is crucial to the success of the project.

- ❑ What materials are needed for the project, and what is your experience with these materials? What software or hardware are you comfortable with, and which ones will require that you rely on others for expertise?
- ❑ Know your budget and guidelines. Complete as much research as possible so that you will be able to stay within your estimate. Set a time frame for completion of various components of the project.

The Designing Process

Graphic design begins with a visual concept—the main idea behind creating the design piece. Before coming up with a concept, you need to plan a strategy and set design objectives that meet your client's needs. Then research information, material, and visuals about your subject, and start writing down your ideas. Make changes and decisions on those ideas with the client, and then generate final comps for the intended media.

Thumbnails

Thumbnails are sketched variations of an idea. Once you have your design idea, thumbnails help create different possibilities for that idea. Create a dozen or more thumbnails, and then narrow them down to about six to ten per concept to show the client. For consistency, make thumbnails the same proportion as the final piece.

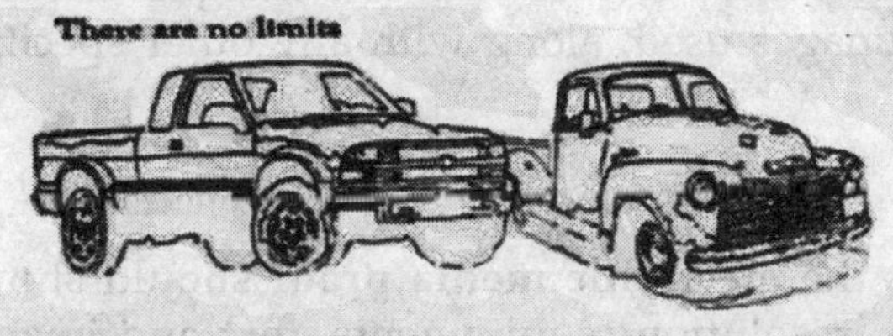

Roughs

Roughs are created as a result of combining specific elements from each thumbnail, or they may be the result of one good thumbnail, A rough is a full-size rendition of your design, including the layout of images and text and overall compositional elements that you show to the client. This version can be created while still at the drawing stage, or it can be done on the computer. The final rough usually must be created on the computer. Generating three to six roughs gives the client a good idea of what the final design will look like.

Comps

Comps show exactly what the final design will look like when printed. The designer must take painstaking efforts to make sure everything is exactly what the client had agreed to in the final rough. This is where all text, colour, imagery, and compositional elements need to come together for the final client approval before going to press, electronic media, or both.

Final Proofs for Press

The client should have the proof that provides instructions for the pressman and finishing operator. The **print proof** should show indications for folding, cutting, bleeding, trapping, registration, and any special requirements. Keep in mind that most ink-jet proofs will not show exact colour but may be close enough for client approval, as long as the client understands before going to press that there may be a slight difference in some colours in the final product. Another final proof will be generated at the print site, provided for and to be approved by the client, so he or she knows precisely what all the elements will look like. The designer should also furnish a disc to the client with fonts and images used, along with any other specific information needed.

Final Electronic Proofs for Electronic Media

For website designers or multimedia designers, the **electronic media proof** should show indications for pixel dimensions, software used, resolution requirements, text and image locations, and information, if needed, for publishing to the web, along with any special requirements. A *final printed proof* is also needed for checking layout of type, imagery, and all elements used, along with the final layout supplied on disc to the client. The client should have the disc contents checked on a calibrated monitor to see as closely as possible what the web page or site will look like. When working with a limited colour palette for web design, the client needs to check carefully to make sure that the colours are as accurate as possible to be displayed on the web. It must also be noted that colours on a Mac and colours on a PC vary slightly in their display.

Typography

Typography is the study and use of text in a document. A designer uses type in titles or headlines and in the body of the document to enhance an ad; it helps to establish a mood or theme in the design or document A **type family**, sometimes referred to as a **typeface**, is a group of fonts that share a basic character construction, like the Arial family, which includes Arial Black, Arial Narrow, Arial Alternative, and so on, similar to having your family of uncles, aunts, cousins, and grandparents. A **font** is a set of characters such as Arial, Times New Roman, Verdana, or Wingdings by themselves, like your immediate family. A **font size** is measured in **points** instead of inches (1 point = 1/72 inch). When you open a document, the default size is usually 12 points. When you need to bold, underline, or italicize type, you are creating a change to that type by applying a **font style**.

Character and Line Spacing

The spacing between characters and lines of text also determines how that type looks on your document. **Tracking** adjusts the spacing between characters and words. Adjusting the tracking of words too tightly in a paragraph can make it difficult to read, whereas adjusting too loosely can create "rivers" of white spacing in a paragraph, especially when type is either left or right justified. Sometimes a designer will create a loose tracking effect on a single word, or a few words, in the title of an ad or magazine cover as an attention getter. **Kerning** is a technique used for pairs of characters in titles or headlines that may need to be brought closer together for a more consistent look. **Leading** refers to the spacing between lines of text. Usually the default leading is 120 percent of the letter size for most documents.

This is a 12 point "Arial Regular" Font

This is a 12 point "Arial Regular" font with an Italicized style.

This is a 12 point "Arial Black" font in the Arial family

This is an18 point size "Arial Regular" Font

In long articles or newsletters, less space between lines of text tends to darken the document, whereas more space will lighten it up. The message or mood you want to convey will determine how you will set up your text and what fonts you will need. The style or arrangement of setting type is called **type alignment**. Left aligned flushes the type to the left and is easy to read; we associate right aligned with professional return addresses on letters. Centred lines of type are used in some headlines or titles, while **justified alignment** places text equally on left and right sides in a column.

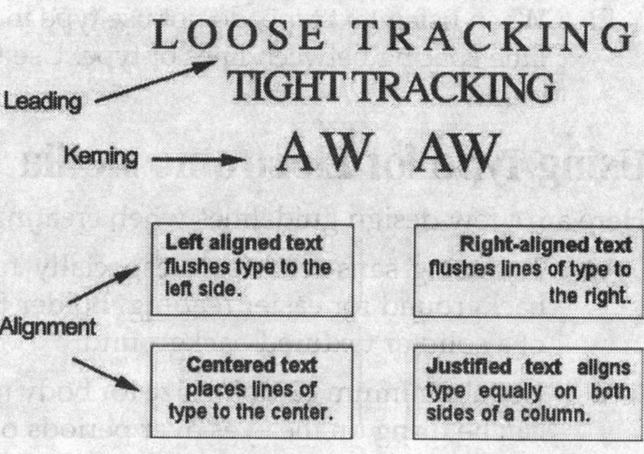

Categories of Type

Two main categories of type are *serif type* and *sans-serif type*. **Serif type** characters contain what look like "feet," or extended strokes, on the tops and bottoms; these are used to convey a conservative look and make it easier to read long articles or bodies of text. **Sans-serif type** has characters without these strokes, and it is more legible for labelling illustrations, headlines, and titles. **ASCII type** is the American standard of type: it is plain text and unformatted and can be read by any application or computer. It uses the extension .TXT. Other type categories include script type, decorative type, and symbol type **Script fonts** are typically used in announcements or invitations and convey the appearance of being created with a pen or brush. **Decorative type** is sometimes used in headlines to create a specific meaning, and **symbol type** is a collection of related symbols, often called *dingbats,* that can be used for bullets, map symbols, or logos. The type you select should be appropriate and must complement your design.

Times Roman is a serif type with extensions.

Arial is a sans-serif type without extensions.

Brush Script MT is a script type used in invitations.

Papyrus is used as a decorative type.

Symbol type (Webdings) for bullets, logos, etc.

Using Type in Print Media

Here are a few design guidelines for starters when creating text documents to be printed:

- ❑ Use the same fonts and sizes for various headings in the same document. If you have to use different fonts, stick with the same type family for consistency.
- ❑ Use 10- or 12-point size serif type minimum for the body of text for easier reading on printedmaterial.
- ❑ Use italics sparingly and infrequently, for emphasis only.
- ❑ When using text type, do not use type in all upper case and do not allow too much or too little spacing between lines of type. Use the default leading on your word processor as a guide.

Using Type for Electronic Media

Here are a few design guidelines when creating electronic documents:

- ❑ Try using sans-serif fonts especially for light-coloured text against a dark or black background for easier reading. Bolder fonts also work better when reversing type out of a solid or textured background.
- ❑ Use a minimum 12-point size for body text, because text is displayed electronically and can be tiring on the eyes over periods of time.
- ❑ Use colour for emphasis of graphic statements. Electronic media is a great means for entertaining visual stimulation.
- ❑ Usually it helps to keep sentences short and use small paragraphs to hold the reader's interest.

Installing Fonts

In Windows, you would open the Fonts folder in the Appearance and Personalisation command in the Control Panel; then from the source window just drag the icon into the fonts folder and it will automatically install:

- ❑ To install your fonts in Windows, select the Start button, then select the Control Panel.
- ❑ Select Appearance and Personalisation link, not the links underneath, then locate the Fonts icon.
- ❑ Click on the Fonts link to open the Fonts folder displaying the fonts on your computer and resize the window to half screen or less.
- ❑ If you download a particular font you like, just drag the icon or the folder

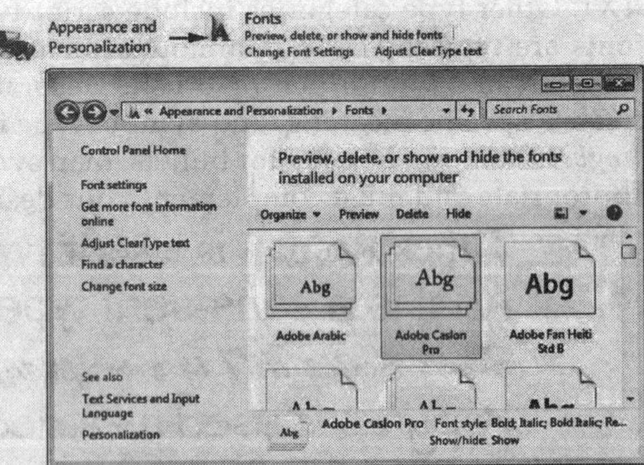

To add font, drag font icon from source to Fonts folder of icons. To delete a font, select font icon and select to delete.

onto the desktop. Resize the window display, then all you need to do is drag the new font icon into the display of Fonts folder. It will automatically install.

- ❑ To delete a font, click on the icon and press delete from the toolbar, or right click the icon and select Delete. Be careful when deleting as it cannot be undone.
- ❑ Close the dialog boxes to get back to the desktop. Your fonts are added to your computer and ready for the text exercises.

Imagery

Images are needed to explain ideas, provide further illustration to text in long articles, and strengthen the mood or idea the designer is trying to convey. We are basically visual learners of our environment. When designing with computer imagery, graphics can be categorised as either *vector images* or *bitmap images*. **Vector images** are lustrations, logos, drawings, or clip art that can be enlarged to any size without affecting the quality of the original image. **Bitmap images,** or **raster images,** are photographs, paintings, or complex designs that use millions of colours to record subtle gradations of tone in the image. They are not capable of being scaled larger than the original size without deteriorating the quality.

Vector Image

Bitmap (raster) Image

Saving Graphic File Formats

Graphic applications allow the designer to save files in specific universal formats for an intended purpose. The file extension determines the type of graphic format saved and how a file may be used. Saving graphic files in these universal formats—extensions such as .EPS, .TIF, .JPG, .GIF, .PNG, or .PDF—gives them the flexibility to be used with other graphics programs for specific purposes.

Understanding the Importance of Colour

Creating a design with appropriate colours is a major factor in client approval. Research on the designer's part is critical to the success of the design. Some colours work better in small quantities than others. A designer must also be wary of design components using dark or light tones in specific quantities that may symbolise positive or negative aspects. Complementary background colours or lettering may be used with products extensively in package design. A bag of apples might have green lettering on the package as its complement to highlight the red colour of the produce, giving a fresher appearance. When working with advertising agencies, whether on a local or global scale, colour is used differently within various cultures. Designers need to be aware of the intended market. For instance, the colour of royalty is purple in America and in Europe, but in China it is yellow. In America white symbolises purity, and people associate it with weddings, whereas in China red is the usual bridal colour.

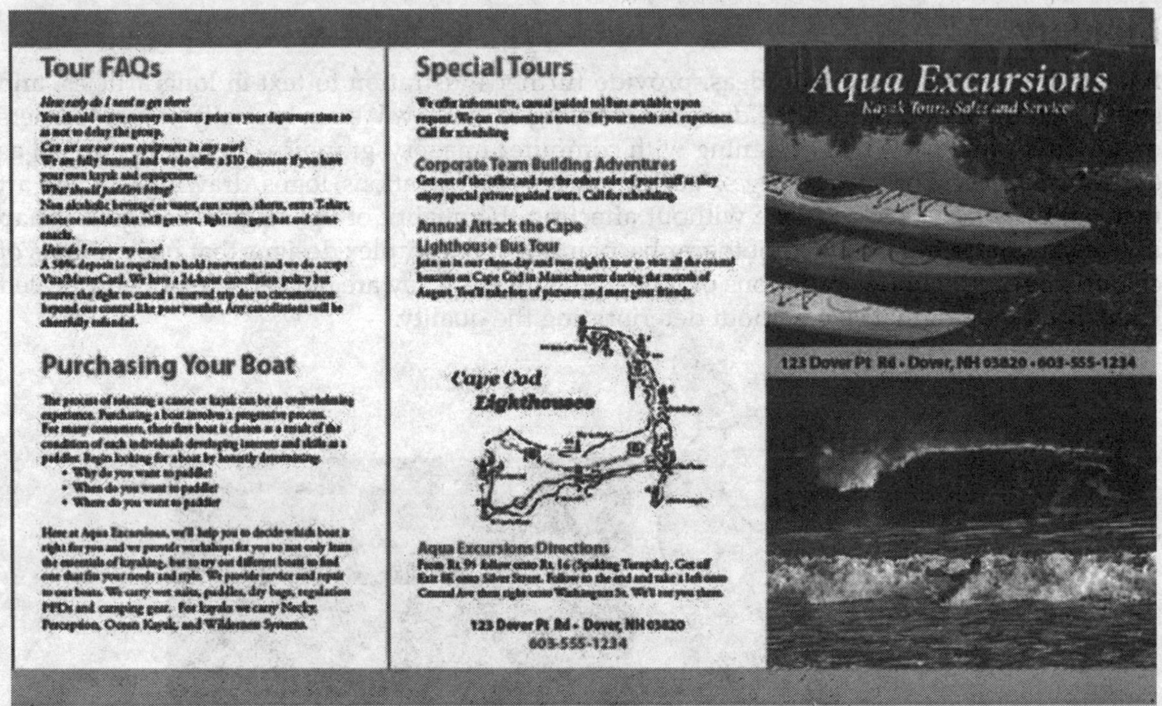

Inside Fold **Back** **Front**

3-Way Folding Brochure (outside page)

Depending on the intended message, colours can have contrary effects. Here are some general concepts regarding the use of colour:

- ❏ White will usually stand for purity, but can also be utilised to generate a feeling of emptiness. Websites sometimes use white backgrounds as a neutral setting for images and for easier readability of text.
- ❏ Black can show value in terms of elegance, such as in tuxedos and gowns. Black can be used as an attention getter as a background with white, or *reversed*, type. Black can also suggest danger or something negative. It is also used as a neutral background in designing web pages that have many photographs.
- ❏ Gray (if a very light gray is used) can provide a subtle background on electronic media, leanding a neutral balance for images and coloured type. On printed media,

it is used very sparingly. Gray can also have powerful negative symbolism, such as stormy weather.

- Red can make the boldest of statements and may draw the viewer's eye more than any other colour. Red can be used in small amounts for emphasis. Red can symbolise love (bright or medium red), strength (middle or true red), or anger (dark red) depending on the tone.
- Pink is a colour used often in the bakery industry. Pink can also suggest high value in packaged goods and is a feminine colour.
- Violet is another colour that is generally used in small quantities. Dark violet, for instance, may suggest royalty.
- Blue, as one of the most widely used colours, has different effects. Lighter shades of blue may signify dream-like fantasies. Medium and dark blues may be used to signify honesty, professionalism, and sometimes spirituality. However, in some instances, blue used as the dominant colour can adversely signify depression, dreariness, or isolation.
- Green signifies nature and can be used for produce, products related to healing, or for environmental issues. Green is also used to represent wealth, perhaps for banking institutions. Contrarily, green can imply jealousy or greed.
- Yellow can produce feelings of warmth and may be used to signify fast service (taxis, fast food). In contrast, yellow can also suggest danger or caution.

Creating Colours on the Computer

Millions of light-emitted colours can be created on the computer by mixing the electronic primary colours: red, green, and blue. These **RGB mode** colours are used for electronic display such as web pages. Computers use an additive process to create colour from the primary colours. The computer's secondary colours are magenta, cyan, and yellow, or **CMYK mode** (K stands for black, which is used to increase contrast). Mix red and blue and you get magenta. White is theoretically created by mixing red, green, and blue at their full intensity. Using computer software, you can convert files from RGB mode to CMYK mode to create colours that will closely match pigment colours used in commercial printing.

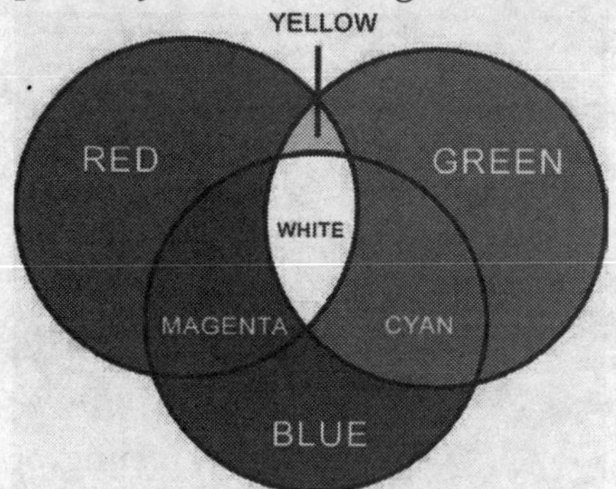

Action Items Overview

Here is a breakdown of what you need to do:

- Determine the layout of images and text, including spacing and margins, for the final size.
- Research what images will be used and what fonts, styles, and sizes will be used.

- ❑ Create three or more thumbnail sketches of how the images will be laid out with the text descriptions (normally, you would create more sketches, but this will do for this exercise).
- ❑ Present your thumbnail sketches to your instructor or peers to get their input.
- ❑ With the sketches narrowed down, create the final, full-size rough combining elements from various sketches. Then show them to your clients for approval.
- ❑ ADVANCED USERS: Identify design elements and principles in various ads.

DTP using MS Word

Introduction

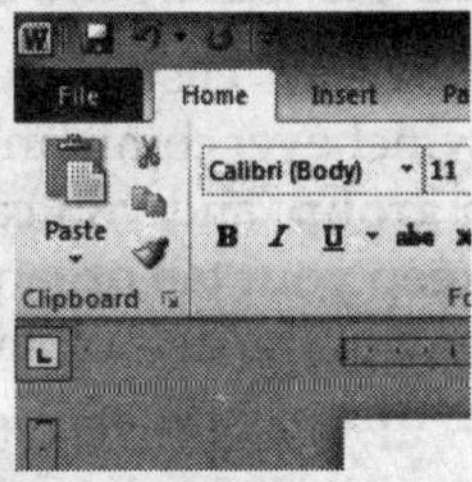

Word 2010 is a **word processor** that allows you to create various types of documents such as letters, papers, flyers, faxes and more. In this lesson, you will be introduced to the **Ribbon** and the new **Backstage view**, and you'll learn how to create **new** documents and **open** existing ones.

Getting to Know Word 2010

Word 2010 is a bit different from earlier versions, so even if you've used Word before, you should take some time to familiarize yourself with the interface. The toolbars are similar to those in Word 2007, and they include the Ribbon and the Quick Access Toolbar. Unlike Word 2007, commands such as Open and Print are housed in Backstage view, which replaces the Microsoft Office Button.

The Ribbon

The new **tabbed Ribbon system** was introduced in Word 2007 to replace traditional menus. The **Ribbon** contains all of the commands you'll need in order to do common tasks. It contains multiple **tabs**, each with several **groups** of commands, and you can add your own tabs that contain your favourite commands. Some groups have an arrow in the bottom-right corner that you can click to see even more commands.

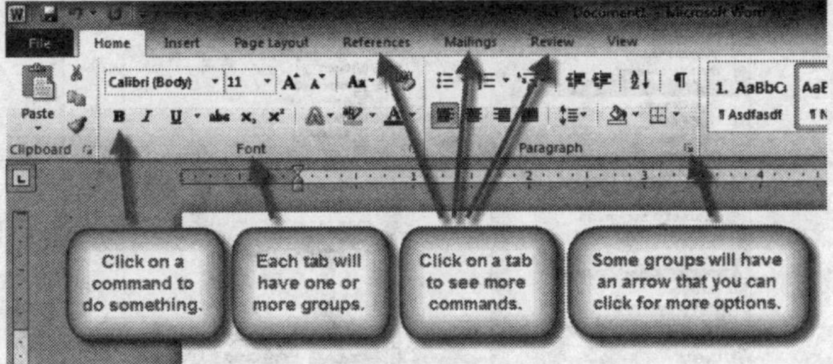

The Ribbon

Certain programs, such as **Adobe Acrobat Reader**, may install additional tabs to the Ribbon. These tabs are called **Add-ins**.

To Minimize and Maximize the Ribbon

The Ribbon is designed to be responsive to your current task and easy to use; however, you can choose to **minimize** it if it's taking up too much screen space.

- ❑ Click the **arrow** in the upper-right corner of the Ribbon to minimize it.
- ❑ To maximize the Ribbon, click the arrow again.

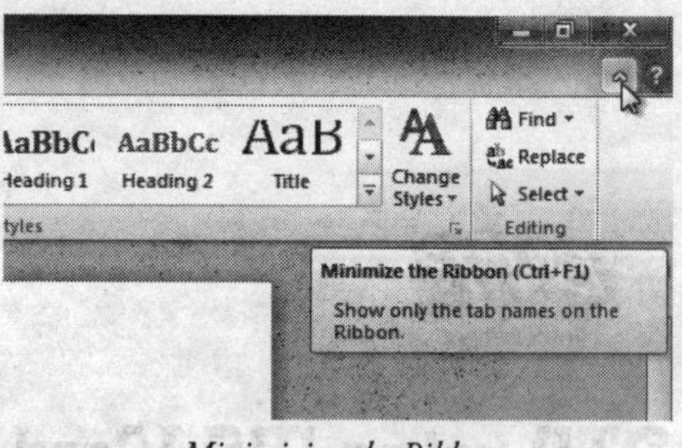

Minimizing the Ribbon

When the Ribbon is minimized, you can make it reappear by clicking on a tab. However, the Ribbon will disappear again when you're not using it.

To Customize the Ribbon

You can customize the Ribbon by creating your own **tabs** with whichever commands you want. Commands are always housed within a **group**, and you can create as many groups as you want in order to keep your tab organized. If you want, you can even add commands to any of the default tabs, as long as you create a custom group in the tab.

Right-clicking the Ribbon to customize it

- ❑ Right-click the **Ribbon** and select **Customize the Ribbon**. A dialog box will appear.
- ❑ Click **New Tab**. A new tab will be created with a new group inside it.
- ❑ Make sure the new group is selected.
- ❑ Select a command from the list on the left, then click **Add**. You can also drag commands directly into a group.
- ❑ When you are done adding commands, click **OK**.

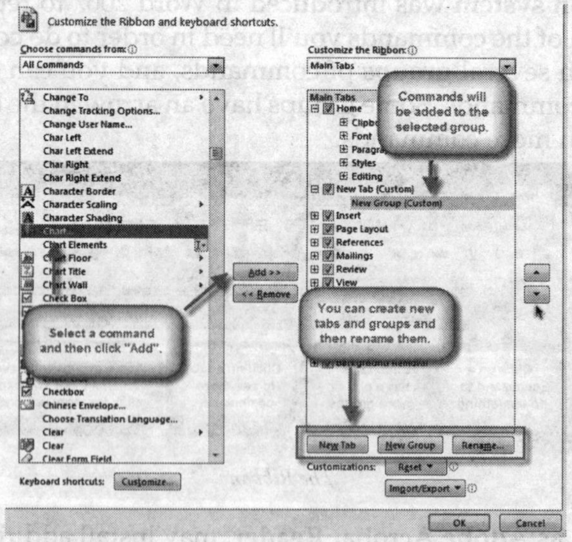

The dialog box where you can customize the Ribbon

If you don't see the command you want, click on the **Choose commands from:** drop-down box and select **All Commands**.

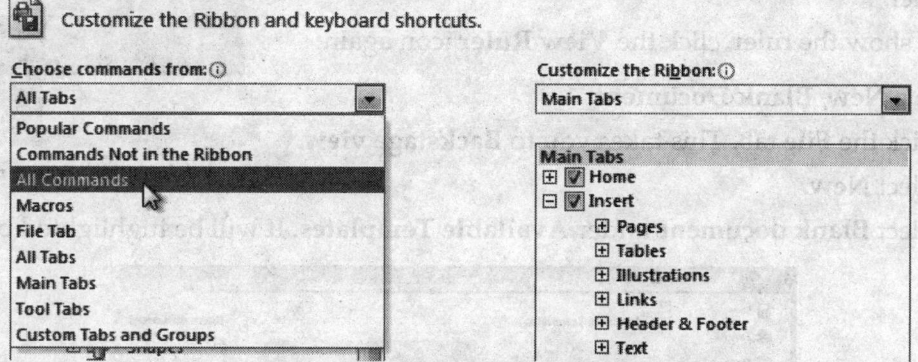

Displaying All Commands

The Quick Access Toolbar

The **Quick Access Toolbar** is located above the ribbon, and it lets you access common commands no matter which tab you're on. By default, it shows the **Save**, **Undo**, and **Repeat** commands. You can add other commands to make it more convenient for you.

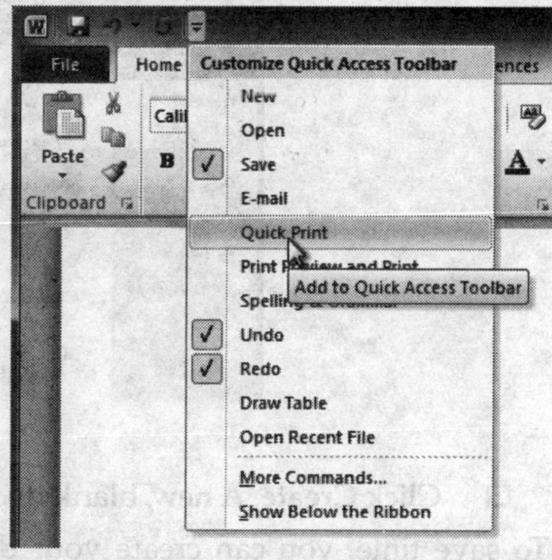

Adding a command to the Quick Access Toolbar

To Add Commands to the Quick Access Toolbar:

- ❑ Click the **drop-down arrow** to the right of the **Quick Access Toolbar**.
- ❑ Select the command you wish to add from the drop-down menu. It will appear in the Quick Access toolbar.

The Ruler

The **Ruler** is located at the top and to the left of your document. It makes it easier to adjust your document with precision. If you want, you can hide the Ruler to free up more screen space.

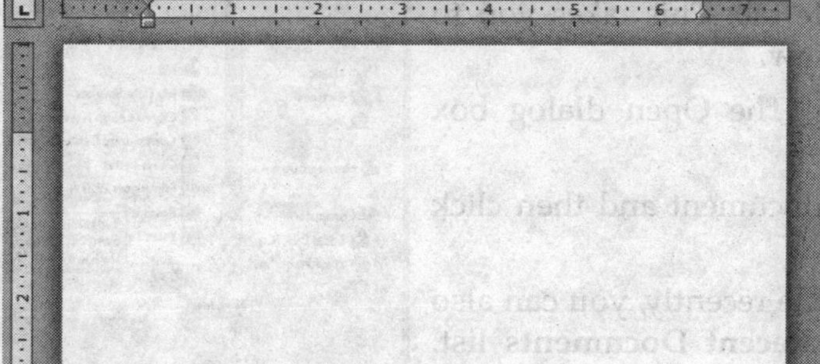

The Ruler

To Hide or View the Ruler:

- ❑ Click the **View Ruler** icon over the scrollbar to hide the ruler.
- ❑ To show the ruler, click the **View Ruler** icon again.

Hiding and viewing the Ruler

To Create a New, Blank Document:

- ❑ Click the **File** tab. This takes you to **Backstage view**.
- ❑ Select **New**.
- ❑ Select **Blank document** under **Available Templates**. It will be highlighted by default.

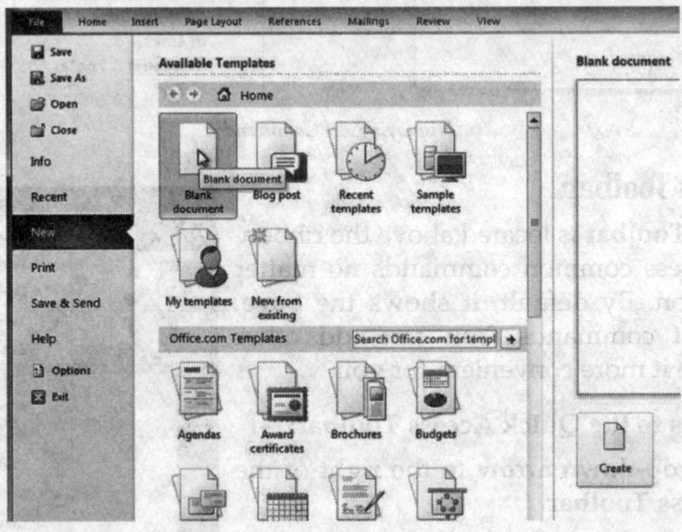

Creating a new document

- ❑ Click **Create**. A new, blank document appears in the Word window.

To save time, you can create your document from a **template**, which you can select from the New Document pane. We'll talk about templates in a later lesson.

To Open an Existing Document:

- ❑ Click the **File** tab. This takes you to **Backstage view**.
- ❑ Select **Open**. The Open dialog box appears.
- ❑ Select your document and then click **Open**.

If you've opened a file recently, you can also access it from the **Recent Documents** list. Just click on the **File** tab and select **Recent**.

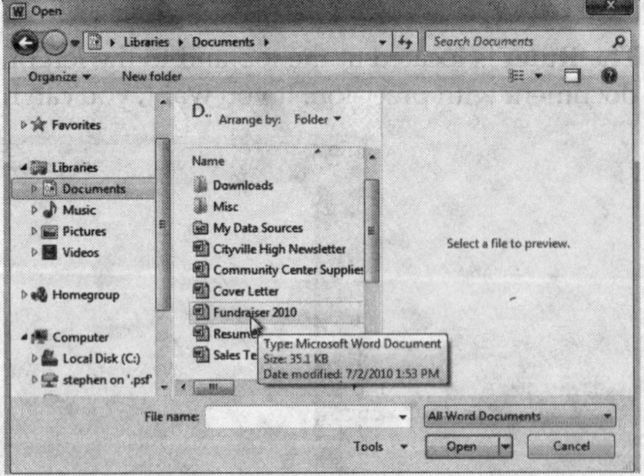

Opening a document

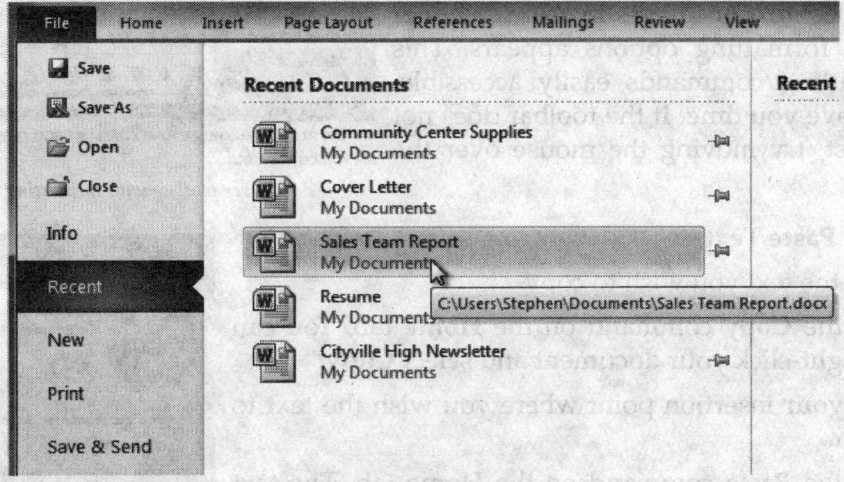

Opening a recent document

Working with Text

To Insert Text:

- ❑ Move your mouse to the location you wish text to appear in the document.
- ❑ Click the mouse. The **insertion point** appears.
- ❑ Type the text you wish to appear.

Insertion point

The insertion point

To Delete Text:

- ❑ Place the **insertion point** next to the text you wish to delete.
- ❑ Press the **Backspace** key on your keyboard to delete text to the **left** of the insertion point.
- ❑ Press the **Delete** key on your keyboard to delete text to the **right** of the insertion point.

To Select Text:

- ❑ Place the **insertion point** next to the text you wish to select.
- ❑ Click the mouse, and while holding it down, drag your mouse over the text to select it.
- ❑ Release the mouse button. You have selected the text. A **highlighted box** will appear over the selected text.

Executive Summary

January 2010 has been a profitable month and the company has shown growth in many arenas. Ad sales are up by 23% and capital expenditures have decreased since 4th quarter in the Sales Department. The sales team hired a new design specialist, the role of VP of sales was filled, a new sales chief position was created, and the sales team accrued 14 new clients, including one national chain. Additionally, online ad sales doubled since July of last year. Statistics indicate that sales in most markets increase with the use of online ads and our clients are reading those statistics and responding to them. Marketing trends indicate that this growth will continue.

Selecting text

When you select text or images in Word, a **hover toolbar** with formatting options appears. This makes formatting commands easily accessible, which may save you time. If the toolbar does not appear at first, try moving the mouse over the selection.

Hover toolbar with formatting options

To Copy and Paste Text:

- ❑ Select the text you wish to copy.
- ❑ Click the **Copy** command on the **Home** tab. You can also right-click your document and select **Copy**.
- ❑ Place your insertion point where you wish the text to appear.
- ❑ Click the **Paste** command on the Home tab. The text will appear.

The Copy command

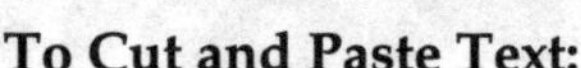

To Cut and Paste Text:

- ❑ Select the text you wish to copy.
- ❑ Click the **Cut** command on the **Home** tab. You can also right-click your document and select **Cut**.
- ❑ Place your insertion point where you wish the text to appear.
- ❑ Click the **Paste** command on the **Home** tab. The text will appear.

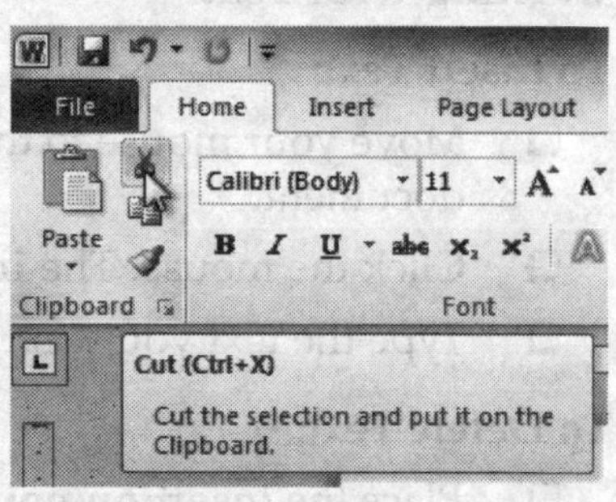

The Cut command

You can also cut, copy, and paste by right-clicking your document and choosing the desired action from the drop-down menu. When you use this method to paste, you can choose from three options that determine how the text will be formatted: **Keep Source Formatting**, **Merge Formatting** and **Keep Text Only**. You can hover the mouse over each icon to see what it will look like before you click on it.

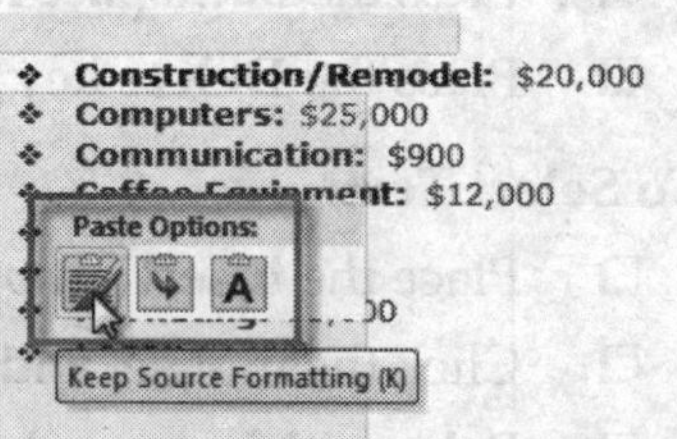

Paste Options

To Drag and Drop Text:

- ❑ Select the text you wish to copy.
- ❑ **Click and drag the text** to the location you wish it to appear. The cursor will have a rectangle under it to indicate that you are moving text.
- ❑ Release the mouse button and the text will appear.

If text **does not appear** in the exact location you wish, you can click the **Enter** key on your keyboard to move the text to a new line.

Dragging and dropping text

Find and Replace

When you're working with longer documents, it can be difficult and time consuming to locate a specific word or phrase. Word can automatically search your document using the **Find** feature, and it even allows you to change words or phrases using **Replace**.

To Find Text:

- ❑ From the **Home** tab, click the **Find** command. The **Navigation** pane will appear on the left side of the screen.
- ❑ Type the text you wish to find in the field at the top of the Navigation pane.
- ❑ If the text is found in the document, it will be highlighted in yellow, and a preview will appear in the Navigation pane.

Clicking the Find command

- ❑ If the text appears more than once, you can click the **arrows** on the Navigation pane to step through the results. You can also click the **result previews** on the Navigation pane to jump to the location of a result in your document.

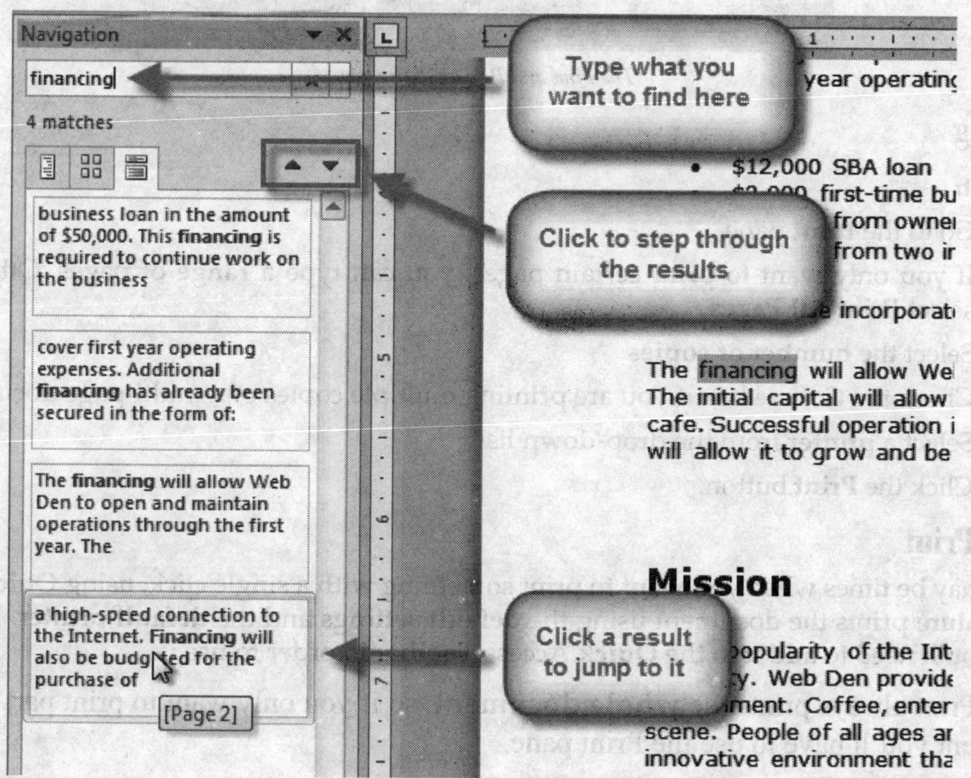

The Navigation pane

- ❑ When you close the Navigation pane, the highlighting will disappear.

To Replace Text:

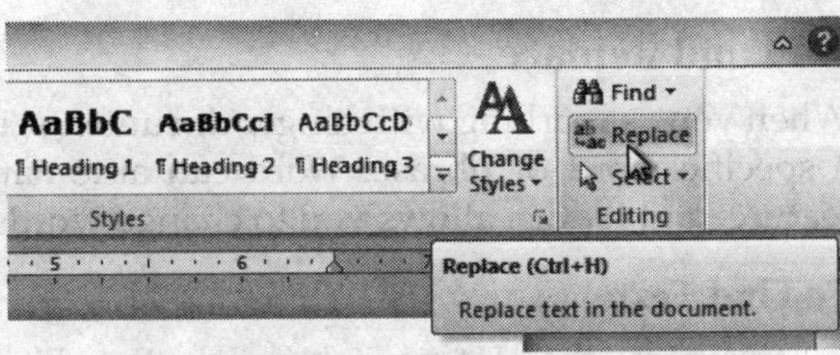

Clicking the Replace command

- ❑ From the **Home** tab, click the **Replace** command. The **Find and Replace** dialog box will appear.
- ❑ Type the text you wish to find in the **Find what** field.
- ❑ Type the text you wish to replace it with in the **Replace with** field.
- ❑ Click **Find Next** and then **Replace** to replace text. You can also click **Replace All** to replace all instances within the document.

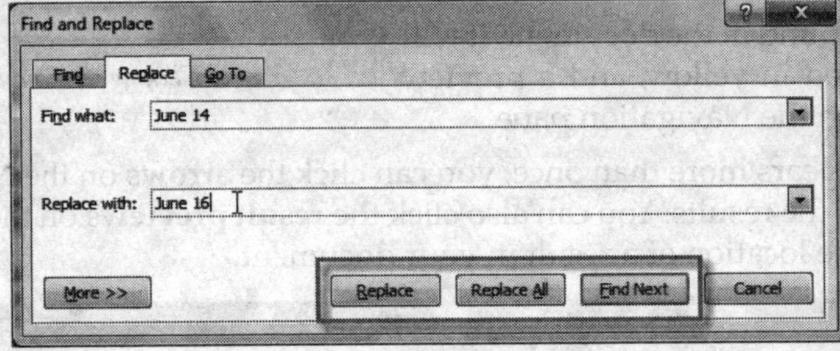

The Find and Replace dialog box

Printing

To Print:

- ❑ Go to the **Print** pane.
- ❑ If you only want to print certain pages, you can type a **range** of pages. Otherwise, select **Print All Pages**.
- ❑ Select the **number of copies**.
- ❑ Check the **Collate** box if you are printing multiple copies of a multi-page document.
- ❑ Select a **printer** from the drop-down list.
- ❑ Click the **Print** button.

Quick Print

There may be times when you want to print something with a single click, using **Quick Print**. This feature prints the document using the **default settings** and the **default printer**. In Word 2010, you'll need to add it to the **Quick Access Toolbar** in order to use it.

Quick Print always prints the **whole document**, so if you only want to print part of your document you'll have to use the Print pane.

To Access the Quick Print Button:

- ❑ Click the **drop-down arrow** on the right side of the **Quick Access Toolbar.**

- Select **Quick Print** if it is not already checked.
- To print, just click the **Quick Print** command.

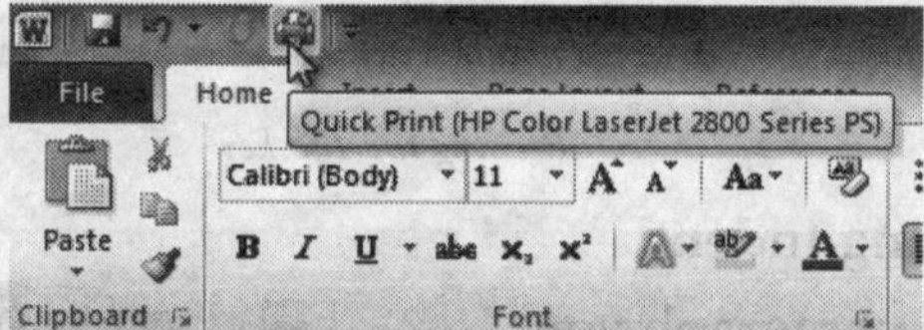

The Quick Print command

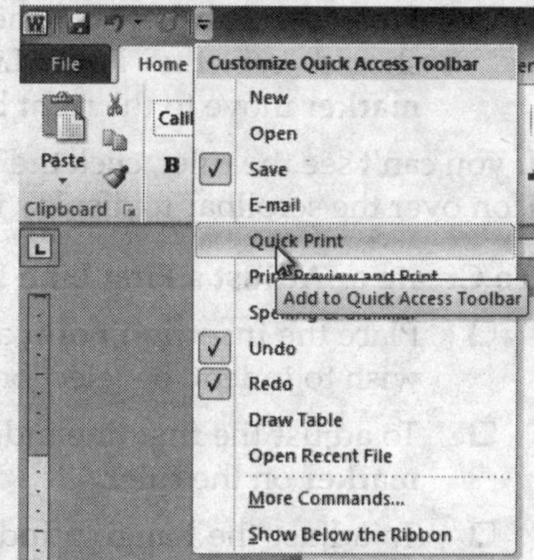

Adding Quick Print to the Quick Access Toolbar

Using Indents and Tabs

There are several ways in Word that you can indent text; however, it's important to use these tools appropriately in order to **indent correctly** each time. This helps the editing process go smoothly, thus saving you time.

In this lesson, you will learn how to use the **tab selector** and the **horizontal ruler** to set **tabs** and **indents**, and how to use the **Increase** and **Decrease Indent** commands.

Indenting Text

In many types of documents, you may wish to indent only the **first line** of each paragraph. This helps to **visually separate** paragraphs from one another. It's also possible to indent every line **except the first line**, which is known as a **hanging indent**.

Dear Mr. Powell:

Thank you for taking the time to meet with me last Thur: position. I enjoyed meeting with you and touring the facility. I w of the showroom and with the competence of the staff at Quality chance to work in such a productive and supportive atmosphere

As we talked about in our meeting, my fourteen years of commissioned floor sales and in the role of Sales Supervisor, wo Furnishings. In that time, I have learned many techniques that w customer satisfaction ratings at Quality Furnishings.

In addition, I wanted to let you know that I have recently Superior Sales Training program at the National Business Institu the program are sure to bolster sales. I look forward to having tl Quality Furnishings.

First Line Indent

Dear Mr. Powell:

Thank you for taking the time to meet with me last Thursday ab enjoyed meeting with you and touring the facility. I was the showroom and with the competence of the staff at Q chance to work in such a productive and supportive atm

As we talked about in our meeting, my fourteen years of sales ex floor sales and in the role of Sales Supervisor, would gre that time, I have learned many techniques that would in satisfaction ratings at Quality Furnishings.

In addition, I wanted to let you know that I have recently receive Sales Training program at the National Business Institut program are sure to bolster sales. I look forward to havi Quality Furnishings.

Hanging Indent

To Indent Using the Tab Key:

A quick way to indent is to use the **Tab** key. This will create a first line indent of 1/2 inch.

- Place the insertion point **at the very beginning** of the paragraph you wish to indent.

Thank you for taking the time to meet with me last Thursday enjoyed meeting with you and touring the facility. I was very showroom and with the competence of the staff at Quality Fu work in such a productive and supportive atmosphere.

Placing the insertion point

- ❑ Press the **Tab** key. On the ruler, you should see the **First Line Indent marker** move to the right by 1/2 inch.

If you can't see the ruler, click the **View Ruler** icon over the scrollbar to display it.

Pressing the Tab key

To Create or Adjust a First Line Indent or Hanging Indent:

- ❑ Place the **insertion point** anywhere in the paragraph you wish to indent, or select one or more paragraphs.
- ❑ To adjust the first line indent, drag the **First Line Indent marker** on the ruler.
- ❑ To adjust the hanging indent, drag the **Hanging Indent marker**.
- ❑ To move both markers at the same time, drag the **Left Indent marker**. This will indent all of the lines in the paragraph.

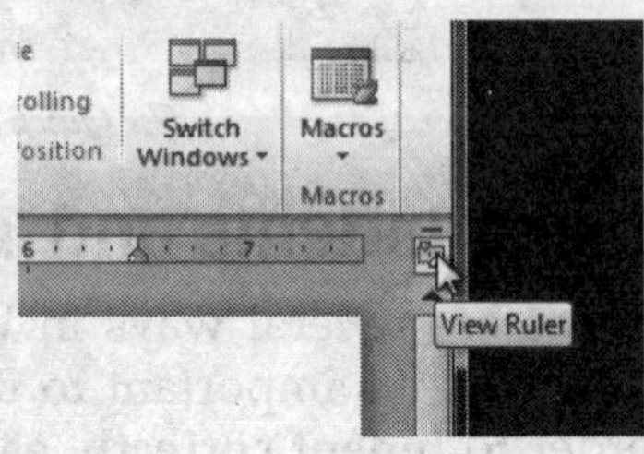

Hiding and viewing the Ruler

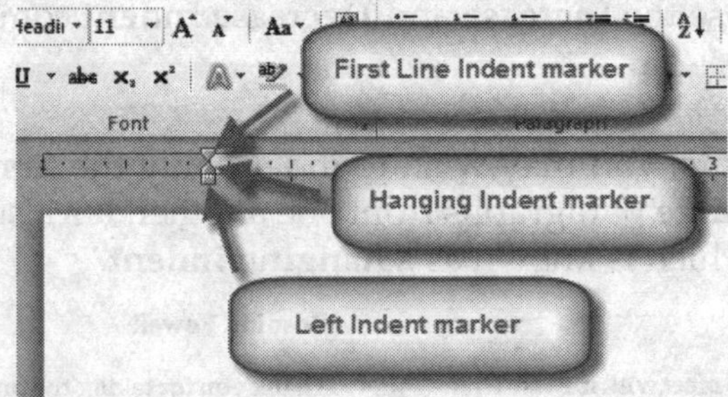

The three indent markers

To Use the Indent Commands:

If you want to indent all of the lines in a paragraph, you can use the **Indent commands** on the Home tab.

- ❑ Select the text you wish to indent.
- ❑ Make sure you are on the **Home** tab.
- ❑ Click the **Increase Indent** command to **increase** the indent by increments of **1/4 inch**.

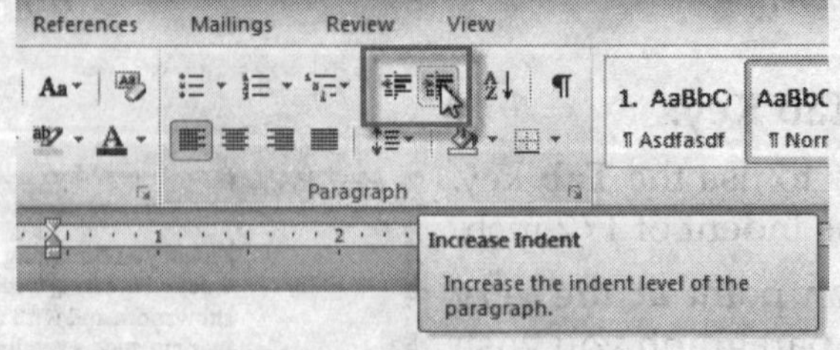

Increasing the indent

- ❑ Click the **Decrease Indent** command to **decrease** the indent by increments of **1/2 inch**.

If you would prefer to type in your indent amounts, you can use the **Indent fields** on the **Page Layout** tab.

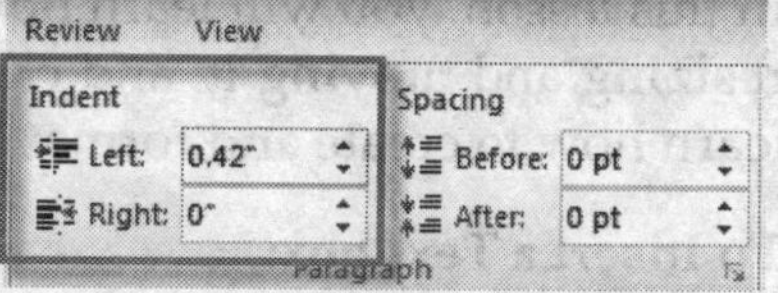

Typing an indent amount

Paragraph Spacing

Just as you can format spacing between lines in your document, you can also choose spacing options between each paragraph. Typically, extra spaces are added between paragraphs, headings, or subheadings. Extra spacing between paragraphs helps to make a document easier to read.

To Format Paragraph Spacing

- ❑ Click the **Line and Paragraph Spacing** command on the Home tab.
- ❑ Select **Add Space Before Paragraph** or **Remove Space After Paragraph** from the drop-down menu.
- ❑ From the drop-down menu, you can also select **Line Spacing Options** to open the Paragraph dialog box. From here, you can control exactly how much space there is **before** and **after** the paragraph.

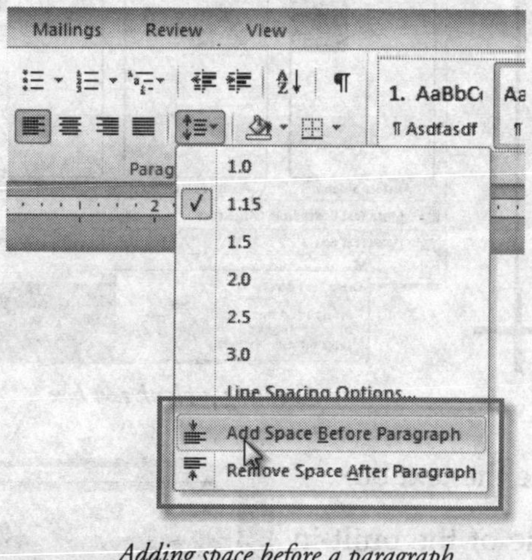

Adding space before a paragraph

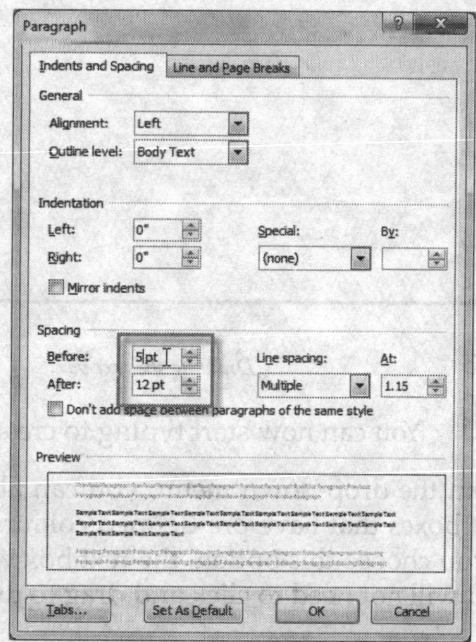

Fine-tuning the paragraph spacing

Text Boxes and WordArt

You may want to **insert a text box** into your document to draw attention to specific text or to have the ability to **easily move text** around within a document. Text boxes are basically treated the same as **shapes**, so you can add the same types of effects to them, and you can even change their shape. If you want, you can format the text inside the text box as **WordArt**, allowing you to apply **3-D effects** and **transformations** to the text itself.

In this lesson, you will learn how to **insert a text box** and format it in various ways including **resizing** and **moving** it, and changing the text box **shape**, **colour**, and **outline**. You will also learn how to create and format **WordArt**.

To Insert a Text box:

- ❑ Select the **Insert** tab on the Ribbon.
- ❑ Click the **Text Box** command in the **Text** group. A drop-down menu will appear.
- ❑ Select **Draw Text Box**.
- ❑ Click and drag on the document to create the text box.

Drawing the text box

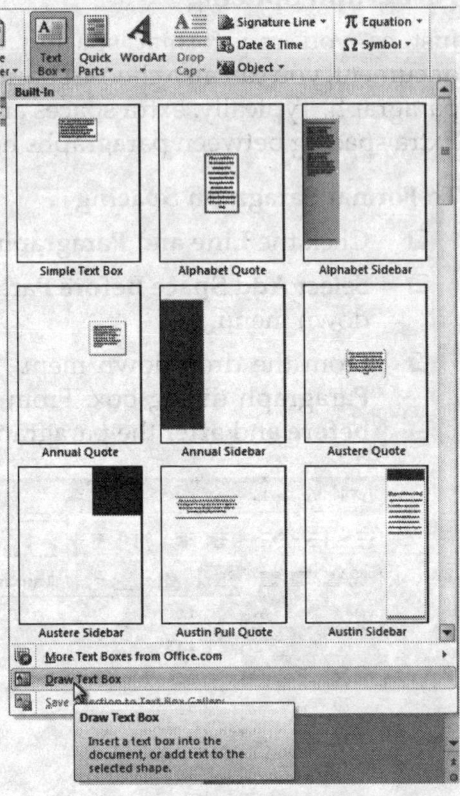

Creating a blank text box

- ❑ You can now start typing to create text inside the text box.

From the drop-down menu, you can also select one of the built-in text boxes that have pre-defined colours, fonts, positions and sizes. If you choose this option, the text box will appear automatically, so you will not need to click and drag to draw it.

To Move a Text Box:

- ❑ Click on the text box.
- ❑ Hover the mouse over one of the edges of the text box. The mouse pointer becomes a **cross with arrows** on each end and looks like this: ✥
- ❑ **Click and drag** the text box to the desired location on the page.

A built-in text box

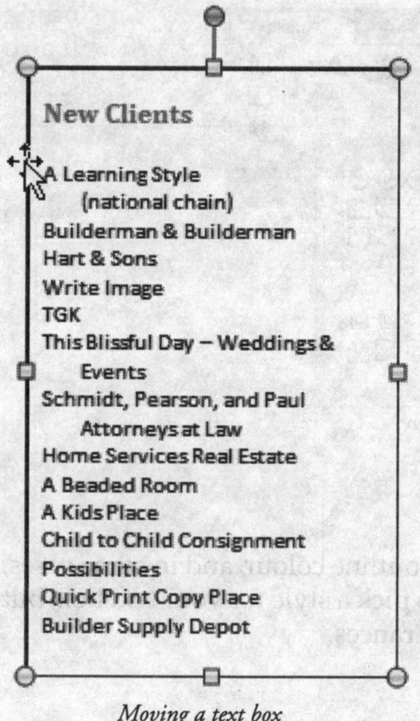

Moving a text box

To Resize a Text Box:

- ❑ Click the text box.
- ❑ Click and drag one of the **sizing handles** on the corners or sides of the text box until it is the desired size.

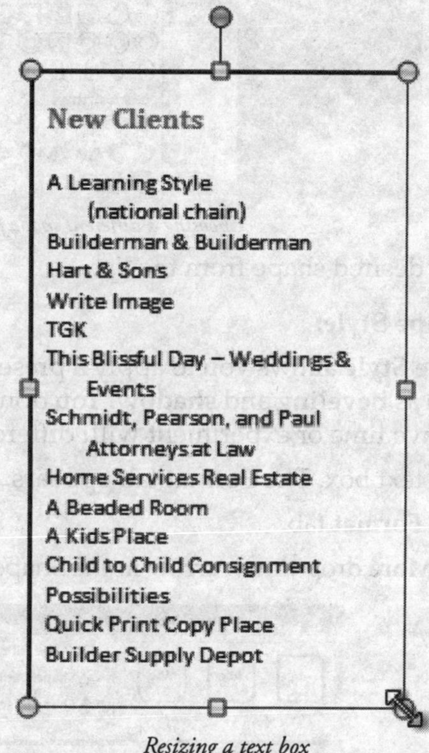

Resizing a text box

If you drag the **sizing handles** on any of the four corners, you will be able to change the **height** and **width** at the same time. The sizing handles on the top or bottom of the text box will only allow you to resize **vertically**, while the handles on the left and right sides will resize the text box **horizontally**.

To Change the Text Box Shape:

- ❑ Select the text box. A new **Format** tab appears with Drawing Tools.
- ❑ Go to the **Format** tab.
- ❑ Click the **Edit Shape** command
- ❑ Click **Change Shape** to display a drop-down list.

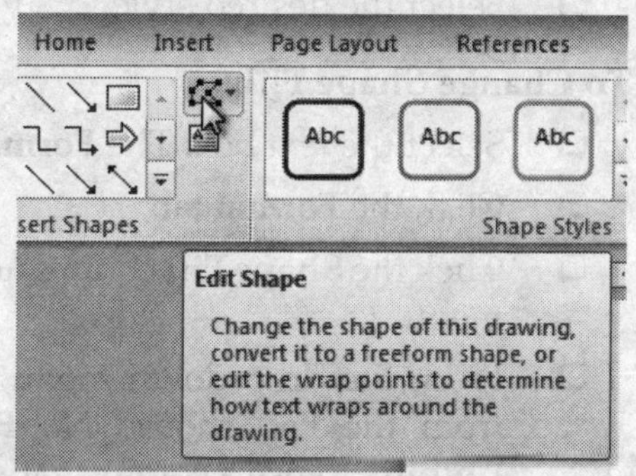

The Edit Shape command

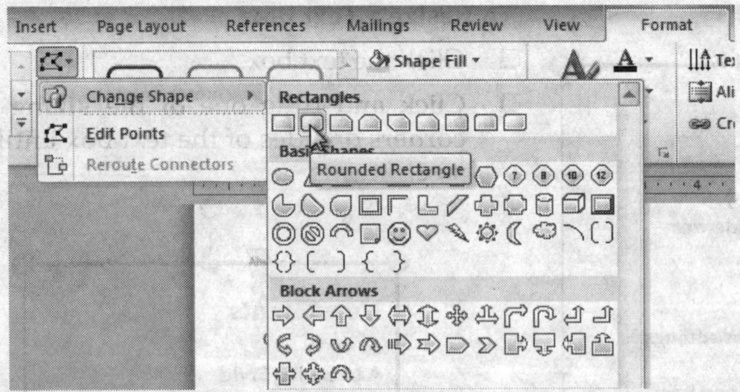

Choosing a different shape for the text box

- ❑ Select the desired shape from the list.

To Choose a Shape Style:

Choosing a **Shape Style** allows you to apply a preset fill and outline colour, and in some cases, other effects such as **beveling** and **shadow**. You don't have to pick a style for your text box, but it can help you save time or experiment with different appearances.

- ❑ Select the text box. The **Format** tab appears.
- ❑ Select the **Format** tab.
- ❑ Click the **More** drop-down arrow in the Shape Styles group to display more style options.

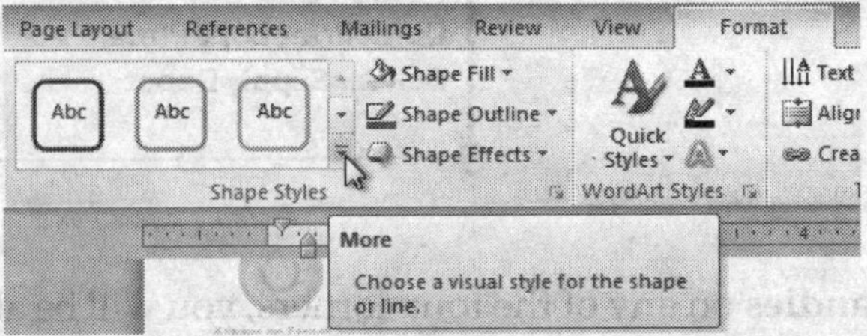

Viewing the Shape Styles

- ❑ Hover the mouse over the styles to see a live preview.
- ❑ Select the desired style.

To Change Shape Fill:

- ❑ Select the text box. The **Format** tab appears.
- ❑ Click the **Format** tab.
- ❑ Click the **Shape Fill** command to display a drop-down menu.
- ❑ From the drop-down menu, you can select a **colour** from the list, choose **No Fill**, or select **More Fill Colours** to use a colour that's not on the list.

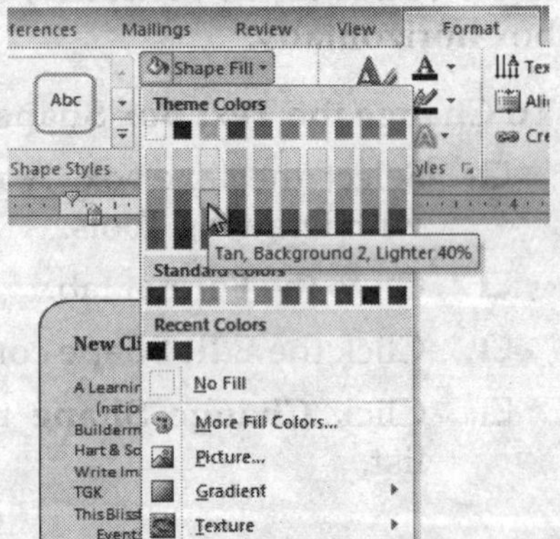

Changing the fill colour

To Change the Shape Outline:

- ❑ Select the text box. The **Format** tab appears.
- ❑ Click the **Shape Outline** command to display a drop-down list.
- ❑ Select a **colour** from the list, choose **No Outline**, or select **More Outline Colours** to use a colour that's not on the list.
- ❑ From the drop-down menu, you can change the outline **colour**, **weight** (thickness), and whether or not it is a **dashed** line.

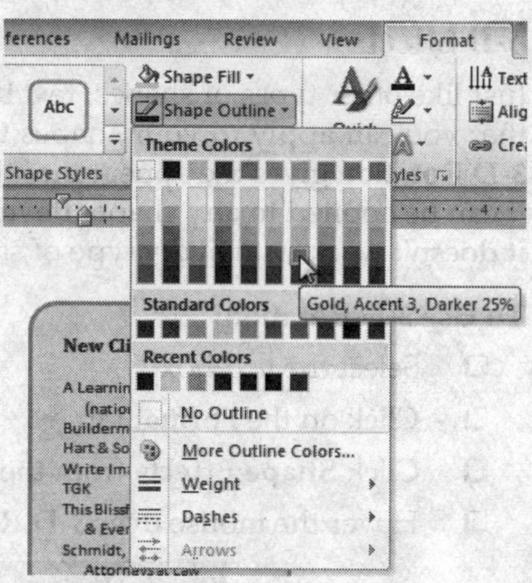

Changing the outline colour

To Change Shadow Effects:

- ❑ Select the text box. The **Format** tab appears.
- ❑ Select the **Format** tab.
- ❑ Click the **Shape Effects** command.
- ❑ Click **Shadow**.
- ❑ Move your mouse over the menu options to see a live preview in your document.

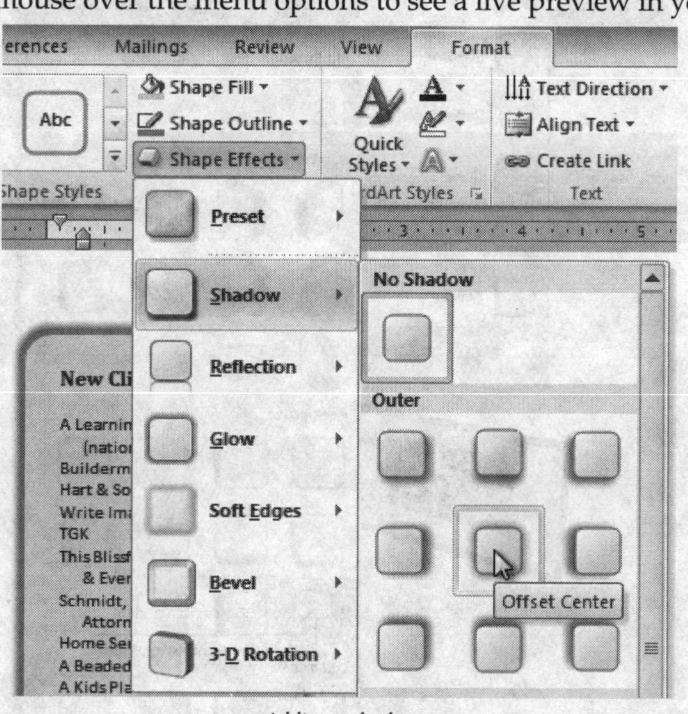

Adding a shadow

- ❑ Click the desired option to select the shadow effect.

To choose a different shadow colour for your shape, select **Shadow Options** from the drop-down menu and click the **Colour** button.

3-D Effects

Just like other types of shapes, text boxes can have **3-D Effects**. There are two kinds of effects that you can apply to your shapes to give them a 3-D appearance: **3-D Rotation** and **Bevel**. **3-D Rotation** gives the appearance that you are viewing the object from a different angle, and it can be applied to any shape. **Bevel** adds thickness and a rounded edge to shapes, however it doesn't work with every type of shape.

To Use 3-D Rotation:

- ❑ Select the text box.
- ❑ Click on the **Format** tab.
- ❑ Click **Shape Effects** from the **Shape Styles** group.
- ❑ Hover the mouse over **3-D Rotation**. A drop-down menu will appear.

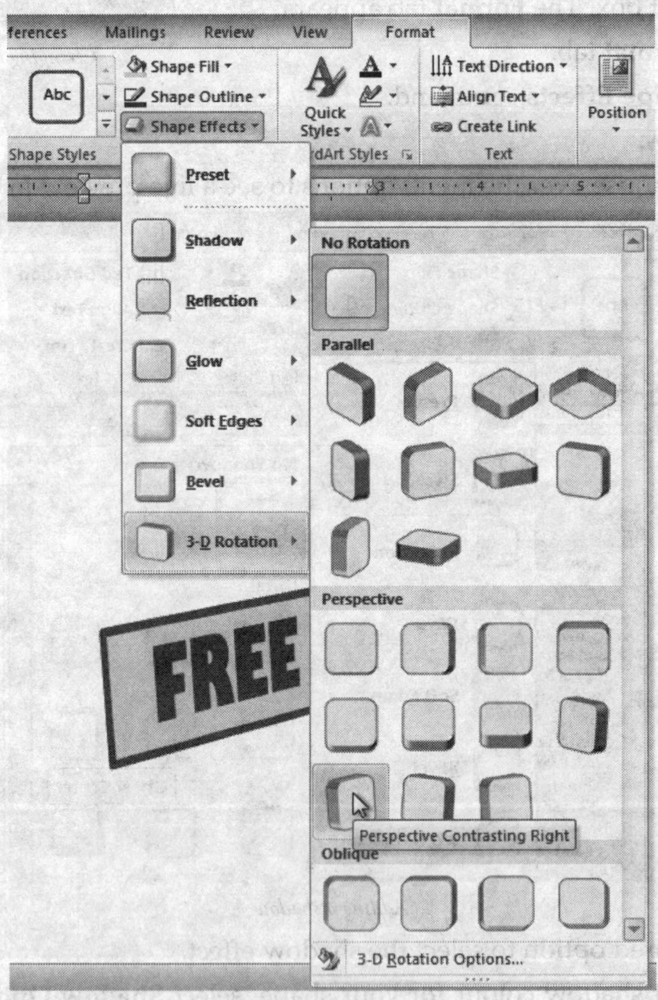

Applying 3-D Rotation to a text box

- Select the desired **rotation preset** from the drop-down menu. You can also click **3-D Rotation Options** if you would prefer to type in custom values.

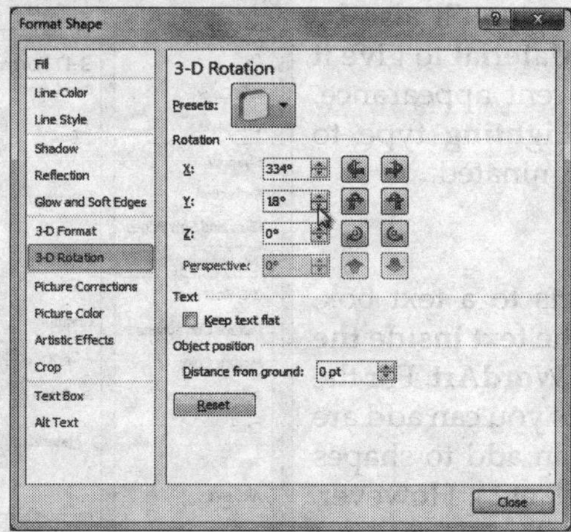

3-D Rotation Options

To Use Bevel:

- Select the text box.
- Click on the **Format** tab.
- Click **Shape Effects** from the **Shape Styles** group.
- Hover the mouse over **Bevel**. A drop-down menu will appear.

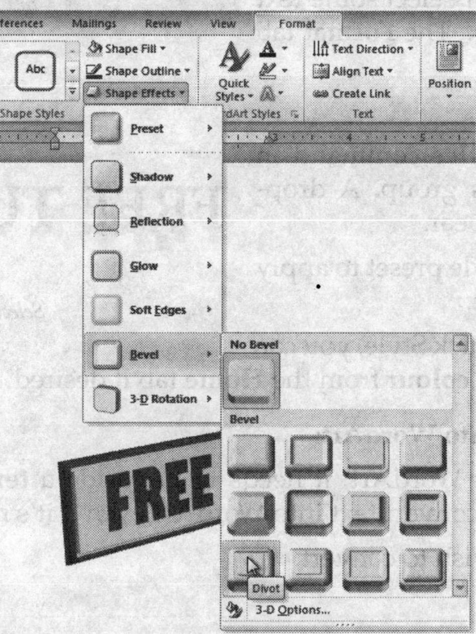

Adding bevel to a text box

- ❑ Select the desired **bevel preset** from the drop-down menu. You can also click **3-D Options** if you would prefer to type in custom values.

If you click on **3-D Options**, you'll also be able to change the shape's **Material** to give it a metal, plastic, or translucent appearance, and you can choose the **Lighting** type to change how the shape is illuminated.

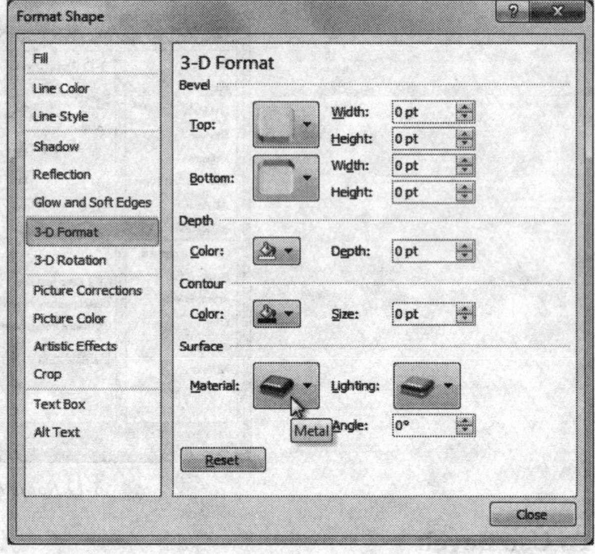

3-D Format Options

Creating WordArt

In addition to adding effects to a text box, you can also add effects to the **text inside the text box**, which is known as **WordArt**. For the most part, the types of effects you can add are the same as the ones you can add to shapes or text boxes (shadow, bevel, etc.). However, you can also **Transform** the text to give it a wavy, slanted, or inflated look.

To Apply a Quick Style to Text:

A **Quick Style** will automatically apply several effects to your text at once. You can then refine the look of your text by adding or modifying text effects.

- ❑ Select the text box, or select some text inside of the text box. The **Format** tab will appear.
- ❑ Click the **Format** tab.
- ❑ Click the **Quick Styles** command in the **WordArt Styles** group. A drop-down menu will appear.
- ❑ Select the desired style preset to apply the style to your text.

Selecting a Quick Style

After you have applied a Quick Style, you can still modify the **font** or **font colour** from the **Home** tab if desired.

To Convert Regular Text into WordArt:

For text to be formatted as WordArt, it needs to be inside a **text box**. However, there is a shortcut that allows you to convert text into WordArt even if it's not in a text box.

- ❑ Select the text you wish to convert.
- ❑ Click the **Insert** tab.
- ❑ Click the **WordArt** command. The **Quick Styles** drop-down menu will appear.

.Converting text to WordArt

- Select the desired **Quick Style**
- Word will automatically create a text box for your text and apply the style to the text.

After converting to WordArt some effects, such as **shadows**, can be added from the **Text Effects** menu in the **Home** tab. When you add effects in this way, it will not place the text in a text box.

To Add or Modify Text Effects:

- Select the text box, or select some text inside of the text box. The **Format** tab will appear.
- Click the **Format** tab.
- Click the **Text Effects** command in the **WordArt Styles** group. A drop-down menu will appear showing the different **effect categories**.

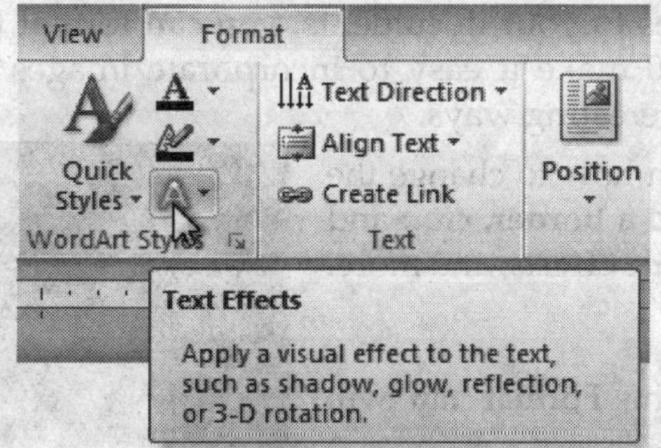

The Text Effects command

- ❑ Hover over an effect category. A drop-down menu will appear. You can hover the mouse over the different presets to see a live preview.

Adding an effect

- ❑ Select the desired effect preset. The effect will be applied to your text. If you want, you can combine several different effects.

Free Tutoring
Cityville High

The finished WordArt

Formatting Pictures

Once you've added pictures to your documents, you can format them in various ways. The **picture tools** in Word 2010 make it easy to incorporate images into your documents and **modify those images** in interesting ways.

In this lesson, you will learn how to change the **picture style** and **shape**, add a **border**, **crop** and **compress** pictures, add **artistic effects**, and more.

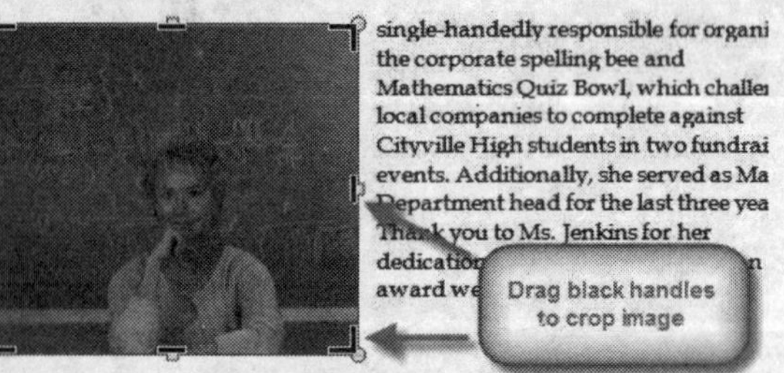

The black cropping handles

To Crop an Image:

- ❑ Select an image. The **Format** tab will appear.
- ❑ Select the **Format** tab.

- ❑ Click the **Crop** command. The black cropping handles appear.
- ❑ Click and drag a **handle** to crop an image.
- ❑ Click the **Crop** command to deselect the crop tool.

Corner handles will allow you to simultaneously crop the image horizontally and vertically.

To Crop an Image to a Shape:

- ❑ Select the image. The **Format** tab will appear.
- ❑ Select the **Format** tab.
- ❑ Click the **Crop** drop-down arrow (below the Crop command). A drop-down menu will appear.
- ❑ Select a shape from the drop-down menu.
- ❑ The image will take the shape that you have selected.

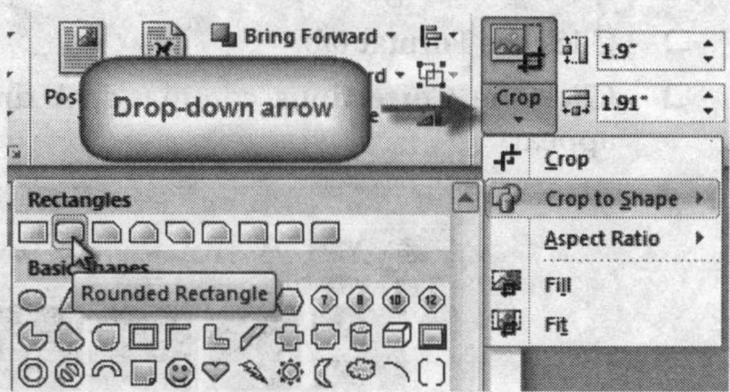

The Crop drop-down arrow and menu

Mary Jenkins Named Teacher of the Year

We are pleased to announce that the 2010 Cityville High teacher of the year is Ms. Mary Jenkins. Ms. Jenkins has worked as a high school math teacher for 16 years and has been with Cityville High for 12 years. In that time she has shown immense dedication to her students and the school. She is single-handedly responsible for

organizing the corporate spelling bee and Mathematics Quiz Bowl, which challenges local companies to complete against Cityville High students in two fundraising events. Additionally, she served as Math Department head for the last three years. Thank you to Ms. Jenkins for her dedication and congratulations for an award well earned!

After cropping to shape

You may want to crop the image to the desired size before cropping it to a shape.

To Add a Border to a Picture:

- ❑ Select the picture.
- ❑ Select the **Format** tab.
- ❑ Click the **Picture Border** command. A drop-down menu will appear.

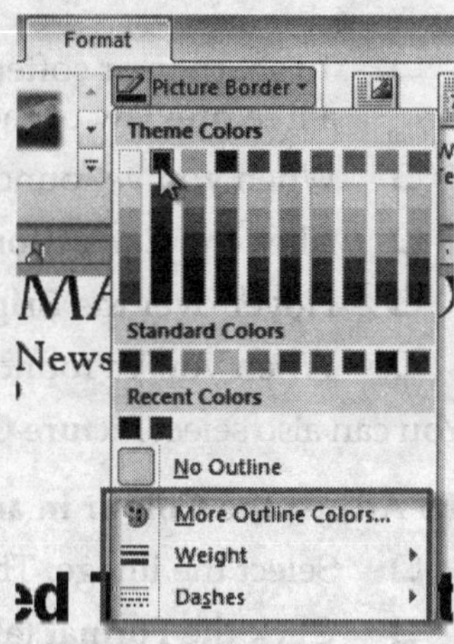

Changing the Picture Border

- ❑ From the drop-down menu, you can select a **colour**, **weight** (thickness), and whether or not the line is **dashed**.

A picture with a blue border

Image Adjustments

To Make Image Corrections:

- ❑ Select the image. The **Format** tab will appear.
- ❑ Click the **Format** tab.
- ❑ Click the **Corrections** command. A drop-down menu will appear.

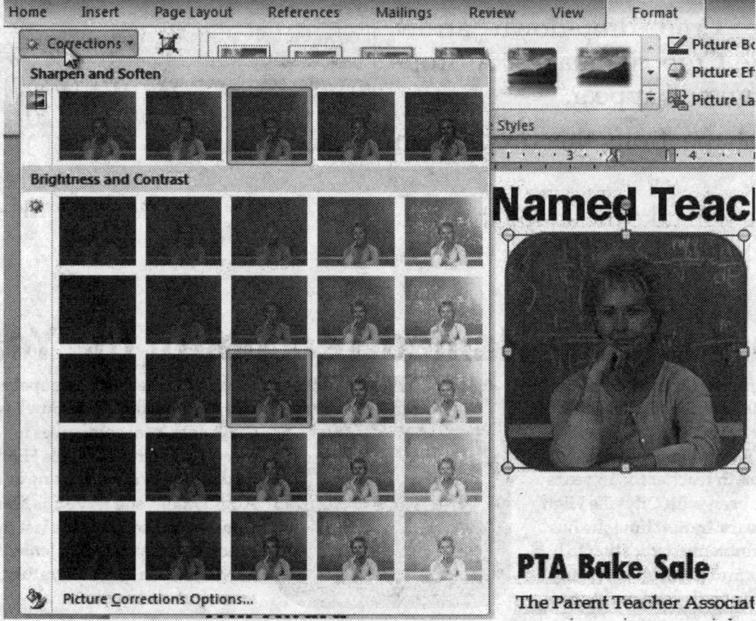

The Picture Corrections menu

- ❑ To sharpen or soften the image, hover over the **Sharpen and Soften** presets. You'll see a live preview of the preset in the document.
- ❑ When you've found a preset you like, click on it to select it.
- ❑ Click the **Corrections** command again.
- ❑ Hover over the **Brightness and Contrast** presets to see a live preview.
- ❑ When you've found one you like, click on it to select it.

You can also select **Picture Corrections Options** from the drop-down menu to refine the settings.

To Adjust the Colour in an Image:

- ❑ Select the image. The **Format** tab will appear.
- ❑ Click the **Format** tab.

- Click the **Colour** command. A drop-down menu will appear.

The Picture Colour menu

From the drop-down menu, you can choose a preset from each of the three categories:

- **Colour Saturation:** Controls how vivid the colours are in the image.
- **Colour Tone:** Controls the "temperature" of the colour, from **cool** to **warm**.
- **Recolour:** Controls the overall colour of the image. Use this option to make the image **black and white**, **grayscale**, or to **colourize** it with a different colour.

You can also select **Picture Colour Options** from the drop-down menu to refine the settings.

Artistic Effects and Styles

To Apply an Artistic Effect:

- Select the picture. The **Format** tab will appear.
- Click the **Format** tab.
- Click the **Artistic Effects** command. A drop-down menu will appear.
- Hover over the different presets to see a Live Preview of each one.
- When you've found a preset you like, click on it to select it.
- To adjust the settings for the effect, click **Artistic Effects** again and select **Artistic Effect Options**.

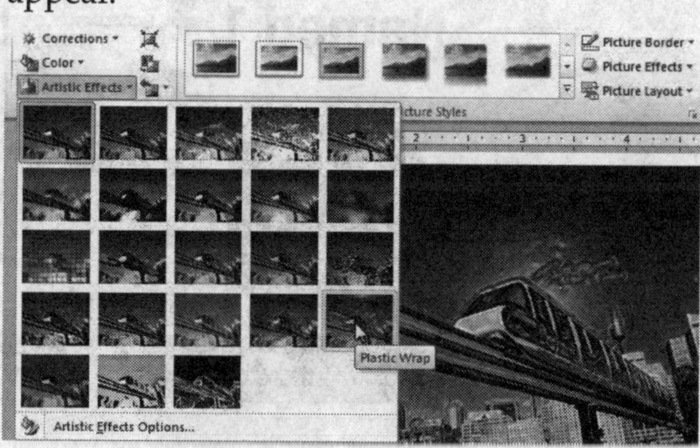

The Artistic Effects menu

Many **Clip Art** images do not allow you apply artistic effects. Generally speaking, the ones that look hand-drawn or painted do not work, while photographs do.

To Apply a Picture Style:

- Select the picture. The **Format** tab will appear.
- Select the **Format** tab.
- Click the **More** drop-down arrow to display all the picture styles.

Viewing the Picture Styles

- Hover over a picture style to display a live preview of the style in the document.
- Select the desired style.
- To refine the picture style, click the **Picture Effects** command to see the **Effects** drop-down menu. You may remember that we talked about the Effects menu in the *Working with Shapes lesson;* you can review that lesson if you'd like more information.

After adding a Picture Style

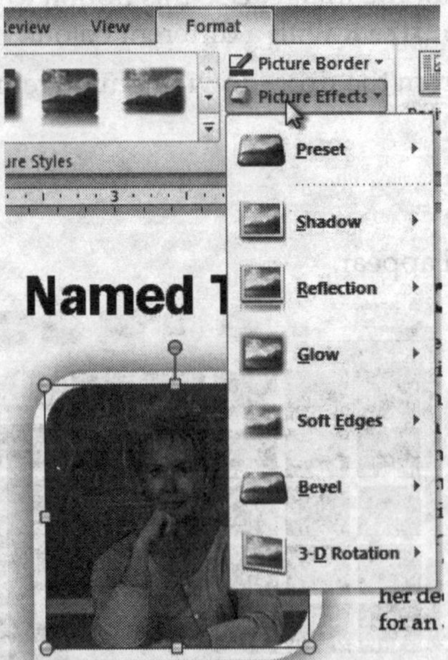

The Picture Effects menu

About Background Removal

With **Background Removal**, Word uses special algorithms to determine which parts of the image are the background and then removes those areas from the image. This can give your images a cleaner appearance, and if you're printing your document, it can also save ink.

Before

After

To Remove the Background from an Image:

- ❑ Click on the image. The **Format** tab will appear.
- ❑ Click the **Format** tab.
- ❑ Click the **Remove Background** command.
- ❑ Word will try to guess which part of the image is the background, and it will mark that area with a **magenta** fill. It will also place a box around the image with selection handles.

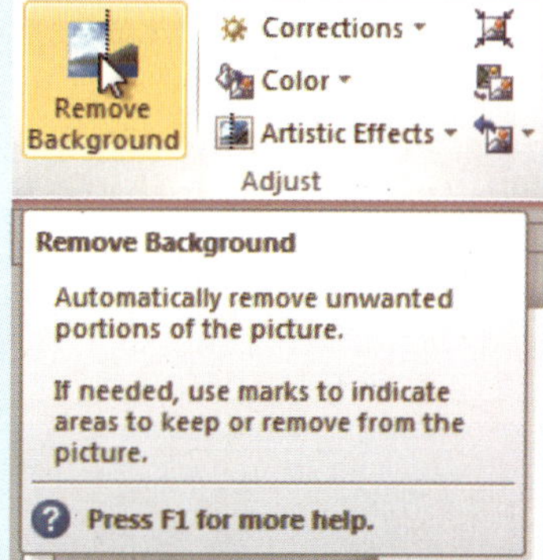

The Remove Background command

Background areas are marked with magenta

- ❑ Drag the selection handles until all of the foreground is inside the box. After you do this, Word may re-adjust the background.
- ❑ At this point, you may need to help Word decide which parts of the image are **foreground** and which parts are **background**. You can do this by using the **Mark Areas to Keep** and **Mark Areas to Remove** commands:

- If Word has marked part of the foreground magenta, click **Mark Areas to Keep** and draw a line in that region of the image.
- If part of the background has not been marked with magenta, click **Mark Areas to Remove** and draw a line in that region of the image.

❑ After you add your marks, Word will readjust the image.

Marking areas to remove

After adding markings

❑ When you're satisfied with the image, click **Keep Changes**. All of the magenta areas will be removed from the image.

The finished image

❑ You can adjust the image at any time by clicking the **Remove Background** command again.

As with **artistic effects**, Background Removal will not work with some **Clip Art** images.

SmartArt Graphics

SmartArt allows you to **visually communicate information** rather than simply using text. Illustrations can really enhance your document, and SmartArt makes using graphics especially easy. In this lesson, you will learn how to **insert a SmartArt graphic**, modify the **colour** and **effects**, and change the **organization** of the graphic.

To Insert a SmartArt Illustration:

- ❑ Place the insertion point in the document where you want the graphic to appear.
- ❑ Select the **Insert** tab.
- ❑ Select the **SmartArt** command in the Illustrations group. A dialog box appears.

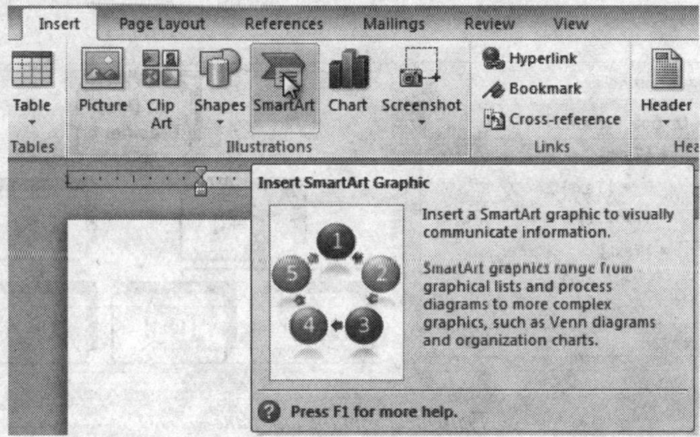

The SmartArt command

- ❑ Select a **category** on the left of the dialog box and review the SmartArt graphics that appear in the **center**.
- ❑ Select the desired SmartArt graphic and click **OK**.

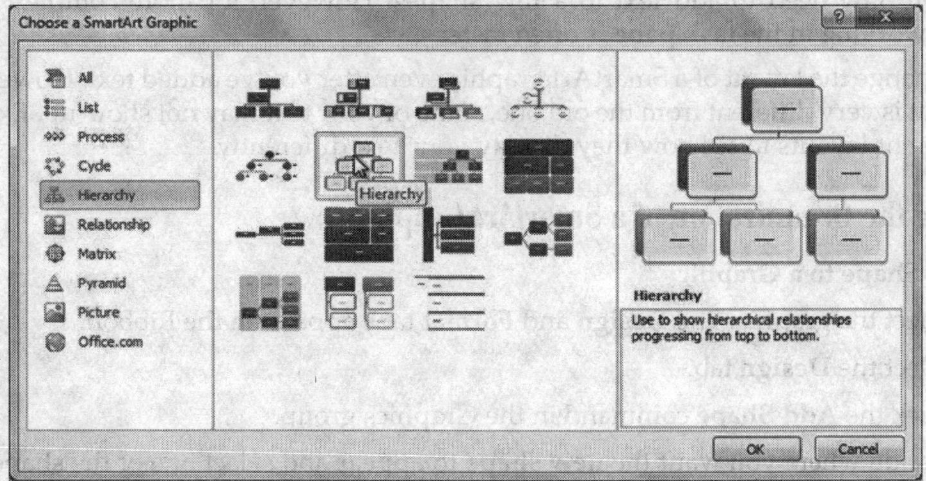

Selecting a SmartArt graphic

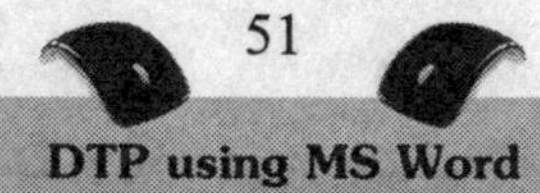

To see more details about a graphic, click on any image, and a larger preview of the graphic with **additional text details** will appear on the **right side** of the dialog box.

To Add Text to a SmartArt Graphic:

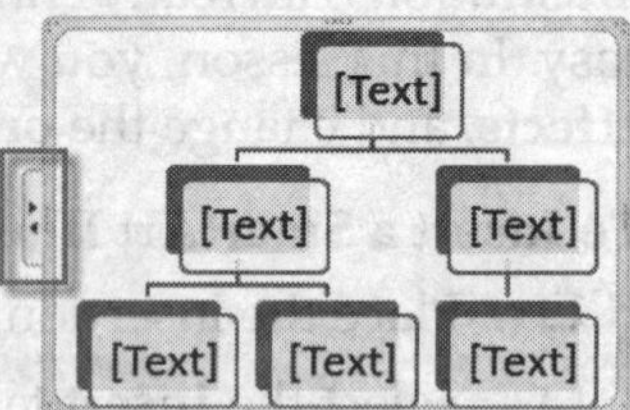

The arrow to open the task pane

- ❑ Select the graphic. A border will appear around it with an **arrow** on the left side.
- ❑ Click the **arrow** on the left side of the graphic to open the task pane.
- ❑ Enter text next to each bullet in the task pane. The information will appear in the graphic, and will resize to fit inside the shape.

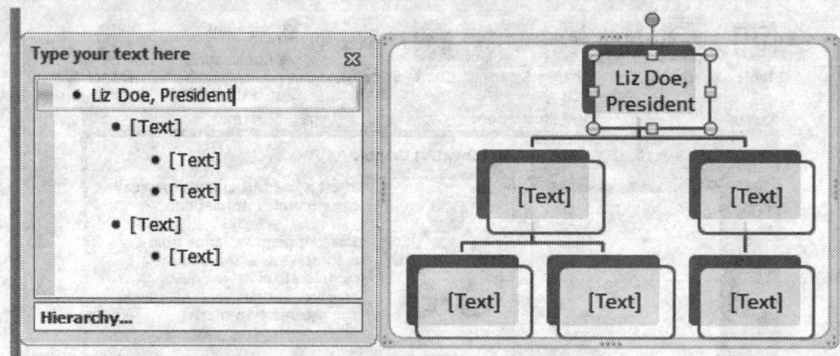

Typing text into the task pane

- ❑ To add a new shape, press **Enter**. A new bullet will appear in the task pane, and a new shape will appear in the graphic.

You can also add text by clicking on the desired shape and then typing your text. This works well if you only need to add text to a **few shapes**. However, for more complex SmartArt graphics, working in the **task pane** is often faster.

You can change the layout of a SmartArt graphic even after you've added text. However, if the new layout is very different from the old one, some of your text may not show up. Experiment with different layouts to see how they display your text differently.

Changing the Organization of a SmartArt Graphic

To Add a Shape to a Graphic:

- ❑ Select the graphic. The **Design** and **Format** tabs appear on the Ribbon.
- ❑ Select the **Design** tab.
- ❑ Click the **Add Shape** command in the Graphics group.
- ❑ Decide where you want the **new shape** to appear and select one of the shapes nearby the desired location.

- ❑ Select **Add Shape Before** or **Add Shape After**. If we wanted to add a superior or a subordinate, we could select the **Add Shape Above** or **Add Shape Below** options.

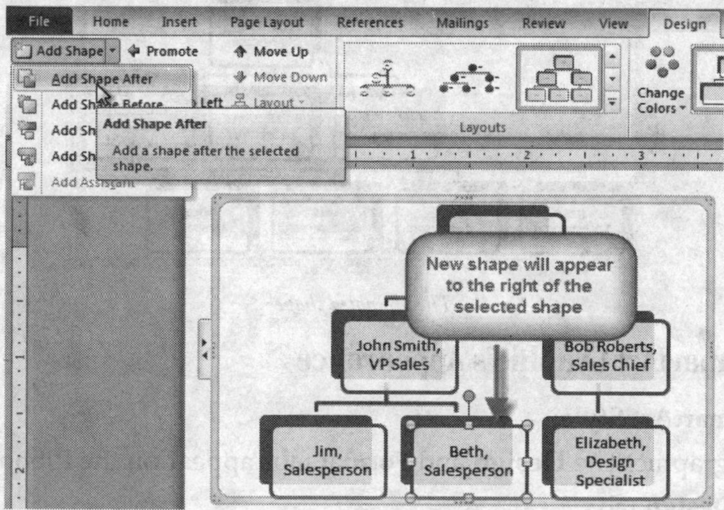

Adding a shape

You can change the layout of a SmartArt graphic even after you've added text. However, if the new layout is very different from the old one, some of your text may not show up. Experiment with different layouts to see how they display your text differently.

To Move Shapes Using the Promote or Demote Commands:

- ❑ Select the graphic. The **Design** and **Format** tabs appear on the Ribbon.
- ❑ Select the **Design** tab.
- ❑ Select the **shape** you would like to move.
- ❑ Click the **Promote** or **Demote** commands in the Create Graphic group.

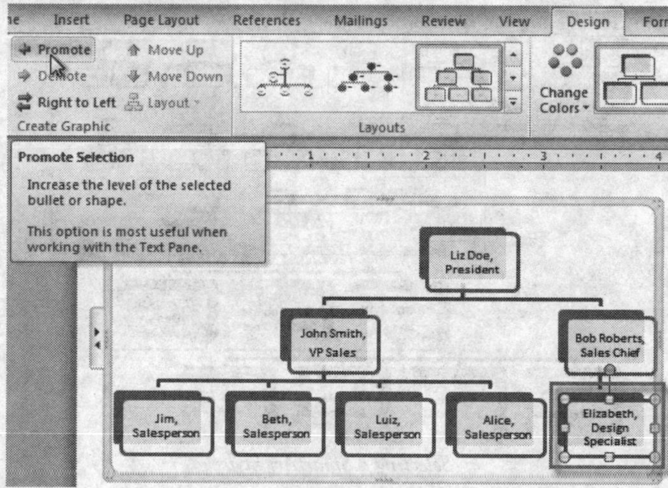

Promoting a shape

- The shape will move up one level.

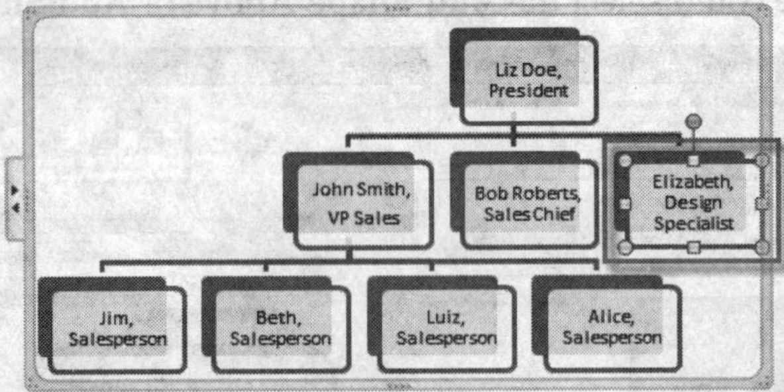

The promoted shape

Modifying the SmartArt Graphic's Appearance

To Change the SmartArt Style:

- Select the graphic. The **Design** and **Format** tabs appear on the Ribbon.
- Click the **Design** tab.
- In the **SmartArt Styles** group, click the **More** drop-down arrow to view all of the styles.

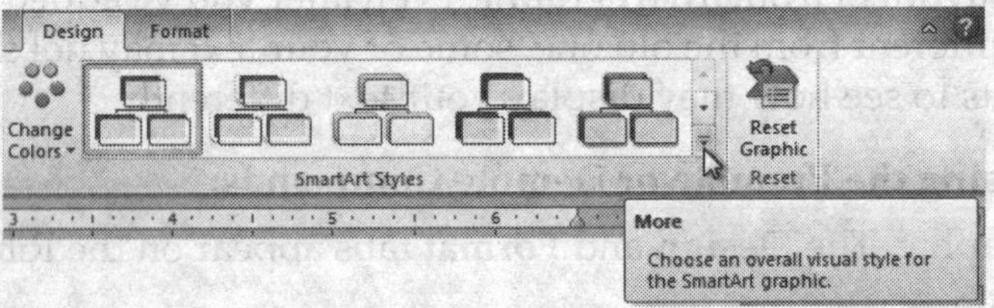

Viewing the SmartArt Styles

- Hover the mouse over each style to see a live preview.

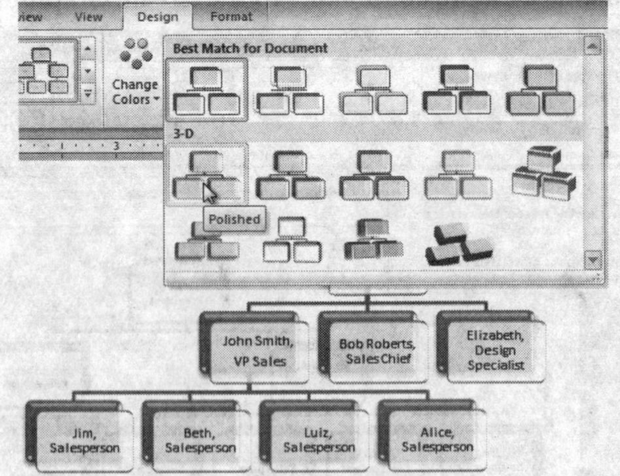

Selecting a SmartArt Style

- Select the desired style.

To Change the Colour Scheme:

Word provides a variety of **colour schemes** to use with SmartArt. The colour schemes use **Theme Colours**, so they will vary depending on which **Theme** you are using.

- ❑ Select the graphic. The **Design** and **Format** tabs appear on the Ribbon.
- ❑ Select the **Design** tab.
- ❑ Click the **Change Colours** command. A drop-down menu appears showing various colour schemes.
- ❑ Select the desired colour scheme.

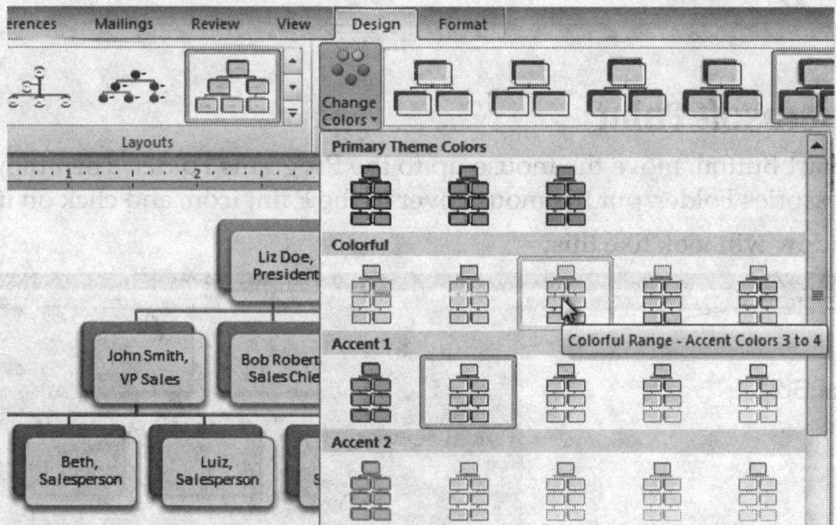

Selecting a new colour scheme

If you want to change the appearance of a **single shape** within the SmartArt graphic, select the shape and click the **Format** tab. You can then modify the **Shape Style, colour, effects** or other settings for that shape.

This is a brief and to the point discussion an how to do DTP using MS Word. It is very simple and with practice you'll master each and every technique easily.

DTP using Microsoft Paint

Launch Microsoft Paint

Click on the Start Button, move the mouse up to the Programs Folder. Then move the mouse up to the Accessories Folder. put the mouse over to the Paint icon, and click on it.

The Paint window will look like this:

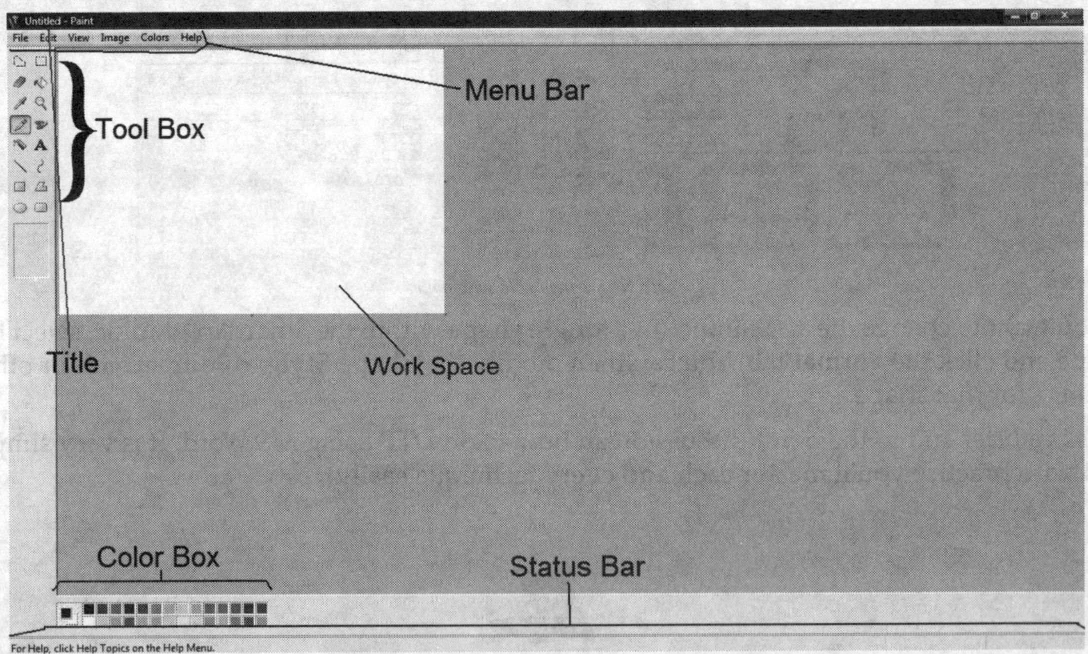

You will need to familiarise yourself with the look and layout of this window, as it is very similar to other paint/image manipulation programs such as Adobe Photoshop. Learning the basic features of Paint will make it easier for you to learn other, more complex programs that much more easy.

First, let's maximise the Paint window by clicking the rectangular button to the left of the X button on the right side of the Paint window's Title Bar. The Paint window should now fill out the entire screen. (If you're very new to using Windows, click on the Title Bar link to learn more about how the Title Bar works.)

You don't really use the Title Bar for anything, but it's good to know about it. Now that you do, you should be ready to learn about using the tools of Paint.

Title Bar

Understanding how to read the title bar is a basic skill in Windows. The Title Bar is indicated by the red circle in the illustration at left. The Icon (at far left) gives you a clue as to what program the window belongs to. In this case, the Icon shows that the window belongs to Microsoft Paint. To the right of the title bar, you'll see some text. The first bit of text is the name of the file that is currently open in this program. Since we've just launched Paint, we see a new (blank) document, which is named "untitled" by default. The next bit of text tells us again that this window is a Paint window, just like the Icon did. It's redundant, but redundancy is common to the Windows interface.

At the right side of the tool bar, you'll see three buttons: From left to right, they are: *Minimise, Maximise/Restore,* and *Close*. If you click on **Minimise**, the window will shrink down and disappear, leaving only the window tab on the task bar (usually located the very bottom of the screen) to let you know that the window is still open. Click tab to bring the window back to its previous size. **Maximize/ Restore** will switch the window between taking up the full size of the screen and some smaller portion of it. When **Restored**, you can re-size the window by clicking along the edge of the window and dragging it to the desired size. You can also move the window about by clicking and holding the Title Bar and dragging the mouse around. When **Maximized**, the window takes up the entire screen and can't be moved around or re-sized. Clicking on the **Close** button will shut the program down completely.

The Tools

Microsoft Paint has an assortment of painting Tools that you can use for drawing shapes and applying colour to areas of your image in various ways. You switch between tools by clicking on the appropriate Icon on the Toolbar, which is located on the left side of the Paint window. The Toolbar looks like this:

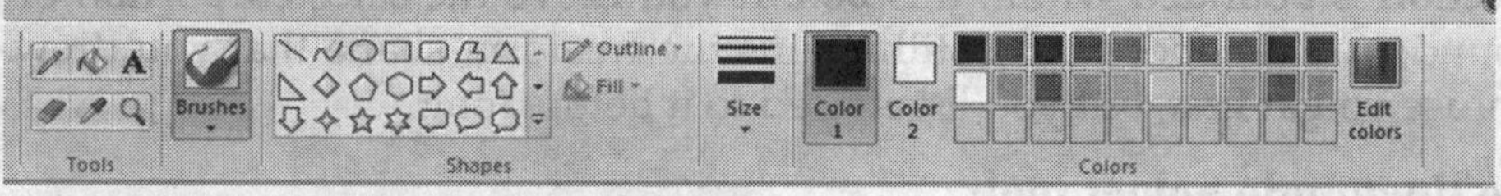

The top row of Icons are the Selection Tools.

The next row has the Eraser tool and the Fill tool Icons.

The third row has the Eye Dropper tool and the Magnifying Glass tool Icons. The fourth row has the Pencil tool and the Paint Brush tool Icons.

The fifth row has the Airbrush tool and the Text tool Icons. The sixth row has the Line tool and the Curve tool Icons.

The seventh row has the Rectangle Drawing tool and the Polygon Drawing tool Icons.

The Eighth row has the Oval Drawing Tool and the Rounded Rectangle Drawing Tool icons.

The bottom portion of the Toolbar changes when you select a tool to reveal additional options or settings for that tool.

Most of the Tools are used to apply colour in some way to a portion of the image. In order to use these tools, you'll first want to make sure that you have selected the correct colour in the Colour Palette.

If this is your first time visiting this page, I suggest that you start out with learning about the Pencil Tool, and then following the links in order from there.

In addition to the various Tools that Paint places at your disposal, you'll also have a number of useful commands that can be accessed through the **Menus**.

Microsoft Paint: Tools

The Selection Tools

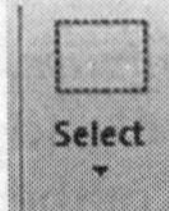

These tools are used to select portions of the image you're working with. These selections can then be moved around, copied, or edited without affecting the rest of the image.

To use the Freeform Select tool:

- ❑ Click on the Freeform Select tool Icon.
- ❑ With the left button, click on your image wherever you want to begin the selection. Drag the mouse around to create the outline of the freeform shape of your selection. Be careful! The mouse is tricky to use. It may help to zoom in using the Magnifying Glass tool. Zoom in close so you can see what you're working with more clearly, and to control the mouse with better precision.
- ❑ When you finish outlining your freeform selection shape, release the mouse button.
- ❑ You will notice that the freeform shape that you had been drawing has just mysteriously turned into a rectangle! What gives? Actually, your freeform shape is still preserved; the selection, however, is outlined in a rectangular-shaped guide box. The freeform selection is bounded within this box. If you move the selected portion of the image around, you'll notice that it still retains the freeform shape that you drew. This may confuse you at first, but you'll get used to it before long.

To use the Rectangle Select tool:

- ❑ Click on the Rectangle Select tool Icon.
- ❑ With the left button, click and hold the button to begin your selection. Where you click will become one of the corners of the rectangular selection area.
- ❑ Drag the mouse diagonally to where you want the opposite corner of the rectangular area to be.
- ❑ Release the mouse button.

The Rectangular selection will also have a rectangular shaped guide box around it. Things you can do with the selected area:

Copy or Cut and Paste: To copy the selection, press Ctrl-C. To cut the selection from the image, press Ctrl-X. After Copying or Cutting, you can Paste the selection by pressing Ctrl-V. By

Pasting multiple times, you can achieve a mosaic or collage-like effect.

Move: Left-click anywhere inside the guide box and hold down the button to "pick up" the selection, and then drag the mouse to move the selection to another area of the image. It will "float" over the rest of the image, allowing you to position it wherever you want it to be. Release the mouse button to "let go" of the selection.

Tip

If you hold down the Shift key as you drag your selection around, it will paste multiple copies of the image, creating a sort of blurred effect.

Stretch: The guide box around your selection can be re-sized. You can resize by clicking on the square-shaped tabs located at the corners and the middle sections of the guide box, holding the mouse button down, and then dragging the mouse to change the size of the selection. Release the mouse button when the selection is the size you want it to be. You can make it bigger or smaller, and achieve a distorted effect by "squashing" or "stretching" the selection to make it either wider/narrower or taller/shorter than its original proportions.

Apply Effects: You can apply any of the effects from the Image Menu directly to the active selection rather than to the whole image.

De-selecting the area: To de-select the area, either activate a different tool by clicking on it in the tool bar, or make a new selection. You can't have more than one selection active at a time. Once the selection is de-selected, it becomes part of the image again, and will cover over whatever it may have been laying over.

Example:

Using selections to combine two separate images. This example uses selections in several ways to achieve interesting results. This page uses a lot of graphics to show step-by-step the procedures used in using the Selection Tools, so I've set it up as a separate page, to decrease the amount of time it takes to download.

After you've finished looking at the example, please proceed to learn about the Menu commands.

You are also missing the Ctrl-drag feature in selection tool description, which is quite significant feature. If you hold down ctrl when you begin to move a selection, it will create an instant copy which you can then position. This is especially useful with the transparent selection mode, you know, those two buttons in the selection mode you don't talk about.

One of the things I use transparent copying for is to create a 50% raster. It takes some patience but starting in zoom helps and it works like this:

- ❑ Draw a 45 degree line (using shift with line tool)
- ❑ Copy the line right next to itself, leaving one pixel gap
- ❑ Select both lines and copy, repeat. You should end up with a raster that has every other pixel white and every other something else.

Transparent copies are also superior to freeform selection in some cases. In your selection tool example you could've painted the edge pixels with background colour before moving it to the new picture. This way you could've avoided the cruft near the edges and made it look like a better fit.

I have mentioned the 50% raster above, there's a very nice use for it in the transparent copying, requiring two steps. The first step is to create a purple-on-white 50% raster using the technique I've described above. Once you have the raster made, use transparent copying to put the raster on top of another image, and you should end up with an image that has every other pixel purple. After this, choose purple as your background colour and keep the transparent mode when you copy it elsewhere. If you followed the steps properly, you should have image with a fake 50% transparency, which you can place on top of another image. For extra smoothness, do this with images that have been scaled up 200% and then scale them down afterwards, and it will no longer be a fake raster, MS Paint will merge the pixels.

Regarding rasters, the black & white mode you can select in the image->attributes menu is perfect for creating transparency masks for the above technique.

Eraser

The Eraser tool is simple to use. Just click on it to select it, then click on the part of the image that you want to erase. "Erasing" changes the erased part of the image back to the background colour of the image file. This is usually white, but can be changed to other colours using the colour palette.

The size of the eraser can be changed by clicking on the Options portion of the Toolbar when the Eraser is active. Use a smaller eraser to go after small details, the larger eraser to wipe out larger areas of the image.

Note: Unfortunately, the eraser does not come in alternate shapes. But, if you want to use a round "eraser" just set your paint brush to the size and use the background colour (paint by using the right-button on the mouse) – it will work just like the eraser! After a while, this might make you wonder why the Eraser is even there. It seems pretty redundant. The best I can figure is it gives you the option of having a separate tool for erasing so that you don't have to continually change the shape and size of the paintbrush when you want to use it for actual colouring.

Example:

Here I used the eraser to isolate the portrait of Andrew Jackson from a $20 bill, and get rid of everything else. When you're doing work like this, the three most important things are a steady hand, patience, and zooming in close with the Magnifying Glass tool.

The Eraser in Paint isn't a simple eraser tool but erasing with right button is a colour replacer tool. Choose the colour you want to replace in foreground, and the new colour in background, and use the eraser tool with right mouse button – now it will only erase the one colour you have chosen in foreground! It is very useful for shading, colouring black lines and many other techniques.

Fill Tool

The fill tool applies colour (or "paint") to a large area of the image. The Icon for the Fill Tool resembles a pouring jar of paint. Just like if you were pouring a liquid in real life, the Fill Tool's "paint" will fill an area's shape with colour.

You have to be careful when using the Fill Tool for this reason: if you click in an unbounded area of the image, the colour will "spill" out and fill more of the image than you originally bargained for, possibly obliterating parts of the image that you wanted to save. Look closely before applying the Fill tool to an area to make sure it is bounded on all sides and that no "paint" can "seep out" and get where it's not supposed to go. If this happens by accident sometime, don't panic. Just Undo the Fill tool by pressing Ctrl-Z, find the "leak" and close it with the pencil or line tool, and then re-apply the Fill.

There are no special options for the Fill Tool.

Example:

In this example, I used the Fill Tool to fill in different regions in this abstract composition with different colours.

Eyedropper

The Eyedropper tool has only one function, but it is a useful one. The eyedropper can be used to "pick up" colours that you've already used in an image. Say you're working with an image with many shades of Green. You want to pick a specific shade, but there are several that are so similar that it's difficult for your eye to distinguish between them. Just click on the eyedropper, and click on the exact portion of the image that contains the colour that you want. The active colour for your paint tools will automatically change to the colour that you picked with the eyedropper. Additionally, the Eyedropper will automatically switch over to the previously selected tool, enabling you to rapidly resuming work on the image with the colour you just selected.

Tip

You can use the Eyedropper tool to select colour for the background colour by using the right button on your mouse.

Magnifying Glass Tool

The Magnifying Glass, or Zoom tool, can be used to get a closer, more detailed view of an image. This is very useful if you're working in close with the fine details of a part of an image. When you activate the Magnifying Glass tool, you'll have an option to select between 1x, 2x, 6x, and 8x magnification. You can click on the part of the image that you want the magnification to centre on. This will not affect the actual image in any way, just how it appears on your screen. Once you zoom in, the magnifying glass will automatically switch back to whatever tool you were using before.

Example:

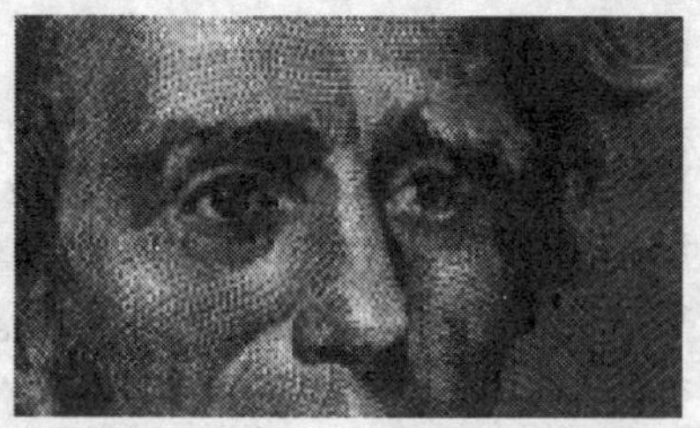

Not too much needs to be said that isn't sufficiently demonstrated by the illustration above. Compare it to the original-sized picture on the Eraser Tool page. With the Zoom Tool, you can get up close and personal with every pixel in your image! If you've got a shaky hand, or need to work with tiny details, the Magnifying Glass will soon become your best friend!

Pencil Tool

The Pencil tool is your basic drawing tool. You can draw in different colours, but other than that there are no other options. The pencil's stroke is a single pixel wide, which makes it useful for working with fine details, but a poor choice for filling in large areas of the image with colour.

Example:

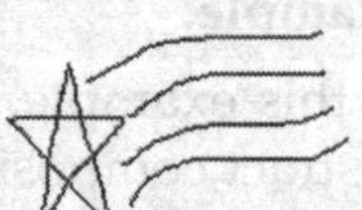

You can do simple line drawings with the pencil if you have the coordination to guide the mouse with great care.

> **Tip**
>
> To draw straight lines, hold down the Shift key as you draw with the pencil. Your pencil line will be limited to horizontal, vertical, or a 45-degree diagonal.

Paint Brush Tool

The Paint Brush tool is similar to the pencil, but has more features. It too can be used in different colours, but the shape and size of the Paint Brush can also be changed. You can use square, round, and slanted shaped brushes, of various sizes, selected in the Toolbar Options.

Example:

You can use the various paintbrush shapes and sizes to create a variety of effects. Draw thick freehand lines like you would do with the pencil, or fill in colour in unbounded areas.

> **Tip**
>
> If you hold down Shift as you paint with the Paint Brush tool, you can make perfectly straight horizontal or vertical strokes. However, unlike the Pencil, you cannot do 45 degree angle diagonal lines with this method.

Airbrush Tool

The airbrush tool is a bit more complicated than the regular paintbrush. Instead of applying colours to the image evenly, it applies it gradually. The "spray" is a semi-random distribution of pixels. Gradually, as the airbrush is left hovering over the same area while it is painting, it will fill up with colour. A skillful artist can use this effect to create subtle differences in tone and variation, and even achieve the illusion that colours are mixing, all by using the airbrush. However, It does take some time to getting used to. The airbrush can paint at three different sizes, selected through the Options portion of the Toolbar.

Example:

Text tool

The Text tool is used to position and enter text into your image. The text may be of any colour or font that you have active on your computer. You also have the option to set the text tool to work so that the background colour is used for the "fill space" around the text, or if the text will be applied with transparent "fill space", allowing the image to show through behind the text.

To use the Text tool, simply select it from the Toolbar, and then drag a rectangle within your image. This rectangle will be the boundaries within which the text will appear. Once you've drawn the text boundary, a floating window will appear, which will enable you to choose the font, size, and formatting (bold, italic, or underline) for your text. Unfortunately, the text formatting will be uniform. If you want to mix fonts, colours, sizes, or formats, you'll have to use the text tool several times, with different settings each time. This means you'll have to be careful in order to make sure that the different applications of text line up properly. You may need to use the selection tool quite a bit to move bits and pieces of text around, and this can be quite tedious. Remember to use the Undo command if you make a mistake, by pressing Ctrl-Z.

As long as the text tool is active, you'll see that rectangular boundary around the edge of the text area. You can move this rectangle around by clicking and dragging on the very border of it, or resize it by clicking on the tab buttons at the corners and midpoints of the edges. But be careful; if you click outside of the boundary accidentally, which is pretty easy to do, the text box will deselect, and the text tool will think you're trying to draw a new text box, and your old text will be set in place.

Once the text is in place, it will no longer behave as text, but rather as pixels. The pixels just happen to be in the proper arrangement to appear to be text in some font; they can't be edited or moved as though a distinct object in the image.

Here's some samples of text created by the Text Tool in various colours, fonts, sizes, and styles. Notice that these words are just graphics; if you try to highlight them with the mouse to Copy them, you'll find that you can't do it. This is because the text in Paint is not "live" once it has been put into the image.

Line Tool

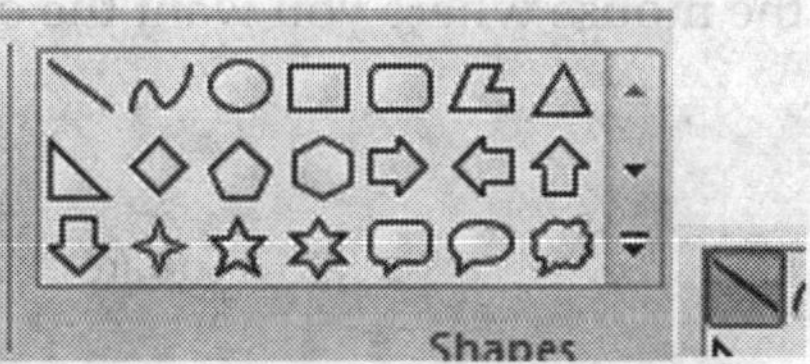

The Straight Line tool is pretty easy to work with. You can change the colour and width of your lines by using the Toolbar Options. All you have to do to draw a line is click on the image where you want one of the line's endpoints to be, then drag over to where you want the other endpoint to be. Then release the button. Easy! But the lines can only be straight.

Example:

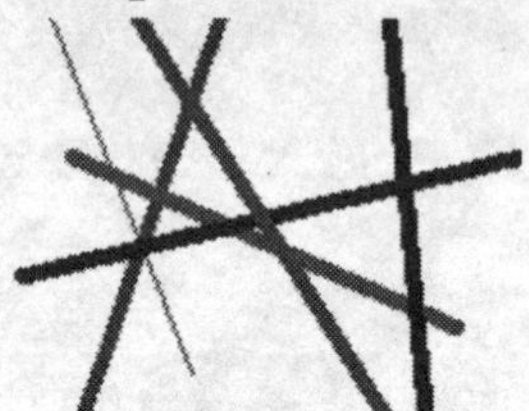

Curve Tool

The Curve tool is trickier to use than the Line tool. It can be difficult to learn how to use, and it is difficult to explain. Your best bet is to experiment with it, but be patient, because it will take a lot of getting used to before you get very good at making curved lines that are the shape that you want.

Like the straight Line tool, the Curve tool can make lines in various thicknesses and colours.

Try experimenting with various techniques for making lines. Try clicking and dragging to make one kind of line, or clicking and releasing two endpoints. Click a third point to determine the curve. Try dragging an already drawn, but still active, multi-point line to distort its curve.

The Curve tool can be very frustrating, especially for beginners, specially since the Undo command can only be used to undo the last change you've made to your image. Just keep practising!

Example:

Look at these curved lines made using the curve tool. The green line has two bends in it (the maximum). The red line just has one curve. Just draw a line like you would with the straight line tool, then click and drag to bend the line and make it curve. The grey loop was created by employing a single click to start a point, then dragging the curved line open to create a full loop.

Shapes

The Shapes tools are all very similar, so we'll look at them all at once.

Rectangle

Rectangle tool draws three types of rectangles: outline, filled with outline, and filled without outline. The interior of the outline rectangle is transparent, whereas the filled types fill the rectangle with the background colour. To draw a rectangle, click on the tool, then click a point on the image where you want one corner to be, then drag diagonally and release the mouse where you want the opposite corner to be.

Tip

To create a square shape, hold down the Shift Key as you draw the shape.

Example:

The Polygon tool is similar to the rectangle, but works a bit differently. To create a polygon, activate the tool from the tool bar. Then, click on the image wherever you want your first vertice to be. A vertice is like a corner. Draw the edges of the shape like you would use the Straight Line tool, then simply connect the last edge to the first vertice and the shape will finish. You have to be pretty precise. If you just miss by a few pixels, the shape will think that you want to continue adding sides to the polygon.

Tip

You can constrain the angle of the line segments of the polygon to 45 degree increments by holding down the shift key as you click to create the next vertex.

Example:

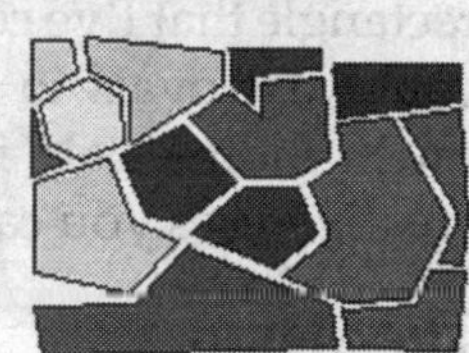

Polygons are great for all creating all kinds of irregular shapes. Unfortunately, it's more difficult to draw a regular polygon, because you have to do each side of the polygon free-hand. But it is still a pretty useful tool. For instance, you can see here how you can use many irregular polygons to create a tile mosaic sort of look.

Oval

The Oval Tool works much like the Rectangle tool. The only difference is that since there are no corners, you will need to guess where the corners would be in order to place your oval where you want it to go. Imagine that the oval you are drawing is being "hugged" by a rectangle that goes around it. Like up the top-most and left-most peaks of the oval's curve to guess where the corner of the imaginary rectangle is and click there. Then, drag down to where the bottom-most and right-most peaks of the oval's curve would be, and click again. Your oval should be about the right size and in the right position if you estimated it correctly. Like the other shapes, you can create ovals that are just empty outlines, filled outlines, or filled with no outline.

Tip

To create perfect circles, hold down the shift key as you draw the shape.

Example:

Here's a picture made in just a few minutes using a number of oval shapes as well as some of the other drawing tools. Notice how the overlapping ovals achieve a sense of perspective with the car's wheels, and for the shape of the car's body itself. I also overlapped ovals to create the crescent moon effect. I also used the Curve and Line tools for some of the details, the Fill tool to fill in spaces with colour, and the Airbrush tool for the exhaust.

Rounded Rectangle

The Rounded Rectangle tool is like a cross between the Rectangle Tool and the Oval Tool. It draws rectangles, but instead of having sharp 90 degree angle corners, they'll be somewhat rounded.

As always, you can create rounded rectangles with empty outlines, filled outlines, or filled with no outline.

Tip

To create rounded squares, hold down the shift key as you draw the shape.

Example:

This is probably the most common use for the rounded rectangle that I've come up with – drawing voice bubbles. You could use ovals to draw voice bubbles, too, but the text fits much more easily into a rounded rectangle. See what other creative uses you can put the Rounded Rectangle tool to!

The rounded rectangle shape is ideal for creating voice balloons!

The Menus

Knowing how to use menu commands is a basic Windows skill. But just in case you're a real beginner, we'll do a quick recap.

Overview

The Menus appear directly beneath the Title Bar in the window. There are six menus in the Paint window, which are circled in red to emphasize.

We call them "Menus" because they work like a menu at a fast food restaurant. When you want to place an order at a restaurant, you look up on the wall for what you want, and if you see it, then you select it. The computer works the same way. You just look in the menu, then select the item that you want. Because a complete list of all the items on the menu would take up a lot of screen space that could be better used for other things, the menu items "hide" most of the time. To bring up a menu in its entirety, just click on the Menu's heading, and the rest of the menu will "pull down".

Here we see the File menu, which we've pulled down (by clicking on the word File, naturally). Now we can see the entire contents of the file menu. Let's take a look at the anatomy of this menu in greater detail.

If you prefer to use the keyboard over the mouse, you'll want to take notice of the ***shortcut features***. To the right of some of the commands you'll see a keystroke command shortcut to the right. For instance, to create a New file, you could click on File to pull down the File Menu, then click on New. Or, you could just press Ctrl-N on the keyboard. Since your hands remain on the keyboard, this can save a few seconds, which may not seem like much but it adds up. This time-saver is of less vital importance in a program like Paint, where you'll be using the mouse a great deal, but it's still good to know about.

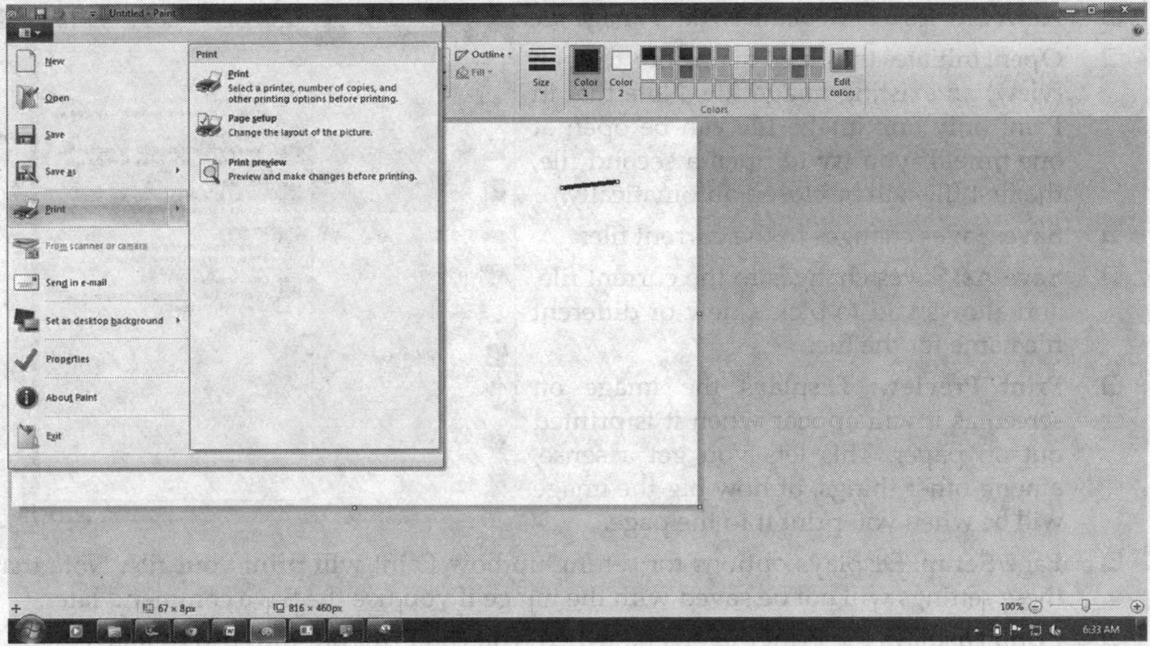

You can also execute menu commands by using the keyboard in a different way. Notice how each menu command has a letter underlined somewhere in it? These are clues to understanding the other keyboard shortcut method. To use this method, all you need to do is press the Alt key, then the letter that is underlined in the command that you want to use. For instance, to look at the Print Preview, you can click on File to pull down the File Menu, then click on "Print Preview". Or, you could press Alt-F, then V.

Just like at most fast food places, if what you want is not on the menu, then you can't get it. Also, some menu items may not be available to you at all times. When this is the case, that item will appear "grayed out". For example, you'll notice that the commands "Set as Wallpaper (Tiled)" and "Set as Wallpaper (Centred)" were not available in the menu above. But they remain listed so you know where they'll be when you're at the point in using the program where those options can be used.

MS Paint: Menus

The File Menu

The File Menu is where you'll find commands that affect the file you're working on in its most basic aspects. This is where you'd go to create a new file, open a file, save a file, or print a file. In fact, most basic phrases that end with "file" will be found… guess where? In the File Menu.

We've already looked at the File Menu in our overview of using menus, so let's get right to it:

When talking about a specific command, we use the arrow notation. For instance, if we wanted to tell you how to open a new file, we might say, "Create a new file." But if we wanted to give more explicit instructions, we'd say something like, "Go to File Open."

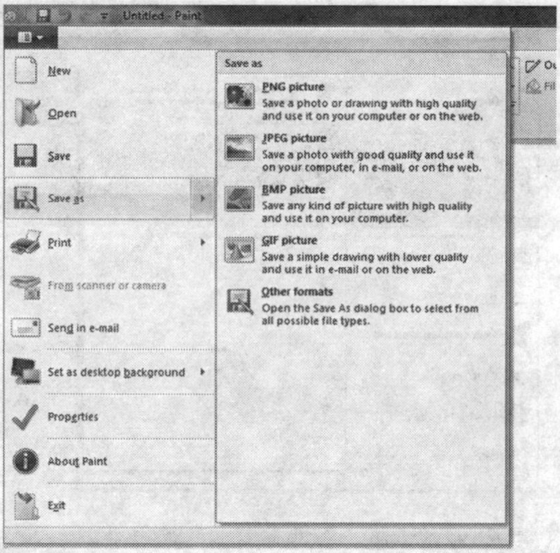

- **New:** Creates a new, blank (white) image file.
- **Open:** Initiates the Open dialog box to open (view) an existing image file. Note that in Paint only **one** image file can be open at one time. If you try to open a second file, the first file will be closed automatically.
- **Save:** Saves changes to the current file.
- **Save As:** Saves changes to the current file, and allows you to pick a new or different file name for the file.
- **Print Preview:** Displays the image on screen as it will appear when it is printed out on paper. This lets you get a sense, among other things, of how big the image will be when you print it to the page.
- **Page Setup:** Displays options for setting up how Paint will print your file. Note that these settings will not be saved with the image if you use the Save command later.
- **Print:** Displays the Print dialog box, where you can Print out the current image file.
- **1, 2, 3:** Opens the 1st, 2nd, or 3rd previous files opened with Paint.
- **Exit:** Shuts down Paint.

Tip 1

While older versions of MS Paint were capable of working only with the .bmp file format, Paint currently handles a variety of image formats, including of the commonly used formats such as JPEG and GIF. This makes Paint appreciably more flexible for working with images and converting from one file type to another.

Tip 2

The Save command may be your biggest friend in Paint, with the possible exception of Edit Undo. But if you combine using Save with Undo, you can reduce your anxiety and work more efficiently. Ordinarily, you can only Undo your last action in Paint. That means, if you want to Undo the second-to-last thing you did, you're stuck. And if you want to go back five or six steps, you may have changed the image so much in the interim steps that the only thing you can do is start over. However, if you Save (or, better yet, Save As) your image after you successfully complete each major change, you'll have effectively worked around this limitation of the Undo command. Each time you save your intermediary work, use Save As to give your file a new name. Each new file that you save will serve as an "undo point" that you can go back to if you really scrwe up and all else fails – if, for some reason, you find that you've made a mistake and can't Undo it, just go back to one of the previously saved files, and begin working again from there. It's a lot smarter to do that than to have to go all the way "back to the drawing board" and re-create your original image and begin again from step one.

Tip 3

If you're going to print your file from out of Paint, be sure to take a look at it with the Print.

Preview mode before you actually print it out. You may notice that the image doesn't fit completely on the page, or that something else is wrong. If you catch it in the Print Preview, it saves you from wasting paper and toner, which can be pretty expensive, as well as time, which is also valuable.

Repeat: Repeat is like the reverse of Undo. It will re-apply the last change that you made to the file you're working on. However, it doesn't seem to be a useable option most of the time. You'll find that it's grayed out most of the time, and not a particularly useful feature.

Cut, Copy, Paste: Cut, along with Copy and Paste are some of the most useful commands in Paint. These are used in conjunction with the Selection tools. First, use either the rectangular or free form Selection tool to select a portion of the image.

The Cut command will remove the selection from the image, just as though you cut it out with a pair of scissors or an x-acto knife. However, the cut portion of the image is not gone. It is stored in the computer's ***copy buffer***, where it can be retained temporarily. Copy works much like Cut, in that it places the selected portion of the image into the copy buffer, but it does not remove the selection from where it originally appears in the image. Paste is how you get stuff out of the copy buffer and back onto the image; it "pastes" the contents of the copy buffer back into the image, where you can move it around before deselecting it.

- ❑ Cut and Paste are good for moving bits of an image around.
- ❑ Copy and Paste are good for duplicating portions of an image to create a motif or pattern or collage-like effect.

Clear Selection: Clear Selection is also used in conjunction with the Selection tools. When you use Clear Selection, whatever is in the selection will be deleted. It's a little trickier than simply using the eraser and zoom, and less precise, but it's quicker.

Select All: This command automatically selects the entire image. You can then use Cut, Copy, Paste, or Clear Selection.

Copy To, Paste From

These commands work with an outside file instead of the copy buffer. The copy buffer is like an invisible file that is associated with the Paint Program itself. This is useful, but limited, because only one thing can be in the copy buffer at a time, and when Paint is shut down the contents of the copy buffer may be lost. Or, if you are working with two programs, such as Paint and Microsoft Word, using the Copy command in one program may overwrite the contents of the copy buffer in the other program. When you're working with copying and pasting a lot, you may find that you wish that you could keep more than one object in the copy buffer at a time.

You must have something selected in order to Copy To. Whatever you've selected gets saved as a separate file. Paste To works in a complimentary fashion, by pasting the contents of some separate file into your active Paint file.

These are useful features, but they require the added step of using a dialog box to save or open a file, and are thus slower than the regular Copy/Paste commands. Only use these if you know you'll be needing a selection frequently as you do your work.

The View Menu

The View Menu isn't particularly useful. You can toggle whether the Tool Box, Colour Box, or Status Bar will be displayed here. You can also set the Zoom here, but since you can do that quicker with the Zoom tool, it's hardly useful. View Bitmap will display the image at full size all by itself with none of the usual Paint window objects to get in the way.

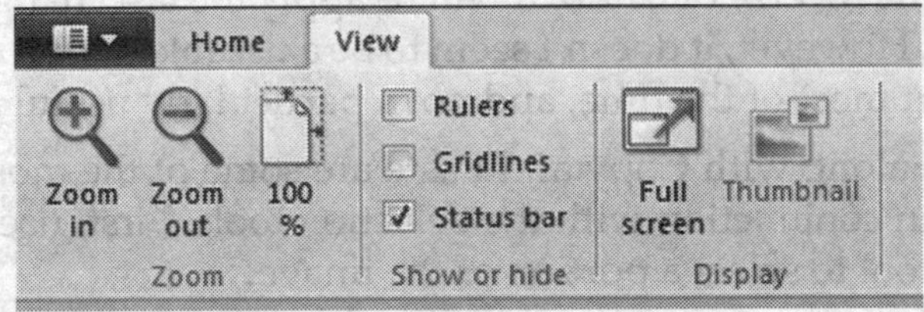

Tip

If you're looking around in the main Paint window for the Tool Box, Colour Box, or Status Bar, and you can't see it, that means they're hidden. To show them, go into the View Menu and make sure that the check mark appears next to each in the menu.

The Image Menu

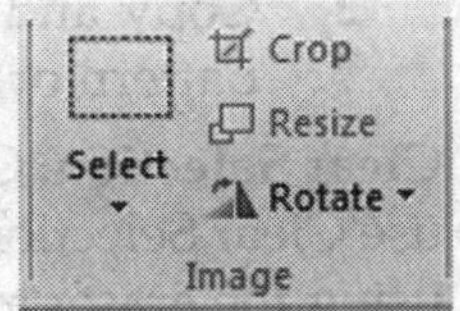

Next to the File and Edit menus, the Image Menu is probably the menu where you'll find the most useful features. You won't use these as often as the File and Edit menu commands, but you can think of the commands in the Image Menu as being your Paint "power tools". You can use these tools to alter your image or selection in a number of interesting and useful ways.

Flip/Rotate:

Flip allows you to "flip" the selection over like a pancake.

You can choose between horizontal or vertical for the direction of your flip. This is good if you need to create a "mirror image" of a selection.

Rotate will rotate the selection. The Rotate command in Paint is not extremely flexible, so you're limited to right-angle rotations (that is, 90, 180, and 270 degrees of rotation.)

Stretch/Skew:

Stretch will let you change the proportions of the selection, making them narrower, wider, shorter, or taller. The ratio of the selection's height and width will change, and will result in some distortion of the image.

Skew is similar to stretch, but it affects opposing edges oppositely. For example, a horizontal skew might shift the top of the image to the right while the bottom of the image stretches to the left. This results in an effect that can be used in making an illusion of 3-d Perspective.

Invert Colours

You'll get an effect similar to a photographic negative.

Attributes: Here is where you can change the basic image attributes such as height and width (which can be measured in pixels, inches, or centimeters), colours (switch between b&w and colour), and transparency (may not be available for all file types.)

Clear Image: Self-explanatory; this wipes out the image, leaving you with a blank file with the same image dimensions.

Draw Opaque: Works with the selection. If unchecked, any background colour (the default is white) in your selection will be treated as transparent. This transparency can be observed by moving the selection around – as the transparent portions of the image move over other areas of the image, you should be able to see those areas peeking through the selection. If unchecked, the background colour will remain opaque when the selection is moved about in the image.

The Colours Menu

The colours menu only has one command in it, Edit Colours.

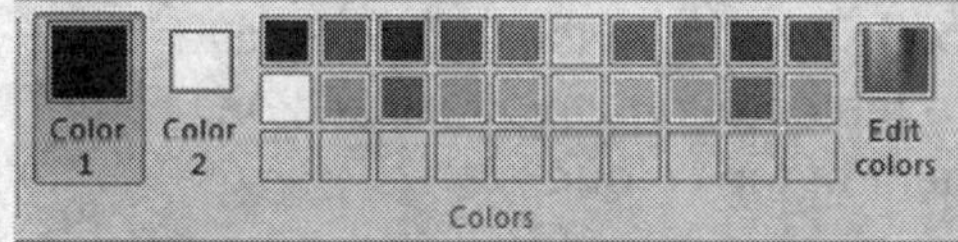

The interface for this command is a bit complicated compared to what we've looked at thus far.

This is the basic Edit Colours window. This will open up on top of the regular Paint window when you select Edit Colours from the Colours Menu.

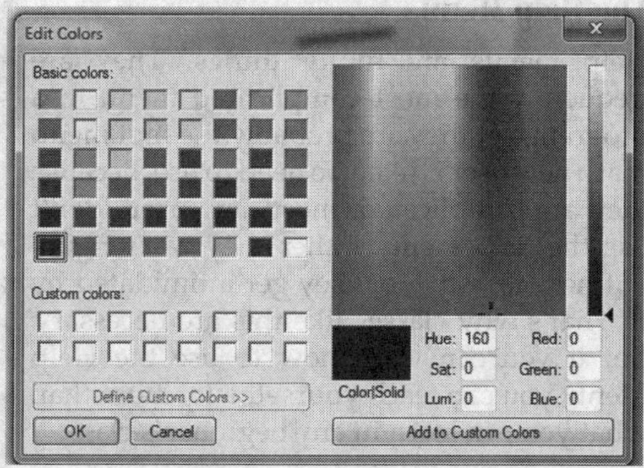

Colour palette

From here, you can customise your colour palette. The Colour Palette is the portion of the Paint window from which you can select which colour you want to use to paint or draw with. Since there are only a relatively small number of colours available through the basic Colour Palette, you'll probably want to pick custom colours at some point if you're doing a lot of actual drawing with the drawing Tools.

To do this, click on "Define Custom Colours". This button will cause the Edit Colours window to expand, and you'll be able to select new colours from the Colour Picker.

As you can see here, the colour picker allows you to pick from a wide variety of shades in the RGB colour gamut. RGB colour is the colour scheme used by mixing the primary colours of light, Red, Green, and Blue, and is the basis for all colour computer graphics.

To pick a colour, you can just click on the region where your desired colour appears. You can adjust the lightness or darkness of the shade by clicking on the shading bar at right. If you know about colour theory, you could enter numbers into the Hue, Saturation, and Luminosity or Red, Green, and Blue boxes. If you don't understand it, it's probably just easier to work with the gamut box.

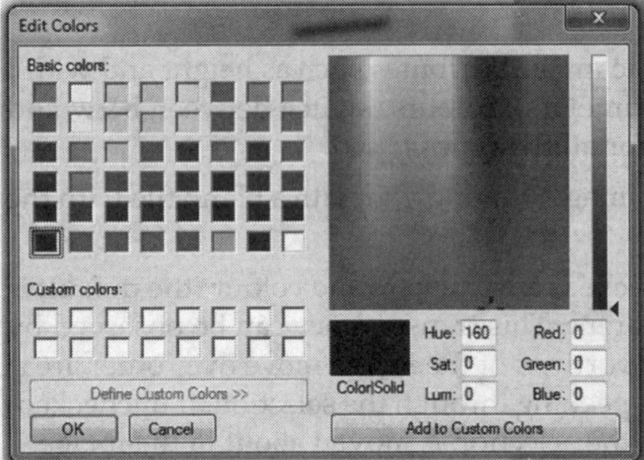

Customizing colour palette

The colour you've currently picked will show up in the box beneath the gamut box. If you like this colour, you can add it to your colour palette by clicking on the Add to Custom Colours button. The new colour will then appear in the Custom Colours palette.

When you are all done, click on OK to resume working in Paint. If you make a mistake and don't want your changes to be saved, click on Cancel.

Tip

To work with an existing colour in the colour picker, click on its swatch in the Colour Palette. The position of the selected colour will automatically change to the colour that you clicked on. You can then make a more gradual adjustment of the colour.

The Help Menu

Help menus are funny things. They are frequently the most complicated menu in a program, yet they are probably the first menu that a new user is likely to need to use. Because they are complicated, most new users don't use the help menu. Either they can't figure out how to use it, or they get intimidated by it. That's why classes like this are necessary. But if you can learn how to use the Help Menu, you can teach yourself a lot more than what you can learn in any beginner's class.

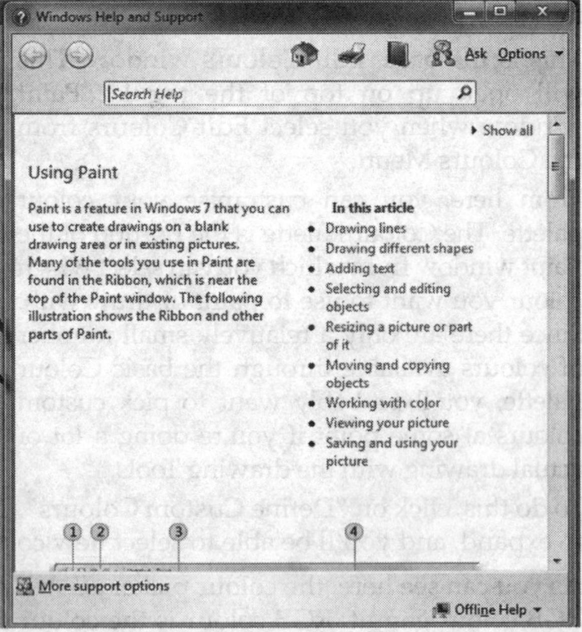

The help menu

Fortunately, as the computer software industry has advanced and matured, they've gradually improved the Help menu's functionality. Today, the Help menu is usually relatively simple to use.

The Help menu only has two sections in Microsoft Paint, which helps eliminate some of the complexity. And, really, only one of these is of any real interest to us. "About Paint" just tells you about the copyright and licensing information… so it's not particularly "helpful."

"Help Topics" on the other hand is where the real show begins. Just click on "Help Topics" to launch the Help Window for Paint.

The Help Topics Window can be displayed side by side with the regular Paint window so that you can refer to it while you're doing your work. As you can see, the Help Window is divided into two "window panes" or "frames." The frame on the left side is your Help Topics index; the right frame is where the actual Help information is displayed when you open up one of the Topics and click the Display button. The Help Topics list can be searched in three different ways: through the Table of Contents, through the Index, or through Searching. I'll leave it up to you to decide which method you prefer, but I think that the Index method is probably the most useful.

The Help Window works a lot like a web page. If you're already familiar with using *Netscape Navigator* here at the library, you should find it easy to navigate the Help Window. Just find the topic you need information about in the Topics list, click on it, and then click the Display button. The help pages related to your topic will then be displayed in the right-side frame. Click on one to get to the information. If you click on the wrong one, or don't find the information you want, just click on the Back button (at the top of the Help Window) to go back a step and go into one of the other help pages, or do another search.

MS Publisher

Introduction

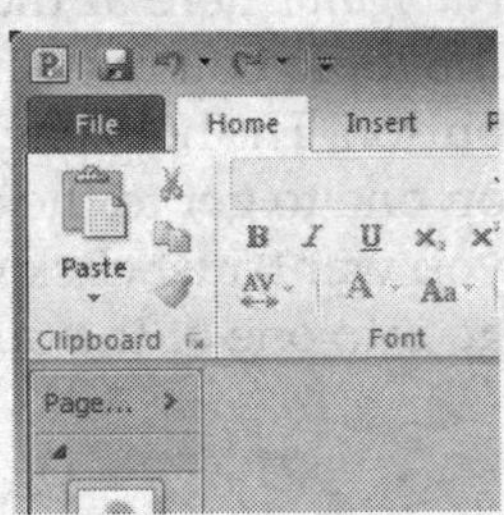

Microsoft Publisher 2010 is a program designed to help you create publications, or documents that you can print and distribute. In this lesson, you'll learn about the advantages and disadvantages of using Publisher 2010. You'll also learn about the Publisher interface, including the Ribbon, rulers and guides, and Backstage view.

Getting to Know Publisher 2010

Even if you've never used Publisher before, you'll probably find its interface familiar, as it has many of the same features as other Microsoft Office programs. However, it does include some features specifically designed for creating publications. If you have used Publisher, you'll recognize these features, but will also notice some slight changes to the 2010 version.

Advantages and Disadvantages of Publisher

Publisher offers templates and other tools to help you create a variety of publications, including **brochures**, **newsletters**, **business cards**, **menus**, and more.

Examples of Publisher 2010 publications

As you might know, you can do most— if not all— of the tasks mentioned above in **Microsoft Word**. So, why not create publications using that program, instead?

One of the advantages of Publisher is that it offers **more control** over certain aspects of your publication. For instance, Publisher offers a work environment that makes it easy to work with documents in a variety of sizes and shapes. It also has a larger variety of tools to help you arrange and align text, images, and other objects within the page margins.

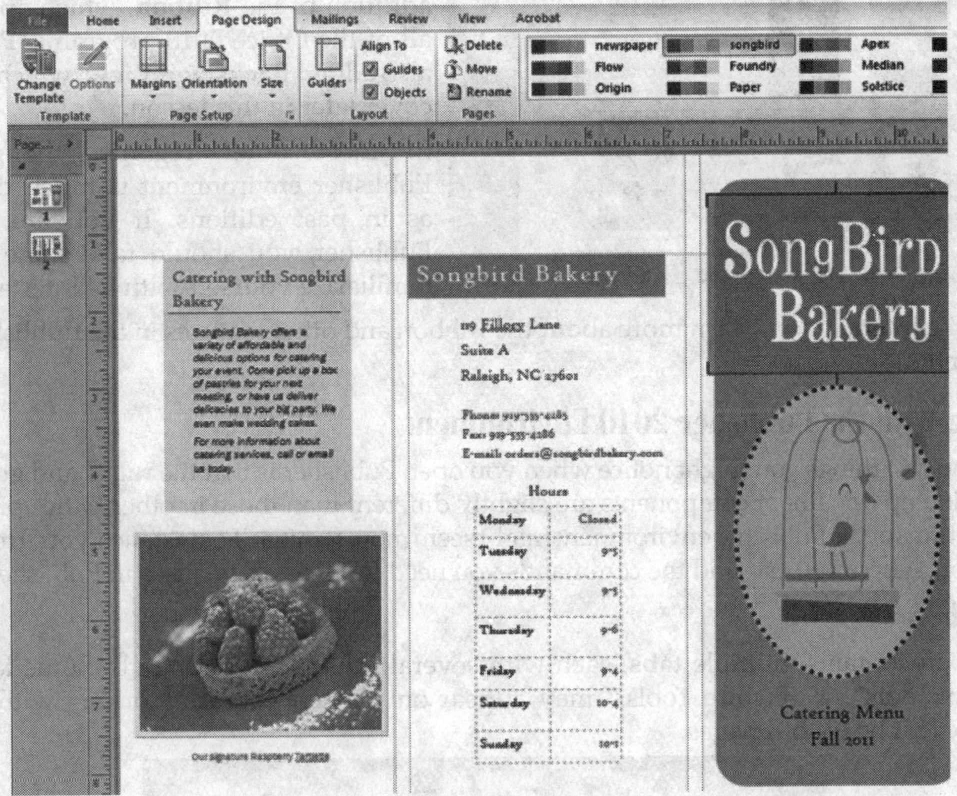

The Publisher interface

However, while Publisher does have certain advantages, it also has the disadvantage of being the **least developed program in the Office 2010 suite**. It does not include the theme colours, advanced image editing tools, or many of the other new features present in Word and PowerPoint 2010. In fact, in terms of these features, Publisher 2010 is more similar to Publisher 2007 and 2003 than it is to other current programs in the Office suite. As you begin to use Publisher 2010, you may find that you prefer to create certain types of publications in Word.

Learning Publisher

While this chapter is an introduction to Publisher, it is not intended for those who are unfamiliar with word processing. In order to learn to use Publisher with our course, **you must already know how to use Microsoft Word**.

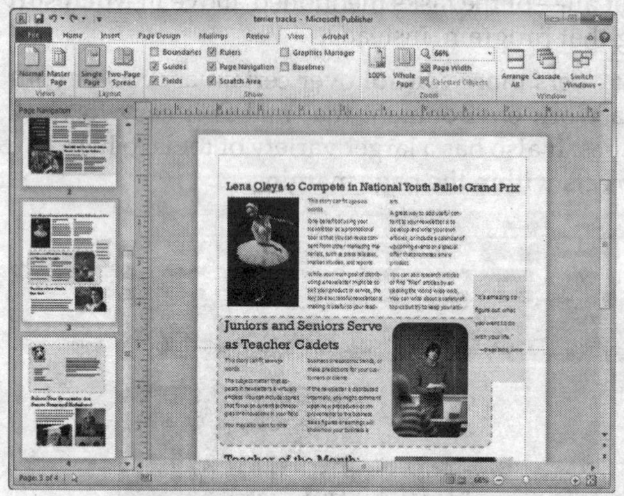

Introduction to the Publisher 2010 Environment

If you are familiar with Publisher 2007 or 2003, you'll notice a few changes to the 2010 interface. The main change is the addition of the **Ribbon**, which appears in all of the Office 2010 programs. Publisher also added **Backstage View**, which we will cover later in this lesson.

In most other regards, though, the Publisher environment is much the same as in past editions. If you are new to Publisher, you should take some time to familiarize yourself with its interface.

Review the interactive to learn more about the Ribbon and other features in the Publisher 2010 environment.

Working With the Publisher 2010 Environment

One of the first things you might notice when you open Publisher is that the rulers and guidelines used to line up document components are slightly different than those in other Office programs. Other features of the Publisher environment might seem more familiar. For instance, you'll recognize the Ribbon, where you can find the commands you need to do common tasks in Publisher.

The Ribbon

The Ribbon contains multiple **tabs**, each with several **groups** of commands. Some tabs, like "Text Box Tools" or "Picture Tools," may appear only when you are working with certain items like text boxes or images.

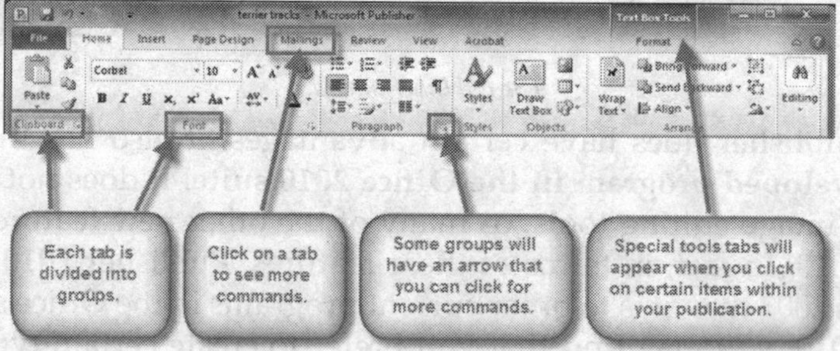

The Ribbon

Viewing Tools

Publisher offers a group of **viewing tools** to help you control the layout of your text, images and objects on the page. These viewing tools are for your editing purposes only. They can be turned on and off and **will not appear** in your printed publication.

- ❑ To access and choose viewing tools, select the **View** tab and locate the **Show** group. Click the checkboxes of the various view options to turn them on and off.

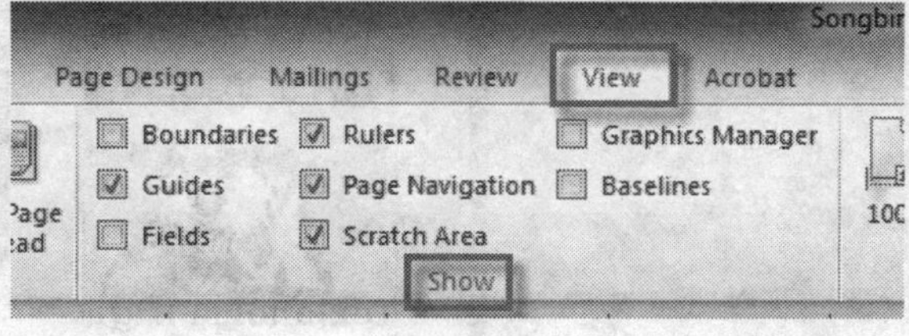

View tools

Publication viewing tools

The publication viewing tools include:

- ❑ **Rulers**

  You can use the rulers to the left and top of your publication to help you line up text, images, and other objects and get a clearer idea of exactly where those objects will appear on the printed page. When you select an object in your publication, a white space will appear on the rulers to show the object's location.

The rulers

- ❑ **Baselines**

  Baselines are evenly-spaced horizontal lines that you can use to line up **text**. You'll learn about automatically aligning text to your baselines in the **Working with Text** lesson.

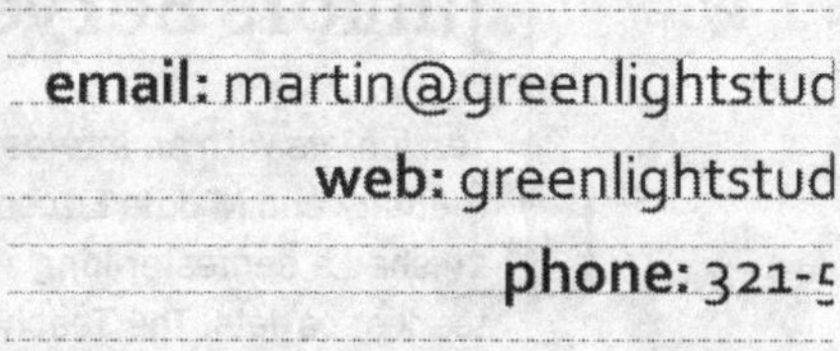

Baselines

- ❑ **Boundaries**

  Boundaries are dark blue dashed borders that appear around your **objects**. Viewing object boundaries can be useful when you are aligning objects or wrapping text.

Boundaries

- ❑ **Guides**

  Guides are thin lines that help you align various objects. There are two types of guides:

  - **Margin guides**, which are blue lines that mark the edges, or margins, of the **printable area** on each page of your publication. Margin guides are automatically created when you set your page margins.
  - **Customizable guides**, which are green lines that you can add anywhere on your publication.

Margin guides

Customizable green guides

To Add Green Guides:

- ❑ **Click** either the horizontal or vertical **ruler**.
- ❑ **Drag** your mouse to your publication, and **release** to add the guide in the desired location.

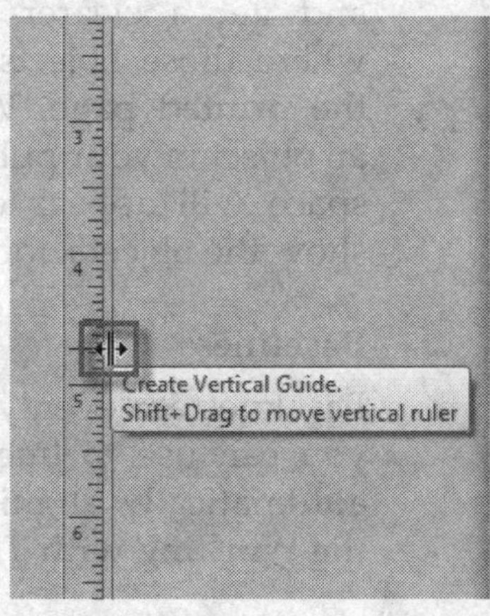

Creating a vertical guide

Dragging the guide to the desired location

- ❑ Your guide will be placed. You can move it at any time by clicking and dragging it.

The added guide

Backstage View

In Publisher 2010, options for **saving**, **printing**, and **creating** publications are all located in **Backstage view**. It is similar to the **Office Button Menu** from Publisher 2007 or the **File Menu** from earlier versions of Publisher. However, unlike those menus, it is a full-page view, which makes it easier to work with.

- ❑ To access Backstage view, click the **File tab**.

Review the interactive below to learn about the different things you can do in Backstage view.

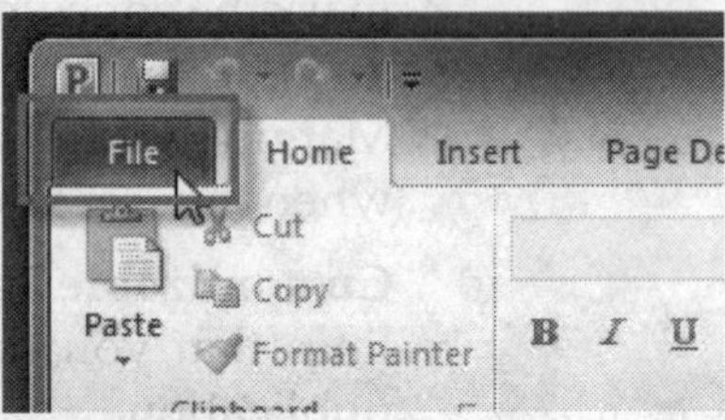

Click the File tab to access Backstage view

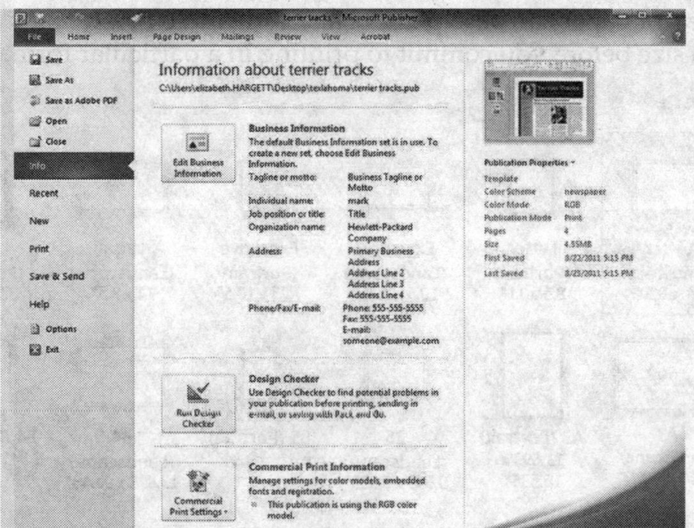

Learn different things in Backstage view

Producing a Publication

Introduction

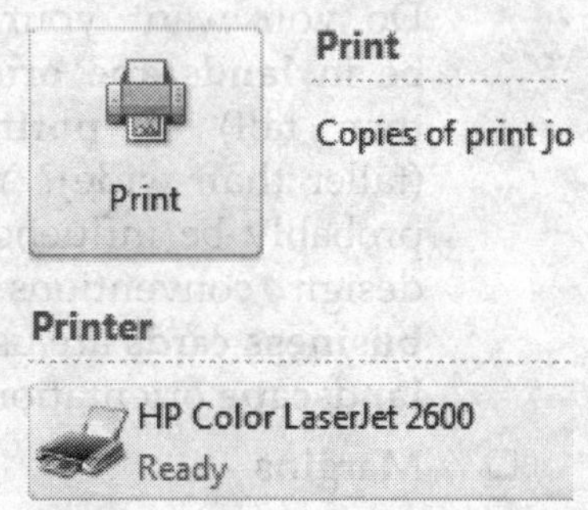

Creating a professional-looking publication takes planning. For instance, before you even begin your publication, you should know whether you plan to print your document or distribute it online. Once you know how you'll present your publication, you can start making decisions about other aspects of it, such as page layout, paper choice, and print option.

Before you create a publication, you should already have an idea of what you want to do with it when it's finished. Will you print and distribute it? Will you publish it online? Knowing the answers to these questions is essential to making decisions about how your publication will look.

In this lesson, you'll learn about the things you need to consider before publishing, like layout, print supplies, and more. You'll also learn about printing your publication and converting it to a PDF.

Page Layout

Some of the first choices you need to make about your publication involve **page layout**. Creating a publication from a **template** takes care of most of these choices for you. However, if you create a publication from scratch or decide to heavily modify a template, there are three components of page layout that you'll have to consider.

- **Size**

  Some publications, like flyers, can be large or small. However, you probably don't want a brochure to be giant. A standard sheet of paper is 8.5 inches wide and 11 inches tall.

Larger sheets of paper can be expensive and difficult to print. Think carefully about your publication size before you commit to printing in a particular format.

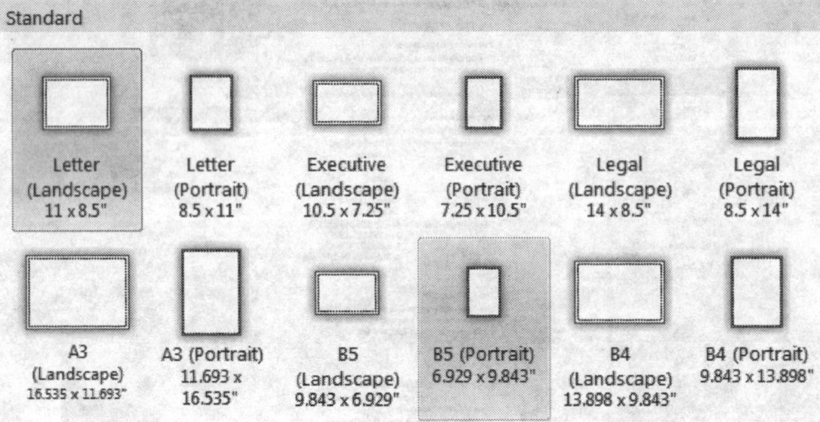

A selection of publication sizes

- **Orientation**

  Do you want your publication to be in **landscape orientation** (wider than tall) or **portrait orientation** (taller than wide)? Your choice will probably be influenced by standard design conventions. For instance, **business cards** are usually printed in **landscape** orientation.

Business cards with different orientations

- **Margins**

  Margins are areas of blank space that line the edges of a printed document. While professional printers can print publications where the text and images stretch out all the way to the edge of the page, most home and office printers require that your publication have margins, even if they are narrow ones.

  The **width** of your page margins can affect the **look** and **feel** of your publication. For example, extremely **wide margins**, like those often found in menus for fancy restaurants, can look sophisticated. However, wide margins don't leave much room for

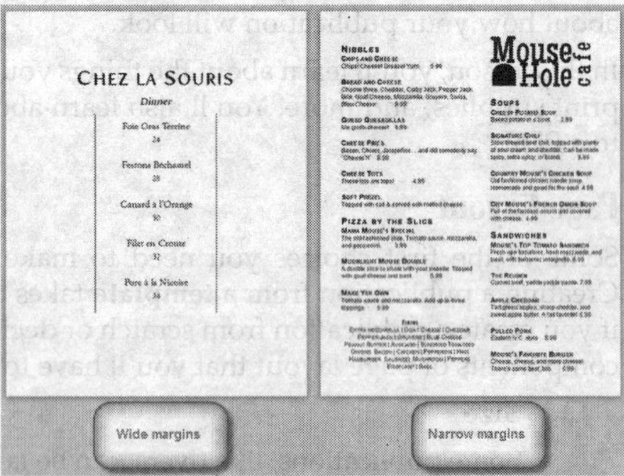

Menus with different sized margins

images and text. In contrast, **narrow margins** give you a large amount of space to work with.

As you plan your publication, it might help to mock up your design on paper. You can also use an existing publication as a model.

A finished brochure and the initial mocked-up design

Producing Printed Publications

If you're planning on printing your publication yourself, your planning doesn't stop when you finish your layout. Before you print your publication, you'll have to make certain decisions about how you want to produce and distribute it.

Paper

- ❑ **Size**

  Your paper must be the same size as your publication layout. Keep in mind that not all printers can handle all sizes of paper. If you don't know whether your printer can use the desired paper size, review the manual that came with your printer or create and print a test page with a few lines of text.

Paper in various sizes

- ❑ **Type**

  Depending on the type of publication you're creating, you might want to consider using something other than standard white paper. For instance, people usually print greeting cards on a **heavier type of paper** called **card stock**. Paper choices aren't just about paper weight, though. For example, if you're printing business cards, you might consider buying **perforated** paper to make separating the cards easier. If you're not sure which type of paper is best for your publication, the employees at your local office supply store may be able to help.

- ❑ **Colour**

  For most publications, white or cream-coloured paper is probably the best choice. However, if you're printing in grayscale or black and white, **coloured paper** can make your publication more attention-getting and visually appealing.

A newsletter printed in grayscale on coloured paper

Print Quality

- ❑ **Colour**

  You have three colour options for your printed publication:

  - **Colour**
  - **Grayscale**, which prints images and details in shades of gray.
  - **Black and white**, which prints all images and text in black ink, without any shading. Many photocopiers only produce black and white images.

Out of these three options, colour often looks the most polished and professional. However, it does have drawbacks. Before you use colour, consider these things first:

- **Expense**. Colour ink cartridges are expensive, and if you're printing many copies of a colour publication, the ink can run out quickly. You can avoid some cost by using colour sparingly.
- **Paper**. If you're planning on using colour in a double-sided publication, you'll probably want to use slightly heavier paper to prevent the colour from showing through. Also, you'll want to stick with white or cream-coloured paper to ensure that the colours show up correctly.

A publication printed almost entirely with colour ink

Colour printing showing through the other side of thin paper

Colour printing on coloured paper

❑ **Printer and copier capability**

Be sure that your printer or copier is capable of printing your publications at the quality you want. This is especially important for professional publications. Do the text and images come out crisp and undistorted? Are the colours accurate? If you are planning on printing a double-sided publication, can your printer do that automatically? If the answer to these questions is no, consider modifying your printer or copier settings or having your publication professionally printed.

Delivery

If you plan to deliver your publication via mail, you should consider how you're going to send it. For instance, if you're planning on mailing many copies of your publication, you should consult with your post office about **bulk mailing** price options, specifications, and restrictions. No matter how many copies of your publication you're mailing, you can choose between two ways of getting your publication ready for delivery.

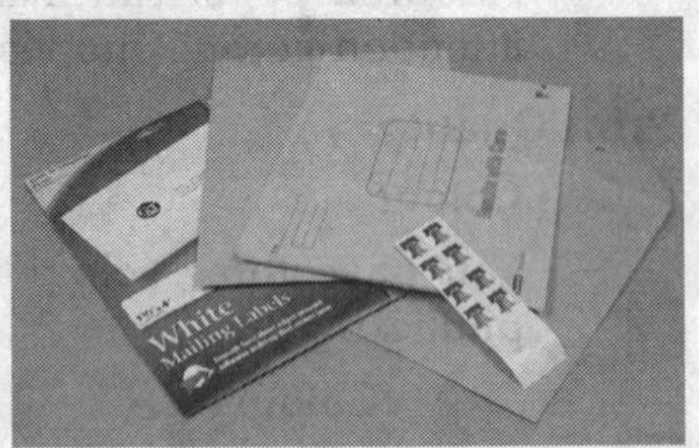

Shipping supplies

❑ **Using Packaging**

For publications that won't fit in a standard envelope, you'll need to use a larger envelope or another package better suited to your needs, like a **tube** if you're mailing a poster, or a **box** if you're sending many copies of your publication to one recipient.

- ❑ **Adding an Address**

  You can send newsletters and similar publications without any envelope at all, using a sticker or staple to keep the pages from unfolding. Make sure to include a space in the publication where you can add the **address**. Many templates for newsletters already include this blank space on the back of the last page.

A newsletter with an address printed on it

Post-Printing Needs

Depending on the type of publication you're producing, you may need to plan to put final touches on your publication just after printing. You may need to arrange time for tasks like:

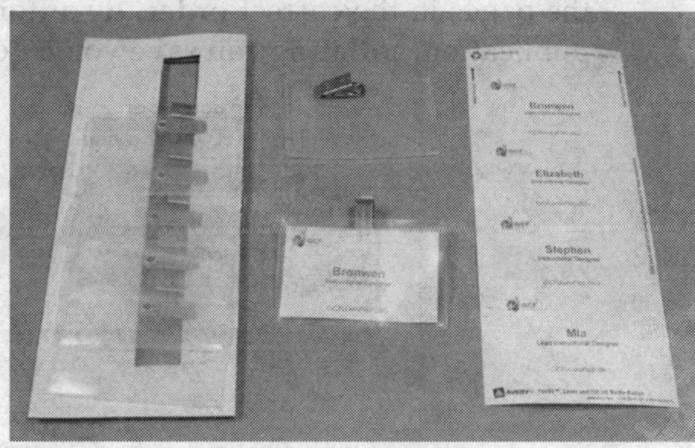
Assembling name badges

- ❑ **Cutting**, for publications like business cards and postcards
- ❑ **Folding**, for brochures, newsletters, and other full-page publications
- ❑ **Stapling**, for multi-sheet publications like newsletters and booklets
- ❑ **Assembling**, for publications like name badges and banners

If you plan on producing many copies of your publication, tools like **paper cutters**, **paper creasers**, and heavy-duty **staplers** can help you assemble your publication more quickly and precisely. Make sure to gather the needed tools ahead of time.

Printing and Publishing

Before you print your publication, take a moment to review the Publisher printing **options** and **settings**. These options give you the ability to control exactly how your publication prints. If you'd rather not print your publication, Publisher also offers a way to publish **electronically**.

Printing Settings

Publisher offers a variety of print settings that you can modify to suit your needs. Among these are two tools for advanced printing tasks: **double-sided printing** and **collating**.

- ❑ **Double-Sided Printing**

  Double-sided printing allows you to print on both the front and back of each sheet of paper. Publisher gives you two choices for double-sided printing: you can flip, or turn, the page on the **long side** of the page or the **short side**.

If you're not sure how flipping the page on each side affects your printed publication, you can preview your double-sided printing with the transparent view slider, which is explained in the interactive below. You can also print a page of your publication and fold, staple, or otherwise prepare it as planned. If the reverse side of your page is upside down, choose the other option.

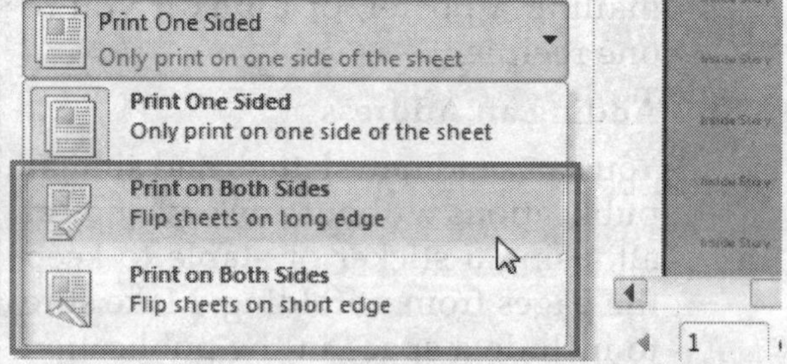

Double-sided printing options

- **Collating**

  The **collated printing** option lets you **assemble** copies of your publication with all the pages in the correct **order**. By automatically grouping individual copies of your publication, **collating** can save you a good deal of time and effort.

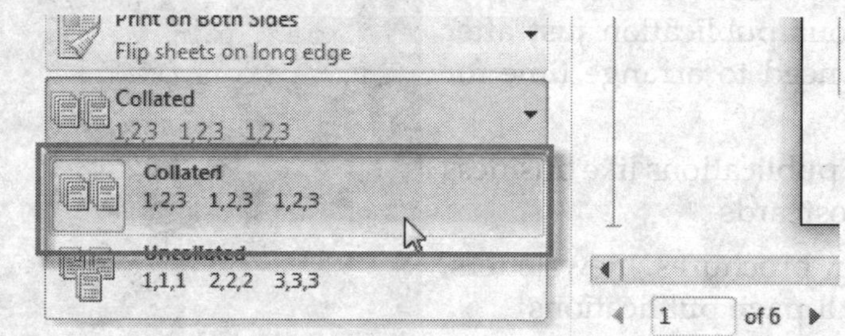

Collating options

Review the interactive to learn about **printing options and settings** in Publisher 2010.

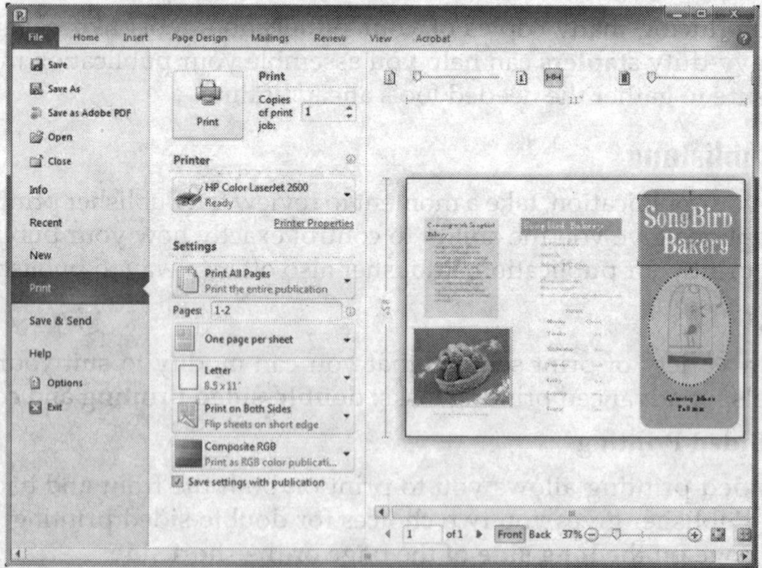

Printing options and settings

Viewing Options

Underneath the print preview, you can use the viewing options to navigate between pages, switch between the front and back views of the current page, zoom in and out, and view multiple pages at once.

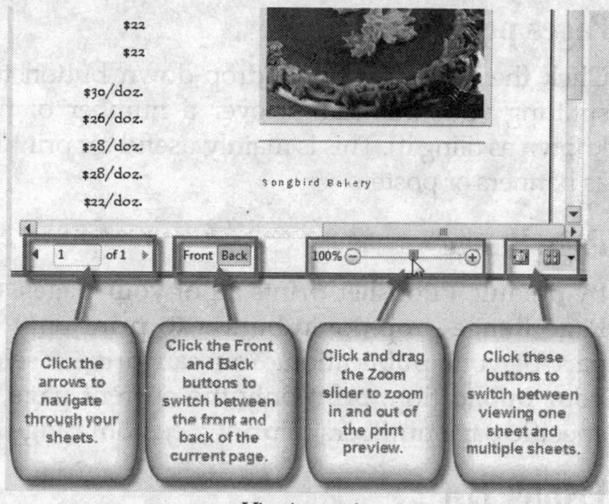

Viewing options

Save Settings

Click Save settings with this publication to make sure that the current publication will always print according to the settings you chose.

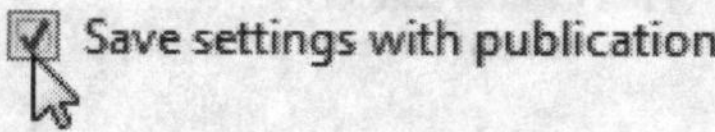

Colour Options

Click the Colour Options drop-down button to choose between printing your publication in colour or grayscale. Remember, you can only print in colour if you have a colour printer installed.

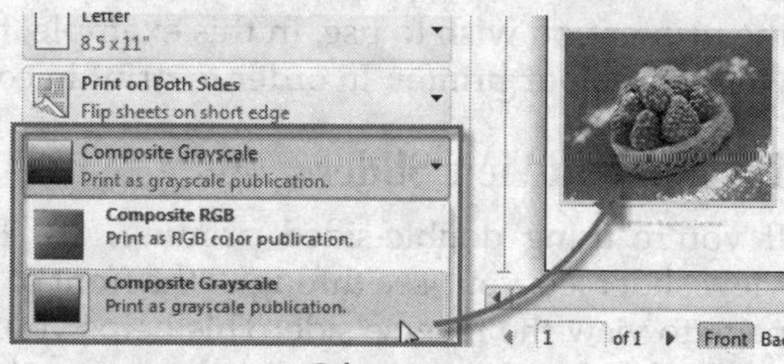

Colour options

Single and Double-Sided Printing

Depending on the type of publication you've created, you may wish to use double-sided printing, which prints on both sides of each sheet of paper. When you print on both sides, you'll have the choice to flip, or turn, the pages on either their long side or short side.

Paper Size

Click the Paper Size drop-down button to choose the size of paper you plan to print your publication on. Only certain paper sizes will be compatible with your publication; incompatible sizes will appear grayed-out. If your printer has multiple printer trays, you may have to manually select the tray where the correct paper is stored. To do this, click Paper Source.

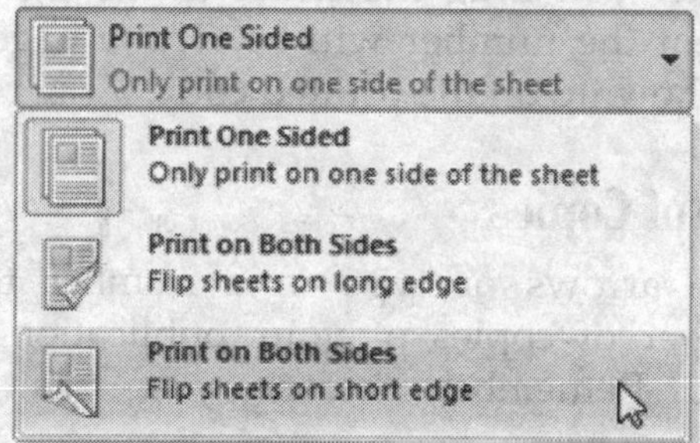

Single and Double-Sided Printing

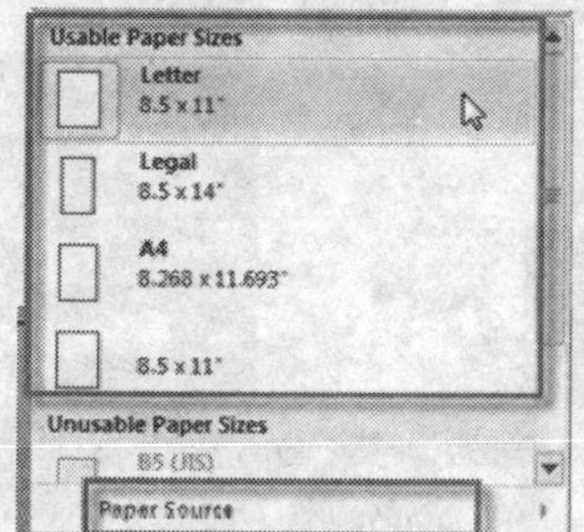

Paper Size

Pages per Sheet

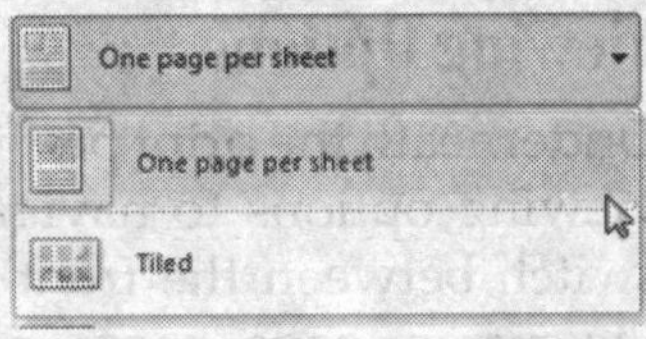

Click the Pages per Sheet drop-down button to view options for splitting your publication over a number of printed sheets (also known as tiling it). This is mainly useful for printing large items, such as banners or posters.

Page Range

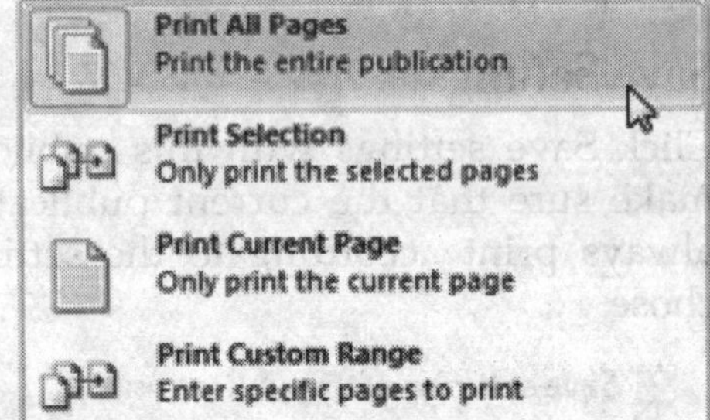

By default, Publisher prints all of your pages. Click the Page Range drop-down button to print only a certain part of your publication. You can print a selection of your publication, print only the current page, or enter specific page numbers to print a custom range of pages.

Printer List

If you have multiple printers installed, you can click the Printer drop-down button to select the printer you wish to use. In this example, there is a printer for black and white printing, as well as a colour printer. In order to print in colour, the colour printer must be selected.

Transparent View Slider

If you're using double-sided printing, the Transparent View slider lets you "see through" the front of the current page to view the reverse side. This helps you make sure that both sides of the page are lined up correctly. Click and drag the slider to move it. The further you drag the slider to the right, the less transparent the reverse side will be.

Transparent View Slider

Rulers

Click the Rulers button to turn on and off the rulers that appear to the top and left of the print preview.

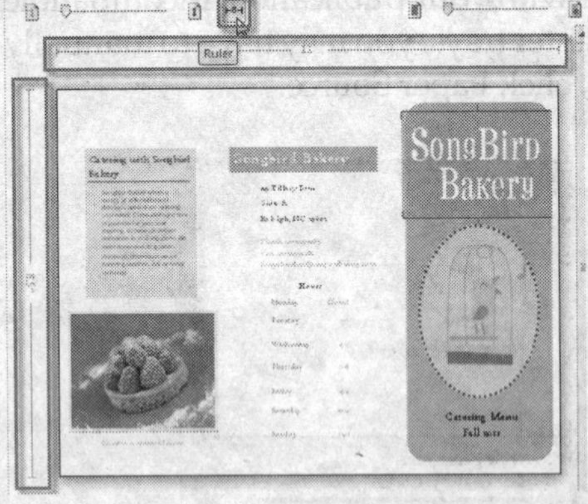

Rulers

Page Numbers Slider

Click and drag the Page Numbers slider to the right to display page numbers on the center of each page. The further you drag the slider to the right, the less transparent the number will be. These page numbers will not show up on the printed copy.

Number of Copies

Print

Copies of print job: 5

Click the arrows or type in a number to indicate the number of copies of your publication you wish to print. Remember, before you print multiple

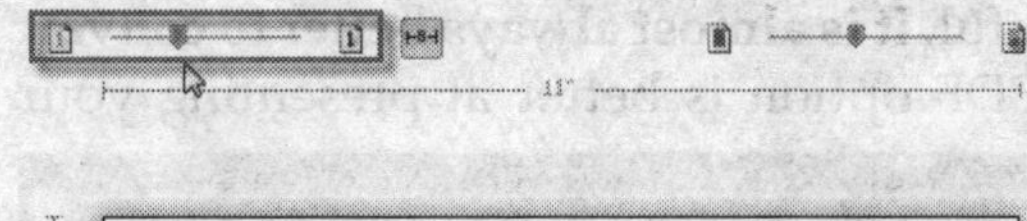

Page Numbers Slider

copies of your publication, you should first print one copy as a test so that you can check your publication for any errors.

The Print Button

When you're satisfied with your printing settings and are ready to print your publication, click the Print button.

Before You Print

Before you print, review your print settings and print a final test copy of your publication. You should also consider running the **Design Checker**. The Design Checker is a tool that helps you **find and fix problems** in your publication that may lead to printing errors.

- ❑ To run the **Design Checker**, go to the **Info** tab in **Backstage view** and click the **Run Design Checker** button. The **Design Checker Pane** will appear to the right of your publication.

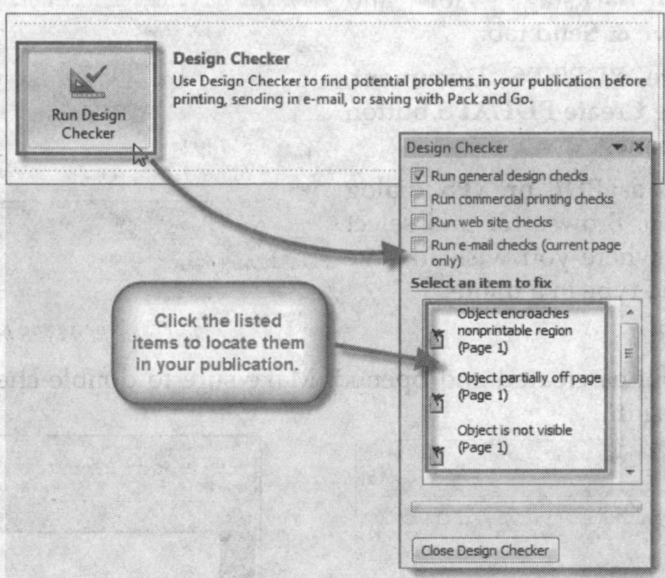

The Design Checker

Publishing Electronically

Depending on the purpose of your publication, you may decide to publish it **electronically** and distribute it **online**. Publisher offers two ways to do this. You can either:

- ❑ Publish as a **PDF** and attach the file to an email or upload it to a website.
- ❑ Publish as **HTML**, which Publisher then **embeds** directly into an email.

Although Publisher promotes the HTML option as useful, **it is almost always better to convert your publication into a PDF**. This is because the PDF option is better at presenting your publication the way you designed it. Publications saved as HTML can lose some of their formatting and may not include custom fonts and images.

However, PDFs aren't perfect either. Depending on the type of publication you're working with, the PDF version may not be easy to browse and read. For example, while you technically can convert a brochure to a PDF, the panels will not be lined up as they would be in a printed and folded version. If you're not sure whether or not your publication is suitable for delivery as a PDF, publish a test copy early in the design process.

A brochure saved as a PDF

To Publish as a PDF

- ❑ Navigate to **Backstage View** and select the **Save & Send** tab.
- ❑ Select **Create PDF/XPS Document**, then click the **Create PDF/XPS** button in the right pane.
- ❑ The **Publish as PDF or XPS** dialog box will open. Browse for and select the location where you wish to save your PDF and type in a **name**.
- ❑ Click **Publish**.
- ❑ Your PDF will be created and opened. Make sure to double-check for any mistakes before sharing it.

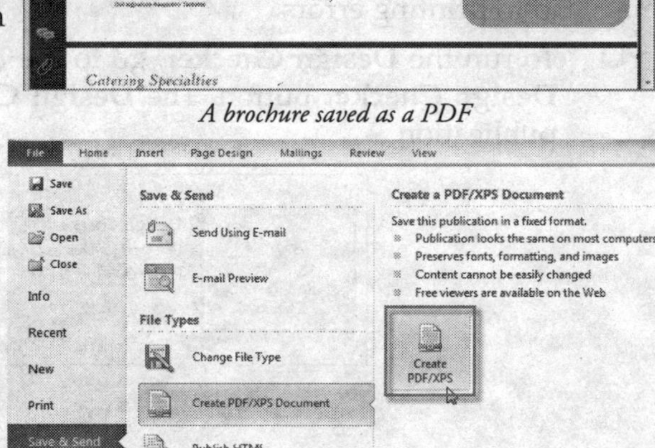

The Create PDF/XPS button

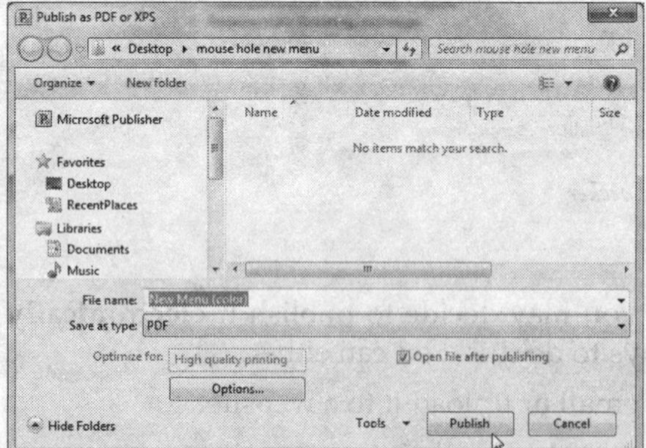

The Publish as PDF or XPS dialog box

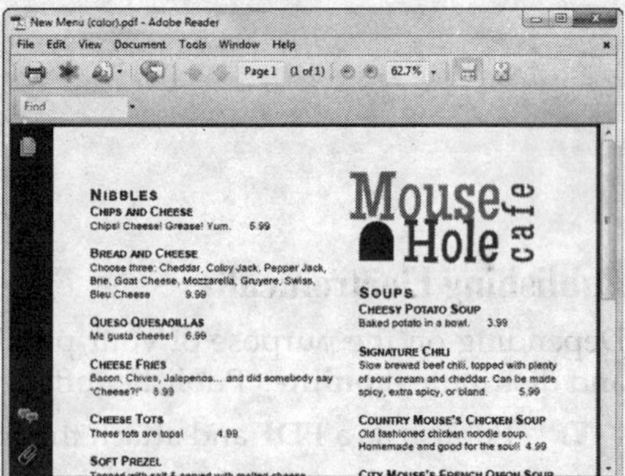

The published PDF

Creating a New Publication

Publisher offers dozens of templates for almost any type of publication you would want to create, including **brochures**, **newsletters**, **greeting cards**, and more. Of course, if you can't find a template that you like, you can always **modify** one to suit your needs, or even create a publication from a blank page. Understanding Publisher's templates and layout tools will help you create publications that look the way you want.

To Create a New Publication from a Template:

- ❑ Click the **File** tab to go to **Backstage view**, then select **New**. The **Available Templates** pane will appear.
- ❑ Select the **type** of publication you wish to create.
- ❑ A selection of templates will appear in the Available Templates pane. Choose from one of two categories:
  - **Office.com templates**, which include templates created by **other users**. User-created templates are indicated with a **User icon** 👤. Although Microsoft does review these templates, you should use caution when downloading them, as they are not guaranteed to be free of viruses and other problems.
  - **Installed templates** created by Microsoft .

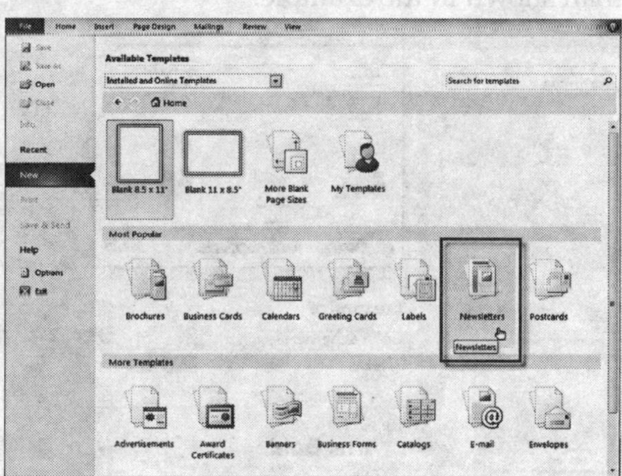

Available template types

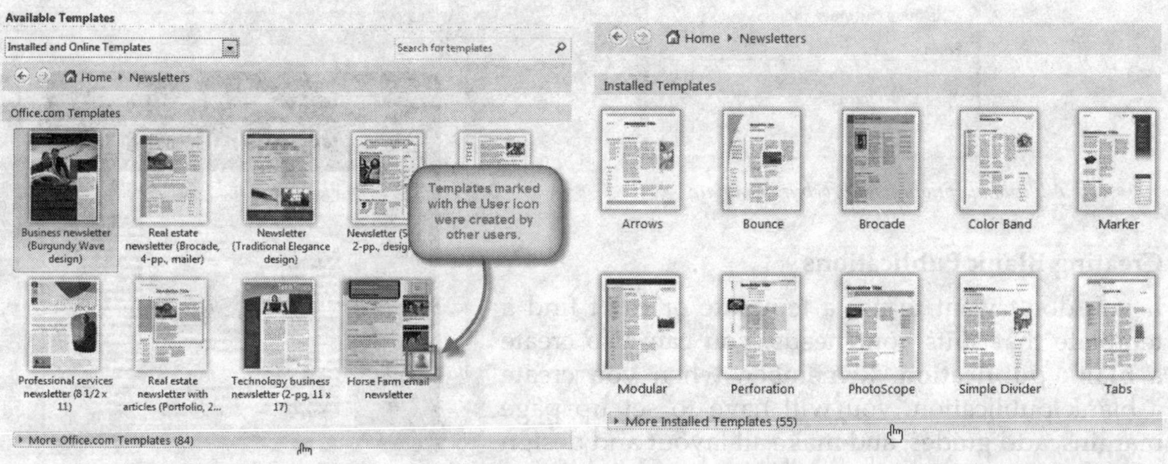

Office.com templates *Templates already installed on your computer*

- ❏ A preview of the selected template will appear in the **Preview** pane on the right. Review the template and modify the template **options** as desired.
- ❏ When you are satisfied with the template, click **Create**.
- ❏ The new publication will be created.

Depending on the type of publication you create, your template may offer more **customization options** than shown in the example.

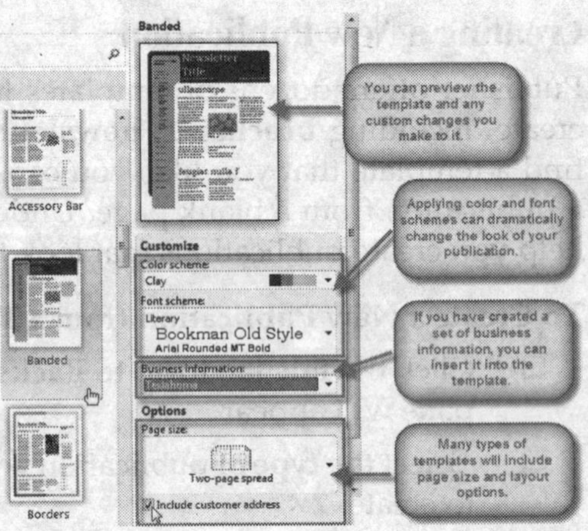

Previewing and customizing the template

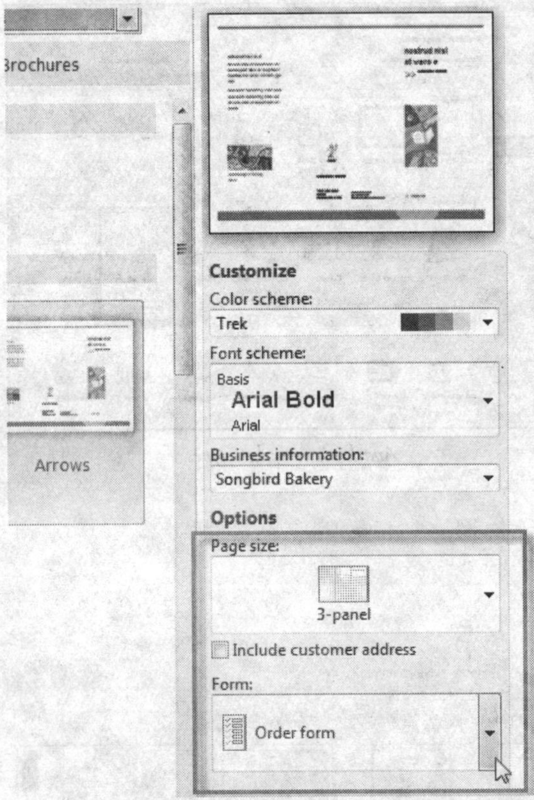

Additional options for a brochure template

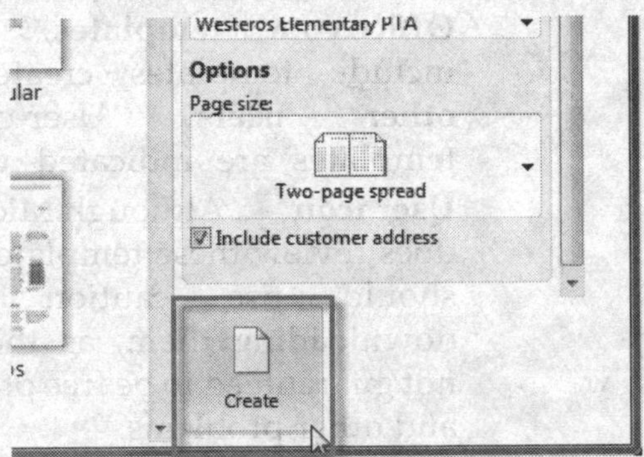

The Create button

The created publication

Creating Blank Publications

If you don't want to use a template or can't find a template that suits your needs, you can also create a **blank publication**. Remember, when you create a blank publication, you will have to set up page margins, add guides, and make all layout and design decisions on your own.

- ❑ To create a blank publication, click the **New** tab in Backstage View and select a **blank page size** in the Available Templates pane.

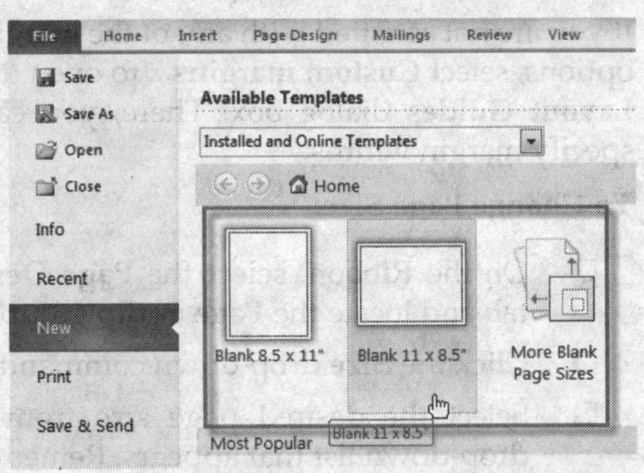

Creating a publication from a blank page

Customizing Your Publication Layout

Whether you chose to create a publication from a template or from a blank page, you may decide to change the publication **layout**. Three components that you can change are **margins**, **size**, and **orientation**. Although you can modify these settings at any time, you should be careful if your publication already contains objects like **text**, **images**, and **shapes**, as you'll have to adjust them to fit the new layout.

To Modify Page Margins:

- ❑ On the Ribbon, select the **Page Design** tab and locate the **Page Setup** group.
- ❑ Click the **Margins** drop-down command.
- ❑ A drop-down list will appear. Select the desired margins.
- ❑ The new margins will be applied.

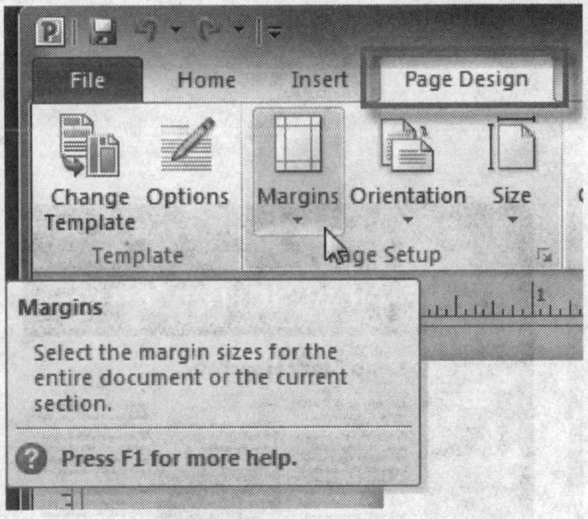

The Margins drop-down command

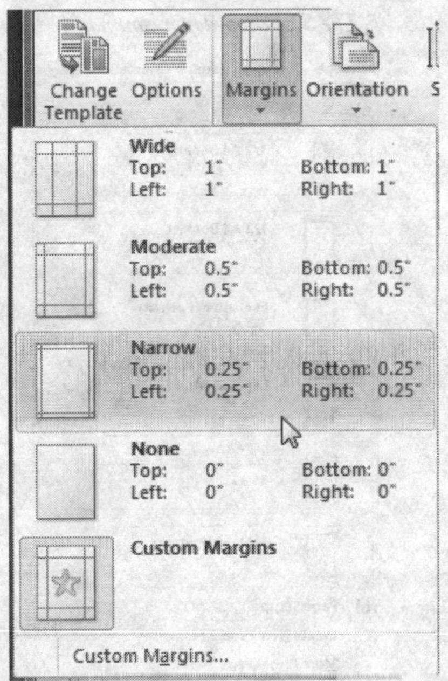

Margin width options

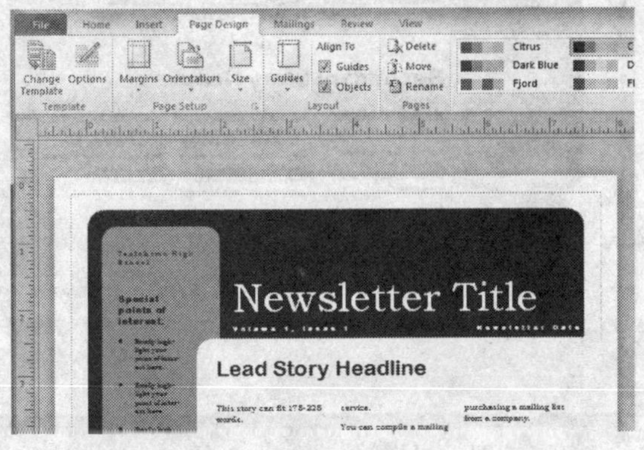

The new, narrower margins have been applied

If you are not satisfied with any of the margin options, select **Custom margins...** to open the **Layout Guides** dialog box. There, you can specify margin widths.

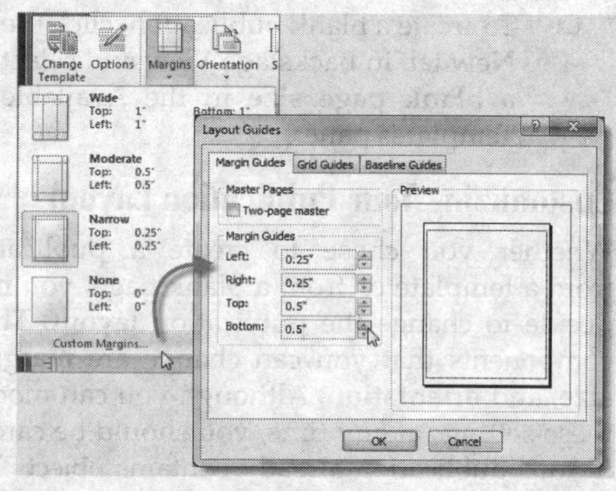
Setting custom margins

To Change Page Size:

- ❑ On the Ribbon, select the **Page Design** tab and locate the **Page Setup** group.
- ❑ Click the **Size** drop-down command.
- ❑ Select the desired page size from the drop-down list that appears. Remember, you should be sure that your printer is capable of handling paper that size.
- ❑ Your publication's page size will be changed.

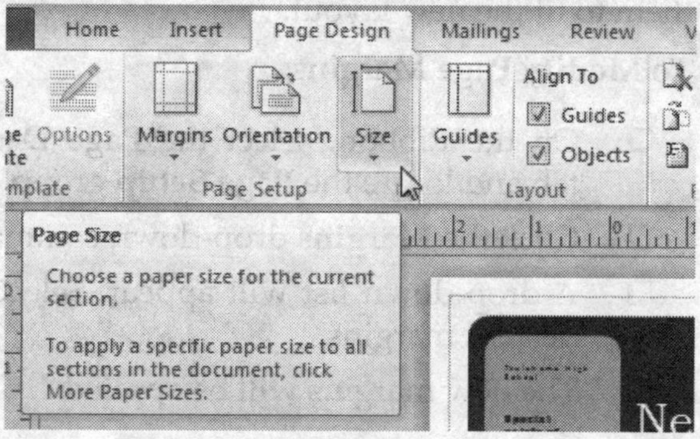
The Size drop-down command

The publication, now on a larger page

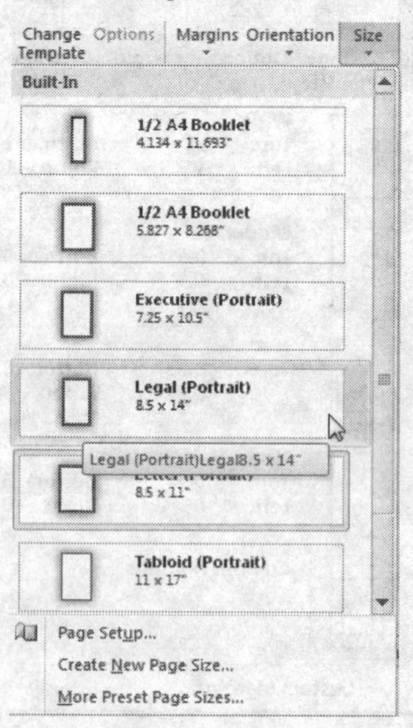
Page size options

If the desired page size isn't included in the drop-down list, select **More Preset Page Sizes...** to view a larger list of page sizes.

More page sizes

To Change Page Orientation:

- ❑ On the Ribbon, select the **Page Design** tab and locate the **Page Setup** group, then click the **Orientation** drop-down command.
- ❑ Select **Portrait** orientation to make your publication taller than wide, or **Landscape** to make it wider than tall.
- ❑ Your publication's page orientation will be changed.

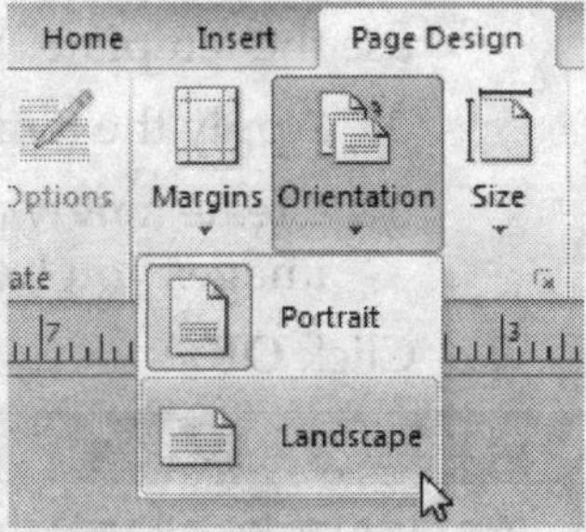

Page orientation options

Depending on the template you chose, changing the page orientation may have a **negative effect** on your presentation. While some templates work equally well in both orientations, others do not.

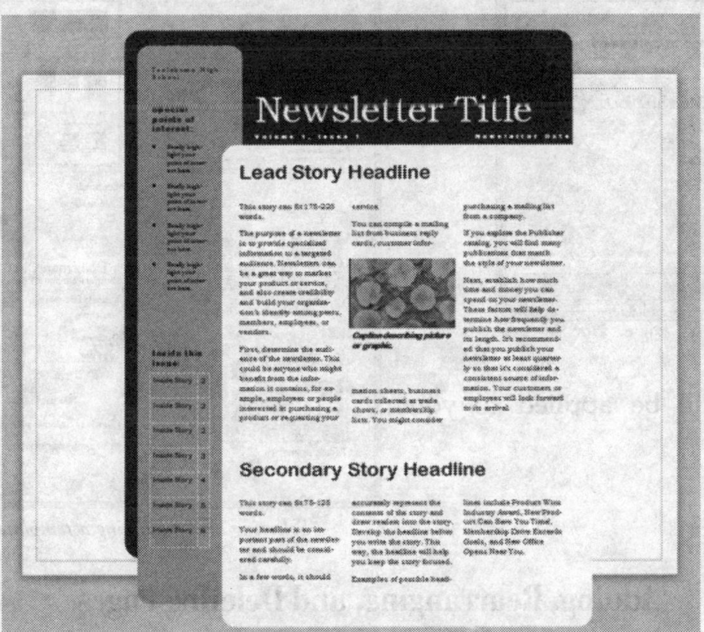

Objects in this template fit poorly with the landscape orientation

Changing or Adding a Template

If you create a publication from a template and later decide that the chosen template doesn't quite suit your needs, you can always **change** it. You can also apply templates to publications that were originally created from blank pages.

To Apply a New Template to an Existing Publication:

- ❑ On the Ribbon, select the **Page Design** tab and locate the **Template** group.

- ❑ Click the **Change Template** command.
- ❑ The **Change Template** dialog box will appear. Select a template to preview it in the **Preview** pane.
- ❑ Modify the template options as desired.
- ❑ When you are satisfied with the new template, click **OK**.
- ❑ A dialog box will appear asking you how you wish to use the template. You can either:
  - Apply the template to the **current** publication.
  - Create a **new** publication that includes the text and images you have added.
- ❑ Click **OK**.

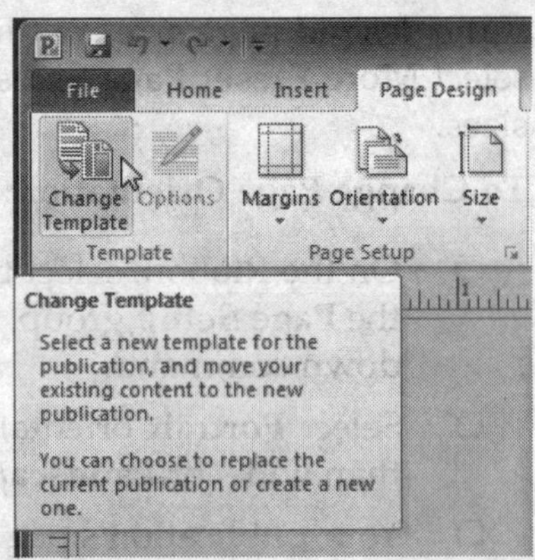

The Change Template command

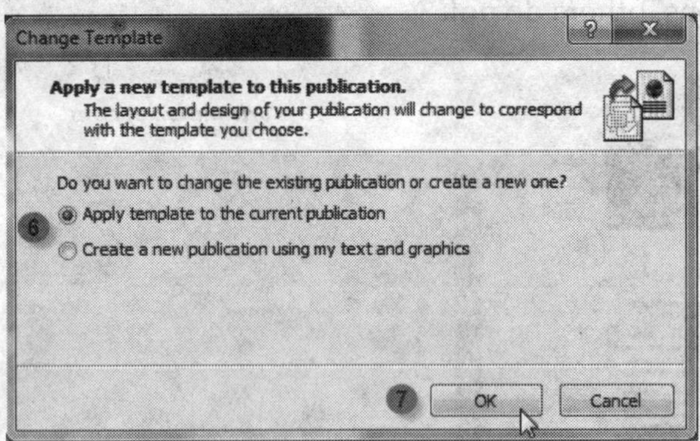

Template options

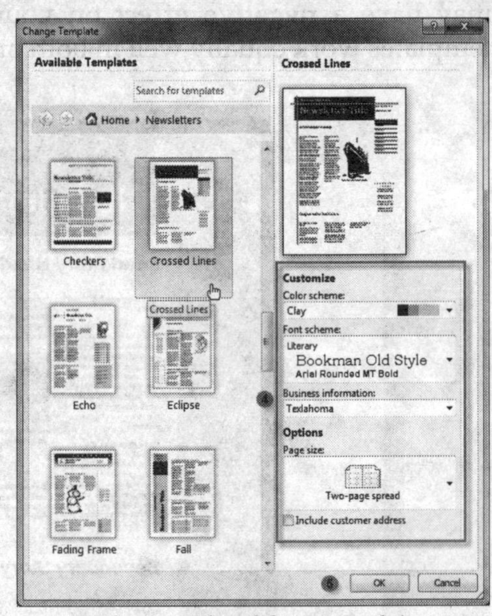

Selecting and modifying a template

- ❑ The new template will be applied to your publication.

The new template

Adding, Rearranging, and Deleting Pages

If you're creating a **newsletter** or another type of publication with **multiple pages**, you might find the **Page Navigation** pane useful. The Page Navigation pane gives you a way to view and scroll through the pages in your publication. It also includes features that let you **add**, **move**, and **delete** pages.

- ❑ To open the **Page Navigation** pane, click the **View** tab on the Ribbon and locate the **Show** group. Then, select the **Page Navigation checkbox**.

To Add a New Page:

- In the Page Navigation pane, right-click any page, then select **Insert Page....**

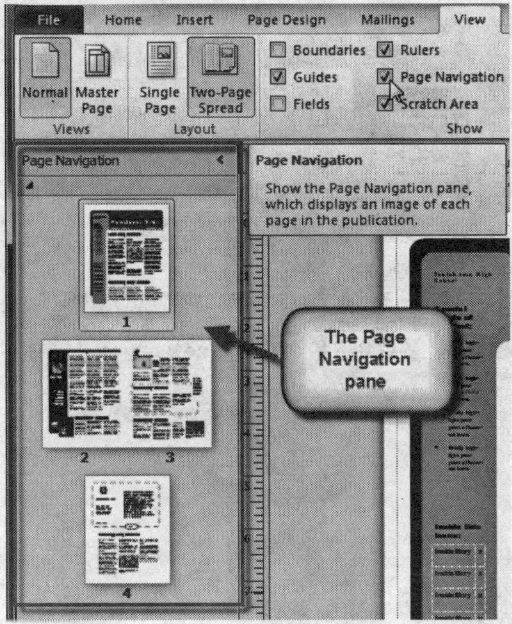

The Page Navigation pane

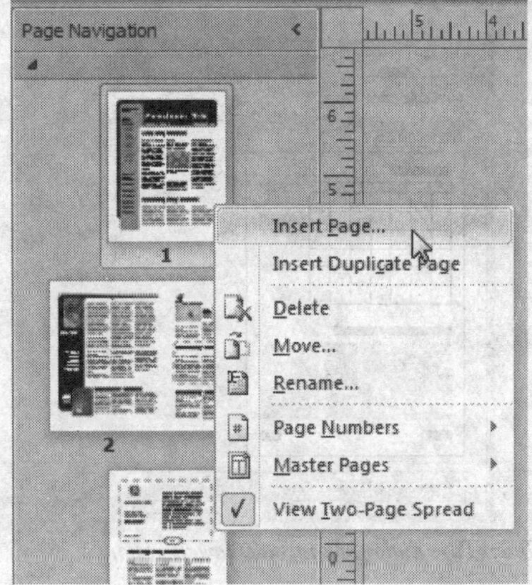

Inserting a new page

- The **Insert Page** dialog box will appear. Specify the **number of pages to insert** and the location where you wish to **insert** them.
- Choose what will appear on the new pages. By default, the pages will be **blank**, but you can also choose to create pages that include **one text box** or pages that are **duplicates** of an existing page.
- Click **OK**.

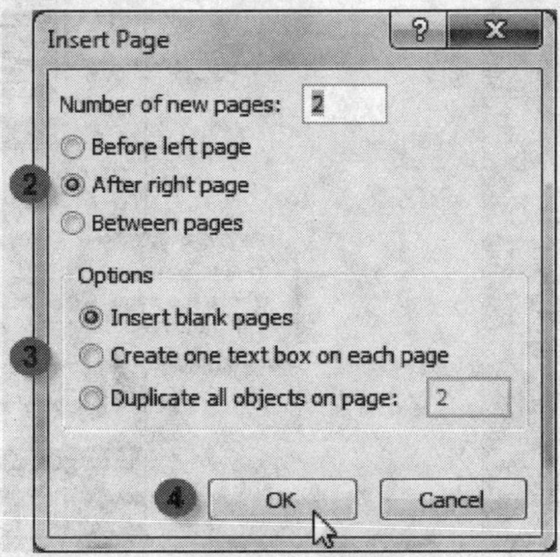

The Insert Page dialog box

- ❑ The new page or pages will be inserted.

Depending on the template you're using, when you add a new page, you may see a dialog box with page layout options.

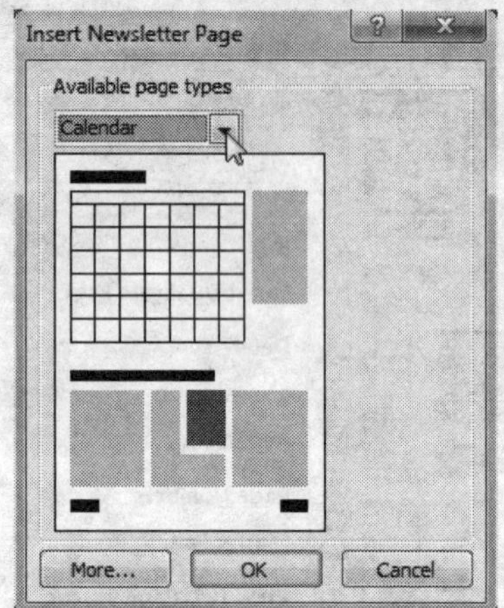

This Insert Page dialog box includes layout options

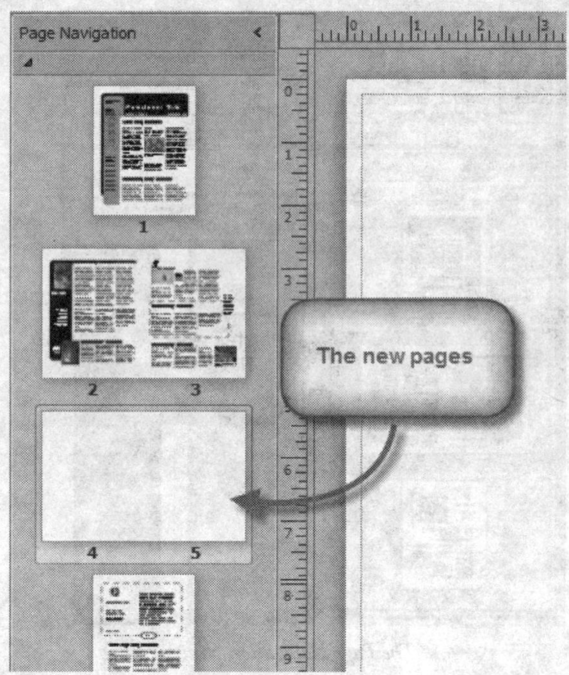

The new blank pages

To Move a Page:

- ❑ In the Page Navigation pane, locate the page you wish to move.
- ❑ **Click** and **drag** the page to its new location, then **release** the mouse.

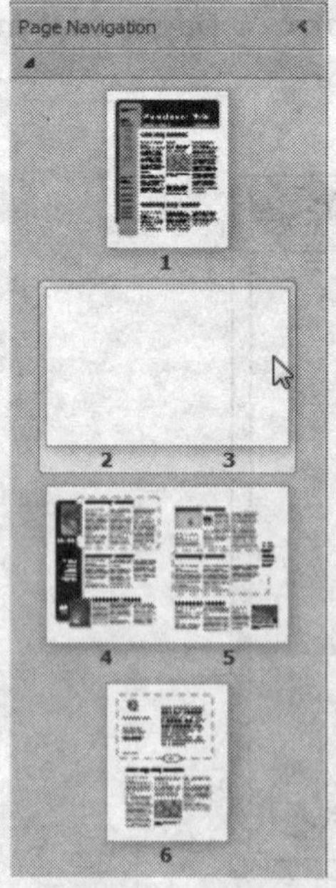

Selecting the page to move

Dragging the page to its new location

- The new page order will be applied.

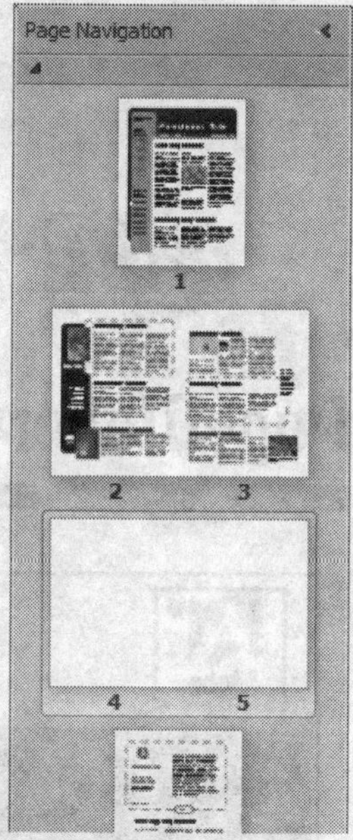

The new page order

To Delete a Page

- In the Page Navigation pane, right-click the page you wish to delete, then select **Delete...** in the list that appears.

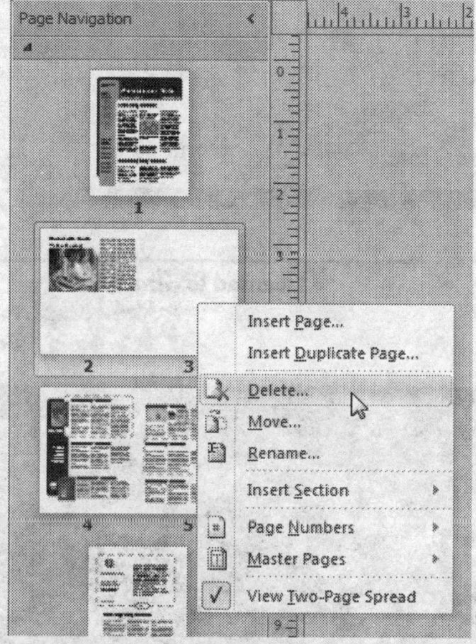

Deleting a page

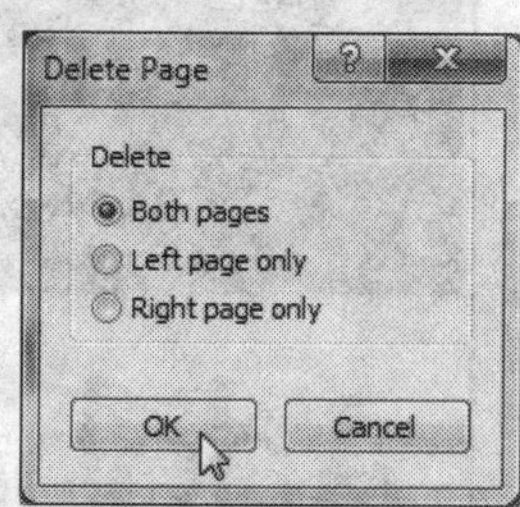

Choosing which pages to delete

- If the page is part of a **two-page** spread, Publisher will ask if you wish to delete one or both pages. Make your selection, then click **OK**.
- The page will be deleted.

Conclusion

Ms Office Publisher is a great Tool for Producing Simple Presentations, brochures etc. Use Ms Office Publish to produce a variety of the Projects.

PageMaker 7.0

PageMaker is a document layout program that has extensive typographic controls, page design capabilities, and customization options. You can add, create, import, and arrange text and graphics and then place them anywhere on the page. PageMaker can also be used as a word processor (complete with a spell check) when in the **Story Editor** mode (found under the **Edit** menu). A word of caution, however: saving a document takes longer in PageMaker than in Word and the file size is larger too. Due to this, it is recommended that you create your text documents in Word, unless your text is relatively short.

PageMaker can be used for single page documents (such as fliers or announcements) or multi-page documents (such as chapters or brochures). In addition, pages can have single or multiple columns, and text can be **threaded** throughout a document (just like a newspaper article that starts on the front page and ends on a different page).

Getting Started with PageMaker

To start a new document, go to **File**, and click **New**. When you create a new PageMaker document, you'll be prompted with the **Document Setup** dialog box. Any of these settings can be changed later on by going to the **File** menu and selecting **Document Setup...**

- ❑ Select a standard page size from the *Page Size* pop-up menu. The dimensions appear automatically in the *Dimensions* boxes.
- ❑ Set the *Orientation* to Tall (Portrait) or Wide (Landscape).
- ❑ **In the Options:** section, click Facing pages if you want left and right pages displayed together (as a two-page spread) and Double-sided if you plan on printing double-sided.
- ❑ **Set Number of pages**: and Start Page #: by entering the desired outcome.
- ❑ **In the Margins**: section, when Double-sided is selected, margins are set as Insideand Outside. The inside margin is on the right side of even numbered pages and on the left side of odd numbered pages. The Outside margins are correspondingly reversed. When Double-sided is deselected, PageMaker changes Inside and Outside to Left and Right margins.
- ❑ Click OK when you've finished setting up your document.

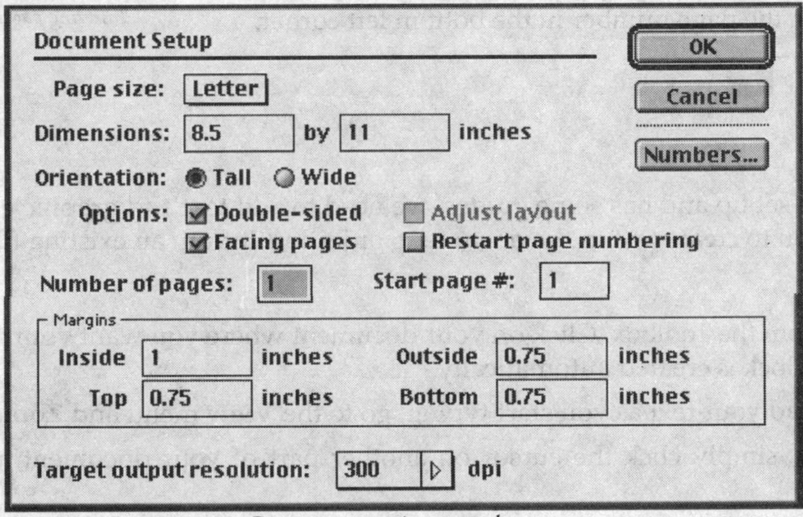

Document setup in pagemaker

Positioning Ruler Guides

- ❑ PageMaker allows you to use nonprinting guides to help you align and position objects on the page. The page already has margin guides – a dotted or coloured rectangle that represents the page margins you specified in the **Document Setup** dialogue box. You can add ruler guides to help position an image, text, etc. so they line up exactly.

- ❑ Under the **View** menu, look to see if there is a checkmark next to the **Snap to Rulers** command. If not, click on it once, and when you check again, the checkmark will be there. When this is checked, the guide will be in line with a tick mark on the ruler.
- ❑ Put your mouse pointer over the horizontal ruler, click and hold, and drag down onto your document to place a horizontal guide. Once you let go, you can move it by clicking and dragging. This process is the same for the vertical guide, and you can create as many guides as you need. You can simply use guides as visual aids, or you can enable the snap-to function by going to the View menu and making sure Snap to Guides i

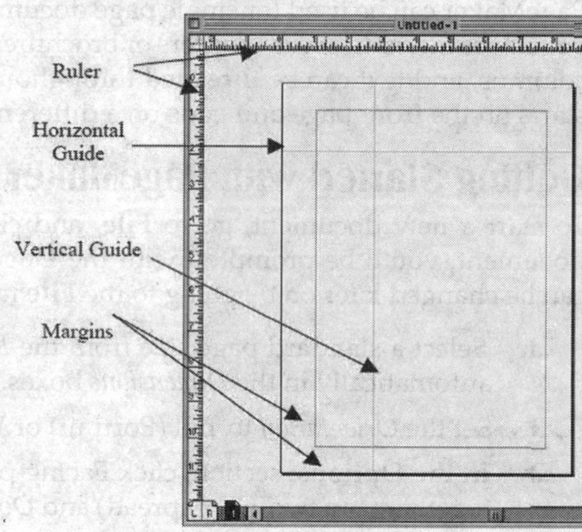

Positioning ruler guides

You can add additional pages in a specific place. Go to Layout, click Insert Pages..., and select the amount of pages desired and where you want to insert them.

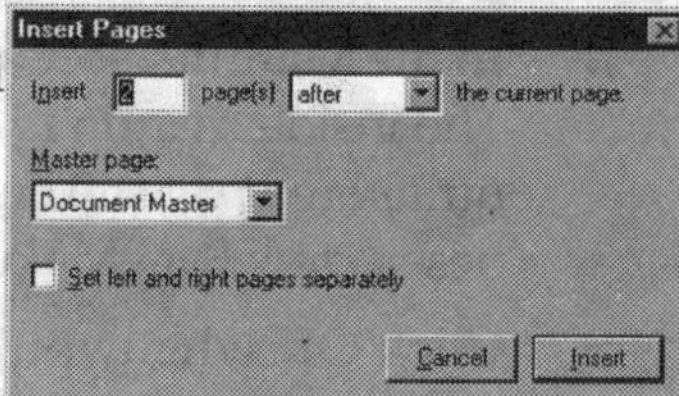

Inserting pages

To navigate through the different pages, just select the number of page to go by clicking the page number in the bottom left corner.

Working with Text

Now that our page is set up and has some guides, we need to add text and graphic elements. PageMaker allows you to create text in the document, or import it from an existing file.

Creating New Text

Select the Text tool from the Toolbox. Click on your document where you want your text, and begin typing. A text block is created automatically.

HINT: If you can't read your text as you start typing, go to the **View** menu and **Zoom In**.

For a new text block, simply click the cursor on another part of your document and start typing again.

- ❑ To **move** a text block, select it by clicking on it once with the Pointer Tool (choose the Pointer Tool from the toolbox). Once it is selected, click and hold, then move it to the new position and release the mouse button.
- ❑ To **resize** a text block, select it by clicking once with the Pointer. Click on the "handles" on the border of the text block and drag until you have the correct new size.

Placing (Inserting) Existing Text

Unlike most programs, PageMaker doesn't have an Insert menu. Even so, you can import text and graphics by using the Place command in the File menu.

- ❑ Go to the File menu and select Place.
- ❑ Navigate to your document and click Open. Your cursor turns into the Place icon. Click in your document where you'd like the text to be placed. Remember, you can always move and resize it.

You can also designate the size of your text block by clicking and dragging a square as you place the text.

Formatting Text

Modifying your text is done in a similar fashion as in Word. The most common characteristics you need to modify (such as font, size, alignment, etc.) are found under the Type menu. Make sure you're using the Text Tool, highlight the text you want to change and go to the Type menu.

Additional text options can be found in the Utilities menu in the plug-ins section (such as Bullets and Numbering, Drop Caps, etc.).

Note....

PageMaker 7.0 can only place Word 6.0/95 documents on the Mac platform. If you are using PageMaker 7.0 on a Windows platform, you can place Word 97 as well as Word 2000 documents. If your Word document is of another version, you should save it as a RTF or Word 6.0/95 (in Word) and then use the Place command in the File menu.

Graphics

To add a graphic to a PageMaker document, you must **Place** it, just like we placed text.

- ❑ Make sure the Pointer tool is selected and go to the **File** menu and select **Place** (if you have the Text Tool selected, the graphic will get placed as part of the text instead of independently).
- ❑ Navigate to the location of your image file.
- ❑ Click OK and the cursor will turn into the Place icon. Click In your document where you'd like the graphic to be placed.

You can move the graphic by clicking and dragging the graphic to its new location. To resize the object, use the Pointer tool to drag the handles.

HINT: To keep the graphic proportionate as you change the size, hold down the shift key on the keyboard as you drag one of the corner handles.

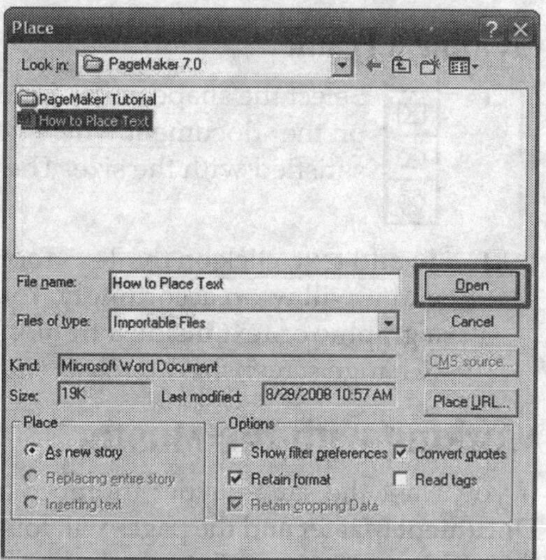

Adding graphics to a document

Wrapping Text around a Graphic

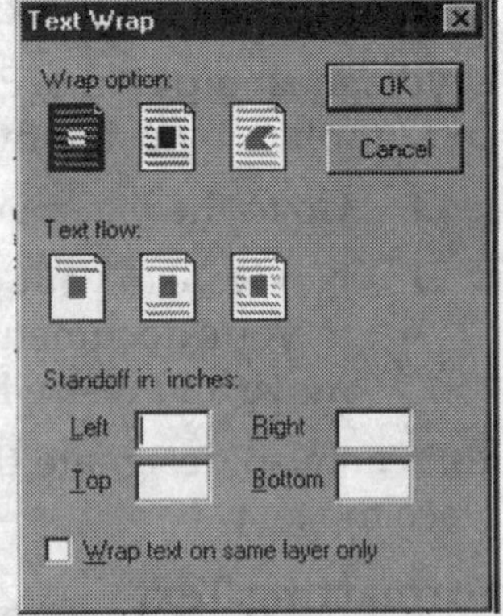

Wrapping text

Similar to Microsoft Word, PageMaker allows you to wrap text around a graphic, or have the text over/under the graphic.

- ❑ Make sure the object is selected. If you can't seem to select it, it could be because your text is on top of it and the graphic is behind your text. Click once on the text block, go to the **Element** menu, then to **Arrange**, and select **Send to Back**. This will send the selected element (in this case, the text block) to the back, so you can now select the graphic.
- ❑ Under the **Element** menu, select **Text Wrap**. You can choose different options for wrapping in the dialog box that appears.

Once you've added wrapping to an object, you'll see additional handles around the object. Use these handles to bring the wrapping closer or further from the object.

Shapes

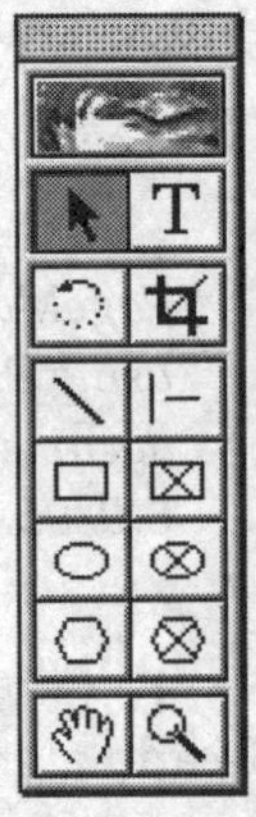

shapes

To add a shape (such as an oval, rectangle, or hexagon) to your document, select the appropriate shape from the Toolbox and click, hold and drag to draw the shape on the page.

To shade your new shape, make sure it's selected and go to the **Element** menu and select **Fill and Stroke**. **Fill** refers to the colour or pattern used for shading, while **Stroke** refers to the border around the shape. If you are planning to put text inside the shape, you should make sure the opacity of the shading colour is light (around 30% or less).

HINT: To offset certain text blocks you can draw a shape around the text and shade it in. When you're finished, you might have to use the **Send to Back** command (**Element** menu, then to **Arrange**) to send the shape behind the text.

Creating a Frame

- ❑ Select the shape of the frame you want to use from the Toolbox. Click on the document where you want the frame to be located and drag until you are satisfied with the size. The frame is now ready to receive content.
- ❑ To add text, click on the Text Tool and then click inside the frame. Start typing your text and it will wrap accordingly. You can also use the **Place** command (**File** menu), to put a graphic or text inside a frame. The text takes the particular shape you have selected. (Change screenshot)

Working with the Master

If you want the same layout (number of columns, etc.) on several pages, you can set up the **Document Master** and the pages will follow that layout. You can have more than one Master – for example, one Master with two columns and one with three. To access the Document Master, click on the **L** and **R** icons in the lower left of your window for a two sided document (for a single page document, make sure you set up the correct side). If you want to make simple changes for your document, such as margins and page orientation, select the **Document Setup** from the **File** menu. **Columns** control the flow of your text on each page. **Autoflow** controls the flow of the text throughout the document. While you can change the number of columns or set the Autoflow on any individual page, if you want the same look throughout the document, do these steps in the Master.

Columns

Go to the **Layout** menu and choose **Column Guides**.

This command creates a specified number of columns of identical widths, fitting them within the margins of the page. If you want PageMaker to automatically reposition existing text or graphics to align with the revised column setup, check the box next to Adjust Layout in the Column Guides dialog box. Refer to the image given below.

AutoFlow

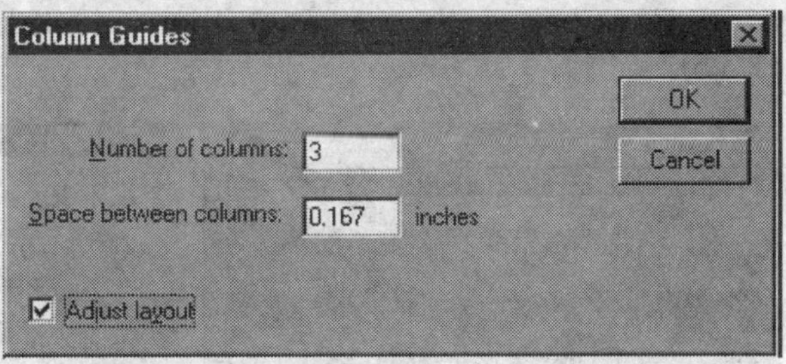

Go to the **Layout** menu and choose **Autoflow**.

If you are placing a long document, you might want it to flow automatically into the necessary number of even pages and/or columns. This can be accomplished using the **Autoflow** feature of PageMaker.

If Autoflow is checked on the Document Master, any text you place will automatically flow into the columns and/or pages that you have in place and new pages will be added if necessary. However, if Autoflow is only checked on an individual page, it won't flow onto the next page and it won't create more pages, you would need to do this manually.

Creating a Booklet

You can also create booklets with Adobe PageMaker. Before you start, you should think about what you would like your booklet to look like and how long you want it to be. PageMaker can create five basic booklets

- **2-up Saddle-Stitch**: made up of sheets of paper folded in half and then stapled in the fold.
- **2-up Perfect Bound**: made up of a series of booklets that are bound along the spine. It is intended for large documents, 20 sheets of paper or more, which none of the other formats can accommodate.
- **2,3 or 4-up Consecutive**: made up of multiple pages on one sheet folded in an accordion-like style.

We will create an 8 page **2-up Saddle Stitch** Booklet.

To start:

- Create a new document by going to the **File** menu, and selecting **New**.

- ❑ In the Document Setup dialog box divide the dimensions of your paper in half.
- ❑ Now select the number of pages you will require.

HINT: There are four pages to every sheet of paper (including the front and back of the page).

Now type or draw the information you would like on each page. Once you have all the information as you like it:

- ❑ Go to the **Utilities** menu select **Plug-ins** and then **Build Booklet**.
- ❑ Select 2-up Saddle Stitch I.
- ❑ Insert any blank pages if your document is an odd number (PageMaker should automatically create them).
- ❑ Select OK.

Printing

Go the **File** menu and click on **Print**. You can select all or a range of pages. If you want contiguous pages, choose range then use a dash (1-3); or for noncontiguous, use a comma (1,3,5).

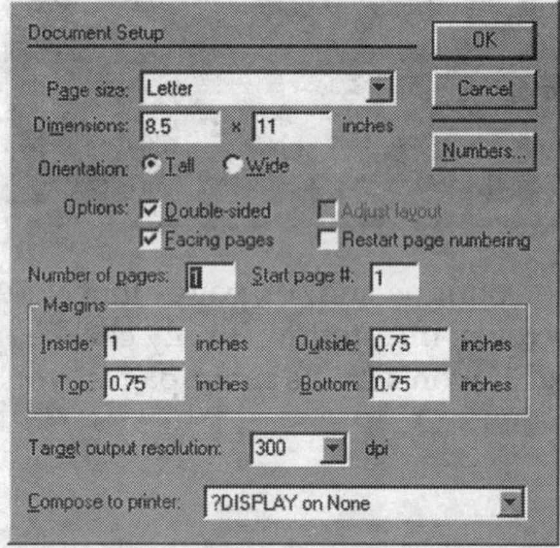

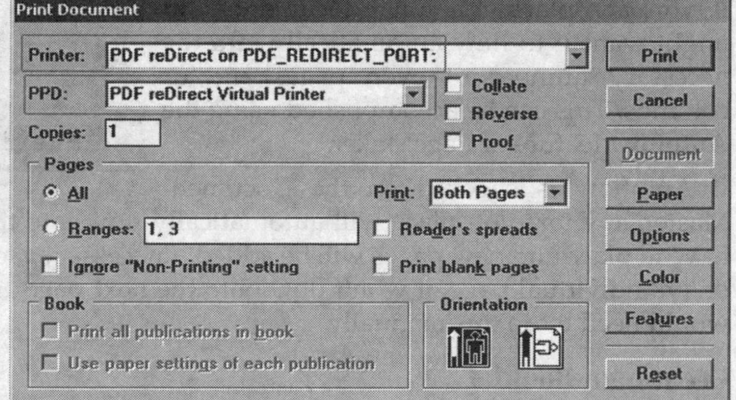

Printing a document

Attention Readers! Now the Adobe PageMaker Features have been merged in Adobe InDesign, Master the Features of InDesign and you need not learn Adobe PageMaker.

Adobe InDesign

Adobe® InDesign® CS5 software is a versatile desktop publishing application that gives you pixel-perfect control over design and typography; and help you to create elegant and engaging pages for print, tablets, and other screens. Use new Adaptive Design Tools to easily repurpose layouts to look great on a variety of pages sizes, orientations, or devices.

Exploring the workspace

The InDesign workspace encompasses everything you see when you first open or create a document: the Toolbox, document window, pasteboard, and other panels. You can customize and save the work area to suit your work style. For example, you can choose to display only those panels you frequently use, minimize and rearrange panel groups, resize windows, and add additional document windows.

The InDesign CS5 Interface

The InDesign interface is very intuitive and easy to navigate. Everything you need to work with and create layout documents is right at your fingertips. The first interface item you should familiarize yourself with is the Welcome Screen.

Shown in Figure next page is the default, essential Workspace for InDesign CS5. These are the main elements you will be working with:

- **Menu Bar:** You can access any of the menu list options by clicking any of the word headings in the menu bar.
- **InDesign Application Menu:** This "Mac only" menu provides access to InDesign's application-specific options, such as Preferences, as well as some other Mac OS X system features such as Hiding and Showing.

  In Mac OS X, you can hide InDesign by Option-clicking anywhere in the desktop area behind the open document. Note that the Application Frame option must be disabled for you to do so.
- **Application Bar:** View options, zoom percentage, screen mode, and arrange options are all available from the Application Bar drop-down lists.
- **Control Panel:** Options for the tool you currently have selected in the Tools panel always appear here.

- **Tools Panel:** You can access any of the InDesign tools by clicking one of the icons shown in the Tools panel.
- **Panels:** All the panels can be accessed under the Window menu in the menu bar. They are listed alphabetically in the main pull-down, but note that some are grouped into submenus within the list. After they are accessed, all panels (other than the Tools panel or the Control panel) appear docked on the right side of your screen, but can also be relocated within the dock, grouped with other panels, or released from the dock and left free-floating.
- **Welcome Screen:** This dialog box appears only when you first launch InDesign. It contains links for opening recent documents, creating new documents, and accessing the InDesign community via the Internet. If you'd prefer not to see the Welcome Screen every time you launch InDesign, enable the Don't Show Again option located in the lower-left corner of the dialog box.

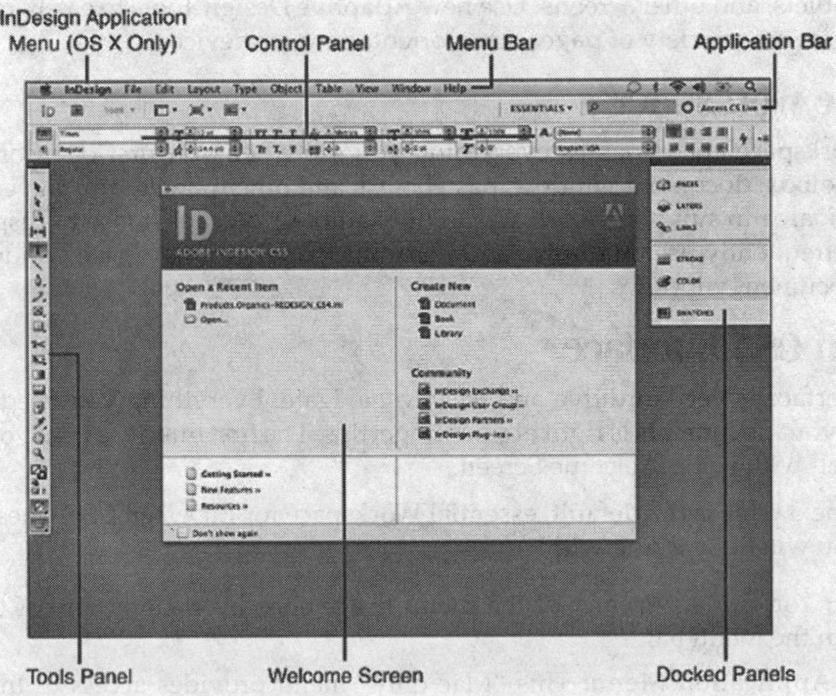

This is the startup Welcome Screen that you see the first time you launch InDesign

In Mac OS X or Windows, you can press Tab to hide all the controls in the interface at once and focus on the document window. Press Shift+Tab to hide all the panels except the Tools panel, the Control panel, and the Application Bar.

The Preferences command, which is located under the InDesign menu in Mac OS X, is located under the Edit menu in Windows.

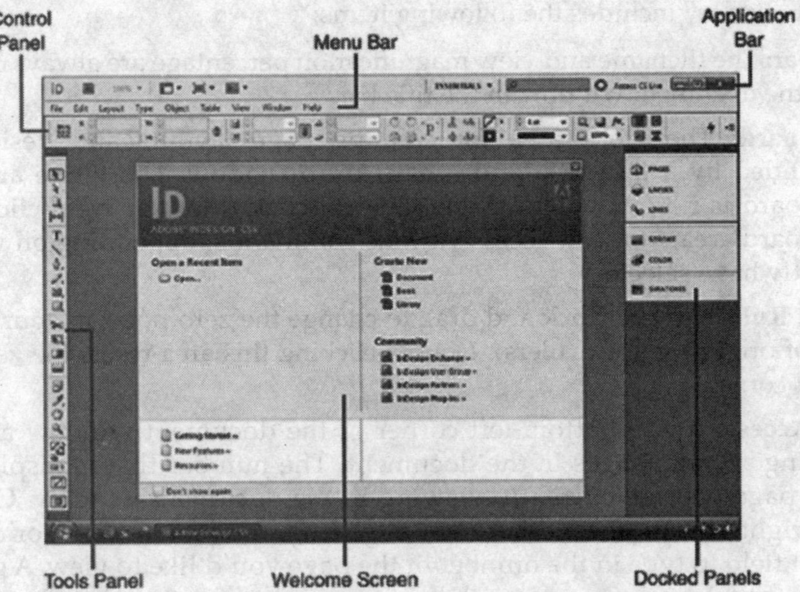

This is the screen you see the first time you launch InDesign CS5 in Windows

The Document Window

Anytime you open or start a new document InDesign places it in its own document window. You can view all the pages in your document within this window (see Figure).

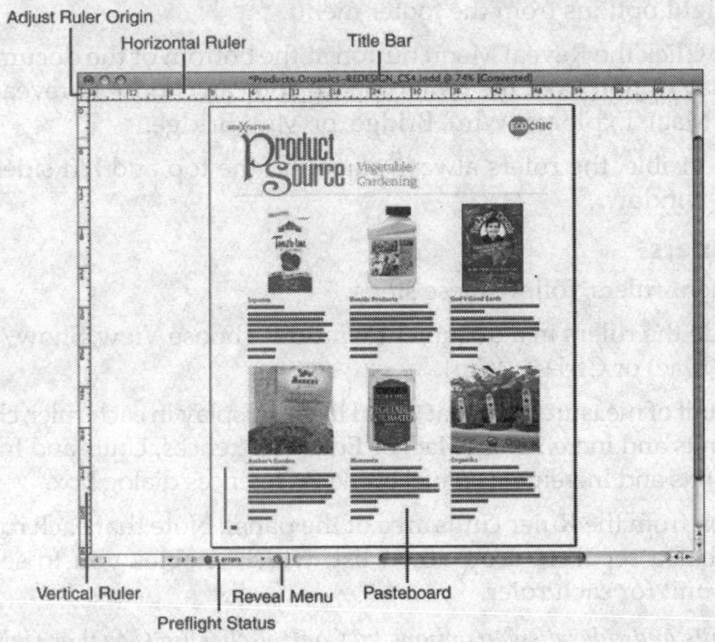

Every document window contains its own set of rulers, as well as controls for accessing specific pages of a document

The document window includes the following items;

- **Title Bar:** The filename and view magnification percentage are always displayed at the top of the document window in the title bar.
- **Pasteboard:** The work area for creating page layouts and designs is always surrounded by a thin rule and a hard drop shadow. The white area outside the pasteboard is not printable. If you Control-click (Mac) or right-click (Win) in the Pasteboard area, you can access various commands, depending on which tool you currently have selected.
- **Adjust Ruler Origin:** Click and drag to change the zero point in your document (the point of origin for your rulers). Double-clicking this area resets the zero point to the top-left corner.
- **Page Access:** In the bottom-left corner of the document window are controls for accessing specific pages in the document. The number that is displayed indicates which page you are currently viewing in the document window. Click the arrow to the right of it to select a different page from the footer menu, or double-click in the text field to type in the number of the page you'd like to view. A group of arrow buttons enables you to access the next spread, previous spread, and first or last page of the document.
- **Preflight Status:** By default, InDesign's Preflight option is always on, which allows InDesign to automatically check for document errors in the background while you work. InDesign displays any Preflight prepress check errors that it finds in the document at the bottom of the window. Click the arrow to the right of the status display to select different Preflight options from the footer menu.
- **Reveal Menu:** Click the Reveal Menu button at the bottom of the document window to choose a display option from the footer menu. You can choose to reveal the document in the Finder (Mac), Explorer (Win), Bridge, or Mini Bridge.
- **Rulers:** When visible, the rulers always surround the top and left sides of a layout in the document window.

Hiding/Showing Rulers

To display the document rulers, follow these steps:

- To show or hide the rulers in a document window, choose View, Show/Hide Rulers or press Cmd-R (Mac) or Ctrl+R (Win).
- To choose the unit of measurement that you'd like to display in each ruler, choose InDesign, Preferences, Units and Increments (Mac) or Edit, Preferences, Units and Increments (Win) to access the Units and Increments panel of the Preferences dialog box.
- Select an option from the Ruler Units area of the panel. Note that each ruler (Horizontal and Vertical) has a separate drop-down list, which enables you to select a different measurement unit for each ruler.

You can also change units and ruler display options by Control-clicking (Mac) or right-clicking in the ruler area and choosing a command from the contextual menu.

The ruler area also enables you to click and drag guidelines (referred to as ruler guides) onto the pasteboard. Hold down Shift as you click and drag to snap the guide to the nearest ruler increment. Double-click in the ruler area to add a guide at that exact measurement point on the page.

Creating New Documents, InDesignCS5

This Section will give readers the basic knowledge on how to set-up a document for print in Indesign CS5.

Opening InDesign & Setting Preferences

Open InDesign and you will be presented with an introduction screen. It is here where we will start to create the new document. But before we create a new document we need to make sure that units used for measuring are set up correctly.

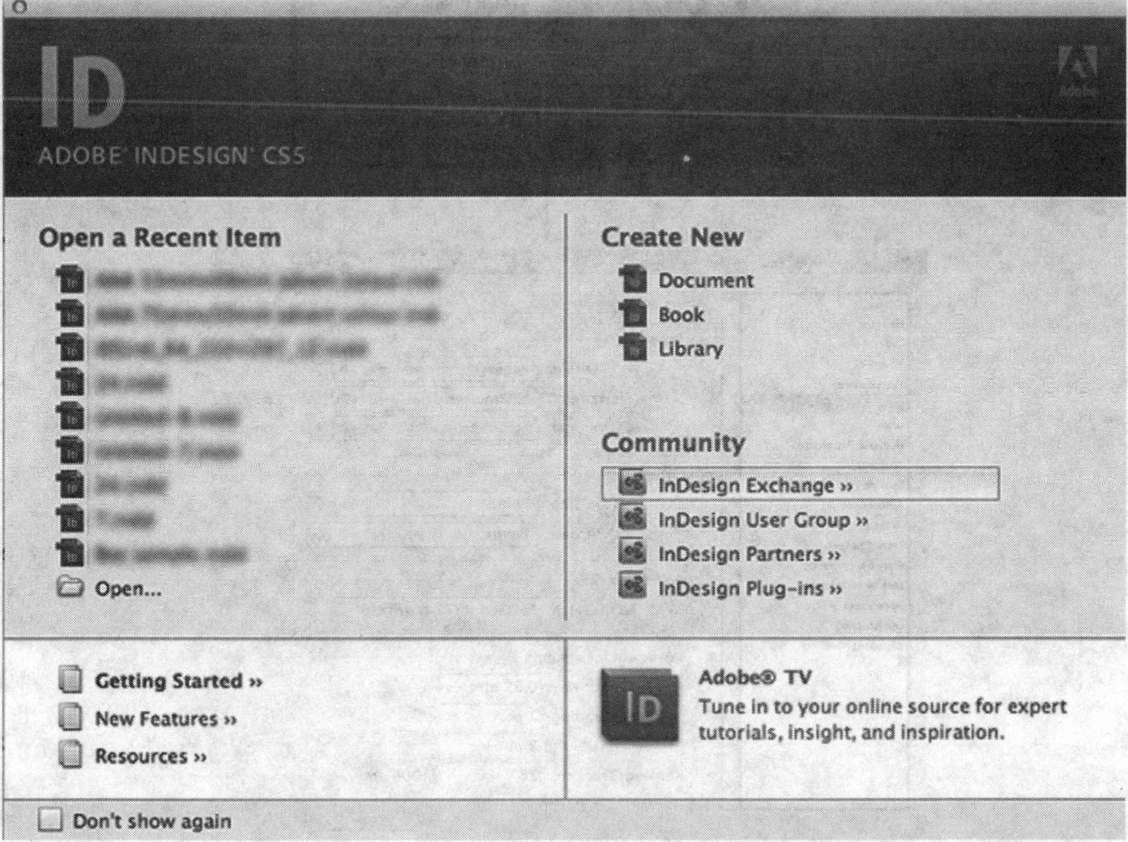

I prefer to work in millimetres for rulers and points for type. To change these values go to **InDesign > Preferences > Units and increments**. Under Ruler Units change the horizontal and vertical values to the desired unit of measurement. You will notice that I skipped the ruler origin. This needs a more detailed explanation which is covered in the next step.

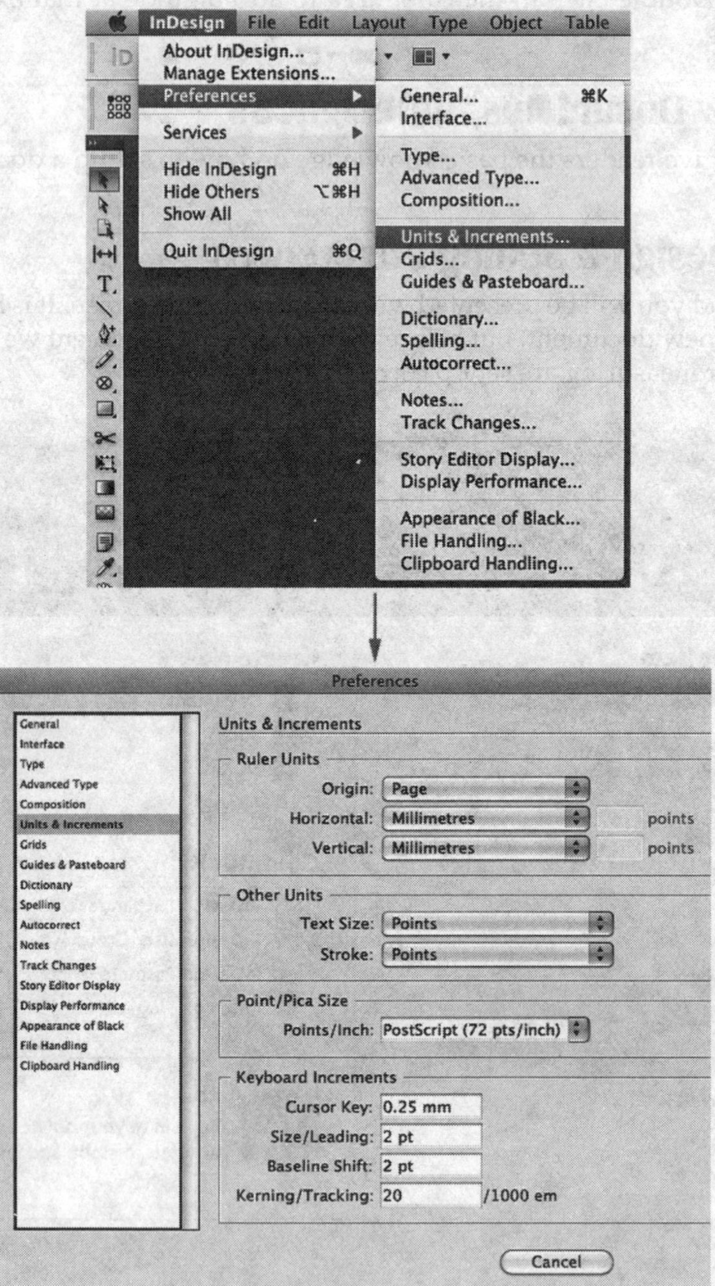

Ruler

The origin of the ruler can be set to spread, page or spine. By selecting spread, the ruler will start from the left hand side of the document and span across the spread of the document.

By selecting page, the ruler will start at the left hand side and stop when it gets to the end of the page and it will start at zero again.

The spine preset is useful when you are using facing pages and of course have a spine. The ruler will start its zero point from the spine and work to the edge of the document.

Creating New Document

Ok, back to the introduction screen. On the right hand side select create new document.

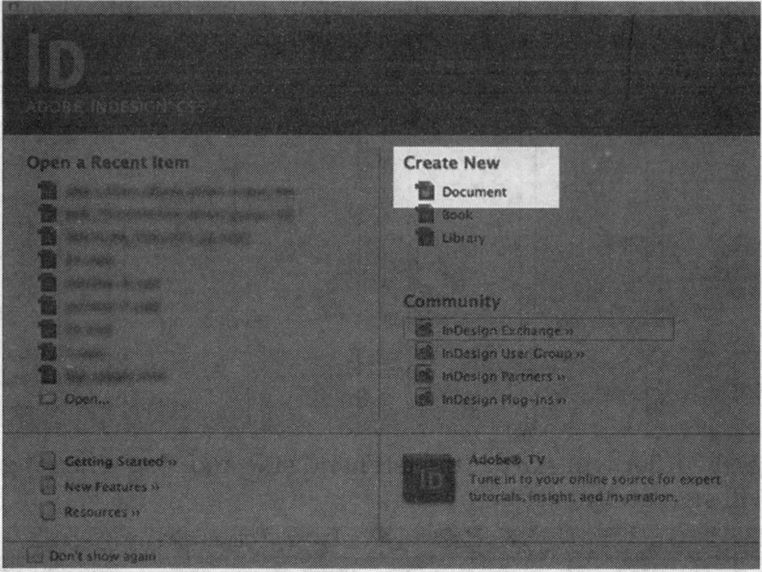

Another floating screen will appear. Now before you format the document it will save time to have a rough idea of the kind of document you want to set (do a sketch for a rough mockup). If you tick Master text frame InDesign will automatically place a text box based on your document setup (three columns, same margins etc).

Selecting Page Size

Within the page size division you have a drop down menu with a selection of popular presets that are used worldwide. In my case A4 is present, so I will select this. If you want to enter a custom size you can do so by typing directly into the width and height boxes. You can also define the orientation to portrait or landscape.

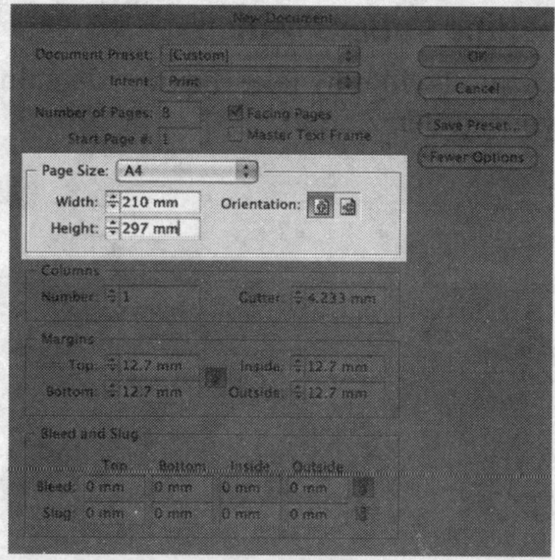

Selecting Columns

As you planned out your design beforehand you know that you need a three column structure. As you have not determined the margins yet you will do it now.

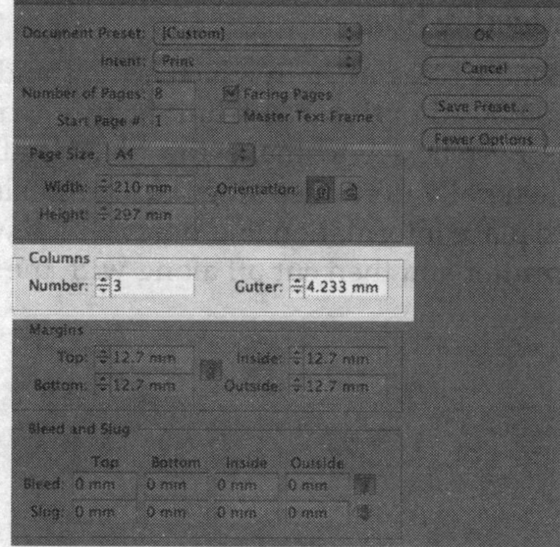

Setting Margin

When setting margins prefer to progress sizes from smallest to largest in the following order: inside, outside, top, bottom. So break down the page as follows: inside: 12.5mm, outside 15mm, top 17.5mm and Bottom 20mm. When entering the values make sure that the link symbol at the centre of the margins column is not ticked. When ticked it will make all the margin settings the same.

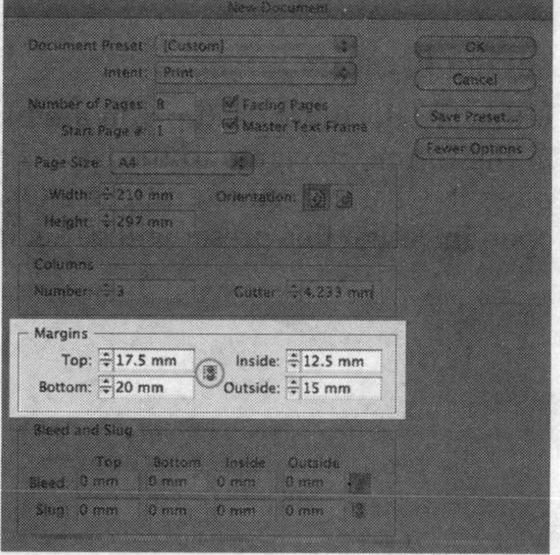

Setting Gutter Position

Ok, you will now take the outside value and half it for your gutter, 7.5mm.

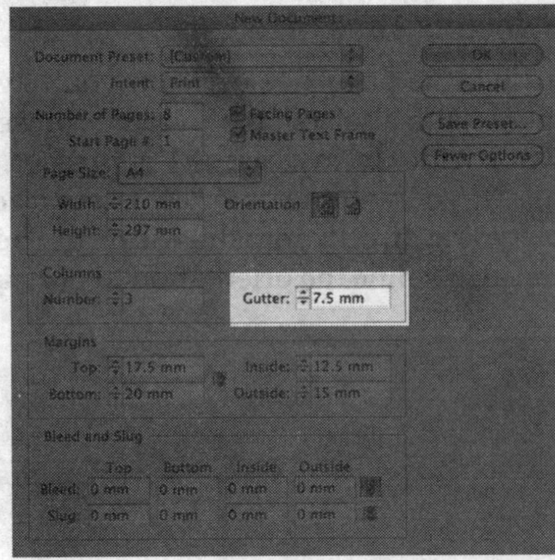

Bleed & Slug

Set the bleed at 3mm which is the standard size. Again the bleed option has a link feature which in this case is best ticked to make the bleed settings the same. Generally don't use slug. However, slug can be used to place information and notes which will be seen by a printer and then cut off along with the bleed.

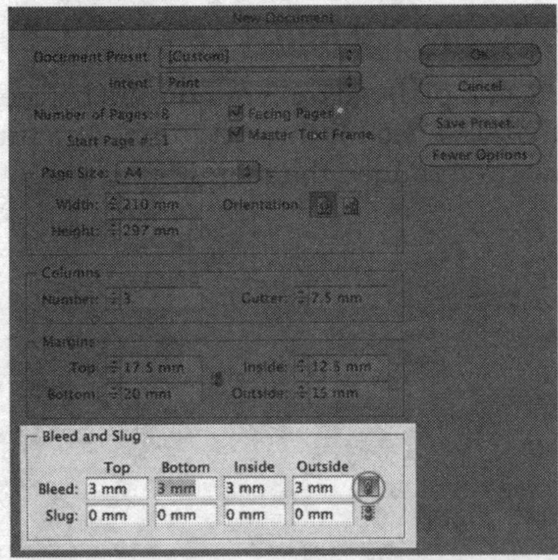

Saving Preset

If this is a document setup you are likely to use again in the future, navigate to the Save Preset button and press it. Give it a name and press OK. Next time you open InDesign this preset will be set up ready.

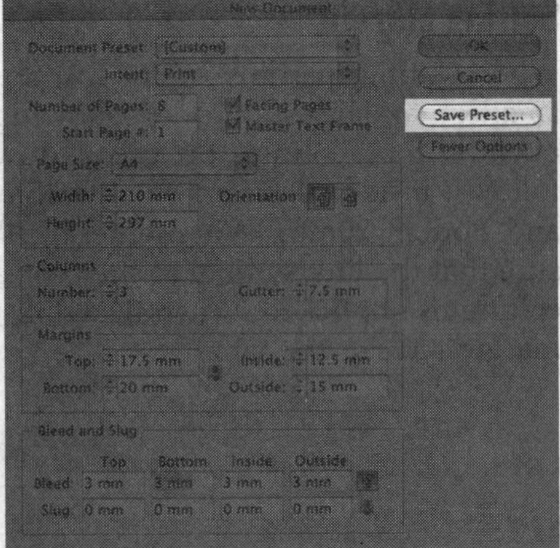

Setting up document Size

If at any time you find you need to change the document size or bleed go to **File > Document Setup**.

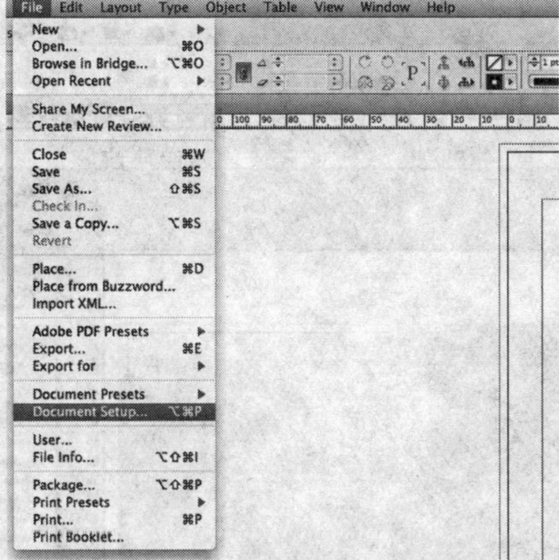

If you need to adjust the margins or columns go to **Layout > Margins and Columns**

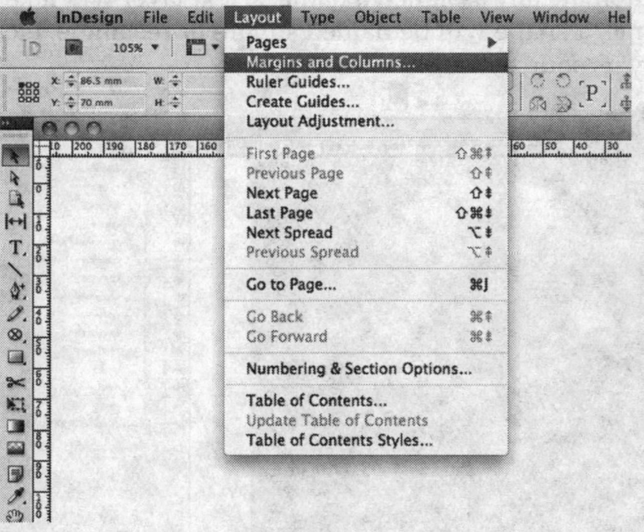

Layers & Panels

The new layers panel added to InDesign CS5 is packed with features that can really speed up your operating pace. The panel now resembles Adobe's Illustrator Layer panel and has borrowed many of its useful features. So if you are new InDesign or have simply overlooked this addition read on.

The Panel

First open an existing document that contains a lot of items. To activate the panel go to **Window > Layers.** Click once on one of the disclosure arrows to reveal the items contained within that layer.

Immediately you will notice that each individual item has been split on to an individual sub-layer. These layers are automatically assigned a name. A text layer will take its name from the beginning of the text frame, a shape will be named square or rectangle, etc. and an imported graphic will be named by its source name.

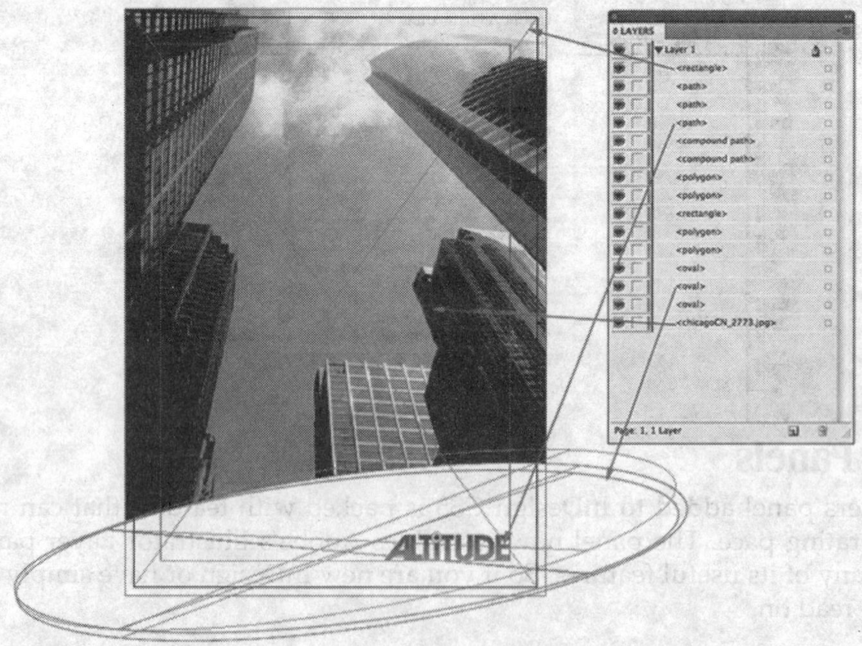

To change the name of a layer, click once on top of the actual name (The cursor will transform to a white hand) and then again, the name will highlight blue, now enter the new name.

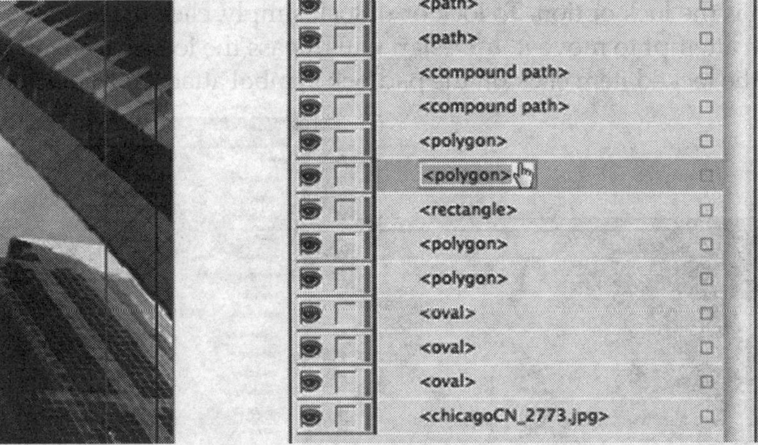

Visibility and Locking

Before the introduction of the Layers panel, InDesign would stack items on top of each other making individual selecting a bit of a headache. Now by using the layers panel it is possible to turn the visibility of the items on or off and in turn locate the item faster. Do this by clicking on the visibility icon indicated below.

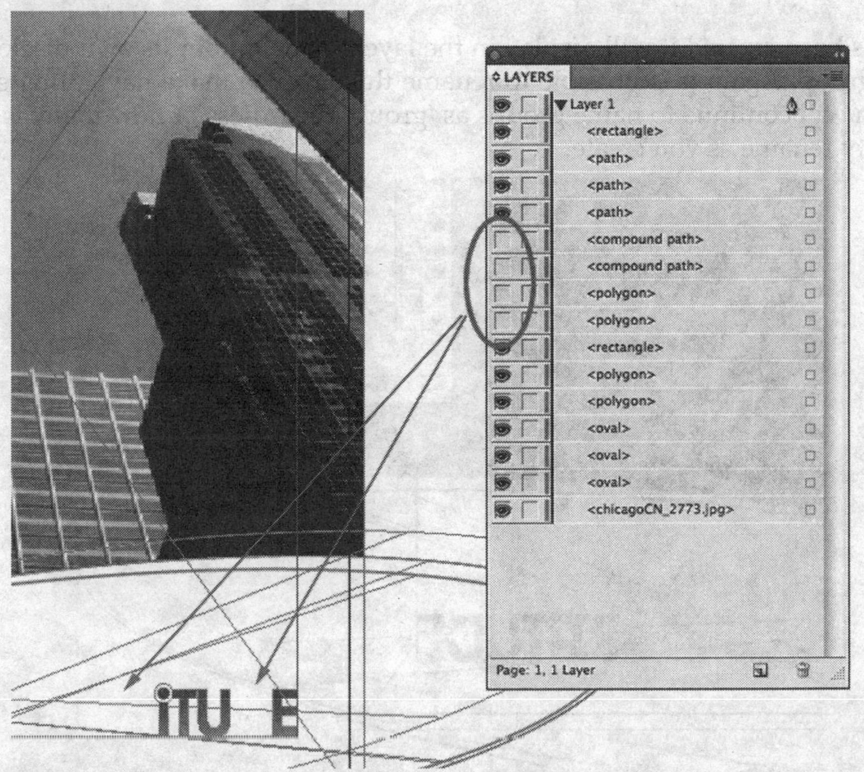

To select or deselect a few items at a time, click once on the visibility icon and drag up or down the line of icons. Alternatively hold down shift to pick out layers not sitting next to each other.

Next to the visibility icon is the lock option. To lock or unlock simply, click in the lock box. When an item is locked and you attempt to move it, InDesign will bypass the locked item and select the item below it. To unlock the locked item click on the padlock symbol attached to the item frame.

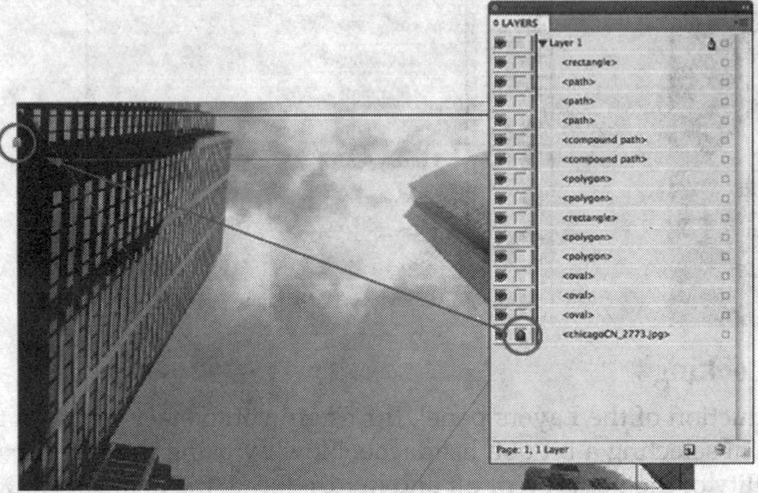

Groups

If a group has been created it will display in the layers panel under its own disclosure arrow and named group. Again it is possible to rename this layer to make navigating easier. Note that InDesign will continue to name groups as 'group' regardless of how many is created, so for your sanity rename as you create.

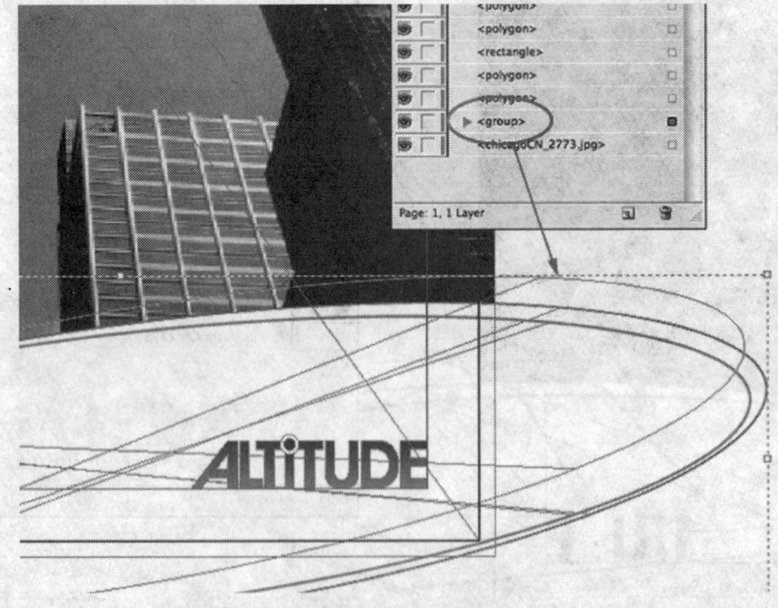

The cool feature about grouping within a layer is the ability to control the groups via the layer panel. In past versions of InDesign if you wanted to add an item to a group you would have to ungroup, select the items and the additional item and group again. Now simply select the item you want to add to the group and drag it into the group layer. This process can be reversed too if you want take an item out of the group, just drag it out.

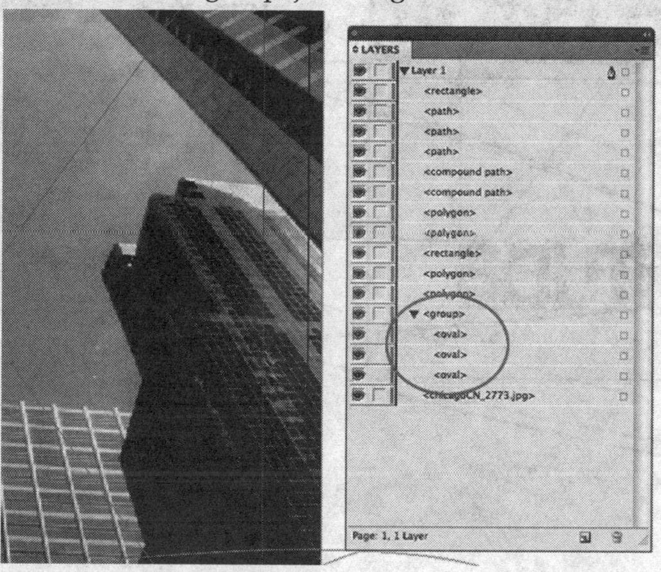

Navigating Items

If there is a particular item you want to locate and edit, use the following method. Find the item in the panel list, **right click > Select** and **Fit Item.** InDesign will automatically select the item, centre it and zoom in close.

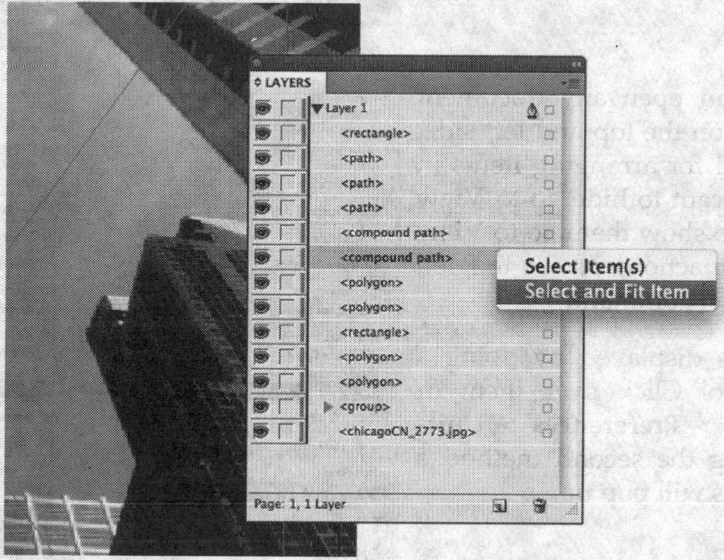

Also it is possible to toggle through individual items by clicking on the square to the left of the layer name. When clicked InDesign will select the frame. However, this method will only highlight the item and it won't be centred.

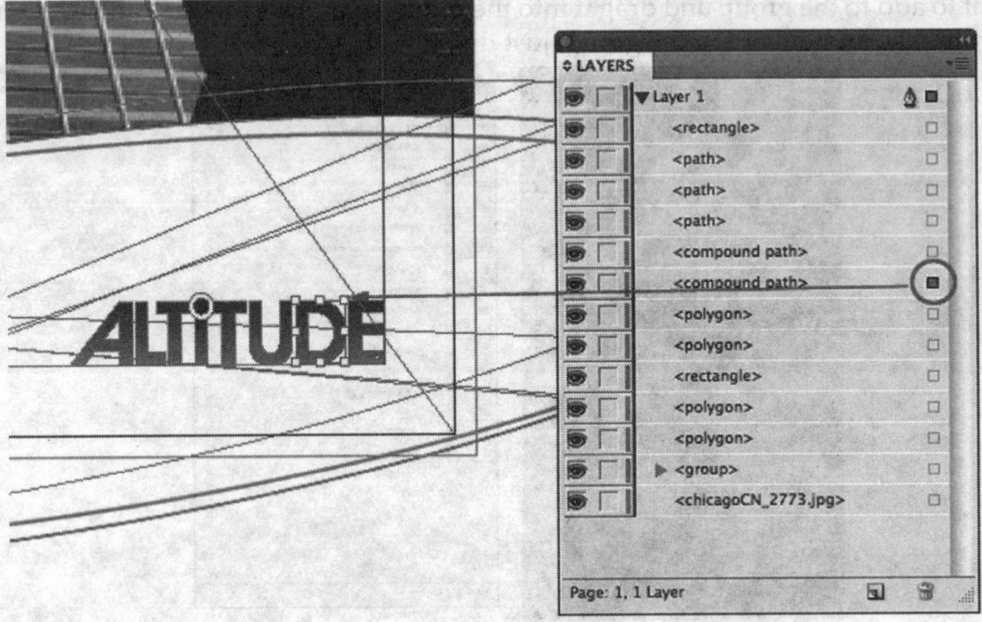

Working with Rulers and Guides in Adobe Indesign

This tutorial will teach you how to improve your InDesign skills, whether you are a beginner or an intermediate user, you will learn some good tips to improve your workspace using rulers and guides.

Rulers

By default when you open any document you'll see the rulers on the top and left side. They are very useful for arranging items in your sheets. If you want to hide go to **View > Hide Rulers** and to show them go to **View > Show Rulers**. Both actions can be toggled with the same hotkey (Command + R).

To change the units displayed by doing a Right Click /Control Click over them or you can go to **Edit > Preferences > Units & Increments**, using the second method a window with options will pop up.

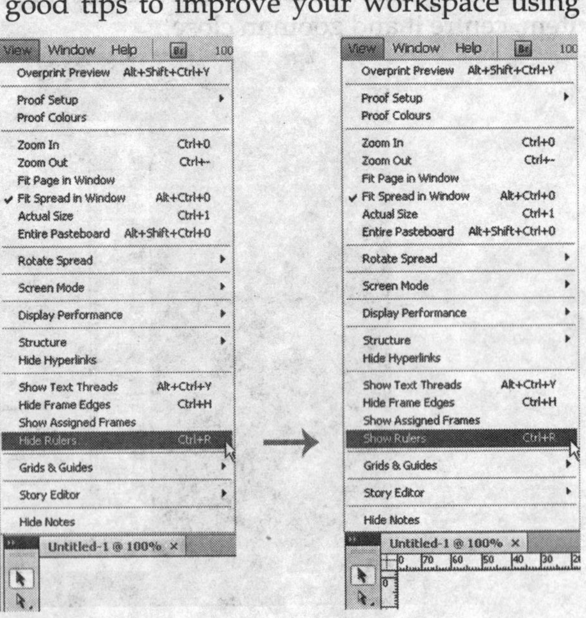

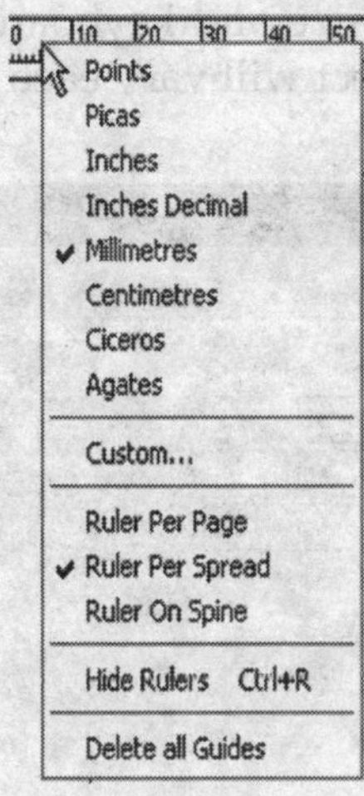
Points
Picas
Inches
Inches Decimal
Millimetres
Centimetres
Ciceros
Agates
Custom...
Ruler Per Page
Ruler Per Spread
Ruler On Spine
Hide Rulers Ctrl+R
Delete all Guides

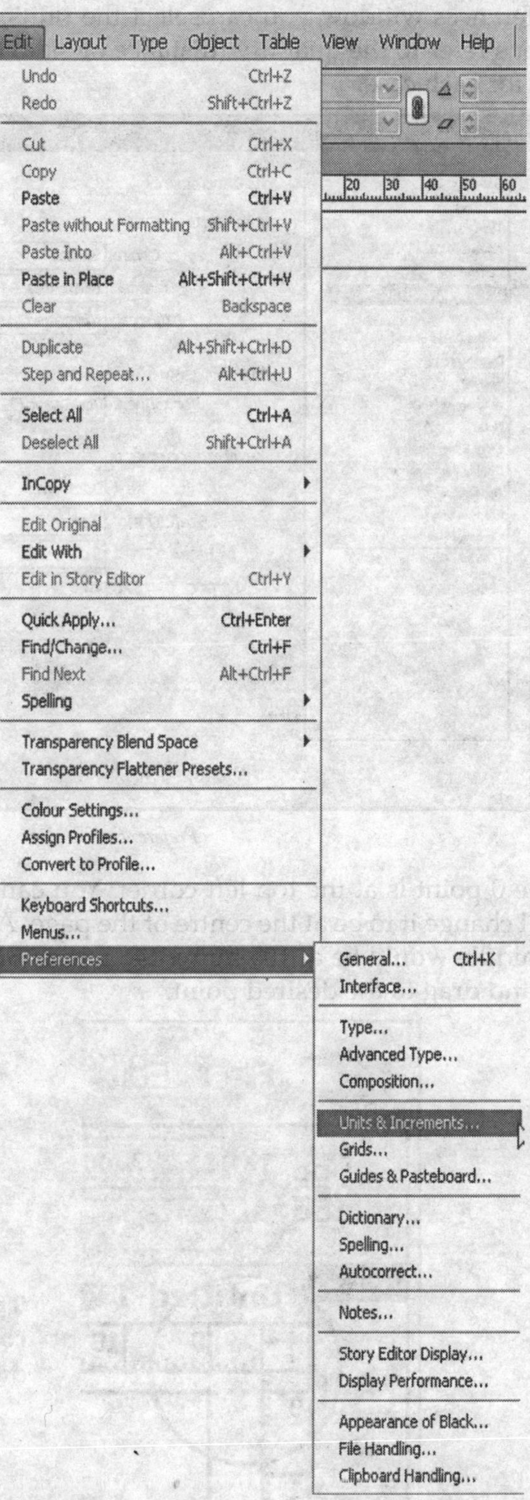
Edit Layout Type Object Table View Window Help
Undo Ctrl+Z
Redo Shift+Ctrl+Z
Cut Ctrl+X
Copy Ctrl+C
Paste Ctrl+V
Paste without Formatting Shift+Ctrl+V
Paste Into Alt+Ctrl+V
Paste in Place Alt+Shift+Ctrl+V
Clear Backspace
Duplicate Alt+Shift+Ctrl+D
Step and Repeat... Alt+Ctrl+U
Select All Ctrl+A
Deselect All Shift+Ctrl+A
InCopy
Edit Original
Edit With
Edit in Story Editor Ctrl+Y
Quick Apply... Ctrl+Enter
Find/Change... Ctrl+F
Find Next Alt+Ctrl+F
Spelling
Transparency Blend Space
Transparency Flattener Presets...
Colour Settings...
Assign Profiles...
Convert to Profile...
Keyboard Shortcuts...
Menus...
Preferences
General... Ctrl+K
Interface...
Type...
Advanced Type...
Composition...
Units & Increments...
Grids...
Guides & Pasteboard...
Dictionary...
Spelling...
Autocorrect...
Notes...
Story Editor Display...
Display Performance...
Appearance of Black...
File Handling...
Clipboard Handling...

With the preferences window you can select the units, point size and keyboard increments. The last options refer to the quantity (distance or size) the object will vary each time you use the keyboard for each case.

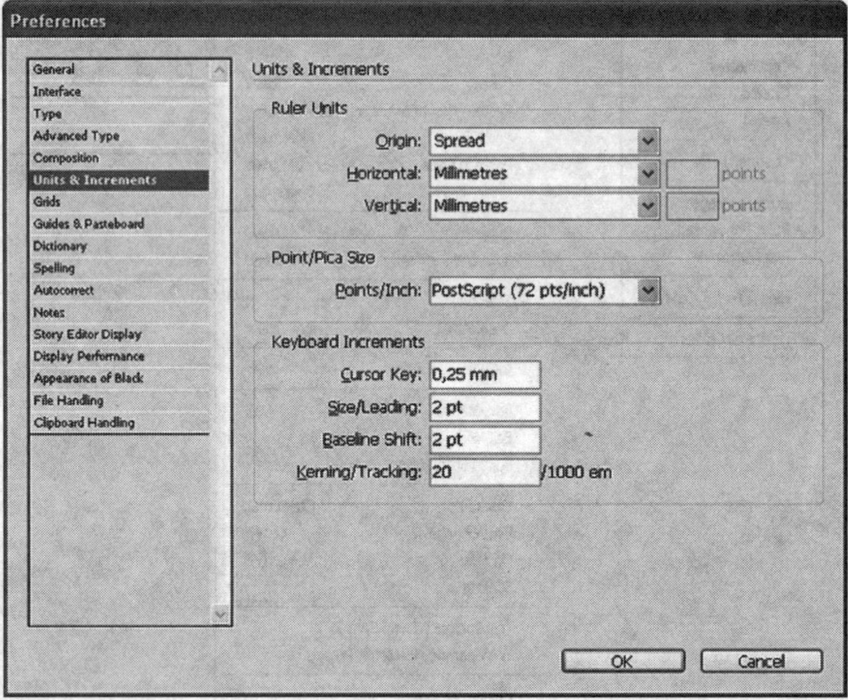

Preferences window

By default the 0 point is at the top left corner. You can change it to any point you want, for example we'll change it to be at the centre of the page. A4 paper dimensions are 210 mm x 297 mm, so the middle would be at 105 mm x 148.5 mm. Simply click over the intersection point of the rulers and drag to the desired point.

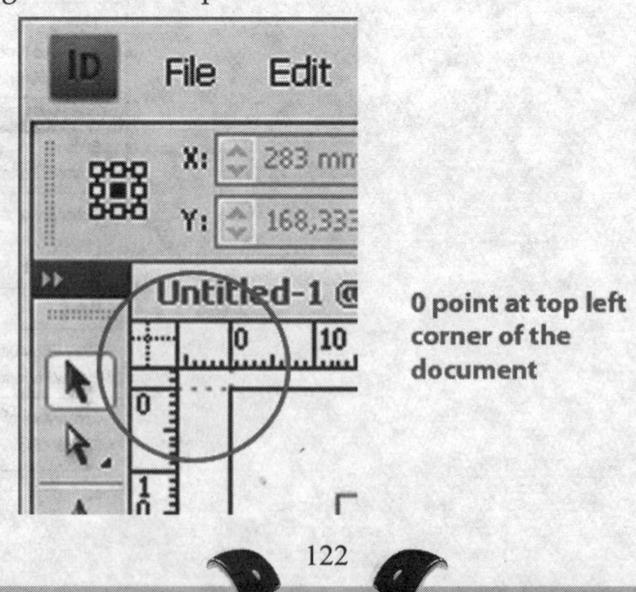

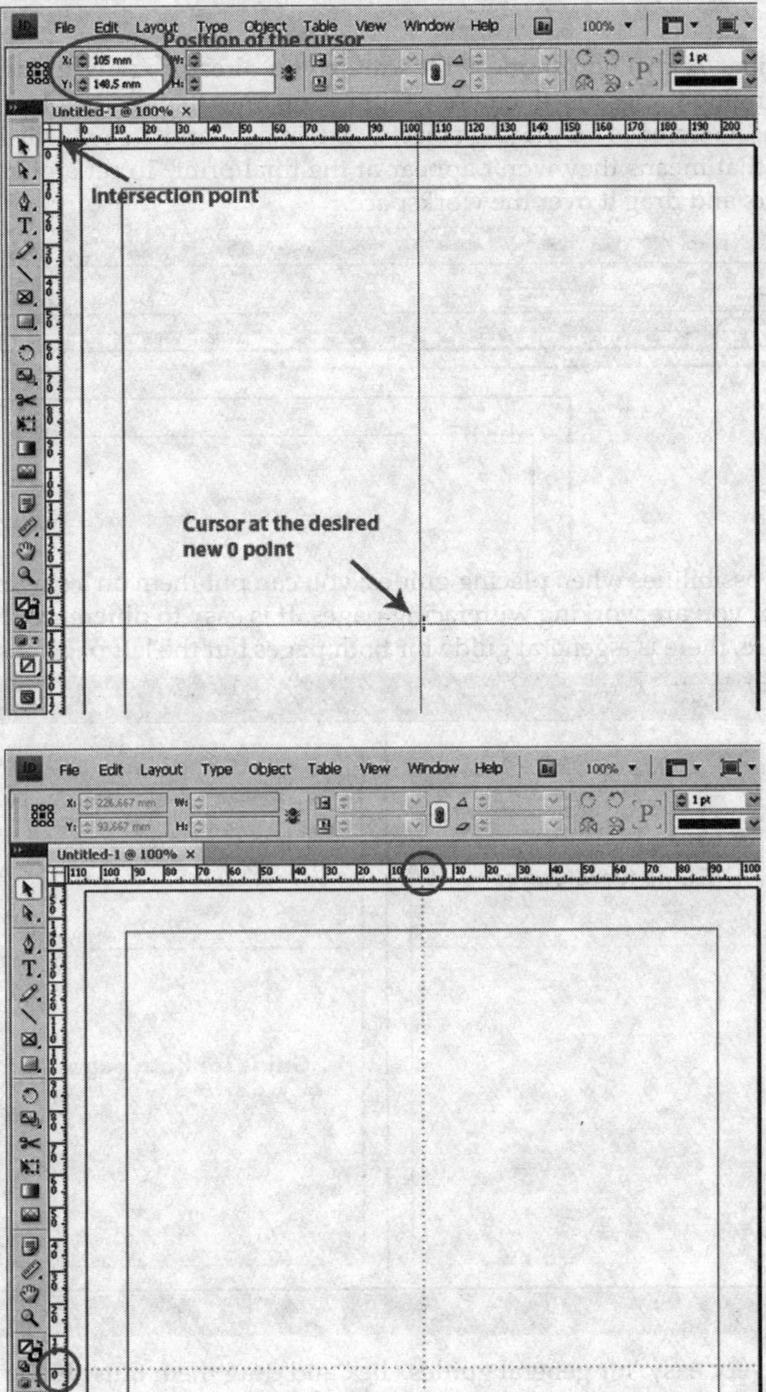

To restore the default 0 point just double click the intersection point of the two rulers.

Guides

If you are familiar with Photoshop or Illustrator you already know guides; they are very helpful for arranging things in a document. Guides are lines that can be placed at any point of the document as a reference for placing objects, text, images and are only visible while editing the document; that means they won't appear at the final print. To set a guide click over any spot of the rulers and drag it over the workspace.

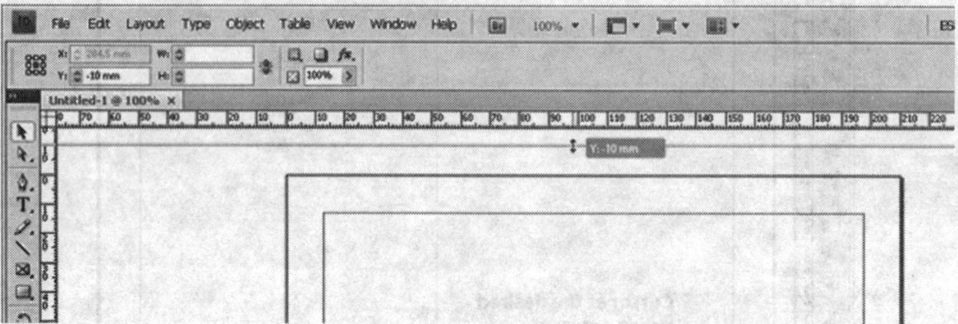

There are two possibilities when placing guides; you can put them on a single page or both at the same time, if you are working with facing pages. It is easy to difference them. Look at the following picture, there is a general guide for both pages but the left page has one only for it.

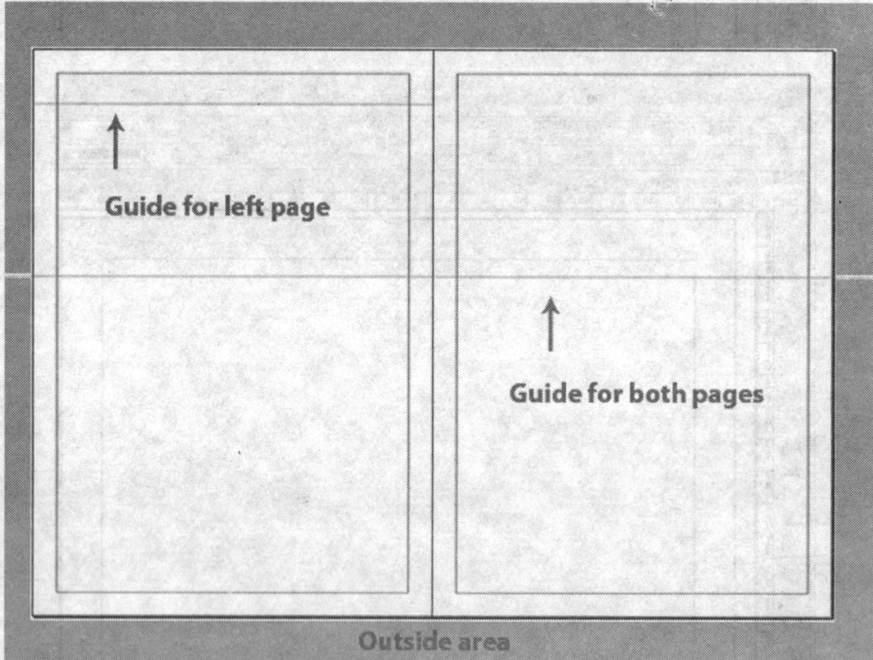

Setting them is very easy: for general guides click and drag them **outside** the document area, and for specific page guides click and drag **inside** the document. This is easy to do when you are working with a distant view. So you may think there is a problem here when you are working on a single page and very close to the document without been able to spot any of the outside area, all the guides you place would only fit that single page, for this cases just press Command when placing the guide and it will be set on both pages.

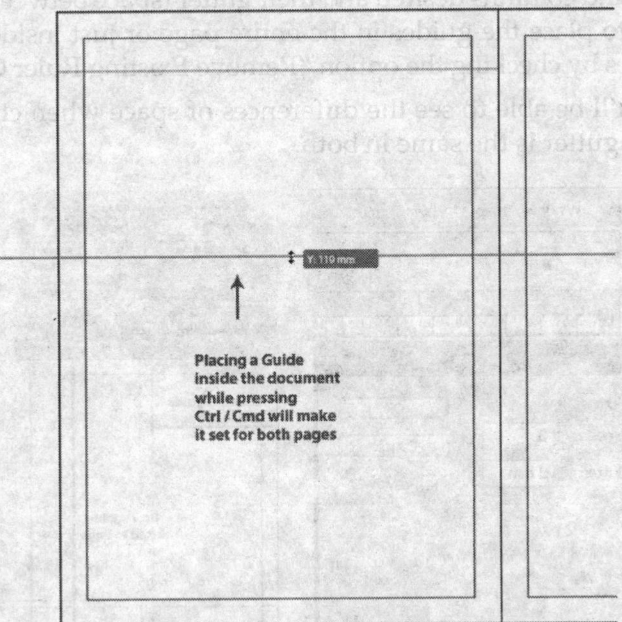

InDesign has some differences compared to Photoshop and Illustrator. Guides are tied to layers. For example when you set some guides in "Layer 1" and you hide that layer the guides will also hide. If you have to place guides in the same position for several pages you should place them in a master page, otherwise you'll see them only in the page you just placed.

You can also place a guide for a specific point horizontally and vertically at the same time. Simply press Command then click over the rulers intersection point and drag to the desired spot. If you did it right you should be able to see both guides and the cursor position at the same time.

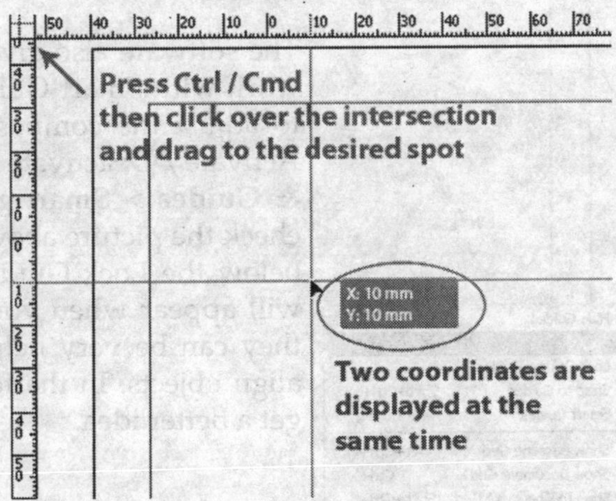

Another feature in InDesign is the possibility to create rows and columns uniformly in the document according to your needs. Go to **Layout > Create Guides**. Here you are asked to input the Quantity of rows and columns desired and their gutter (space between rows / columns). You are given the choice to place the guides in the entire page or just inside the margins. You can replace existing guides by checking the option "Remove Existing Ruler Guides".

See the example, you'll be able to see the differences of space when choosing to fit guides to Page or Margins, the gutter is the same in both.

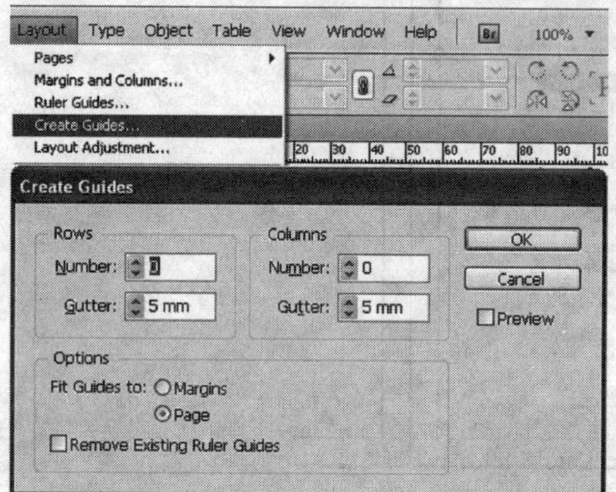

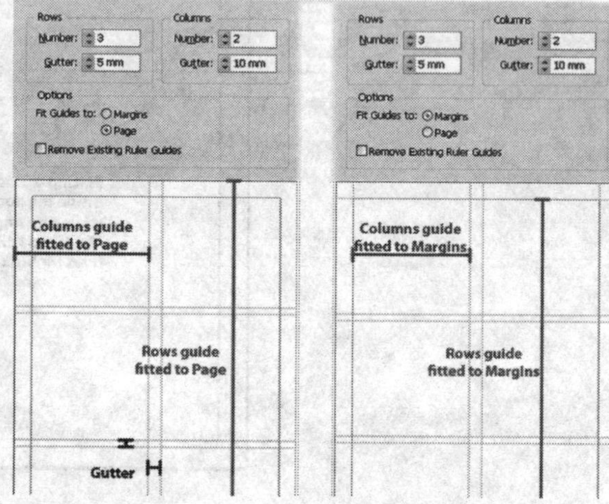

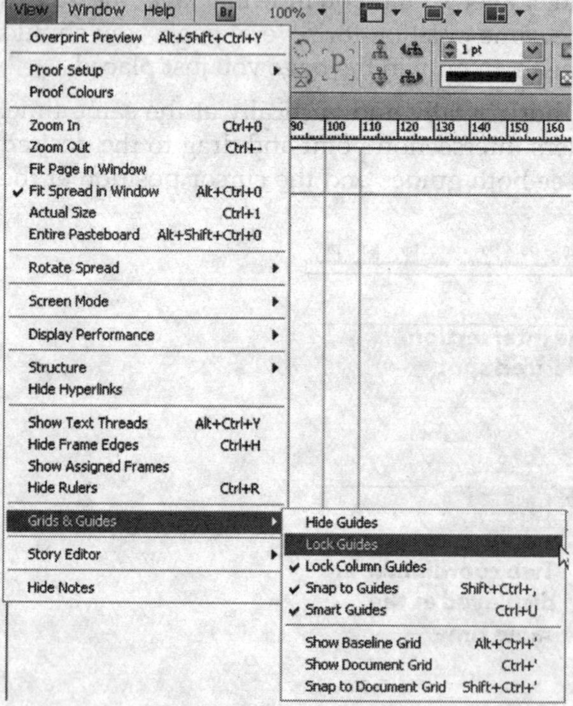

To avoid moving the guides accidentally it is highly recommended to lock them. Go to **View > Grid & Guides > Lock Guides**. If a check mark is next to this option then the guides are already locked. To unlock them follow the same route and un-check the option.

The software also gives you the possibility to work with Smart Guides; these can help you to adjust the composition of your work. To Activate / Deactivate them, go to **View > Grid & Guides > Smart guides** (Command + U) check the picture above, it's just some options below the Lock Guides toggle. Smart guides will appear when you are moving an object; they can be very helpful when you want to align objects. In the following pictures you'll get a better idea.

First picture, we have a square and a circle.

Second picture, when you move any object you'll see a reference copy until you drop it to the desired spot, once dropped the reference will vanish. In this picture the square is moved towards the circle, notice two Smart Guides had appeared, one violet which indicates the square is aligned to the centre of the document and the green says the centre of both shapes are aligned. It may seem there are two squares but the one from the left is the reference of the original square position.

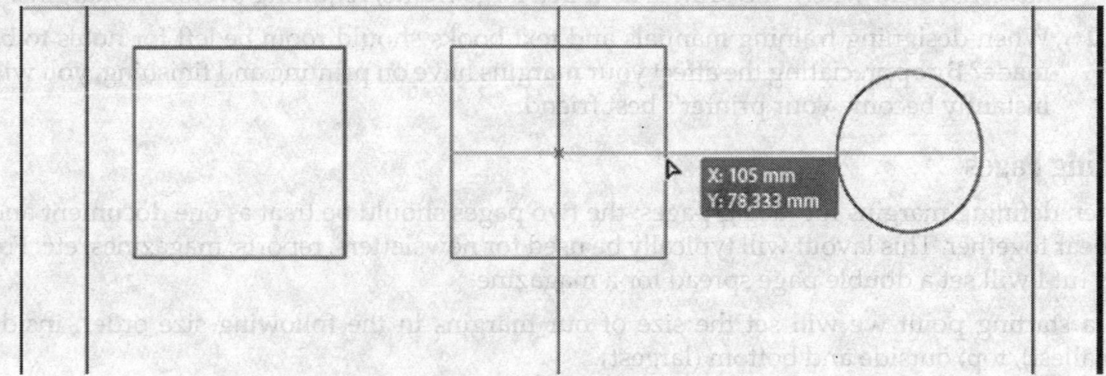

Third picture, the green guide indicates both shapes are aligned along the top, and again the square from the left is just the reference copy.

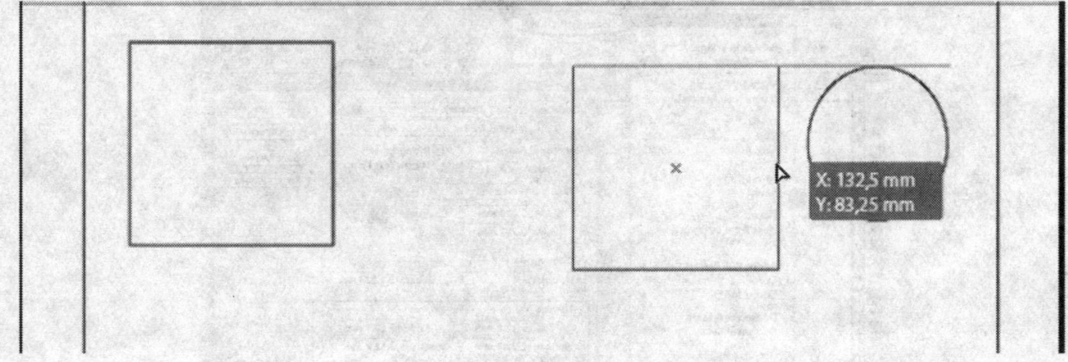

Setting Margins using Indesign

As you will have heard countless times, white space is a very important element to a successful layout. A large proportion of white space will typically be occupied by margins. The purpose of this tut is to give new InDesign users the knowledge on setting up margins and their functions relating to two main layout types, which are single and facing page layouts.

Getting Started

Before the margins are defined, it is important to understand their function. Visually margins cage the content and support the structure of a layout. They provide a resting place for the readers' eyes as well as supporting the tone of design. Also there are some common practical functions to consider:

- ❑ How much room is needed for holding the print, so the reader doesn't obscure any content?
- ❑ How is the print going to be finished? ring bound, stapled, etc.
- ❑ Are there any safe zones set by the print house. One example would be a street poster/ advertisement where the print is held in a large frame, requiring oversized margins.
- ❑ When designing training manuals and text books should room be left for notes to be made? By appreciating the affect your margins have on printing and finishing, you will instantly become your printer's best friend.

Facing Pages

When defining margins for facing-pages, the two pages should be treat as one document and appear together. This layout will typically be used for newsletters, reports, magazines, etc. For this tut I will set a double page spread for a magazine.

As a starting point we will set the size of our margins in the following size order: inside (smallest), top, outside and bottom (largest).

Start by going to **File > New > Document.** Within the floating palette three quarters of the way down is the margin section.

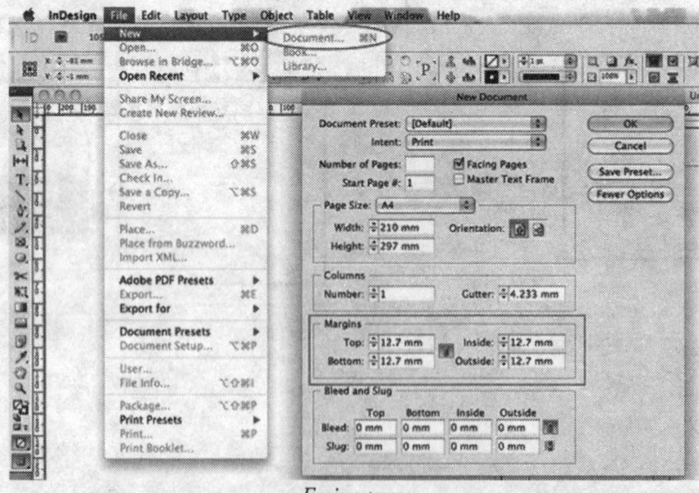

Facing pages

I am going to start by setting the outside margin to 15mm. The inside margin will be half the size of the outside at 7.5mm. The bottom margin will be three times the inside at 22.5mm and finally the top is half the size of the bottom margin at 11.25mm. If the 'make all the same' chain is activated click it once to deactivate.

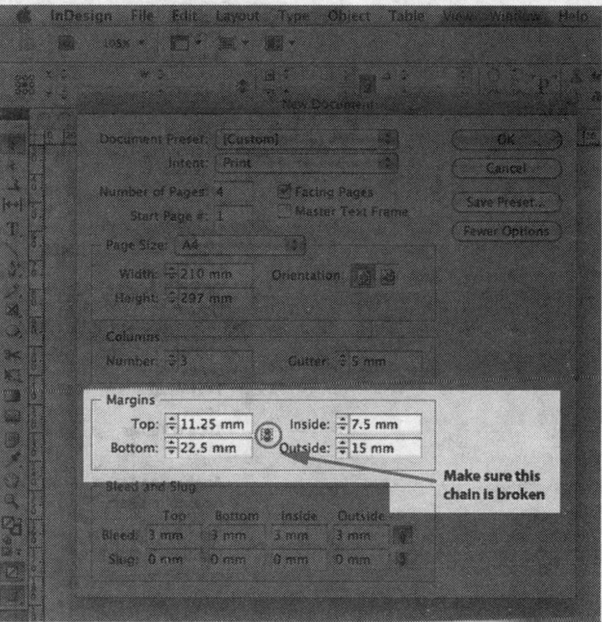

Setting the outside margin

As a designer you should use this technique as a starting point only. Use these methods to find the best margin set up that fits your brief requirements and functions.

Single Page

A single page layout can be a poster, flyer, sign, advert or similar design. For the purpose of this tut I am going to set an A4 poster, which will be displayed within different sections of a large office on notice boards, etc.

Again start by going to **File > New > Document**.

For the top margin I am going to be generous and give the reader a bit of lead in space, about 12.5mm. As this is a single page layout I want to retain the balance, so I will set both the left and right margins at 15mm. Finally the bottom margin will be set at 25mm. These margins will act as a safe zone and I will not be placing any important information within this area. The safe zone will lend itself to practical use, for example the poster might be held up by drawing pins or clipped into a frame.

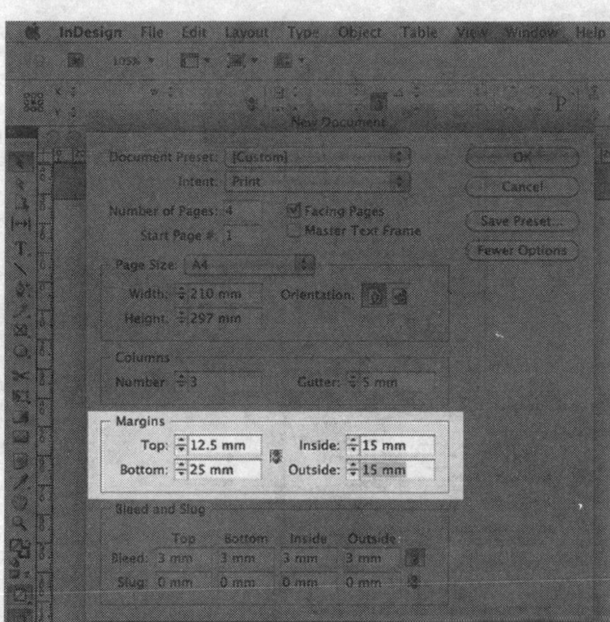

Changing Margins

Once the margins are set, define the other boxes as I have done in the screen shot below or set them to your own requirements.

Changing Margins

Once you have set your margins using the new document palette, it is possible to redefine them. Make sure you select the pages you want to edit. Check this by opening the Pages palette, if it is not open go to **Window > Pages**.

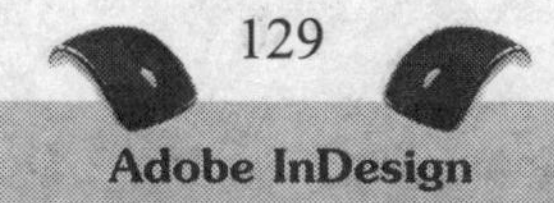

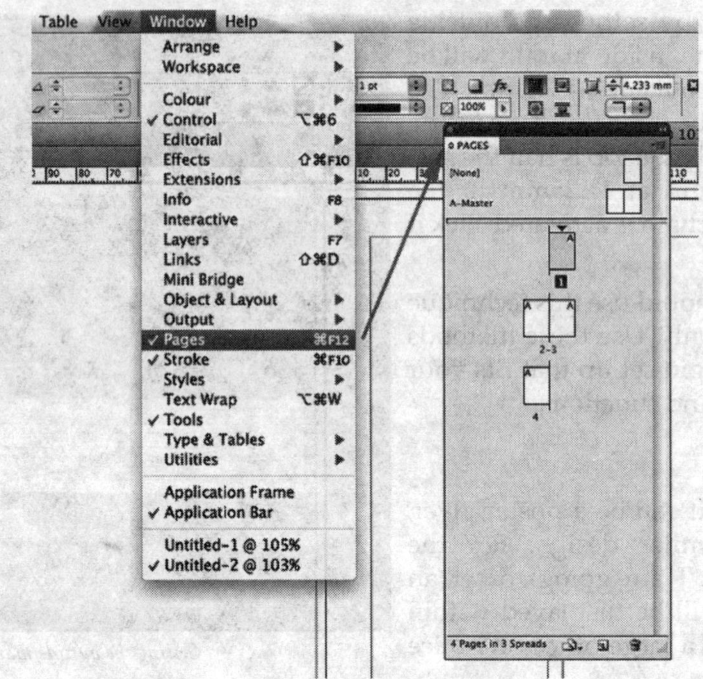

Once the palette is open hold down Shift and click the pages you need and go to **layout > Margins and columns.** Within this option box you can edit your measurements. By using this method it is possible to have different margin set-ups on each individual page, just select one or a number of pages still holding down shift and go into the Margins and Columns palette. The pages which were not selected will remain the same.

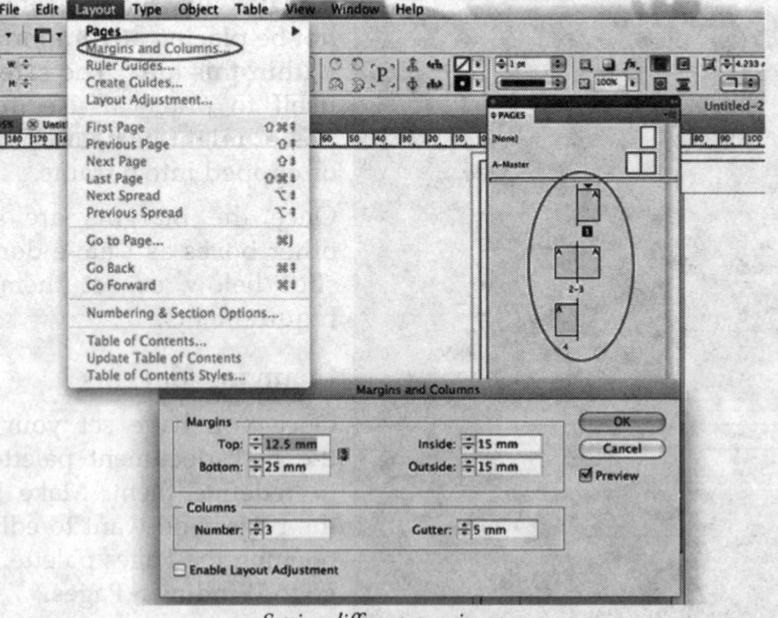

Setting different margin setups

Taking the points from this tut into account, it is ultimately up to you, the designer, to decide on the best structure for a project. Remember to give some careful thought to the function of the margins and in turn they will strengthen your designs.

Importing Type Using Indesign CS5

Importing type into InDesign can seem like a straight forward process, either copy and paste or use the place option. It is definitely a process designers take for granted. This tut will illustrate the capabilities InDesign offers when importing type using the "Show import options" feature. In turn this will give insight on how you – the designer – can take full control over importing and placing type.

Methods of importing type

Here are some common methods of placing type within InDesign:

- **Direct input:** Select the Type Tool, draw a text box, select your typeface, size, colour, etc. and start typing.
- **Copy and paste:** Content can be copied and pasted from a variety of sources (PDFs, text documents and the internet to name a few)
- **Importing a word processor file (Word, OpenOffice etc):** A file can be added using the Place option (**File > Place**)

For the purpose of this tut we are going to focus on method 3.

Importing a Text Document

Step 1

Start by importing a text document. Importing an Word doc. Go to **File > Place** and navigate to where your file is located. Select it but don't hit the "Open" button just yet.

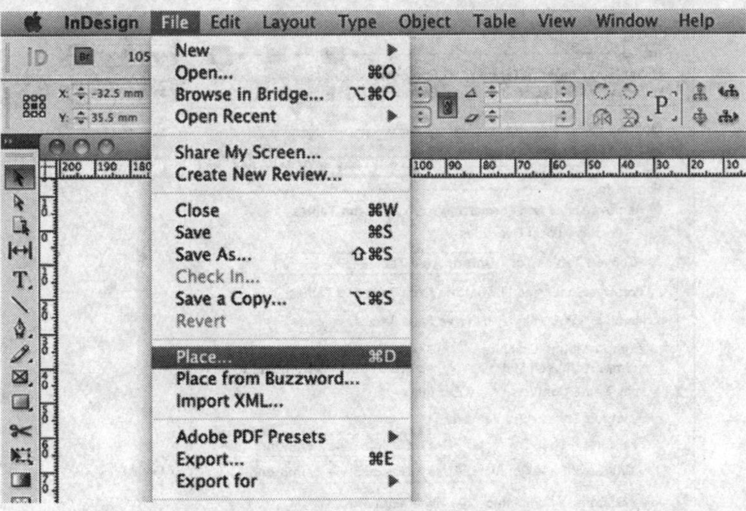

Step 2

To the bottom left of the "Place" floating window you will see a tick box titled "Show Import Options". Tick this box, then press "Open". InDesign will then present you with a new window.

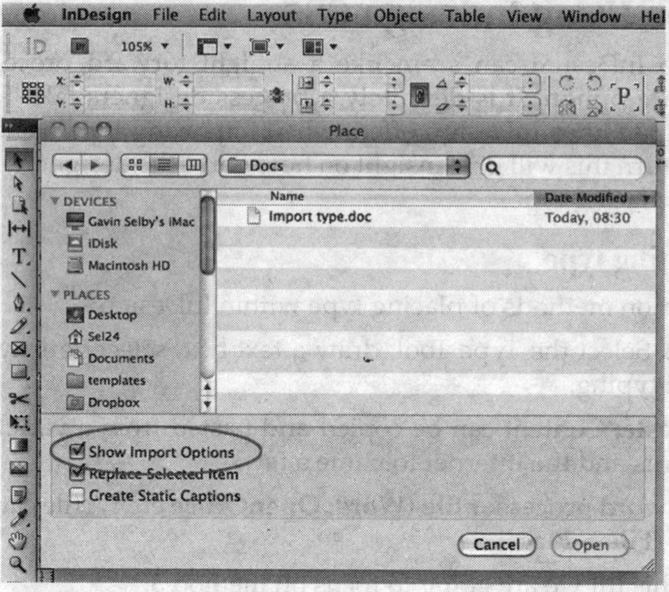

Step 3

The "Import Options" box is divided into three sections, **Include, Options** and **Formatting**. The Include box is pretty self-explanatory and here you can choose to omit or include various formatting. The option to omit Footnotes has proved to be helpful on a number of occasions.

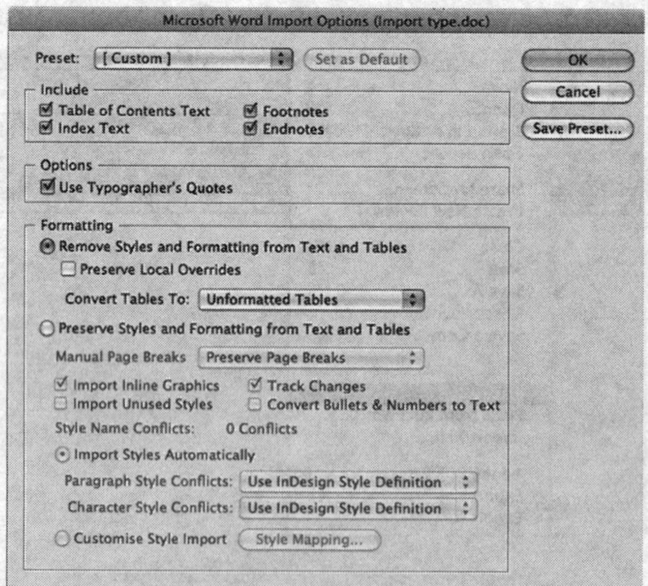

Step 4

The options box contains just one tick box, "Use Typographer's Quotes". Here you can choose to use curly quotes or use straight quotes, a choice that has caused great debate among designers.

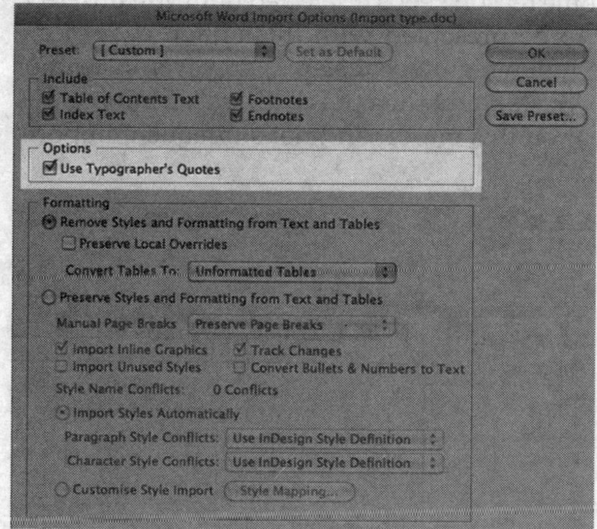

Typographer's Quotes turned ON

“Type”

Typographer's Quotes turned OFF

"Type"

Step 5

The formatting box is a bit more daunting. However, the gem here is the "Remove Styles and Formatting" option. As many designers will have experienced, word docs can cause unusual and unwanted formatting when importing into InDesign. Within this box you can take full control over the text or simply import unformatted type. Do this by selecting / unselecting the tick options.

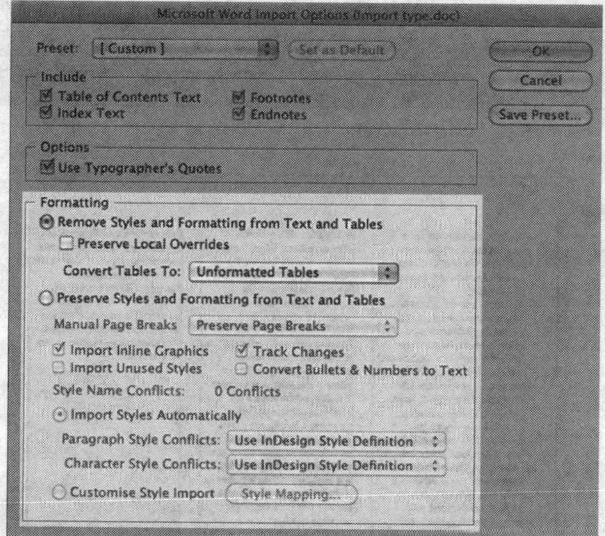

Step 6

Now the next time you go to import an element (image or type) using "Place", the Import Options box will appear automatically by default. Indesign remembers that you have ticked the "Show Import Options" box before and for some reason keeps it selected until you unselect. This can become annoying if you don't want to be presented with this option every time you import. A way of avoiding this is to do the following: Repeat step 1, however instead of ticking the "Show Import Options" box hold down shift and then press "Open". By doing this the "Show Import Options" box will only appear on this import and not subsequent imports unless of course you hold down shift again.

Step 7

Once you have clicked "Open" your cursor will be loaded with the text from the document. Click once within the InDesign document to place the content.

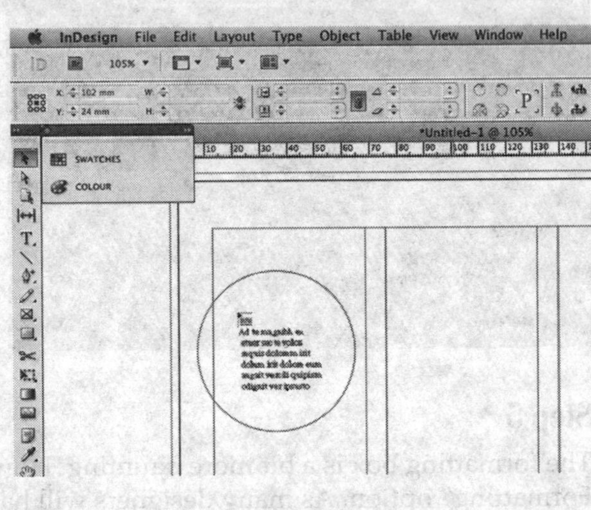

Step 8 – Extra Tip!

If you click your loaded cursor on a column structure, the width of the text frame will mimic the width of the column. But make sure that your guides are turned on **View > Grids and Guides > Show Guides**. You can see from the example below that my text frame automatically split across the 3 column structure.

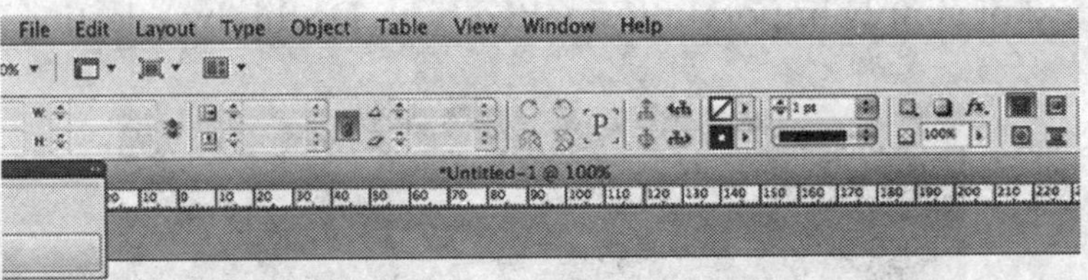

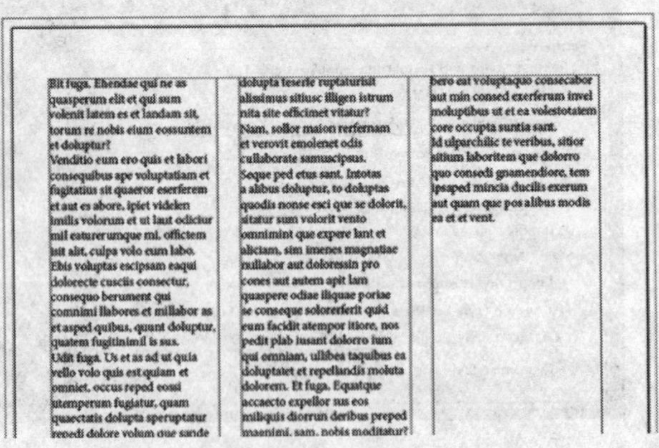

You now have the basic knowledge on controlling the text you import. I recommend that you use these techniques as a starting point to developing your skills further by experimenting with the different options available within the Import Options box.

Using Em Dashes, En Dashes & Hyphens within Indesign

When using dashes you have three options available, a **hyphen**, an **en dash** and an **em dash**. Choosing the right dash for the job in hand is usually overlooked and misunderstood. This Quick Tip will outline the differences between the three dashes as well as advice on when and how to use them correctly within your designs.

The Hyphen

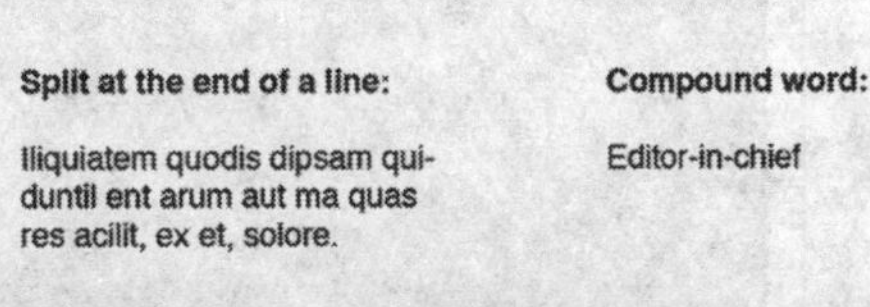

First up is the Hyphen. It has two main functions, to divide a word that needs to be split at the end of a line and to join a compound word.

On a standard English keyboard the hyphen can be found to the right of the zero.

Indesign will hyphenate your body copy automatically if the "Hyphenate" tick box is selected, it can be found within the paragraph panel. If it is not activated go to **Window > Type and Tables > Paragraph**.

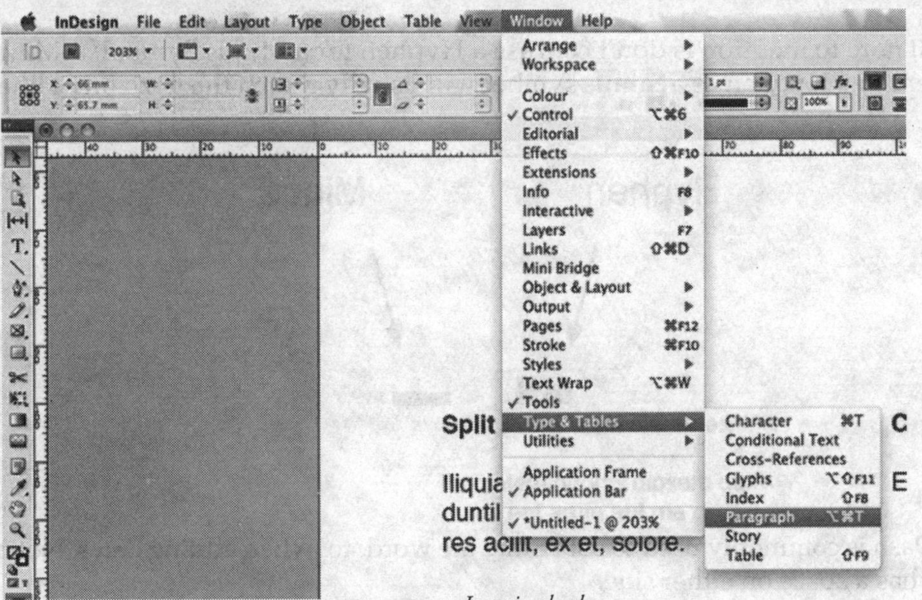

Instering hyphen

The tick box is located at the bottom left of the palette. Activate the tick if it isn't already. However, some designers like to have full control over the hyphenation and prefer to add their own. To deactivate automatic hyphenation simply select your text box/boxes and deselect the option on the paragraph palette.

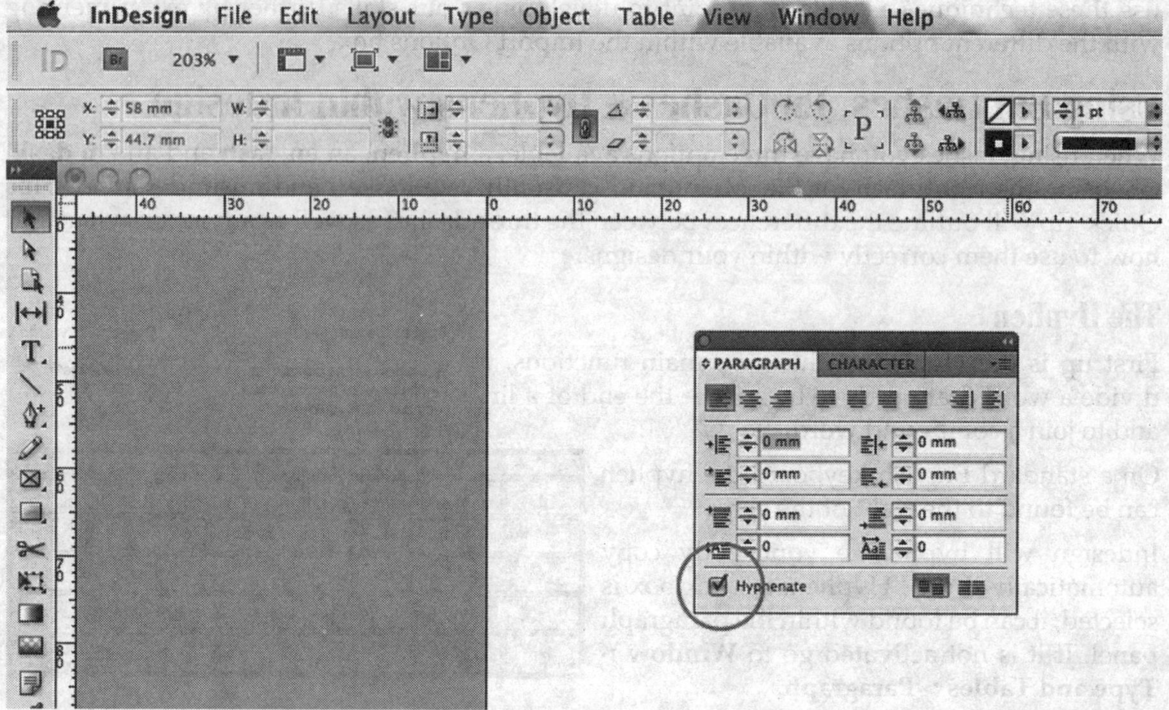

One final note to mention is don't confuse a Hyphen for a Minus Symbol. A Minus Symbol is different to a Hyphen as a minus symbol will usually match the horizontal line on a plus sign.

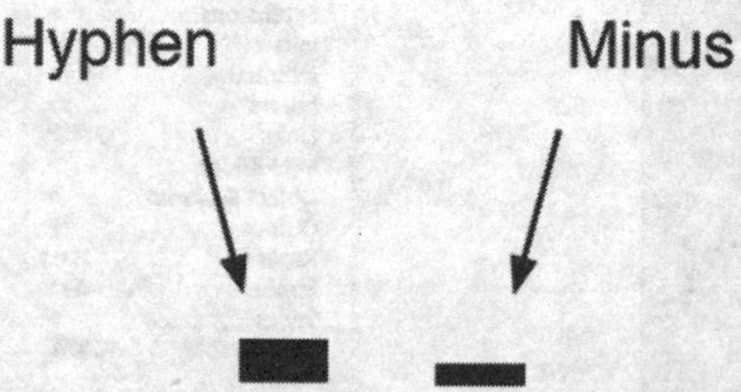

En Dash

The En Dash is commonly used to substitute the word 'to' when adding dates. Notice how the En Dash has a space on either side.

November 24 – 25, 2011

Unlike a Hyphen the En Dash is not visible on the keyboard and must be activated. The shortcut is Option + Hyphen or you can go to **Type > Insert Special Character > Hyphens and Dashes > En Dash.**

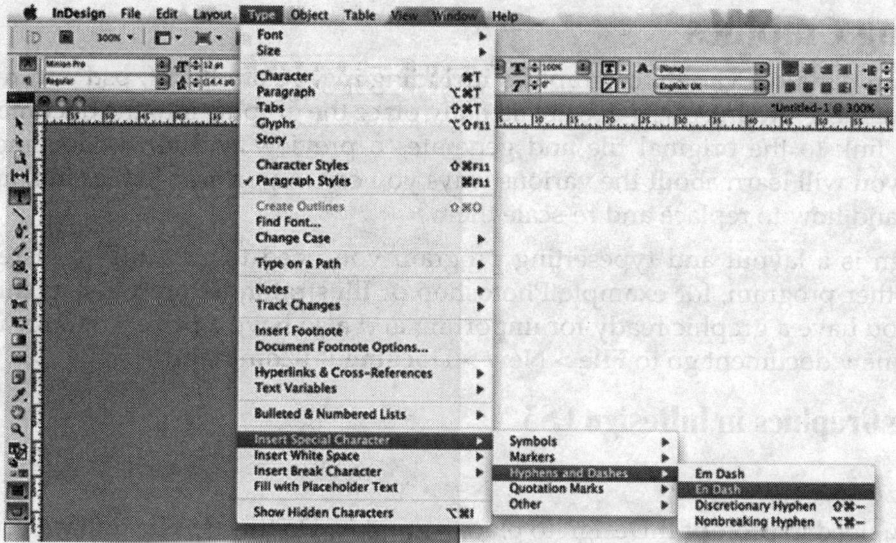

Inserting en dash

Em Dash

The Em Dash is used to indicate a break or interruption in thought or to separate a sentence from a bullet point. The Em Dash has no space on either side.

• Vectortuts website—A place for superb tutorials

Like the en dash the em dash is not visible on keyboard and must be activated. The shortcut is **Option + Shift + Hyphen** or you can go to **Type > Insert Special Character > Hyphens and Dashes > Em Dash**.

Glyphs

There is another way of selecting dashes. Go to **Type > Glyphs** and a new floating palette will open. The glyphs palette will display a visual reference to all of the characters within the typeface you have selected. As there is a lot of content to scroll through lets narrow down our search. In the drop down menu titled 'Show' select Punctuation, within this option the dashes can be found. By hovering your cursor over each of the glyphs InDesign will display their names.

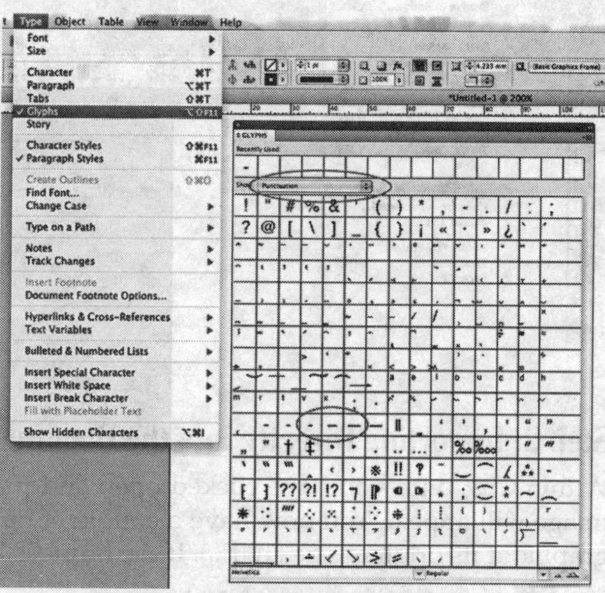

Selecting dashes using glyphs

Once you start to notice the different ways Dashes are used, you'll be able to spot them in everything you read.

Importing Graphics

InDesign can handle a variety of graphics including jpg, eps, pdf, tiff, psd and most Adobe formats to name a few. InDesign doesn't actually place the graphic into the document. Instead it makes a link to the original file and generates a preview within the document. In this Quick Tip you will learn about the various ways you can import image files into an InDesign document and how to replace and re-scale them.

As InDesign is a layout and typesetting program you need to edit and prepare your files within another program, for example Photoshop or Illustrator. Before we start this tut make sure that you have a graphic ready for importing and also have a project open ready for use. To create a new document go to **File > New > Document (Command + n)**.

Importing Graphics in InDesign CS5

Step 1

To start you need to prompt InDesign to place a graphic. Do this by **File > Place (Command + d)** navigate to where your graphic is located, select and click open. When importing graphics you can either import into an existing frame by selecting the frame with the Selection Tool (V) before starting step 1 or import the graphic directly into the document, which will automatically create a frame for the graphic to sit in.

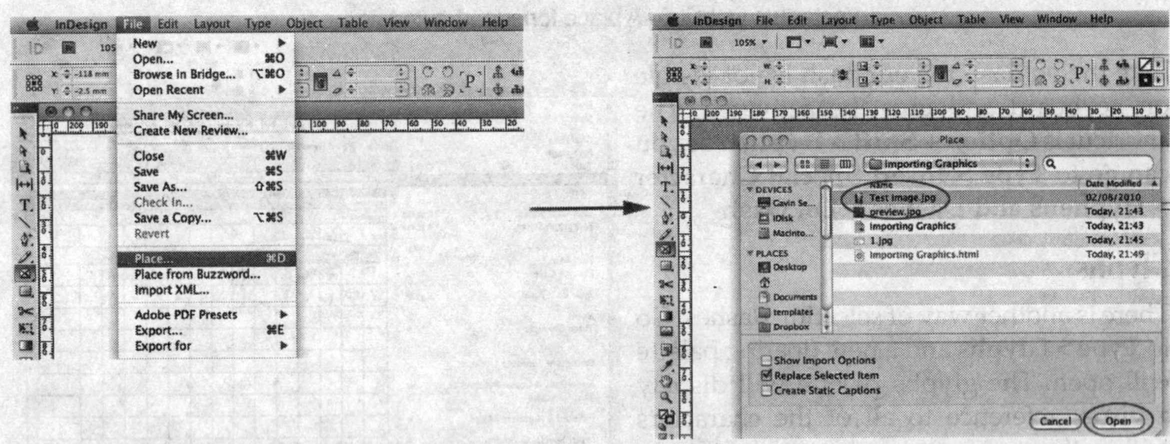

Step 2: Importing Directly into the Document

Within CS5, once you have clicked open and placed a graphic, a small transparent preview image will appear. You now have a couple of options. Firstly, clicking once will import your graphic at its original size (100%). If the frame is hanging over the edges of the working space use the Selection Tool to drag one of the corners to resize. Hold down shift to constrain the proportions.

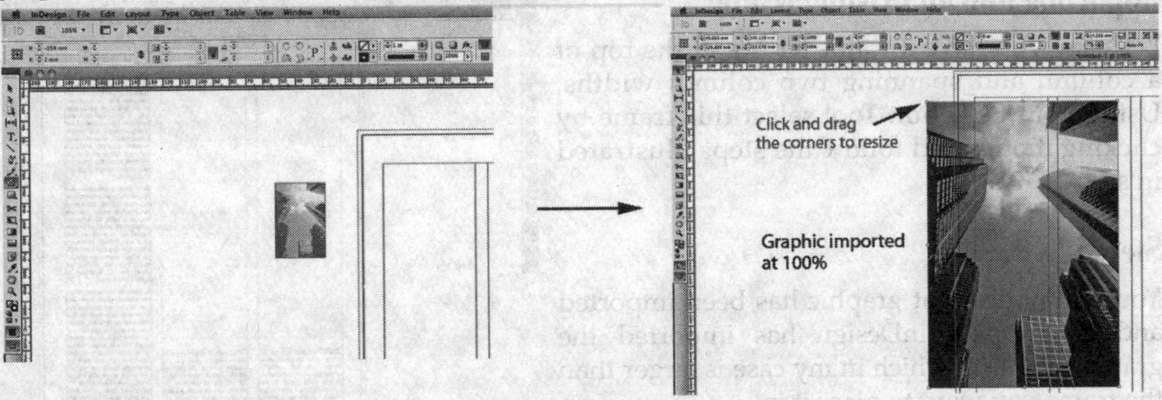

Step 3

Secondly, by clicking and holding down your mouse button, you can size the bounding box to suit the layout. After selecting open, click on the document and don't release the click. Drag your mouse to the required size and then release.

Tip

Holding down Command after you clicked once and while you are dragging will constrain the proportions.

Step 4

Importing into an Existing Frame

Let's say you have a frame sitting at the top of a column and spanning two column widths. Using your Selection Tool select this frame by clicking it once and follow the steps illustrated in step 1.

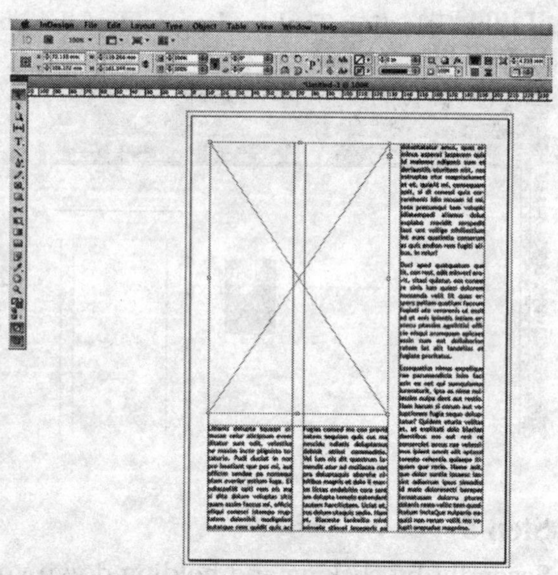

Step 5

You will notice that graphic has been imported and is cropped. InDesign has imported the graphic at 100%, which in my case is larger than the frame you want to place it in.

Step 6

To fit the graphic correctly, activate the Control Dock by going to **Window > Control.** I have highlighted the buttons that are needed below. If they are not visible select your frame with the Selection Tool. The Control Dock sits at the top of your screen above your document.

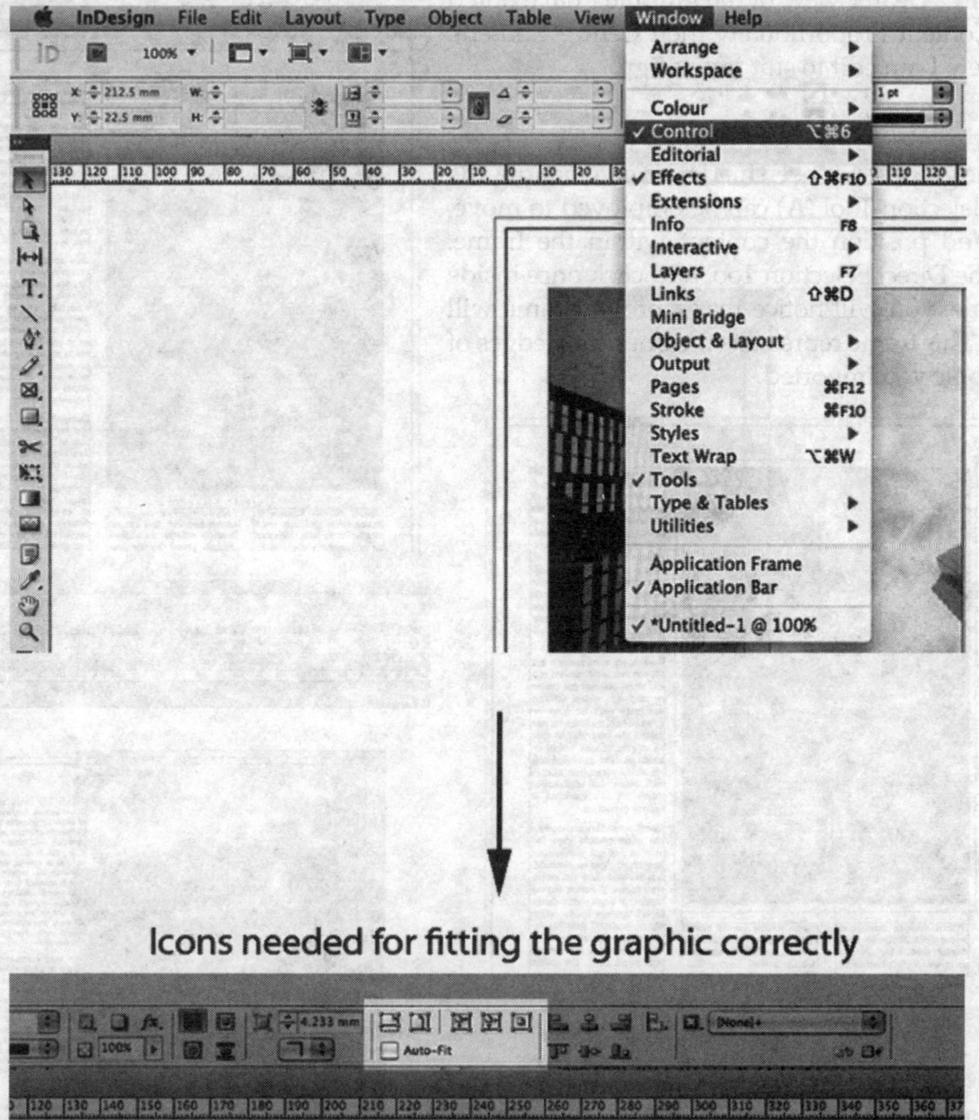

Tip

By hovering over each button with your cursor a text description will appear for each icon.

Step 7

To obtain a clearer view of the graphic I have opted to Fit Content Proportionally then Centre Content. From here I can edit to suit my design.

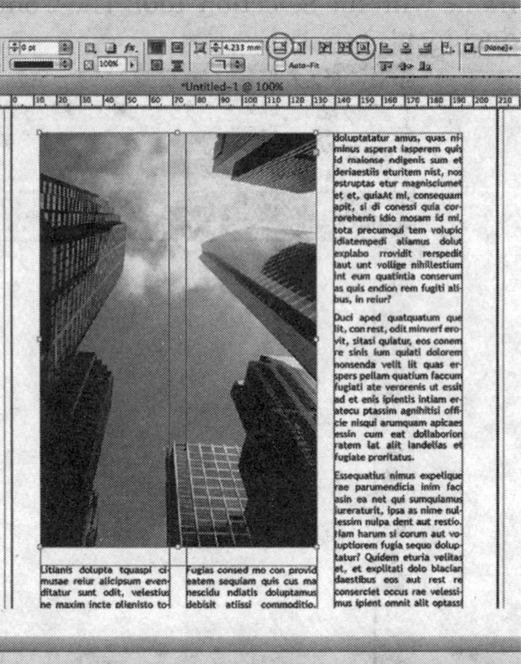

Step 8

Once the graphic has been made easier to handle, the Direct Selection Tool (A) can be employed to move, resize and position the content within the frame. Select the Direct Selection Tool and click once inside the frame, you will notice that a brown frame will appear. This frame represents the bounding edges of the graphic you imported.

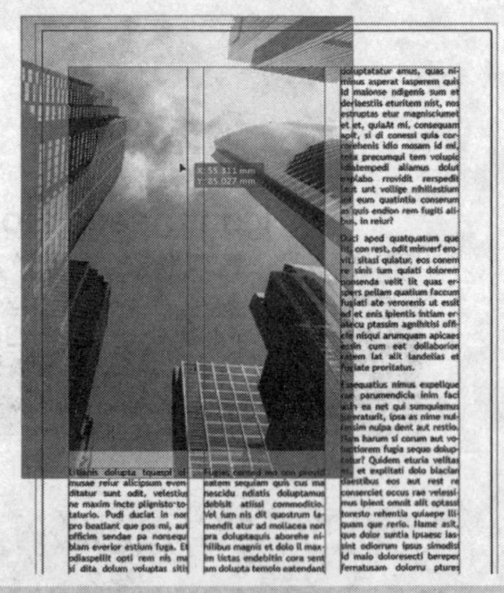

Step 9

Hover above the brown frame and the Hand Tool will appear. To edit, either click and drag to change the position, or resize by dragging on of the corners out or in.

Tip

Hold down shift to constrain the proportions. The image next page is an example of clicking and dragging, notice how InDesign displays a preview of the graphic.

By following these steps you now have the basic knowledge to import and handle graphics.

Threading Text in InDesign CS5

Threading text within InDesign can hugely improve the experience of editing and amending copy while working on layouts. The process of threading text is linking two or more text frames allowing text to flow from one separate frame to another. Let's take a look at the basics.

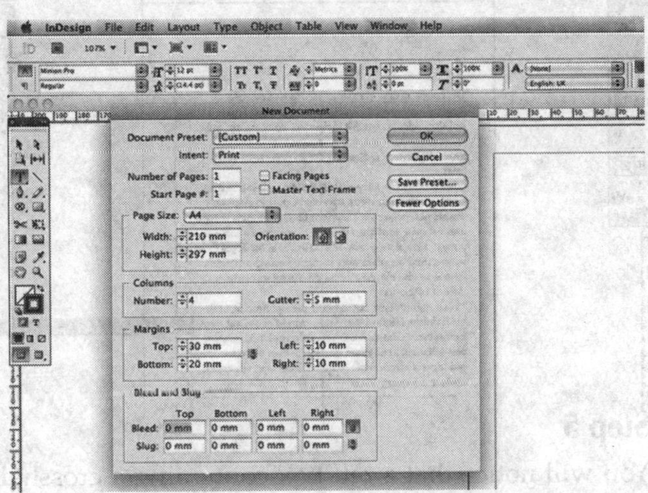

Step 1

Create a new document by going to **File > New > Document** and set the number columns to two or more and the remaining values to suit.

Step 2

Select the type tool (T) from the tool box and draw a text frame over two columns by clicking and dragging over the area you want to cover.

Step 3

Go to **Type > Fill** with Placeholder Text.

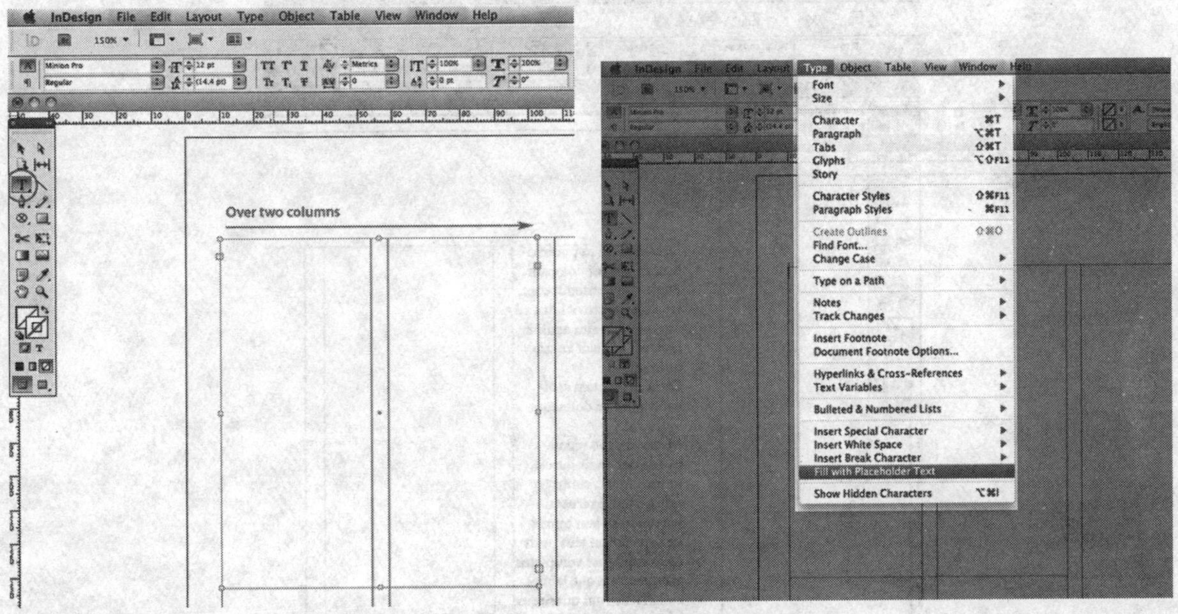

Step 4

Now reduce the text frame to one column. Do this by selecting the Selection Tool and dragging the middle handle that sits on the vertical edge of the frame until it snaps to one column.

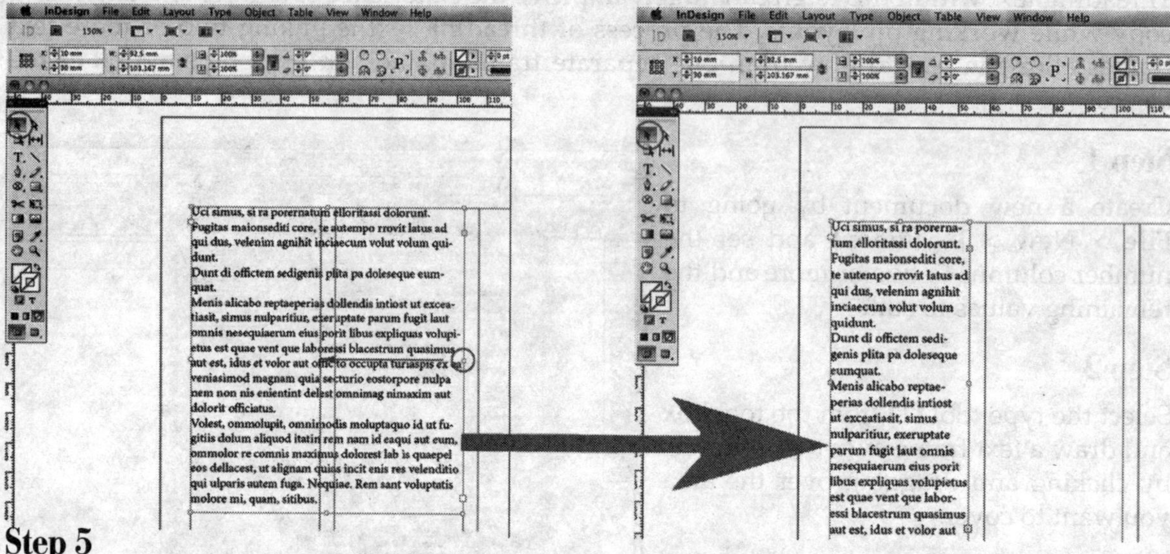

Step 5

You will notice that a red box containing a crosshair has appeared at the bottom right hand side of the frame. This indicates that there is text overflowing and missing from view. Now draw another text frame as detailed in step two.

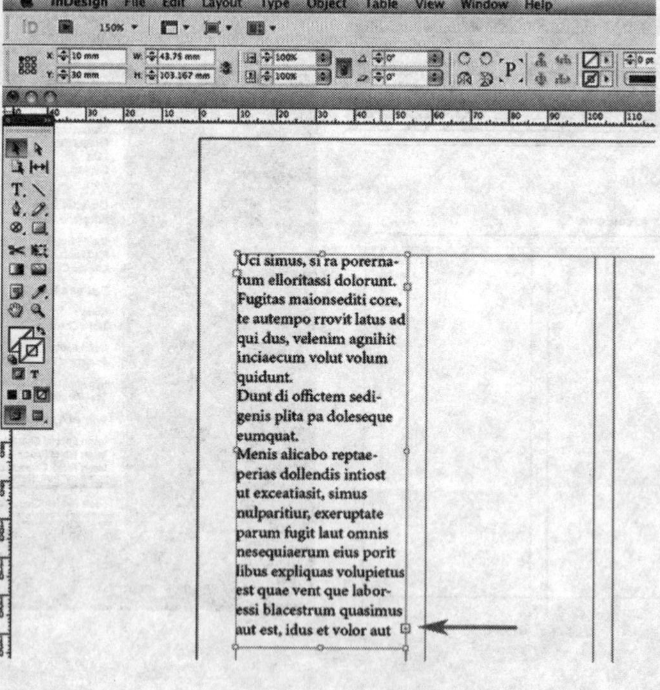

Step 6

Using the Selection Tool, click once on the red box (out-port) in the first frame. You will notice that the cursor will change its appearance to a thread icon and a small preview paragraph will appear, the text is now ready for threading.

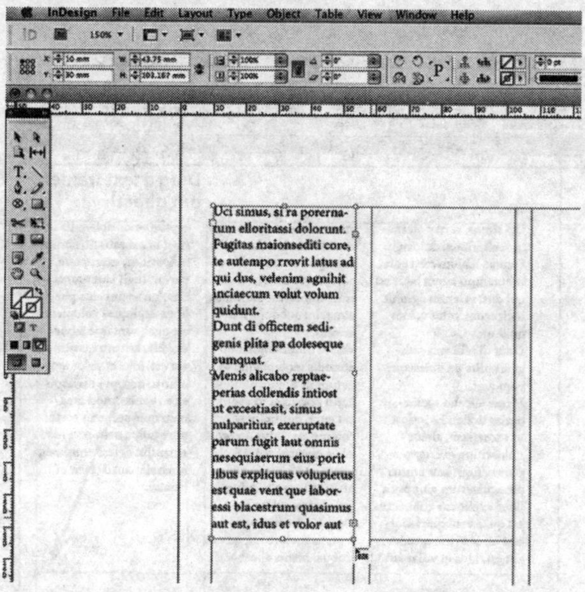

Step 7

With the cursor still loaded hover over the second text frame, the cursor will change to a link icon. Click once and watch as the text is flowed into the second frame.

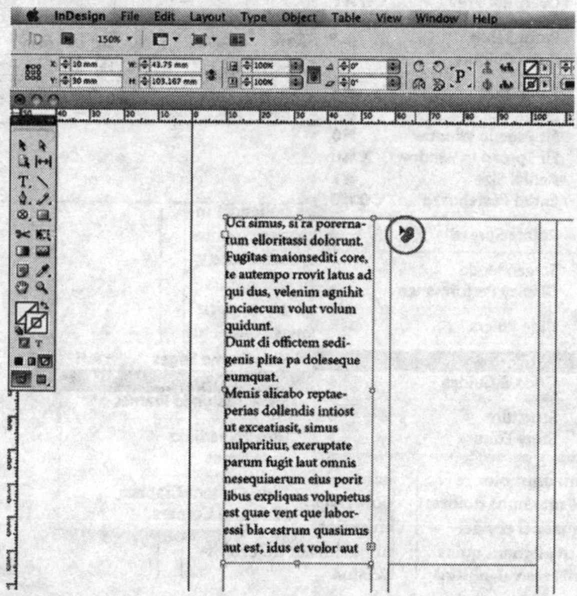

Step 8

At this point you might still be left with an indicating red box on the second text frame. Instead of creating a new text frame with the text frame tool, select the Selection Tool, click on the red box and click and draw a frame with the loaded cursor. The new frame will contain the reminder of the text.

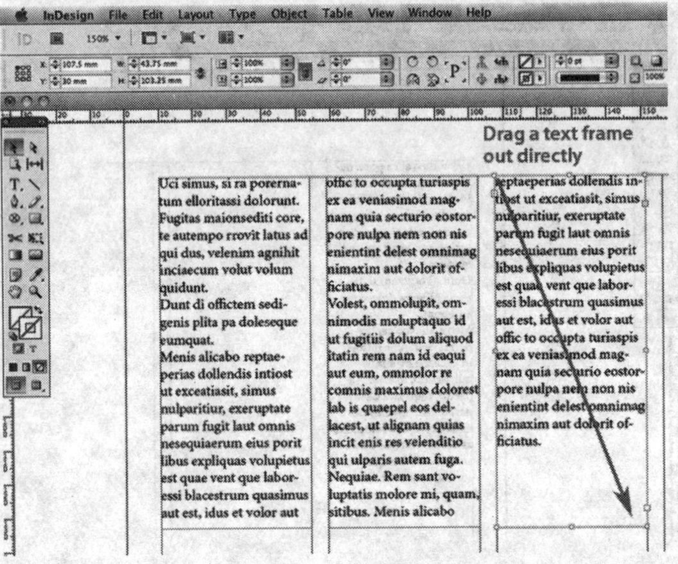

Step 9

To view text threads go to **View > Extras > Show Text Threads**.

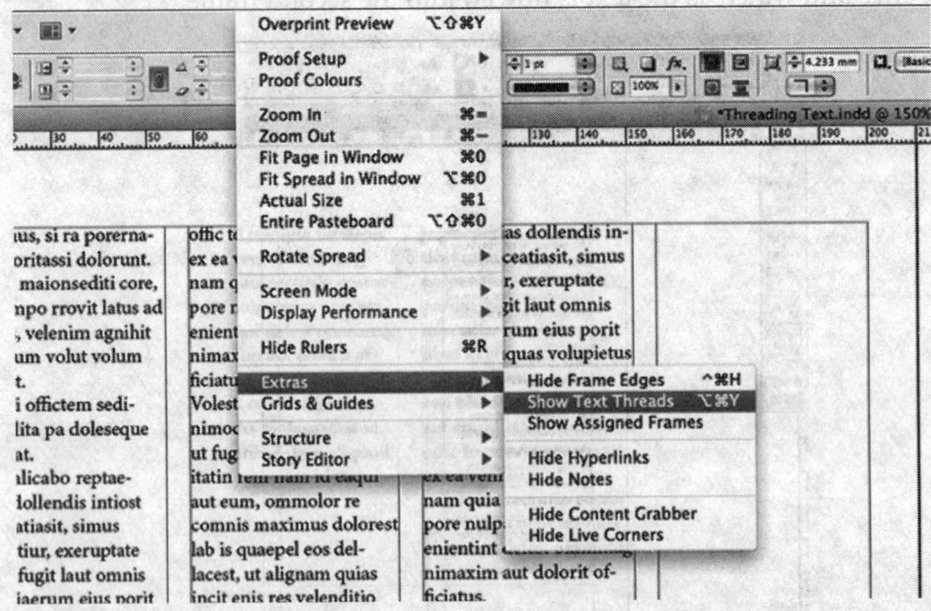

Viewing threads can be useful when working with text heavy documents.

Uci simus, si ra porernatum elloritassi dolorunt. Fugitas maionsediti core, te autempo rrovit latus ad qui dus, velenim agnihit inciaecum volut volum quidunt.
Dunt di offictem sedigenis plita pa doleseque eumquat.
Menis alicabo reptaeperias dollendis intiost ut exceatiasit, simus nulparitiur, exeruptate parum fugit laut omnis nesequiaerum eius porit libus expliquas volupietus est quae vent que laboressi blacestrum quasimus aut est, idus et volor aut offic to occupta turiaspis ex ea veniasimod magnam quia secturio eostorpore nulpa nem non nis enientint delest omnimag nimaxim aut dolorit officiatus.
Volest, ommolupit, omnimodis moluptaquo id ut fugitiis dolum aliquod itatin rem nam id eaqui aut eum, ommolor re comnis maximus dolorest lab is quaepel eos dellacest, ut alignam quias incit enis res velenditio qui ulparis autem fuga. Nequiae. Rem sant voluptatis molore mi, quam, sitibus. Menis alicabo reptaeperias dollendis intiost ut exceatiasit, simus nulparitiur, exeruptate parum fugit laut omnis nesequiaerum eius porit libus expliquas volupietus est quae vent que laboressi blacestrum quasimus aut est, idus et volor aut offic to occupta turiaspis ex ea veniasimod magnam quia secturio eostorpore nulpa nem non nis enientint delest omnimag nimaxim aut dolorit officiatus.

Step 10

To undo a thread use the selection tool and double click on the in-port of the text frame you wish to unthread.

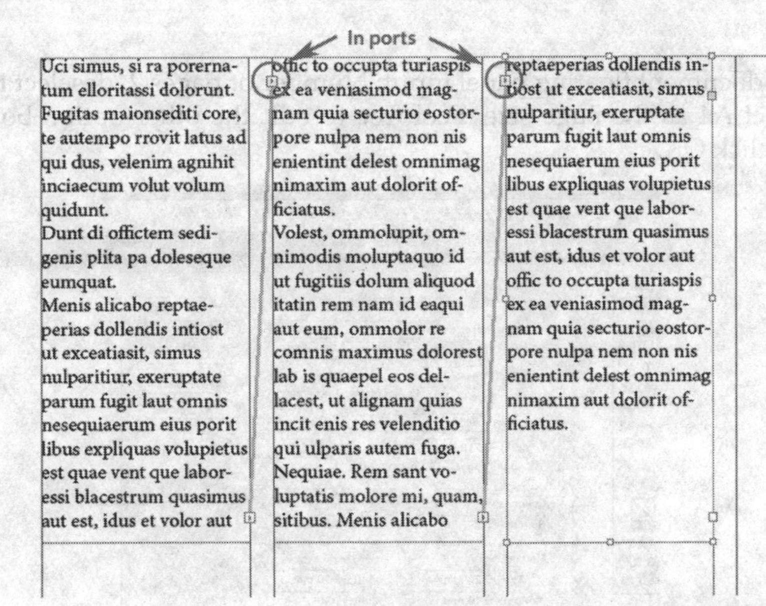

Learning the basics of text threading will help to keep layouts and text frames simple and easy to edit.

The Page Tool in InDesign CS5

Step 1

For this tutorial we are going to set an A4 and A5 page alongside each other in the same file. Create a new document by going to **File > New > Document**.

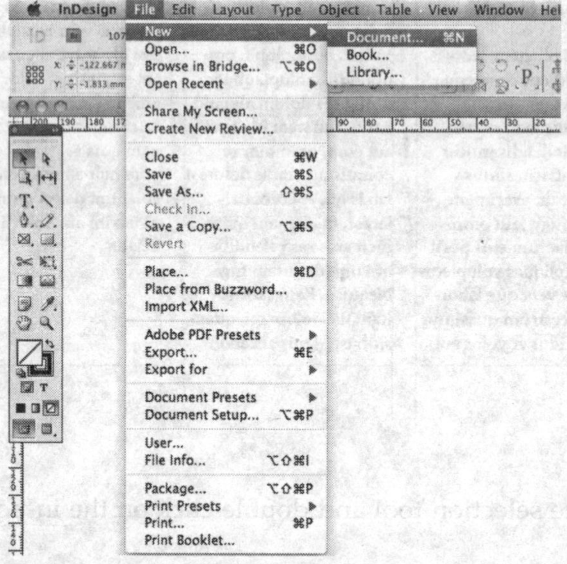

Step 2

Within the new document floating panel input: Number of pages 2, deselect the Facing Pages option and select A4 as the page size. Feel free to edit the other option boxes to suit your project. Finally click OK.

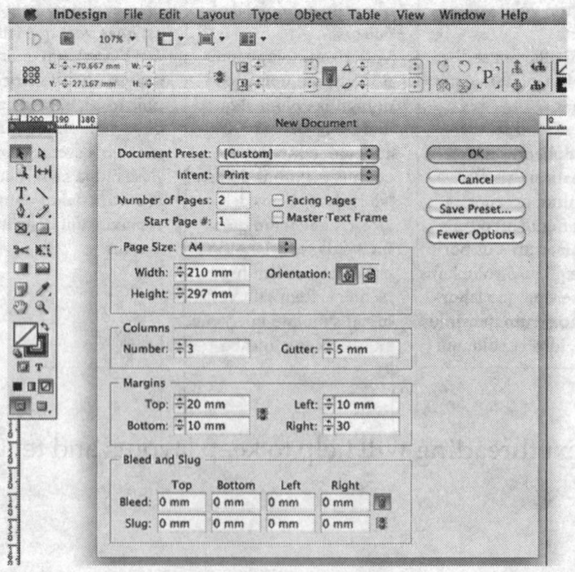

Step 3

If it isn't already active open the pages panel by going to **Window > Pages**.

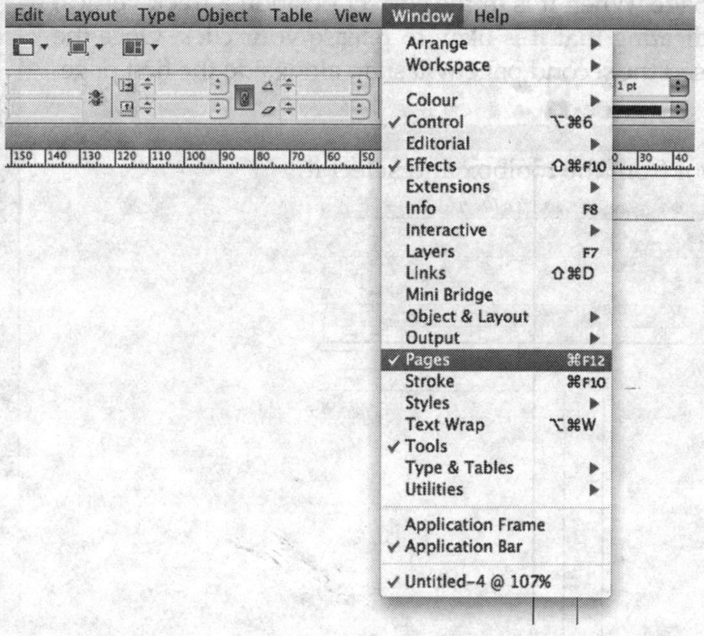

Step 4

Go into the options menu located at the top right hand corner of the Pages Panel and deselect **'Allow Document Pages to Shuffle'**.

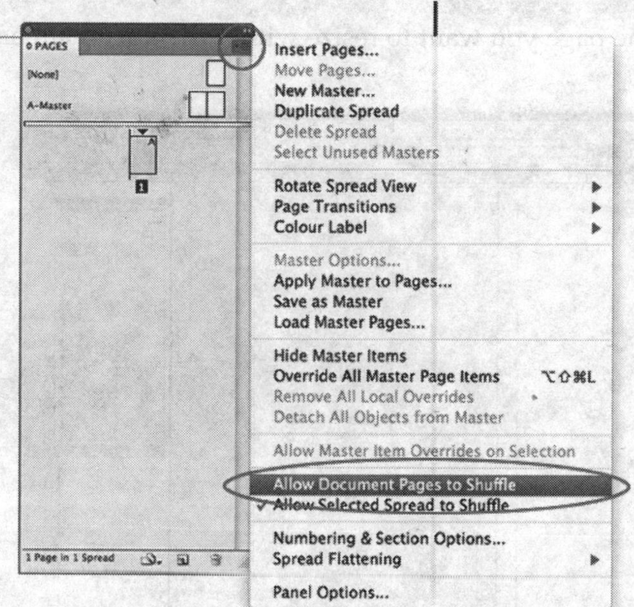

Step 5

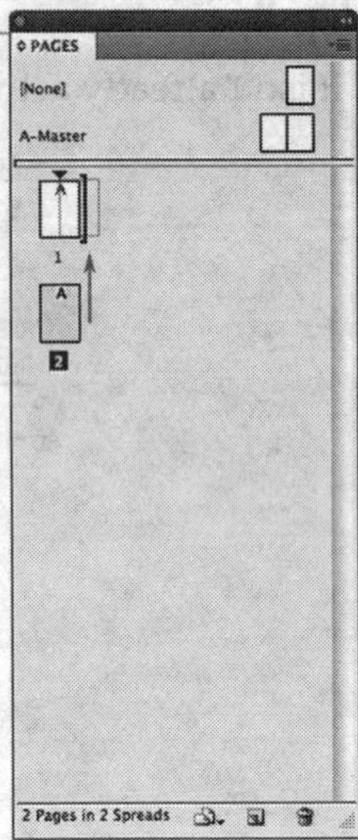

Within the pages panel click and hold on the second page and drag it alongside the first page. When it is in the correct position a thick vertical line will appear indicating that it is okay to release your click. Once the click has been released the second page will snap alongside the first page.

Step 6

Locate the Page Tool from the toolbox and select it.

Step 7

Hover above the page you want to resize within the document and click once. The page will highlight blue.

Step 8

In the Control Panel a set of options will appear. Here you can control the size of the page, orientation and the point it registers to. You will also notice that there is a drop down menu with sizes preloaded.

Below is an example of the set up and how it looks on screen. If you haven't already saved your document by do it going to **File > Save**.

That is it! Now you have a template for designing an A4 document which, when finished can be adapted to an A5 document in one neat file. These basic steps can be used on a variety of setups, from book dust jackets to gatefold magazine covers.

Creating Quick Grids and using Live Distribute with InDesign CS5

The following information will help you create fast grids as well as explaining how to distribute frames quickly.

Step 1

Create a new document by going to **File > New > Document** or use **Shortcut Command + N** and set up your document by entering the specific values for each section.

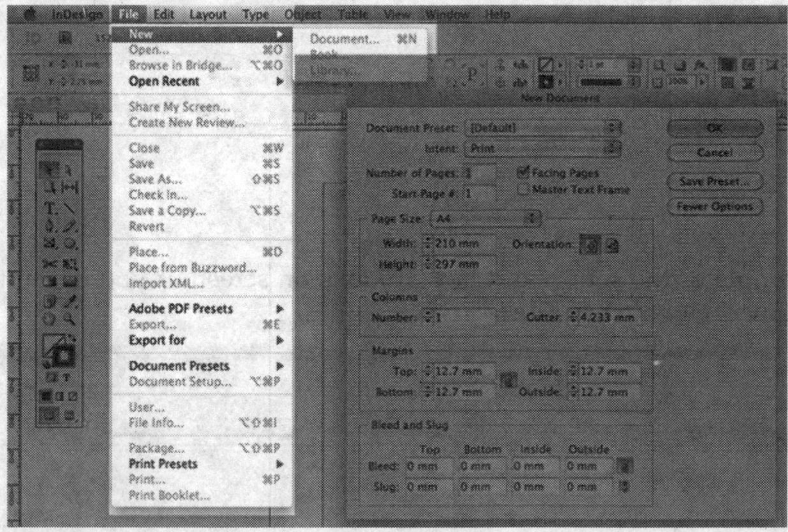

Step 2

From the Tool Box select the Rectangle Frame Tool (F).

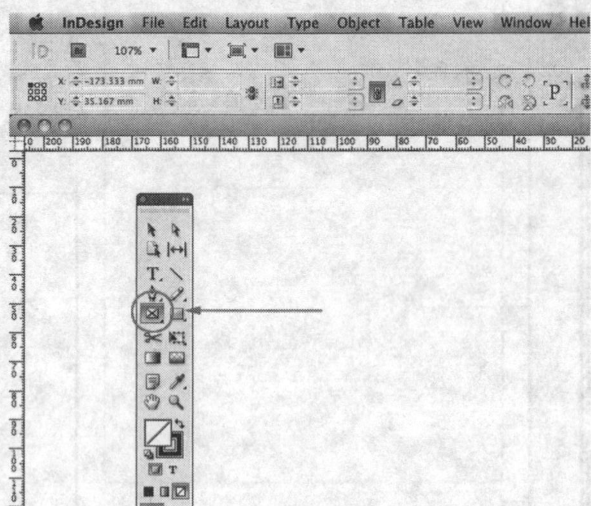

Step 3

Click within the document and drag out the cursor to create a large square or rectangle. Don't release the click, instead press your right arrow key a couple of times. You will notice that the box divides itself into columns according to the amount of times the arrow key was pressed.

Still holding down the mouse, press the up arrow key to set the number of rows. Once you are happy with your grid release the mouse click. (Additionally all of the methods in step 3 will also work on text frames)

Note....

While holding down your mouse click you can delete the amount of rows and columns by using the left/down arrow keys.

Step 4

After releasing mouse click the frames should be still selected, so let's import some images. Go to **File > Place** or use Command + D and navigate to where your images are saved. Hold down the Command button and select the images you want to use by clicking on them individually. Finally click Open.

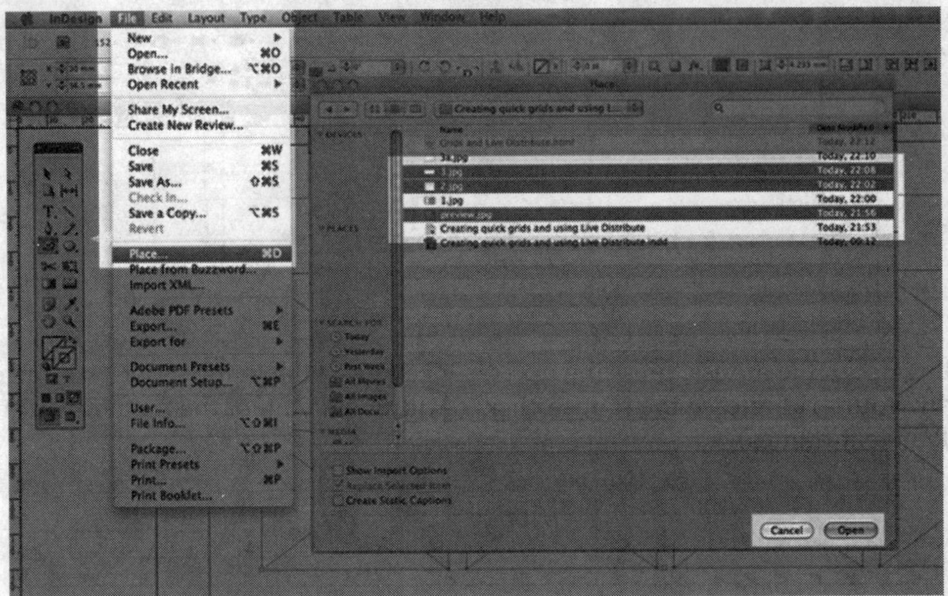

Step 5

The cursor should now be fully loaded with the images ready to import. Add the images by clicking on the frames one by one.

Step 6

Now fit the images proportionally and centre them. Do this by selecting the frames and pressing the quick buttons on the Control Bar illustrated below.

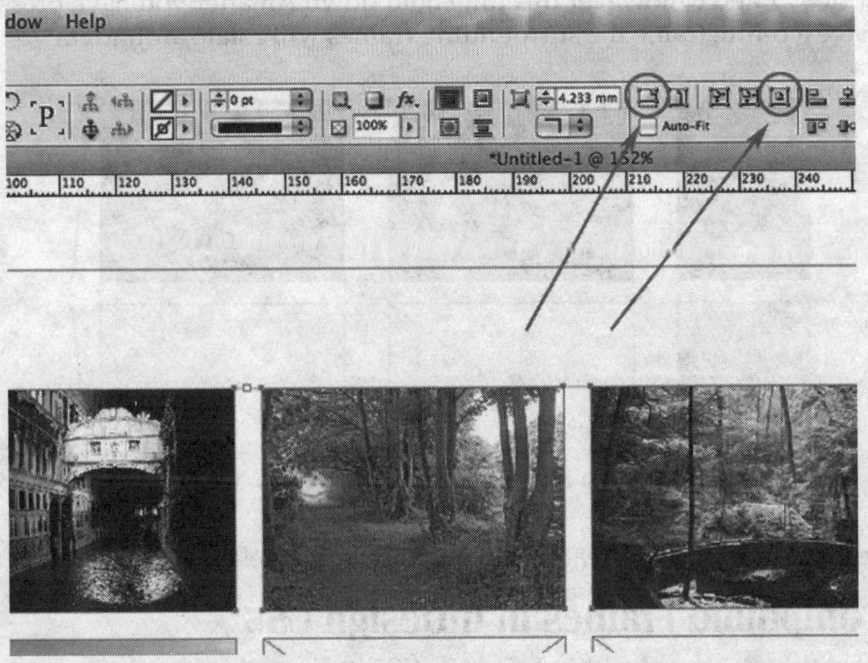

Step 7

The grid is now set up, so let's take a look at the Live Distribute feature. Select the Selection Tool (V) from the Tool box. Select all the frames you want to distribute and pull out the side handle on the right hand side of the collective frame and then hold down the space bar. Instantly you will notice that all the frames will be distributed equally and aligned.

Step 8

This method can also be used on the corner handles too. Simply resize from the corner frame using the instructions detailed in step 7. To distribute from the centre use the same methods described in steps 7 and 8, however this time hold down Alt after you have pressed the space bar. If you have a centre frame the surrounding frames will rotate around it.

Use these brilliant Indesign CS5 features to enhance and quicken your operating skills.

Create Compound Frames in InDesign CS5

By using the pathfinder panel within InDesign CS5 it is possible to create a compound frame that can be used to import an image to create a unique effect. Find out more about Compound Frames here.

Step 1

Start by creating a number of frames to work with. Select the Rectangle Frame tool from the Tool box or use Shortcut = F, click and drag to create the frames.

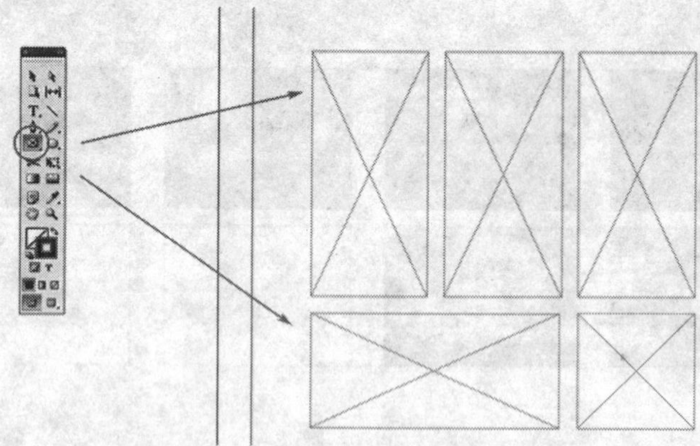

Step 2

Go to **Window > Object and Layout > Pathfinder.** You will be presented with a floating panel.

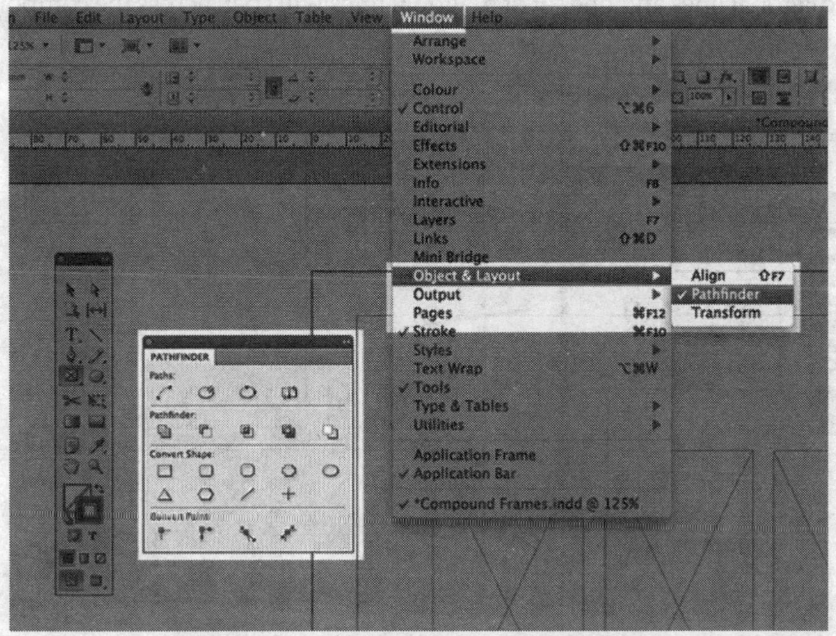

Step 3

Using the Selection Tool, Shortcut = V, select the frames you want to compound.

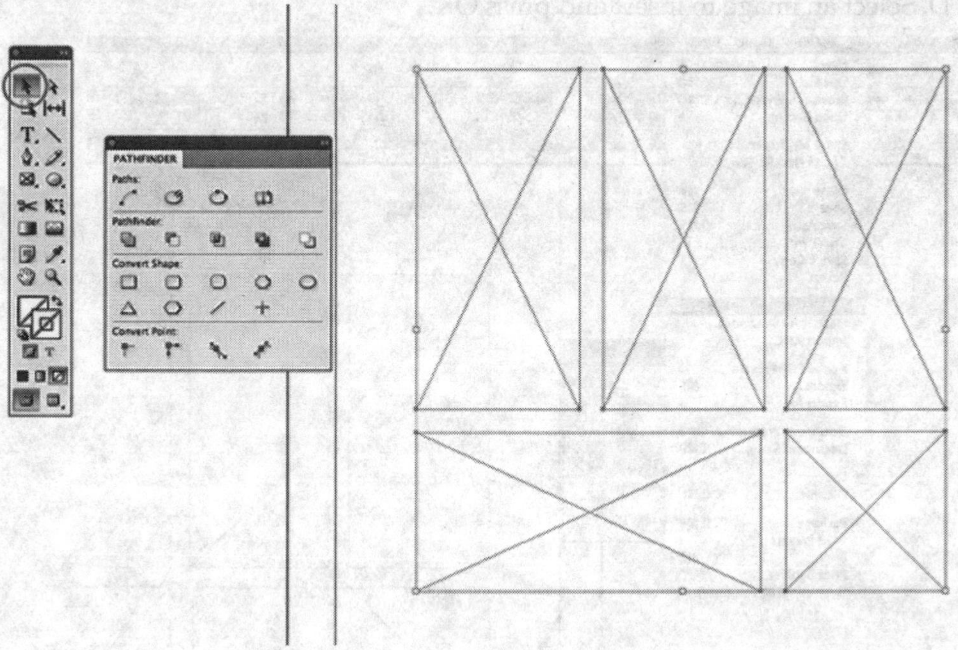

Step 4

On the pathfinder panel locate the Add button and press it to compound the frame. The frames will lose their diagonal lines and one set of diagonal lines will span across the compounded frames.

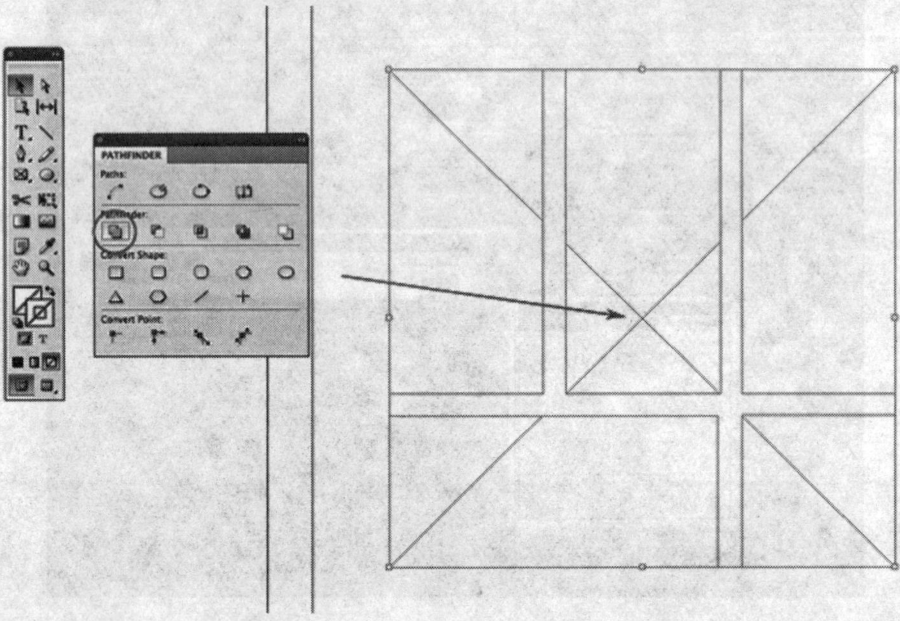

Step 5

Leaving the frame selected place an image by going to **File > Place** or by using shortcut Command + D. Select an image to insert and press OK.

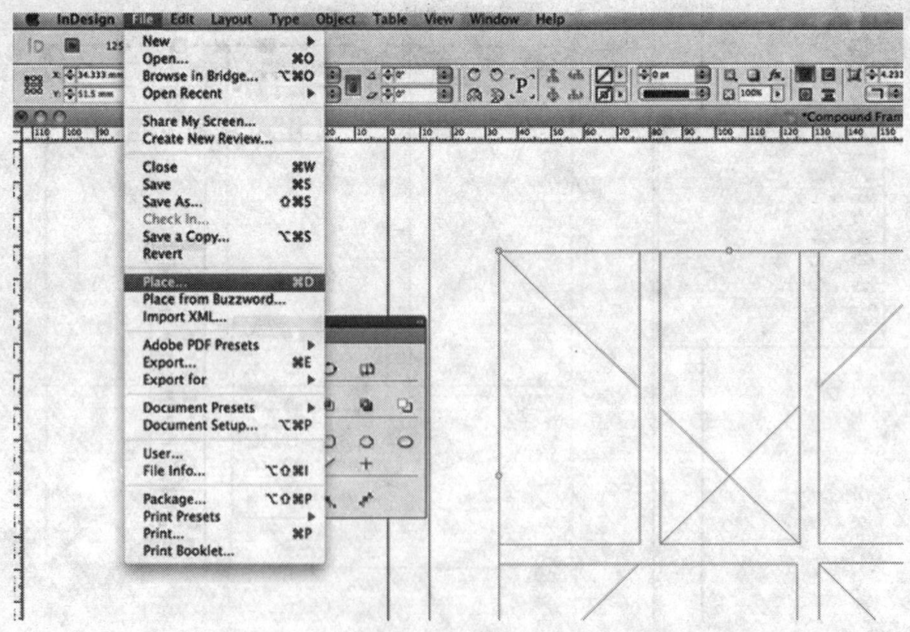

Step 6

To change the position of the imported image select the Direct Selection Tool and click inside the frame. A hand cursor will appear, use this to click and drag the image.

Step 7

Additionally the image can be modified by using the Fitting Options by going to **Object > Fitting**.

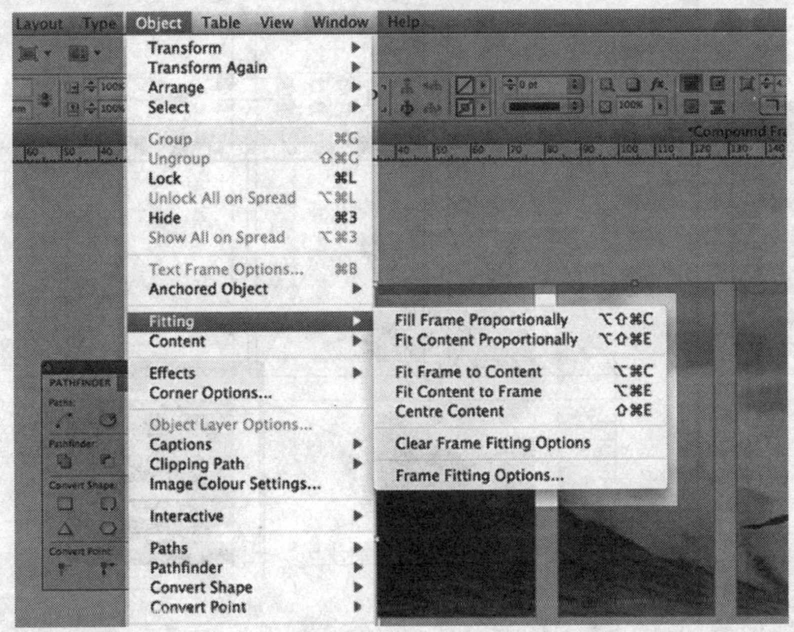

Step 8

To release a compound frame, select the Selection Tool, click once on the compound frame and go to **Object > Paths > Release Compound Path.**

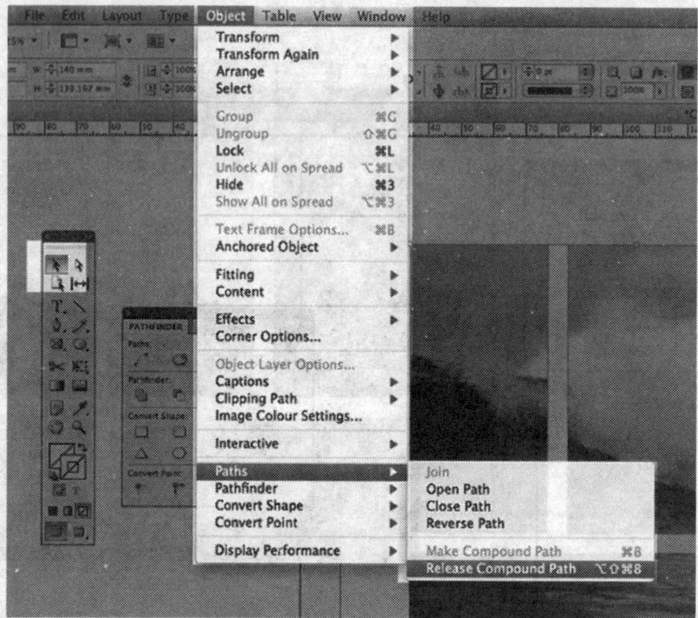

Once released the image will be contained in one frame and the rest will be left empty.

Try this technique in your next project to add a new visual effect to your layouts and designs. It works great when more than one compound frame is used in a single design.

The Gap Tool in Indesign CS5

The Gap Tool can be used to adjust the white-space in-between and around page items. This tool holds the ability to allow the user to work quickly with item with heavy layouts as well as viewing real-time changes.

Step 1

The Gap Tool is an awesome tool in its own right, however, combining it with the Auto-Fit feature enhances its potential.

Step 2

The Gap Tool is located in the Toolbox. It can also be selected by using shortcut, U.

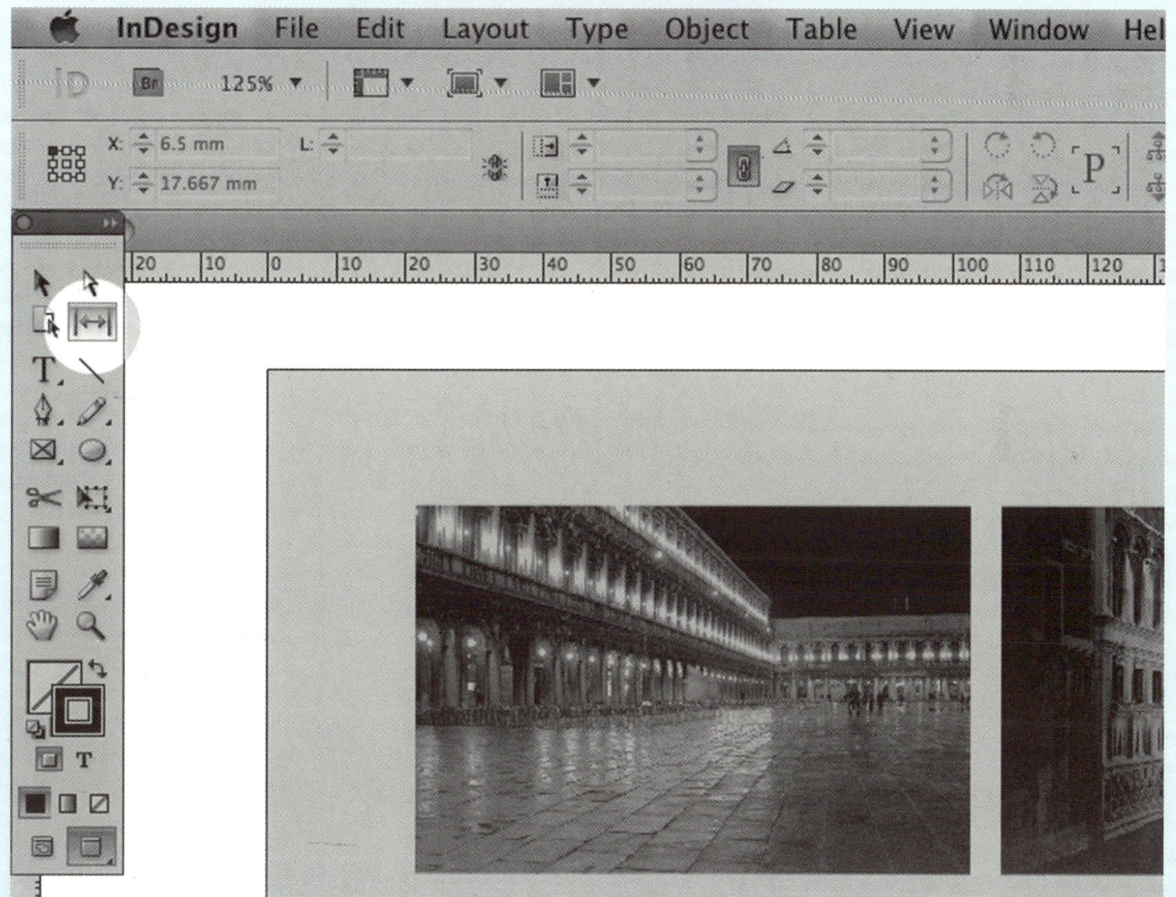

Step 3

Once the Gap Tool has been selected move the cursor and hover above an existing gap. The cursor will change to the gap icon and the white space in-between the items will be highlighted in light grey.

By hovering above the white space between the edge of an item and the edge of a document the Gap Tool will select this gap too.

Step 4

Continue to hover above a gap, click and drag in any direction. Immediately the surrounding frames attached the gap will resize as well as retaining the same Gap width. The tool will work on the horizontal and vertical gaps and the space in-between the images to the edge of the page. Note that because the Auto-Fit feature is active all the images within the frames will resize in tandem with the gap changes.

Gap moved to the left

Modifier Keys

To restrict the Gap Tool to affect only items on the opposite sides of the cursor hold down Shift and drag to desired size.

By holding down command the Gap Tool will resize the gap only.

Hold Option to move all the items attached to the gap.

And hold **Option + Shift** to confine to two items attached to the gap. Additionally the Gap Tool works on text frames as well as image frames.

Using the Gap Tool with the Auto-Fit feature creates a powerful partnership for constructing fluid layouts within InDesign CS5.

Working with Track Changes in Indesign CS5

The Track Changes panel is a handy feature that gives the user the ability to view all significant changes made to an existing story. Changes can be kept for reference or discarded once checked and approved. The feature can also be useful when there is more than one contributor working on the same document.

Step 1

To open the Track Changes panel go to **Window > Editorial > Track Changes**. You will be presented with a floating panel.

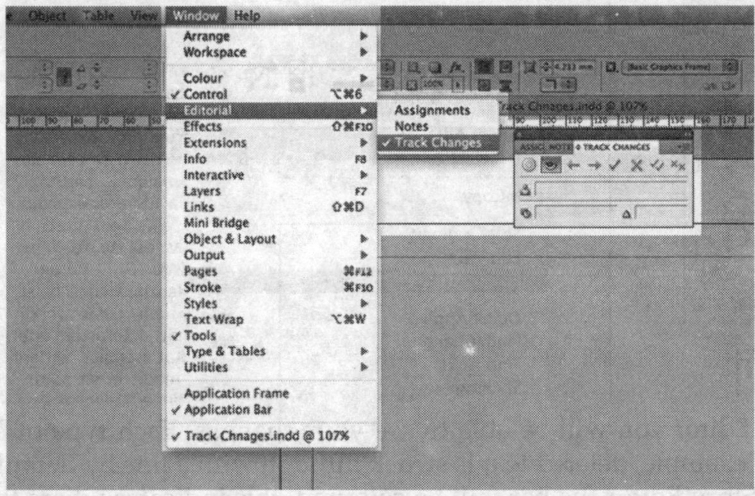

Step 2

Select the Type tool from the toolbox and click once in your text frame. Go back to the Track Changes panel and hit the Enable button. For the purpose of the tut make some changes to your text. For example, delete a character and add a word somewhere. You will notice that nothing has changed, don't worry; the Track Changes feature doesn't display within the document.

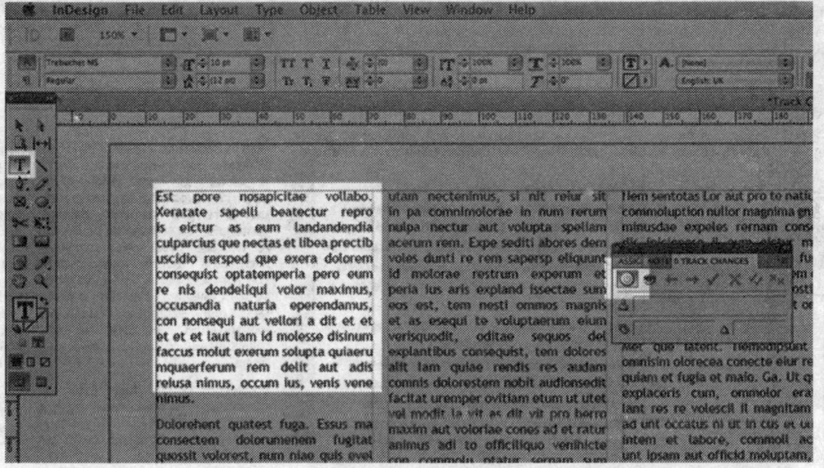

Step 3

To view your changes open the Story Editor, this can be found by going to **Edit > Edit in Story Editor**.

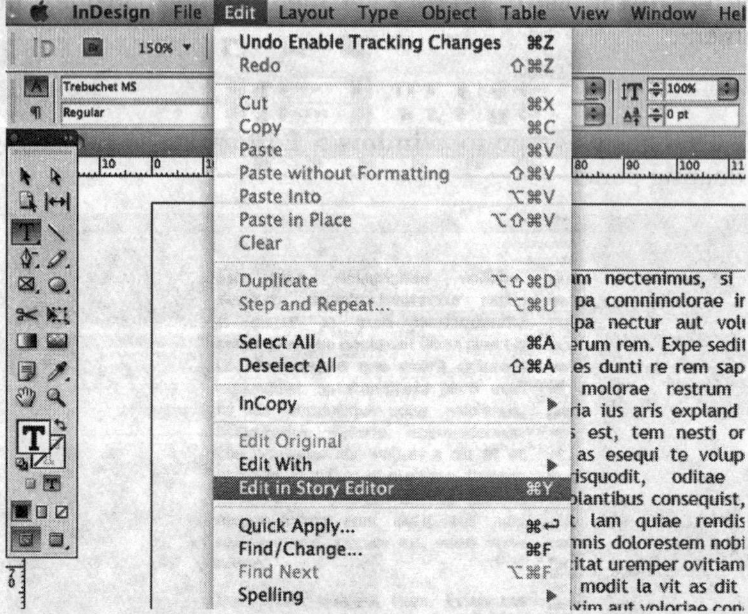

Within the Story Editor you will be able to see your changes. Each type of edit has its own characteristic, for example, deleted text is struck through with a line by default. Down the left hand side of the Story Editor the bar will be coloured, this indicates where the changes have been made.

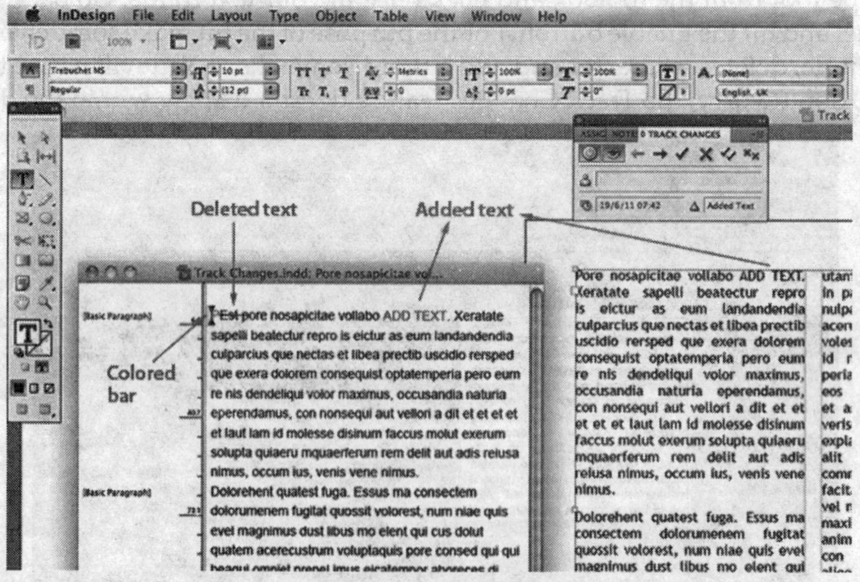

Step 4

Characteristics can be changed via Preferences. Go to **InDesign > Preferences > Track Changes**. The panel is divided into two main parts, Show and Change Bars. The Show box contains all the options for how the changes are displayed. To distinguish each type of edit I am going to use the following settings:

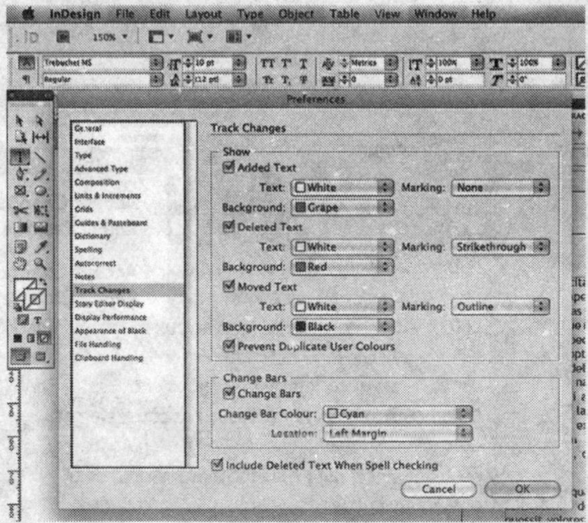

I prefer to use something other than white for the background so that the changes pop out and can't be missed. For the Change Bars option I have left it as the default colour Cyan and Location left. Once the preferences have been determined, click OK.

Step 5

Open the Story Editor again **(Command + Y)** to take a look at the changes. Your preference choices will be reflected here.

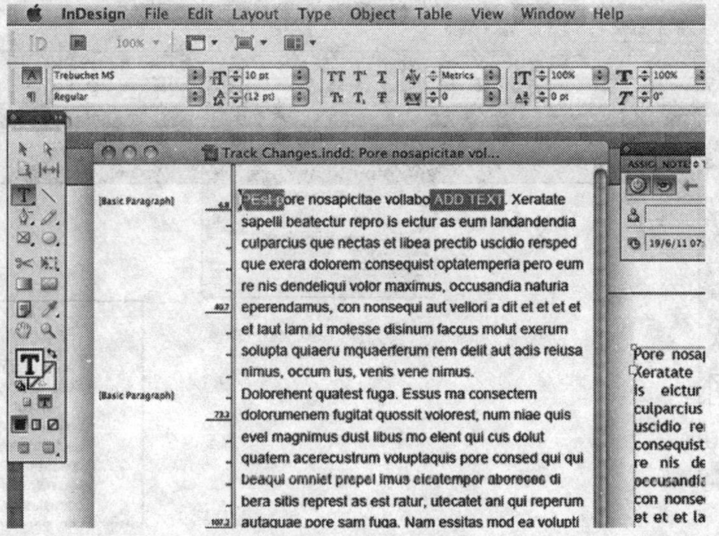

The edits you have made to your text will remain in the Story Editor until you action them. Right click on one of the edits, a floating panel will be appeared like this:

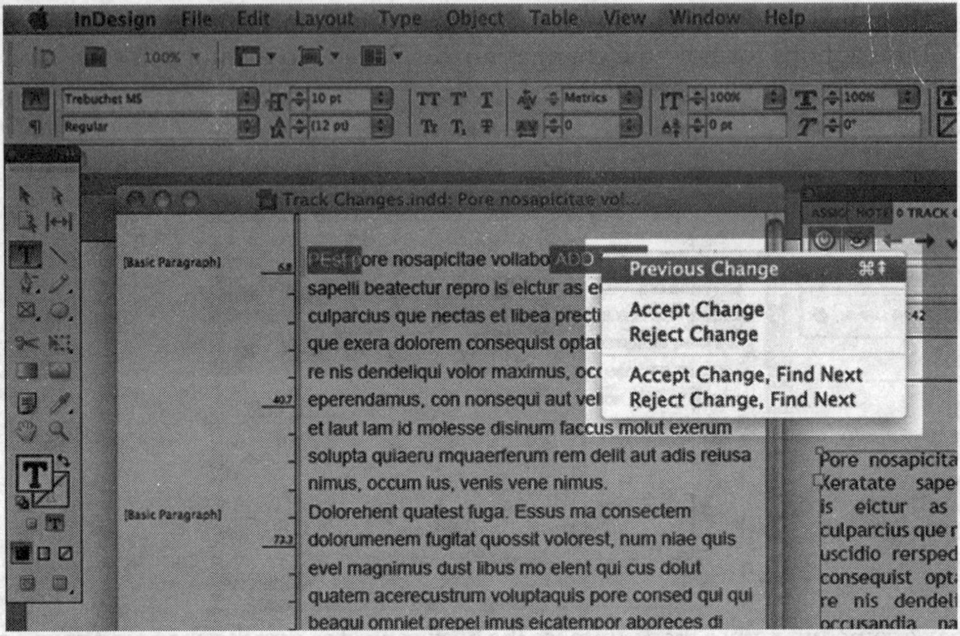

You have two options, to Accept or Reject the changes. It is possible to navigate throughout the changes yourself or use the Accept/Reject, Find next option. Once actioned the changes will disappear from the Story Editor.

These options can also be found in the Track Changes panel in the form of buttons and using them will link directly to the Story Editor. Hover above each button with the cursor to read a short description.

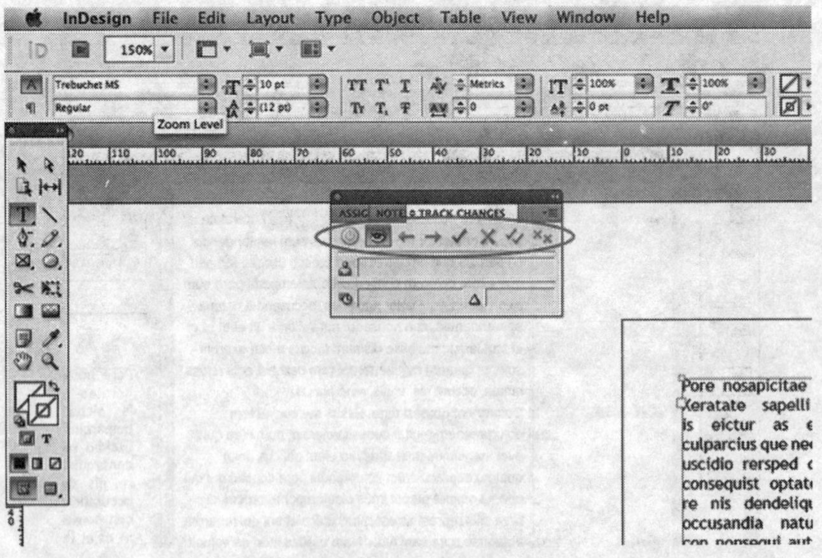

Additionally further options can be located in the fly-out menu on the Track Changes panel. In one way or the other they relate Accepting/Rejecting changes.

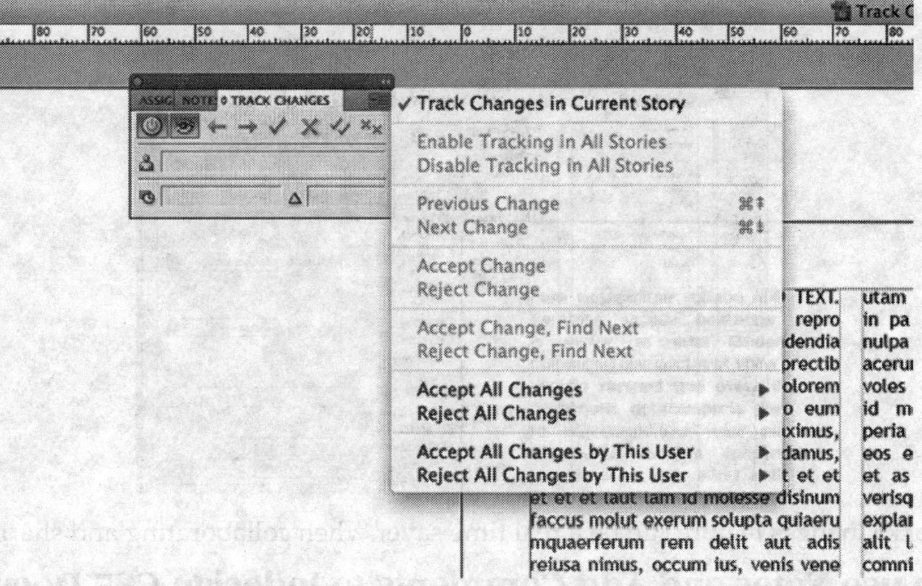

Step 6

If you are working with multiple users on a project, a useful feature is to dedicate a colour to each user. Then whenever a user makes amends, their own unique colour will mark where they have changed the content. To do this, go to **File > Users**. Add a name and specify a colour and click OK.

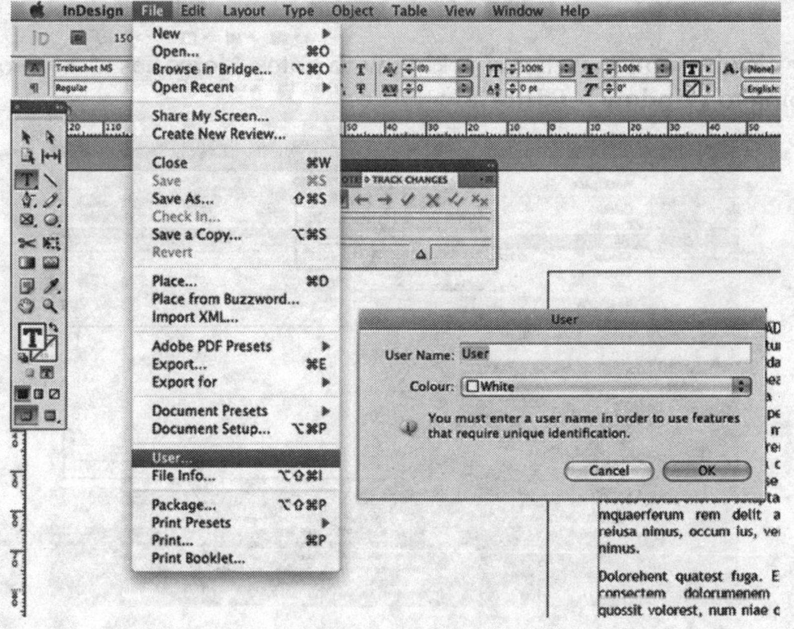

Now go back to the Track Change preferences and specify where you want the user colour to be used.

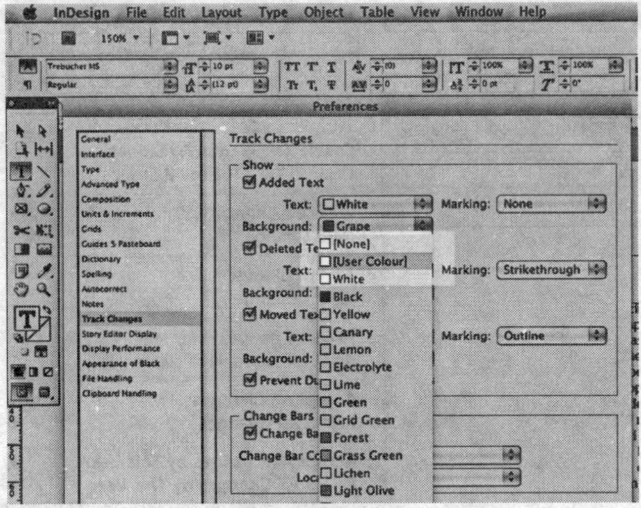

Using Track Changes feature can be a real time saver when collaborating and sharing files.

How to use Notes and Add Comments to Indesign CS5 Documents

The notes mode is perfect for adding comments to existing copy within an InDesign document. Notes can be added, but are not visible in the body of the text, instead these notes are hidden and can be viewed in the Notes panel or Story Editor. If you usually keep notes in a separate document this Quick tip could save you some valuable time.

Location

There are a few viewing options when working with notes. Notes has its own panel which can be found by going to **Window > Editorial > Notes**.

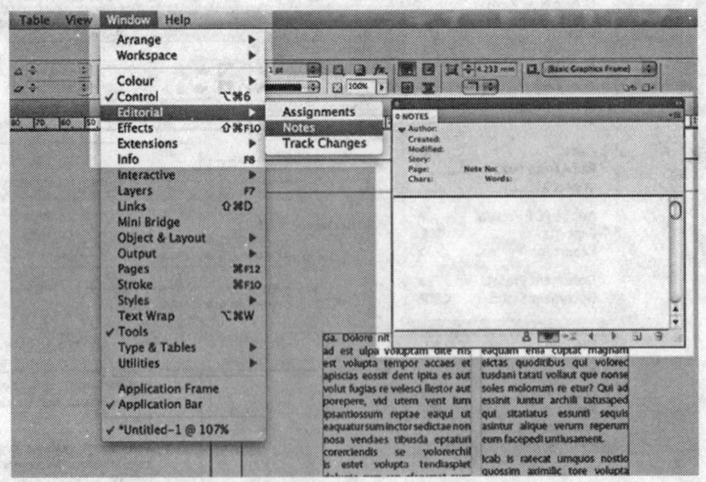

Alternatively, click once in an existing text frame and go to **Type > Notes**. Here you will be presented with options relating to Notes in a drop down menu.

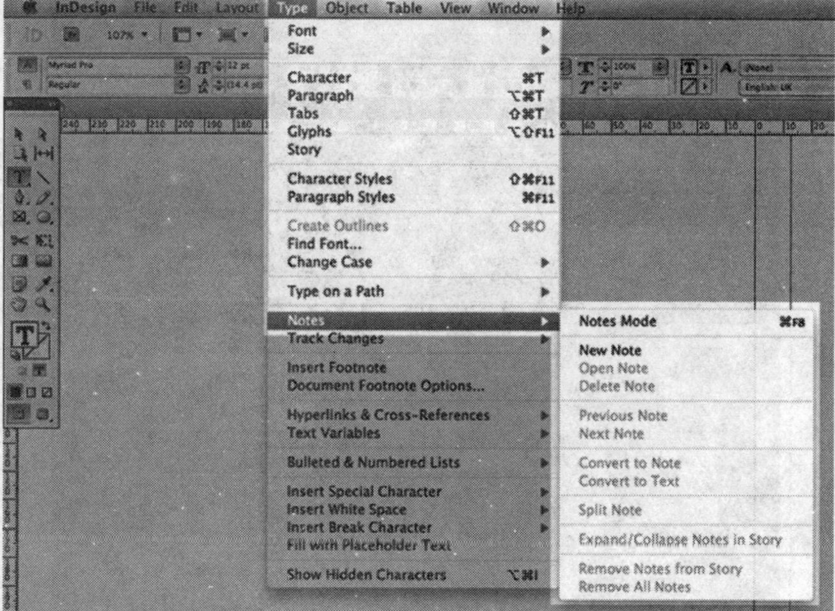

Adding notes

To input a note, use the Type tool and click at a point where you want the note to be positioned. Navigate to the Notes panel and press the New Note button. Now add your note within the Notes panel.

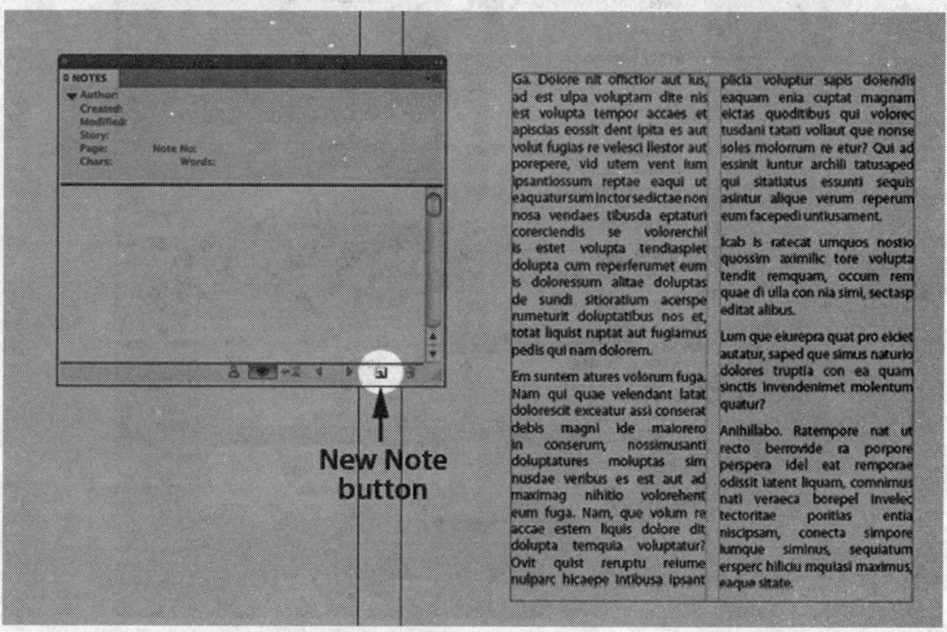

You can also add a new note by right clicking on the spot you want to add the note to and scroll down to New Note.

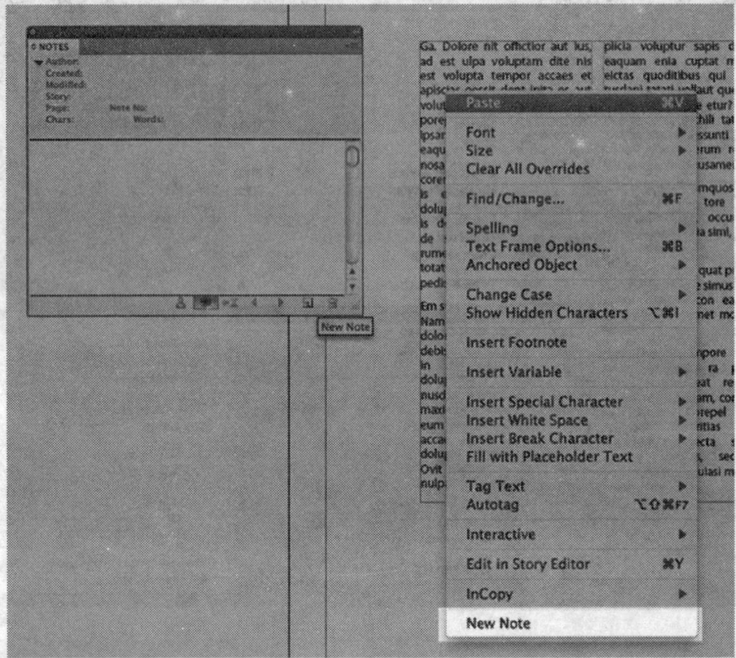

To view note markers within the Layout view go to **View > Extras > Show Notes**. A barbell will appear within the Layout view indicating where you added the note.

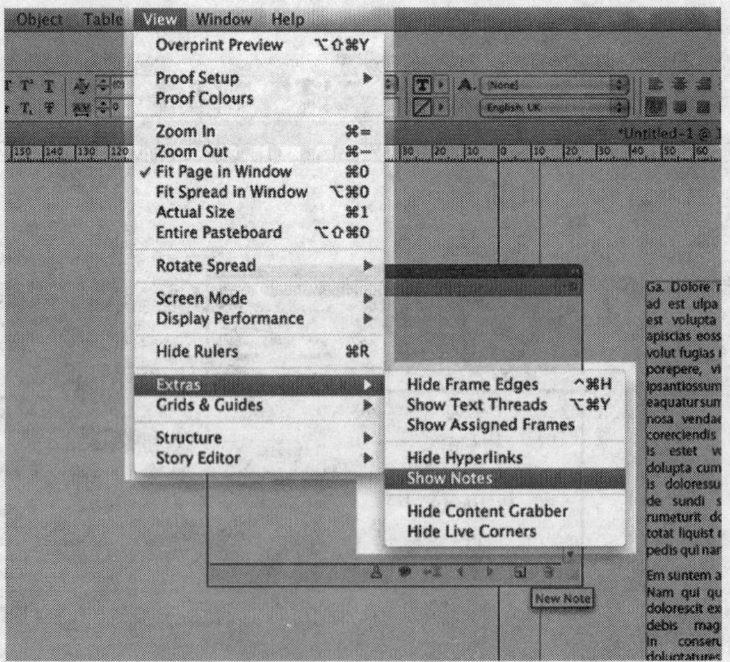

To change the colour of the barbell go to **InDesign > Preferences > Notes.** Use the drop down menu to select your preferred colour and click OK.

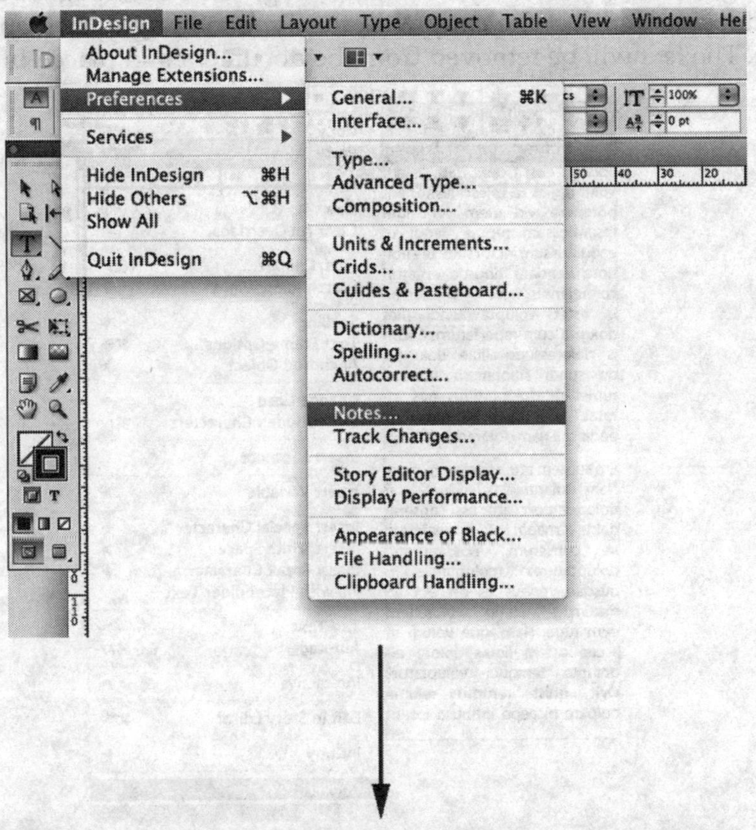

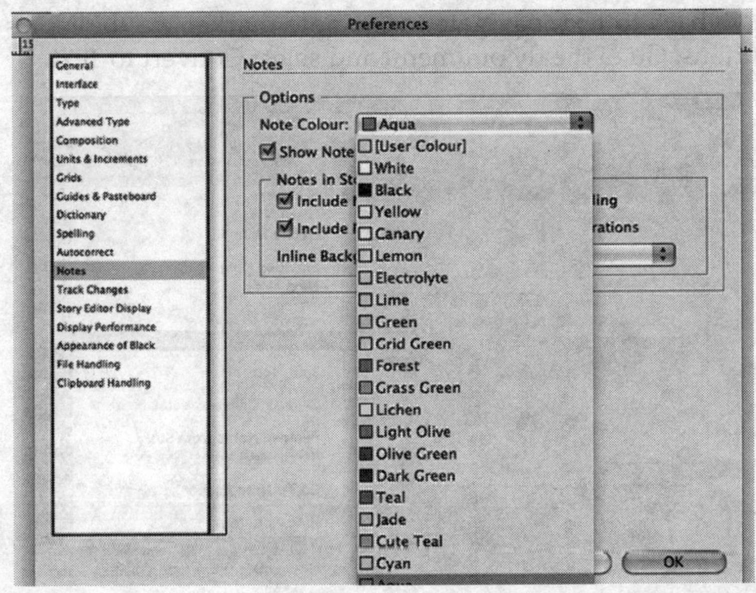

Converting text to a note

If you are deleting text but there is a possibility it might be needed again use the following method to avoid losing it. Select the copy with the Type tool, right click and scroll down to Convert to Note. The text will be removed from the document and placed in the Notes panel.

To convert the note back to text, navigate to the note marker via the Notes panel using the next/previous buttons. Go to the fly out menu and select Convert to Text.

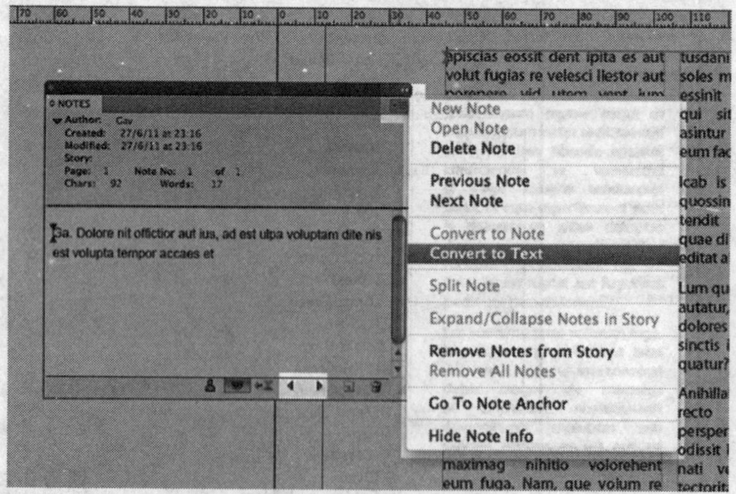

Viewing notes

As mentioned earlier you can view your notes by using the 'next/previous' buttons via the Notes panel. Additionally notes can be viewed via the Story Editor. To do this click once in the text frame with the Type tool and use shortcut **Command + Y**. The Story Editor will open and the notes will be contained within a box between two arrows. It is worth mentioning that you can use the Notes panel 'Go To Next/previous' buttons to navigate through the notes in the Story Editor window.

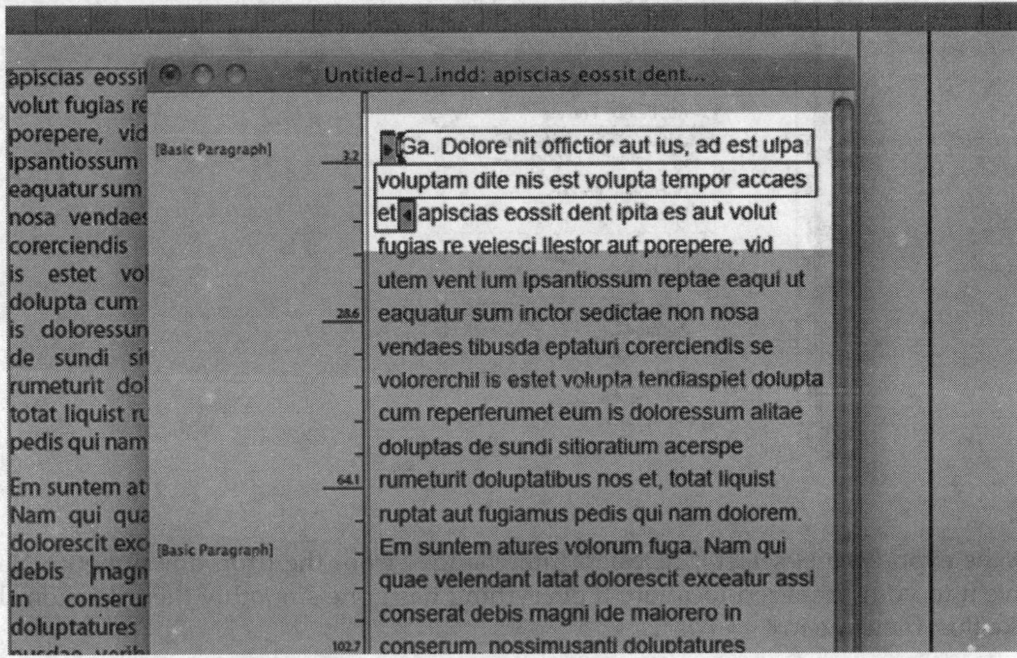

Whether adding notes for yourself or communicating with a colleague, this feature is great for keeping design notes and layouts together in a single file.

How to Fix Corrupt Indesign Files

If you regularly use InDesign, you may find that from time to time a file may be corrupt and glitch. In this Quick Tip you will learn a technique that may help recover your file in just a few easy steps.

Introduction

If you have a file that won't open, keeps crashing or doesn't preview properly try this Quick Tip to solve the problem.

Step 1

If you can Open the File but it's Corrupted.

Ok, let's start by opening the corrupt file. Once open go to **File > Export**

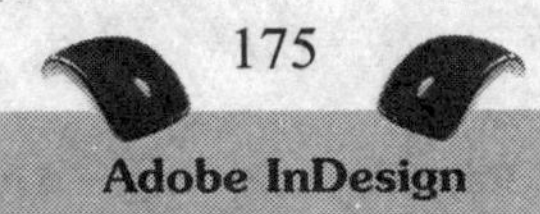

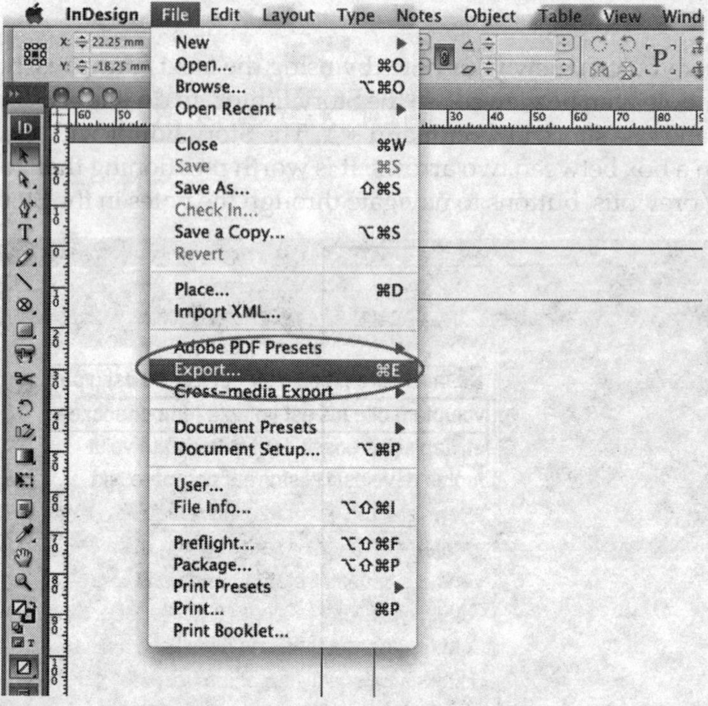

Step 2

Within the export panel select "InDesign Interchange" from the drop down menu. Name it and save it to your preferred location. If everything has gone smoothly the extension should look like this: filename.inx

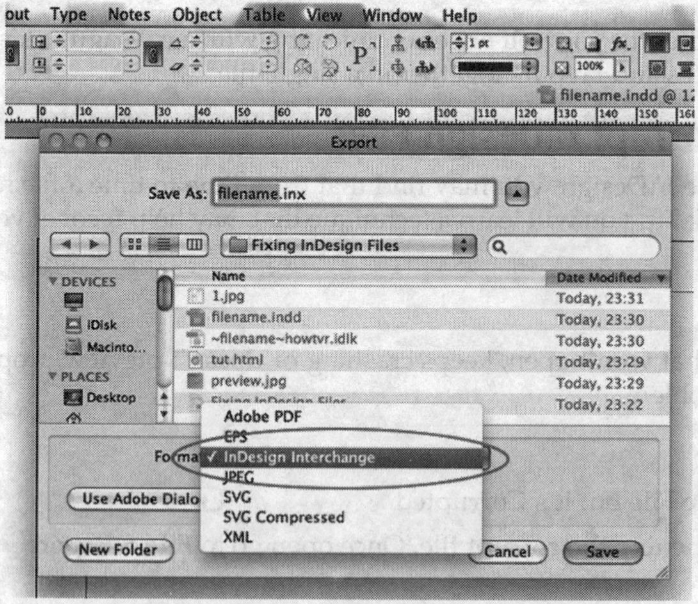

If You Are Using CS5

Within InDesign CS5 the IDML format has replaced the Interchange INX format, so instead of selecting "InDesign Interchange", select "InDesign Markup".

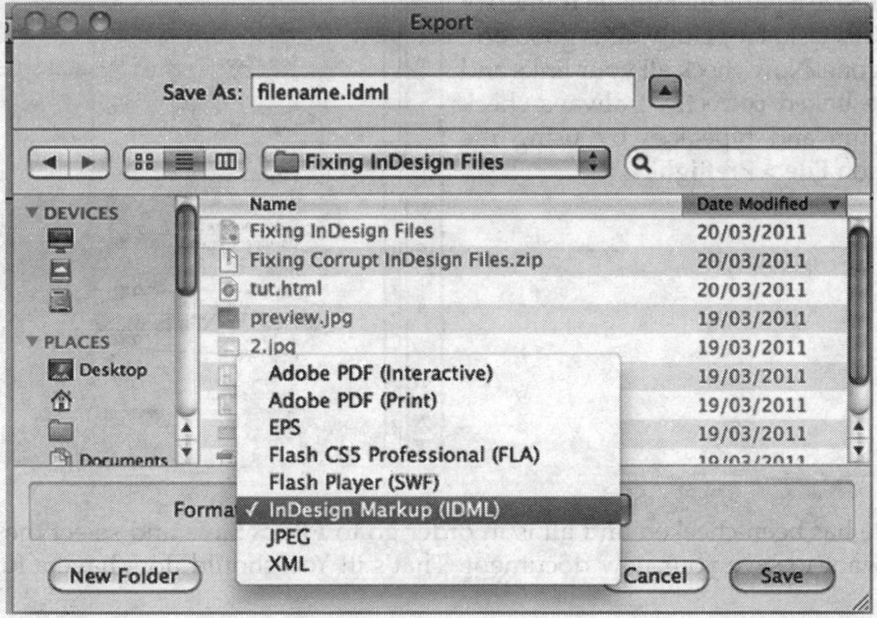

Step 3

Now close the corrupt file and open the new .inx file you just created. When the .inx file opens within InDesign you will notice that it is classed as an "Untitled Document". More importantly all of the original content / design should be present and bug free.

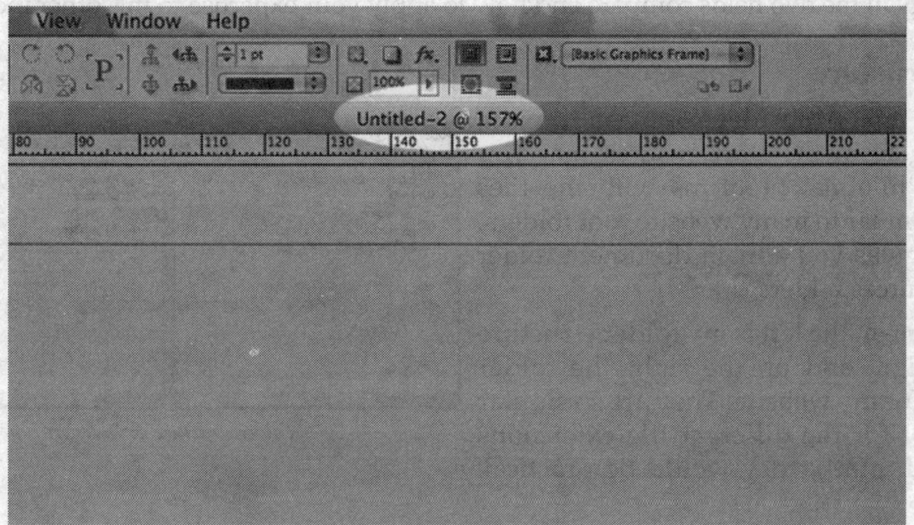

Step 4

Double check that the bug has been removed. So for example, if InDesign kept crashing when you tried to resize a particular image frame, try performing this task. Hopefully all is good and the bug has gone. Now check all your links and typefaces are linked correctly. I always check images, colours and typefaces by using the preflight option **File > Preflight**.

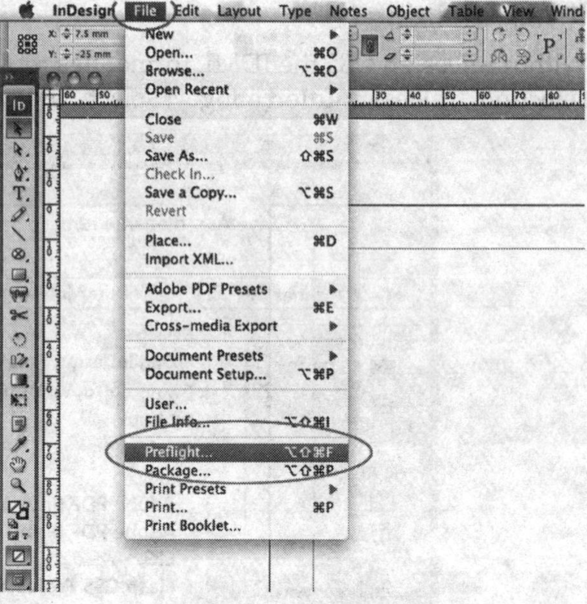

Step 5

When the file has been checked and all is in order go to **File > Save** and select the destination where you want to save your new document. That's it! You should now have a fully restored InDesign file.

Adobe InDesign For Web Developers & Designers

Adobe InDesign is the primary application of print designers for laying out multiple pages and assembling print documents. This article gives you, the Web-based developer, a look at some of the tools in InDesign that translate directly into what you currently use. We'll look at how the terminology in the two fields compare and how to apply your expertise to this other industry.

Folder Structure

As with any Web development project, organizing from the start ensures that you will have minimal problems with the files later on. Similar to many website root folders, InDesign gives you a main document folder and a resources folder:

In the figure on the left is my folder structure for InDesign, and on the right the folder structure for my website. They are so similar that, if not for the different file extensions (.indd and .html), they would be practically the same.

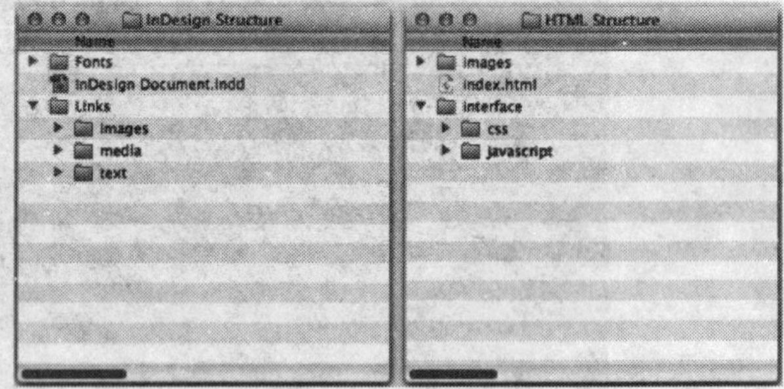

Folder structure in Indesign

Setting up the Document

Setting up an InDesign document is similar to setting up a mobile website. You specify the height, width and purpose of the document. For print-based items, set the "Intent" to "Print." If you will be using the file for an eBook or digital publication, then specify "Web." If you will be using the document for both, then specify "Print" to ensure that the colours are maintained properly.

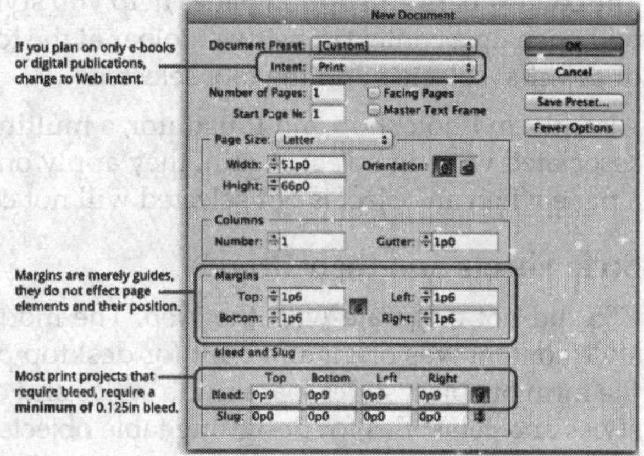

Setting up a document

The margins in InDesign are guidelines that are positioned on the page and are not like Web margins that affect objects on the page.

Main Tools

If you're familiar with Photoshop and Illustrator, then you are used to finding the main group of tools on the left side of the workspace, at least by default. InDesign is the same. The way you interact with and build objects on the page, though, works slightly different than Adobe's other design software. Containers are needed in order to place images, vector objects and textual content on the page.

You can import vector objects directly into the document, but you will usually be importing files into content boxes that you position in the layout. This should come easily to you because Web design operates on the same principle: creating DOMs that contain images or text, and then positioning them in the layout. The one major difference is that, while objects are positioned in a Web document relative to their structure (unless otherwise styled), objects on an InDesign layout are always given an x and y position based on the overall page (by default, the top-left corner, similar to absolute positioning).

Because we are working with a vector- and object-based layout, one of the main tools you will use for the majority of your editing is the Selection tool, which gives you control of position and size. It also is used to select an object in order to change its properties. This is quite different from Photoshop, in which you edit individual layers. To change the colour of an object, you need to select it first using the Selection tool, and then adjust it using one of the various ways to change colour.

These content boxes can be created with various tools. The Type tool enables you to create a box for text. The Rectangle Frame tool creates a box to add an image or linked resource. The Rectangle tool is not assigned to any particular kind of content. These three frame types allow you to build the layout any way you want.

In spite of both the Rectangle and Rectangle Frame tools, many designers who were trained on older software use only the Frame tool. The one difference between them is that the Frame tool shows a placeholder (an x). The Rectangle tool merely allows for a cleaner workspace but does not affect the final output.

The context bars and option panes help you style the content. As in Photoshop, various objects will open up a context-sensitive toolbar at the top, allowing for quick editing based on the type of object(s) selected and the tool selected.

Also like in Photoshop and Illustrator, a multitude of panes are available to control the values associated with an object. Again, they apply only to selected objects. Selecting an option from a pane when an object is not selected will not cause any objects to change.

Style Sheets and their Origins

CSS did not originate with the Web. The model of defining a set of instructions in order to style content was originally built for desktop publishing applications. In InDesign, this takes the form of object styles, paragraph styles and character styles. There are also table styles, row styles and cell styles for designing table objects, but we'll stay away from these in this lesson.

Styles in InDesign work similar to Web-based CSS but have one major difference: you cannot group multiple style sheets of the same type. For example, you cannot apply multiple paragraph styles to one paragraph. However, you can apply a character style sheet to content in a paragraph that already has a style sheet applied to it.

Shortcuts and menu locations for the panes are given below. But the panes will already be open on the right side of your workspace if you have selected Window→Workspace→Advanced or have selected the "Typography" option. These function exactly like the panes in Illustrator and Photoshop: you can snap them together and arrange them to your liking, and they contract to icon format.

Object Style Sheets

Draw a content box on the page using the Rectangle tool. With the box selected, you can modify the content box—including the border, background and corner effects—as you would a div object. If you give it, say, a background colour, a drop shadow and rounded corners, you can save that style by selecting a new "Object Style" in the Object Style pane when the object is selected (Window→Styles→Object Styles, or Command/Control + F7). You can give the style a name (much like a class name) and modify any of the style properties you've assigned.

After saving this new style, you'll still need to apply it to the object. This may sound redundant; however, you've only created a new style based on the properties of the selected object. By clicking on the new style with the object selected, you will apply that style. Think of it like addingclass="object_style" to an HTML element after you've set up the CSS.

Paragraph Style Sheets

Select the Text tool, and click in the newly styled box. Add a few paragraphs of content (you can cheat by going to Type→Fill With Placeholder Text). With your cursor in the first paragraph, you can start changing some of the properties of what, in Web terms, would be the <p> tag by using the Paragraph pane (Window→Type & Tables→Paragraph, or Command/Control + Alt + T).

Notice that options for modifying font size, letter spacing and weight are not available. This is because these aspects relate to the characters of the paragraph. While a paragraph style can and most likely will include instructions for these values, the Paragraph pane does not provide access to them.

Let's create a paragraph style via the Paragraph Style pane (Window→Styles→Paragraph Styles, or Command/Control + F11). This opens a new window that gives you God-like control over all aspects of the text. Name your style, and jump to the "Basic Character Formats" option on the left.

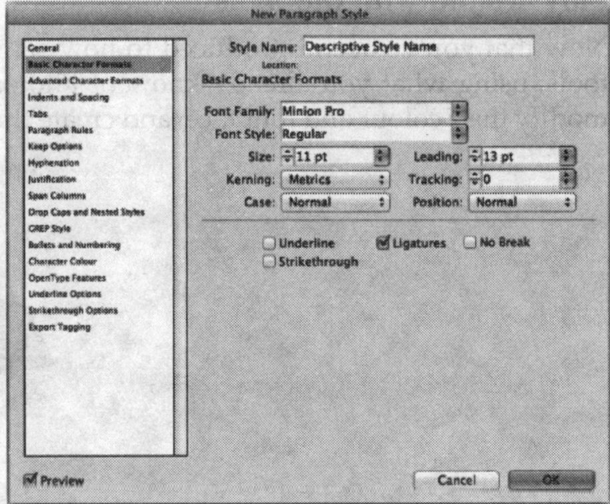
Paragraph style

This is what I meant when I said that character properties could be defined in the paragraph style. Change the font size, weight and spacing here, and click "OK." As you did with the object styles, you will still need to apply it to the paragraph you are working with. To do this, put your cursor in the paragraph text or select a portion of it, and then click on the paragraph style's name. If you have selected the entire object using the Selection tool, then the paragraph style will be applied to all of the content.

Character Style Sheets

With the Type tool still selected and your cursor in the paragraph, highlight a portion of the text. Using the Character pane (Window Type & Tables Character, or Command/Control + T), adjust the properties of the characters. You can add italics or bold or change the font family.

Once more, let's create a style that incorporates these modifications. In the Character Styles pane (Window Styles Character Styles), create a new "class." Name it something relevant, save it, and then apply it to the highlighted text. This would be akin to adding a little <span> tag to some text in a paragraph, which allows you to apply styles to that text independent of the parent element.

CSS vs. Style Sheets

We've just gone over a lot here. The reason we went over these three things is to illustrate that, unlike CSS styling, I cannot add a second style sheet of the same type to an element. In CSS, I can do something like this 1 <div class="orange_box rounded"></div>

This would apply two styles to the same object (the orange box). InDesign attributes of a given type (whether object, paragraph or character) must be contained in a single style. Higher-level styles are overwritten by child items. For example, character styles overwrite paragraph styles, which in turn overwrite object styles; but you cannot apply multiple styles to a single object, etc.

As in CSS, I could overwrite an object manually. For instance, I could apply a style sheet that gives a paragraph a font size of 11 points and a leading (line height) of 14 points, but then manually change the leading to 16 points by adjusting it in the Character pane. This would result in Web code like:

```
<p class="standard_body" style="line-height: 16px;"></p>
```

As you can see, we end up with code that would be considered poor practice by most people. However, it does allow us to customize as issues arise.

Play around with the Tools

Now that you've been introduced to how set up a document, start playing around with the tools, using what you already know of Photoshop or Flash. Position elements on the page, modify their colour and font face, and create the layout for a product that you've already built.

Adobe Photoshop

Are you interested in creating, modifying, combining, and/or optimising digital images on your computer? This chapter introduces you to Adobe Photoshop CS5, a popular software application for working with digital images.

Getting Started

Photoshop enables you to create, modify, combine, and optimise digital images. You can then save the images to print, share via e-mail, publish online, or view on a handheld device, such as an iPod.

You've heard of Photoshop, right? Of course you have – you wouldn't be reading this book otherwise! You've probably heard of Photoshop's sidekick, Fireworks, too, but you might not be quite sure of what it does or where it fits in.

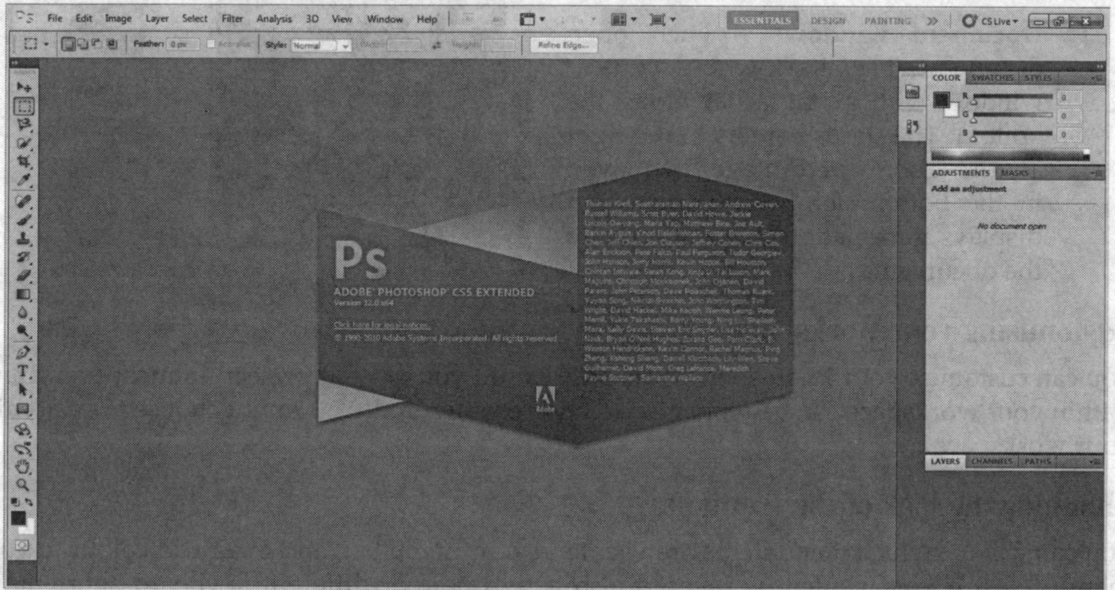

Photoshop is the most commonly used tools in the web designer's arsenal. From the preparation of initial design comps to generating optimised graphics for a web page, most web designers rely heavily on these two programs.

In this introductory chapter, we'll cover some of the basic tools and tasks that we'll draw on in the later chapters. We'll also discuss some of the shortcuts and time-savers that we use frequently. So what are you waiting for? Open up Photoshop and let's go!

The Photoshop Workspace

Photoshop's "out of the box" workspace consists of the following components:

- **Menu bar** – You will probably already be familiar with the menu bar from other programs. This runs across the top of your Photoshop window, and contains various menu options for Photoshop's tools.
- **Options bar** – The options bar sits beneath the menu bar and holds contextualised options for different tools. It also contains the workspace menu, where you can save and load arrangements of palettes.
- **Toolbox** – By default, the toolbox sits to the left of your Photoshop window, and contains shortcuts to Photoshop tools.
- **Palettes** – Individual "panes" that hold information or options for working with your file, known as palettes (or panels), float on the right-hand side. Each palette is labeled with a tab, and can be minimised, closed, grouped with other palettes, or dragged in and out of a panel dock. In the example that follows, the Navigator palette contains a thumbnail of the image that allows you to zoom in or out of the image quickly, and to change the part of the image displayed on the screen.
- **Document windows** – Each open document has its own document window with a status bar along the bottom. The status bar sits to the right of the zoom percentage displayed in the bottom left-hand corner, and displays information that's specific to the document.

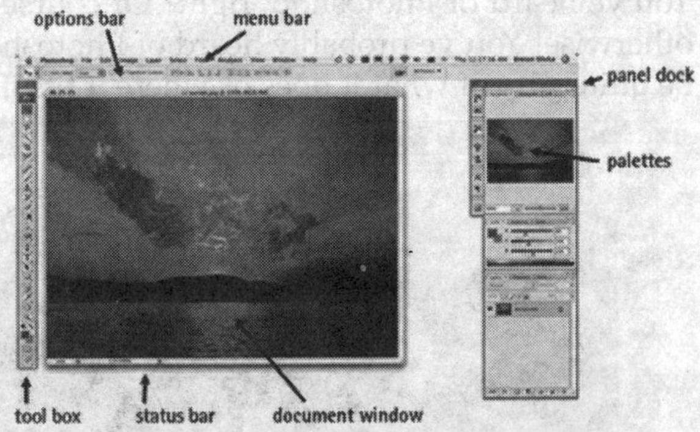

Photoshop workspace

Customising your Workspace

You can customise your Photoshop workspace to suit you or your project – almost everything within your workspace can be repositioned and reconfigured! You might choose to customise your workspace by:

Changing the look of the menu bar

You can change which menu items are visible in your menu bar, and even add colour to your menu items. If you wanted, you could also assign new or different keyboard shortcuts to menu commands (which I don't recommend until you feel very comfortable with Photoshop or have a compelling reason to do so!). Go to **Edit > Menus** and use the dialog box to modify the menu bar and palette menus.

Moving the options bar

If you want to move the options bar, you can do so by clicking on the handle on its left side and moving it around. The options bar will "dock" to the top or bottom of the screen automatically if moved near those areas.

Moving the toolbox

The toolbox is extremely portable, and can be moved to any location on your screen. Move the toolbox by clicking on the light gray area at the top of it and dragging it around. You can switch between different toolbox layouts by clicking the double arrow along the top of the toolbox.

Rearranging palettes

There are many ways to rearrange your palettes. You might want to separate a palette from its palette group, and move it into another group. You can do this by dragging the palette tab out of its original group and into the new group. You may want to expand or collapse a dock, by clicking on the double arrows at the top of the dock. You might also decide to drag some of your palette tabs out of their dock, and close the rest. To display a palette that has been closed, go to Window and select the palette you want to show.

Displaying different information in the document window status bar

The status bar displays the document file size by default. The file size is shown as two numbers separated by a forward slash: the first number is an approximation of the image file size with all layers merged (known as "flattening" the image), and the second number is an approximation of the total file size of the image with layers intact. If all this sounds new to you, don't worry – we'll be discussing layers shortly. You can set the status bar to display different information, such as the document dimension in pixels, or the version number of the file. To do this, click on the arrow icon next to the status bar, select Show and choose the information you'd like to see.

Displaying information in document status bar

Saving your Customised Workspace

As you become more proficient with Photoshop, you may discover that you use certain sets of palettes for different types of projects, and that there are some palettes that you don't use at all. Photoshop allows you to save and load different workspaces – different arrangements of palettes, menus, and even different keyboard shortcuts – to help you work more efficiently.

After you've customised your workspace to your satisfaction, select the Workspace menu in the options bar, click Save Workspace and enter a name for your workspace, such as Creating Thumbnails or My Default Workspace. You can then load your different workspaces by opening Workspace and selecting your custom workspace from the menu list.

Working in Photoshop

Now that you've been introduced to the Photoshop workspace and have a basic idea of where everything is, let's start getting our hands dirty.

Creating New Documents

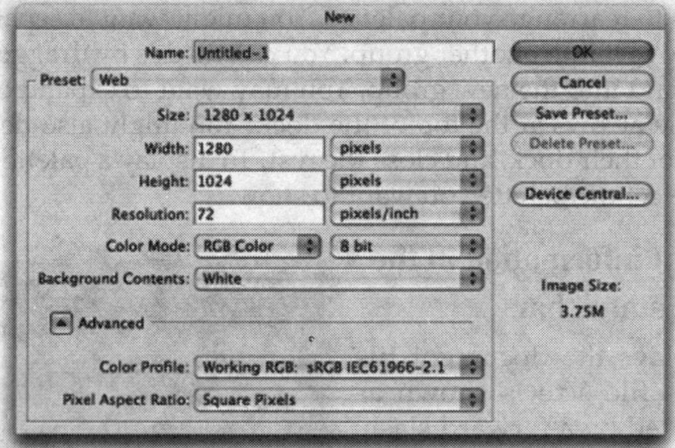

Creating a new document

The New dialog box

You can create a new document by selecting **File > New** from the menu bar, or pressing the keyboard shortcut **Ctrl-N** on a PC or Command-N on a Mac. The New dialog box will appear, where you can specify the document size and other settings.

Opening Files

Open files by selecting **File > Open** from the menu bar, or pressing Ctrl-O (Command-O on a Mac). You can select and open multiple files by holding down Ctrl (Command on a Mac) and clicking on all the files you require in the file dialog box.

Saving Files

Save a file by selecting **File > Save,** or pressing **Ctrl-S** (Command-S on a Mac). For a newly-created document, this will save your work in Photoshop Document (PSD) format. If you would prefer to save a copy of the document, you can use **File > Save As** or pressing **Ctrl-Shift-S** (Command-Shift-S on a Mac) instead.

Snappy Presets

If you're designing for a website with a minimum screen size of 800Ã—600 pixels, I'd recommend you start with a 750Ã—550 pixel document. The smaller dimensions give you a better estimate of your actual screen area after you take into account scroll bars and menu bars. Also, be sure to set the resolution at 72dpi to reflect the actual screen resolution. If you want easy access to these dimensions for other new documents, it's probably a good idea to click Save Preset and give the settings a name like Web Page. The next time you create a new document, you will be able to load your Web Page settings from the Preset list.

Saving Files for the Web

Photoshop files themselves can't be embedded into a web page. You will need to export your file and save it in a web-friendly format. There are three formats for web graphics: GIFs, JPEGs, and PNGs.

GIF

The GIF format (pronounced "jiff" or "giff" depending on which side of the tracks you grew up) can have a maximum of 256 colours. GIF files support transparency and animation, and work best with graphics that have large areas of the same colour, as shown in the logo below.

JPEG

The JPEG format (pronounced "jay-peg"), works best with photographic images or images that have more than 256 colours and gradients, such as the flower on the opposite page. Images saved in JPEG format are compressed, which means that image information will actually be lost, causing the image to degrade in quality.

PNG

The PNG format (pronounced "ping") is similar to the GIF format in that it supports transparency and works best with solid-colour images like the logo shown to the right, but it's superior to the GIF format as it has the ability to support true levels of transparency for coloured areas. Transparent PNGs are currently not in widespread use on the Web because older versions of Microsoft Internet Explorer do not support them; however, they're often used in Macromedia Flash movies. PNGs can produce a better quality image at a smaller file size than can GIFs. Photoshop allows you to save an image as a PNG-8 file (which works the same way as a GIF would with 256 colours) or a PNG-24 file (which allows for millions of colours as well as variable transparency).

Double-clicking Power

As if keyboard shortcuts weren't quick enough, Windows users have even more ways to open and save files, such as: holding down Ctrl and double-clicking the work area to create new documents, double-clicking the work area to pull up the Open dialog box to open files holding down, Alt and double-clicking the work area to open existing files as new documents, holding down Ctrl-Shift and double-clicking the work area to save documents holding down Shift and double-clicking the work area to access Adobe Bridge — Adobe's "control centre" and file browser. The work area is the gray area behind the document windows. If your shortcuts aren't working, check that you are clicking on an empty spot on the work area, and not in one of the document windows or Photoshop tools! Alas, Photoshop on a Mac does not have a work area, so Mac users won't get to enjoy the goodness of double-click shortcuts.

Example of an image that should be saved as JPEG

To save for the Web in Photoshop, select **File > Save for Web & Devices**… or press **Ctrl-Alt-Shift-S** (Command-Option-Shift-S on a Mac). This will bring up the Save For Web dialog box shown overleaf, which will show you a preview of the image that will be exported, with its optimised size in the bottom left-hand corner. You can adjust the settings for the image using the options in the pane on the right. Choose whether you want to save the file as a GIF, JPEG, PNG-8, or PNG-24, and have a play with the other settings, keeping an eye on the optimised file size. Try to strike a balance between the quality and file size of the image. When you're happy with your result, click Save and give your image a filename.

If you tried the above exercise, you're probably quite pleased with yourself for saving an image of reasonable quality at a file size significantly smaller than the original. You managed this by altering the settings in the right-hand pane, but what do these settings actually do?

GIF/PNG-8

- ❑ **Colours** – Adjusting this setting reduces the number of colours used in the image. This will usually make the biggest difference in the final image.
- ❑ **Dither amount and type (No Dither, Diffusion, Pattern, Noise)** – This setting has nothing to do with being nervous or agitated (although it's quite possible that you may have been a few moments ago!). Dither refers to a compression technique in which the pattern of dots is varied to give the illusion of a colour gradient. Changing the dither will result in a more noticeable degradation for images that involve a large number of colours blended together.
- ❑ **Transparency** – If you want transparent areas in your graphic, check this box. We'll look more closely at transparency later.
- ❑ **Matte colour** – For transparent images, the matte colour is used to help blend the edges of your image into the background of the web page. For non-transparent images, the matte colour defines the background colour of the image. Using matte colour with transparent images is covered in more detail in later Chapters.

JPEG

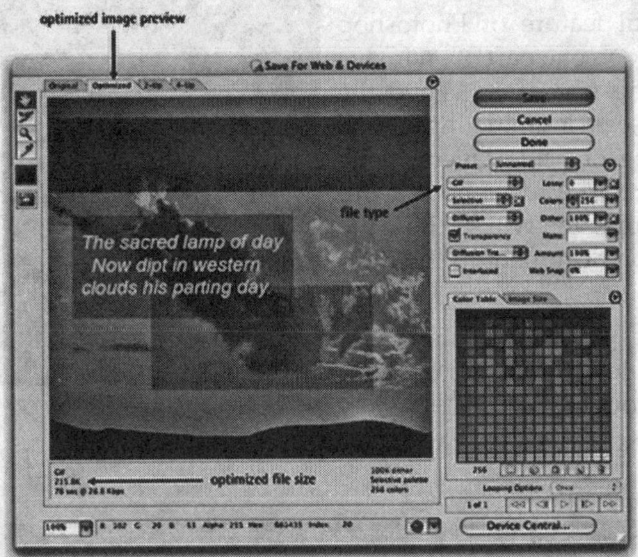

Quality – Changing the value in the Quality drop-down box alters the level of compression for the image. Reducing the quality may result in blurring or pixelation, but too high a setting will produce a large file that will take users too long to download. A good approach is to decrease the quality value gradually until you notice the degradation of your image becoming unacceptable. A reasonable compromise will be somewhere around this point.

Saving Files for the Web in Fireworks

Optimise palette in Fireworks

You can optimise images for the Web in Fireworks using the Optimise palette, shown at right. Set the file type and options in the Optimise palette in advance, and when you're ready to export your web image, select **File > Export** or press **Ctrl-Shift-R** (Command-Shift-R on a Mac). Fireworks will save the image based on the settings that you've defined.

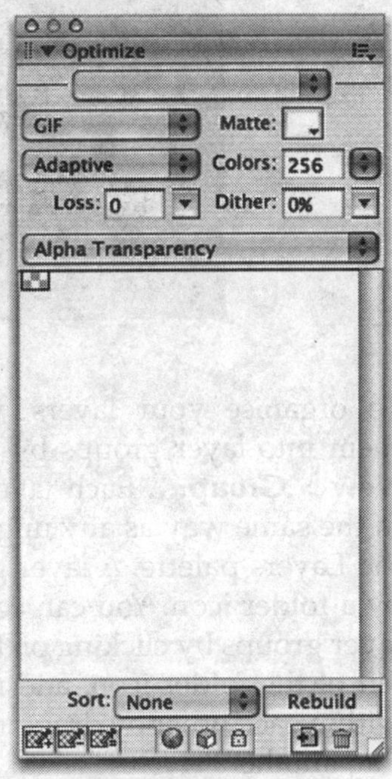

Optimise palette in fireworks

Why Two Tools?

Considering that it's possible to save files for the Web in Photoshop, it's perfectly reasonable for you to wonder why you would need Fireworks. While it's true that both programs can perform many of the same tasks, there are certain things that Fireworks can do that Photoshop can't. Fireworks also makes web-specific tasks easier, and since it's a smaller program that doesn't contain the full suite of Photoshop effects, it loads more quickly than Photoshop. As you work through this book you'll come to learn which tool is more suitable for particular tasks.

Photoshop Layers

Photoshop layers

Layers are a powerful feature of Photoshop that allow you to work on one part of an image without disturbing the rest of it. While the concept of layers may seem intimidating at first, once you get the hang of using layers you'll wonder how you ever survived without them! In the following examples you will see how the layers in the Photoshop document to the right stack together.

The transparent parts of any layer, shown by the checkered grid, allow the layers beneath that layer to show through.

You can show and hide each layer in an image by clicking on its corresponding eye icon in the Layers palette.

Sharing layers

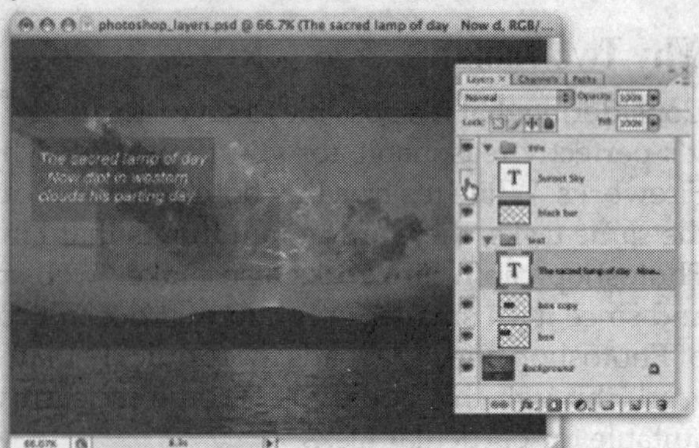
Organizing layers

To organise your layers, you can arrange them into layer groups by going to **Layer > New > Group….** Each layer group displays in the same way as any ungrouped layers on the Layers palette. A layer group is signified by a folder icon. You can collapse or expand layer groups by clicking on the triangle to the left of the folder icon, and nest layer groups within each other by dragging one folder icon into another.

Layer Shortcuts and Tasks

Rename layers by double-clicking on the layer name

Change the transparency of a layer by changing its opacity with the Opacity slider, or typing a value into the Opacity box (which is visible when you have the Selection, Move, or Crop tools selected).

Duplicate a selected layer by pressing Ctrl-J (Command-J on a Mac). You can also duplicate a layer by dragging it while pressing the Alt (Option) key.

Select multiple layers by holding down Ctrl (Command on a Mac) and clicking the layer names. This forms a temporary link between the selected layers that allows you to move them as one unit, delete them all, and so on.

You can also link layers together. Select layers by clicking on them while holding down Shift or Ctrl (Command on a Mac). Once you have selected all the layers you wish to link, click the Link Layers button at the bottom-left of the Layers palette (signified by the chain). Linking layers allows the link relationship to remain even after you select a different layer (unlike the process of simply selecting multiple layers).

To unlink all the layers, select one of the linked layers and go to **Layer > Unlink Layers.** To unlink a single layer, select the layer you wish to remove from the link and click its corresponding link icon; the other layers will stay linked. To temporarily unlink a layer, hold down Shift and click on its link icon (a red "X" will appear over the link icon). Reactivate the link by holding down Shift and clicking the link icon again.

Rearrange layers by dragging the layer above or below other layers. Use the "move down" shortcut Ctrl-] (Command-] on a Mac) and the "move up" shortcut Ctrl-] (Command-]) to move selected layers up and down. Shift-Ctrl-[and Shift-Ctrl-] will bring layers to the very top or the very bottom of the stack.

Select a layer by using the keyboard shortcuts Alt-[and Alt-]. These keystrokes let you move up and down through the layers in the Layers palette.

Create a new layer by pressing Shift-Ctrl-N (Shift-Command-N on a Mac). This will bring up the New Layer dialog box. Want to create new layers quickly without having to deal with the dialogue box? Simply press Shift-Ctrl-Alt-N (Shift-Command-Option-N).

Merge a layer into the one beneath it by pressing Ctrl-E. If you have selected layers, this shortcut will merge those selected layers together.

Quick Keyboard Shortcuts

Naturally, most of the tools in the toolbox have a keyboard shortcut. You can learn each tool's shortcut by hovering your cursor over a tool for a few seconds: a tooltip box will appear, displaying the name of the tool and its shortcut. If additional tools are available in the flyout menu, you can cycle through them by pressing Shift-[keyboard shortcut]. Keyboard shortcuts can save you valuable time – pressing "V" to bring up the Move Tool is certainly a lot quicker than moving the cursor over to the toolbox to select it. It may not seem all that significant right now, but the time you take to access tools will add up over the course of a project! For your convenience, whenever I mention a tool, I'll list its shortcut in parentheses, e.g., the Move Tool (V).

Photoshop Toolbox

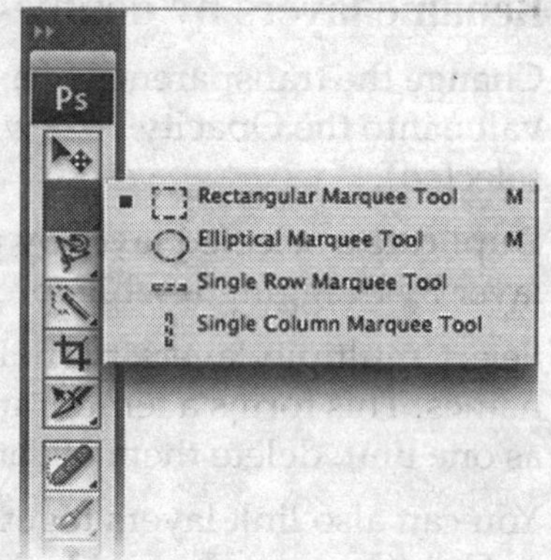

Hidden tools in toolbox

You've probably been hanging out to get stuck into the very nifty Photoshop toolbox. In this section, you will be introduced to some of the most frequently used tools found in the toolbox. I'll discuss some of the other tools in later discussions as we apply them to solutions.

Finding the hidden tools

You'll notice that some of the tool icons have small black triangles in their bottom right-hand corners. These icons contain hidden treasures! The triangle indicates that there are more related tools available; if you click on the tool icon and hold it down, a "flyout" menu will appear, displaying the additional tools.

Secret Selections

Selections can have varying levels of transparency, known as the degree of opacity. It's actually possible to make a selection with an opacity of 100% in one area, but only 20% in another area. If a selection contains any pixels for which the opacity is more than 50%, they will be displayed with a border of dotted lines. Photoshop won't visibly outline areas with less than 50% opacity (though they will still be selected). Selection tools automatically select at 100% opacity. We'll learn about creating transparent selections using Quick Masks and alpha channels later in this chapter.

Selection Tools

You can use the selection tools to select certain areas of your document for editing. If you use a selection tool, only the area that's selected will be affected by any changes you make. You can "feather" selections (specify a fuzzy radius for them) using the Feather field in the options bar. The example below shows two rectangles: one created by filling in a selection with a feather of zero pixels, and one that's created by filling in the same selection with a feather of five pixels.

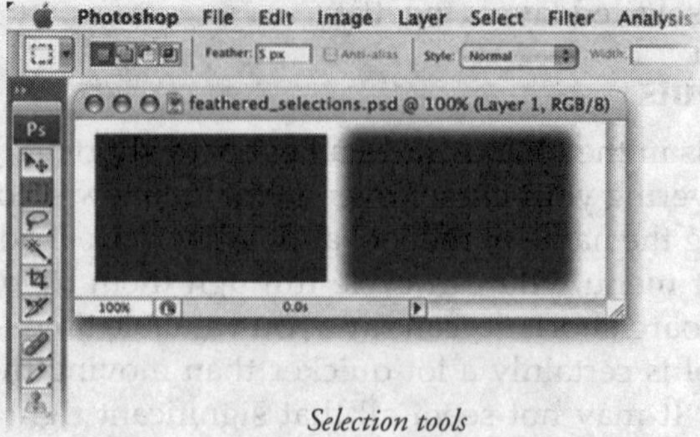

Selection tools

The Marquee tools

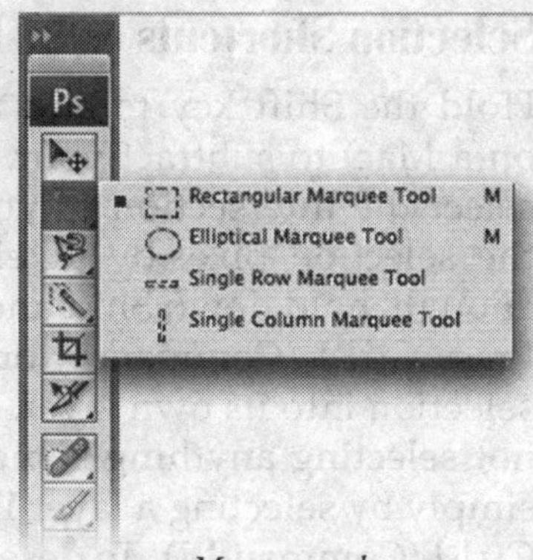

Marquee tools

Marquee tools (M) are used to create rectangular or elliptical selections, including selections that are "single row" (one pixel tall, stretching across the entire width of the document) and "single column" (one pixel wide, stretching through the entire height of the document). To make single-row or single-column selections, click with the appropriate tool on the image area where you want to select a row or column.

Lasso tools

You can use the Lasso tools (L) to create freeform selections. The Lasso Tool comes in three different forms:

Lasso Tool (L) – Click and drag the Lasso Tool to draw as selection area. Releasing the mouse button will close the selection by joining the start and end points with a straight line.

Polygonal Lasso Tool (L) – Click at different points to create vertices of a polygonal shape. Close the selection by moving your cursor to the beginning and clicking once, or pressing the Enter key.

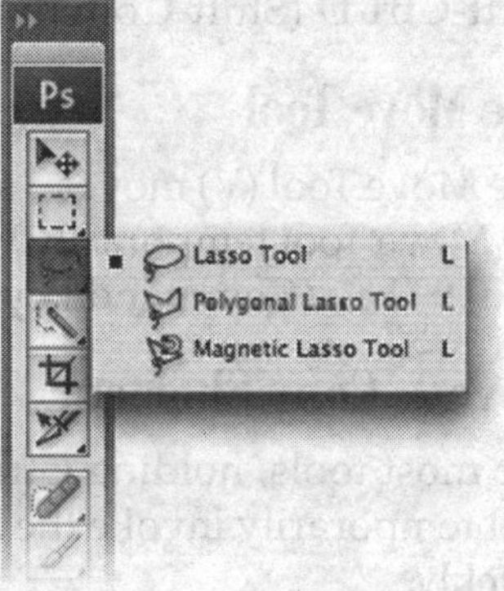

Lasso tools

No Selection Sometimes Equals All Selected

If you've made a selection, only the pixels within the selection are active and can be worked on. Some tools can be used without making a selection at all. However, be aware that if you have not made a specific selection, Photoshop will assume that you are working on the entire layer and any changes you make will affect all pixels in the layer.

Magnetic Lasso Tool (L) – If you think you need help with making your selection, try the Magnetic Lasso Tool. Photoshop will attempt to make a "smart" selection by following the edges of contrast and colour difference. Click once near the "edge" of an object and follow around it – Photoshop will automatically lay down a path. You can also click as you follow the line to force points to be created on the path. Close the selection by pressing the Enter key or clicking at a point near the beginning of the selection.

Magic Wand

The Magic Wand Tool (W) selects areas of similar colour. You can change the tolerance (how close the colour values should be to the sampled colour in order to be selected) of a Magic Wand selection, and choose whether you want the selection to be contiguous (pixels that are touching) or not (in which case, matching colours across the entire document will be selected).

Magic wand

Selection Shortcuts & Tasks

Hold the Shift key to add another selection to the first. Hold the Alt key (Option key on a Mac) to subtract your new selection from the first. Hold Shift-Alt (Shift-Option) to select the intersection of your first and second selections. Use the arrow keys to move the selection pixel by pixel. If you feel that this doesn't move your selection quickly enough, hold down Shift and use the arrow keys to move the selection ten pixels at a time. Press Ctrl-J (Command-J on a Mac) to copy the selection into its own layer. To cut the selection into its own layer, press Shift-Ctrl-J (Shift-Command-J. Now that you know that not selecting anything sometimes means that everything is selected, it makes sense that simply by selecting a layer in the Layers palette, you can copy the entire layer by pressing Ctrl-J (Command-J). To deselect a selected area, click outside of it with one of the Marquee tools, or press Ctrl-DA (Command-D on a Mac). To reactivate your last selection, press Shift-Ctrl-D (Shift-Command-D).

The Move Tool

The Move Tool (V) moves a selected area or an entire layer. You can invoke the Move Tool temporarily when using most other tools by holding down the Ctrl key (Command key on a Mac).

Move tool

Move & Copy Shortcut

For most tools, holding Ctrl-Alt (Command-Option on a Mac) and dragging a selected area will temporarily invoke the Move Tool, allowing you to move and duplicate the selected layer quickly.

You can also duplicate a layer by holding down the Alt key (Option key on a Mac) while using the Move Tool, as shown in the image below.

Using move tools

The Crop Tool

Crop tool

The Crop Tool (C) is used to trim images. Create a selection using the Crop Tool, then double-click the centre of the selection, or press Enter, to crop the image to the size of the selection.

To cancel without cropping, select another tool or press the Esc key.

Using crop tool

Crop outside the Box

You can use the Crop Tool to resize your canvas. Expand your document window so that it's larger than the image area, and create a crop selection that includes the image and extends onto the gray areas "outside" the image. Applying this crop will resize your canvas to include those extended boundaries, making your canvas larger.

Drawing and Painting Tools

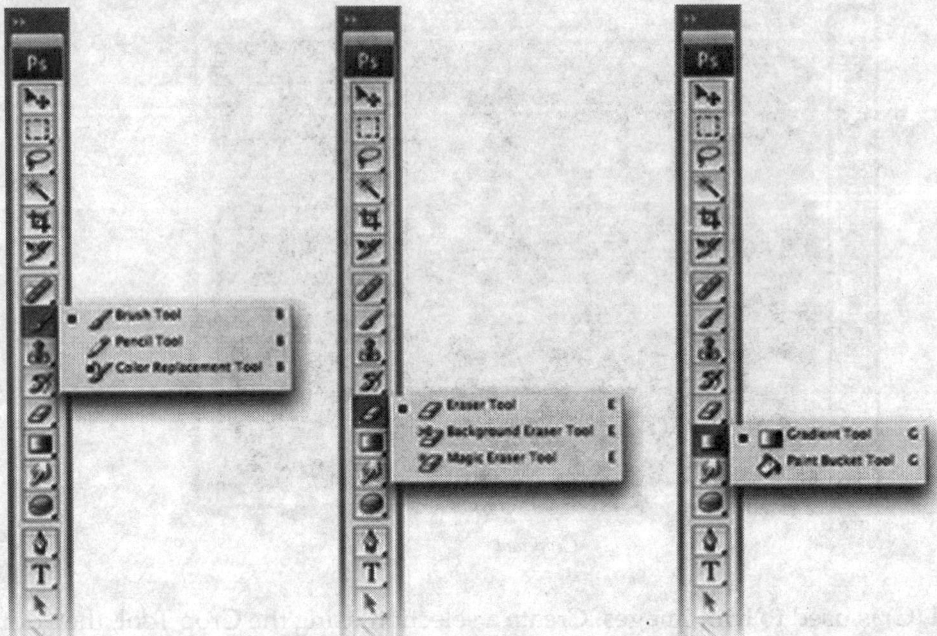

Drawing and painting tools

Apart from its extraordinary photo editing abilities, the multi-talented Photoshop also provides drawing and painting tools that allow you to create your own shapes and backgrounds.

Brush

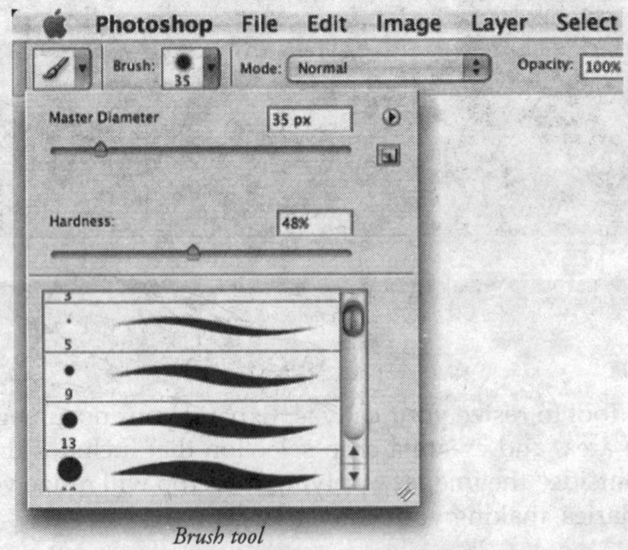

Brush tool

The Brush options

The Brush Tool (B) is suitable for soft-edged painting or drawing. Draw strokes by clicking and dragging the mouse over the canvas. You can change the brush size and other settings in the options bar at the top of the window.

Pencil

The Pencil Tool (B) is suitable for hard-edged drawing or painting and has similar options to the Brush Tool for setting its size, opacity, and more. The Pencil Tool is often used for drawing on, and editing individual pixels in, zoomed-in images.

Eraser

The Eraser Tool (E) removes pixels from the canvas. You can choose between Pencil, Brush, or Block mode from the Mode drop-down menu in the options bar.

Aliased Vs Anti-aliased

Unlike the Brush Tool, the Pencil Tool's edges are aliased. The term aliased refers to the edges of an object being "jagged," in contrast to an anti-aliased object, in which the edges are "smooth." In the two examples shown here, the top shape in each example was created using the Pencil Tool, while the bottom shape was created using the Brush Tool. Notice the difference in the "jaggedness" of the edges of these curves. We'll look more closely at anti-aliasing when we discuss the Text Tool.

Aliased and anti-aliased

Paint Bucket

The Paint Bucket Tool (G) fills a selection with a flat colour. To use the Paint Bucket Tool, click once in the area that you wish to fill. If the chosen area is not within a selection, the Paint Bucket Tool will fill all similarly-coloured pixels within the vicinity of the clicked area.

Gradient

The Gradient options

The Gradient Tool (G) fills a selection with a blend of two or more colours, known as a gradient. You can easily create your own gradient, or use any of the preset gradients available in Photoshop.

Display the gradient presets and tools by clicking on the small triangle on the right-hand side of the Gradient Tool. Apply a gradient by setting your desired colours, choosing your gradient style, then clicking and dragging the cursor over the area to be filled.

Gradient tool

I find that I use the first two gradients — the foreground-to-background gradient, and the foreground-to-transparent gradient — most often. The former will blend your foreground colour into your background colour, while the latter will blend your foreground colour into a transparent background, giving it a "fading out" effect.

Text Tool

The Text Tool (T), true to its name, creates text layers. This one's easy to use — just select the Text Tool, click on the canvas, and start typing! You can also click and drag to create a rectangular text area that will force text to wrap within its boundaries. You can change the font size, colour, and other text properties using the options bar along the top of the window.

When the Text Tool is active, you can move the cursor outside of the text area. The cursor will change from the "text insert" cursor to the "move" cursor, and you'll be able to move the text layer around.

It's worth noting that when the Text Tool is active, you can't use keyboard shortcuts to access other tools. This may seem like an obvious thing to point out now, but it won't always be so apparent — especially when your text mysteriously starts spurting strange characters because you've been trying to use the shortcut keys!

To finish using the Text Tool, press Ctrl-Enter (Command-Return on a Mac). You can then resume your regular keyboard shortcutting!

Shape Tools

You can create shapes simply by clicking and dragging Photoshop's Rectangle, Rounded Rectangle, Ellipse, Polygon, Line, and Custom Shape tools (U).

The specific options for each shape tool are displayed in the options bar, and you can access additional options by clicking on the arrow to the right of the Custom Shape button. For example, the Line Tool has options for displaying arrowheads, and for controlling the shapes and sizes of those arrowheads, as shown in the example below.

If you look at the options for each shape, you'll notice that there are three different methods you can use to create a shape:

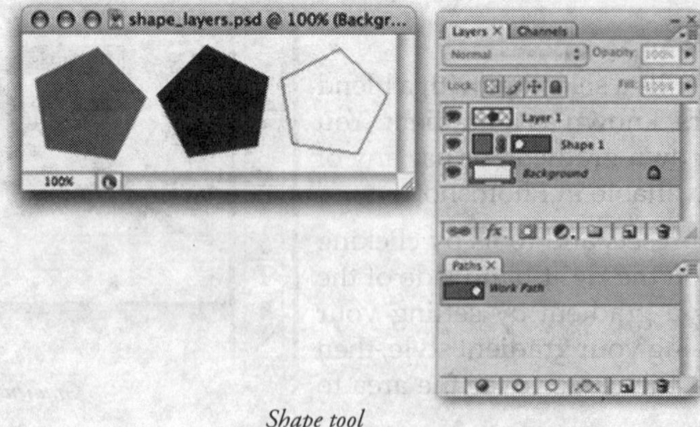

Shape tool

Different ways to create shapes

Your shape will be created as a solid-coloured layer covered with a vector shape mask. Confused? Think of the mask as a sheet of dark paper that has a *hole* (your shape) cut out of it so that the colour shines through the hole. To change the colour, double-click on the colour block in the Layers palette as shown in this example. To change the vector shape mask, use the vector editing tools.

- ❑ As a path – Your shape will be created as a path in the Paths palette.
- ❑ As filled pixels – Your shape will be created on whichever layer is currently selected

Selecting Colours

Set foreground and background colours by clicking on the appropriate tile and choosing a colour from the Colour Picker, as demonstrated in the example below.

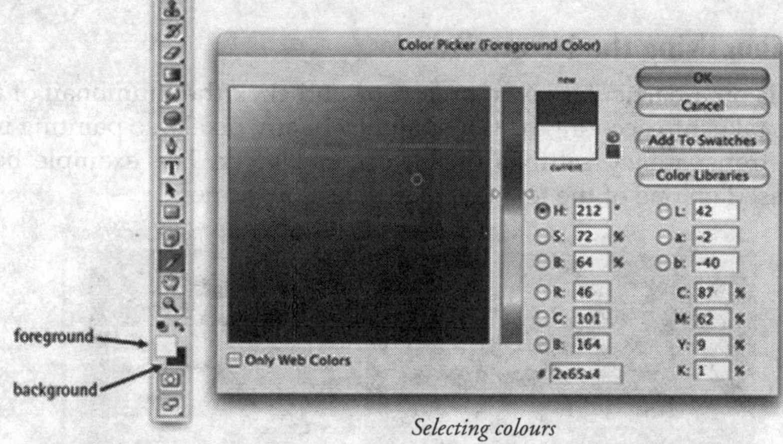

Selecting colours

Selecting foreground and background colours using the Colour Picker.

Colour Picker Shortcuts

Press X if you want to switch the foreground and background colours. Press D if you want to revert to a black foreground and white background.

Eyedropper

The Eyedropper Tool (I) lets you sample another colour from your image, and set this as the foreground colour. In fact, it's actually possible to sample colours from anywhere in your display and even from other applications outside of Photoshop. Simply click inside the document window, then drag the cursor to the colour you wish to sample. Click to select that colour.

The Eyedropper Tool also allows you to set the background colour. To do so, hold down the **Alt key** (Option key on a Mac) as you select colours using the eyedropper.

The Paint Brush, Pencil, Paint Bucket and any of the other painting or drawing tools can temporarily be turned into the Eyedropper Tool by holding down Alt (Option).

The Hand Tool

The Hand Tool (H) moves your canvas, which is handy when you're zoomed in to an image, or have a very large document open.

What's even handier is the fact that you can invoke the Hand Tool while you're using any other tool (except the Text Tool) by holding down the spacebar. This is a neat way to position your image exactly where you want it without having to chop and change between tools to do so.

Other Useful Tasks & Shortcuts

Zooming

Zooming right into your image is the only way to make subtle changes at the pixel level. Use **Ctrl +** to zoom in and **Ctrl –** to zoom out. You can also zoom using the slider on the Navigator palette.

Making a Selection Using the Layers Palette

To select the pixels on a particular layer, press Ctrl and click the thumbnail of the layer. This selection will also take into account the transparency of any pixels, so painting in the selection will recreate the transparency settings of the original layer. The example below shows a selection made based on one of the text layers in sunset document.

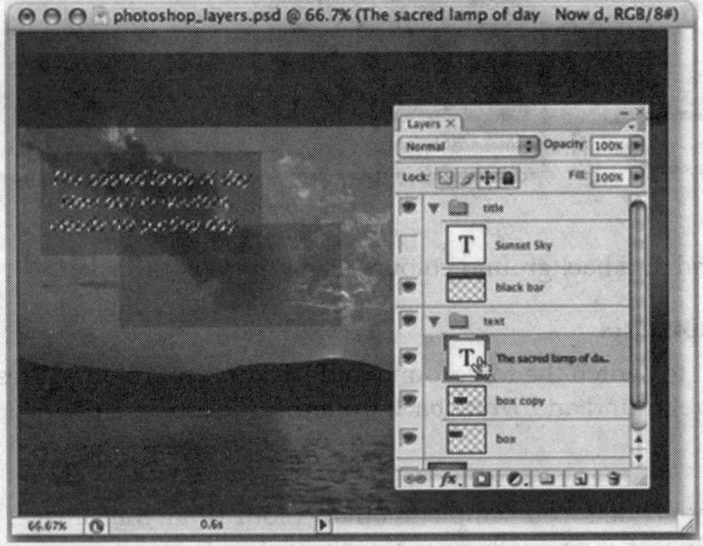

Using layer palette

Making a Selection Using a Quick Mask

Quick Masks are one of those closely guarded trade secrets that professional designers use all the time, but beginners often are wary of trying because they seem complicated at first. Well, they're not!

A Quick Mask is an alternative way of making a selection. The usual way to use a Quick Mask is to go into Quick Mask Mode (Q) and, using a tool such as the Brush Tool, painting the things you don't want to select. This is called painting a "mask," and the resulting reverse-selection will display as the transparent red colour. You can edit this red layer – honing the mask shape, for instance – using the drawing and painting tools. Those alterations won't affect your image, though: they impact only on your final selection. Switching back to Standard Mode (Q) will complete your selection.

Why would we use this technique instead of those trusty selection tools that we've all come to depend on so heavily? Well, Quick Masks have a couple of advantages over the standard selection tools:

- They allow you to control the level of transparency of your selection.
- It's easier to colour an object in, than it is to carefully draw a line around it.

Initially, it can be difficult to get your head around the fact that you aren't painting on your image: you're just painting the selection. But once you master that concept, you'll feel confident to be able to make a selection quickly on any shape, no matter how difficult it seems!

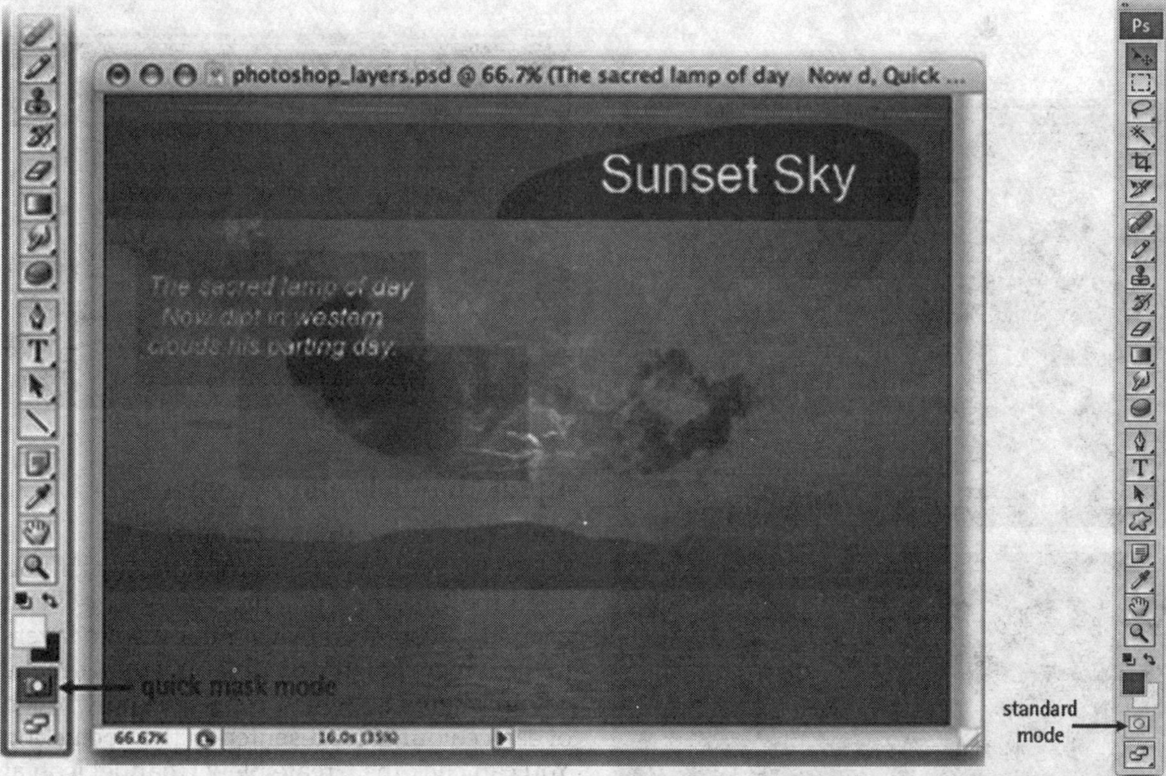

Quick mask mode

Quick Mask Options

Set Quick Mask Mode so that it lets you paint in the selected areas rather than the non-selected areas. To alter your settings to do the same thing, double-click on the Quick Mask Mode icon and change the Colour Indicates: option to Selected Areas.

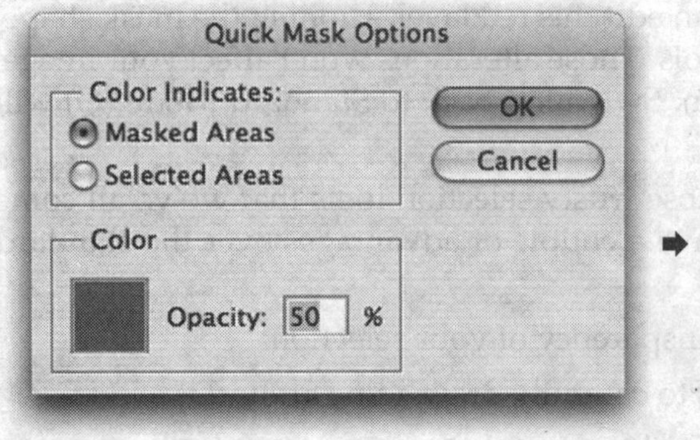

Painted areas are now selected=

Alpha Channels and Selections

You can use alpha channels to create selections and save them for later use. If you open the Channels palette, you'll see several channels, displayed in a similar way to layers in the Layers palette. By default, you'll see the colour channels, which represent how much of each colour is represented in the document. You can click the Create New Channel icon at the bottom of the palette to create your own alpha channel.

Creating a new alpha channel

You can then use any of Photoshop's painting or drawing tools to create a grayscale image that will represent your selection – white areas represent selected areas, black areas represent deselected areas, and grays represent the levels of transparency in the selection.

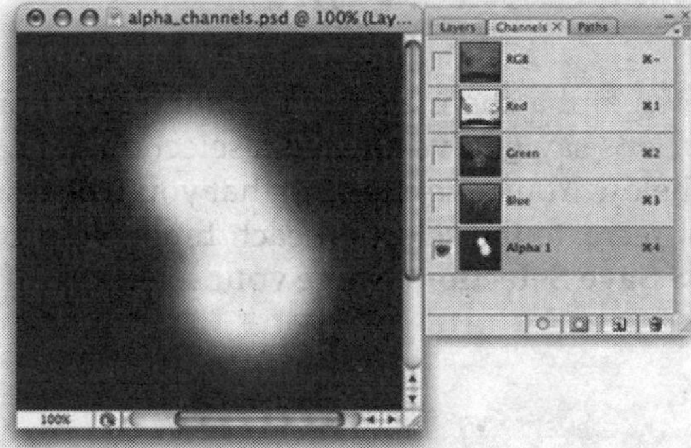

To turn your alpha channel masterpiece into a selection, simply hold down Ctrl and click the channel's thumbnail (hold Command and click if you're on a Mac).

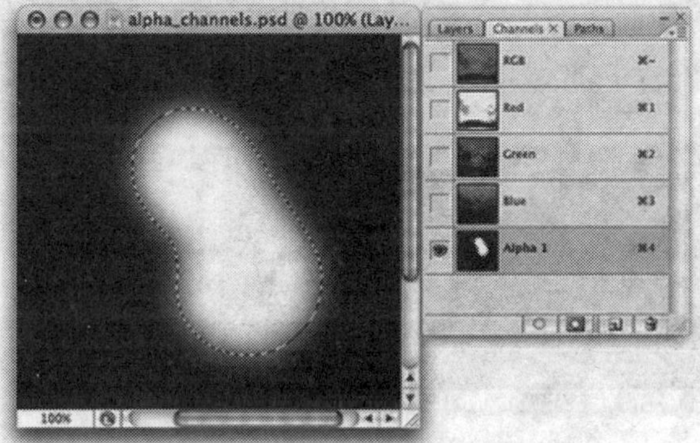

To return to the normal image view, click on the Layers palette tab, and select any layer. Your selection will still be visible.

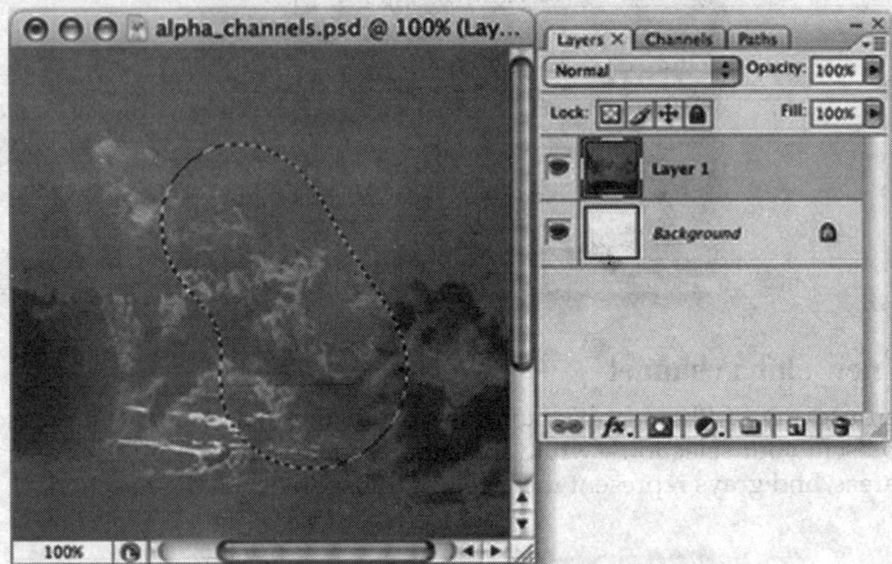

You can also create your own alpha channels from existing selections – a capability that can be very useful! *For example*, let's say you've created a selection of an island silhouette like the one shown in the example below. You have a feeling that you'll be reselecting this island pretty often, but you'd rather not recreate the selection each time. No problem! Once the selection has been made, use **Select > Save Selection**. Name your selection (in this example, Land), and click OK.

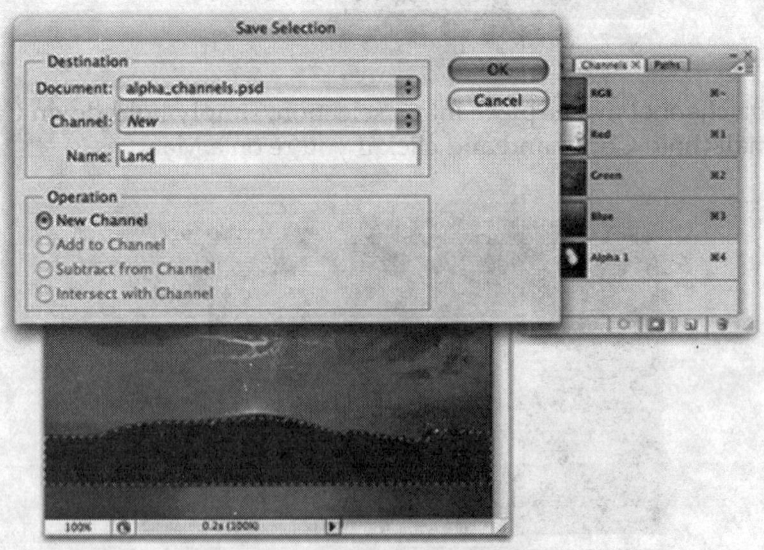

If you go to the Channels palette, you'll see a new selection at the bottom of the list, named Land in the following image – that's your saved selection. Now you can reload your Land selection as many times as you need to!

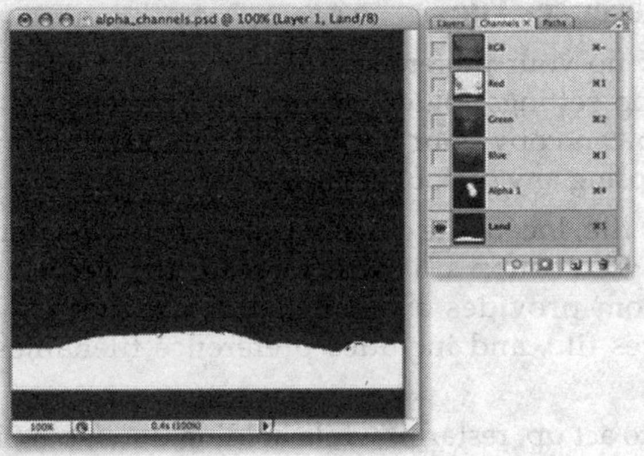

The History Palette

The History palette is your key to time travel (in Photoshop, anyway). It lists the most recent steps that you've made, and allows you to undo your actions by rolling your image back to a previous state. You can set the number of steps that are stored in the memory by selecting **Edit > Preferences > Performance (Photoshop > Preferences > Performance on a Mac**) and changing the value in the History States text box.

Like most of Photoshop's other tools, the History palette has a set of useful keyboard shortcuts for quick access:

Ctrl-Z (Command-Z on a Mac0) lets you undo and redo the previous step.

Ctrl-Alt-Z (Command-Option-Z) steps back through the History palette.

Shift-Alt-Z (Shift-Option-Z) steps forward through the History palette.

As only a limited number of history states are available, there may be cases in which you want to save a "snapshot" of your document so that you can revert to it later if required. To do so, click on the small triangle on the top-right of the History palette and choose New Snapshot…. You can save a snapshot of the whole document, the current layer, or merged layers.

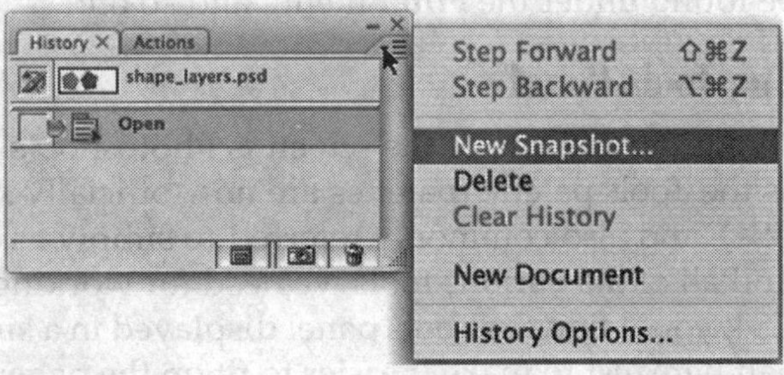

History palette

When Photoshop Stops Working

If Photoshop stops working on your system, the first thing to do is reset the preferences file. The preferences file (which you can customise by going to **Edit > Preferences** on a PC, or Photoshop > Preferences on a Mac) holds Photoshop settings and can often become corrupted.

The location of the preferences file depends on the operating system and version of Photoshop you are using. For Photoshop CS3, the preferences file is named Adobe Photoshop CS3 Prefs. psp. The preference file for other versions of Photoshop will have a similar name.

Backing up Your Preferences File

It's a good idea to back up your preferences file by copying and pasting it into a location outside of the Photoshop settings folder. Then, if the preferences file Photoshop is using becomes corrupted, you can copy your backup back into the settings folder to replace the corrupted file, without losing any of your settings.

To reset the preferences file, locate the current preferences file, delete it (while Photoshop is closed), and restart Photoshop – it will recreate the preferences file using default settings. Creativepro.com provides a detailed tutorial that explains how to find and replace your preferences file, and includes preference filenames for different versions of Photoshop.

If Photoshop continues to act up, restart it while holding down the **Shift-Ctrl-Alt** keys (Shift-Command-Option on a Mac), and click OK when asked if you wish to delete the Photoshop settings file. Unfortunately, this will also delete your custom actions, tools, and other settings, but the good news is that it should fix your Photoshop problems.

User Interface in Photoshop

We have talked about the Interfaces already. Now let's look over the Each one in detail.

The Menu Bar

At the very top of the screen as always is the **Menu Bar**, a common feature of most programs these days. Clicking on the various menu headings brings up a list of related options and commands. For example, the **File** menu is where we find options for opening, saving and closing Photoshop documents. The **Layer** menu contains options for working with layers. Photoshop's many filters can be found under the **Filter** menu, and so on:

The Tools Panel

Along the left side of the screen is Photoshop's **Tools panel**, formerly known as the Tools palette (palettes are now officially known as panels in Photoshop CS4), and also commonly referred to simply as the Toolbox. This is where we find all of the various tools we need for working on our images. In Photoshop CS4, you'll find the Tools panel displayed in a single column, but I've split it in half here just to make it easier to fit on the page:

Again, there's a couple of tools shown here that are exclusive to the Extended version of Photoshop CS4 (the **3D Rotate** and **3D Orbit** tools directly above the Hand Tool), but the majority of the tools are available in both the Standard and Extended versions and most have been around in Photoshop since forever.

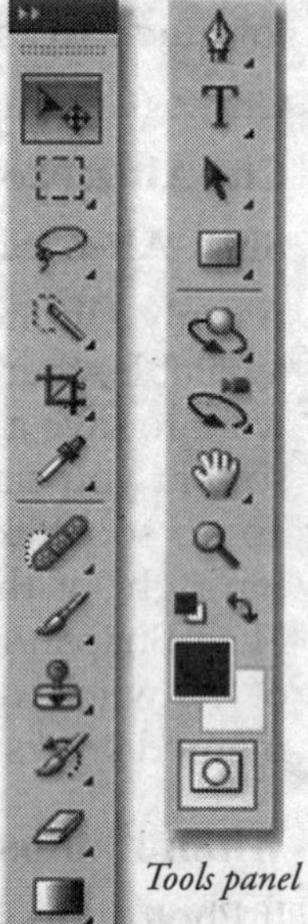

Tools panel

Menu bar

Single Or Double Column Layout

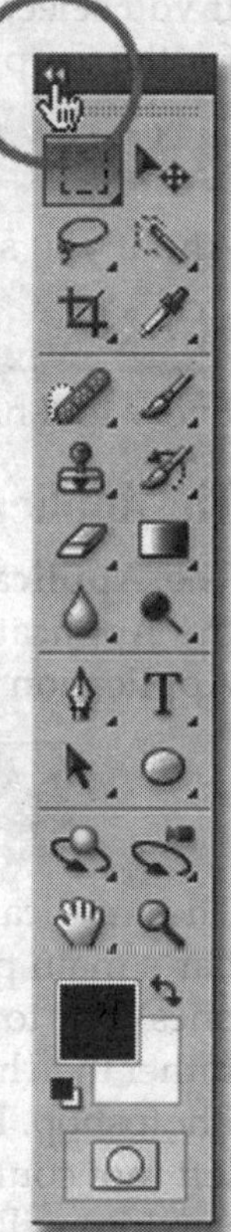

Photoshop CS4, like CS3, gives us a choice of how we want the Tools panel displayed. We can leave it in the default single column, or if you prefer, you can click on the small double-arrow icon at the top of the panel which will switch it to a double column layout, handy if you've upgraded from Photoshop CS2 or earlier and you can't get used to the new single column design. Click again on the icon to switch back to a single column:

Photoshop CS4, like earlier versions, comes with so many tools that if Adobe tried to display them all at once, the Tools panel would need its own scroll bar. So instead, Adobe has grouped many related tools together, with one tool in the group visible in the Tools panel and the others hidden behind it. Whenever you see a tool in the Tools panel with a small arrow to the bottom right of the icon, it means there are additional tools behind it waiting to be selected, and if you click and hold your mouse button down on one of these tools, a fly-out menu will appear showing you the additional tools. For example, by clicking and holding on the **Rectangular Marquee Tool** at the top of the Tools panel, a fly-out menu appears giving me access to the **Elliptical Marquee Tool**, the **Single Row Marquee Tool** and the **Single Column Marquee Tool**. Simply move your mouse cursor over the name of the tool you want, then release your mouse button to select it:

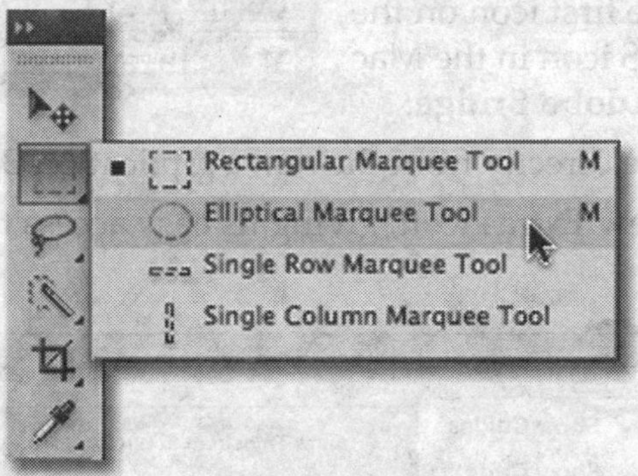

Click and hold on some tools in the Tools panel to access additional tools behind it.

Click and hold on the other tools in the Tools panel to see all of the tools available to us in Photoshop CS4.

The Options Bar

Directly related to the Tools panel is the **Options Bar** at the top of the screen. On a Windows system, the Options Bar is located below the Menu Bar. Here, the Options Bar is displaying options for the **Move Tool**:

If you select the **Crop Tool** from the Tools panel, the Options Bar changes to display options for the Crop Tool:

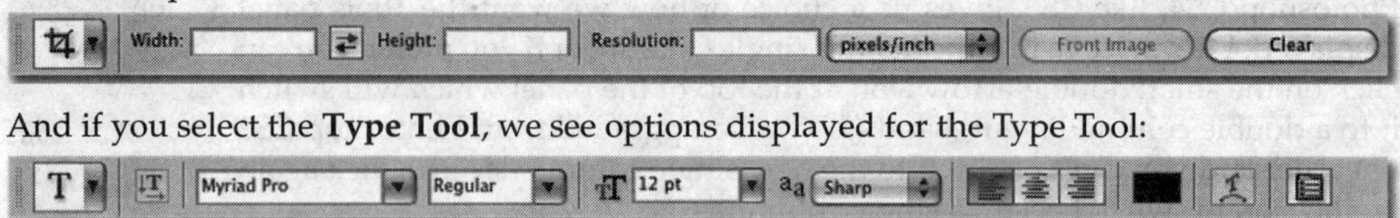

And if you select the **Type Tool**, we see options displayed for the Type Tool:

Every tool has its own set of options which will always be available in the Options Bar.

The Application Bar

The **Application Bar** is a new tool in Photoshop CS4. On a Windows system, you'll find the Application Bar combined with the Menu Bar at the top of the screen. On a Mac, the Application Bar is separate and located directly below the Menu Bar:

The Application Bar itself may be new, but many of the options you'll find here are not. The bar's main purpose is not really to wow us with new features (although there are some new ones) but to give us a central location for some commonly used features, tools and options rather than having them scattered throughout Photoshop. For example, the first icon on the left (not counting the blue PS icon in the Mac version) will quickly open **Adobe Bridge**:

We can launch Adobe Bridge directly from the new Application Bar in Photoshop CS4.

To the right of that is the **View Extras** icon, giving us easy access to Photoshop's Guides, Grid and Rulers.

Use the View Extras icon to quickly turn the Guides, Grid or Rulers on or off.

Next is the **Zoom Level** icon which allows to quickly choose from four preset zoom levels – 25%, 50%, 100% or 200%. You can also type your own zoom level directly into the input box if none of the presets work for you:

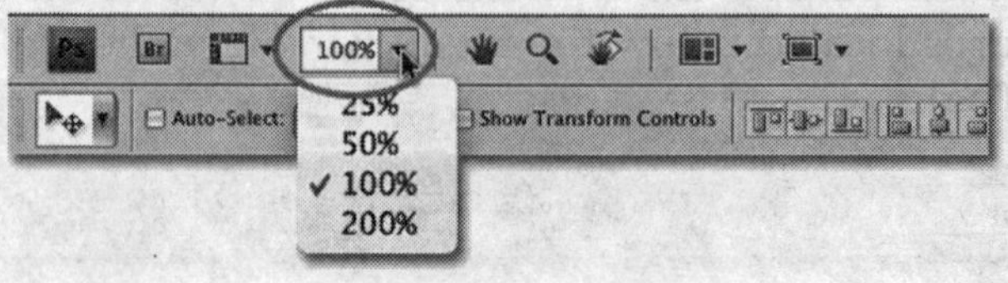

The Zoom Level icon gives us four preset zoom levels to choose from, or type your own into the input box.

Also found in the Application Bar are Photoshop's standard **Hand** and **Zoom Tools** which have traditionally been (and still are) found at the bottom of the Tools panel:

Both the Hand Tool and Zoom Tool from the Tools panel are now available in the Application Bar.

The New Rotate View Tool

Next, we come to a brand new feature in Photoshop CS4, the **Rotate View Tool**, which also happens to be available in the Tools panel (click and hold on the Hand Tool in the Tools panel and select the Rotate View Tool from the fly-out menu). We'll take an in-depth look at this new feature in another tutorial, but essentially, the Rotate View Tool allows us to rotate our view of the image on screen as if we were rotating a photo on a desk or table, which can make it easier to paint or edit certain areas. What's great about it is that since we're only rotating our view of the image, not the image itself, no pixels are harmed by the rotation and the image will still save, print and export upright. Again, we'll look more closely at the new Rotate View Tool in another tutorial:

The new Rotate View Tool allows us to rotate our view of the image without actually rotating the image itself.

New Multi Document Layouts

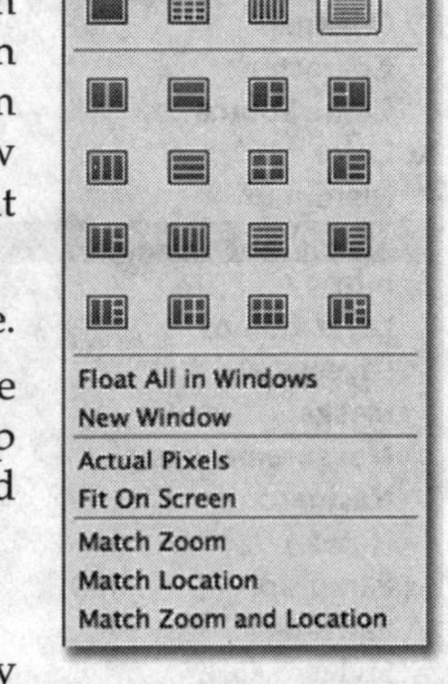

Also new in Photoshop CS4 is the **Arrange Documents** icon which gives us lots of new layouts for viewing multiple documents on screen at once. You'll also find some standard viewing options from the Window menu like Match Zoom and Match Location, but the new multi document layouts are a great new feature and one we'll look at in more depth later:

Photoshop CS4 gives us many ways to view multiple documents at once.

Finally, rounding out the options in the new Application Bar is the **Screen Mode** icon, allowing us to quickly choose between Photoshop CS4's three screen modes – **Standard, Full Screen with Menu Bar** and **Full Screen Mode**:

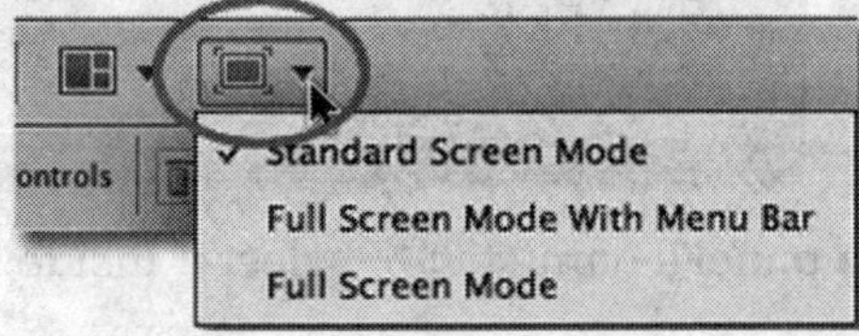

You can quickly switch between screen modes directly from the Application

Bar in Photoshop CS4.

The Panels

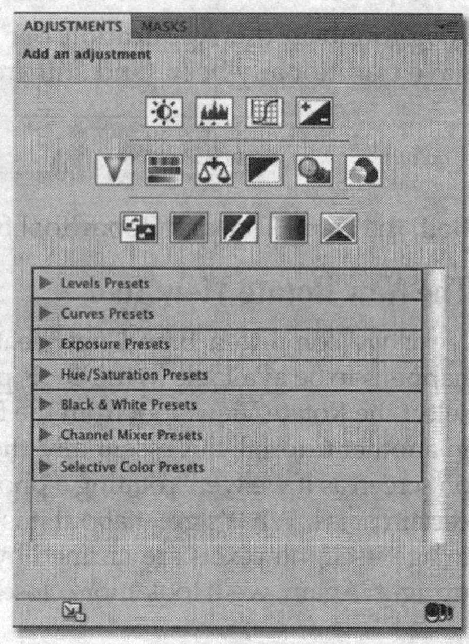

Along the right side of the screen in Photoshop CS4 is where we find the **Panels** column (panels were known as palettes in earlier versions of Photoshop). Panels give us access to all kinds of commands and options for working on our images, from organising layers and viewing individual colour channels to choosing colours, stepping back through history states, working with text, viewing information about our images, and so much more. Most of the panels in Photoshop CS4 are the same ones that have been available in earlier versions of Photoshop, but some, like the **Adjustments Panel**, are brand new to CS4.

By default, only a handful of panels are displayed on the screen to begin with, but you can access any of Photoshop's panels at any time simply by choosing the one you want from the **Window** menu up in the Menu Bar. A checkmark beside a panel's name means it is already open on the screen. Selecting a panel that is already open will close it. A couple of the panels listed below are available only in the Extended version of Photoshop CS4, but most are available in the Standard version:

3D
Actions ⌥F9
✓ Adjustments
Animation
Brushes F5
Channels
Character
Clone Source
✓ Color F6
Histogram
History
Info F8
Layer Comps
✓ Layers F7
Masks
Measurement Log
Navigator
Notes
Paragraph
Paths
Styles
Swatches
Tool Presets

To keep things organised and save screen space, most of Photoshop's panels are grouped in with other related panels. This is known as a **panel group**, if you didn't already guess that on your own. For example, the Layers, Channels and Paths panels are grouped together by default. To select the panel you want from the group, simply click on the panel's name tab at the top:

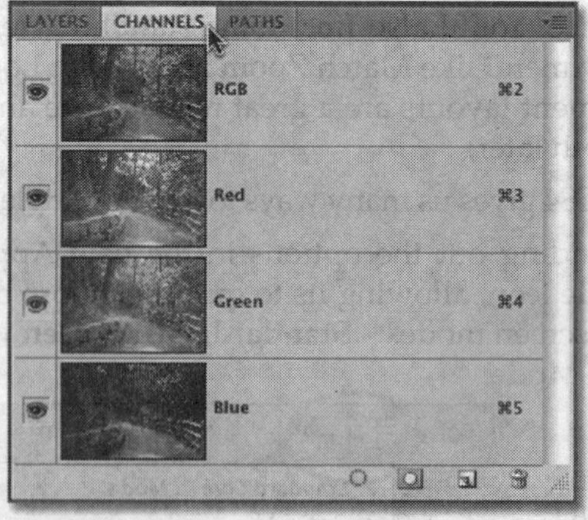

Click on a panel's name tab to select it inside the panel group.

All panels come with various options and commands that are specific to that panel. You can access these options by clicking on the panel's **menu icon** in the top right corner. Unfortunately, it's not the most obvious thing on the screen and many Photoshop users don't even know it's there, but you should click on each panel's menu icon to see what options and commands are available for it:

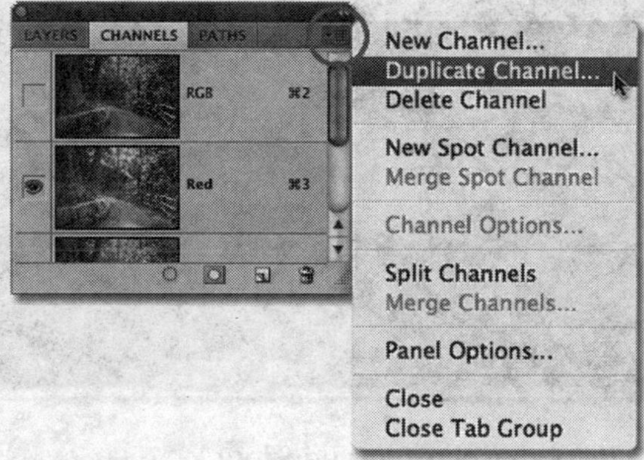

Click on a panel's menu icon to view a list of related options and commands.

We'll look at all the different ways we can arrange and organise Photoshop CS4's panels in another tutorial.

Workspaces

In the top right corner of the screen is an option that allows us to quickly select from various **workspaces**, either ones that are built in to Photoshop CS4 or custom workspaces we've created ourselves. Workspaces allow us to set up different panel arrangements, menus and even keyboard shortcuts for different tasks. For example, you may want certain panels open when editing images and other panels open when painting with Photoshop's brushes or when working with type. Workspaces allow us to set up the screen any way we want, save it, and then quickly select it again any time we need it! Photoshop CS4 comes with several built in workspaces. The **Essentials** workspace is selected by default but you can access the complete list of available workspaces, including any custom ones you've created, by clicking on the word Essentials and selecting a new workspace from the list that appears:

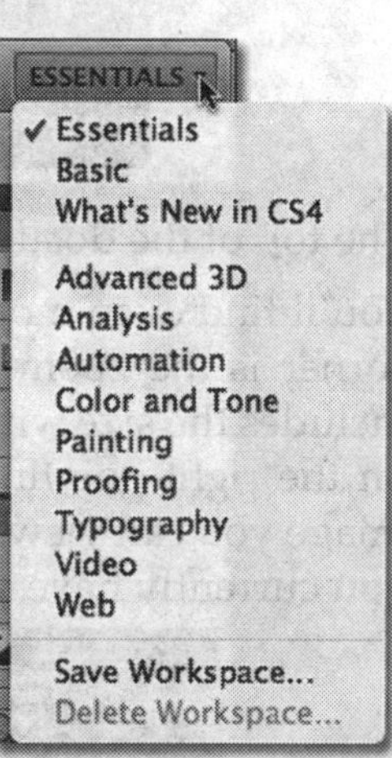

Workspaces in photoshop

Click on the word "Essentials" in the top right corner of the screen to view all the available workspaces.

The Document Window

The largest and most obvious interface element in Photoshop is the **document window**. The document window is where we view our images and where we do all of our editing work:

Each image appears inside its own document window.

Document windows in Photoshop do much more though than simply display the image. They also tell us quite a few things about the image. At the top of the document window, you'll find the name of the image, followed by the current zoom level, the colour mode, and the current bit depth:

The top of the document window gives us information about the image.

You'll find even more information at the bottom of the document window. In the bottom left corner is the zoom level once again, followed by the current file size of the image, which includes the size with all layers intact and the size if you were to flatten the image. If you click on the right-pointing arrow, then choose **Show**, you'll see a whole list of details about the image you can view, including the document dimensions, colour profile, and even which tool you currently have selected from the Tools panel:

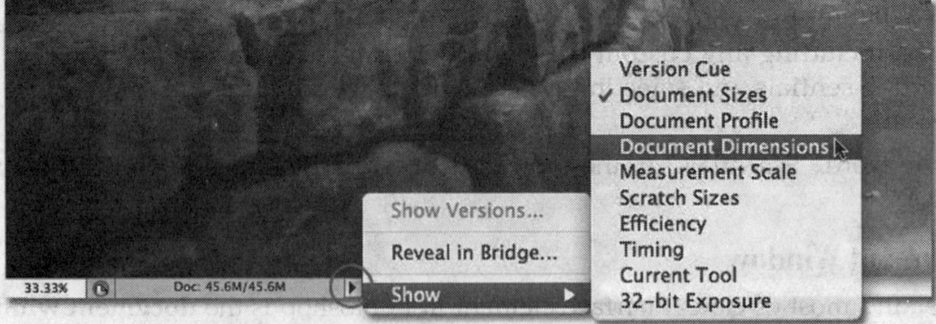

Much more information about the image is available at the bottom of the document window.

The Tool Box

Now let us learn about toolboxes

Anatomy of the Toolbox

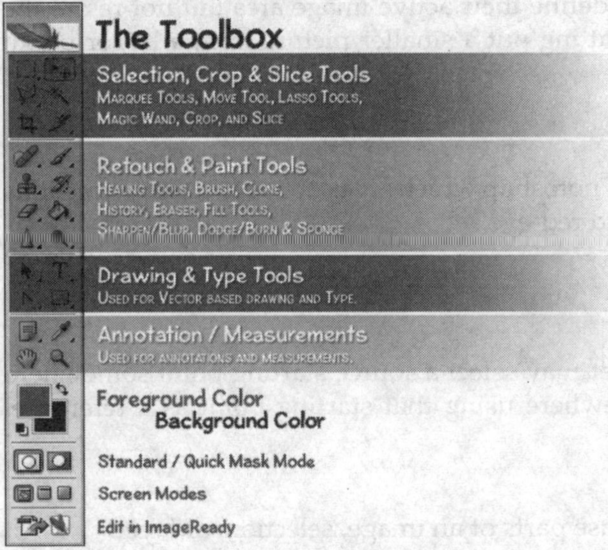

The toolbox in Photoshop is split up into 4 unique categories so that finding the right tool is never a hassle. Those categories are:

- ❑ Selection, Crop & Slice Tools
- ❑ Retouch & Paint Tools
- ❑ Drawing & Type Tools (Vector Tools)
- ❑ Annotations & Measurement Tools

In addition to these 4 sections, a few other components make up the toolbox, most notably, the Foreground and Background colours.

Now that you see how the tools are all organised, let's take a look at some of the most vital tools Photoshop has to offer. This is really just a cursory glance of the toolbox, but you ought to now have an understanding what some of the tools are capable of.

Selection Tools

The Marquee Tools are used for selecting objects such as rectangles, squares, and ellipses.

The Move Tool is used to move selections, objects, and layers.

There are several Lasso Tools which are used to make irregular selections. There is a *polygonal lasso tool* for polygon selections, and a *magnetic lasso tool* which automatically follows edges of objects.

The **Magic Wand Tool** selects an area of similar colours in a single click (*such as the white in the cloud logo*).

The **Crop Tool** allows users to redefine their active image area but not resize the ENTIRE image. It's sort of like cutting out a smaller picture from a larger photo with a pair of scissors.

Retouch Tools

There are several **healing tools** in Photoshop which are used to repair imperfections in images, or handle blemishes and red-eye.

With the **Clone Stamp Tool**, a user may select a source starting point somewhere on an image, and then paint elsewhere using that starting point as a reference, effectively cloning the source.

The **Eraser Tool** can be used to erase parts of an image, selection, or layer.

The **Sharpen Tool** is used to sharpen edges in an image, while the Blur Tool burs edges. The Smudge Tool smudges an image, similar to using finger paint.

The **Dodge Tool** lightens parts of an image while the Burn Tool darkens. The Sponge Tool is used to saturate, or de-saturate parts of an image.

The **Brush and Pencil** tools are used to paint strokes in graphics. These tools can be highly customised for very effective painting.

The **Fill Tools** are used to fill entire layers, selections and areas with a solid colour, or gradient.

Vector Drawing & Type Tools

The **Type Tools** are used for creating and setting type in an image. Both vertical and horizontal type can be created.

The **Pen Tools** are used to create clear shapes and paths which can be used as vector objects that can be scaled to any size.

Custom Shapes are vector objects that can be created on the fly from a list of presets (including user created shapes).

Foreground / Background Colour

A foreground colour and background colour can be set to be used to paint with, colour text, and fill objects among other things. This view provides an easy way to see what colours are currently selected, and allows for easy switching between two different colours.

Using Tools

To actually use a tool varies from case to case. To Select a Tool from the toolbox, simply click it once. If the tool displayed has a black arrow in the bottom right corner, that means that there are more tools of that type hidden underneath it. To select one of these hidden tools, *hold down the mouse button while over it*, and then release once you're over the tool you'd like to select.

Retouch & Healing Tools

Photoshop offers a large selection of tools and features for retouching photographs and images. Here, you'll learn how to use the common touch-up tools.

Spot Healing Brush Tool

The **Spot Healing Brush** is primarily used to quickly remove blemishes, imperfections or other unwanted elements from an image. To use it, *paint* over an imperfection you'd like to get rid of using a suitable brush (*brushes can be selected and modified in the options bar*). The Spot Healing Brush Tool will automatically try to repair the imperfection by sampling the surrounding area.

Careful! Although the Spot Healing brush can be a great tool for quick fixes, it's not always guaranteed to work if the area surrounding the imperfection is busy. Generally speaking, the surrounding area should be an approximate match in colour & texture to what you want to take place of the unwanted element in your image.

Healing Brush Tool

The **Healing Brush Tool** performs a similar function to the spot healing brush tool mentioned above. Instead of automatically trying to determine the lighting, shading, and texture from the surrounding area, the healing brush tool lets you manually select a source, and then paint over an imperfection. To select a source, **hold alt and click the desired part of the image**. Then paint over the area you wish to replace. As with the Spot Healing Brush Tool, settings such as brush size can be controlled in the *options bar*.

Patch Tool

With the **Patch Tool**, an entire area can be repaired with pixels from another area. Just like the healing brush tool, the patch tool will try to correct lighting, shading, and texture. To use the patch tool, first **draw a selection** with any of the selection tools (or the patch tool, which will function as a lasso tool). Then, using the **patch tool**, **drag that selection** over the destination you want to use to repair that area.

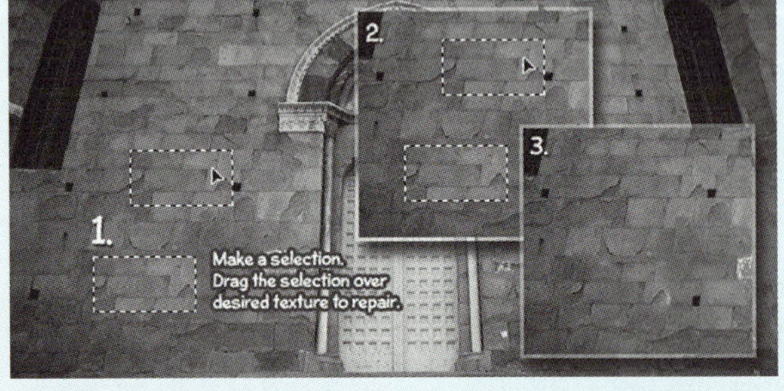

Clone Stamp Tool

The final tool we'll cover in this tutorial is called the **Clone Stamp Tool**. The Clone stamp tool allows you to paint with a sample of an image.

Keep in mind that you are not healing/repairing an image when you use the Clone Stamp Tool. Therefore, **lighting and shading will not be maintained** when you paint over an area. What you see is literally what you get when you paint from a given source, making it very useful in certain situations.

Blur & Sharpen Tools

The **Blur** and **Sharpen Tools** allow us to manipulate edges by making them softer or harder. They do exactly what you would expect them to do; blur and sharpen.

Both tools have similar attributes such as *Strength* (increase or decrease the strength of the tool, or how much it will blur) and the *brush*, all of which can be adjusted in the *Options Bar* for each tool. To use the blur or sharpen tool, simply set up the brush to your specification, hold down the mouse button, and hover over the areas you'd like to alter in your image.

You should have a pretty good feel of the basic retouching tools by now. The next step in mastering Photoshop is usually learning how to use the painting tools to compliment your photo mastering abilities!

Pen Tools

Let's Learn Using Pen Tools:

Click on the canvas to create paths with straight segments, click and drag to create paths with Bezier curves.

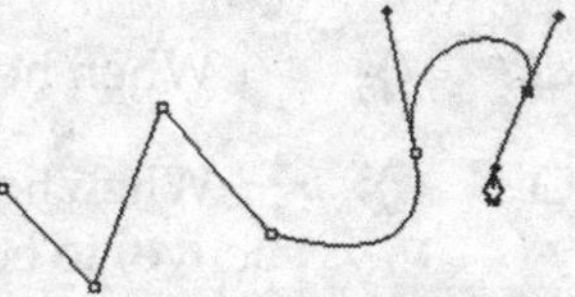

Freehand Pen too : Click on the canvas and drag to draw paths freely, as though using a brush.

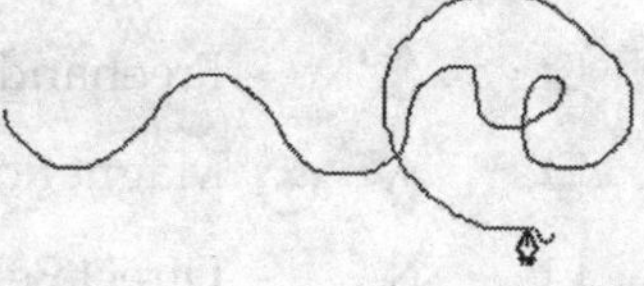

Add Anchor Point tool: Click on a path segment to add anchor poi

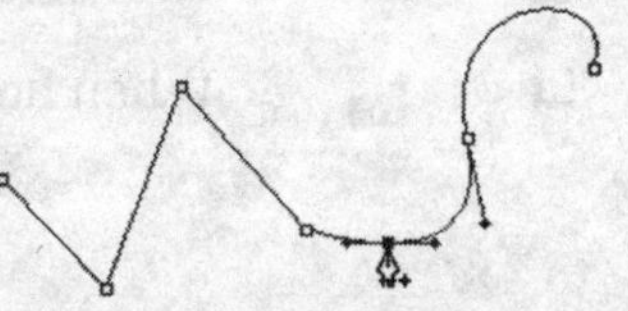

Delete Anchor Point too : Click on anchor point to remove from pa

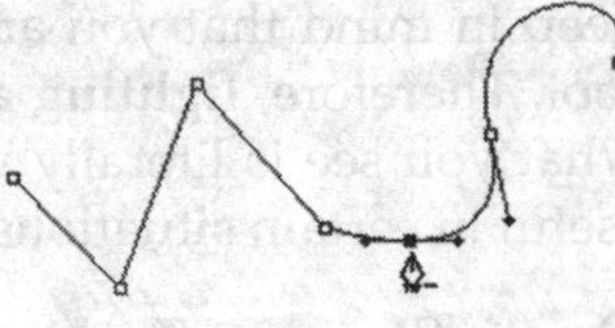

Convert Point tool: Click on an anchor point and drag to create bezier handles where there were none, click on an anchor point with handles to a remove them.

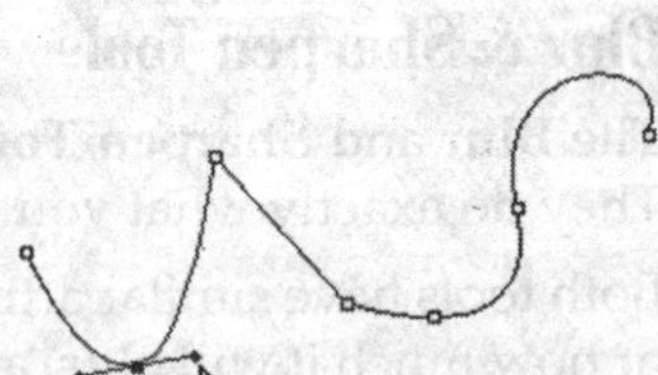

Before we go ahead, we should learn following controls for better practising.

Lets Acquaint ourselves with the Cursors

The Pen tool takes on different forms depending on what you're doing when you are using it. Each one intuitively makes you aware of the action you are about to perform.

(*Caps Lock* to toggle between pointer and cross hair in some cases)

- Prepared to begin path
- while midway through creating or editing a path
- When mouse is pressed
- Add an anchor point to path
- Remove anchor point from path
- When hovered over begin point of path; to close path
- When hovered over endpoint of existing path; to continue path, or (if path is active) to edit that point
- Prepared to convert existing anchor point
- Freehand Pen Tool
- Magnetic Freehand Pen Tool
- Direct Selection Tool; Pen Tool with *Command* pressed
- Path Selection Tool; Pen Tool with *Command* + *Alt* pressed
- When hovered over canvas with *Ctrl* pressed; prepared for options menu

Learn Secondary Mouse Controls (with path selected and Auto Add/Delete checked)

- *Pen tool hover over anchor point*: changes to Delete anchor point tool
- *Pen tool hover over path segment*: changes to Add anchor point tool

Keyboard Controls used while using Pen Tool

- Hold *Ctrl* and click on canvas. Opens up an options menu.
- Hold *Shift* to constrain movements to 45 , 90 , 135 or 180 while creating or editing anchor points and handles.
- Select anchor point with Direct selection tool and click *Delete*. Anchor and adjoining path segments are deleted leaving two paths.
- Pen tool + *Option (Alt)*: changes to Convert anchor point tool.
- Pen tool + *Option (Alt)* while editing bezier curve: splits curve (unhinges handles).
- Pen tool + *Command* whilst creating path: changes to Direct Selection tool allowing repositioning of previously drawn anchor points.

Options

The Options Bar (*Window* > *Options*), usually located at the top of your screen, provides the most important options for whichever tool is selected. This is also true of the Pen Tools and their options are outlined below:

- **Presets:** Allows presets to be saved for whichever tool is selected. Define the options as discussed below and save as a Preset to quickly come back to those settings later.

- **Shape Layers:** While this is selected, paths created will contribute to a shape, visible within the *Paths* palette and within the *Layers* palette as a vector mask.

- ❑ **Paths:** While this is selected, paths created will contribute to a path, visible within the *Paths* palette.

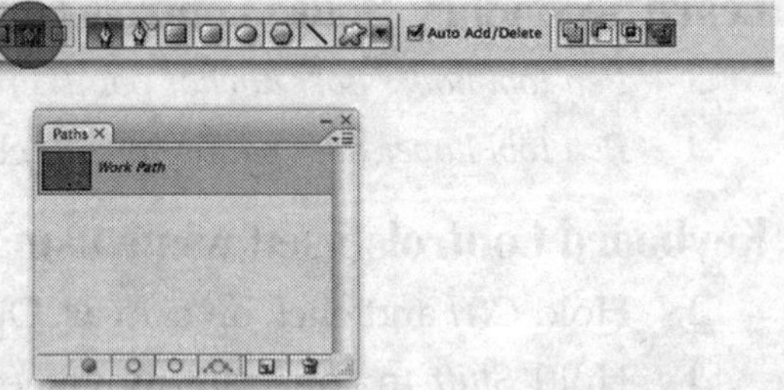

- ❑ **Fill Pixels:** The third path type option, available while one of the shape tools is selected. While this is selected, paths created will become filled areas.

- ❑ **Pen Tool:** Selects the Pen Tool.

- ❑ **Freehand Pen Tool:** Selects the Freehand Pen Tool.

- ❑ **Rubber Band:** Available from within the Pen Options dropdown while the Pen Tool is selected. Rubber Band gives a visual of the path you're about to create, without you having the cursor pressed on the canvas.

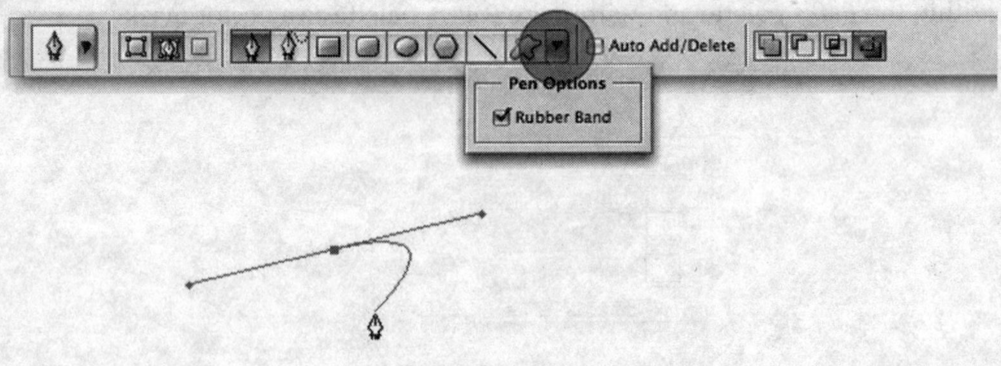

- **Curve fit:** Available from within the Freehand Pen Options dropdown while the Freehand Pen Tool is selected. Value entered determines the accuracy to which bezier handles will be added to your freely drawn path. The higher the value, the more accurate your result will be. A value of between 0.5 and 10 pixels is required.

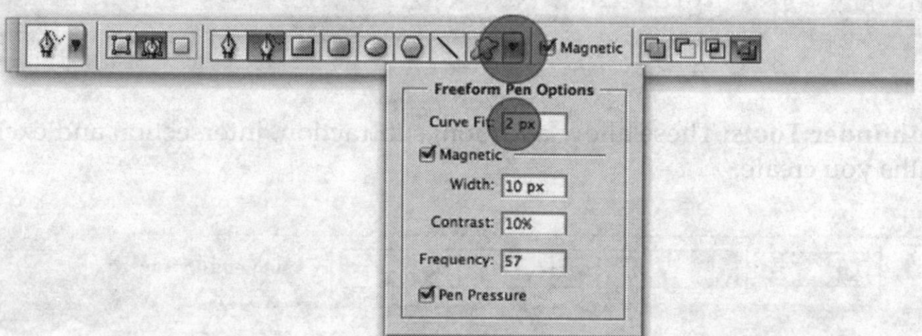

- **Magnetic:** Available from the Options bar and within the Freehand Pen Options dropdown while the Freehand Pen Tool is selected. When selected, paths drawn will *magnetise* to pixels. The Magnetic settings, as shown below, determine the width of the area the path is prepared to jump across, the contrast of the pixels necessary to attract the path and the frequency of anchor points added to the path.

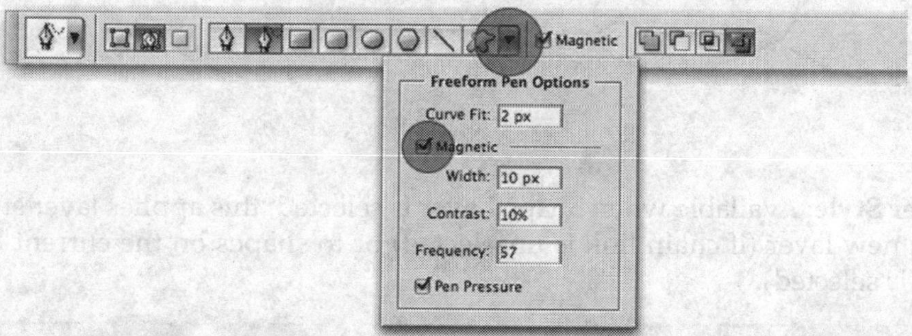

- **Pen Pressure:** Available from within the Freehand Pen Options dropdown while the Freehand Pen Tool is selected. When selected, the pressure applied to a graphics tablet (if you're using one) influences the pen width.

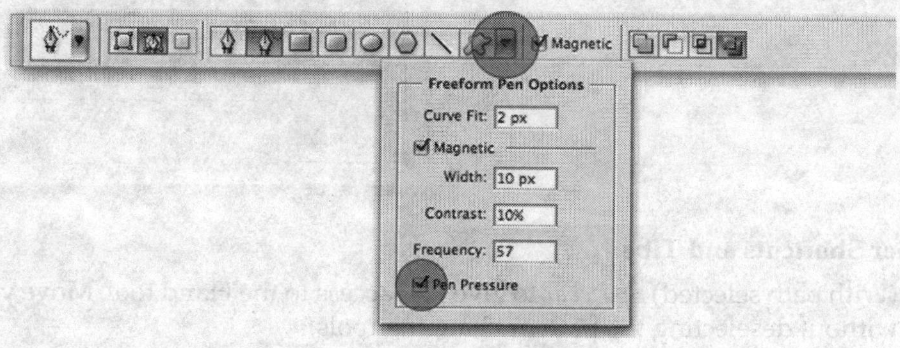

- **Auto Add/Delete:** Available when the Pen Tool is selected; allows adding and removing of anchor points with the normal Pen Tool *(see Secondary Mouse Controls)*.

- **Pathfinder Tools:** These allow addition, subtraction, intersection and exclusion of the paths you create.

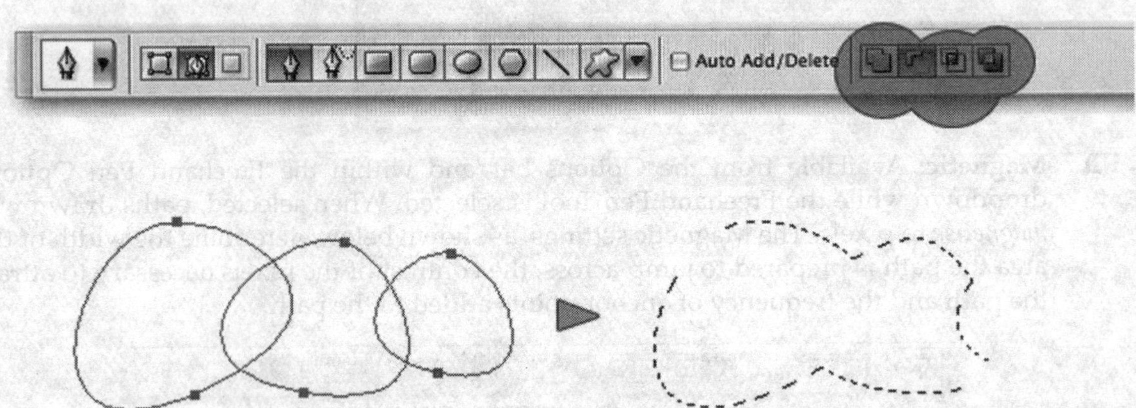

- **Layer Style:** Available when Shape Layer is selected; this applies layer styles to shapes on a new layer (if chain link is unselected) or to shapes on the current layer (if chain link is selected).

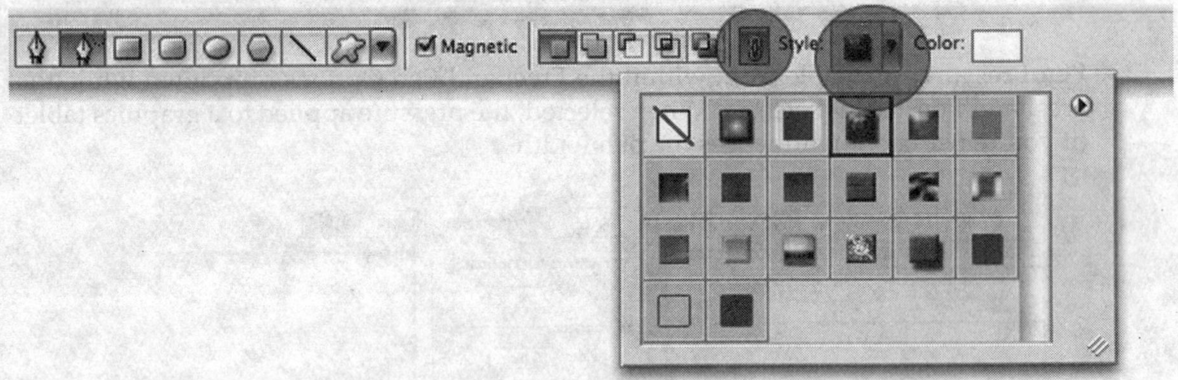

- **Other Shortcuts and Tips**
  - (With path selected) *Spacebar* to give you access to the Hand tool. Move your screen without deselecting the path or changing tools.

- Go to View > Snap To > Grid to allow precise creation of curves with the Pen Tool.

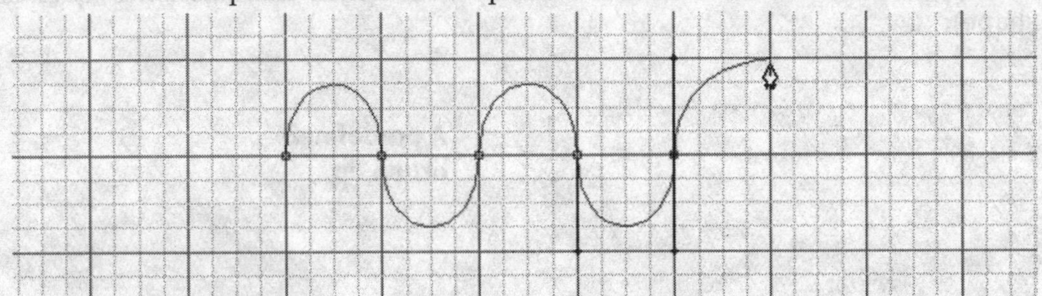

❑ **Best Practice Suggestions**

- Drag handles from the first anchor point when beginning a curved path.
- Drag your handles around just one third of the curve you're creating for a smooth path.

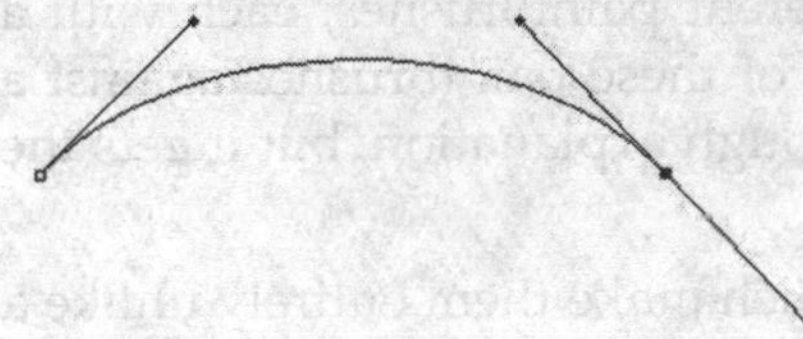

- Position anchor points on a curve where the paths begin to change direction, not in the middle of its curve.

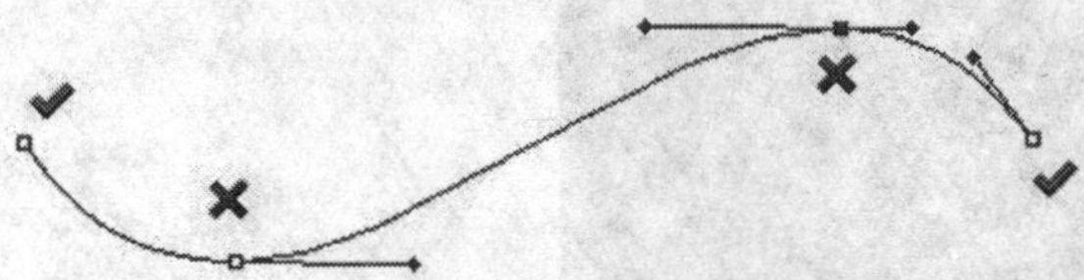

- Be sparing with your use of anchor points, fewer points = neater path.

Photoshop Painting Tools

In Photoshop, the painting tools are used to paint strokes, and fill areas with colour or with colours that blend together. Knowing how to use the paint tools is a must for any designer/ artist who wishes to use Photoshop.

We have discussed a bit about it earlier; lets learn more.

The Brush Tool

In order to use the **brush tool** to its full extent, it's important to understand *what* exactly a brush is in Adobe Photoshop. A **brush** uses **brush presets** that are predefined (or user defined). A **brush preset** is any brush tip with defined characteristics (such as size and shape).

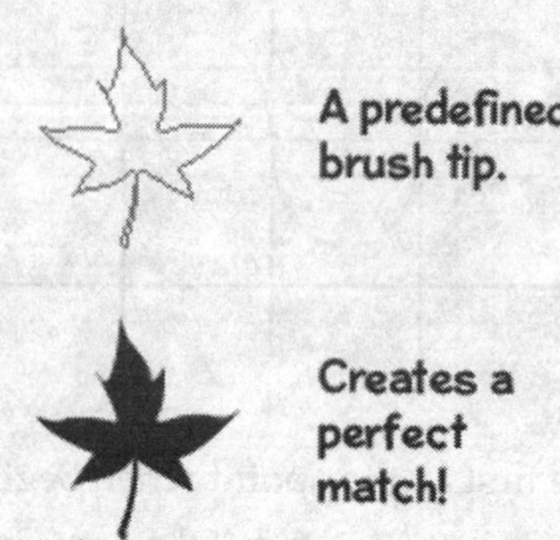

Think of brushes in Photoshop as a large collection of different paintbrushes, each with a different shaped tip. Imagine when you press the tip of one of these paintbrushes against a canvas, the shape of the tip is imprinted immediately. It's a rough explanation, but it gets the *basic idea* across.

Brushes in Photoshop have plenty of other characteristics which make them entirely unlike a real world paint brush. By manipulating these attributes, we can create entirely new brushes that act in unique ways. You could create a brush that changes in shape and size as you are painting, a brush that scatters itself in random directions, and even a brush that becomes more and less transparent while creating strokes. The possibilities are literally endless.

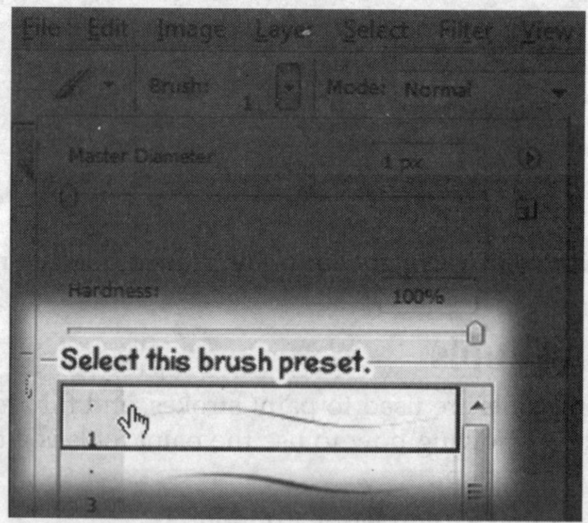

Let's Create a Quick Brush for demonstration purposes

Create a new document, 200px by 200px with a white background. Select the **Brush tool**, and in the options bar select the first brush preset from the *brush preset picker* (activated by clicking on the small down arrow next to the current brush).

Go ahead and give this brush preset a whirl in your active image area. Select a foreground colour you'd like to paint with, point your cursor to where you'd like to start painting, hold down the mouse button, and create a stroke.

Modifying Brushes

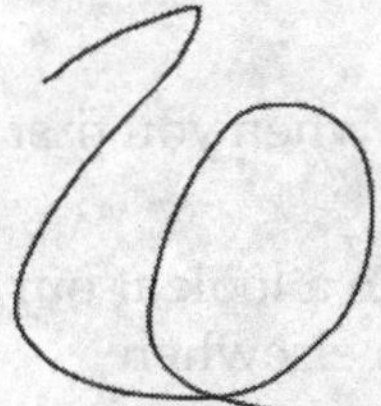

This brush preset creates a 1px *hard* stroke. We can modify some of the characteristics of this brush to create something entirely different.

To modify a brush preset, you're going to need to access the **Brush Palette**. To open the brush palette, go to ***Window > Brushes***. Here's a quick overview of the palette.

a. Brush Settings *– Various settings for the selected brush tip.*

b. Brush Stroke Preview *– A preview of the current brush stroke will look when used.*

c. Selected Brush Tip *– The currently selected brush tip.*

d. Brush Tip Shapes *– A list of all brush tip shapes available.*

e. Brush Options *– Options for modifying the currently selected brush tip. Changes will not be permanent unless a new brush preset is saved.*

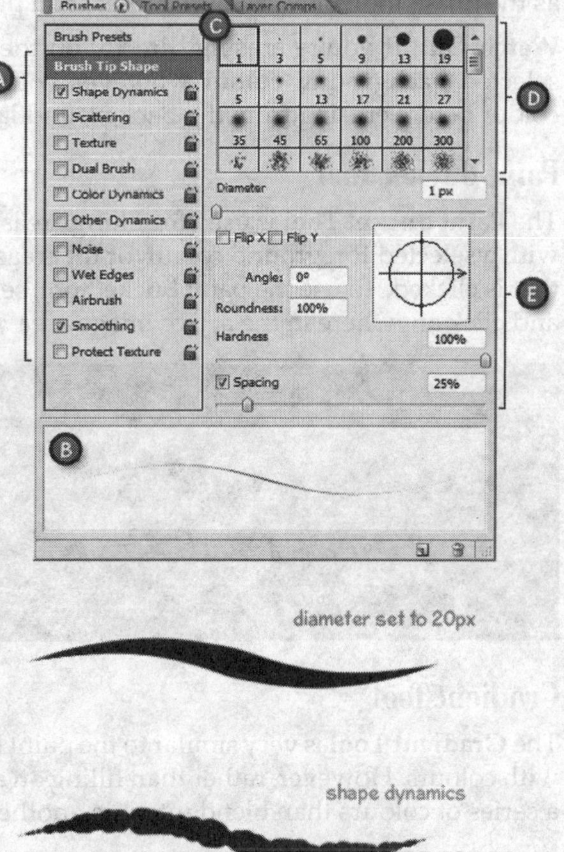

From the **Brush Tip Shape** settings, a user can select a brush tip shape from a list of available shapes (predefined or user defined).

By clicking any of the various **brush settings** on the left, a panel of *options* will be displayed that can adjusted to your own preference.

In the **Brush Tip Shape** area, set the diameter of your brush to 20px. By changing the diameter, you affect the size of the brush.

Now go to **Shape Dynamics** and set the *size jitter* option to 100%. By changing shape dynamics, you're adjusting how a brush mark changes during a stroke.

Finally, go to **Scattering**, and set *scatter* to 300% with a *count* of 1. Scattering will affect placement and number of brush marks.

Try painting with your brush now, and you ought to see a huge difference from when you first started! Modifying brushes is really that simple!

If you're interested in learning more about brushes, then you may want to take a look at our guide on installing new brushes in Photoshop which you've downloaded from elsewhere.

Eraser Tool

We're not going to go into too much detail with the eraser tool, simply because you should already have a pretty good understanding of how it works. *How so?*

Well, like many other tools in Photoshop, the **Eraser Tool** uses brushes which effect the size, shape, and hardness of the tool. Essentially, the eraser tool is controlled in the exact same way as the brush tool, only it erases rather than paints.

Watch Out! If you're erasing directly on the **"Background"** layer, you'll leave the currently selected **background colour** wherever you erase. Always be sure to set your background colour before erasing from the Background layer.

Paint Bucket Tool

The **Paint Bucket Tool** is used for filling areas with solid colours. It can be used to fill selections with a selected foreground colour, or fill areas that are similar in colour to the part of an image that is clicked. To use the paint bucket tool, select a foreground colour you'd like to paint with, and click anywhere in the active image area you'd like to fill.

Gradient Tool

The **Gradient Tool** is very similar to the paint bucket tool, in that it fills entire areas or selections with colours. However, rather than filling an area with a solid colour, the Gradient Tool creates a series of colours than blend into one another.

When the gradient tool is selected, a preset gradient can be selected from the **gradient picker**

in the options bar. A gradient can then be created in the active image area by clicking and holding the mouse button, and dragging in the direction you'd like the gradient to go. Release where you'd like the gradient to stop.

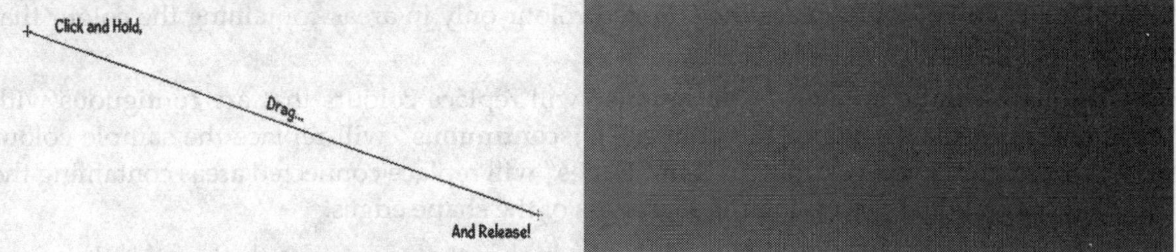

There are 5 different **gradient styles** which can be selected to create different effects. You can set them from the Options Bar.

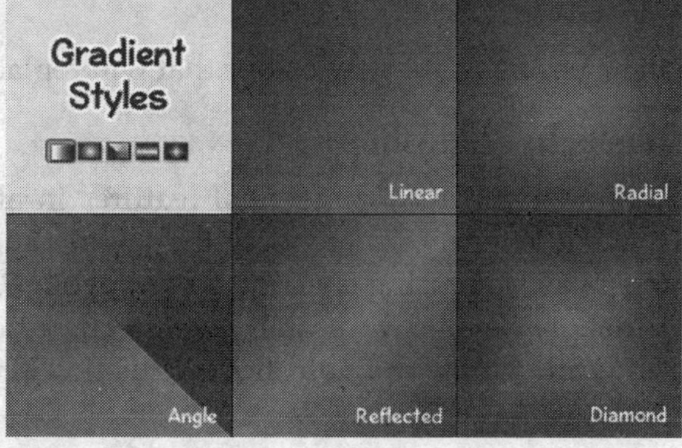

Enjoy Practicing These Skills….!

Photoshop Colour Replacement Tool

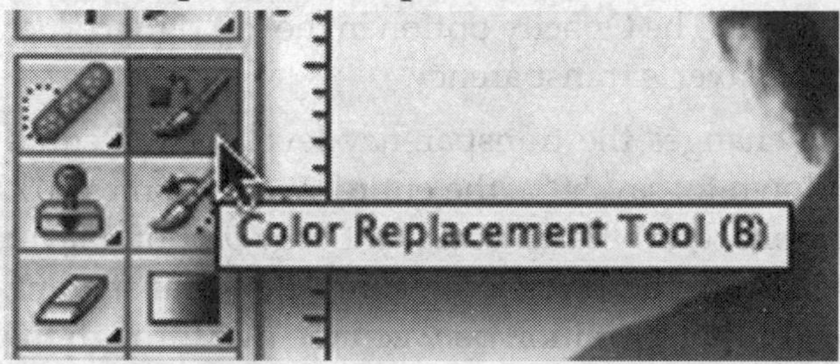

Some tools don't get enough attention; this tool might be one of them. This tool **works like a regular paint brush**; it manipulates the colour on your image while the underlying texture stays unaffected. Because of this, you can apply a colour change in a more precision way.

If you select the tool in the Toolbox, you'll get to see the various options in the Options bar like different Modes to work with in which the **Replace Colour Tool** can be applied: Hue, Saturation, Colour and Luminosity. The Hue will apply the replacement in the most subtle way, while the Colour mode might result is a far too vibrant effect.

Sampling determines the source for the colour replacement. "**Continuous**" means you will be continuously sampling as you go. "**Background Swatch**" uses the background swatch as a pre-defined sample colour. Only areas containing the current background colour will be replaced. "**Once**" will replace the targeted colour only in areas containing the colour that you've first clicked.

You also have **Limits** options. "**Contiguous**" will replace colours that are contiguous with the colour immediately under the pointer "**Discontinuous**" will replace the sample colour under the pointer wherever you go. "**Find Edges**" will replace connected areas containing the sampled colour while preserving the sharpness of the shape edges.

The **Tolerance** is a bit like with other tools, the higher the percentage the broader the range and the more colours will be replaced. Check the **antialiasing** option to get softer edges, although it could give you a less precise result. You can use the "**Find Edges**" options to limit the antialiasing.

The foreground colour will be used as your new colour that will replace the unwanted colour.

Understanding Layer Masks In Photoshop

Now we're going to look at one of the most essential features in all of Photoshop – **layer masks**. We'll cover exactly what layer masks are, how they work, and why you want to use them. If you've been staying away from using layer masks with your Photoshop work because you thought they were somehow beyond your skill level, well, if you know the difference between black and white and can paint with Photoshop's Brush Tool, you already have all the skills you need!

So what are layer masks then? Well, if the term "mask" is what's confusing you (and who could blame you), replace the word "mask" in your mind with "transparency", because that's exactly what a layer mask does. It allows you to control a layer's level of transparency. That's it, that's all. There's nothing more to them than that. The Opacity option in the top right corner of the Layers palette also allows you to control a layer's transparency.

But here's the difference. The Opacity option changes the transparency level for the entire layer at once. If you lower the Opacity level down to, say, 50%, the entire layer becomes 50% transparent. That may be fine for some situations, but what if you want only *part* of a layer to be transparent? What if you want the left side of the layer to be completely transparent, the right side to be completely visible, with a gradual transition between the two through the middle of the layer? That's actually a very common thing to do with a layer in Photoshop, allowing you to fade from one image to another. But you can't do that with the Opacity option since as I said, it's limited to controlling the transparency of the entire layer at once. What you would need is some way to control the transparency of different areas of the layer separately. What you would need is a layer mask.

Let's learn with an example. Here we have a couple of wedding photos which would work well blended together. Here's the first one:

And here's the second one:

In order to blend them together, whether I'll be using a layer mask or not, I need to have both photos inside the same Photoshop document, so with each photo open in its own separate document window, I'm simply going to press V on my keyboard to select my Move Tool and then click inside one of the documents and drag that photo into the document containing the other photo:

Dragging one photo into the same Photoshop document as the other photo with the Move Tool.

Now both photos are in the same Photoshop document, and if we look in the Layers palette, we can see that each one is on its own separate layer, with the photo of the couple facing towards the camera on top and the photo of the couple walking away from us into the woods: ➡

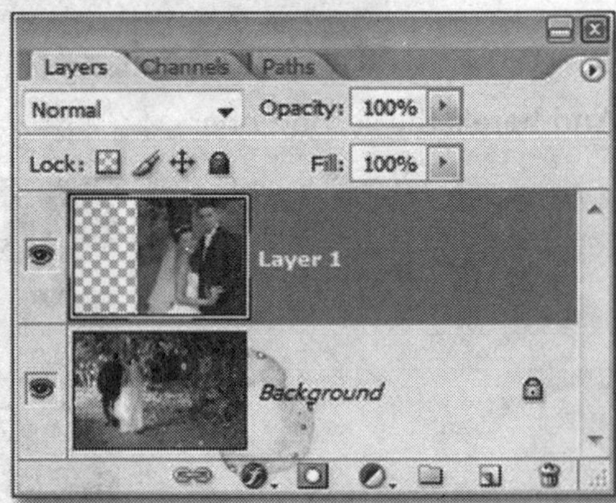

Now, we have to blend these two photos together. Well, let's see what happens if you simply try lowering the opacity of the top layer. If you lower it to about 70% just to see what sort of effect you end up with: ➡

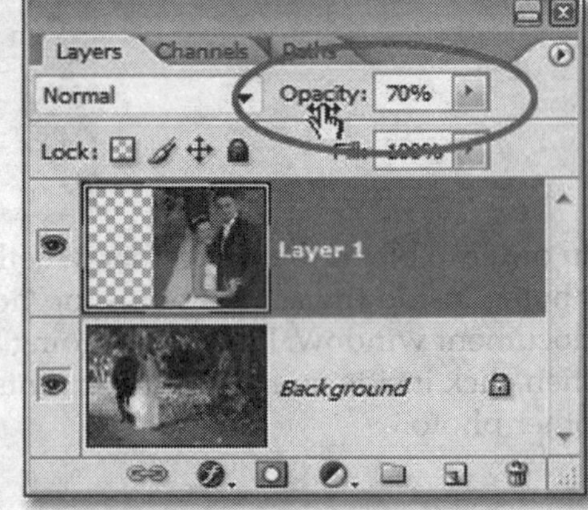

Here's the result:

After lowering the opacity of the top layer (which again contains the image of the couple facing towards the camera on the right), the image on the bottom layer of the couple walking in the woods is now showing through the image above it.

So far in our quest to blend our two photos together, we've tried lowering the opacity of the top layer with disappointing results, since all that basically did was fade the entire image. What I really want is for the couple in both images to remain fully visible, with the blending of the two images happening in the area between the bride walking away from us on the left and her looking towards us on the right. Now I use Photoshop's Eraser Tool. I'll use the Eraser Tool with nice, soft edges to erase the part of the image on the right that I don't need. This should really work.

Press E on the keyboard to quickly select the Eraser Tool. To soften the edges, hold down the Shift key and press the left bracket key a few times. you can also increase or decrease the size of the Eraser as needed using the left bracket key on its own to make the Eraser smaller and the right bracket key to make it larger (the same keyboard shortcut works with any of Photoshop's brush tools). Now you have your Eraser at the right size and with soft edges. Now go ahead and erase away parts of the left side of the top image so that it blends in with the image below it:

After finishing up with my Eraser, here's the result:

As we have discussed at the beginning of this discussion, layer masks allow us to control the transparency of a layer, but unlike the Opacity option which controls overall transparency, layer masks allow us to set different levels of transparency for different areas of the layer (although technically, you *could* use them to control the overall opacity as well, but the Opacity option already handles that very well and layer masks are capable of so much more).

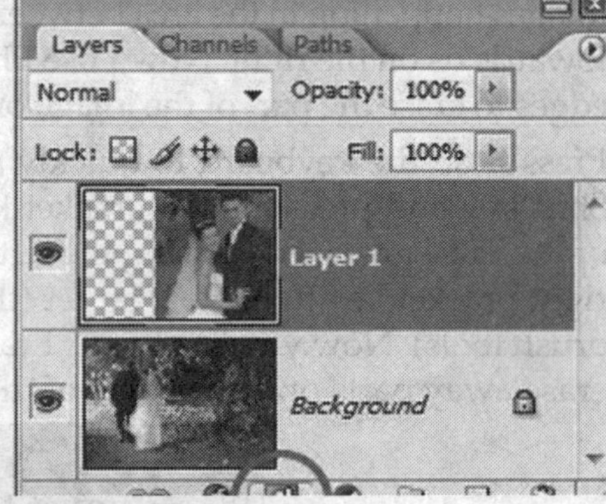

How do layer masks work? To add a layer mask, you first want to make sure that the layer you're adding it to is selected in the Layers palette, otherwise you'll end up adding it to the wrong layer. Add a layer mask to a layer by selecting the layer in the Layers palette and then clicking on the "Layer Mask" icon.

Once you've clicked on the icon, nothing will seem to have happened in your document, and that's because by default, layer masks are hidden from view. After all, the whole point of them is to show and hide different parts of the layer and it would be pretty difficult to do that if the mask itself was blocking our view of the image. So how do we know, then, that we've added a layer mask if we can't see it? Easy! Look back over in the Layers palette, to the right of the preview thumbnail on the layer you added the mask to, and you'll see a brand new thumbnail. This is your layer mask thumbnail, and it's how we know that a layer mask has been added to the layer:

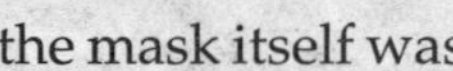

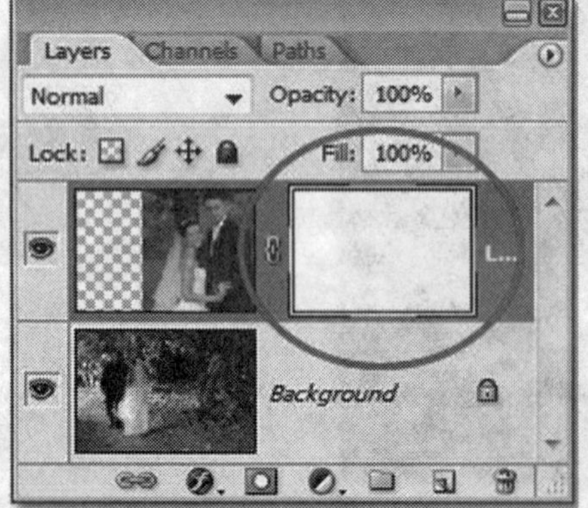

Notice that the layer mask thumbnail is filled with solid white. That's not just some random, meaningless colour that Photoshop users to display layer mask thumbnails in. The reason why the thumbnail is filled with white is because the mask itself is currently filled with white, even though the mask is currently hidden from view. If you want a proof that the mask really is there in your document and really is filled with white, simply hold down **Alt** and click directly on the layer mask thumbnail in the Layers palette:

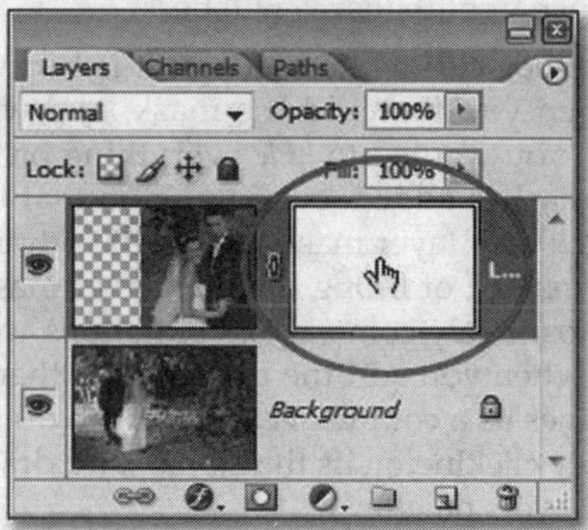

Doing this tells Photoshop to show us the layer mask in our document, and sure enough, there it is, filled with white:

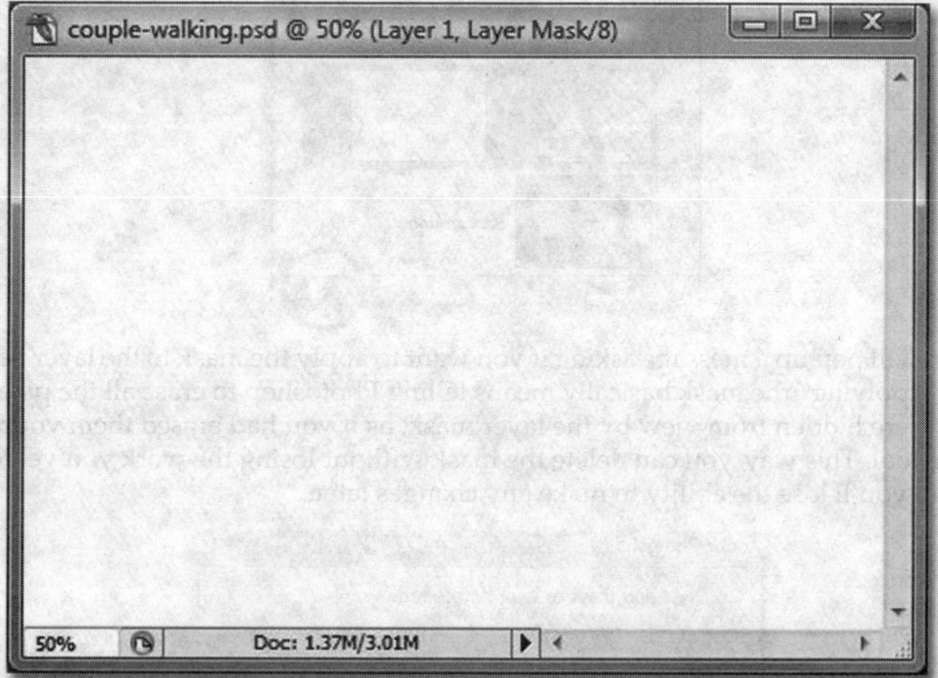

The layer mask is now blocking our image from view though, so once again hold down Alt and click on the layer mask thumbnail to hide the mask.

Layer masks use only white, black, and all the shades of gray in between, and they use these three colours (white, black and gray) to control the transparency of a layer. White in a layer

mask means 100% visible. Black in a layer mask means 100% transparent. And gray in a layer mask means some level of transparency depending on how light or dark the shade of gray is. 50% gray will give us 50% transparency. The lighter the shade of gray, the closer it is to white and the less transparent that area of the layer will be. The darker the shade of gray, the closer it is to black and the more transparent that area will be.

The reason layer masks are filled with white by default is because usually you want to see everything on your layer when you first add the mask, and white in a layer mask means 100% visible. What if instead, you wanted to *hide* everything on the layer when you add the mask, so that as soon as the mask is added, everything on that layer disappears from view? Well, we just learned that black on a layer mask means 100% transparent, so we would need a way to tell Photoshop that instead of filling the new layer mask with white, we want it to be filled what black. You'll most likely come across situations where it makes more sense to hide everything on the layer when you add the mask rather than leaving everything visible, and fortunately, Photoshop gives us a couple of easy ways to do that. First of all, I'm going to delete my layer mask by simply clicking on its thumbnail and dragging it down onto the trash bin icon at the bottom of the Layers palette:

Photoshop will pop up a message asking if you want to apply the mask to the layer before you delete it. "Applying" the mask basically means telling Photoshop to erase all the pixels on the layer that were hidden from view by the layer mask, as if you had erased them yourself with the Eraser Tool. This way, you can delete the mask without losing the work you've done with it, although you'll lose the ability to make any changes later.

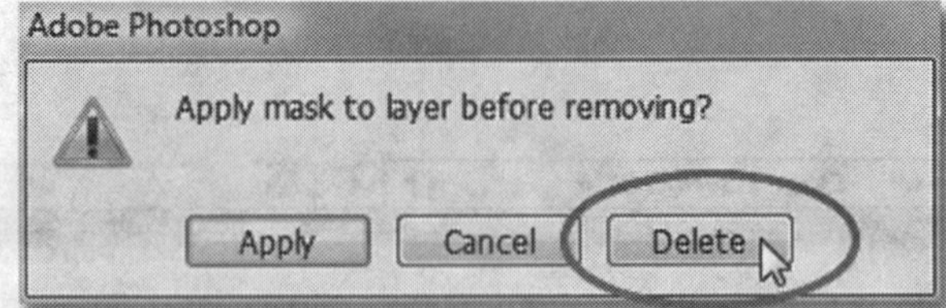

In most cases, you'll simply want to delete your mask and start over, but there are times when you may want to apply the mask to the layer before deleting it, which will erase all the pixels on the layer that were hidden by the mask.

Now that I've deleted my mask, both the mask itself and its thumbnail in the Layers palette are gone: ➡

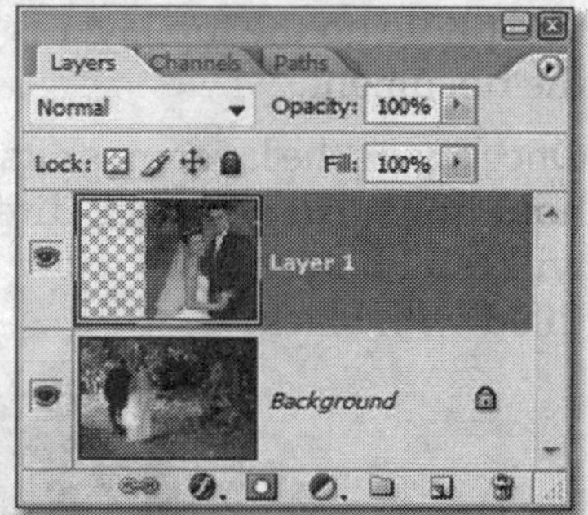

When you delete a layer mask, its thumbnail in the Layers palette also disappears.

This time, I want to add a mask to the top layer and have Photoshop hide everything on the layer as soon as the mask is added, which means the mask will need to be filled with black instead of white. The "getting paid by the hour" way to accomplish this would be to go up to the Layer menu at the top of the screen, choose Layer Mask, and then choose Hide All (remember last time, we chose "Reveal All"). The faster and easier way though is to hold down your Alt key and click on the Layer Mask icon at the bottom of the Layers palette: ➡

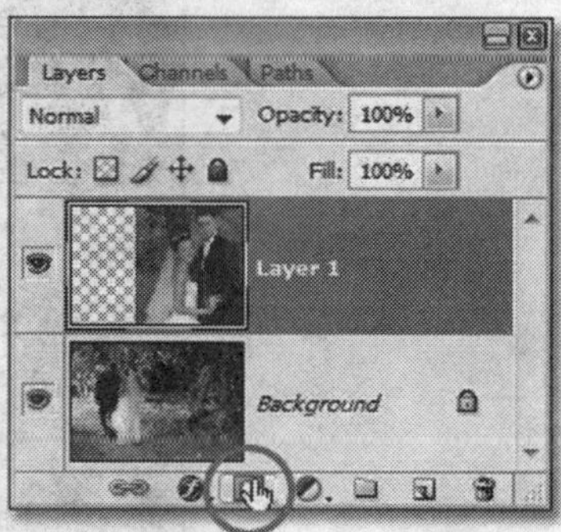

Either way you choose to do it, Photoshop adds a new layer mask to the currently selected layer, just as it did before, but this time, it fills the mask with black instead of white. We can see this in the layer mask thumbnail which is filled with solid black ➡

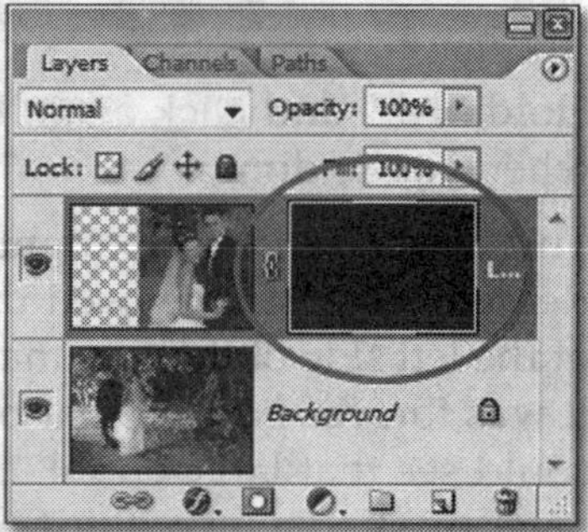

And, unlike the first time we added a layer mask where nothing seemed to have happened to our image, this time the top layer (the photo of the couple facing the camera) is completely hidden from view, leaving only the image below it visible:

The photo on the top layer is now 100% transparent, leaving only the photo below it visible in the document.

Once again, the layer mask itself is hidden from view, but if you want to see it in your document, hold down Alt and click directly on the layer mask's thumbnail in the Layers palette, which will tell Photoshop to show you the mask in the document window. This time, the mask is filled with black:

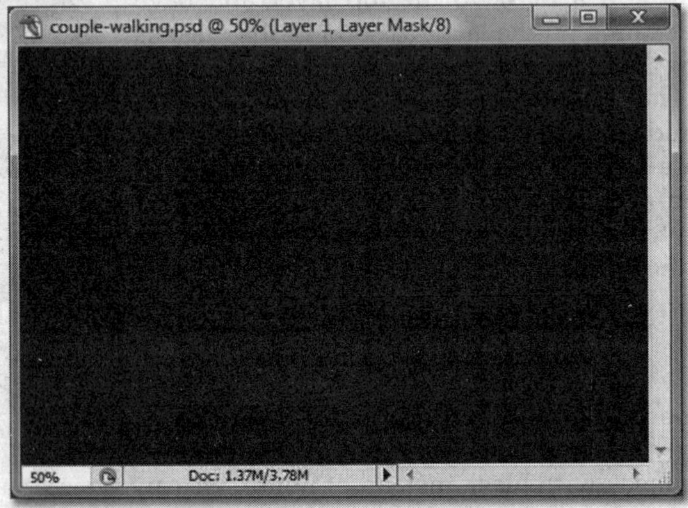

Hold "Alt" and click again on the layer mask thumbnail to hide the mask in the document when you're done.

This is where the important difference between the Eraser Tool and layer masks comes in. Remember when we used the Easer Tool to blend the images together by erasing away part of the left side of the top image? The Eraser Tool physically deleted that part of the image and it was forever gone at that point, and if we looked in the top layer's preview thumbnail, we could see that large chunk of the image missing on the left. This time though, we've used a layer mask to hide not just part of the left side of the image but rather the entire image, yet if we look in the layer's preview thumbnail, the image is still there, completely intact:

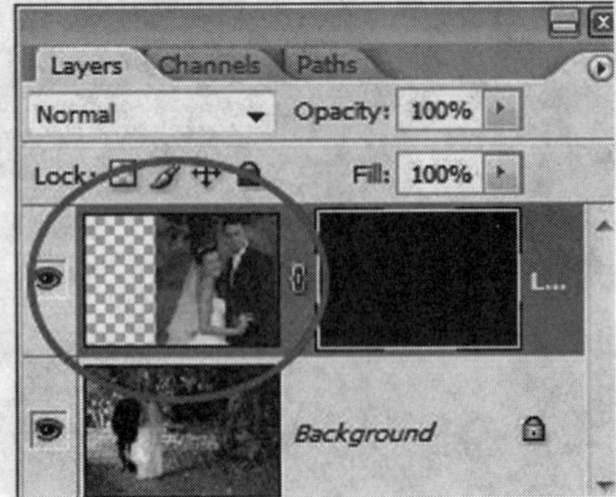

Where the Eraser Tool deleted the contents of the layer, the layer mask simply hides it from view! To prove that the photo on the top layer is still there, I'm going to fill the layer mask with white. To fill a layer mask with white, or do anything at all with a layer mask, you first need to select the mask so that you're working on the mask itself and not the actual layer, and to select it, all you need to do is click directly on the mask's thumbnail in the Layers palette:

Filling the layer mask with black

You can switch between selecting the layer itself and its layer mask by clicking on the corresponding thumbnail. You can tell which one is currently selected by which thumbnail has the white highlight border around it, as we can see around the layer mask thumbnail in the image above.

To fill the mask with white, I'll go up to the Edit menu at the top of the screen and choose Fill, which brings up Photoshop's Fill command dialog box. For Contents I'll choose white:

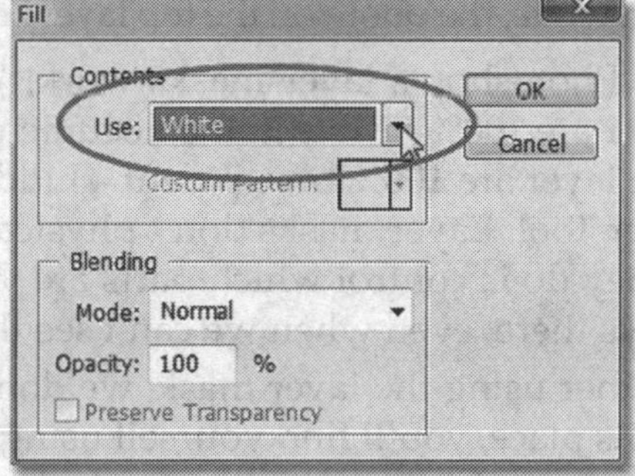

With white chosen as my fill contents, I'll click OK in the top right to exit out of the dialog box and have Photoshop fill my layer mask with white. I can now see in the Layers palette that the mask thumbnail is filled with white:

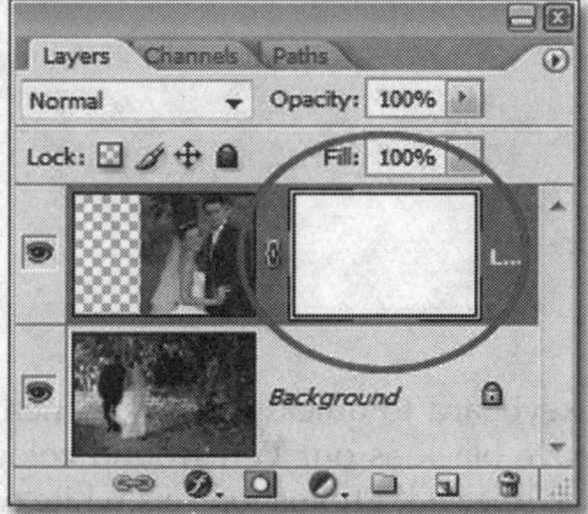

And with the mask now filled with solid white, my photo on the top layer is completely visible in the document once again, proving that even though the image was hidden from view a moment ago when we filled the layer mask with black, it was always there, untouched and unharmed:

After filling the layer mask with white, the photo on the top layer becomes fully visible once again.

And that's the basics of how Photoshop's layer masks work! When the mask is filled with white, the contents of that layer are 100% visible in the document, and when the mask is filled with black, the contents of the layer are 100% transparent – hidden from view but not deleted as was the case with the Eraser Tool. Layer masks don't physically alter or affect the contents of the layer in any way. All they do is control which parts are visible and which are not. The contents of the layer are always there, even when we can't see them.

To blend the two images together using the layer mask, we don't use the Eraser Tool. In fact, while the Eraser Tool still has its place, you'll find yourself using it less and less as you become more comfortable with layer masks. Instead, we use Photoshop's Brush Tool, and with our layer mask filled with white as it currently is, which is making the entire layer visible, all we need to do is paint with black on the layer mask over any areas we want to hide.

Let's discuss with examples:

You could also press B on the keyboard to quickly select it. Then, since we want to paint with black, we need to have black as our Foreground colour, and by default, whenever you have a layer mask selected, Photoshop sets white as your Foreground colour, with black as your Background colour. To swap them so black becomes your Foreground colour, simply press X on your keyboard. If I look in the colour swatches near the bottom of my Tools palette, I can see now that black is my Foreground colour:

Now we resize the brush to the same general size used with the Eraser Tool by once again using the left and right bracket keys, and I want my brush to have nice, soft edges so I get smooth transitions between the areas of the layer that are visible and the areas that are hidden, and I can soften my brush edges by holding down Shift and pressing the left bracket key a few times. Then, with my layer mask selected (I know it's selected because the layer mask thumbnail has the white highlight border around it), I'm going to do basically the same thing I did with the Eraser Tool, except this time I'm painting with black on the layer mask over the areas I want to hide rather than erasing anything:

After spending a few more seconds painting away the areas I want to hide, here's my result, which looks pretty much the same as it did after I used the Eraser Tool:

If we look at the layer mask thumbnail in the Layers palette, we can see where I've painted with black, which are now the areas of the top image that are hidden from view:

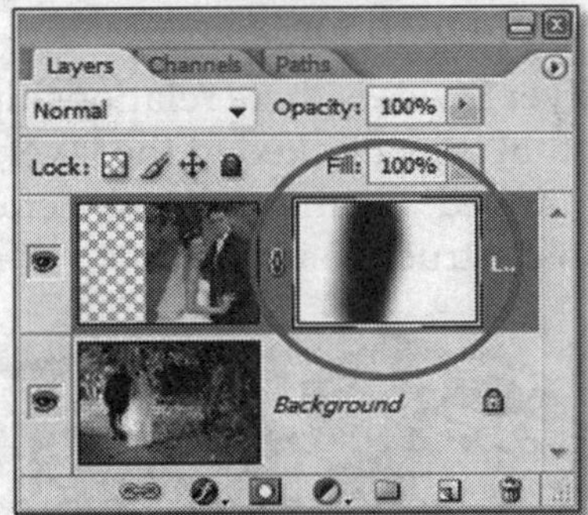

The layer mask thumbnail now shows the areas we've painted with black.

If you make a mistake when you are painting and accidentally show or hide the wrong area, all you need to do is press X to swap your Foreground and Background colours, paint over the mistake to undo it, then swap your Foreground and Background colours once again with X and continue on. And here, after a couple of minutes worth of work painting the veil and the tree trunk back into the image, you'll get the final result:

That's the basics of how layer masks work in Photoshop!

Layer Styles in Photoshop

Effects can be added to individual layers in Photoshop that automatically change as a layer is modified. The combination of effects on any given layer is called its Layer Style. We'll teach you how to use and make your own layer styles in this tutorial.

What are Layer Styles?

Layer styles are special effects that can be quickly and easily applied to individual layers in Photoshop to drastically change the appearance of something in very little time. They can be preset, customised, or even saved and used for later.

One of the useful properties of Layer Styles is there relationship to the layer contents. Since the style is actually a separate entity that is just linked to the layer, it will continually update itself as a layer contents are edited or moved. Furthermore, the effects can easily be adjusted after applying them, making them non-destructive in nature.

Some shapes and text with and without layer styles applied

Using Layer Style Presets

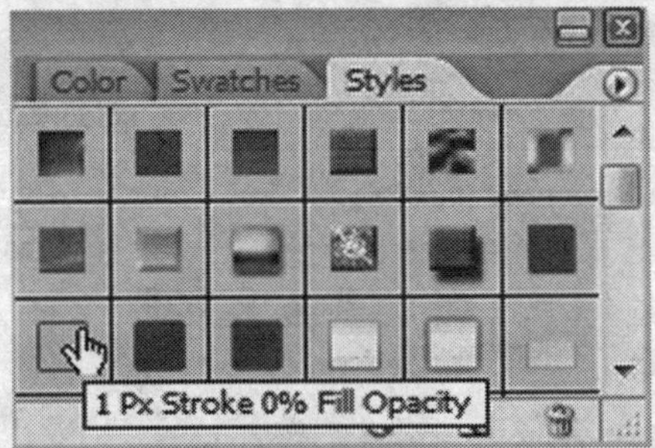

Photoshop comes packed with a good number of **Layer Style Presets**, all which are accessible through the **Styles Palette** (*Window > Styles*). To apply a **Layer Style**, select the Layer you'd like to work with in your document from the ***Layers Palette***, and then select the *Layer Style* which you would like to apply.

Some Text

A Text Layer Before and After a Layer Style Preset is applied to it.

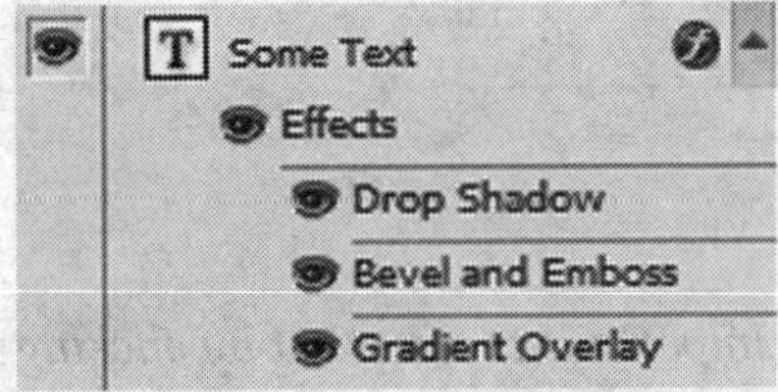

After applying a *Layer Style*, the effects in the layer can be seen, adjusted, disabled or reenabled from the *Layers Palette*. Layers with effects applied to them will have a small round icon with an *'f'* in it. To expand or collapse the effects applied to a layer, click the arrow to the right of this icon.

When layers effects have been expanded, you can quickly disable specific effects within the layer style by clicking the *eye* icon next to the effect. Just like a layer, these effects can become visible again by clicking the blank area (*where the eye would reside*) when an effect is disabled.

Making Quick Changes

You can make quick changes to a layers style by double clicking the **'f'** icon to pull up the **Layer Style Options**. From here, you can completely customise your layers style.

Creating your own Effects and Styles

To add your own layer effects, and create your own styles, go to ***Layer > Layer Style > Blending Options***, or ***Right Click your Layer,*** and ***select Blending Options***. This will bring up the **Layer Style Options**.

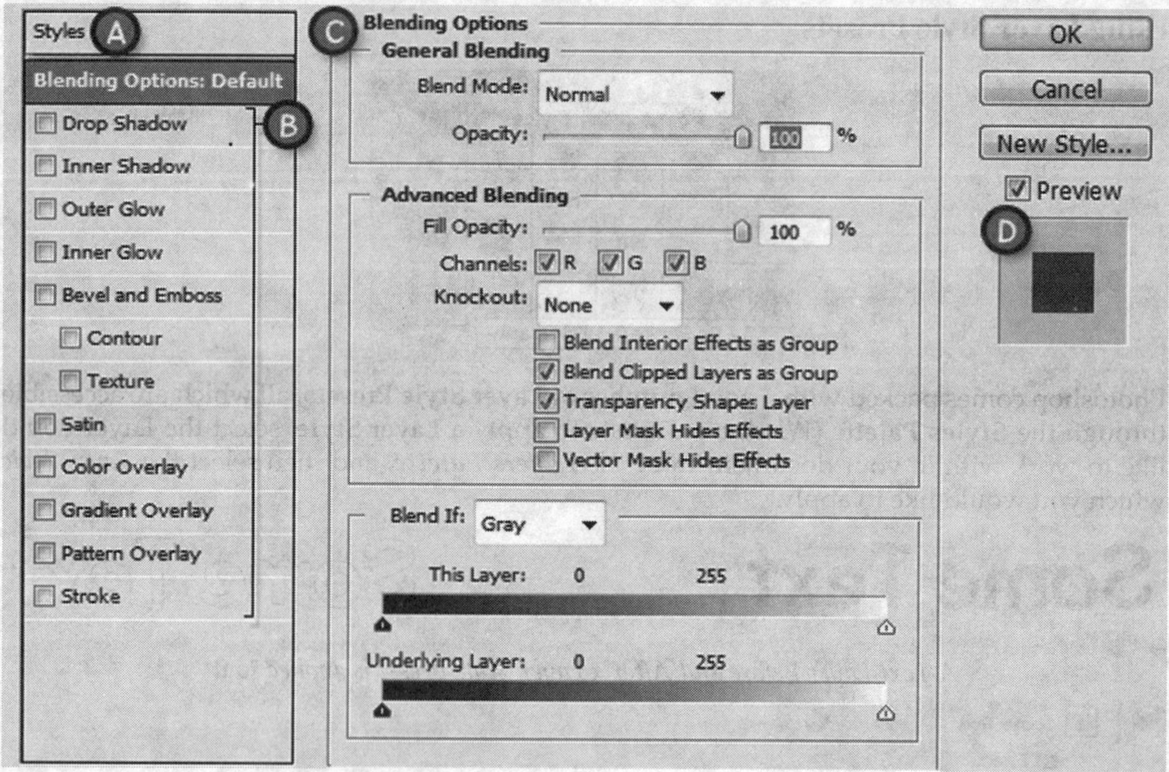

a. **Style Presets** – *List of the Style Presets.*

b. **Effects** – *The various effects that can be used in a layer style. It's important to note that by clicking on the name of any of the effects will enable that effect, and display the options for the individual effect.*

c. **Options / Settings** – *When the name for an effect is checked, it's options will be shown here. When* ***Blending Options*** *is selected, settings such as Opacity, Fill, and other advanced options will be displayed.*

d. **Layer Style Preview** – *A preview of the Layer Style.*

Effects (**b**) can be enabled by checking them, and likewise, disabled by un-checking them. To edit an effect, you need to **click the name** (*rather than checkbox*). The effects settings will be displayed in the **Options** area (**c**), where they can be easily adjusted. To apply a set of effects and options, simply press **OK**.

Layer Effects

Styles can be built with the following effects:

- **Drop Shadow** – Creates a shadow behind the layers contents.
- **Inner Shadow** – Creates a shadow on top of the layers contents.
- **Outer Glow** – Creates a glow behind the layers contents. Cannot be distanced like the drop shadow.

- ❑ **Inner Glow** – Creates a glow on top of the layers contents. Again, cannot be distanced like the inner shadow.
- ❑ **Bevel and Emboss** - Used to create unique highlight and shadow effects on a layers contents.
- ❑ **Satin** – Gives the layer contents a satin-like, glossy appearance.
- ❑ **Colour Overlay** – Fills the layer contents with a solid colour.
- ❑ **Gradient Overlay** – Fills the layer contents with a gradient.
- ❑ **Pattern Overlay** – Fills the layer contents with a pattern.
- ❑ **Stroke** – Creates an outline on layer contents using a solid colour, gradient, or pattern.

Let's try it out to make sure we've got a clear understanding of all this. We're going to test our abilities by creating a basic layer style for some text. Go ahead and **create a new document** in Photoshop, and use the **Type Tool** to add some large, black text.

Right Click the text layer, and **Select** ***Blending Options***.

First we're going to add a **Drop Shadow**. Check the *Drow Shadow Effect*, and click on it to bring up its options. Set things up as shown in the diagram below:

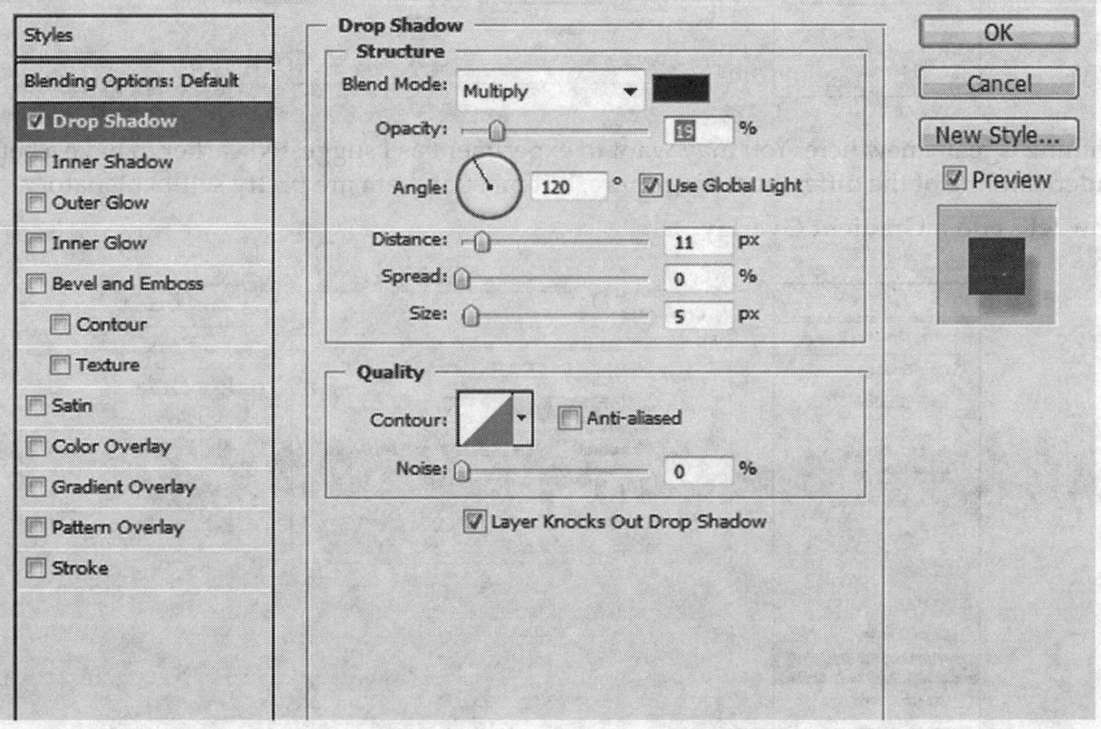

As you're making adjustments, you should be able to see changes being made in your actual document. Keeping an eye on your document while adding effects will allow you to better determine how to adjust settings with your mouse by clicking on the wheel. Doing so will change the angle of your shadow.

Now let's add a **Bevel and Emboss**. We're going to create a bevel that is subtle, so that it doesn't draw too much attention, but at the same time pops our text a bit. Again, mimic the settings shown in the diagram below.

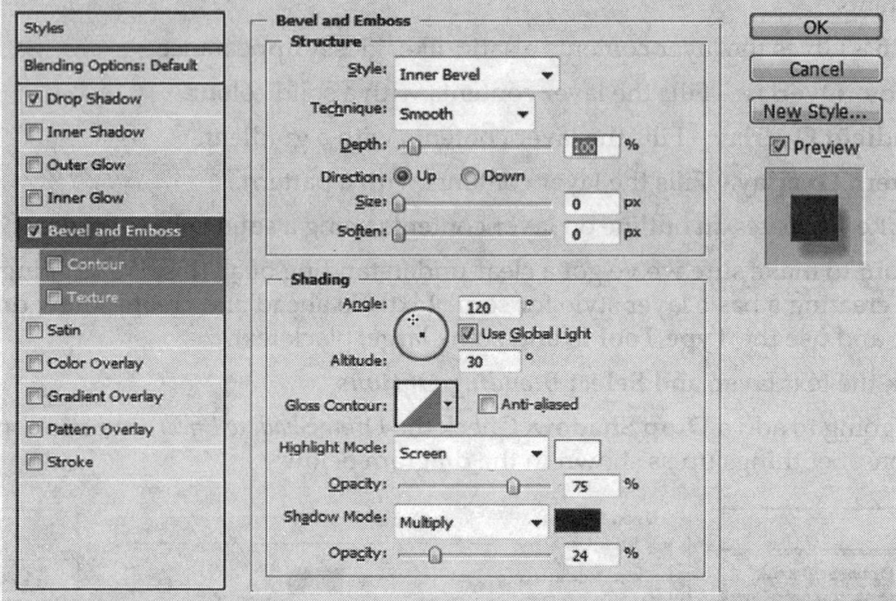

Nothing is really new here. You may want to experiment as I suggested earlier to have a better understanding of the different settings here, but most of them are pretty self-explanatory.

Now let's add a **Gradient Overlay**.

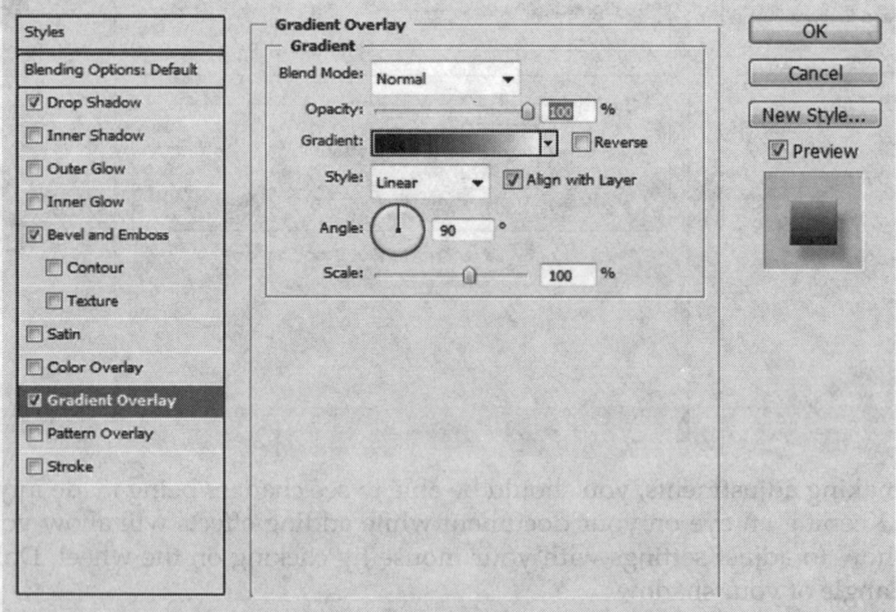

By default, the Gradient Overlay will probably use a *Foreground to Background* gradient, which is not exactly what we are looking for (unless we've setup the Foreground and Background Colours in Photoshop specifically for this step). That's OK though, because we can easily adjust the gradient from here.

Click on the gradient shown in the **Gradient Picker** (*Black fading to White in the above diagram*). This will bring up the **Gradient Editor**. From the *Gradient Editor*, you may choose a gradient preset, or create a new custom gradient of your own. Towards the bottom of the editor is the current gradient, with ***Opacity Stops*** (*Determine how opaque the gradient is at a specific point*) and **Colour Stops** (*Determine what colours are used in the Gradient*). We can add, delete, and modify stops by clicking anywhere above or below the gradient, or by clicking on the stops themselves.

We only want to modify the current colour stops. Double Click the first colour stop, and apply the colour *#50a2e7*, and then apply the colour *#75cefc* to the right most stop. **Click OK** to Apply the Gradient.

Click OK to apply the layer style you've created.

Working with Layer Styles – Understanding Bevel and Emboss

This versatile effect helps create a feeling of depth by adding highlight and shadow to layer shapes. Depending on where these highlights and shadows are placed, a 3D effect can be quickly generated.

The **bevel effect** makes an object look as though it has been chiselled away, and is great for giving hard, sharp edges. The **emboss** options are a bit softer and make objects seem to rise out of the document or look as though they have been stamped into the page. In addition to deciding on a **bevel or emboss**, you also have control over the size of the effect, the direction of light and shadows and the shape of the edges. The option to apply a texture is also worth investigating and opens up even more options.

With the **Layer Style** window open and the **Bevel and Emboss** checkbox checked, go to the **Style** drop-down menu in the middle section to pick whether you go for a bevel or an emboss.

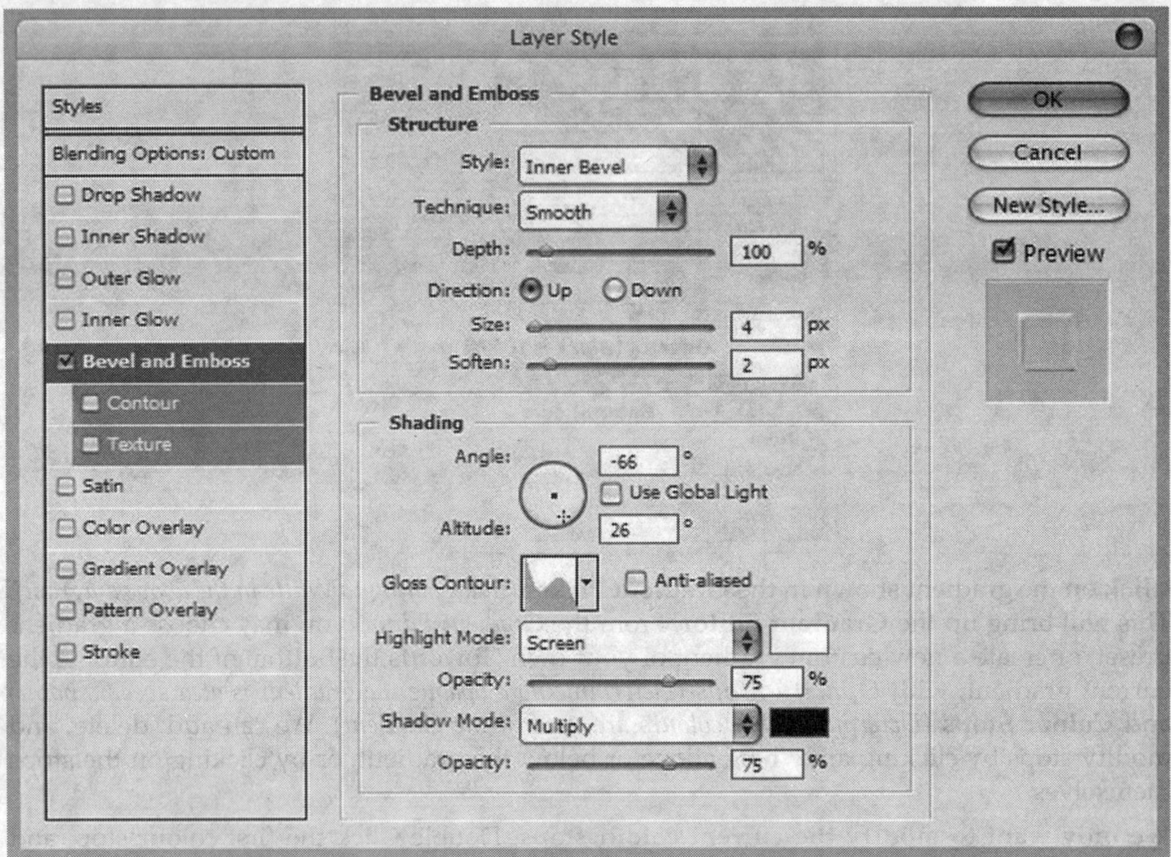

Bevel and Emboss options:

Style – This is where you choose the type of beveling that you want to apply. **Outer Bevel** adds a bevel outside the layer boundary, giving the impression of the layer being raised from its background.

Inner Bevel adds the bevel inside the layer boundary instead, making the layer itself look beveled and 3D.

Emboss adds a bevel across the layer boundary, giving the impression of the layer being stamped on the underlying layers.

Pillow Emboss adds shading to both the inside and outside of the layer boundary to make the layer look like it's embedded in the underlying layers.

Stroke Emboss adds embossing to the layer's Stroke effect only.

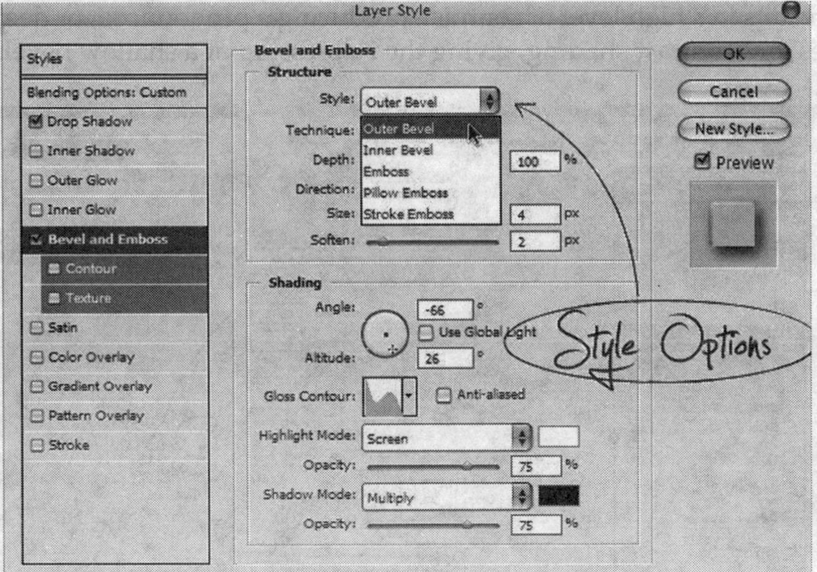

Technique – This option lets you tweak the method that Photoshop uses when forming the beveling effect.

Smooth applies a small amount of blur to the effect to produce a softer result.

Chisel Hard hugs the contours of the layer boundary much more accurately, preserving features from the layer contents, making it great for type layers.

Chisel Soft is a compromise between **Chisel Hard** and **Smooth**. It usually doesn't follow the contours as accurately as **Chisel Hard**, but it produces a gentler effect.

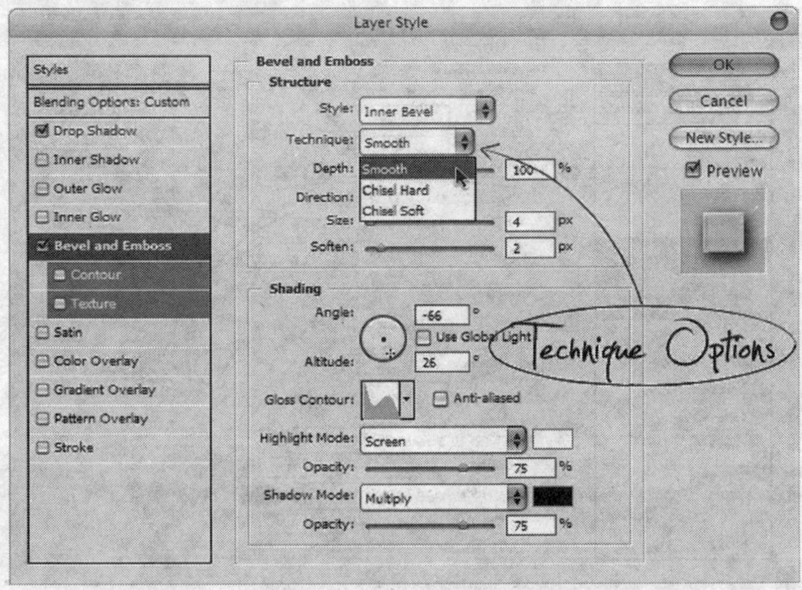

Depth – This option specifies the contrast of the shading used for the effect.

A high value results in a high level of contrast, producing a pronounced, or deep, bevel. A low value produces low-contrast shading, giving the impression of a shallow bevel.

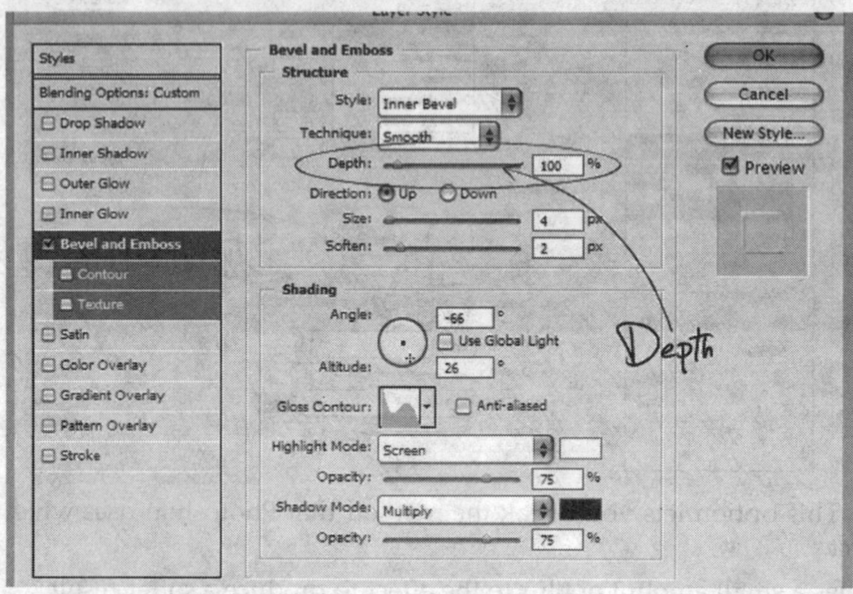

Direction – This option controls whether the beveling effect makes the layer appear raised (**Up**) or indented (**Down**). It's equivalent of rotating the **Angle** setting by **180 degrees**.

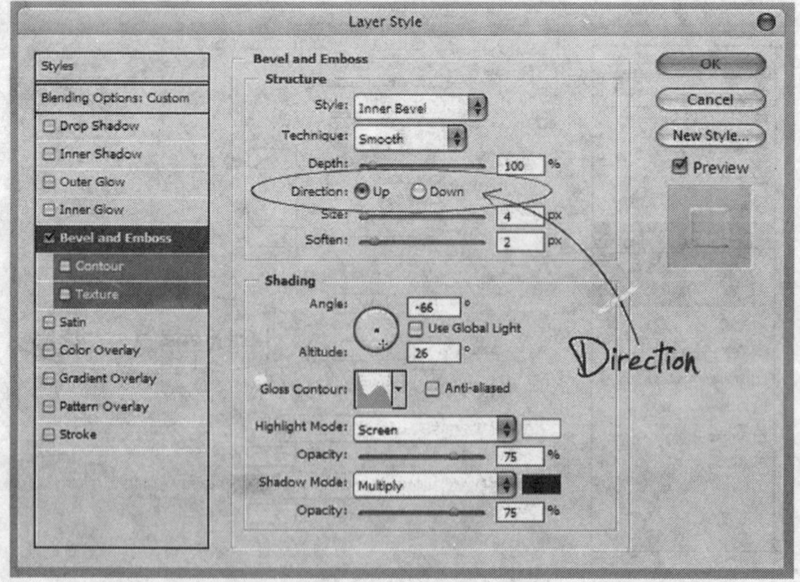

Size – Use this option to control the size of the bevel in pixels. Click and drag the slider to change the size, or type a value in the box to the right of the slider.

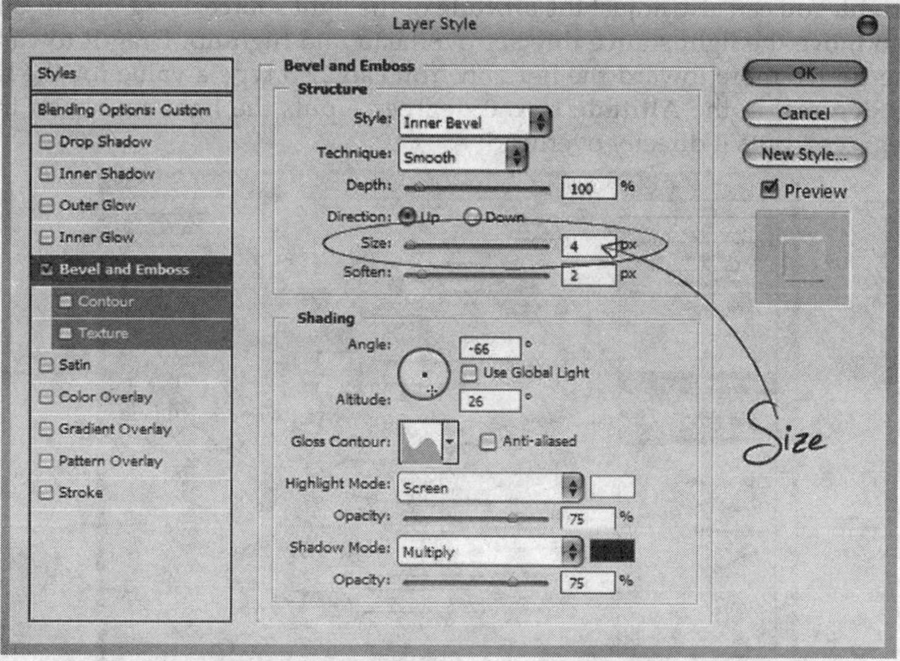

Soften – This option is great for smoothing over artifacts caused by using either of the **Chisel** techniques. It adds a touch of blurring to the effect to help smooth things out.

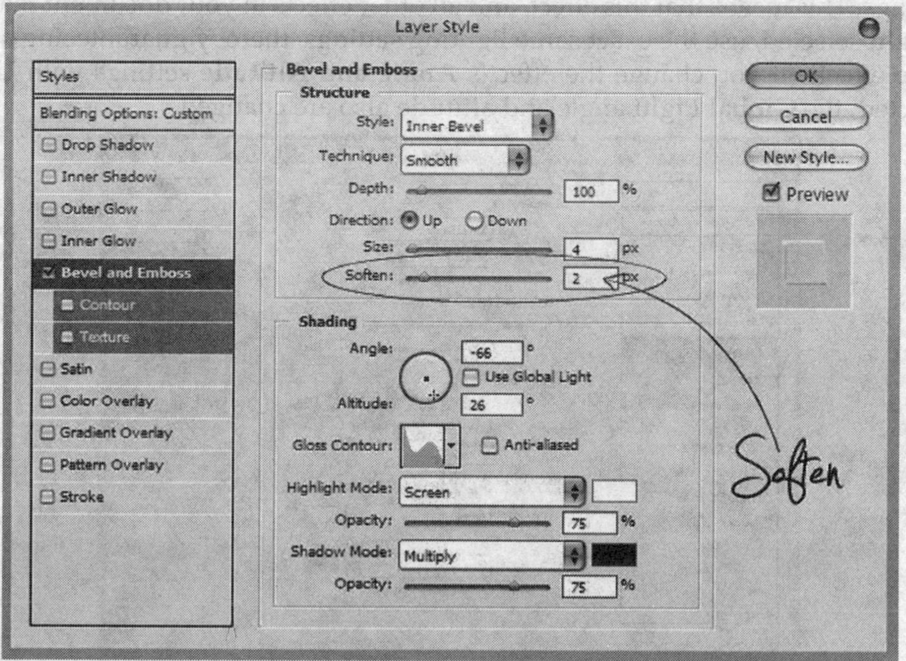

Angle and Altitude – Use the **Angle** option to adjust the direction of the light source used for the bevel effect. Click and drag the little crosshair in the circle, or type a value in the **Angle box** to the right. You can also adjust the **altitude** of the light source. Drag the crosshair toward the centre to move the light source directly overhead and high up. Drag it toward the edge to move the source more toward the horizon. You can also type a value for the light source **altitude**, in degrees, in the **Altitude box, 0 degrees** – puts the light source on the horizon, while **90 degrees** – puts it directly overhead.

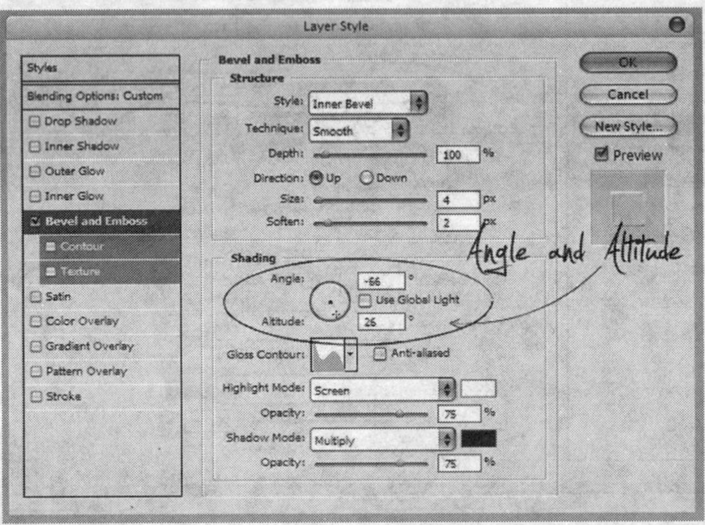

Use Global Light – This option locks the effect's **Angle and Altitude** settings to the **Global Light** settings. This means that this effect, and all other effects in your document that have **Use Global Light** selected, use the exact same lighting settings, thereby guaranteeing a consistent look to the effects. If you change the effect's **Angle and Altitude** settings with **Use Global Light** selected, the **Global Light** angle and altitude also are changed.

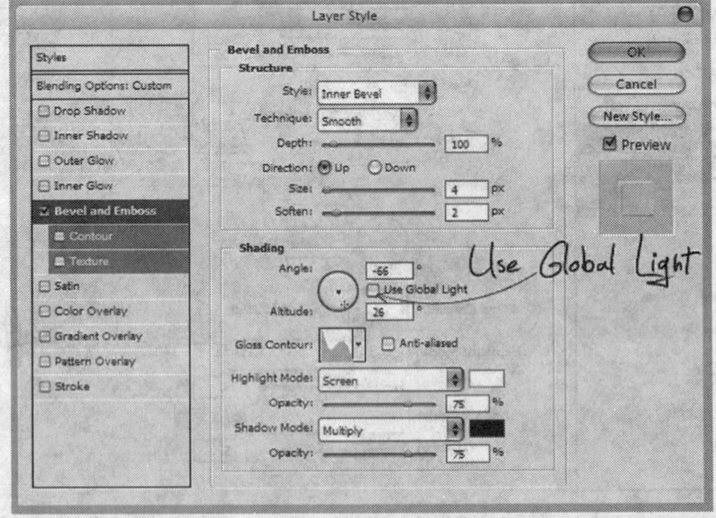

Gloss Contour – This option controls how the highlights and shadows that make up the effect are mapped across the range of the effect. Choose a preset contour by clicking the downward-pointing arrow next to the box, or create your own contour by clicking the graph in the box. The **Input values** along the bottom of the graph represent the areas in shadow in the effect (on the left) to the areas in the light (on the right). The **Output values** up the side of the graph represent the amount of shadow (at the bottom) or highlight (at the top) to apply. So the default **Linear gradient** exactly maps shadowed areas to shadows, and lit areas to highlights. By varying the curve within the graph, you control how the "dark" and "light" areas of the bevel are shaded.

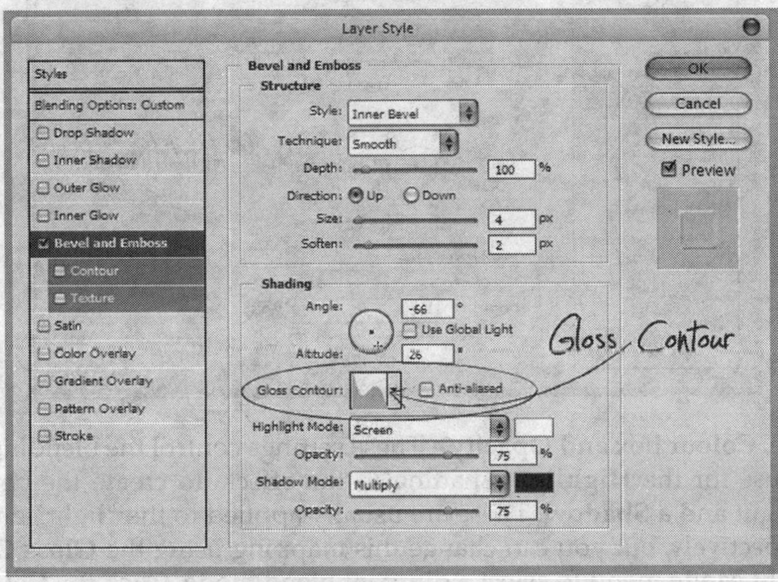

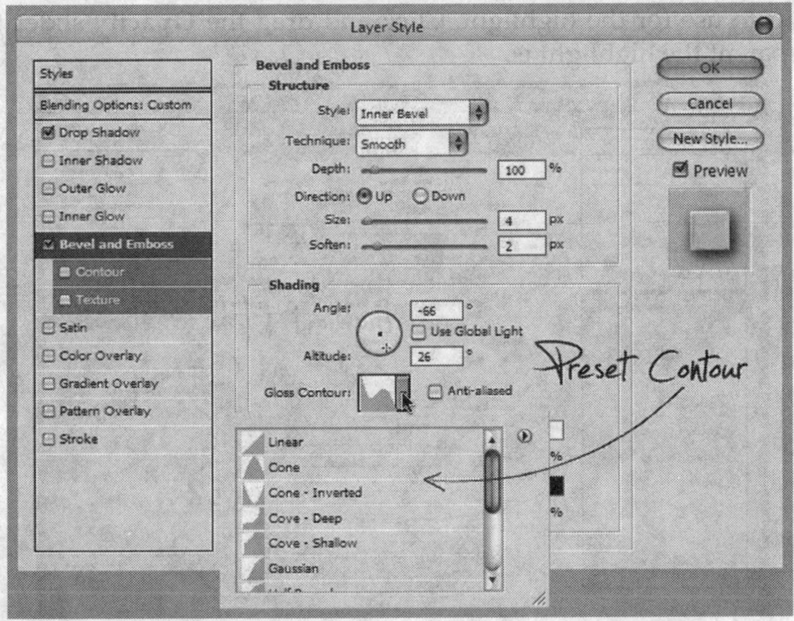

Anti-Aliased – If you use a fairly complex **Gloss Contour** graph, with lots of spikes, then you'll probably notice that the glossy effects appear jagged in the image, particularly if your original layer is quite small or detailed. By selecting the **Anti-Aliased** option, you can smooth out these transitions, resulting in a less jagged effect.

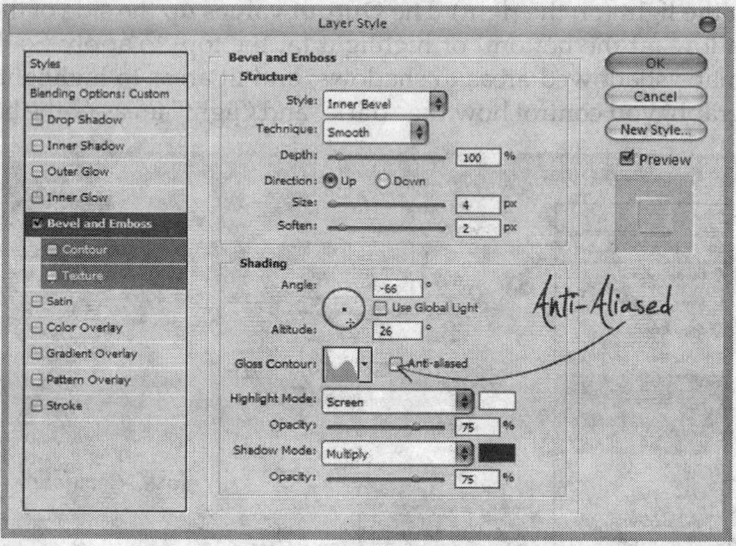

Highlight Mode, Colour box and Opacity – These settings control the blending mode, colour, and opacity to use for the **Highlight** shading in the effect. To create the bevel, Photoshop applies a **Highlight** and a **Shadow**. These are usually applied to the "light" and "dark" areas of the effect, respectively, but you can change this mapping using the **Gloss Contour** option. Use the **Highlight Mode** menu to select a different blend mode. Click the **Colour box** to pick a different colour to use for the highlight. Click and drag the **Opacity** slider to control how opaque or transparent the highlight is.

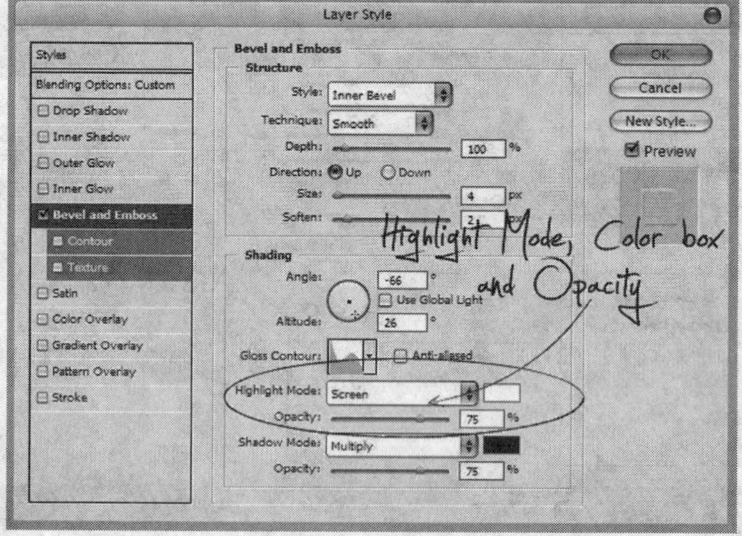

Shadow Mode, Colour box and Opacity – These controls apply to the **Shadow** shading used for the effect and behave much like their **Highlight** counterparts described previously.

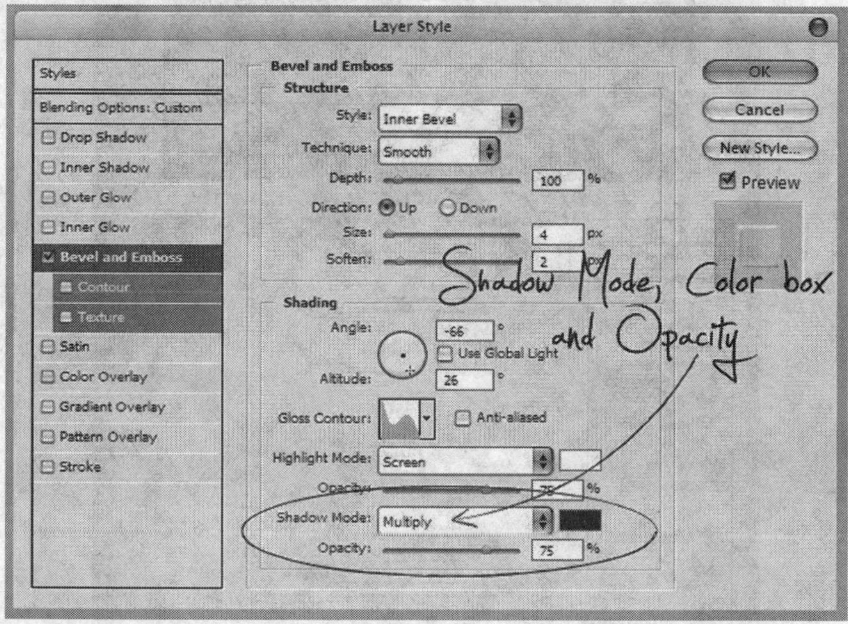

By adding an **Inner Bevel** to text, we've managed to create a pretty realistic 3D effect. Examples of **Bevel and Emboss** in action (**text colour – white, Fill – %**):

Outer Bevel

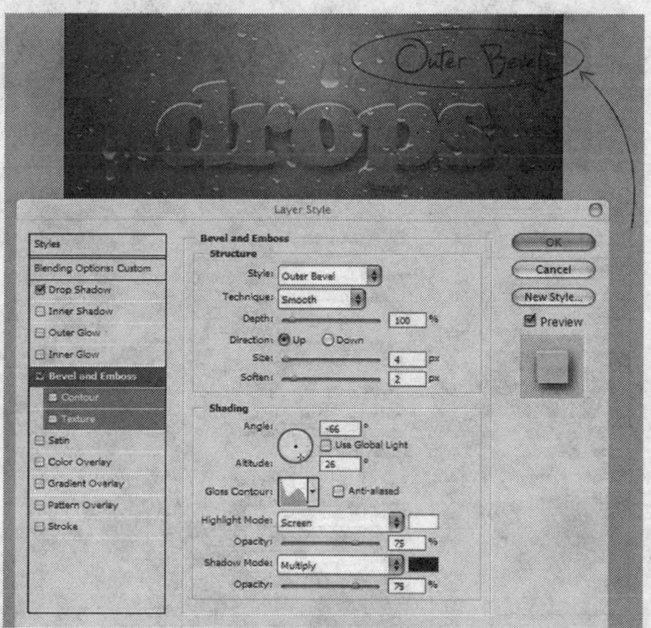

Inner Bevel

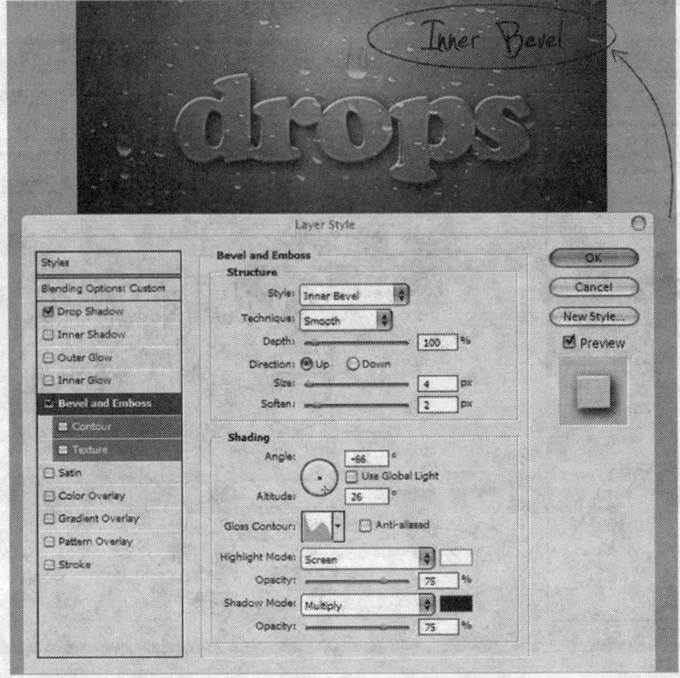

Emboss

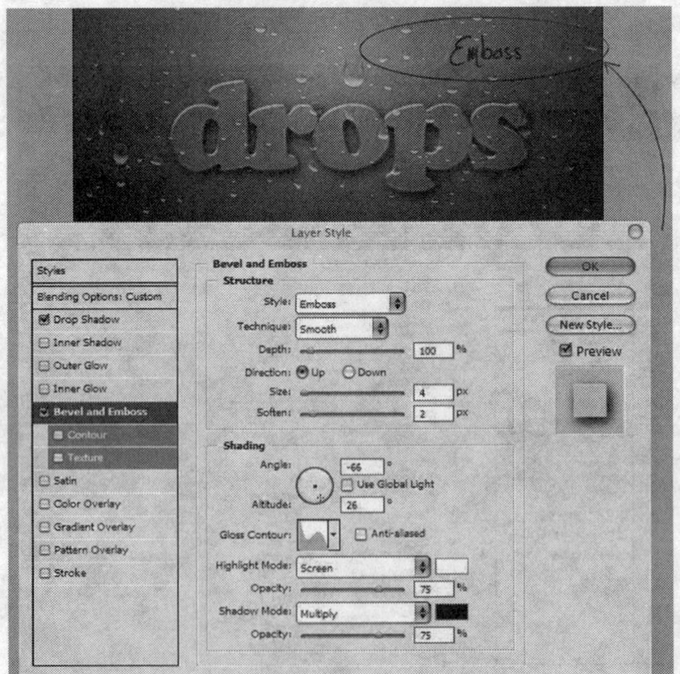

Pillow Emboss

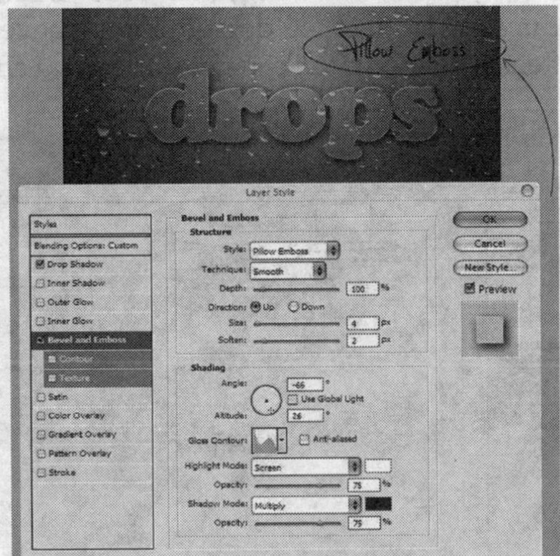

Stroke Emboss

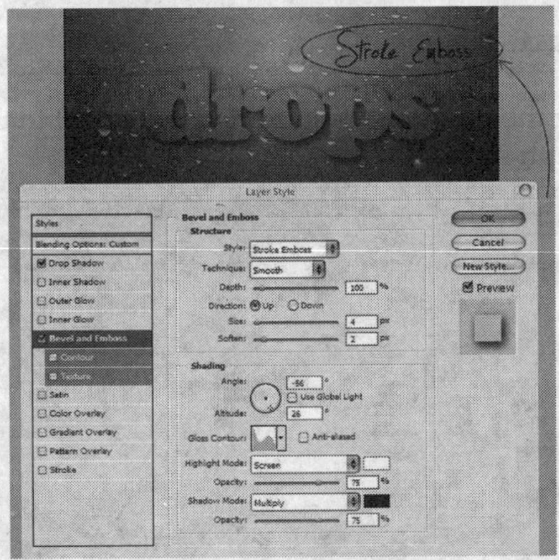

The **Bevel and Emboss** effect has two sub-effects: **Contour** and **Texture**.

Contour allows you to sculpt the shape of the bevel itself, while **Texture** lets you apply a pattern as a bumpy texture to the layer contents.

Select the check box to the left of **Contour** or **Texture** to enable the sub-effect, or click the sub-effect name itself to both enable the sub-effect and edit its options.

The Contour options:

Contour – The contour you choose here affects the shape of the raised and lowered parts of the bevel effect around the edge of the layer contents. Think of the bevel as a 3D shape viewed from above, with the contour being a cross-section of that shape as viewed from the side; if you could cut through the bevel at any point with a saw, you'd see your selected contour shape. The default contour, **Linear**, produces a standard, 45-degree sloping bevel—which is the same as not enabling the **Contour** sub-effect at all—but you can get some great effects with the other presets.

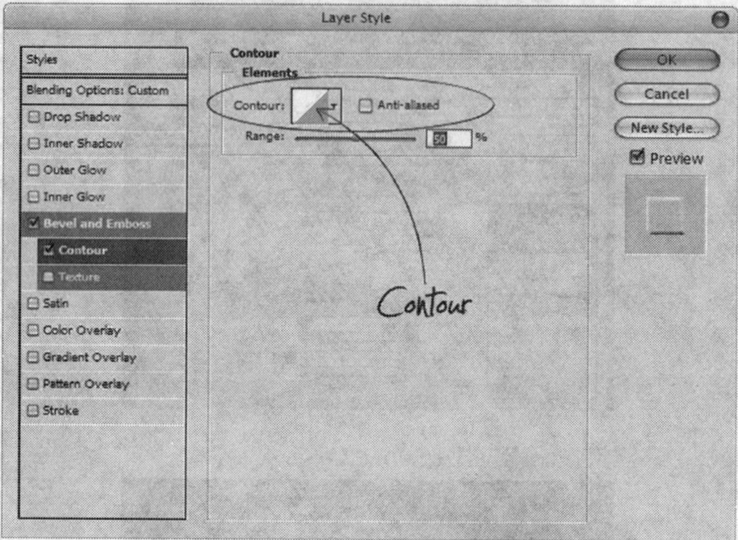

Choose a preset by clicking the downward-pointing arrow next to the box, or create your own contour by clicking the graph in the box.

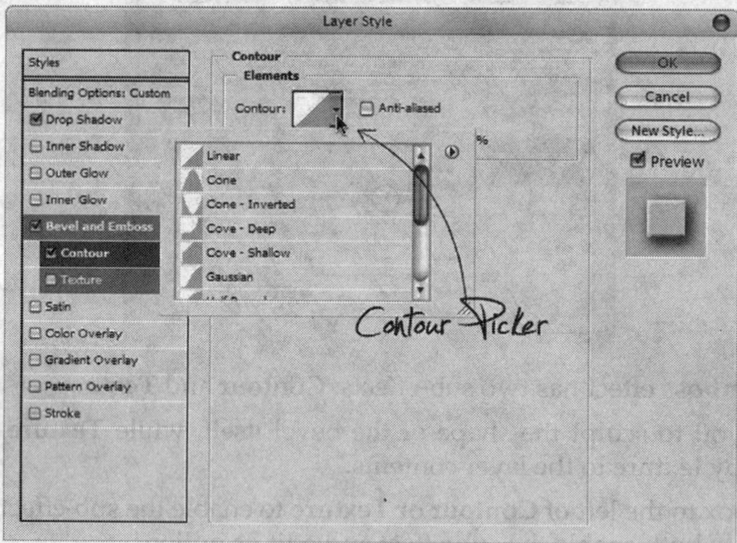

Anti-Aliased – The **Anti-Aliased** option is particularly useful for this effect, because it's very easy to produce quite jagged-looking bevels, especially with some of the spikier contours. Simply select this option to smooth out all those nasty jagged bits, and create a nice smooth beveling effect.

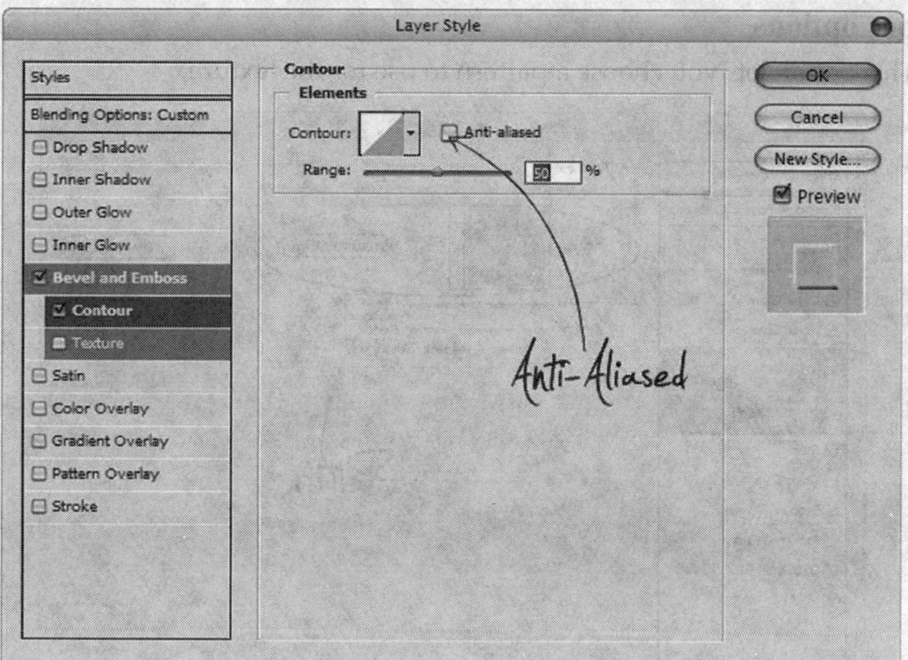

Range – Use this option to adjust the position and size of the contour within the bevel's cross-section. For value of 0, the contour is pushed to one edge of the bevel and only takes up a tiny proportion of the bevel, for value of 100 percent, the contour stretches to fill out twice the width of the bevel.

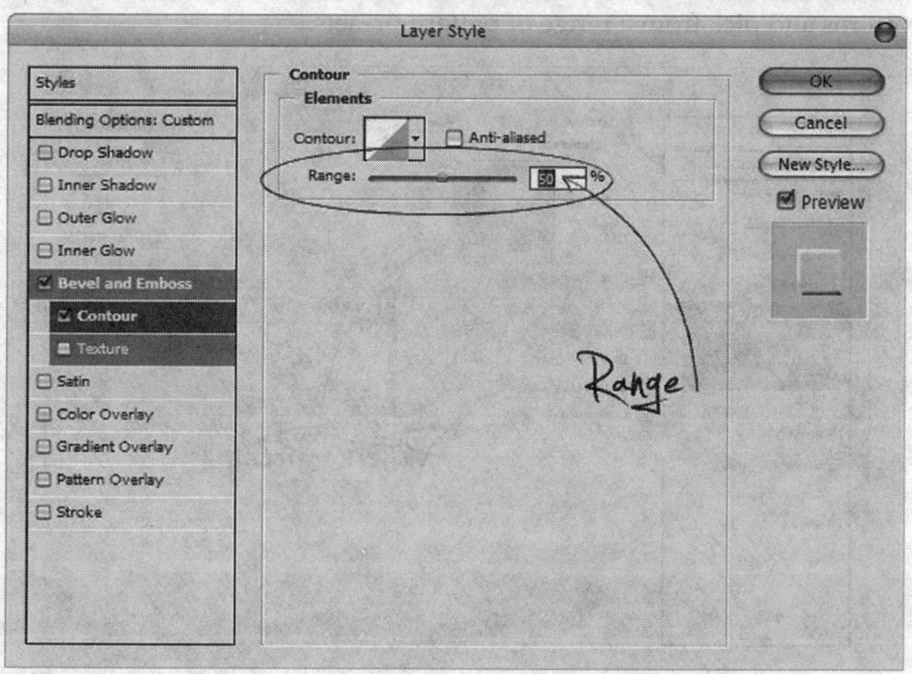

The Texture options

Pattern – This option lets you choose a pattern to use for the texture.

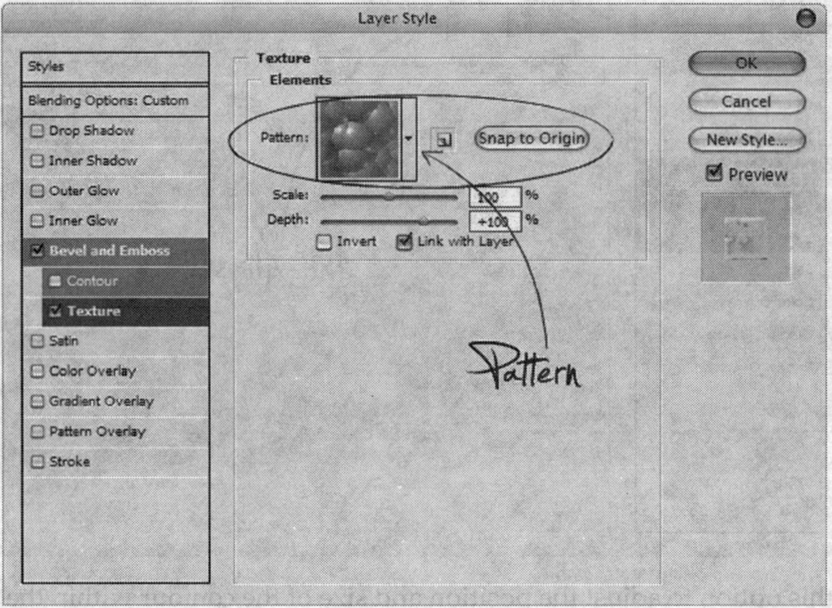

Click the pattern to display the pop-up **Pattern picker**, then click the pattern you want to use. You can also click the triangle in the top right of the **Pattern picker** to bring up the palette menu – this lets you create and delete patterns, change the appearance of patterns in the palette, load and save patterns and pick from a range of pattern presets.

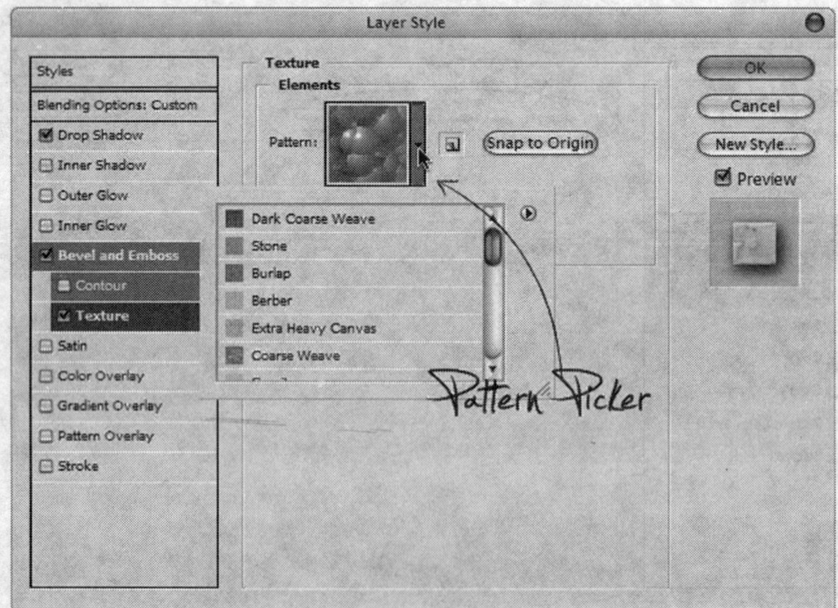

Snap To Origin – If you have moved the texture from its original position by clicking and dragging it in the document window, you can move the texture back to its default position by clicking this button.

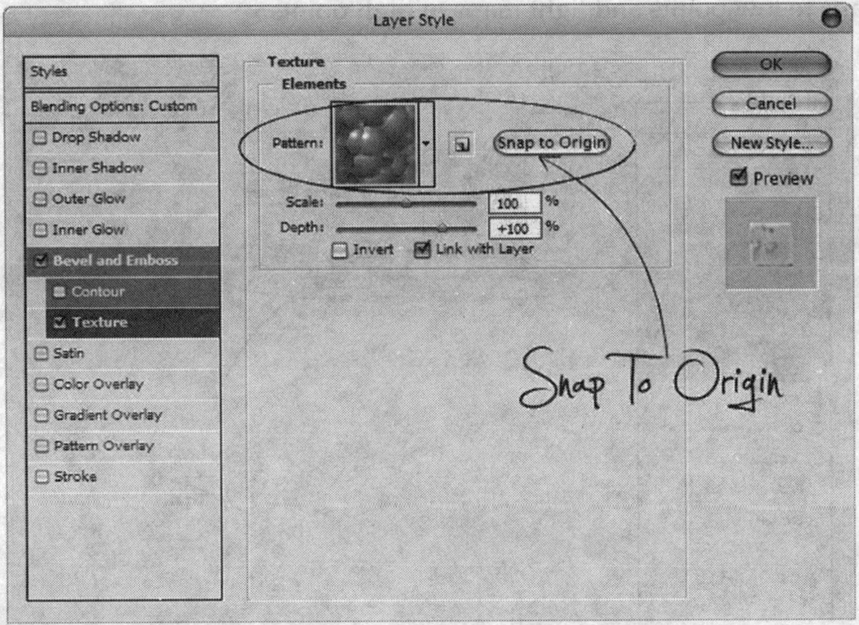

Scale – By clicking and dragging this slider you can control the size of the texture as it appears in the effect. This is useful because the resolution of the pattern probably won't match the resolution of your document.

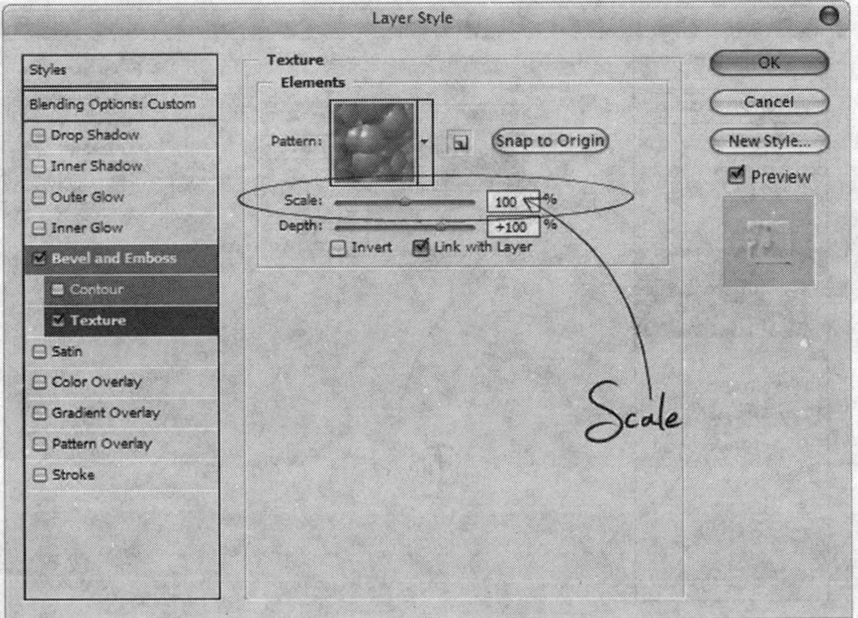

Depth – This option lets you control how much the texture is "raised" or "lowered." Positive values raise the texture, so that dark pixels in the pattern correspond to high points in the texture and light pixels correspond to dark points; negative values reverse this mapping, so that dark maps to low points and light maps to high points.

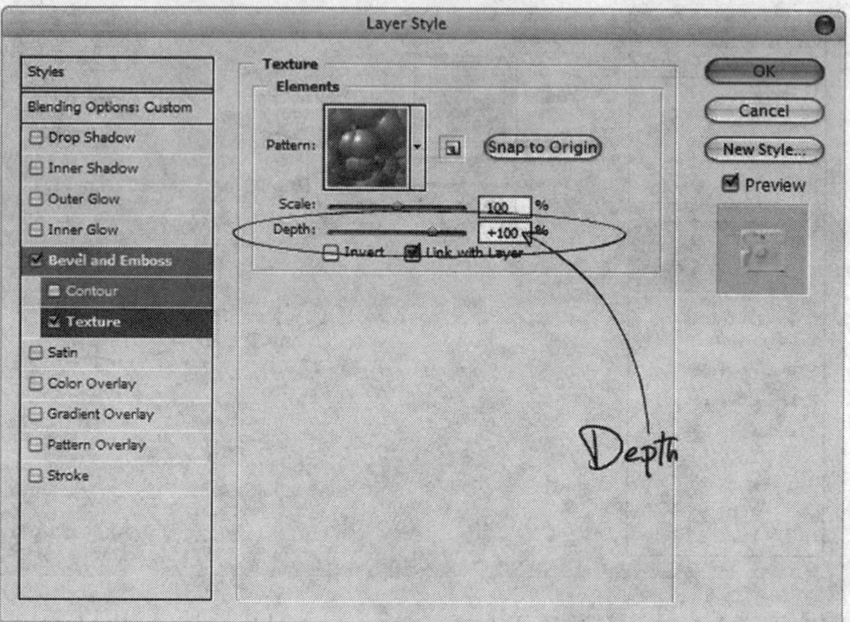

Invert – This option simply inverts the high and low points of the texture, so that dark pixels of the pattern map to low points in the texture and light pixels map to high points.

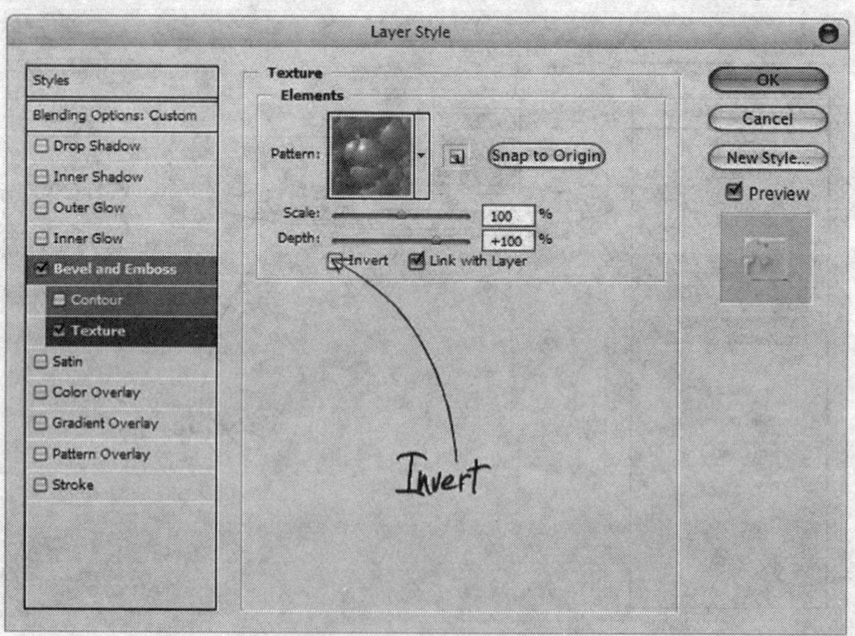

Link with Layer – Selecting this option causes the texture to move with the layer contents when using the **Move tool**, which is usually what you want to happen. Disable this option, and the texture remains fixed relative to the document window.

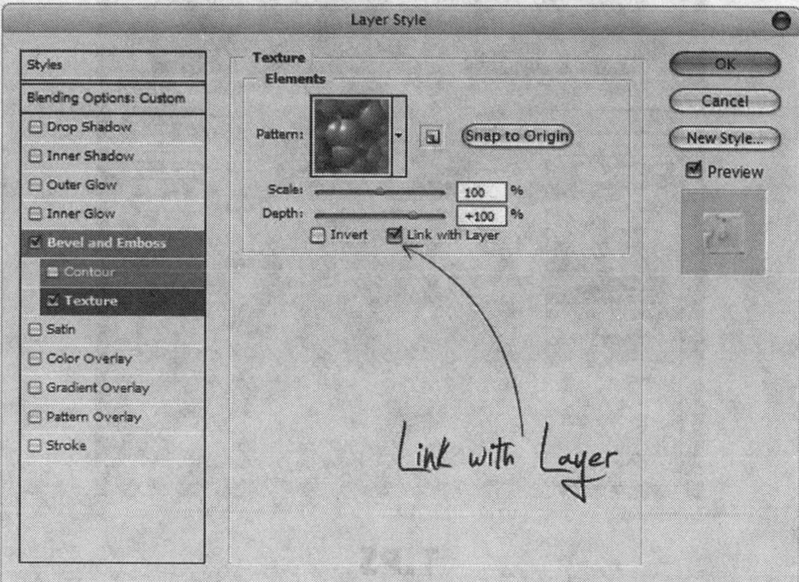

Examples of **Contour and Texture** in action:

In the first example the **Rounded Steps** contour is applied to the text using the **Contour** sub-effect, while the second example uses the **Texture** sub-effect to apply the **Bubbles pattern** as a texture to the text.

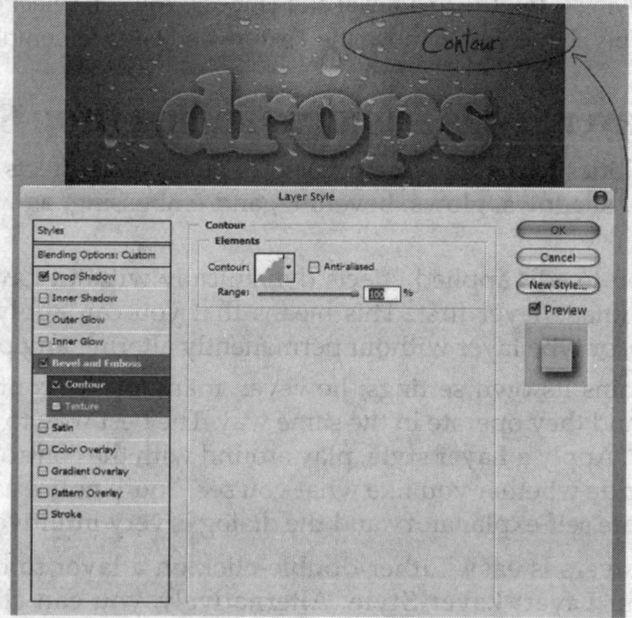

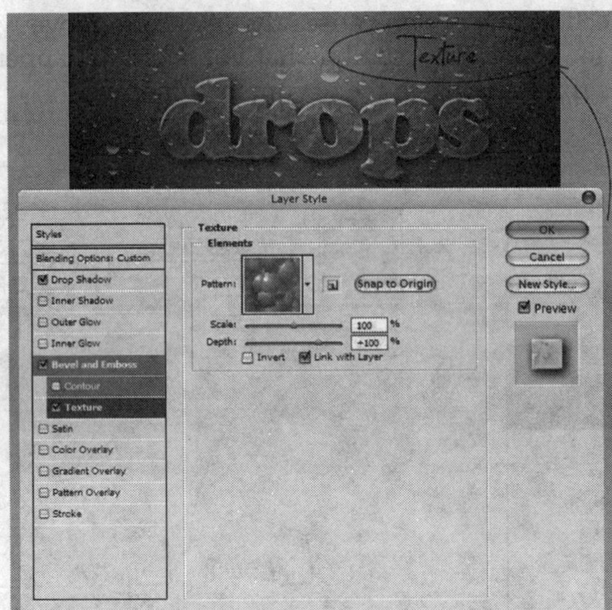

TIPS

1. You can apply **Bevel and Emboss** effects to text layers as well as shape layers. In fact, the effect is probably most successful with text, especially the emboss options.
2. The shape of the Bevel, as defined by the chosen **Contour**, is most obvious when using the **Chisel Hard** technique.
3. When you're applying a **Texture** to a **Bevel and Emboss**, you can select the **Link with Layer** checkbox. This allows you to move the **Texture** and layer in complete unison.

Working with Layer Styles – understanding Drop Shadows

Adobe Photoshop includes **Layer Styles**, a number of automated effects that you can apply to layers, including drop shadows, glows, bevelling, and embossing, as well as a colour filling effect.

Layer styles allow you to edit applied effects dynamically without having to create a smart object version of the image layer first. This means that you can apply editable effects to a selected image, shape, or type layer without permanently altering any pixels.

Each layer style contains its own settings; however, many of the controls are available for more than one effect and they operate in the same way. The best way to become familiar with them is to experiment. Apply a **Layer style**, play around with the control settings, and use the **Preview** option to decide whether you like what you see. You'll notice as you experiment that many of the controls are self-explanatory and the dialog is very intuitive.

Applying effects to layers is easy. Either double-click on a layer to open the **Layer Style** dialog, or go to menu **Layer>Layer Style**. Alternatively, you can click **Add Layer Style** button at the bottom of the Layers palette (the one with the *fx* icon), and choose an effect from the list.

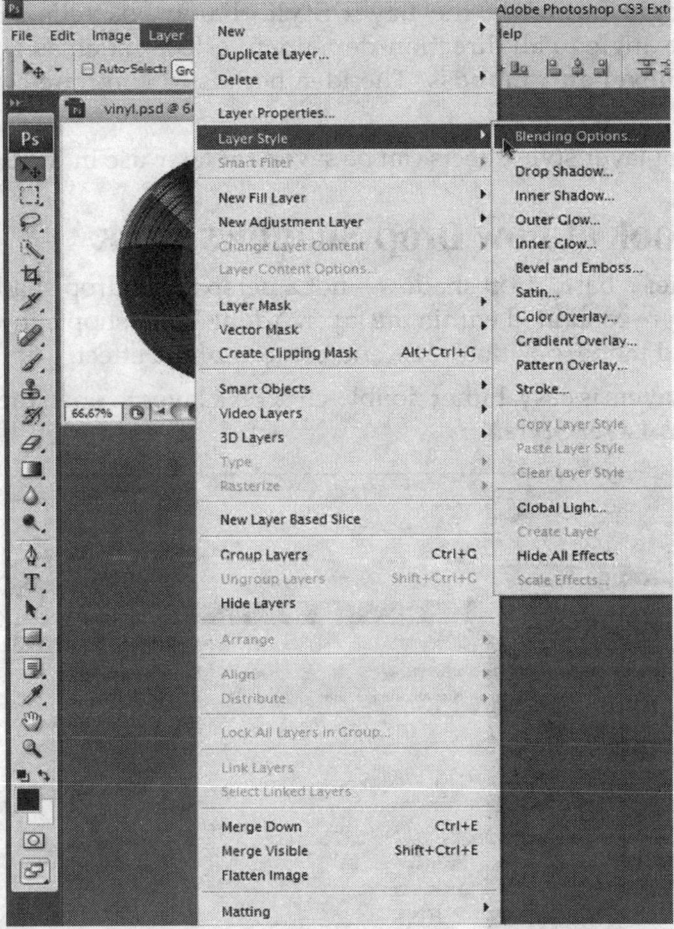

Some things to take note of when working with layer style effects and the **Layer Style** dialog:

- **Layer styles** cannot be applied to the **Background layer**.
- **Layer styles** can be applied to only a single selected layer at a time – not to multiple selected layers or to layer groups.
- **Layer styles** are attached to the layer. Therefore, when you move the layer in the **Layers palette**, the effects tag along.
- Type layers remain editable even after a layer style effect is applied.
- **Layer styles** can be copied from one layer to another.
- Adobe Photoshop displays applied **Layer style** effects as items in the **Layers palette**.
- Clicking the eye icon next to each effect's name in the **Layers palette** temporarily disables the layer style. Click the eye next to the word **Effects** to temporarily disable all the applied layer styles for that layer.

- Lowering the **Fill** percentage in the **Layers palette** reduces the **Opacity** of the layer, but not the applied **Layer styles**.
- **The Global Light** option in the **Layer Style** dialog box tells Adobe Photoshop to apply the same angle to all direction-dependent effects, such as **Drop Shadow, Inner Shadow**, and **Bevel and Emboss**. The idea here is to simulate consistent real-world lighting.
- Combinations of layer style effects can be saved for later use in the **Styles palette**.

Take a close look at how Drop Shadows work

Drop Shadow applies a basic drop shadow—not a perspective drop shadow—to the images, type, or shapes that are contained within the layer. Adobe Photoshop allows you to specify the colour, opacity, blend mode, position, size, and contour of the effect.

Applying effects to layers is easy. Either double-click on a layer to open the **Layer Style** dialog, or go to menu **Layer>Layer Style**.

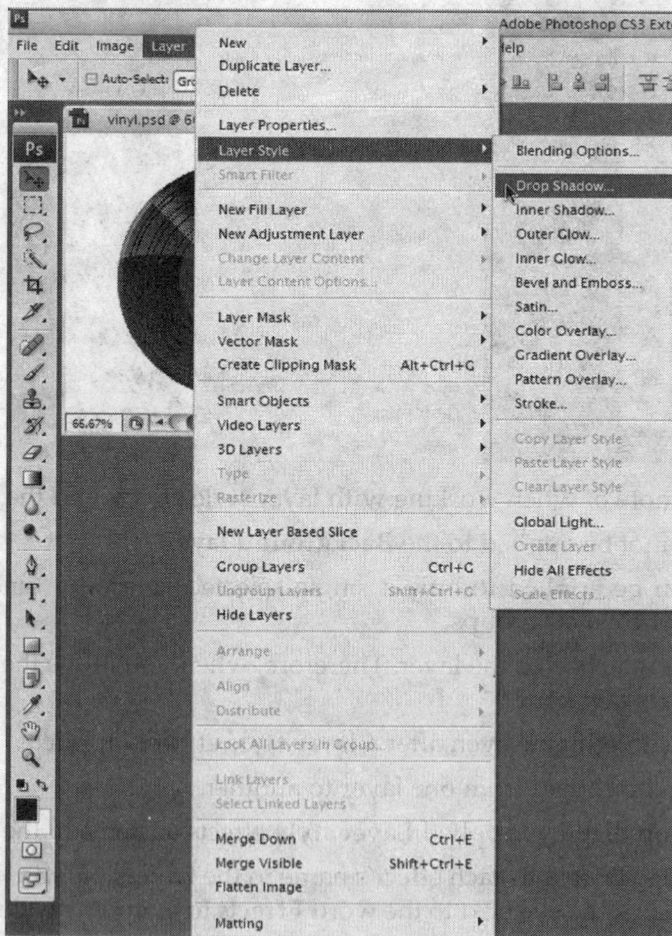

Alternatively, you can click **Add Layer Style** button at the bottom of the **Layers palette** (the one with the *fx* icon), and choose an effect from the list.

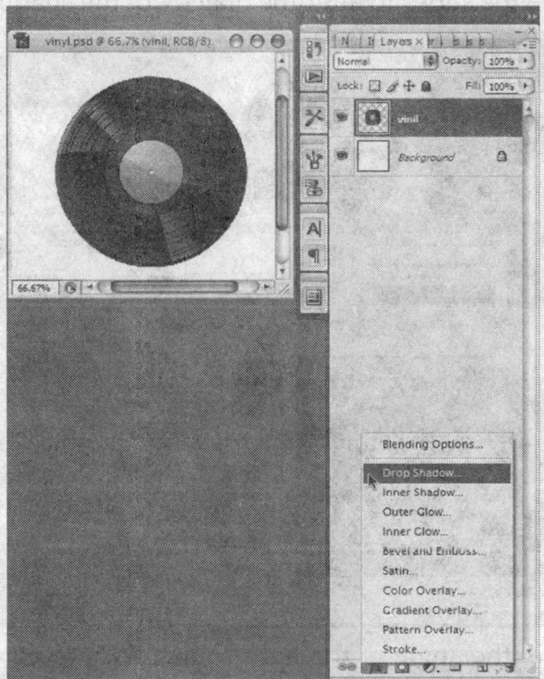

Once the **Layer Style** window opens, pick the **Drop Shadow**, apply settings and click **OK**.

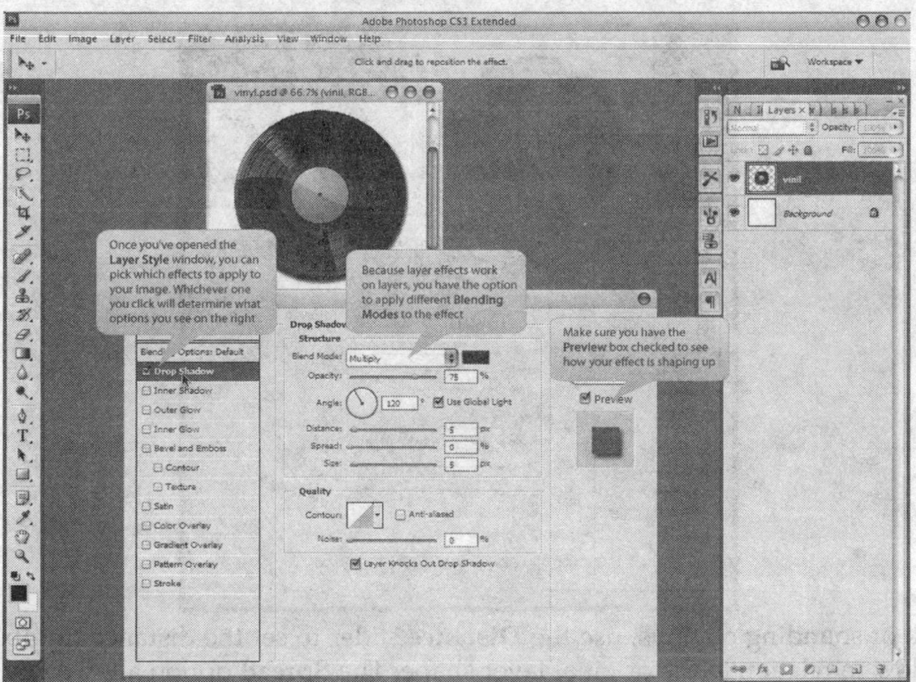

The top part of the **Drop Shadow** settings allow you to set a blending mode for the effect as well as the colour of the shadow. Just double-click the black rectangle to bring up the **Colour Picker**. You can also move the slider to alter the opacity of the shadow.

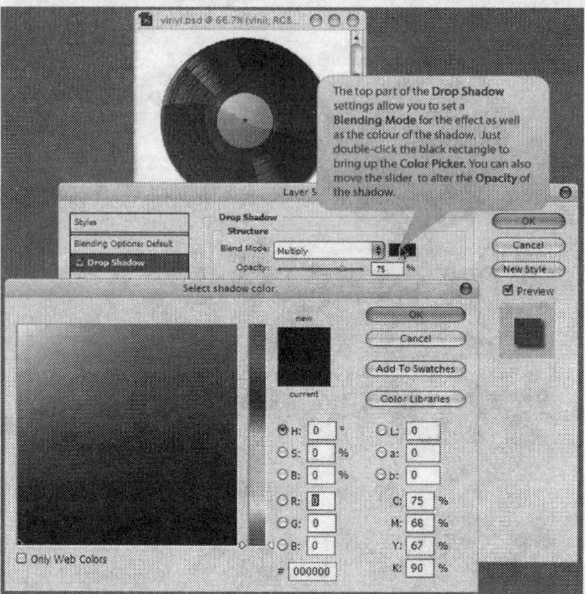

Use the **Angle** circle to set the angle of the light source. Whatever angle you choose will be in relation to the original layer shapes. If you keep the Use **Global Light** option checked, the effect will use the current angle setting from **Layer>Layer Style>Global Light**.

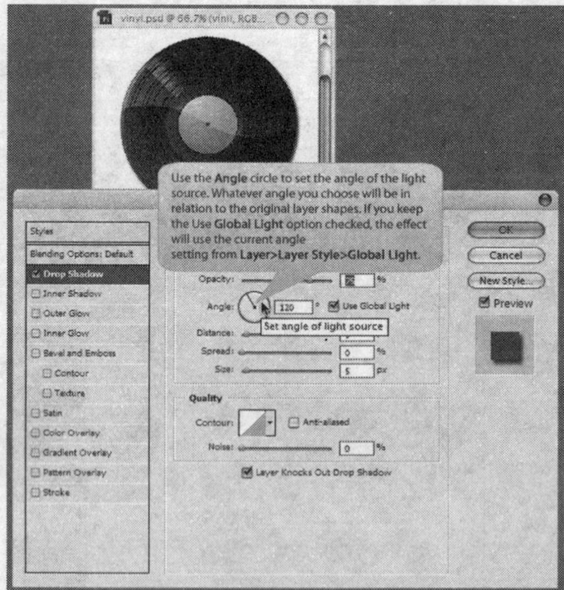

At the risk of sounding obvious, use the **Distance** slider to set the distance (in pixels) of the drop shadow in relation to the original layer shape. The **Spread** option allows you to control where the shadow starts to fade, while the Size slider controls the size of the shadow, again in pixels.

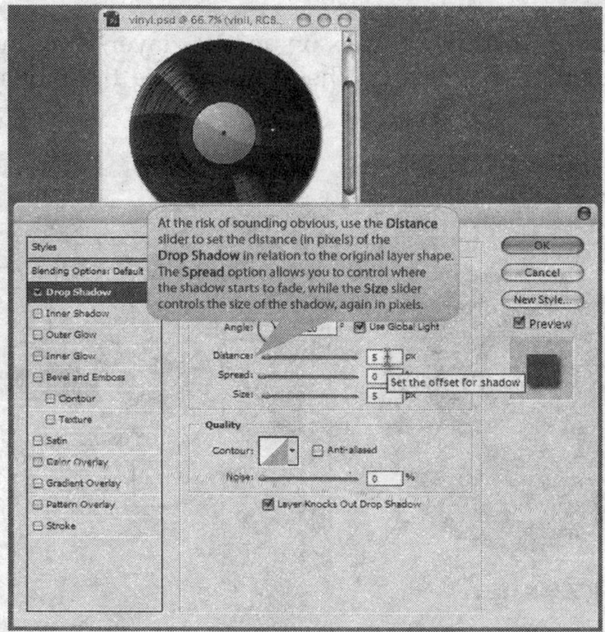

The **Quality** area of the dialog allows you to set different contours. These beauties control the edge shape of the shadow and can dramatically alter the effect. Keep the **Anti-aliased box** checked to soften the edges between the shadow and other parts of the image, and also experiment with the **Noise** slider.

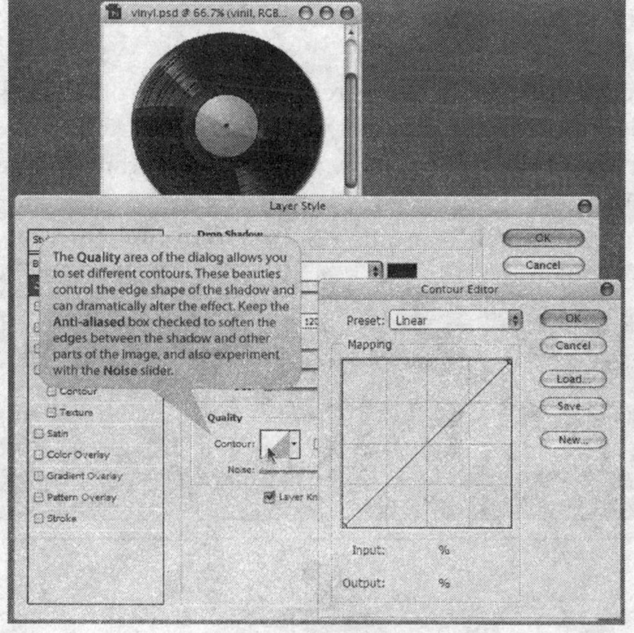

When working with **Drop Shadows**, it's worth keeping the **Layer Knocks Out Drop Shadow** option checked. This will prevent the shadow from showing through layer pixels that have a low **Fill** opacity

Tip: To use the same **Drop Shadow** settings on another layer, drag the **Drop Shadow** layer in the **Layers palette** to the other layer. When you release the mouse button, the shadow attributes are applied.

Points to Remember

- ☆ choose the "Once" option for the more dangerous areas and the "Continuous" for the safer areas
- ☆ used the "Hue" mode for a more subtle replacement (the others will create pretty drastic results)
- ☆ used the "Colour" mode in combination with a less vibrant colour to enhance the pink colour of the shirt
- ☆ used the "Background Swatch" sampling option to resolve the grey areas

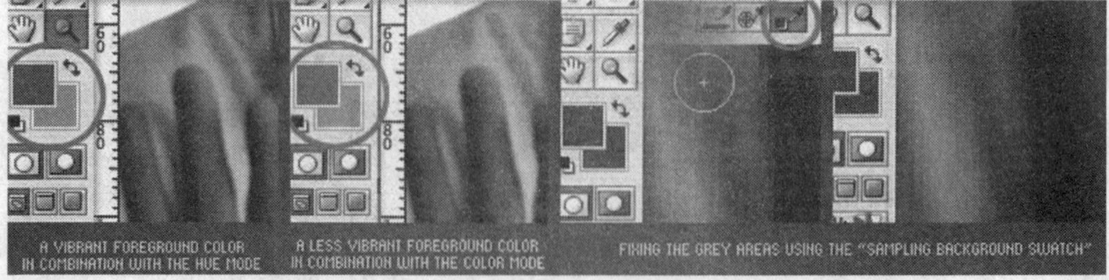

Adobe Illustrator

Illustrator is a vector drawing program. It is often used to draw illustrations, cartoons, diagrams, charts and logos. Unlike bitmap images that store information in a grid of dots, Illustrator uses mathematical equations to draw out the shapes. This makes vector graphics scalable without the loss of resolution.

Advantages of Vector Graphics

- Scalable without resolution loss
- Lines are crisp and sharp at any sizes
- Print at high resolution
- Smaller file size
- Good for drawing illustrations

Disadvantages of vector graphics

- Drawings tend to look flat and cartoon
- Hard to produce photo realistic drawings

Common Uses for Illustrator

- Designing Logos

- ❑ Drawing Maps

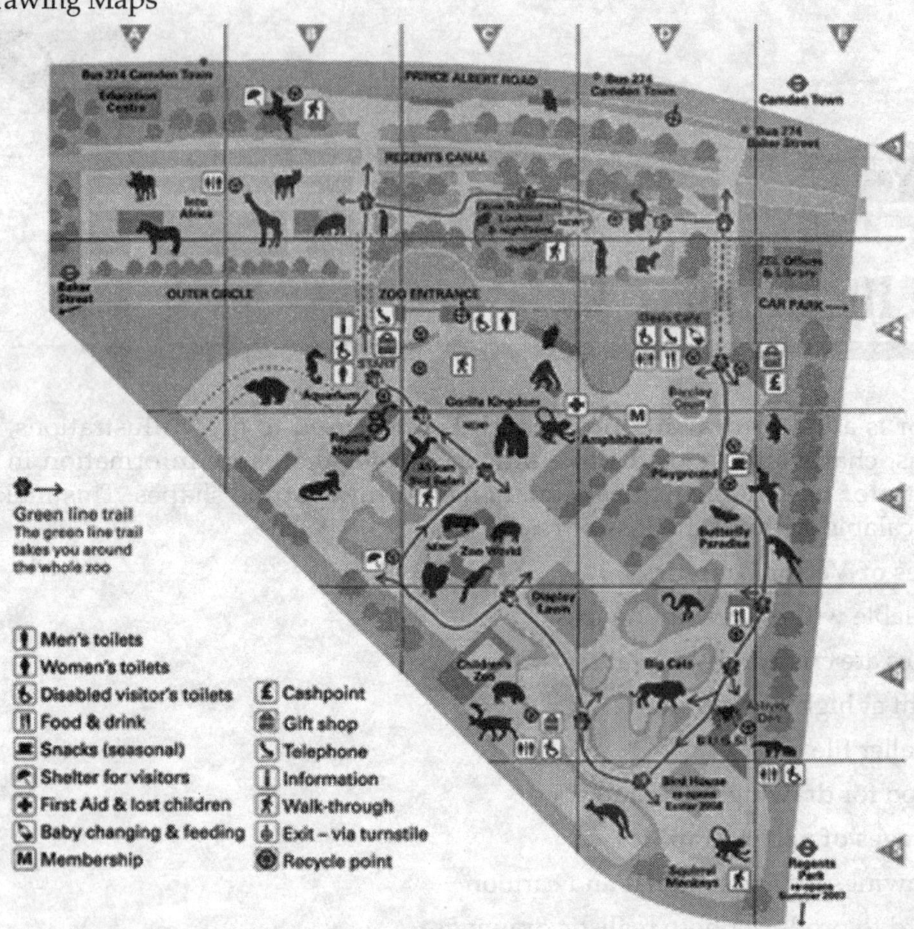

- ❑ Drawing Illustrations

- Infographics

- Photorealistic Drawings

- Packaging Design

These are just a few examples of what Illustrator can do. If you have experience with Photoshop, you can bring your illustrations into Photoshop and enhance its effects. That's how a professional does it. In the next discussions, I will be covering the basics of Illustrator so that you can produce your first vector art!

Getting Started in Illustrator

Let's learn to start Working in Illustrator

Create New Document

Go **File>New Document** to create your first document. Type in a Name for the document and click Advanced to select RGB for Colour Mode as we will be working for the screen. Click Ok after that.

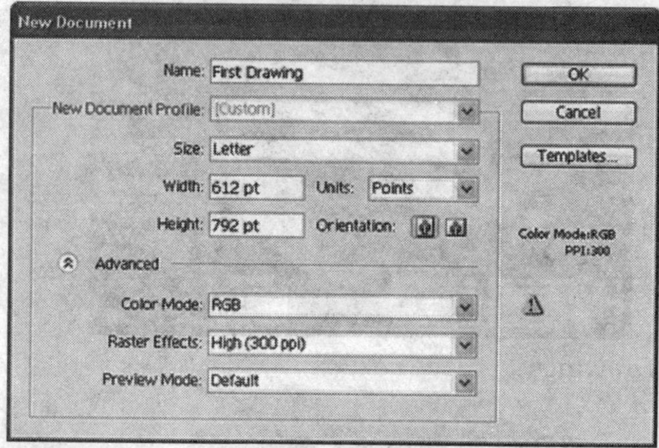

Illustrator Workspace

Below is the workspace and some common terms for calling it. If you are using the Adobe Illustrator CS3, you will notice to new design for Floating Palette. The rest looks about the same.

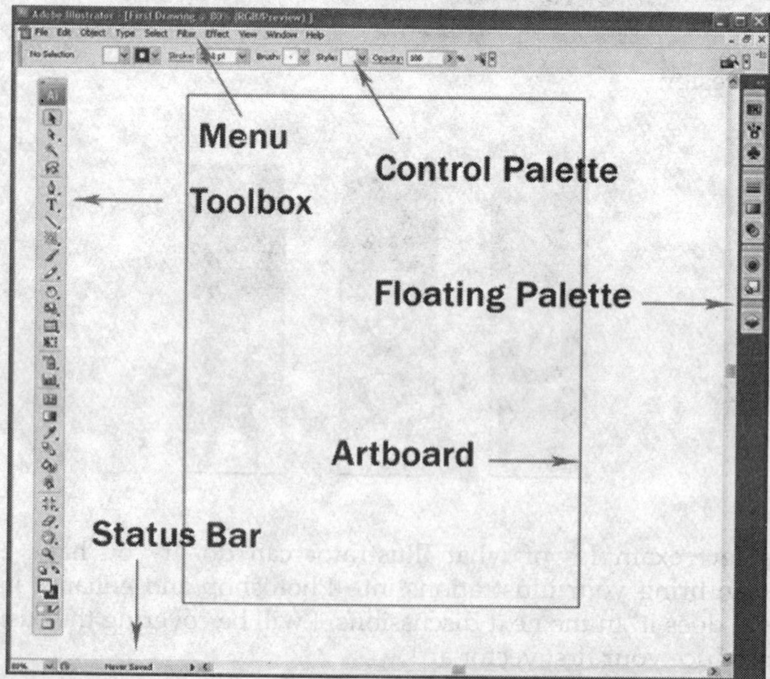

Toolbox

This is the handy toolbox which we will use most often. By default, it comes in one single column as shown in the screenshot below. To switch it back to the old 2 columns toolbox, you can simply click the top left mini arrow to toggle it into 2 columns. Some of the tools like Rectangle have more tools hidden. To expand, just click and hold the icon to reveal all the similar tools under that group.

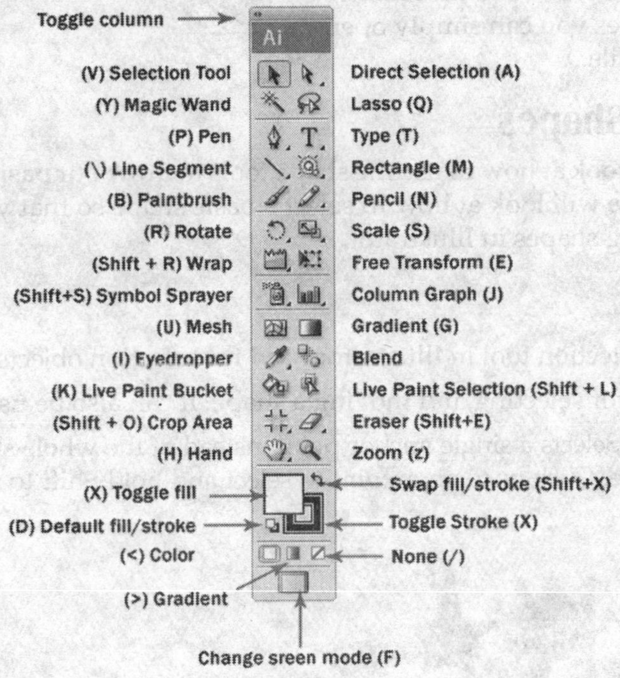

Floating Palette

This is the floating palette which contains properties for our shapes. It is commonly used for changing colours and stroke width.

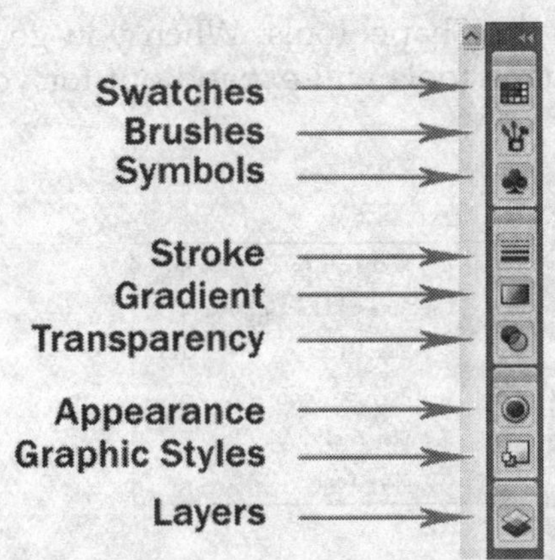

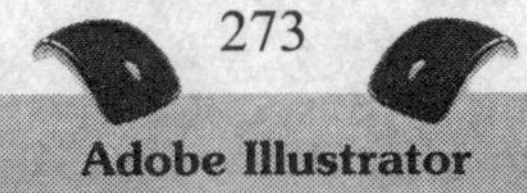

Saving AI Files

Let's select the type and click on the art-board and type some text. After that go to **File>Save.** Select Adobe Illustrator (*.AI) for file type and name it "First Drawing". Click Ok after that. Leave the rest of the settings at default. You have successfully saved your first file. To make any more changes you can simply open the Adobe Illustrator file.

Illustrator ROCKS!

Drawing Basic Shapes

In this lesson, we will look at how to use the shape tools to draw our basic shapes in illustrator. But before we start, we will look at how to select a basic shape so that you have no problems in selecting and editing shapes in Illustrator.

Selection Tools

There are 2 types of selection tool in Illustrator used for selection objects.

Selection Tool: Used for selecting and moving a shape. It can also be used to resize a shape.

Direct Selection Tool: Selects a single anchor point instead of the whole shape. Used for editing anchor point of a shape. Click once on a point to select and hold Shift to select multiple anchor points.

Selection Tool

Direct Selection Tool

Shape Tools

Now we will move on to the Shape Tools. When you go to the Tool Palette and hold the Rectangle Tool, a list of shape tools will expand out for you to pick. We will start with the default Rectangle Tool.

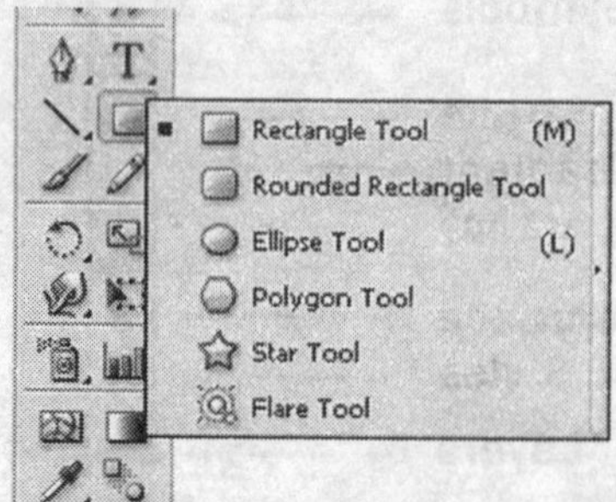

Understanding Fill & Stroke

Click and drag out a Rectangle as shown in the figure. By default, it has a white fill and black stroke. (Stroke is the border of the shape)

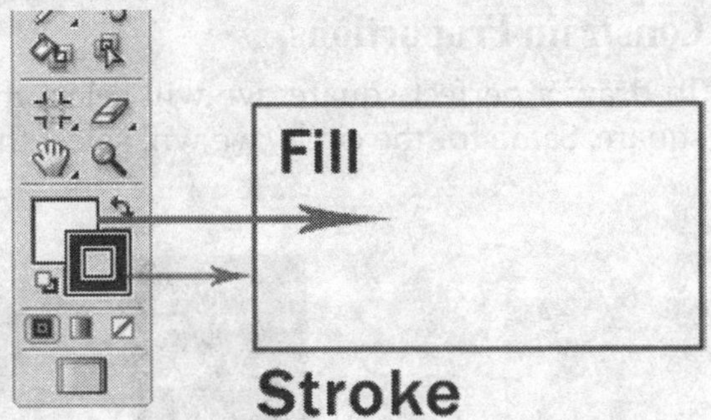

Changing Fill Colour

Let's start changing the fill colour for the rectangle. Double click the Fill from the Tool Palette. It will pop up the Colour Picker. Drag the slider to blue and select a deep blue colour. Click Ok after that.

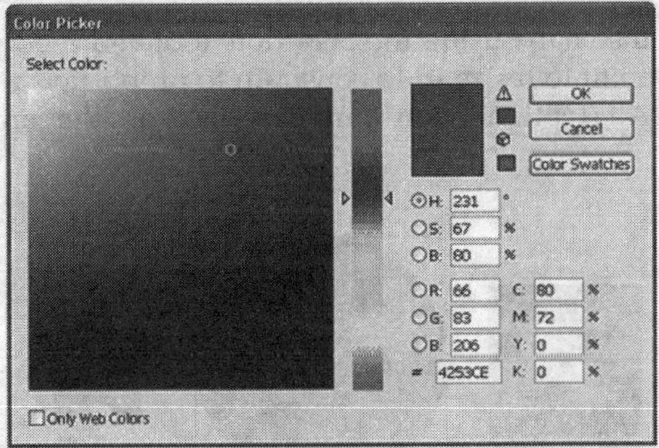

Removing Stroke

Click the Stroke in the Tool Palette once to swap it above Fill. Click the 'None' icon boxed up in red to set the Stroke to None. The black stroke will disappear.

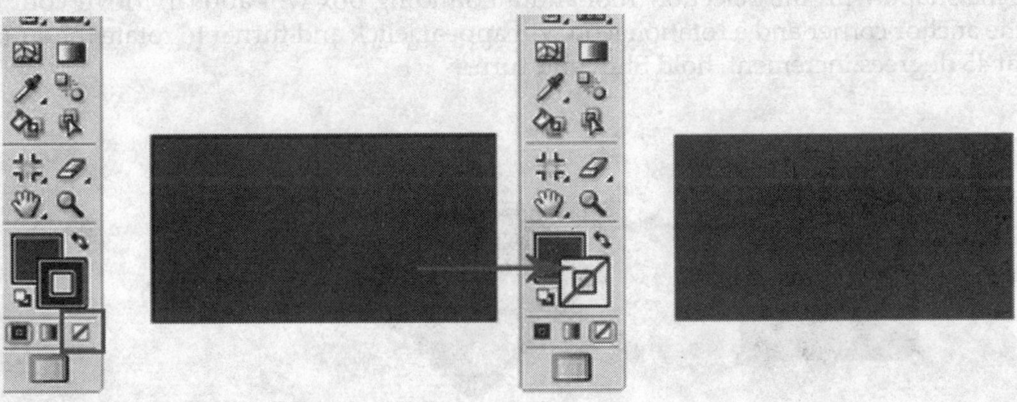

Constrain Proportions

To draw a perfect square, we will select the Rectangle Tool. Hold Shift and drag to draw a square. Same for the circle, we will select the Ellipse Tool and hold Shift to drag out a circle.

Hold Shift to constrain proportion

Resizing Shapes

To resize shapes, select the shape using the Selection Tool and a bounding box will appear. Drag the corner anchor point to resize it. To constrain to proportion while resizing, hold Shift as you resize. Also hold Alt/Option if you want to resize from the same position.

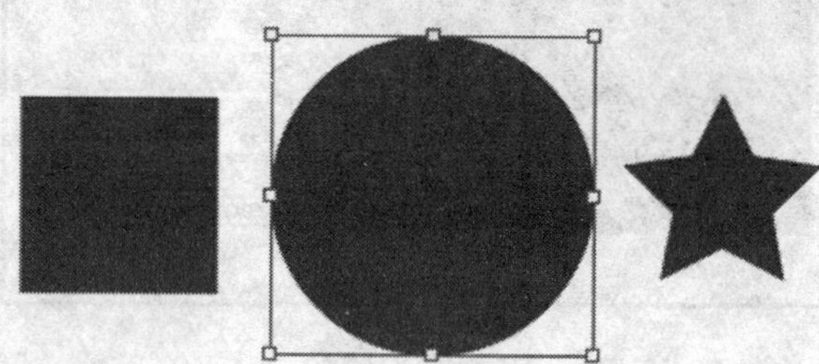

Rotating Shapes

Select the shape with the Selection Tool and a bounding box will appear. Move your cursor near the anchor corner and a rotation icon will appear, click and turn it to rotate the square. To snap at 45 degrees increment, hold Shift and turn.

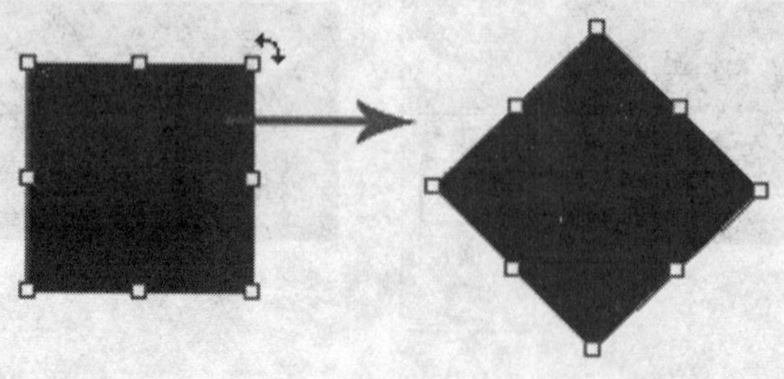

More Options for Shape Tools

Select the Star Tool. Click once on the art-board and an option will pop up. Enter the same values below and click Ok. It will draw a star burst shape. This method can be used to bring out more options for shape tools.

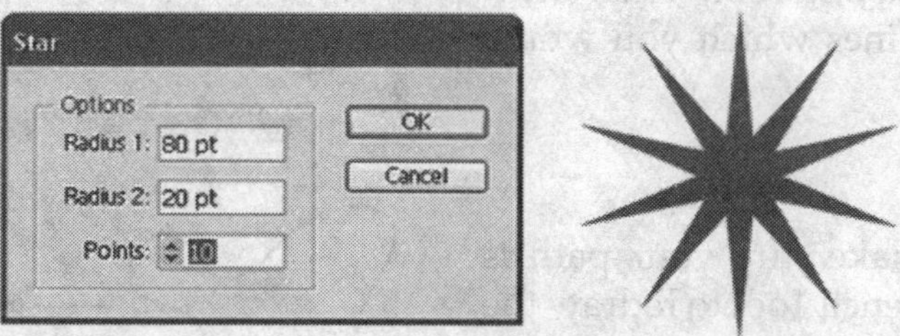

Almost all the objects found in our daily life can be built from combining using the basic shape tools. Later, we will learn about Compound Paths which will help us create more complicated shapes by adding and subtracting from the basic shapes.

Drawing with Pencil Tool

We can quickly draw shapes and lines using the Pencil Tool. This lesson will show you some of the tricks in drawing smooth and fluid lines.

Drawing a Line

Select the pencil tool and click and drag to draw a free hand line drawing.

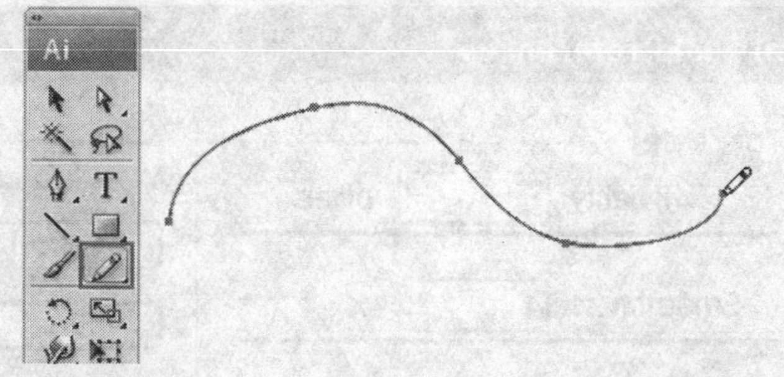

Closing Paths with Pencil Tool

To close a path, hold Alt as your Pencil Tool reaches the start point. A circle icon will appear next to the Pencil Tool to indicate path closure.

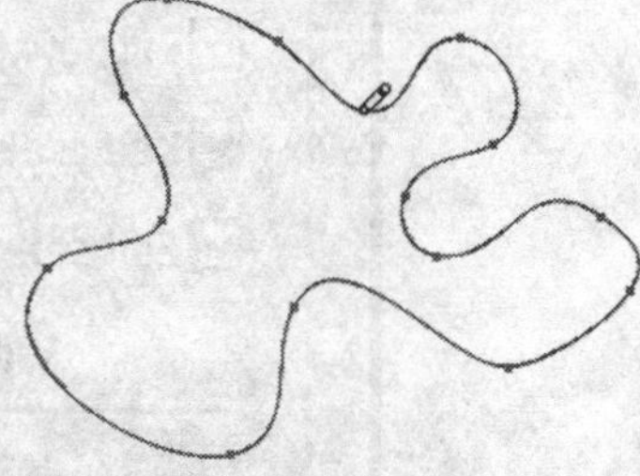

Smoothing Jaggy Lines

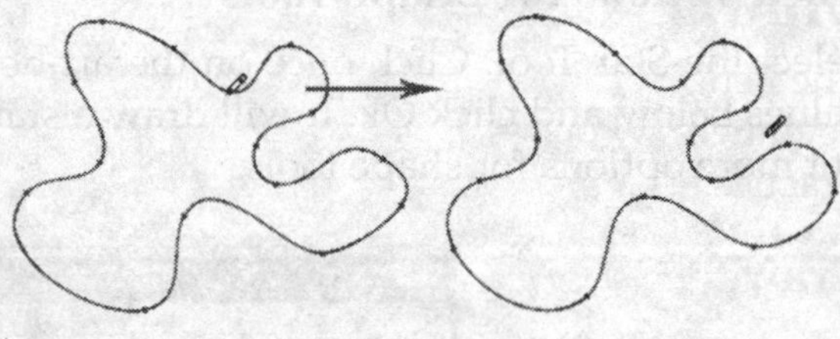

Normally when you draw with the Pencil Tool, the path looks jaggy. To smoothen the parts that are jaggy, simply hold Alt to turn the Pencil Tool to Smooth Tool. Then draw over the area of the lines which you would like to smoothen.

Reshaping Path

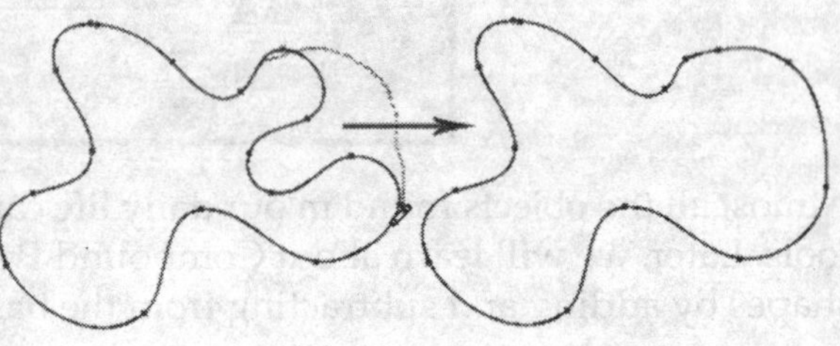

To reshape a path, make sure your path is selected and use the Pencil Tool to redraw the parts you would like to reshape. Note that the start and end path must be close to the original path to make it work.

Pencil Tool Preferences

You can turn on the Pencil Tool Preferences by double clicking on the Pencil Tool. You can change the fidelity and smoothness to find a combination that works for you.

Fidelity: Determines how close the path is drawn to your mouse movement. Set it at a higher fidelity if you are not good at drawing with your mouse.

Smoothness: The higher you set for smoothness, the less anchor point it produces. Thus, producing a smoother line.

Pencil Tool Preferences

Tolerances

Fidelity: 4 pixels

Smoothness: 4 %

OK

Cancel

Reset

Options

☐ Fill new pencil strokes

☑ Keep selected

☑ Edit selected paths

Within: 12 pixels

Drawing with Pen Tool

The Pen Tool will be the hardest tool to learn in Illustrator. It usually takes weeks to learn and beginners always end up in frustration while figuring how it works. So don't give up and practice it every day and soon you will be able to draw any shape.

Drawing Straight Lines

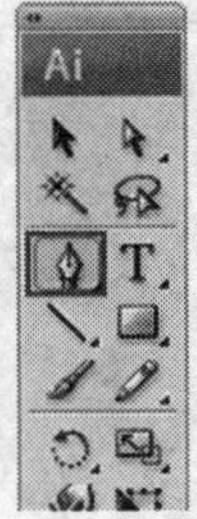

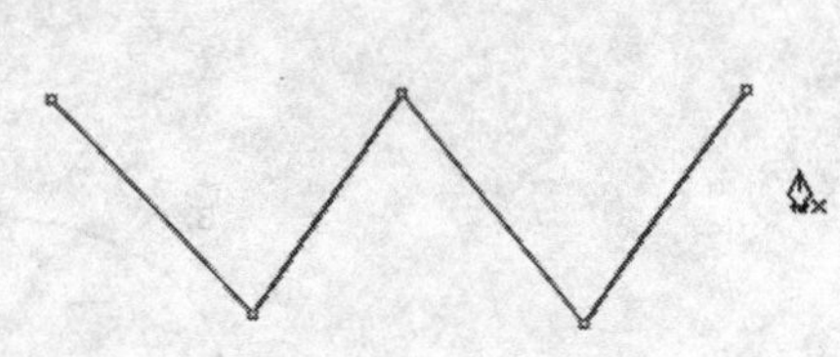

Select the Pen Tool and click once to add the first anchor point. Move your mouse to the next position and click again to create the second point. The two anchor points will be connected together. Continue doing this to create a W shape as shown. To draw a new line, click the Selection Tool (The Black Arrow Icon) and click back the Pen Tool again.

Closing a Path

To close a path, click back the starting point to close the shape.

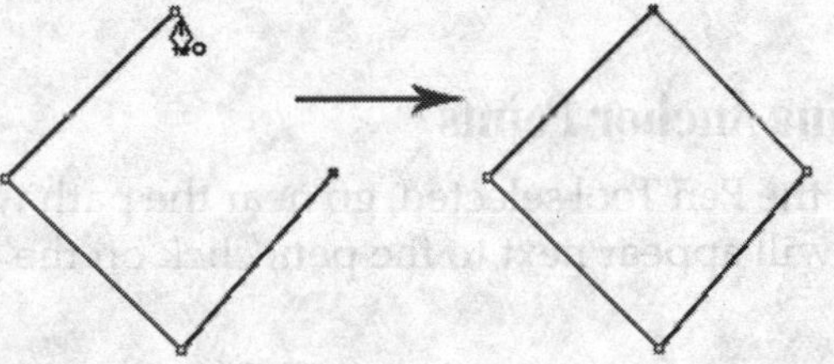

Drawing a Curved Line

Click and drag to put out the handles to create a smooth anchor point.

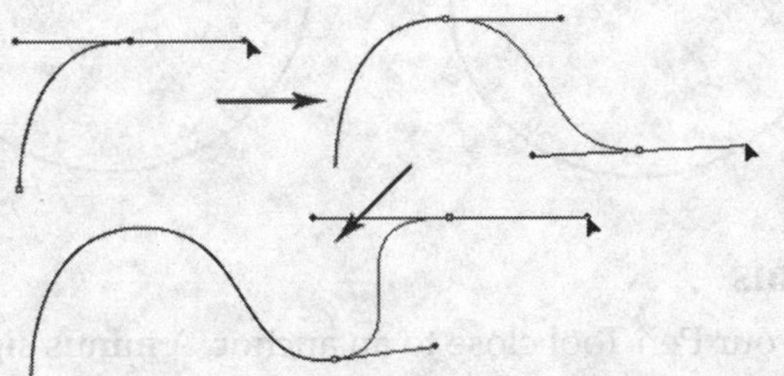

Changing Path Directions

Click and drag to create a smooth anchor point. Without releasing your mouse, hold Alt and drag the handle up to change the path direction.

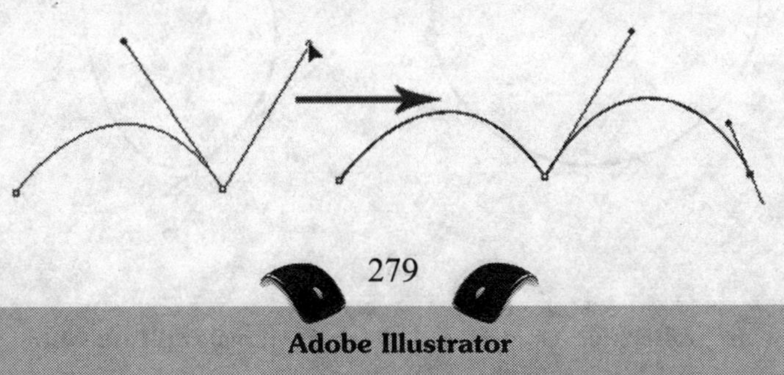

Drawing a Circular Path

Click and drag to create a smooth anchor point. Continue adding points and click back the starting point to close the path.

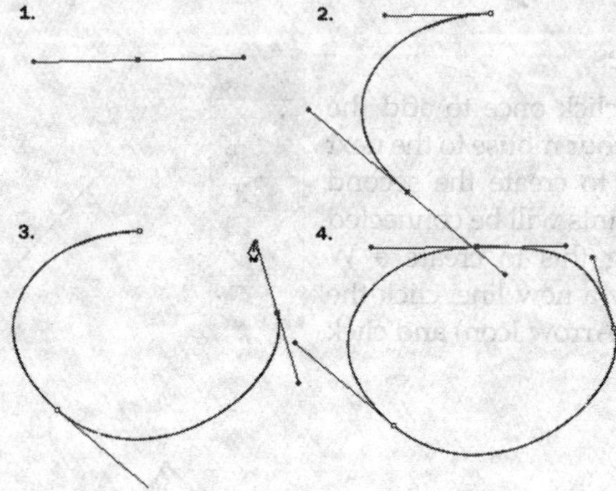

Adding Anchor Points

With the Pen Tool selected, go near the path where you want to add a new anchor point. A plus sign will appear next to the pen, click on the path to create a new anchor point.

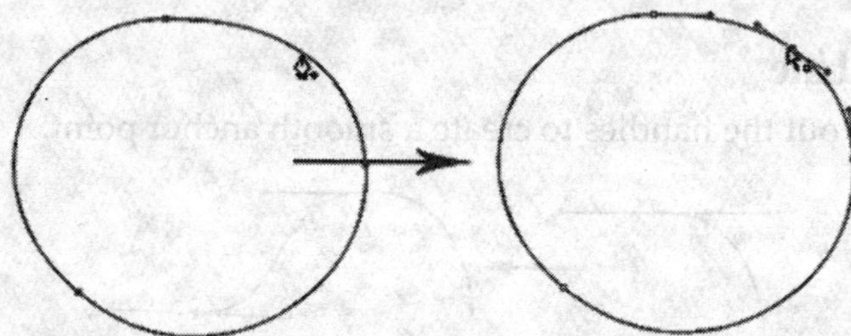

Removing Anchor Points

To remove point, move your Pen Tool close to an anchor. A minus sign will appear next to the pen. Click on the anchor point to delete it.

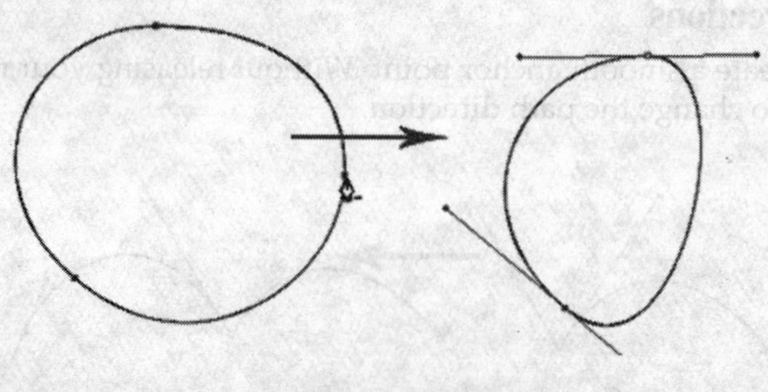

Converting Anchor Points

To convert a smooth anchor point to a sharp anchor point, move your Pen Tool near the anchor and hold Alt and your Pen Tool will change to an arrow shape. Click on the smooth anchor to convert it to an anchor point. Click and drag on the anchor point again to change it back to a smooth anchor point.

Moving Anchor Points

Select the Direct Selection Tool and click and on anchor you want to move. Click and drag to change positions.

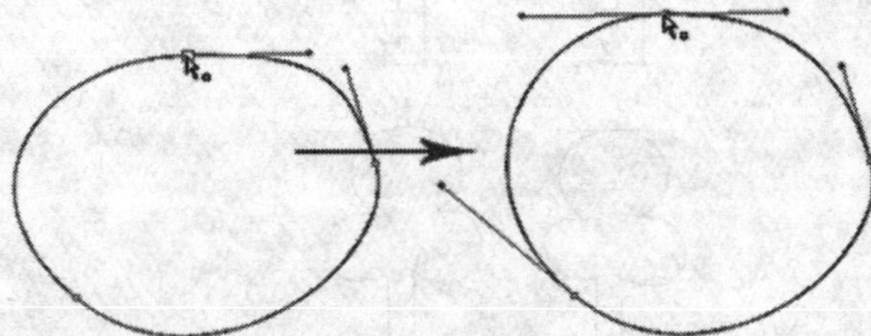

Changing Anchor Directions

With the Pen Tool, you can quickly change the anchor directions. Hold Ctrl to quickly change the Pen Tool to Direction Selection Tool. Select the anchor point you want to edit. The anchor handle will appear. Now release Ctrl and hold Alt to change it to Convert Anchor Tool. Click and drag the handles to change the direction.

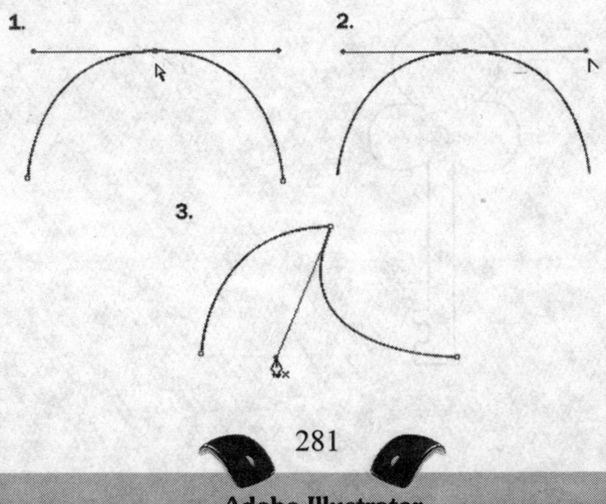

Drawing an Old Key

After learning the concepts of how the Pen Tool works, we will apply what you have learnt to create this ancient old key shape. For the right angles, hold Shift before adding anchor point to constrain it to 90-degree.

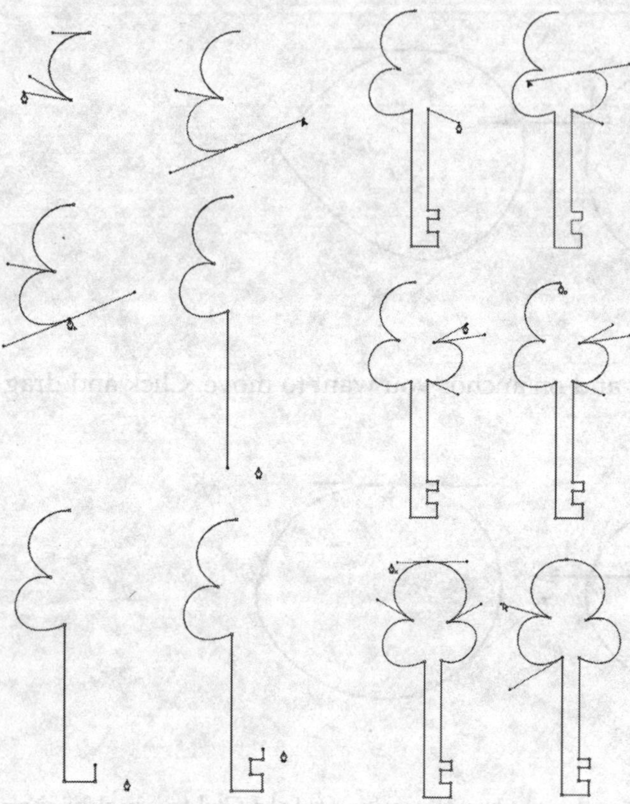

Final Illustration

This is the final illustration.

Tips for Using Pen Tool

- Use as little anchor points has your need to create your shape
- Add anchor points where there is a change in direction of the line/curve
- Use shortcuts like Alt/Option or Ctrl/Command to quickly swap to other tools to edit your path
- Hold shift to lock your path while adding a new anchor point for 45-degree increments.

Using Brushes

Using the Brush Tool, you can add styles to your lines. It can also be used to mimic calligraphy, crayon and brush strokes. This will help you add more life to your line works.

Applying Brush Stroke

Select the Brush Tool and draw your object. Then go to your Brushes Palette and select the crayon brush to apply the effect.

Calligraphy Brush Stroke

To apply a calligraphy brush stroke, draw your path and select the calligraphy brush. Increase the Stroke to make it thicker.

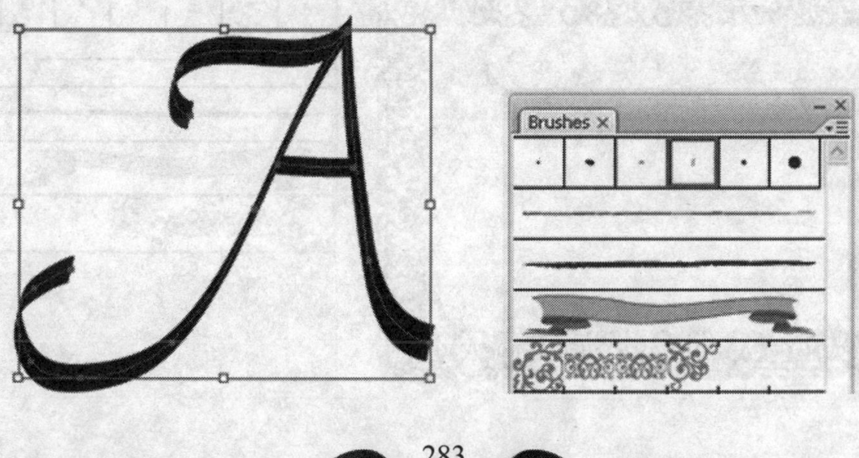

Calligraphy Brush Options

To make changes to your calligraphy brush, you can double click the Calligraphy Brush to pop up the calligraphic brush options. Drag the brush to change the angle in the thumbnail. Change the Diameter makes it thicker.

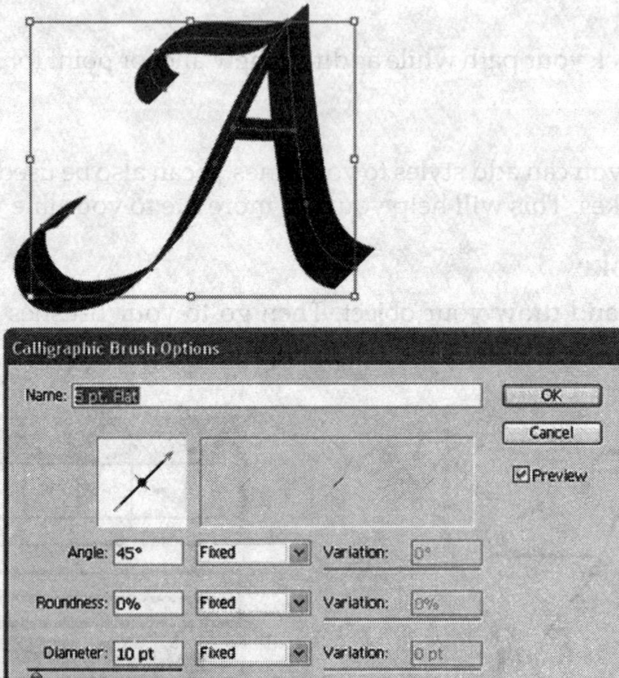

Create a Border Pattern

Draw a rectangle and pick the border pattern. This will create a frame for it.

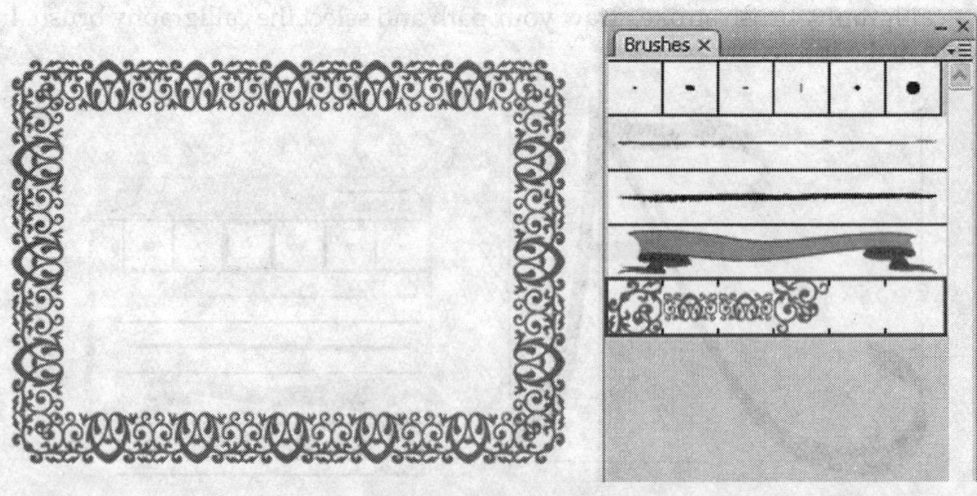

Creating a New Pattern Brush

Draw a Star and drag it to the Brushes Palette. A New Brush selection appears. Choose New Pattern Brush for it.

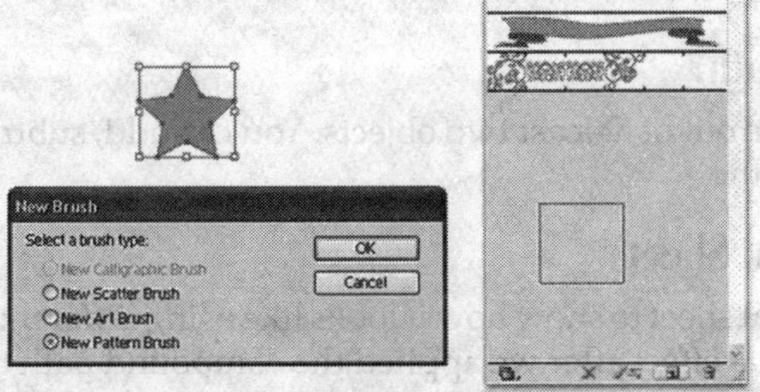

Applying Pattern Brush

Draw a circle and apply our new brush stroke.

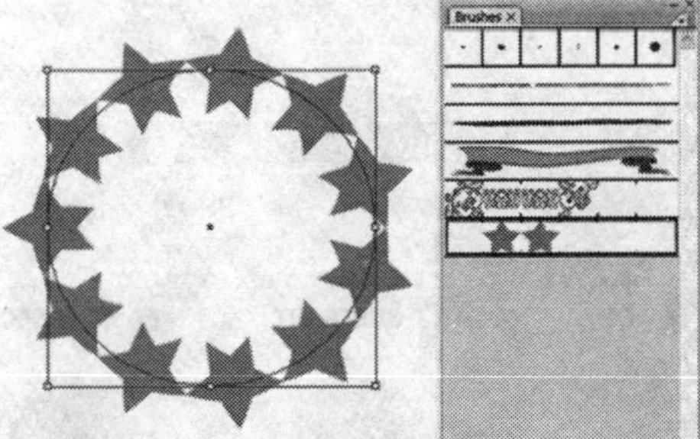

Next draw a line path and apply the brush stroke. Double click the star brush from your brushes and set Scale and Spacing to 20% to get the effect below.

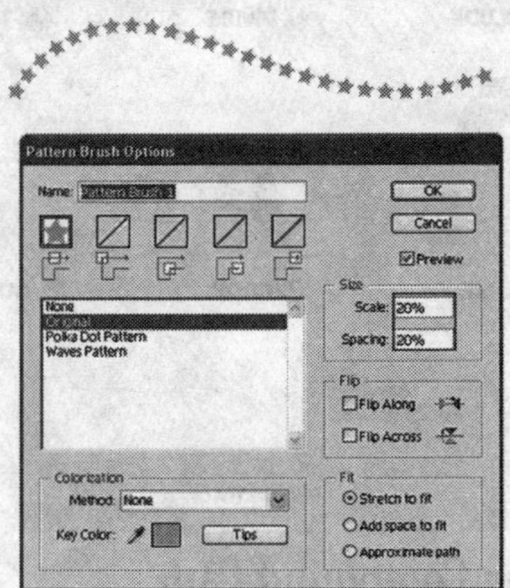

Brushes are very good for aligning objects and creating borders. So experiment with it and have fun!

Creating Compound Paths

Almost all objects in our daily life can be built with basic shapes. By drawing shapes using our basic shape tool, we can use compound path to combine or subtract shapes to create what we need.

What is Compound Path?

Compound path is made out of at least two objects. You can add, subtract and intersect shapes to form a compound path.

Compound Path Cheat Sheet

We have compiled a cheat sheet to show how it looks like using different functions of compound path. You can see the final effect after we applied the compound path to three coloured circles.

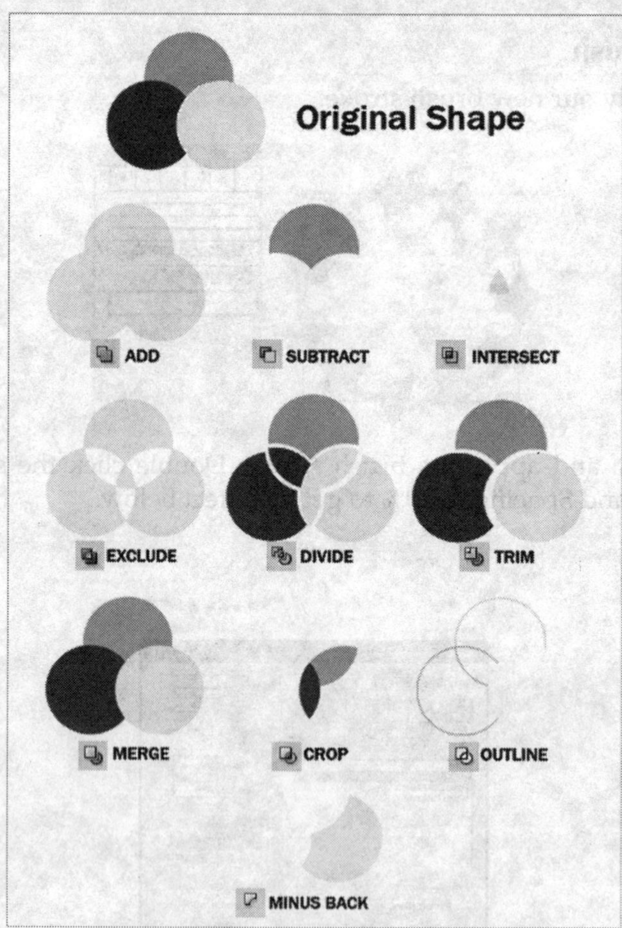

Creating an Ancient Key using Compound Path

In this section, we will discuss you how to create an ancient key using compound paths rather than using Pen Tool in our previous tutorial.

Turning on the Grids

Go to **View>Show Grid** to turn on the grids, then go and turn on Snap to Grid. With the grid and snapping turned on, you can easily snap objects to the grid.

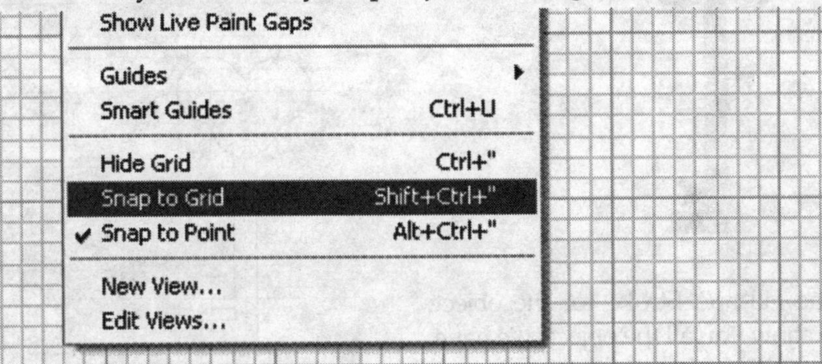

- First draw a Circle using your Shape Tools, hold Alt as you click and drag a new copy beside it.

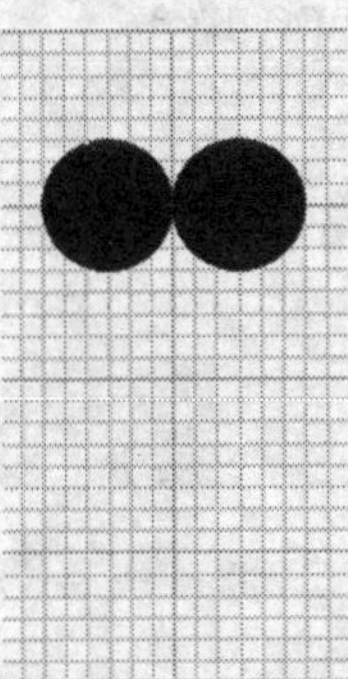

- Duplicate a new circle and place it on top.

- Next, select the Rectangle Tool and continue building up your key shape.

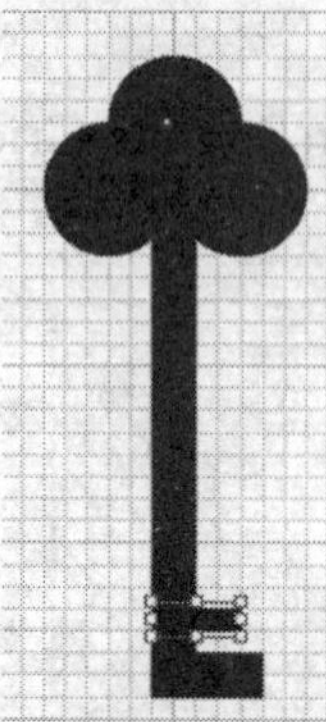

- Swap the Fill and Stroke for the object, this will show you all the objects we have.

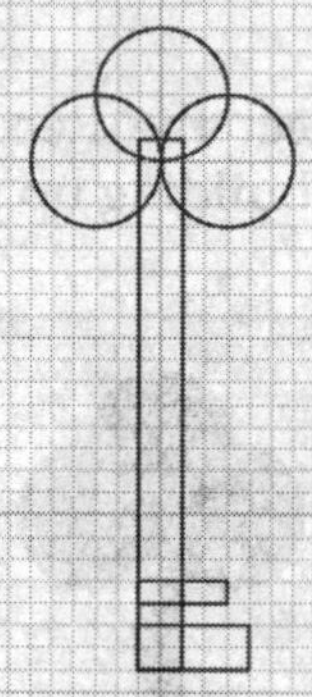

- Using the Selection Tool, select the whole shape and go to **Window>Pathfinder** to bring up the Pathfinder. Select Add to shape to combine the objects.

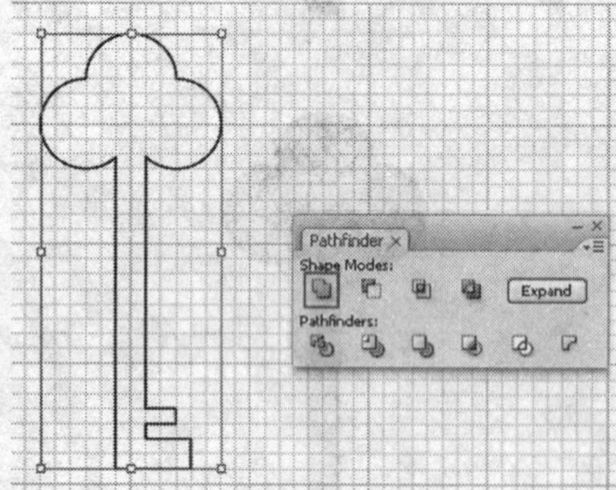

- You can still make changes to the compound path at this stage. Try moving the top circle below to see how it works. To do this, double click with the Selection Tool to go into isolation mode to move the individual shapes.

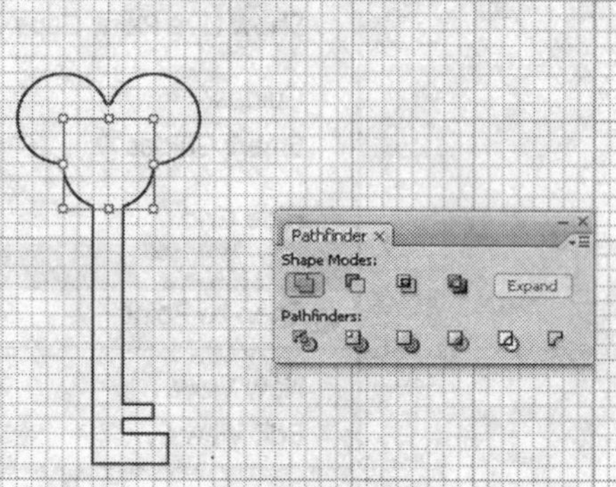

- Next we will swap it back to black fill again, draw a circle in the middle which we will punch a new hole there. Select both shapes and select Subtract from shape area.

Here is the final illustration.

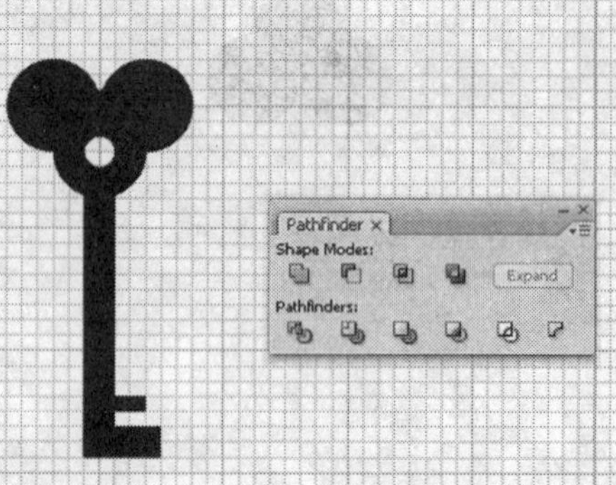

Practice these skills.

Working with Colour and Strokes

Filling Colour Using Swatches

To fill an object, open up your Swatches Palette. Select your object and pick any colour from the swatches.

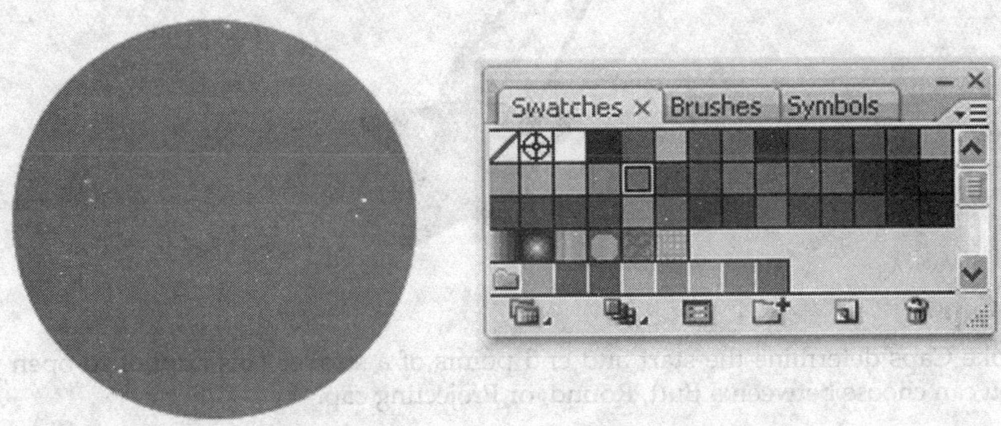

Filling Colour using Colour Picker

Another way to fill colour is by double clicking on the Fill in your Tool Palette. A Colour Picker window will appear and you can pick your colour.

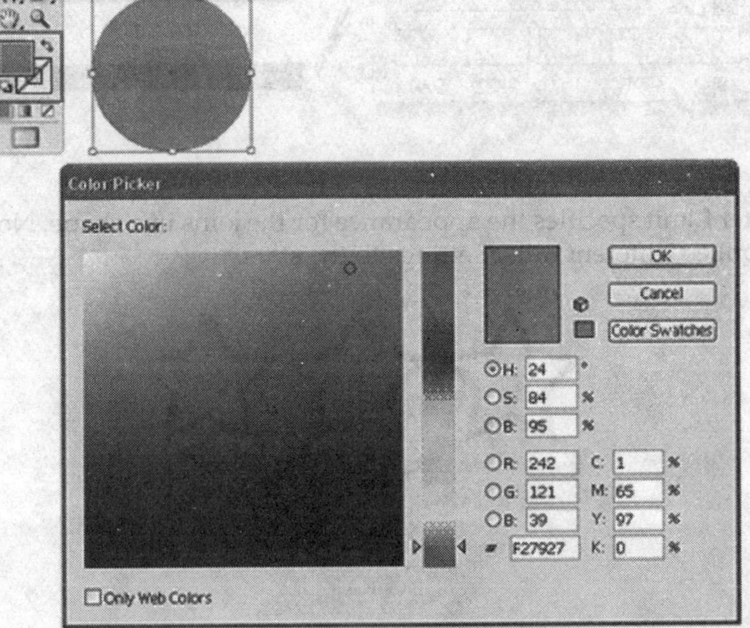

Changing Fill and Stroke Using Control Palette

You can also easily change fill, stroke colour and stroke width by accessing your Control Palette at the top of your art-board.

Stroke Caps

The Stroke Caps determine the start and end points of a stroke. This applies to open paths only. You can choose between a Butt, Round, or Projecting cap.

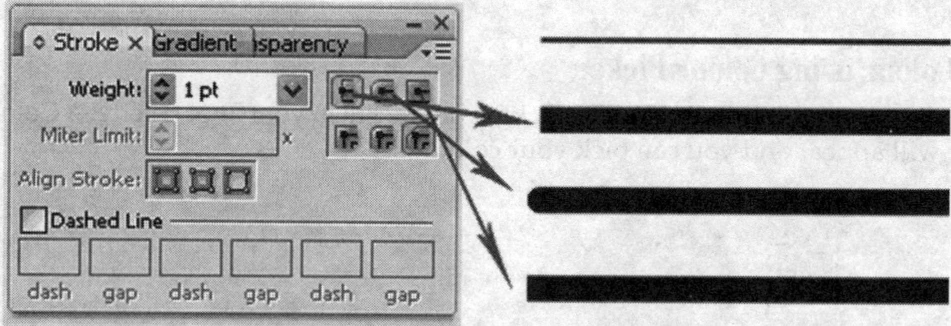

Miter Limit

The stroke's Miter Limit specifies the appearance for the joins in a shape. Notice how the joins look after we applied different miter settings to the stars.

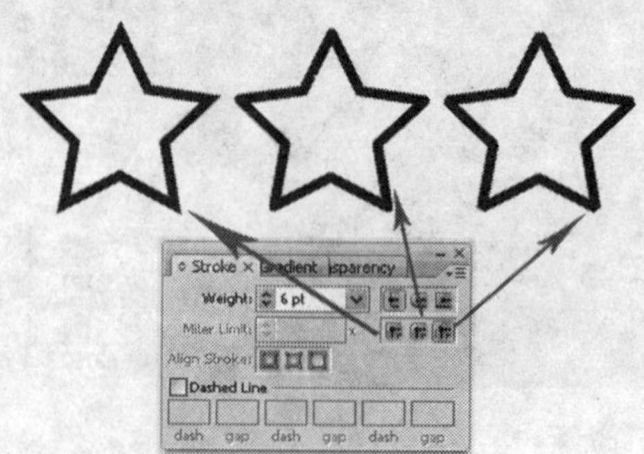

Applying Gradient to Objects

To apply gradient to your object, go to the Tool Palette and set it to Gradient Fill.

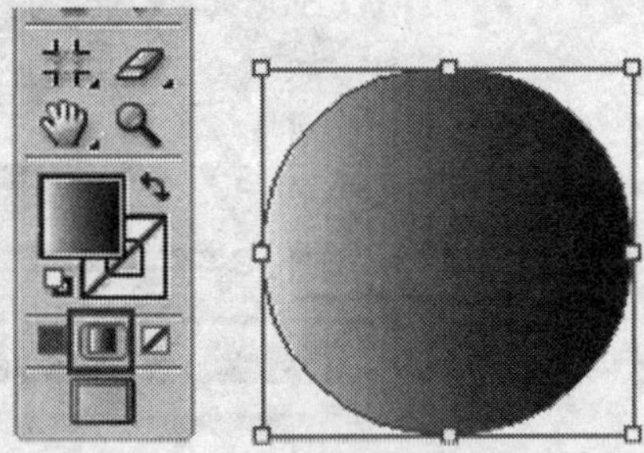

Open up your Gradient and Colour Palette. By default it is a Grayscale gradient. Click Options icon at the corner and change it to RGB mode.

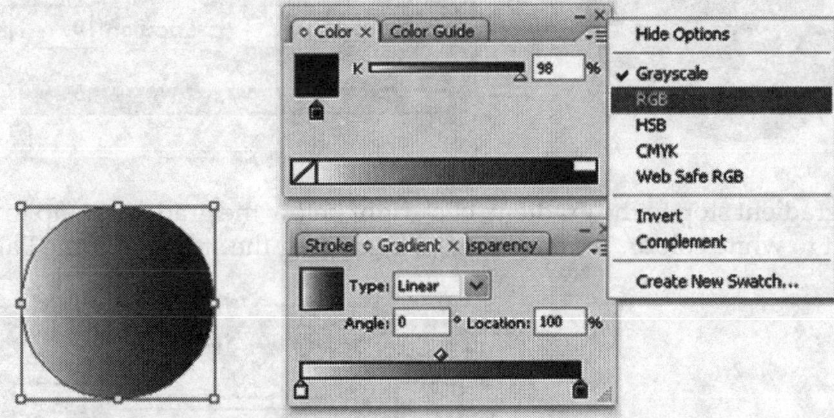

After we switched to RGB there will be a slider and a colour chart to pick the colour. Choose a dark blue for it.

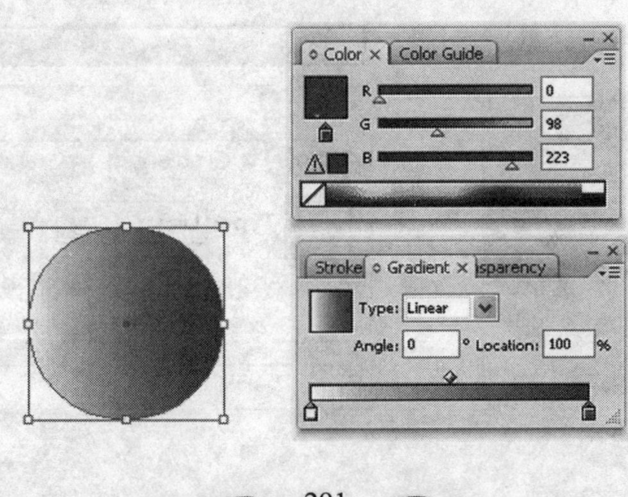

Do the same for the start point, change it to RGB and choose a light blue.

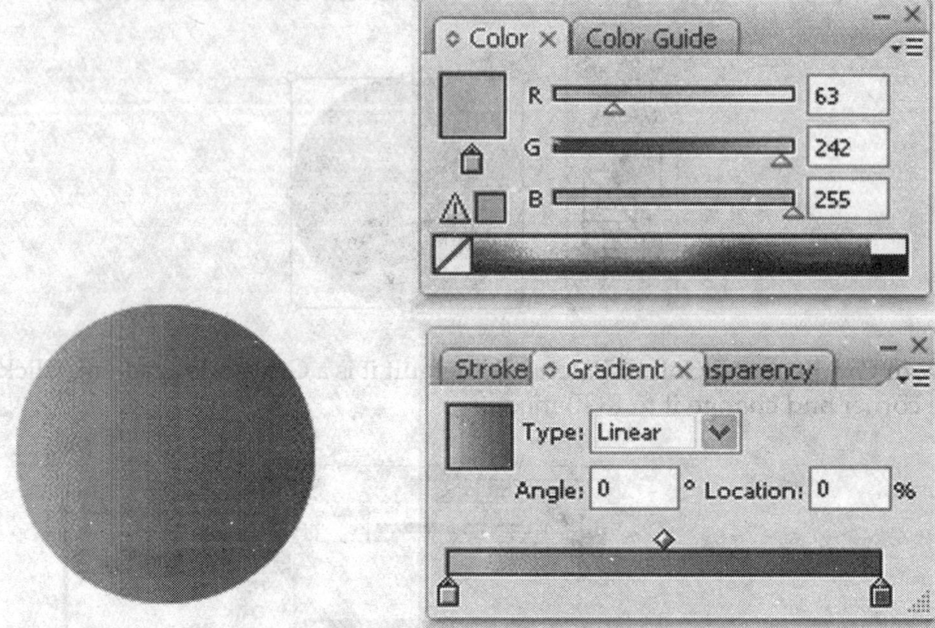

To add a new gradient stop to the gradient, click right below the gradient ramp to create a new stop. Change it to white colour. To remove it, you can drag the stop out of the Palette.

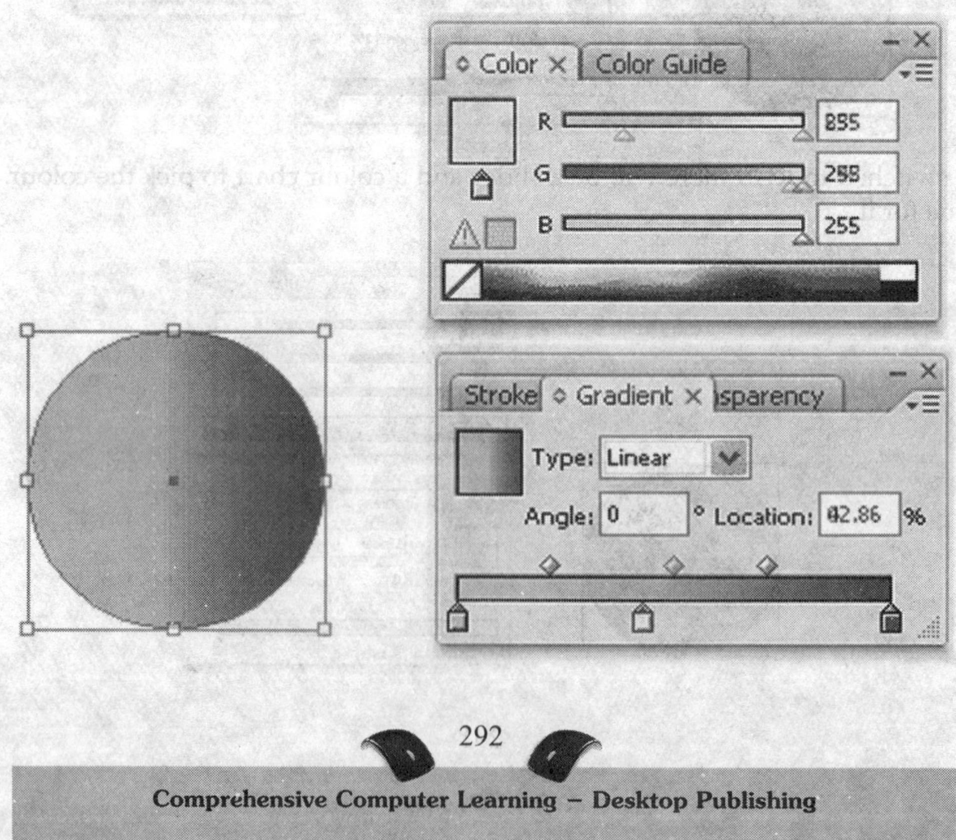

To change the direction of the gradient, select the Gradient Tool from the Tool Palette. Click and drag in the direction you want the gradient to follow.

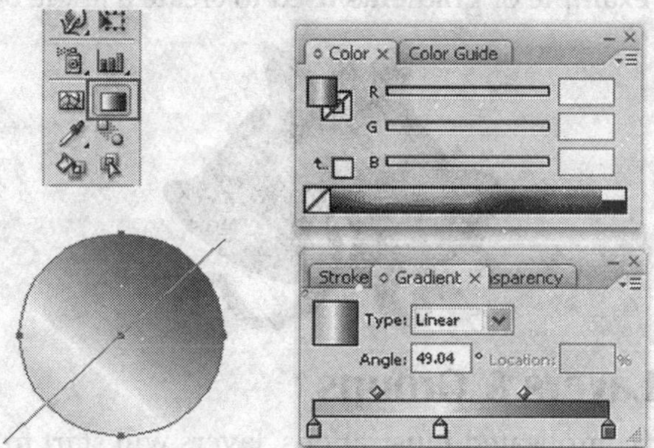

Radial Gradient

To set it to radial gradient, choose Radial instead of Linear.

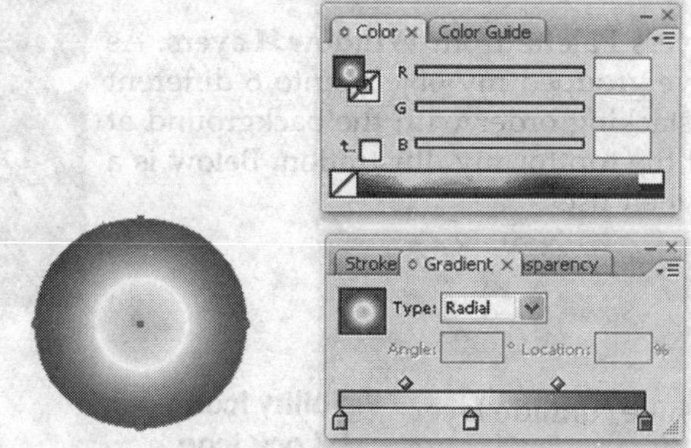

Pattern Fill

To create seamless pattern fill, we can choose the pattern fill from the Swatches.

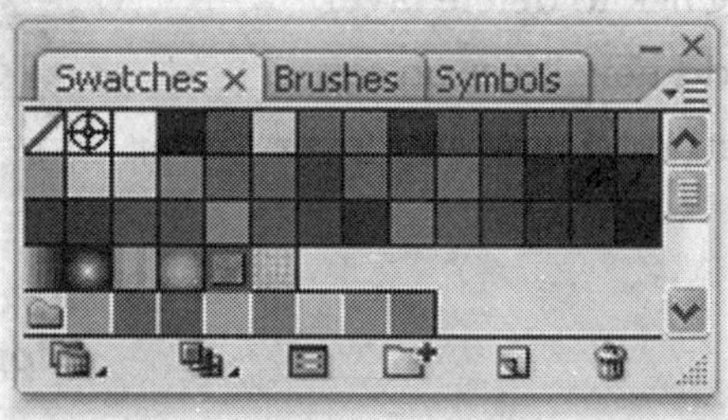

Using radial and linear gradient, we can achieve a lot of realism to our artwork. Radial patterns can add depth and volume to circle, and linear pattern can be used to create volume for cylinders. Here is an example of gradients used to create a jingle bell.

Editing Objects, Layers & Groups

As you start working on complicated illustrations, layers will start to build up. And you will have to group and arrange them so that you can move and edit the layers easily. Here we will discuss with an example of an illustration.

Layers Palette

You can access your Layers Palette from **Window>Layers.** As you can see below, I have grouped my objects into 6 different layers. You can see the stacking order with the background at the bottom and towel at the top for my illustration. Below is a list of layer settings and their uses.

Visibility Icon: Click to hide/unhide layer

Lock Icon: Click the lock to lock the layer

Layer Name: Double click to rename it

Target Indicator: Click to select layer

Delete Layer: Click to delete layer

New Layer: Add new layer on top

New Sub-layer: Add new sub-layer under Layer 1

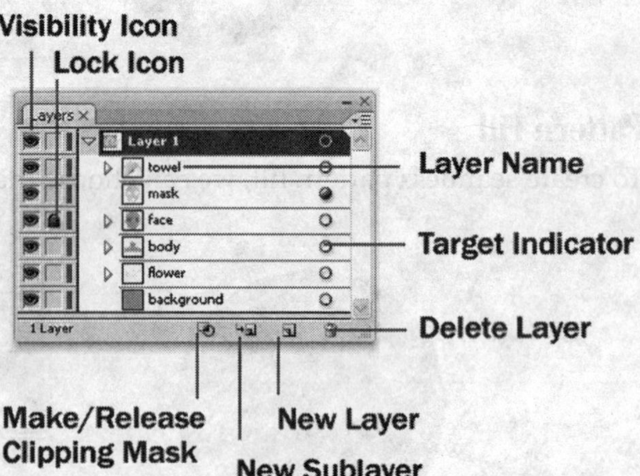

Arranging Objects

To bring a layer on top, select the layer and drag it to the top. Now the flower is at the top layer and covers the whole picture.

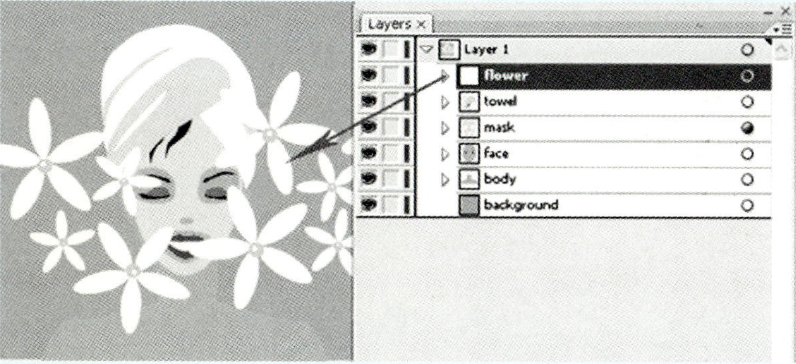

Grouping Objects

By grouping objects, you can move them together rather than spend time selecting all the objects individually. Here is an example of a flower made up of 6 layers. By selecting the object and grouping them by pressing Ctrl+G, I am able to group them together and move. To edit the grouped object, double click to go into isolation mode to edit the objects. If you want to ungroup them, press Ctrl+Shift+G.

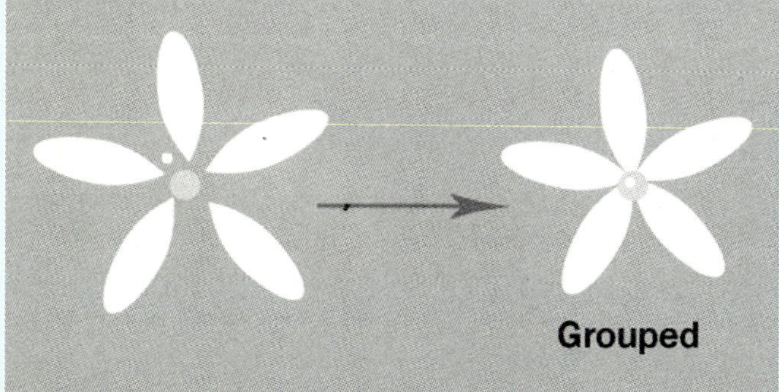

Next, I duplicate a few more of my grouped flower and group them again to form my flower layer.

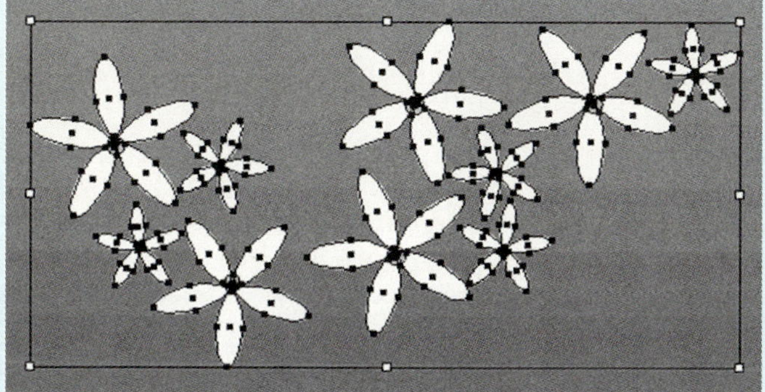

Appearance Palette

The Appearance Palette shows what effect is applied to a layer. You can Add New Fill or Add New Stroke to the whole layer or individual objects. Go **Windows>Appearance** to open up your Appearance Palette. Let's see how it looks when we apply a new fill. Click the option icon and choose Add New Fill.

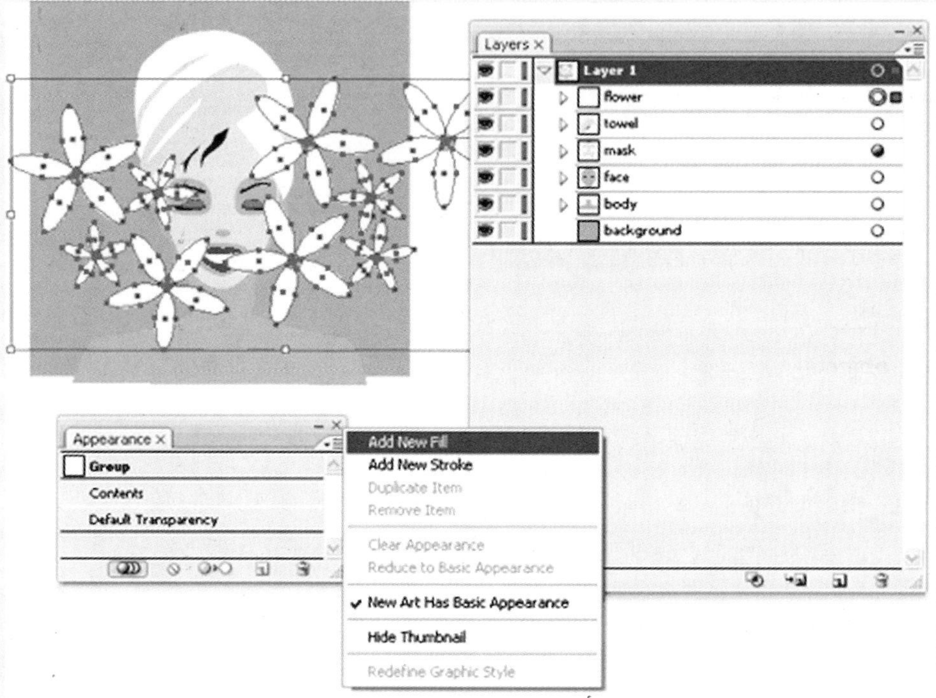

After we set the Fill with pink colour, it turns the whole layer to pink.

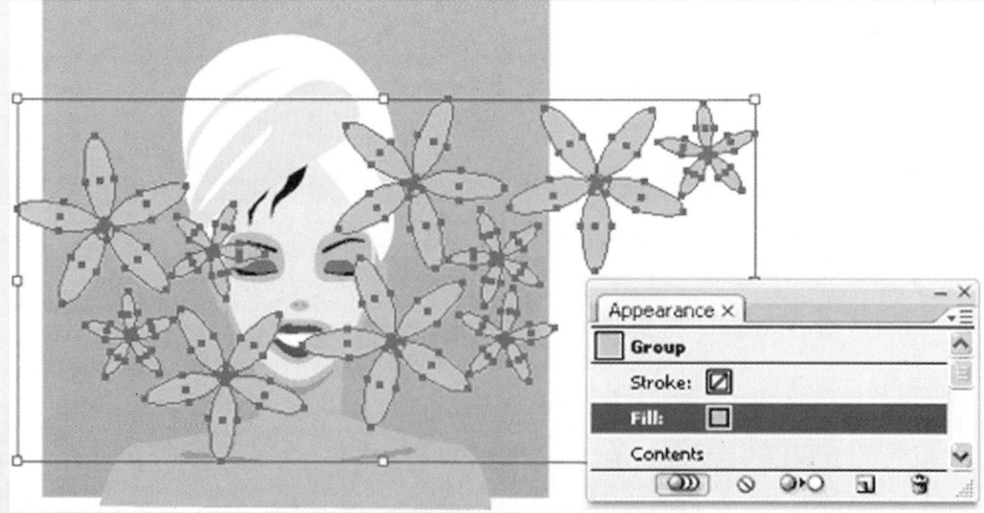

Transparency & Graphic Styles

Transparency effects open the door for designers to create eye catching effects. You can add transparency to drop shadows or apply blending modes to objects to enhance your illustrations.

Adding Transparency

You can add transparency in Illustrator by lowering the opacity of objects so that underlying artwork becomes visible. Go **Window>Transparency** to open up your Transparency Window. Stack a few objects and set it to a lower opacity of 50% for the underlying colour to show through.

Blending Modes for Objects

If you are familiar with Photoshop, you may have heard of Blending Modes. Blending modes let you vary the ways that the colours of objects blend with the colours of underlying objects.

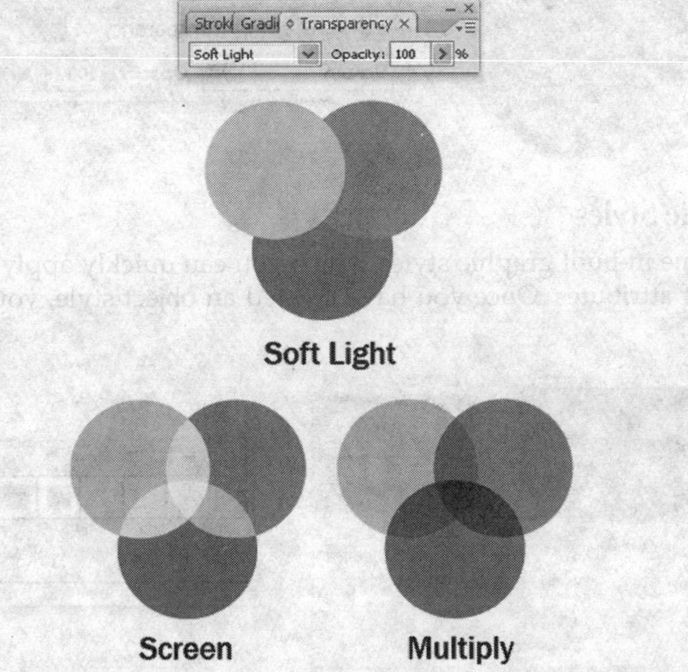

Here we have an example of 3 popular blending modes to show you the effect.

Button Reflection Using Screen

First draw a circle and apply a gradient of light to dark orange to it.

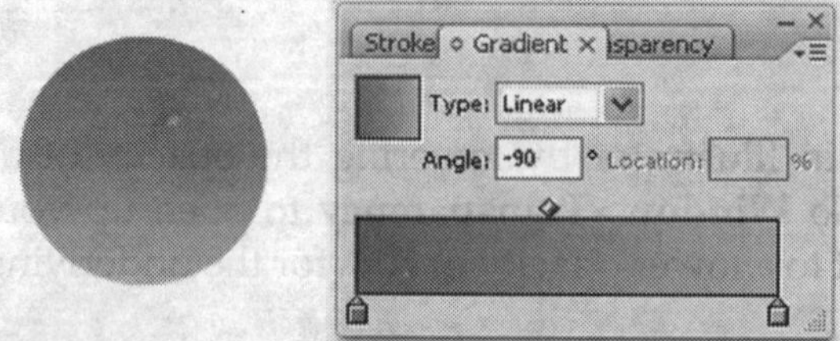

Draw another circle on top and apply a gradient from black to white.

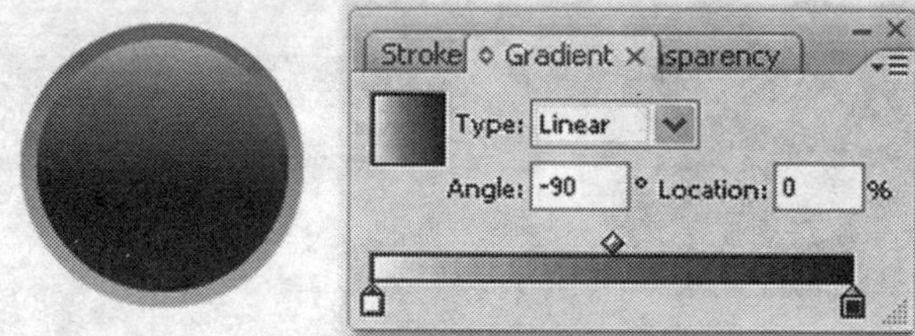

Finally, select the black to white circle and change the blending mode to Screen. And you're done!

Applying Graphic Styles

Illustrator has some in-built graphic styles which you can quickly apply to your objects. It is like a saved set of attributes. Once you have created an object style, you can apply it across different objects.

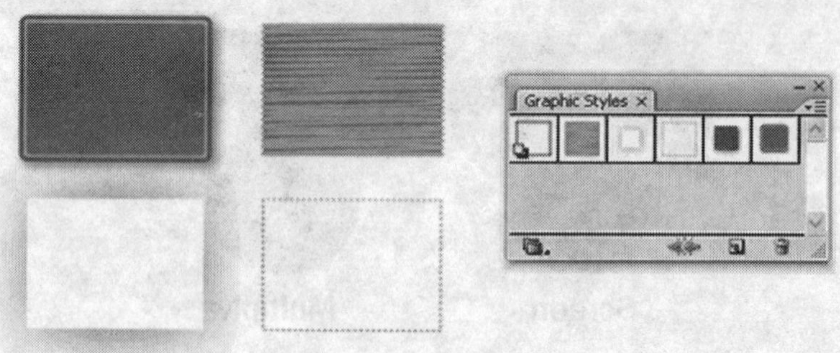

To see the attributes of an graphic styles, go **Window>Appearance**. Here we can see that there are 3 fills with effects (fx icon) applied. We will learn more about using effects in the later lessons.

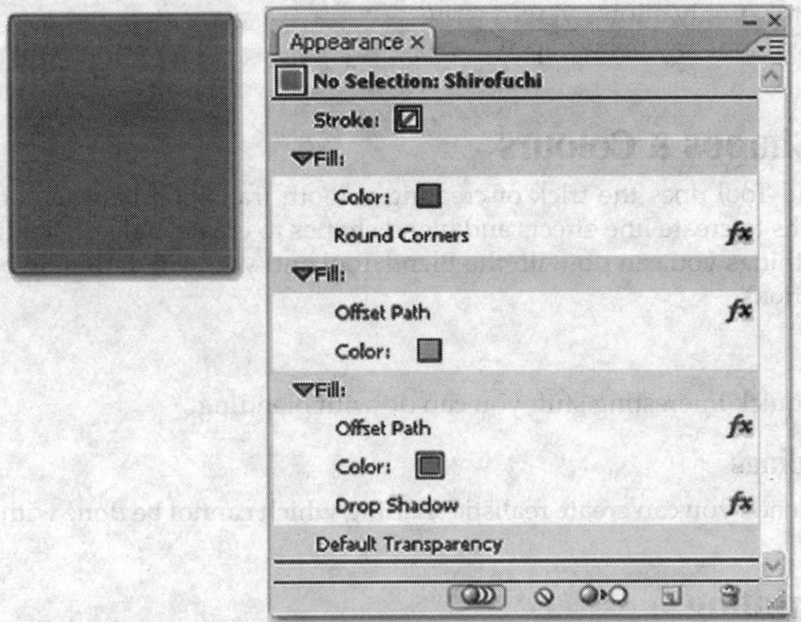

Transforming & Moving Objccts

In this lesson, you will learn how to quickly resize and rotate objects using the Transform functions. I will be showing some useful transform tricks to create random rotating objects using Transform each function.

Resizing Objects

Select the object with Selection Tool and a bounding box will appear. Select the corner handle and resize while holding Shift to constrain proportion.

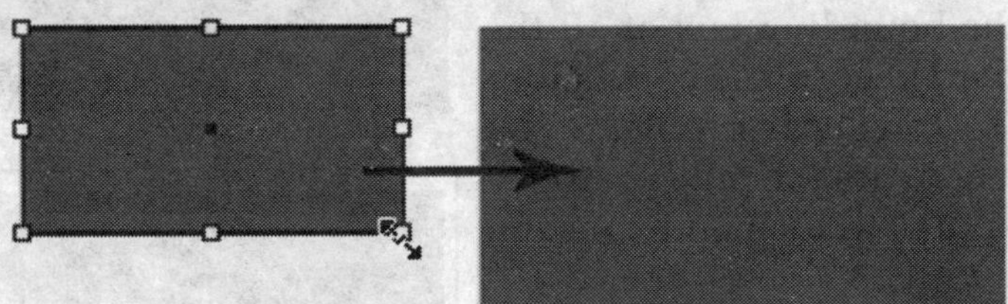

Basic Text

The type tool allows some simple common text formatting. You will learn about columns, wrap text and text on a path. This will help you create aesthetic type effects on brochures and newsletter covers.

Typing Text using Point Text

To create a point text, simply click once on the art-board using the Type Tool and type out your text. Point text only allows you to write a one line text without any text wrap.

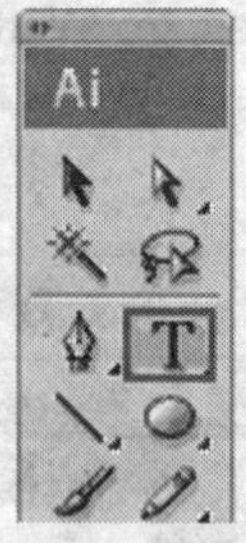

Typography is fun...

Blending Shapes & Colours

Illustrator Blend Tool does the trick of creating smooth transition between objects. You can blend open paths to create line effects and blend shapes to create realistic shadings. There are many creative things you can do with the Blend Tool and you will definitely be using it a lot in your illustrations.

Blend Effects

Here are some quick interesting stuff you can do with blending.

Realistic Shadings

With smooth blends you can create realistic shading which cannot be done with gradient.

Saving & Printing

In this lesson, you will learn how to crop your artwork for exporting to JPG for website or printing. We will also cover about EPS file which is the universal format for saving vector graphics.

Savings Files Using Crop Area

When you try to export your file to a JPG, sometimes you may notice white areas around the image. This is due to the hidden images under the mask (see example below). Illustrator exports the bounding box of all the objects in the art-board regardless of whether it is masked away. To solve this problem, you will need to define a crop area to tell Illustrator this is the area to export rather than exporting the whole graphic.

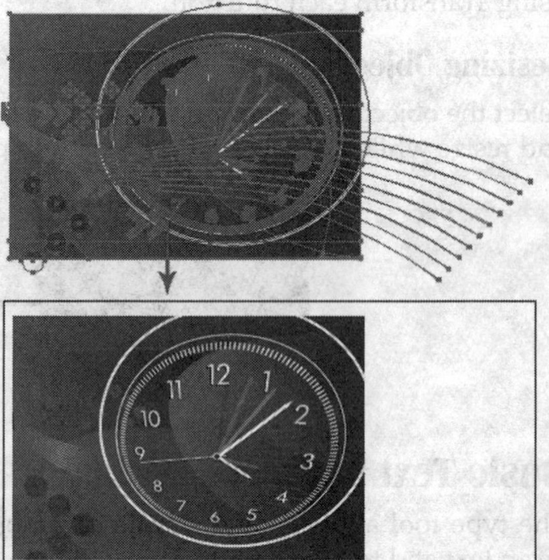

Designing a Logo

Designing a logo is a common task in Adobe Illustrator. In this discussion, we will sum up what we have learnt so far in Illustrator to create your own custom logo. I will show you the process in drawing a logo and hopefully you have more confidence after this tutorial.

Drawing the Honey Farm Logo

First scan the sketch of your logo and save it as a jpeg.

Next, we need import it to Illustrator. Go **File>Place** and select your picture. Make sure Template is checked to place it as a template. When you open your Layers Palette, you will see that it is locked and the colours are faded out. This makes it perfect for tracing.

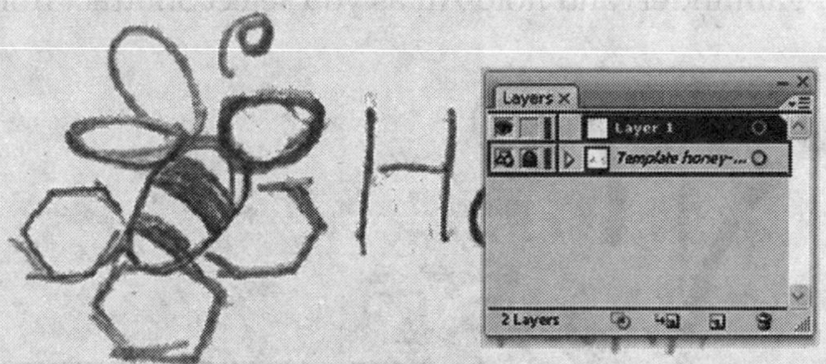

We will start with the bee's body. Draw an oval shape. Edit the points using the Direct Selection Tool to form the body of the bee.

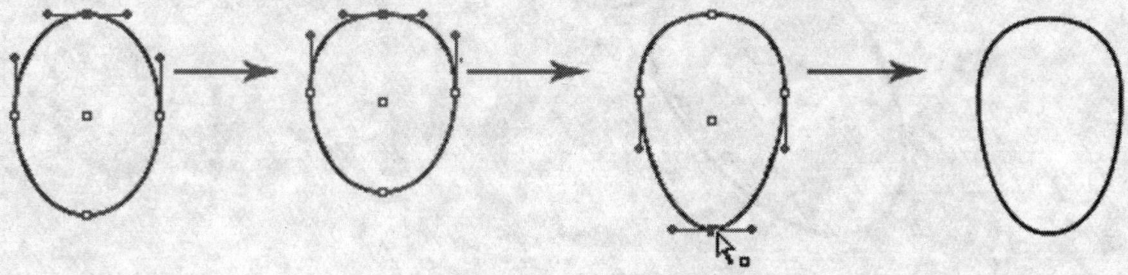

Next, draw a circle shapes for the head. Edit the points to make it slightly pointed.

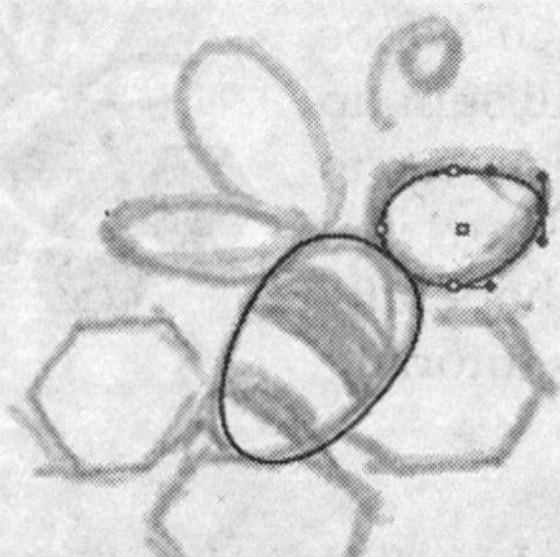

To draw the antennae, I use an oval and draw a thick line using Pen Tool connecting to it.

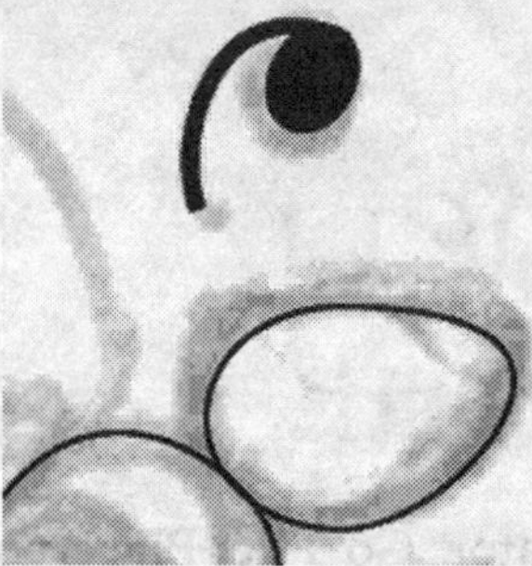

Next, draw 2 ovals and rotate it to form the wings. Select the bigger wing and press Ctrl + C to copy. Press Ctrl+F to paste infront. Now, hold Shift and select the small wing. Open up your Pathfinder (Window>Pathfinder) and hold Alt as you select Subtract from shape area.

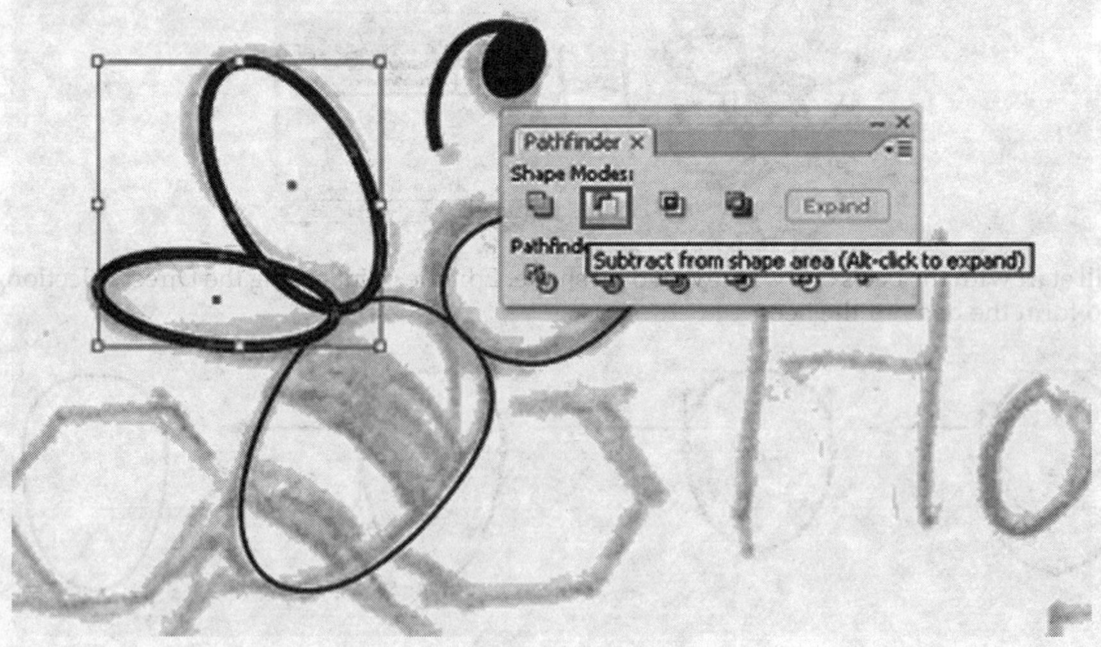

The overlapping part of the wing will be subtracted.

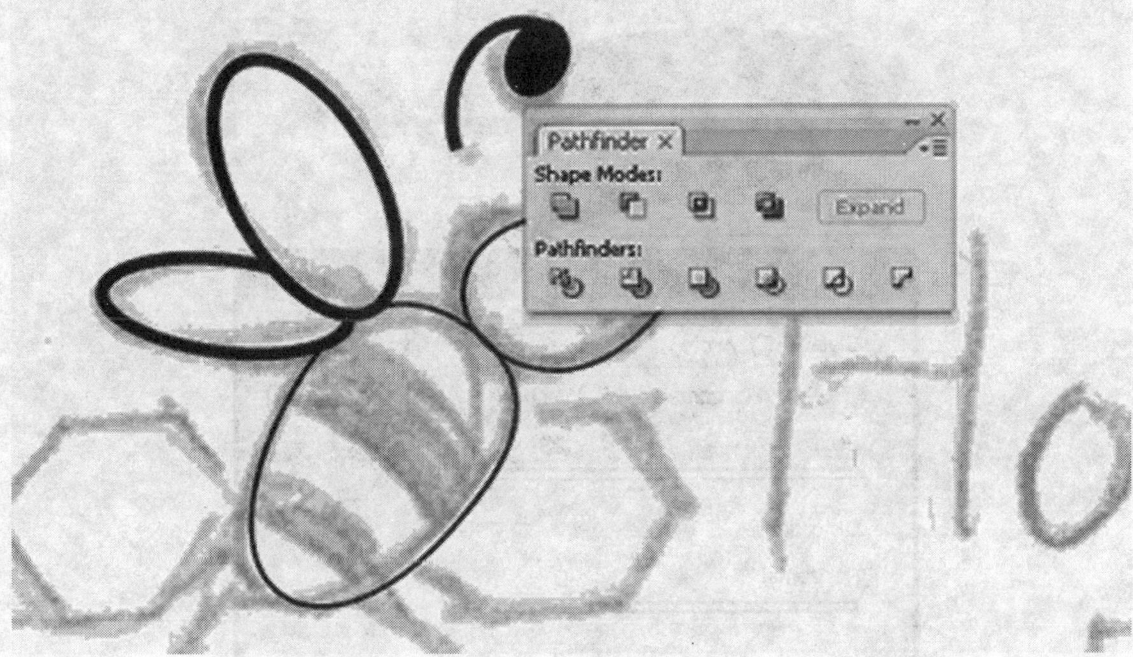

We will move on to create the body stripes. Draw 2 rectangles with the height of the stripe thickness.

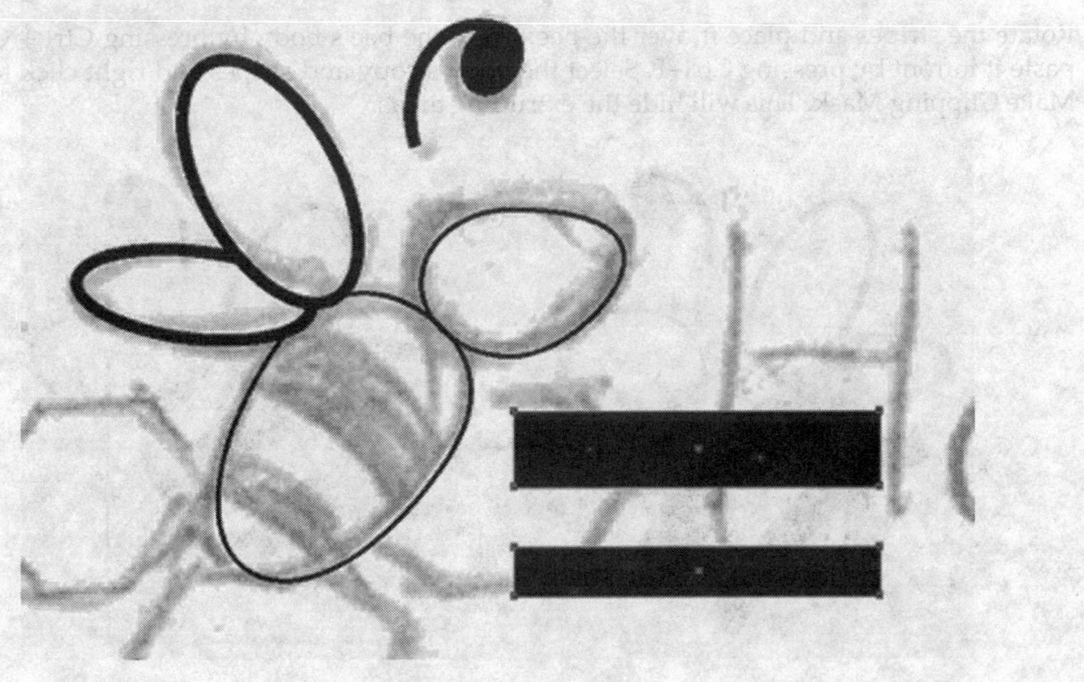

Select both rectangles and go **Effect>Warp>Arc**. Set Bend to 23% to bend the rectangle. Go **Object>Expand Appearance** to expand the effect.

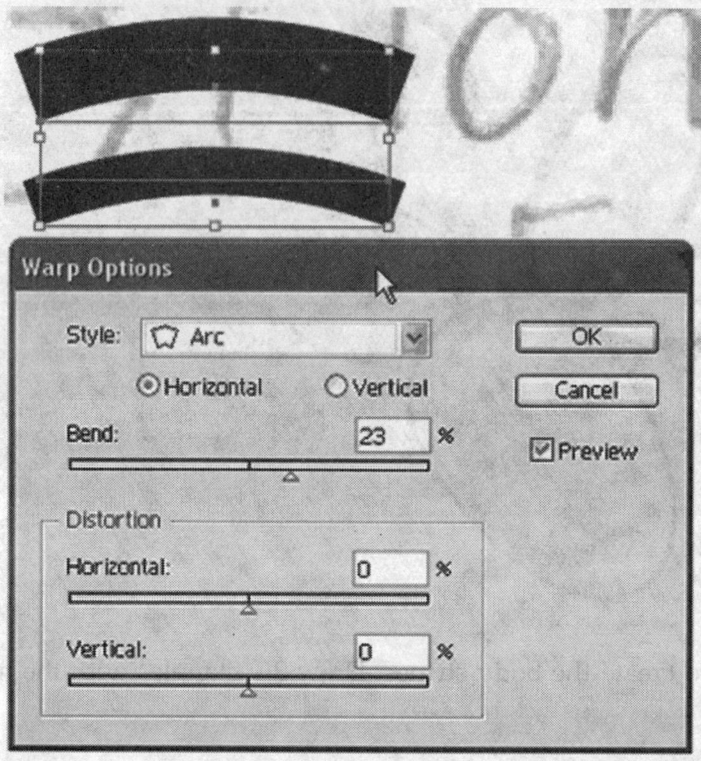

Rotate the stripes and place it over the bee. Copy the bee's body by pressing Ctrl + C. Then paste it infront by pressing Ctrl+F. Select the body's copy and stripes and right click to select Make Clipping Mask. This will hide the extruding areas.

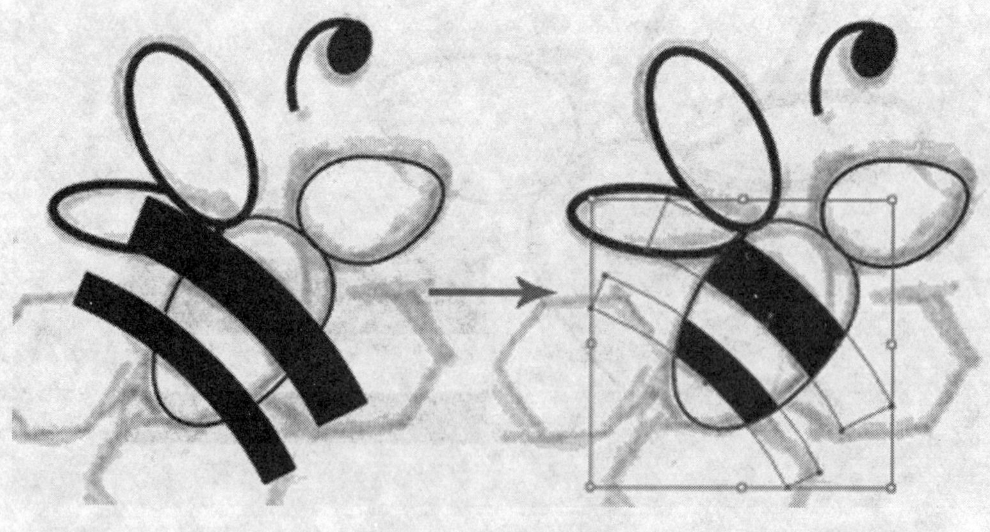

Select the Polygon Tool and hold Shift as you drag a polygon on the canvas. Hold Alt and drag the first polygon to make another copy of it. Do this until you have 3 copies of it.

Select all 3 polygons and swap it to black fill. Then group it by pressing Ctrl+G.

We will now crop away the overlapping areas of the polygons. Select the bee's body and go to **Object>Path>Offset Path** and set the Offset value to 10pt. Send the new path to the top by pressing Ctrl+Shift+].

Select both the offset path and polygons and open up your Pathfinder (Window>Pathfinder). Hold Alt as you select Subtract from shape area.

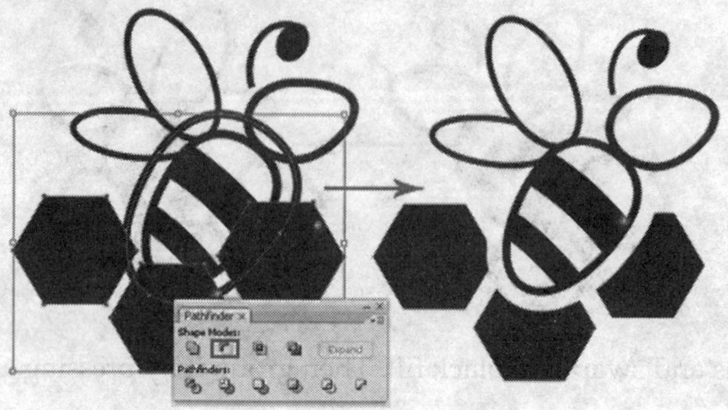

Final Touch ups

Finally, we will add in the text for our final logo. Notice that I have increased the strokes for the bee's body to make sure that the line doesn't fade out when printing. Also zoom out to see whether it still looks clear and sharp when it is small. Print out a copy at different sizes to see how it will look in letterheads and continue tweaking until you are satisfied.

Cleaning up the Logo

Save a copy of your logo so that you still have the original copy to work with if you need to make any adjustments. Now select your text and outline it by pressing Ctrl+Shift+O to convert it to paths. This will prevent missing fonts on other computers.

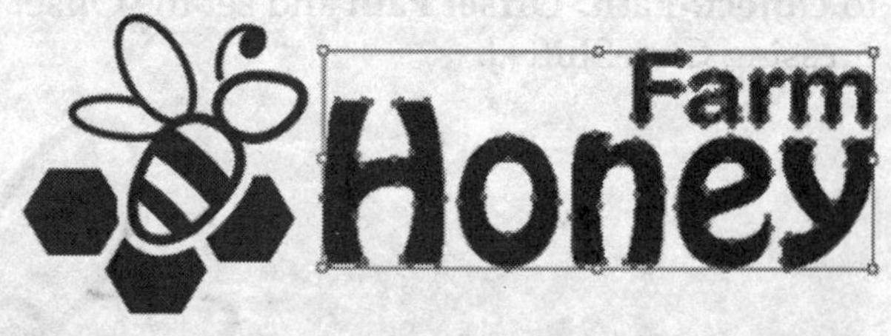

Next, select the bee stripes and go to Pathfinder and select Trim to trim away the edges.

Select the paths of your bee that are made contains line strokes and go to **Object>Expand** and click OK. We will need to expand it to maintain the same stroke thickness or else the proportions get distorted when we rescale the logo.

After we expanded the bee, hold Shift and select the bee stripes. Go to Pathfinder and hold Alt as your select Add to shape area. This will combine the bee shapes together.

Finally, we will add in the colours for the logo and we are logo is done.

That's it! Now you can enjoy using various techniques of Illustrator in designing purposes.

Adobe Acrobat Reader

What is Adobe Reader?

Adobe Acrobat is used to create, review, and modify PDF files. You can use PDF as a way to share documents created with the Adobe Creative Suite. Because PDF is a common file format, you can use it to share Creative Suite files for review, approval, or final publication. When you use a program in the Creative Suite, such as Illustrator or InDesign, to create a document, others would need the same software to open or edit the files. By converting your documents to PDF, they can easily be shared with others who might not have the same software as you because PDF files can be viewed by users on virtually all types of computers and operating systems.

PDF provides a common file format for viewing files, regardless of what software program was used to create them. Additionally, Acrobat provides extensive tools for reviewing, commenting, and marking files so that you can easily collaborate on a project without modifying the original document, along with tools to make PDF files interactive, merge related documents together, and secure files to restrict viewing or editing.

Because the software to view PDF files is free, you can be assured that those receiving your files don't need to purchase any special software. In fact, the odds are quite good that most users already have some type of free PDF viewing software, such as Adobe Reader.

PDF has become a popular way to share files because it provides a true reproduction of an original document. PDF is used by the Internal Revenue Service to distribute tax forms online. Many financial services firms and insurance companies use PDF because the electronic documents can be secured, and they accurately represent documents that have been approved for distribution. Graphic artists even use PDF files to send books, like the one you're reading now, to the printing plant.

Although PDF files provide a high-quality representation of an original file, they're more than just a picture of a document. PDF files retain the high quality appearance of text while keeping the text searchable. Logos and illustrations created with Adobe Illustrator retain a high quality appearance when converted to PDF, and intricate details from bitmap images, such as those edited with Adobe Photoshop, can also be maintained. PDF files allow you to distribute a high-fidelity electronic document. When creating a PDF file, you can choose settings that make the file suitable for high-quality printing or make the file smaller and more suitable for posting to a Website or sharing as an e-mail attachment.

Although Acrobat is part of the Creative Suite, it's not a design tool – rather, it's a tool for distributing documents created in other software programs and enhancing these documents for online distribution. You generally don't use Acrobat to build new documents. Acrobat is a medium for sharing files, not for creating them. With Acrobat, you can:

- ❑ Share documents with users who don't have the same software or fonts that you use.
- ❑ Review and mark PDF files that others send to you. With Adobe Acrobat, you can enable a PDF file to be reviewed by users with the free Adobe Reader software.
- ❑ Combine documents created in other programs. You can use Acrobat to merge PDF files together into one document, even files that may have been originally created in different programs.
- ❑ Create a PDF portfolio. You can combine various file formats into a single PDF package and yet retain the files in their original file formats.
- ❑ Edit Adobe PDF files to make minor changes to text or graphics.
- ❑ Apply security to PDF files when you don't want them changed or you want to restrict viewing to certain individuals.
- ❑ Add interactivity to PDF files by enhancing them with sounds, movies, animations, and buttons.
- ❑ Create interactive forms to collect information electronically, avoiding the need for manual data collection.

Viewing modes

Acrobat provides several viewing modes that control how the document is displayed. For example, you can choose to display the pages of a book or a magazine side-by-side, or view only one page at a time. You can choose which viewing mode is used by choosing **View Page Display** and selecting the viewing option you want.

The viewing modes are:

- **Single Page:** This mode displays only the current document page on screen and doesn't show any adjoining pages. When you scroll to the top or bottom of the current page, other pages aren't visible at the same time as the current page.
- **Single Page Continuous:** With this mode, you can see the current document page, and if you scroll to the top (or bottom) of the current page, the adjoining page is also visible. If you reduce your page viewing magnification, many document pages are visible.
- **Two-Up (previously known as Facing):** Use this mode to see pages as a *spread,* where you can view both the left and right sides of adjoining pages at the same time. When you have documents with pictures or text that spans a pair of pages, use this option to see the pages presented side-by-side in Acrobat. As with the Single Page mode, other pages that go before or fall after the spread aren't visible – only the one pair of pages is visible on-screen, regardless of the magnification or scrolling.
- **Two-Up Continuous (previously known as Continuous-Facing):** If you have a document with many pages containing text or pictures on their adjoining pages, you can use this mode to scroll from one pair of visible pages to the next. When the Two-Up Continuous view is selected, you can see adjoining page spreads. This option is identical to the Two-Up option, but it also shows pages above or below the spread you're presently viewing.
- **Full Screen mode (View Full Screen Mode):** You can use the Full Screen mode option to hide all menus, toolbars, and other parts of the Acrobat interface. This option is useful if you want to focus on the document being displayed, not the program being used to view it. Use this mode, for example, when you've a converted PowerPoint file to a PDF document and want to deliver the presentation with Acrobat. If you're viewing a document in the Full Screen mode, press the Esc key to return to the regular viewing mode.

  When using the Full Screen mode, you can select **Edit Preferences** and choose Full Screen to define attributes that change the way the file displays. You can set the display to advance automatically from one page to the next at a certain interval, choose from many different page transition types, and define the background colour.
- **Reading mode (View Reading Mode):** The many toolbars and buttons of Acrobat can get in the way of the document you wish to review. Use Reading mode to temporarily hide all the toolbars and buttons, making it easier to focus on the content of the PDF file.

Navigation panels

Acrobat offers a variety of panels that are helpful when navigating through PDF documents. The navigation panels are displayed along the left side of your Document window as small icons.

Converting Photoshop and Illustrator files to PDF

Both Adobe Photoshop CS5 and Adobe Illustrator CS5 can save documents directly in the Adobe PDF file format. To do so, simply choose **File⇨Save or File⇨Save As**. Then, from the

File Type drop-down list, choose Adobe PDF (Illustrator) or Photoshop PDF (Photoshop). In these programs, you can create PDF files without Adobe Acrobat or Acrobat Distiller because they've integrated PDF creation capabilities.

Converting InDesign documents to PDF

Like Photoshop and Illustrator, the ability to convert InDesign documents to PDF is integrated into the application. With Adobe InDesign, you can choose **File⇨Export** and select Adobe PDF from the File Type drop-down list. InDesign provides a significant number of options for controlling the size and quality of the resulting PDF file. Many of these options are similar to those available for PDF Maker for Microsoft Office.

Adding Bookmarks

Creating bookmarks that link to a page

By navigating to a page, and to a specific view on a page, you can establish the destination of a bookmark link. With a PDF document open, follow these steps:

- ❑ If the Bookmark icon isn't visible, choose **View⇨Navigation Panels⇨Bookmarks.**
- ❑ The Bookmarks panel appears on the left of the Document window.
- ❑ In the Document window, navigate to the page that you want as the bookmark's destination.
- ❑ Set the magnification of the view that you want by using the MarqueeZoom tool to either zoom in or zoom out.
- ❑ In the Bookmarks panel, click the Options icon (it shows gears) and from the menu that appears, choose New Bookmark.
- ❑ Change the name by typing something more descriptive
- ❑ Test your bookmark by scrolling to another page and viewing it in the Document window; then click your saved bookmark in the Bookmark panel.

Creating bookmarks that link to external files.

Although bookmarks are most commonly used to link to content within a PDF file, you can also use bookmarks to create links to other documents. To create a link to an external file, follow these steps:

- ❑ Choose **Options⇨New Bookmark** in the Bookmarks panel.
- ❑ Replace the Untitled bookmark entry that appears in the Bookmarks panel with an appropriate title for the bookmark.
- ❑ Choose **Options⇨Properties** from the Bookmarks panel menu. The Bookmark Properties dialog box appears. With this dialog box, you can change a bookmark so that it links to any type of file. In this example, we use a PDF document, but the bookmark could be a link to another PDF file, a Photoshop file, or even a Microsoft Excel file. Just remember that this bookmark creates a relative link. The linked file must travel with the PDF document in order for the link to work.

- In the Bookmark Properties dialog box, click the Actions tab, choose Open a File from the Select Action drop-down list, and then click the Add button. The Select File to Open dialog box appears.
- Click the Browse button, choose a file to which the bookmark will navigate, and then click the Select button.

Using bookmarks

To display the Bookmarks panel when a file is opened, follow these steps:

- Choose **File⇨Properties**.
- In the Document Properties dialog box that opens, select the Initial View tab
- From the Navigation drop-down list, choose Bookmarks Panel and Page and then click OK.

Adding Interactive Links

To add an interactive link to your PDF document, follow these steps:

- Locate an area of a page where you want to add a link and then choose **View⇨ Toolbars⇨Advanced Editing** to display the Advanced Editing toolbar.
- Select the Link tool and then click and drag to select the region that you want to link to.
- The Create Link dialog box appears.
- Choose an action that the link will perform:
  - **Go to a Page View**: This option is the default, where you can scroll to the page that is the destination of the link.
  - **Open a File:** Alternatively, you can choose to link to another file; click the Browse button to locate the file.
  - **Open a Web Page:** If you choose this option, you're choosing to link to a Web address. In the Address text box, enter the complete address of the Website to which the link should direct viewers. To create a link to an e-mail address, type mailto: followed by an e-mail address.
  - **Custom Link:** Use this option to choose from other types of links in the Link Properties dialog box.
- Click Next and follow the instructions in the next dialog box before clicking OK.

Adding Buttons to Simplify your PDF Files

To add a button to your PDF document, follow these steps:

- Choose **View⇨Toolbars⇨Advanced Editing.** The Advanced Editing toolbar appears.
- Click the OK Button tool and drag where you want the button to appear in the document.
- Type in an appropriate name for your button in the Field Name dialog box that appears.
- Click the Show All Properties button to see the Button Properties dialog box.

- In the General tab, you can enter a name for the button in the Name text box and provide a ToolTip in the ToolTip text box. A ToolTip is the text that appears whenever the mouse cursor is positioned over the button.
- In the Appearance tab, establish how your button will look by setting the following options:
  - **Border Colour/Fill Colour**: Click the square to the right of the appropriate attribute in the Borders and Colours section of the Appearance tab and then choose a colour from the Colour Picker.
  - **Line Thickness and Style**: These options don't appear unless you change the border colour from None (red diagonal line) to another selection.
  - **Font Size/Font**: Change the size and font of the button text by making a selection from the Font Size and the Font drop-down lists.
  - **Text Colour:** Change the colour of the text by clicking the colour square and choosing a colour from the Colour Picker.
- In the Options tab, make these selections:
  - **Layout:** Use the Layout drop-down list to specify whether you want to use a label (text that you enter in Acrobat that appears on the face of the button) or whether you want an icon (an imported button graphic that you may have designed in Photoshop or Illustrator).
  - **Behaviour**: Choose Push from the Behaviour drop-down list to create different appearances for a button so that it changes based upon whether the mouse cursor is positioned over the button. The button appearance can also change when clicked.
  - **State**: To specify the different appearances (see Behaviour, discussed in the preceding paragraph), click the State on the left side of the Options tab and then choose the Label or Icon status for each state.
  - **Label:** If you choose to use a label, enter the text for it in the Label text field.
  - **Icon:** If you choose to use an icon, specify the location of the graphic file by clicking the Choose Icon button. You can create button icons in either Photoshop or Illustrator.
- In the Actions tab, choose an action from the Select Action drop-down list and then click the Add button.

  Actions are applied to buttons similar to the way in which they're applied to links and bookmarks:
  - To choose actions that are a part of the menu commands, such as printing a document, closing a file, or navigating to the next or preceding page, choose the Execute Menu Item action and then specify the command to be accessed.
  - You can also choose the activity that causes the action to occur, known as the *trigger*. The default trigger is *Mouse Up*, which causes the action to occur when the mouse button is depressed and then released. You can choose other actions, such as the mouse cursor merely rolling over the button without the need to click it.
- After you make all your changes in the Button Properties dialog box, click Close.

Text and Graphics

The tools for editing text and graphics are located on the Advanced Editing toolbar

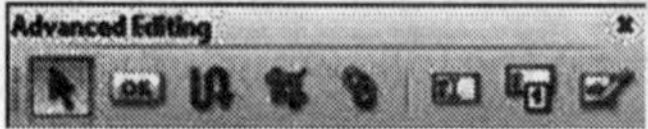

For text tools, you have three choices:

- ❏ **Touch Up Text tool:** Used to manipulate text.
- ❏ **Touch Up Object tool:** Used to manipulate objects.
- ❏ **Touch Up Reading Order tool:** Used to correct the reading order or structure of the document.

You have a few ways to accomplish text edits:

- ❏ Choose the Touch Up Text tool, click within the text that you want to change to obtain an insertion point, and then start typing the new text.
- ❏ Click with the Touch Up tool in your text and press the Backspace or Delete key to delete text.
- ❏ With the Touch Up tool, drag to highlight text and enter new text to replace the highlighted text.

Using Commenting and Annotation Tools

Text Edits tool

The Text Edits tool is actually six separate text commenting tools. Use these tools to replace selected text, highlight selected text, add a note to selected text, insert text at cursor, underline selected text, and cross out text for deletion.

To use the Text Edits tool, follow these steps:

- ❏ Choose the Text Edits tool and drag to select text that requires a change or comment.
- ❏ Click the arrow to the right of the Text Edits tool to access the drop-down list containing your six choices.
- ❏ Choose an option from the list of available editing choices:
  - Replace Selected Text: Replaces the selected text.
  - Highlight Selected Text: Highlights the selected text.
  - Add a Note to Selected Text: Allows you to add a note to the selected text.
  - Insert Text at Cursor: Places a cursor at the end of the selected text.
  - Underline Selected Text: Underlines the selected text.
  - Cross Out Text for Deletion: Crosses out the selected text.

The Stamp tool

You can use stamps to identify documents or to highlight a certain part of a document. Common stamps include Confidential, Draft, Sign Here, and Approved.

To apply a stamp to your document, follow these steps:

- ❑ Select the Stamp tool from the Comment & Mark-up toolbar.
- ❑ Click the arrow to the right of the Stamp tool and from the menu, choose the stamp you want to apply to the document.
- ❑ Drag within your document at the location where you want the stamp to appear.

The Highlight Text, Underline Text, and Cross Out Text tools

To highlight text, follow these steps:

- ❑ Select the Highlight Text tool from the Comment & Mark-up toolbar.
- ❑ Drag over the text that you want highlighted.
  The text is now highlighted.

To underline text, follow these steps:

- ❑ Select the Underline Text tool by selecting **Tools⇨Comment & Mark-up Tools ⇨Underline Text**.
- ❑ Drag over the text that you want underlined.
  The text is now underlined.

To cross out text, follow these steps:

- ❑ Select the Cross Out Text tool by choosing **Tools⇨Comment & Markup Tools⇨Cross Out Text Tool**.
- ❑ Drag over the text that you want crossed out.

The Attach File tools

Follow these steps for file and sound attachments:

- ❑ Choose **Comments⇨Comment & Markup Tools⇨Attach a File** as a Comment. A pushpin icon appears.
- ❑ Click where you want the attachment noted. The Add Attachment dialog box appears.
- ❑ In the Add Attachment dialog box, browse to the file that you want to attach and click the Select button. You can attach text, graphic, or sound files.
- ❑ Select the type of icon to represent the attached file and then click OK.

The drawing tools

There are three shape tools, two line tools, and a pencil in the Comment & Mark-up toolbar. Use the drawing tools to add lines, ovals, rectangles, and other shapes to your PDF file. These shapes can call attention to specific portions of a document.

To use the Cloud Shape tool, follow these steps:

- ❑ Select the Cloud Shape tool from the Comment & Mark-up toolbar.
- ❑ Click in your document to begin the shape.
- ❑ Click again in another position to set the length of the first part of the cloud and then click again to begin shaping your cloud.

Click as often as you like to create your shape.

- ❑ When you're finished with your shape, double-click to close the cloud shape.
- ❑ While the Cloud Shape tool is selected, click the shape you created and drag the corner points to resize, if necessary.

To use the rectangle and oval shapes, follow these steps:

- ❑ Select either the Rectangle or Oval Shape tool from the Comment & Mark-up toolbar.
- ❑ Click and drag in your document to draw the shape.
- ❑ While the drawing tool you chose is selected, click the shape you created and drag the corner points to resize, if necessary.
- ❑ After creating the shape, right-click (Windows) or Control-click (Mac) the shape and choose Properties from the contextual menu to change the colour and thickness of the line values; when you're finished, click OK.

The Text Box tool

When creating notes that you want to prominently display on a document, you can use the Text Box tool.

Follow these steps to add a text box to hold your comments:

- ❑ Select the Text Box tool from the **Comment & Mark-up** toolbar.

  A text field is placed directly on the document.
- ❑ Drag to add the comment.
- ❑ Right-click (Windows) or Control-click (Mac) and choose Properties from the contextual menu to set the colour of the text box that contains the note.
- ❑ Make your choices to modify the appearance of the text box and then click OK.

The Callout tool

The Callout tool creates a callout text box that points to a section of your document with an arrow. The callout text box is made up of three parts: the text box, the knee line, and the end point line. You can resize each part individually to customise the callout area of your document.

To use the Callout tool, follow these steps:

- ❑ Select the Callout tool from the **Comment & Mark-up** toolbar.
- ❑ Click where you want the arrowhead point to be.
- ❑ Drag up or down or to the side to position the text box and begin typing.

  You can click the text box and then use the anchor points on the line to resize the box.
- ❑ Right-click (Windows) or Control-click (Mac) and choose Properties from the contextual menu to set the colour of the callout text box. You can change the size, colour, and font characteristics of the text in the callout text box.
- ❑ Make your choices to modify the appearance of the callout text box and then click OK.

The Pencil tool

With the Pencil tool, you can create freeform lines on your documents. These lines can be useful when you're trying to attract attention to a specific portion of a page. Just follow these steps:

- ❑ Select the Pencil tool from the **Comment & Mark-up** toolbar.
- ❑ Click and drag to draw on your document.
- ❑ Edit the colour and thickness of lines created with the Pencil tool by right-clicking (Windows) or Control-clicking (Mac) the line and choosing Properties from the contextual menu. Alternatively, you can press Ctrl+E (Windows) or Ô+E (Mac) to access the Properties toolbar.
- ❑ Make your choices and click OK.

Sharing comments

You can share your comments with other reviewers who have access to the same PDF document by following these steps:

- ❑ Make sure that the Comments List is visible by clicking the Comments tab on the bottom left of the Document window.
- ❑ Select the comment that you want to export by clicking it (Shift+click for multiple selections).
- ❑ From the Comments List window, choose **Options⇨Export Selected Comments.** The Export Comments dialog box appears.
- ❑ Browse to the location where you want the comments to be saved and give the saved file a new name.

You now have a file that includes only the comments' information, and not the entire PDF file.

Securing Your PDF Files

Applying Password Security to Your PDF Documents

- ❑ With a PDF file open, click and hold the Secure button on the Security taskbar and choose Encrypt with Password.

  Click OK when the dialog box appears, verifying that you want to apply security to this PDF. The Password Security - Settings dialog box appears, as shown in the figure:

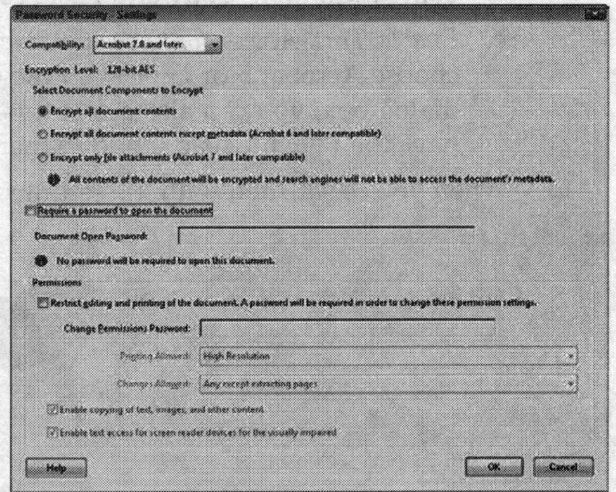

- ❑ Choose Acrobat 7 from the Compatibility drop-down list.

  Although Acrobat 9 and later provides more robust security, few people are using version 9 of Acrobat, making it difficult to distribute the file with this high level of security.

- ❑ Select the Require a Password to Open the Document check box.
- ❑ Enter a password in the Document Open Password text box.
- ❑ Click OK.
- ❑ Confirm the password, click OK again, and the dialog box closes.
- ❑ Save, close, and then reopen the PDF file.

To limit editing and printing of your PDF document, follow these steps:

- ❑ With a PDF file open, click and hold the Secure button on the Security taskbar and choose Encrypt with Password. The Password Security – Settings dialog box opens.

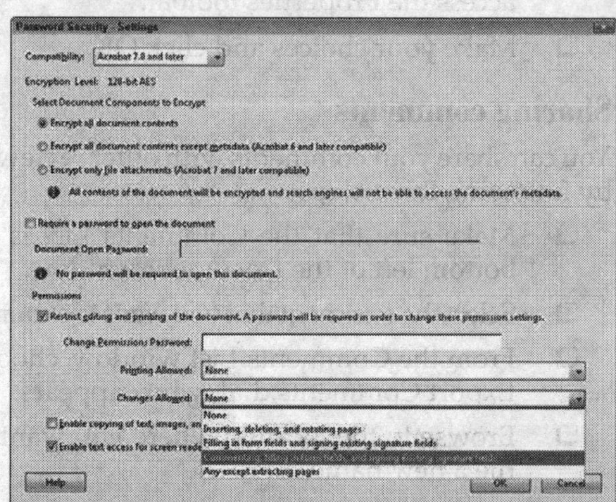

- ❑ In the Permissions area, select the check box labelled Restrict Editing and Printing of the document.
- ❑ In the Change Permissions Password text box, enter a password.
- ❑ Choose whether users can print the document by selecting from the Printing Allowed drop-down list.
- ❑ Choose from the Changes Allowed drop-down list to restrict editing. (see Figure ⇨)
- ❑ Select the last two check boxes if desired:
  - *Enable Copying of Text, Images, and Other Content:* When deselected, this option restricts copying and pasting of text and graphics from a PDF file into other documents. Selecting this option lets users extract text and images from a file by using the simple Copy and Paste commands.
  - *Enable Text Access for Screen Reader Devices for the Visually Impaired:* When you choose Acrobat 5 or later from the Compatibility drop-down list at the top of the dialog box, you can also select this check box to allow visually impaired users to have the PDF file read aloud to them.
- ❑ When you're satisfied with the settings, click OK.

Adobe Flash

Introduction to flash

Adobe Flash was created in 1996 as a way to display rich media on a webpage. In the mid-90s, most websites were a collection of static pages that displayed only text and images. When Flash was introduced, it opened a new world of animation and interactivity to the Web. People were able to create moving animations and clickable interactive graphics that went beyond the capabilities of standard HTML and CSS.

Flash was – and still is – owned by a single company, which is now Adobe. This means that Flash is a proprietary software, and is not an open standard on the Web.

Here are some of the **pros** for using Flash on a website:

- Quickly create rich interactive graphics using a timeline-based software tool.
- Utilise a number of pre-built libraries and classes to build sophisticated projects that might otherwise take longer to build from scratch.
- A cross-browser compatible tool that works the same on Internet Explorer, Firefox, Mozilla, Opera and Chrome.
- Good for construction of data-intense animated data visualisations that need to access an online database.

Here are some of the **cons** when using Flash:

- ❑ Does not work on a multitude of mobile smartphone devices.
- ❑ Many touch-screen devices (i.e. tablet computers) require different types of interaction that aren't often supported by most Flash projects. For example, the difference between a mouse roll-over, and a tap, touch or swipe.
- ❑ Does not conform to the open standards of the web as defined by the World Wide Web Consortium, thus it does not promote a standardized open Internet.
- ❑ Issues regarding accessibility of content for persons using special tools like screen readers.
- ❑ In some cases, intensive use of Flash graphics can drain the battery life on many laptops and mobile devices.
- ❑ Not as optimised for search engines (SEO). Flash is a closed multimedia construct on most webpages making it difficult for some search engines to properly index.

Drawing in Flash

Vector vs. Raster

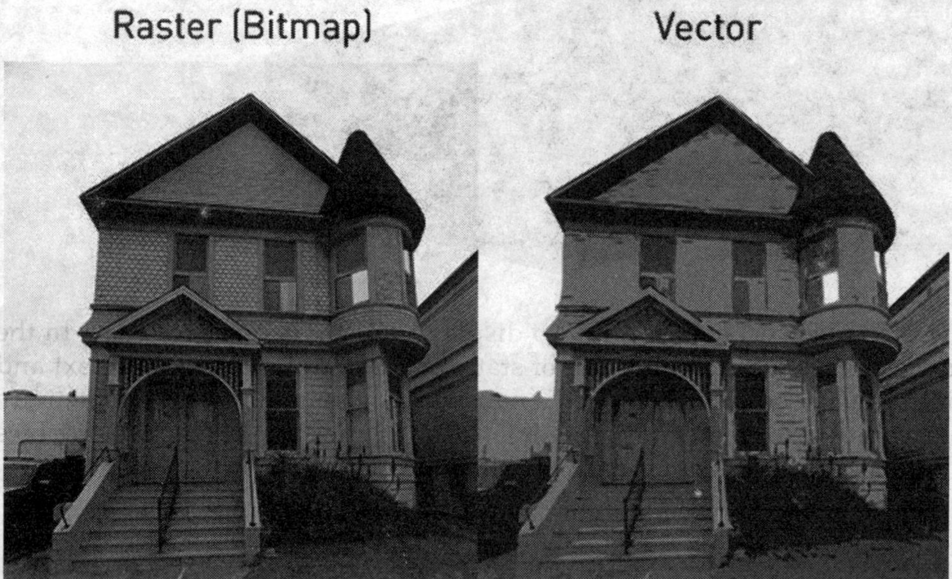

It is important to understand the difference between vector graphics and raster (Bitmap) images. Vectors are colour-shape-based line art, while bitmaps are photographic images made up of pixels.

Vectors are made up of lines called **paths**. These lines are connected by dots called **anchor points**. Vectors are not made up of pixels, and thus their size can be changed without losing any quality. Vectors don't take up much memory, but they can be taxing on a computer's processor the more complex they become. Vectors are designed to be simple shapes, graphics or animations.

Bitmaps are photographic images that are comprised tiny squares called pixels. Bitmaps lose quality when they are resized, especially when their size is increased from their native size. Newer algorithms in the way Adobe resizes bitmaps have allowed quality loss to be minimal in many cases where the percentage change in size is a small. Bitmaps take up much more memory (and increase loading time on a webpage) however, they are not as taxing on processing.

Tools

There are dozens of tools in Flash that one can use for various purposes in creating art. We will go over a few essential tools to start with.

Selection tool

Sub-selection tool

The first are the two arrow tools; the **Selection Tool** (black arrow) and the **Sub-selection Tool** (white arrow). The Selection Tool is used for selecting and moving elements on the stage. It can also be used to bend and modify vector shapes. The Sub-selection Tool (white arrow) is only used for selecting drawing paths in shapes. The Selection Tool is generally used much more often and is the default tool for most tasks. The Sub-selection Tool is only used in specific cases when drawing or modifying vector shapes.

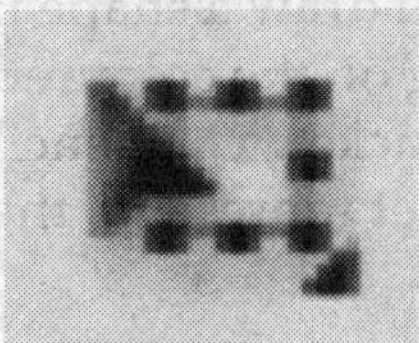

The **Free Transform** tool is used to change the size of an object on the stage. When using the Free Transform tool, you must first click on an object on the stage to select it, and then use the eight black handle points that appear around the box to change the shape of your object. When selecting objects with the Free Transform Tool, a small white circle will appear, usually in the centre of the object. This is called the reference point, and can be moved with the mouse. This reference point will determine how the tool rotates and scales the object. It is also possible to skew an object by moving the cursor just outside the bound of the box.

The **Lasso Tool** is used for selecting object on the stage. It is done by drawing a circle around the objects you wish to be selected. It can also be used for selecting portions of a shape.

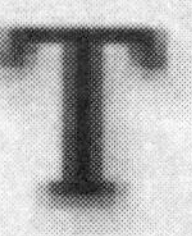

The **Text Tool** is used to create text boxes for entering text. The tool can be used by simply clicking the stage once to create a default text box (which can be resized later) or by clicking and drawing a text box to a desired shape. Static text boxes can only be drawn to a specified width and always start out as one line of text. This means you won't be able to give your text box a height. As you type, you can press return to create additional lines of text. Dynamic text boxes can be given a height.

The **Shape Tool** is for drawing some basic preset shapes, like a rectangle, circle or polygon. Click and hold down on the tool item to select the shape type you want. There are settings in your property inspector for specifying characteristics of the rectangle and oval tools when you draw them. The primitive version of those shapes allows you to continuously edit those properties after you've drawn the shape (such as the rounded corners on the rectangle, and the shape of an oval). You will need to either break apart or convert the primitive shapes in order to further edit them.

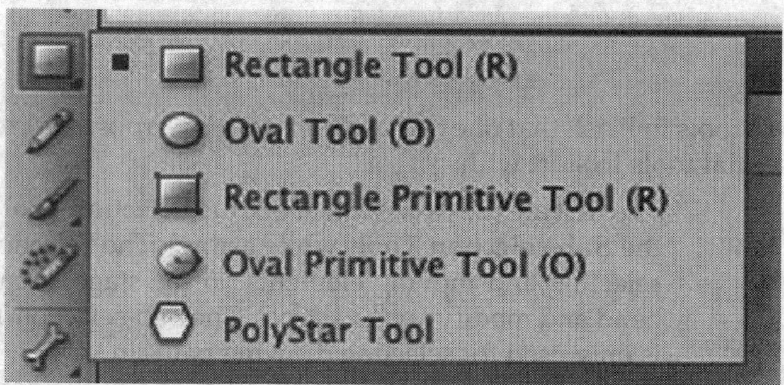

The **Colour Picker Tools** allow you to specify the colours of shapes either before you draw them, or you can change the colour after you draw a shape if it's currently selected. The colours can be selected by clicking on the coloured boxes just below the icon of a pencil and the icon of a paint bucket. The pencil icon represents the colour for the stroke, and the paint bucket represents the colour for the fill.

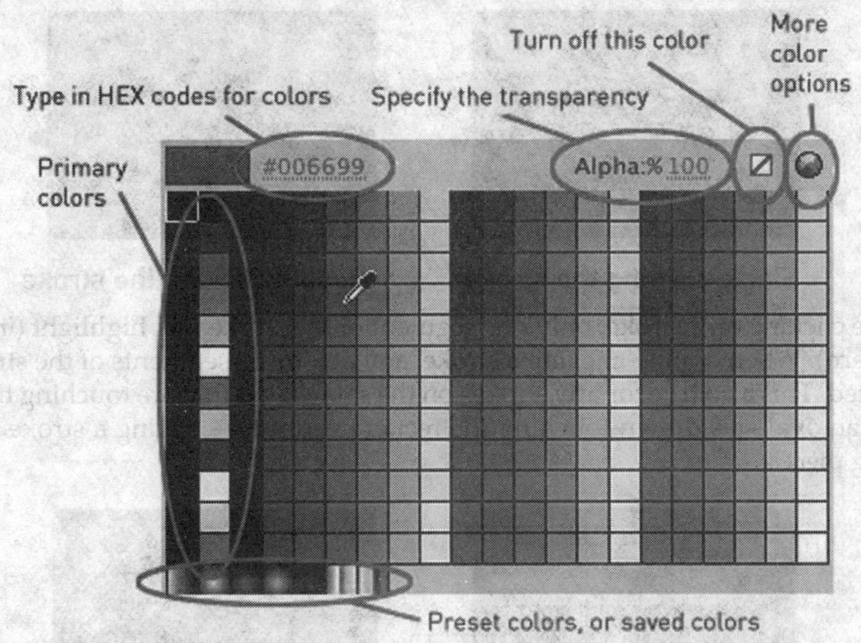

The **Colour Picker pallete** has several options for choosing a colour. Of notable interest are the options along the top of the window which allow you to turn off the colour, or specify an Alpha (transparency) setting. If you have the six-digit colour hexadecimal colour code, you can type it in by clicking the code at the top of this box.

Parts of Basic Shapes in Flash

There are two parts to drawing basic shapes in the Flash. The **stroke** is the outline, and the **fill** is the colour shape itself. It is important to realise that the stroke and fill are two independent parts of a shape, and can be drawn separately.

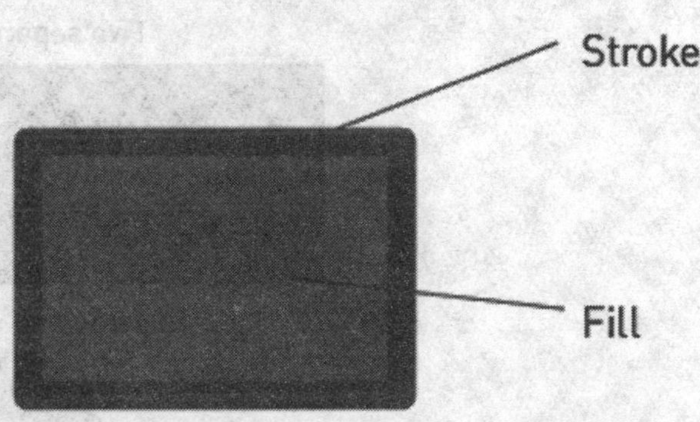

For people who have never used vector-based drawing software, shapes can seem oddly non-intuitive. It is important to understand all of the quirks to drawing in Flash, and why shapes respond to certain actions. With a little practice, shape manipulation can become like second nature.

Selecting Shapes

The first thing to understand about shapes is how they respond to selection with the **selection tool** (black arrow tool). Draw a rectangle on the stage, and use the selection tool to click on the various portions of the shape.

Single clicking the stroke Double clicking the stroke

When single clicking on a stroke, only one segment of the stroke will highlight (indicated by a stipple pattern). When double-clicking a stroke, any adjoining segments of the stroke will also be highlighted. This also true for any strokes on the same layer that are touching the shape. For example, if an oval was drawn touching the rectangle, double-clicking a stroke would select all adjoining pieces.

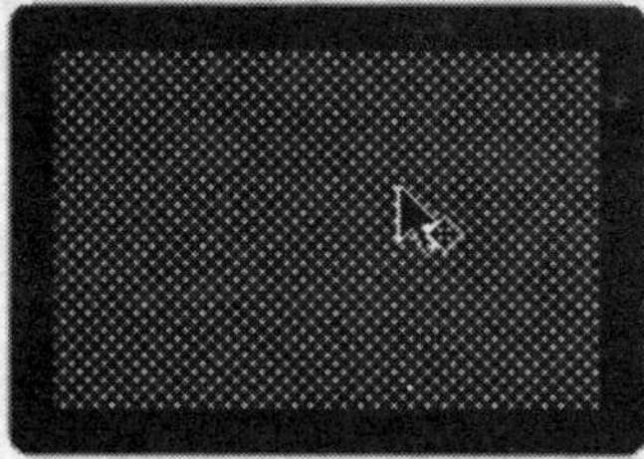

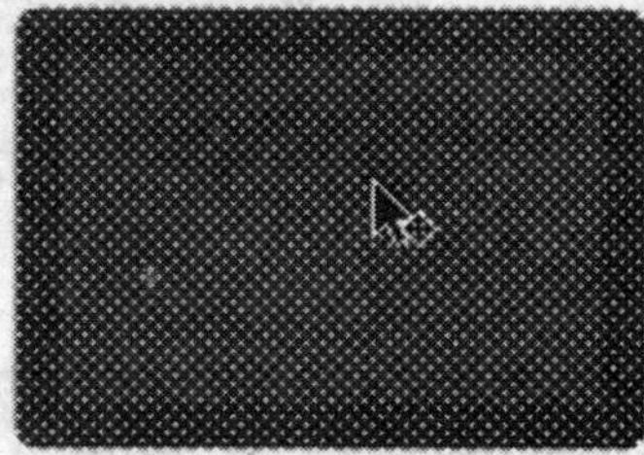

Single clicking the fill Double clicking the fill

Fills operate a little differently in Flash. Single clicking a fill will select and highlight the entire fill area. However, double clicking a fill will select the fill as well as any adjoining strokes. Double-clicking the fill is an easy way to select an entire shape if you wish to move it around on the stage.

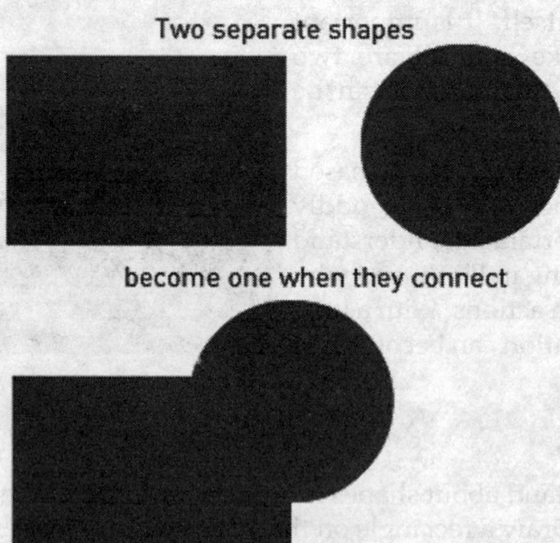

Two separate fill shapes will become one fill shape if they are moved on top of each other and are deselected. This is important to note when drawing, as it can often be counter-intuitive to what most people expect.

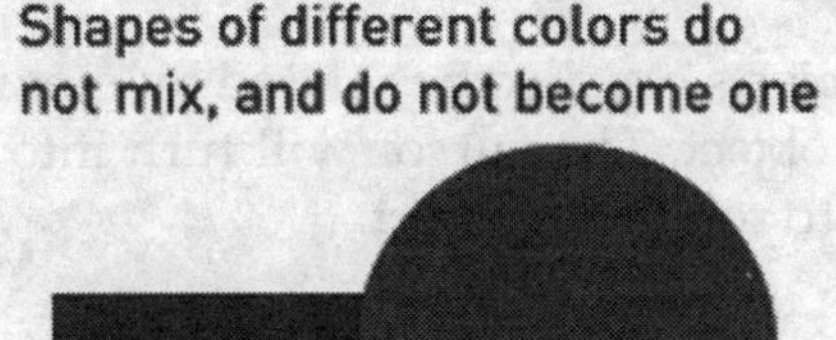

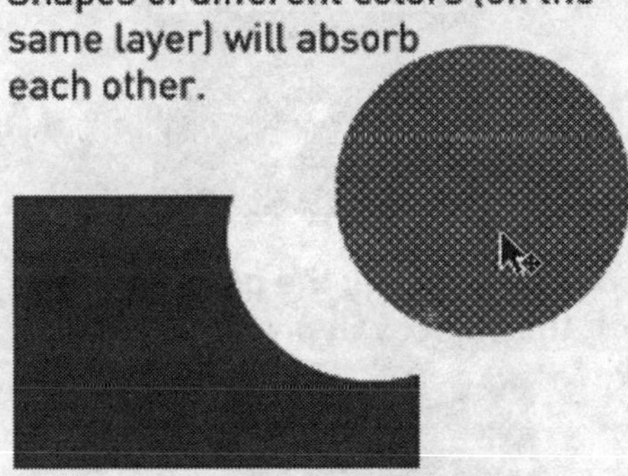

Shapes of different colours do not mix in the same fashion. Instead, they will absorb, or remove other shapes. The most recently selected shape is what takes precedence.

This characteristic of fill shapes (either connecting or absorbing other shapes) can be prevented if you wish by grouping objects into a number of different containers, such as a drawing object, a group or a symbol.

Modifying Shapes

There are a number of ways to modify shapes in Flash. The most basic method is to use the **Free Transform tool** to select a shape and adjust its size, rotation or skew properties.

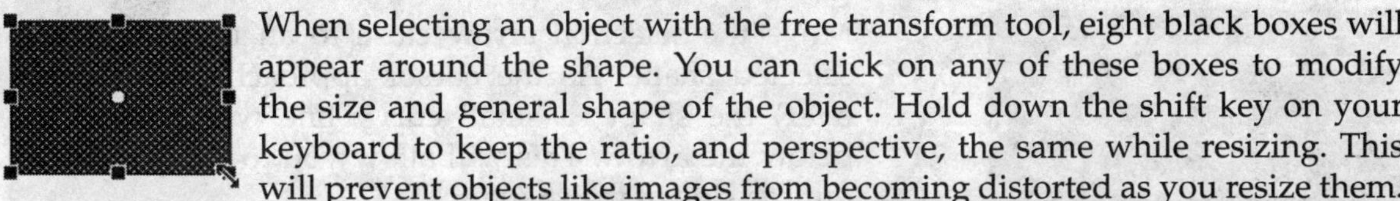

When selecting an object with the free transform tool, eight black boxes will appear around the shape. You can click on any of these boxes to modify the size and general shape of the object. Hold down the shift key on your keyboard to keep the ratio, and perspective, the same while resizing. This will prevent objects like images from becoming distorted as you resize them. You can also flip an object by grabbing one side and moving it past the opposite side of the shape (however, this is only noticeable with objects like images.)

Shapes can be skewed by moving the mouse cursor just outside the object between the centre box and a corner box. Click and drag to skew the shape.

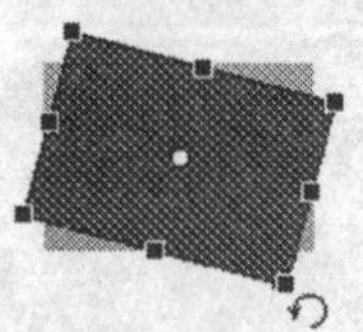

Shapes and objects can also be rotated by moving the cursor just outside the corner of the object. The cursor will turn into a small circular symbol, and you can drag to rotate the object.

The white dot in the centre of the object is called the **reference point**. It can be moved by clicking on it and dragging it anywhere on or even outside the shape.

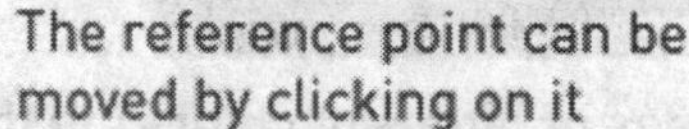

It will specify the point where the object will pivot

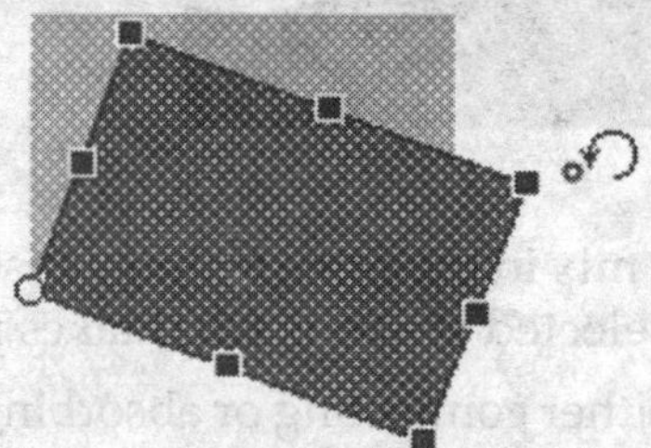

Bending Shapes with the Selection Tool

You can also modify shapes using only the Selection Tool (black arrow tool). This is useful for reshaping fills, or bending a stroke. Modifying shapes can be a little tricky. It takes practice to really get it down.

Move the selection arrow close to an un-selected shape. As the cursor approaches (but is not over) the shape, a small curvy line will appear just below the arrow. This will allow you to click and drag out the side of the shape.

This allows you to reshape the edges of the object into curves. It is also possible to push an edge into the shape.

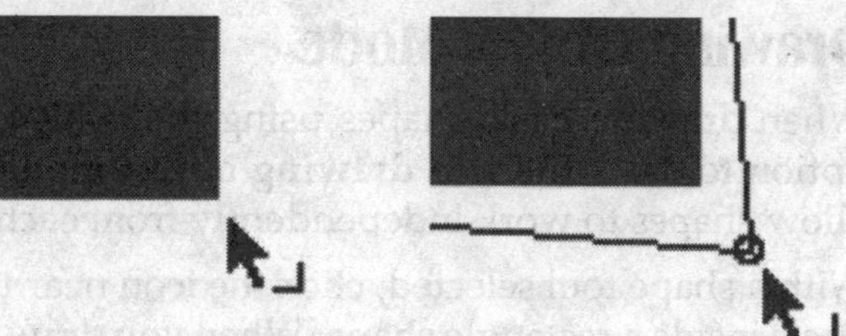

You can also modify the corners of a shape in much the same fashion. When you move the selection arrow cursor just outside a corner of the shape, you will see a small corner symbol appear next to the arrow. This signifies that you can click and drag the corner point to a new location.

Modifying Shapes with Sub-Selection and Pen Tools

You can modify shapes with fine-grain precision using the sub-selection or pen tools. These tools allow you to change the paths that make up the shape at a fundamental level. All shapes in Flash are made up of lines and points in a connect-the-dots fashion. Some of the dots, called anchor points, are designed to be curved (known as bezier curves) and will have handles. Others are corner points and have straight lines connecting them. Lastly, some points are both, they have a curved line on one side, and a straight line on the other.

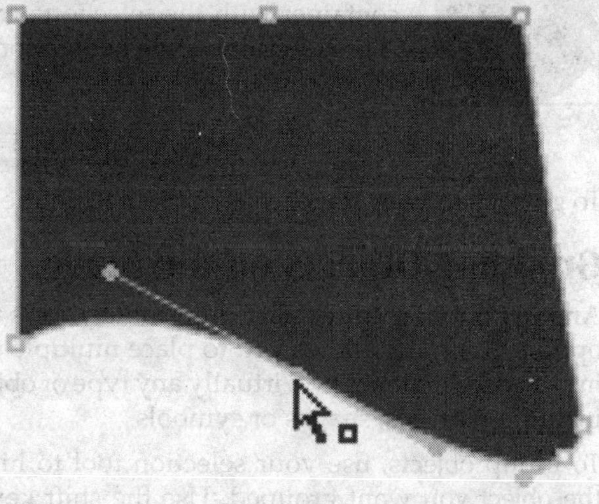

Using the sub-selection tool (the white arrow) click on the edge of a shape to see its paths. You can click on the small green anchor points and reposition them. If an anchor point is a bezier curve, some handles will appear when you select it. You can click the handles and drag them to modify the curve of the shape.

To add anchor points, delete anchor points or change an anchor point from curve to corner, you will have to use the pen tool options.

The **Pen Tools** are the animators' most used tools. The first two tools, the Pen Tool and Freeform Pen Tool, are used by illustrators and animators to create shapes from scratch. Usage of these tools goes beyond the scope of this lesson. The last three tools, Add Anchor Point, Delete Anchor Point and Convert Point are used to modify existing shapes.

Grouping Objects

Flash has numerous ways to group objects on the stage. Grouping objects can serve a number of benefits, depending on the type of grouping you use. This page will cover some of the basic ways by which you can group objects, and end with the most important group type: symbols.

Drawing Object Mode

When drawing basic shapes using the ovals or rectangle shape tools, you have an option to draw them in **drawing object mode**. Drawing objects are containers that allow shapes to work independently from each other.

With a shape tool selected, click the icon near the bottom of your tool palette that looks like a circle inside a rectangle shape. When you draw shapes with this option turned on, every shape will automatically be placed in a separate grouping box. This will allow you to place shapes over other shapes without the effects of having them affect each other.

A rectangular box will appear around any object you draw. This is the container that holds the object. If you wish to edit your shape, you must double-click the container with the selection arrow to go inside the drawing object container. A bread-crumb style navigation will show you that you are inside a drawing object container.

To go back to your stage, click on Scene 1 in the navigation bar.

Grouping Objects on the Stage

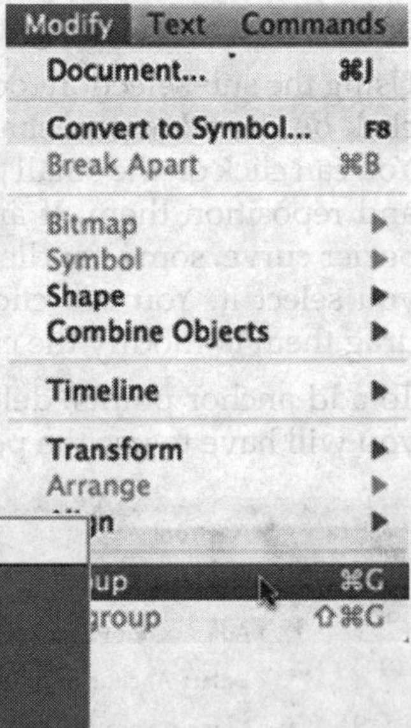

Another option to put objects into containers is using the Grouping option. Grouping allows you to place multiple objects on the stage into a generic container. Virtually any type of object can be grouped, including images, shapes or symbols.

To group objects, use your selection tool to highlight all parts of the object you want grouped. Use the shift key to select multiple objects, or click and drag a selection box around the objects you want to select. Next, select **Group** from the **Modify** menu at the top of the screen and this will group all currently selected objects.

With multiple objects grouped, you can treat the grouped container as one object. It can be rotated, resized or adjusted as if it were a single object. To ungroup object, simply use the ungroup option also found in the modify menu.

Breaking Apart

Grouping objects seems simple at first, but can quickly get complicated when you have groups inside of groups. Flash has a mechanism called break apart which will reduce an object to a simpler form. In the case of grouping, it will gradually ungroup the objects until they return to shapes.

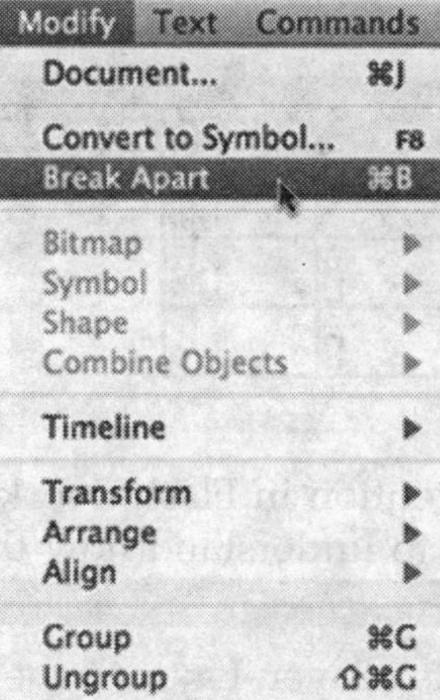

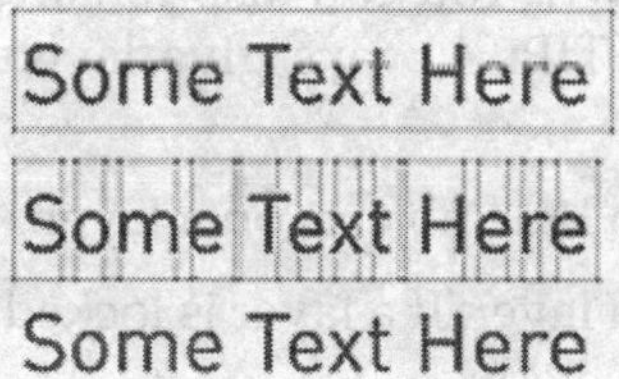

Some care should be taken with breaking apart groups. The break apart option will convert objects like text and images into shapes. In the case of text, breaking apart will first separate all of the letters of a text box into their own text box. Doing another break apart will convert the letters into shape fills.

Building flash templates

Understanding File Types

There are three types of files you will generally encounter when working with Flash:

- **.FLA** – This is the authoring file which requires the Flash program. It contains all of the images, text and graphics that exist in your Flash project.
- **.SWF** – This is the published Flash "movie." You have to embed this in a Webpage or upload it to a Content Management System.
- **.FLV** – This is a Flash video file. You cannot play this video by itself unless you create a player in Flash to hold this movie file.

Working with Flash Layout

At first appearance, the Flash environment looks to be a cross between Photoshop and Premiere. You will see a timeline at the top of your screen, and there is a white "stage" area in the middle where the work is displayed. While Flash may appear similar to both programs, it is a mistake to think that Flash works like either of the previous two programs mentioned.

The biggest difference is that Flash is a "frame-based" program, so the timeline does not represent actual time, rather each square represents an individual frame that can be

manipulated. Flash originally began as an animation program, but has evolved to support displaying interactive graphics and rich media in the form of audio, video, graphics and text.

Timeline

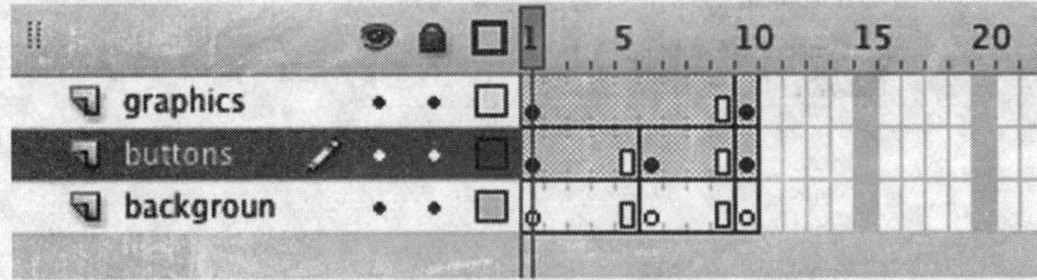

The timeline is a very unique convention in Flash. Working in the timeline can be tricky to a first-time user. Taking a moment to understand how the timeline works will save a lot of trouble in the long run.

- ❑ **Layers** – Each row represents a layer. Layers have a hierarchy, so if one layer is above another, objects on higher layers will cover objects on layers below it. You can re-order layers by simply clicking and dragging the layers up or down. You can also rename layers by double-clicking on the text that describes them. TIP: Always give layers relevant names.
- ❑ **Hiding** – Click on the small black dot beneath the eye icon to hide objects on a layer.
- ❑ **Locking** – Click on the black dot beneath the padlock to lock a layer. If a layer is locked, nothing on that layer can be changed, selected, moved or affected.
- ❑ **Frames** – Each square on the timeline represents one frame. The time it takes to display a frame depends on the framerate of your project.
- ❑ **Keyframes** – Keyframes are denoted by the solid black dots. A keyframe means there is content on the stage in that frame. Each keyframe is independent, so if there is content on one keyframe, another keyframe might have something completely different.
- ❑ **Gray Frames** – Gray frames are simply a continuation of the keyframe directly preceding them. Nothing changes in gray frames until the next keyframe.
- ❑ **Small White Boxes in Gray** – This denotes the end of a keyframe. In reality, it means nothing. Simply ignore these boxes.
- ❑ **Blank Keyframes** – These are the small white circles. It represents a keyframe with no content.
- ❑ **Red Playbar** – This represents the section of the timeline that is currently on display in the stage. You can grab this red square and drag it back-and-forth through the timeline.

Selecting (highlighting) frames on the timeline is tricky. You can click and drag to highlight frames, but once frames are highlighted, you are forced to drag them on the second click. You can de-select them by clicking elsewhere if you want to redo your selection. The easiest way for first-time users to highlight frames is to hold the shift key and click all the frames you want to select.

Library

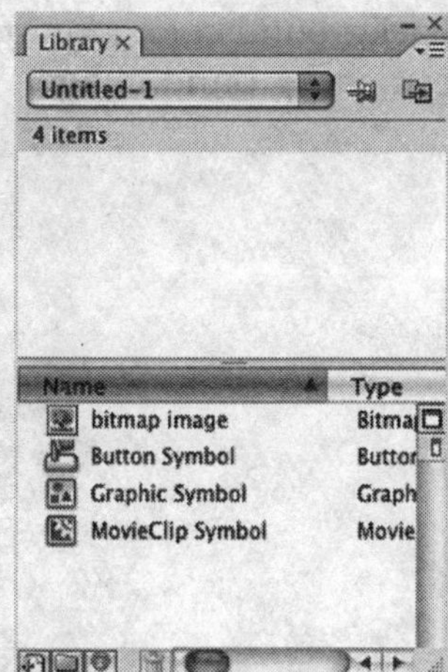

It's best to think of the Library as a bin that holds all of your media. Anything you import into Flash will automatically be displayed in the Library. You can click and drag things out of the Library and onto the stage.

Property Inspector

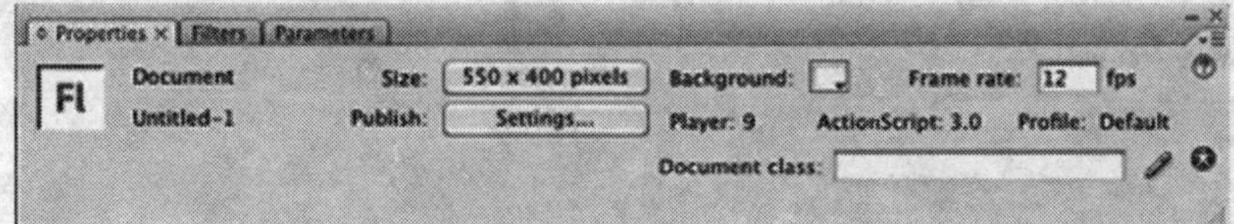

One of the staples of the Flash program is the property inspector. This panel is contextual, which means the options on this window pane **will change** depending on what you last clicked on.

For example: To see properties for the timeline, click on the timeline. To see and adjust the properties of an object on the stage, click on that object and the property inspector window will change to reflect the settings related to that clicked object.

Setting up a Flash project

In this Section, you will be guided through all of the steps to create a simple Flash template that consists of three sections. It's important to understand that Flash should be used as a publishing tool, not an editing one. This means, building your project in Flash should be the last step in the multimedia creation process.

Setting image sizes

Before you begin building a project in Flash, you want to make sure you have correctly sized all of your images in Photoshop **before** you import them.

Don't resize images in Flash because it may cause images to appear jagged or distorted, similarly to how an image might appear if it is resized on a Webpage. This requires you to know how your Flash project will appear before you start building it. Generally people first build comps or mockups in Photoshop to size images and understand the size relationships between the different elements.

In our tutorial sample media, we have already gone through the process of correctly sizing all of the images to match the output.

Setting the Stage

First, click anywhere in the stage to bring up the stage properties in your property inspector pane. Click on the "**size**" option, and this will allow you to set the document size and

background colour, among other things. Make your project **600 x 400** pixels, the same size as our background image.

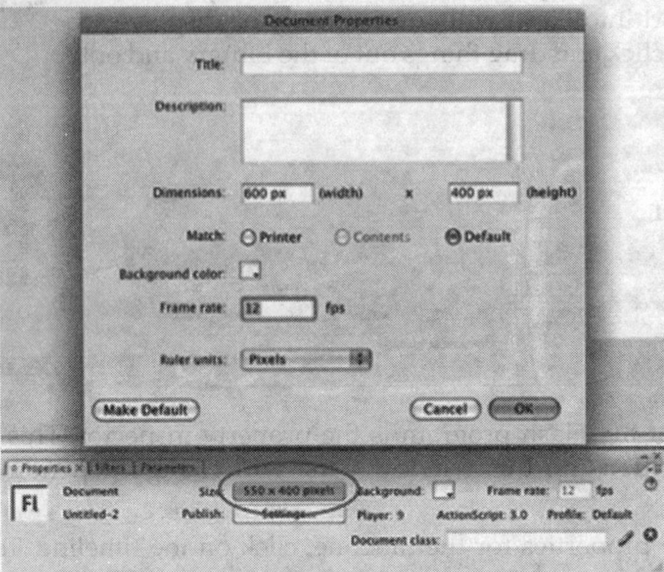

In most cases, you will check with the Web team first to see how large to publish your Flash project. You should decide this before building your project.

Importing your photos

To import your photos, simply go to the File menu and click "**Import -> Import to Library**".

You can pick multiple photos to import at the same time by holding down the **shift** key and selecting multiple photos. Go ahead and import all of the photos from the images folder in our tutorial sample.

Creating a Background

Having a background image or graphic is a very popular style in Flash multimedia projects. In this step, drag the background.jpg image to your stage.

To align your image with the stage, open the "**align**" pane under the window menu.

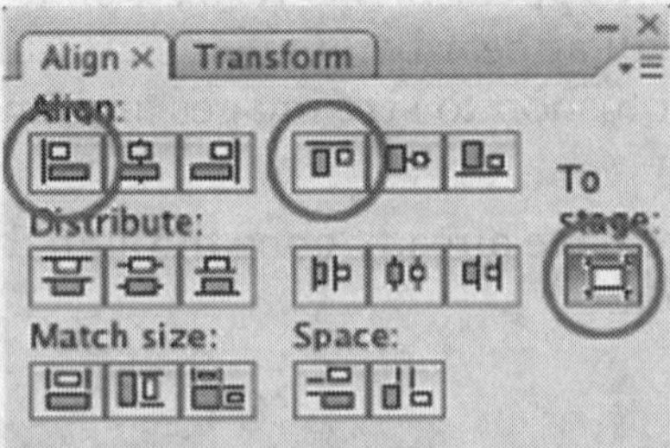

To align, you must first set the **To stage:** option to "**on**," then click the buttons to align to the left edge of the stage and the top edge of the stage.

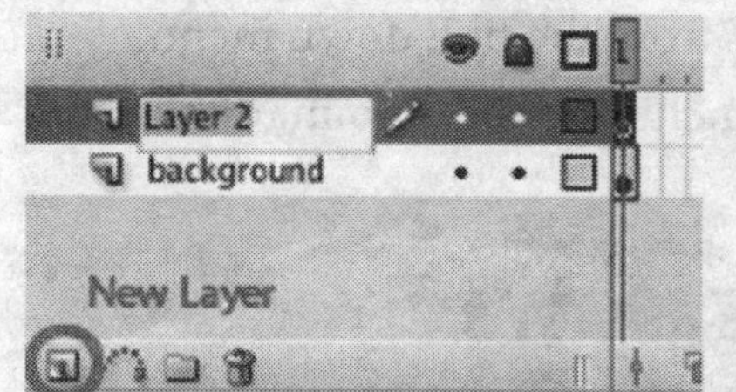

Next, double click on name of the layer up in the timeline and name it to "**background**." You might have noticed that the keyframe on this sole layer has now turned black to indicate that there is something on that keyframe. Next, click the little page icon to create a new layer, which is where we will put our title.

Name the new layer "**title**." (**Important!** After you create the title layer, LOCK your background layer. Why? Accidentally placing content on the wrong layer is very easy to do in Flash. Lock your layers when you're not using them to prevent you from accidentally selecting them or putting content on them.)

Creating a graphical title for your project

You want the title to be attractive and easily descriptive. Titles are typically not as long as headlines in a newspaper, but serve a very similar purpose. You can also rely on subtext to describe your project in greater detail.

Use the text tool to draw a box on your stage. And type in "**Disappearing in Darfur.**"

When you click on the text tool, you might have noticed your properties box has changed to show you all of the options related to text. Here you can change the colour of your text, the font, and the style.

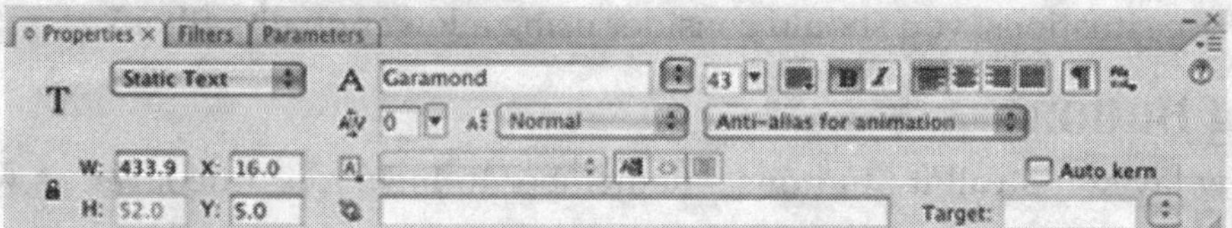

You want to make sure you are using **Static Text** (like it sounds, it is text that never changes). This is the most common form of text you will use for titles, captions, or text that is "**static**" and unchanging.

(**Fonts**: Unlike Web design, you are free to use ANY font you want. Flash converts all fonts into something called "vector outlines" so go wild! But follow standard graphic design principles. Weird or crazy fonts are best for titles and simple easy to read fonts are best for blocks of text.)

Adding Filter Effects to your Text

You can add effects, such as drop shadows, to your text by clicking on the **filters** tab in your property inspector:

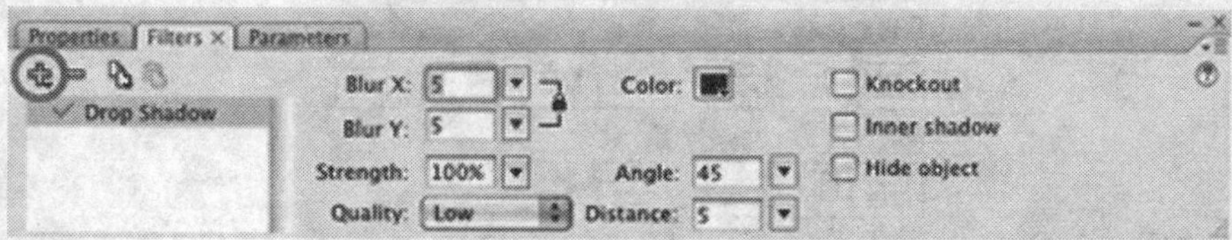

Press the small plus symbol "+" and choose "**Drop Shadow**" from the pull down menu.

Here you can adjust all of the settings for the drop shadow, including the amount of blur, the angle of the shadow, and the distance from the text.

(**Note on Quality**: Most filters have quality settings. Setting them to the highest quality seems like the natural thing to do, but doing so can make your project very "process intensive" which means older or slower computers might struggle to display these graphics. Generally this not an issue unless you have several filters (10 to 100) running at the same time on different pieces of text. In these situations, you should consider using a lower quality filter.)

Inserting Buttons

Create a new layer and call it "**buttons**." Remember to **lock** your title layer, as we won't be using it again.

(Putting everything on its own layer not only helps to organise your project, it also makes it possible to find and select things. Having too many elements on one layer makes it difficult to find or select objects when they overlap each other.)

Now grab each of the **button1_up.jpg, button2_up.jpg, button3_up.jpg** and drag them to the right side of the stage one at a time, so they are stacked vertically.

You can space the images out evenly by selecting all of them and using the align pane. This time we are not aligning them to the stage but, rather, to each other. So we turn off the **To stage:** option.

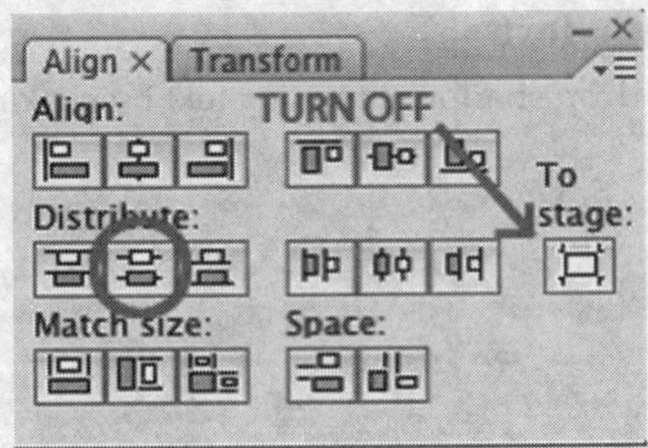

You can use the middle **Distribute** option or the left **Space** button to space out the three buttons. You can also align each button to their left or right edge. In order for this to work, all three buttons have to be selected (you will see a grey strip surrounding them).

The next step is to convert the three images into button symbols.

Converting to Symbols

The idea of "symbols" is by far the most confusing part in the process of learning Flash. It is best to think of symbols as containers that hold things. In this discussion, we will primarily be using the button symbol.

Click on only **ONE** of your three button images, making sure only one is selected. Then in the top menu click on **Modify** then choose **Convert To Symbol**.

Don't be fooled, this wording is a little deceptive. You are not actually converting the image into a symbol, rather you are placing it **inside** a symbol container.

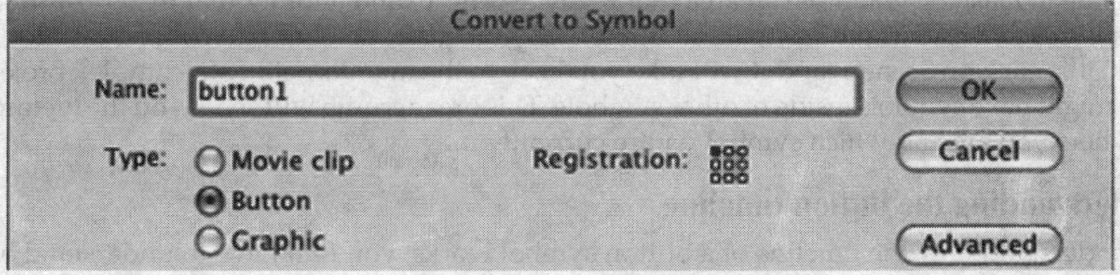

Choose **button** for the symbol type, and give your symbol a relevant name. This name is for your reference only.

You might have noticed a new addition to your Library: the button symbol you just created. It might seem redundant to keep the button1_up.jpg image in your Library now that you have converted it to a symbol, but deleting the image from your Library will only remove the image from the symbol container, and you'll be left with an empty button symbol!

You will know you have successfully converted your button to a symbol when you see a blue line surrounding your image and a small circle in the centre. Repeat the steps above for each image, converting each one to a **button symbol**.

Editing Button Symbols

Once you have "converted" each of the three images into button symbols, you can edit the properties of each symbol by double-clicking it to enter **symbol-editing mode**.

Double-click on the first button, and you'll notice that your timeline has completely changed! Don't worry, you're simply seeing the timeline INSIDE the button.

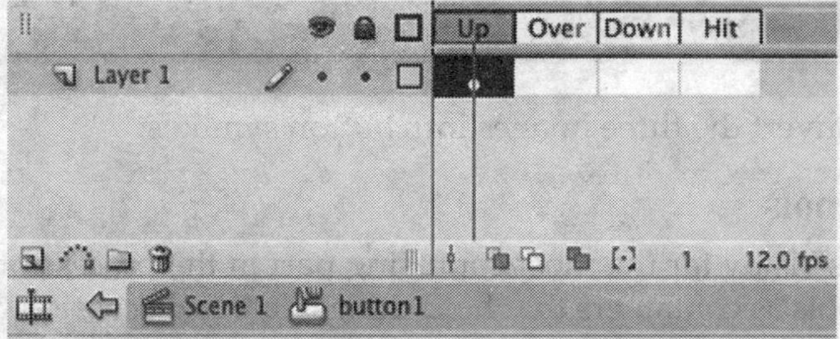

Note....

The image above represents Flash CS3. In Flash 8 the breadcrumb appears above the timeline.

How do you know you're inside the button? If you look just below the timeline (above the timeline in Flash 8), you'll see an area that reads "**Scene 1**" and another that reads "**button1.**" This is called breadcrumb navigation. Scene 1 is your main timeline. If you ever want to go back, just click on Scene 1, and it will take you back to the main timeline. In complex projects, you might have symbols inside of other symbols. This breadcrumb will show you the hierarchy of where you are and which symbol you're currently in.

Understanding the Button timeline

To understand how the timeline of a button symbol works, you first have to understand how most clickable links work on a Website. They have certain properties depending on how you interact with them. When you encounter a link on a Webpage, several things happen depending on what you do with your cursor:

- You initially see the link or button displayed.
- You move your mouse OVER the button or link, and it changes to indicate that it is clickable. Maybe it changes colour, gets brighter, or a text description appears.
- And sometimes you will see a different colour when you click down on the button.

On the button symbol timeline, you'll see four sections or states. Up, Over, Down and Hit.

- **Up** – The up state is what you see when you first go to the project. It is the default state.
- **Over** – This is the state you'll see when you move your mouse arrow over the button.
- **Down** – This is the state you'll see when you click down on the button.
- **Hit** – This is a special state that is never visible to the public. It specifies which area will activate the button. In most cases, you can ignore this state and Flash will deal with the hit state for you. But this state allows for the possibility of creating "hotspots" or invisible buttons for more complex projects.

First, let's rename the only layer to **"image"**. After that, click on the frame representing the "over" state, and click **Insert →Timeline → Keyframe**. You can also right-click to insert a keyframe.

You now have two **Keyframes** that are independent of each other. Each one represents a different state. While the red play head is currently on the **over** state, click on the button image on your stage, and then in your property inspector click on **swap**.

This allows you to swap the photo on that keyframe for another photo. The advantage to using **swap** is that the new photo will be placed in the same exact location as the previous photo. If you were to manually delete the photo, and grab another copy from your library, then you might have a tough time remembering the exact position it was in.

Choose **button1_down.jpg**. This is the same photo, but in colour.

After you swap the image, grab the red playhead and drag it back and forth between the **UP** and **OVER** states. You'll see your image change from black and white to colour. This shows you the change that will occur when you move your mouse over the image in the published project.

In fact, let's test it now. You can test a project at any time by going to **Control Test Movie**. Or you can press the shortcut key which is Ctrl + Enter (command + return on a Mac). Try moving the mouse arrow over the image you modified with an **OVER** state.

Now close the window, and repeat the steps above giving each of your three images an **OVER** state. Remember, you can go back to the main timeline by clicking on **Scene 1**.

Creating "sections" of your project using the timeline

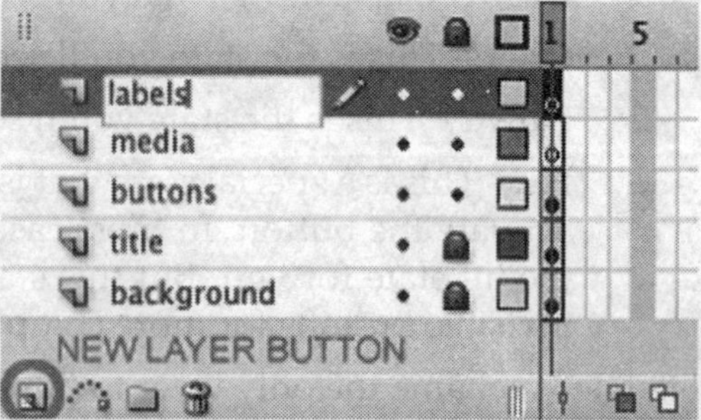

Now that you have three buttons with rollover properties, it is time to actually make these buttons DO something. Each button will take you to a different section of your project where you will have some media waiting.

Create two new layers. Name one **"media"** and the other **"labels."** The media layer will hold all of the videos, photos, and audio in your project. The labels layer simply exists to give names to each section.

Highlight frame 40 of all layers. You can do this one of two ways, either by clicking on frame 40 in the top layer and dragging down or by highlighting the top frame first, then holding the shift key down and clicking on the bottom layer. Your timeline should look like this:

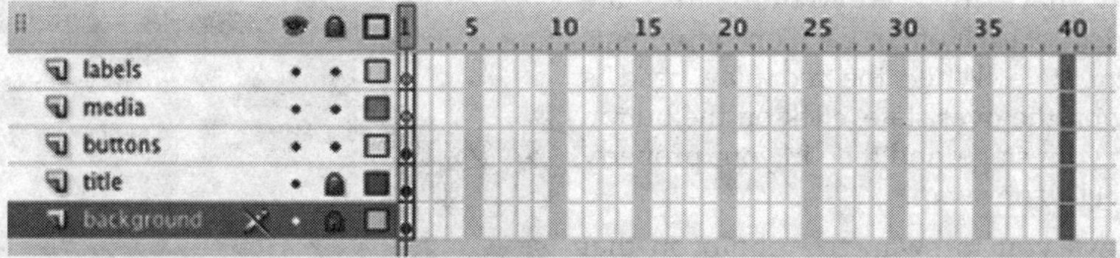

Now go to the **Insert** menu and click on **Timeline** and insert a **Frame**. (This option is also available if you right-click on the selection.)

Now that you have stretched your project out so that it is 40 frames long, we will be creating sections of the project that hold different media types.

Highlight **frame 10** only on both the **media** and **labels** layers, then insert a **keyframe**.

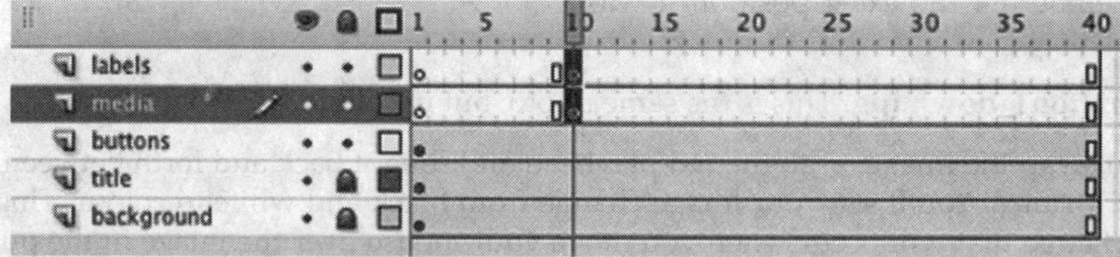

Do the same for frame 20 and frame 30.

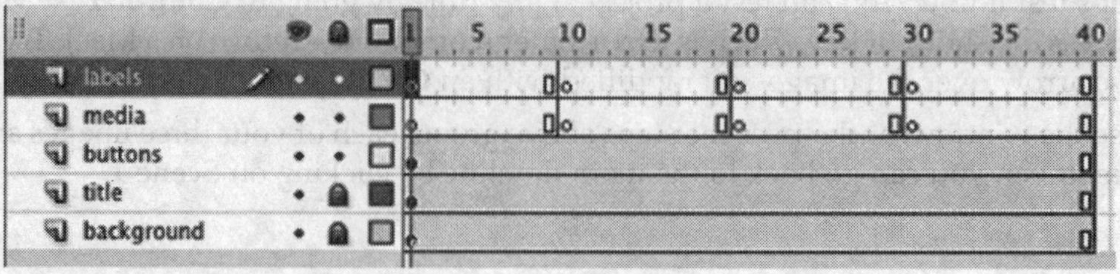

Each of these will represent different sections of your project. Let's label the sections, so we know which is which.

With the first frame on the **labels** layer highlighted, look at your property inspector, and you will see a section that allows you to insert a **frame label**.

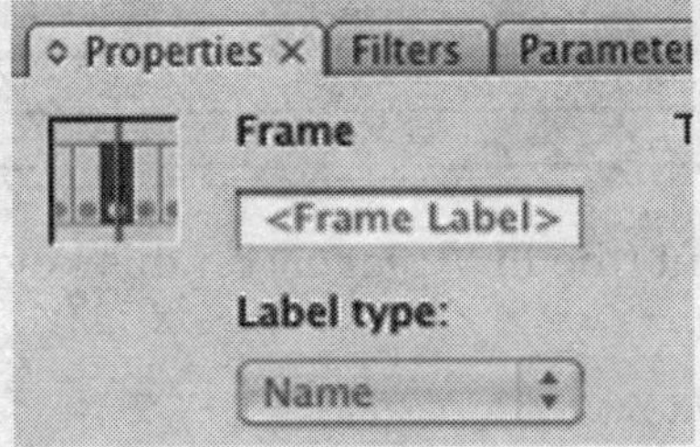

Let's call this first section "**opening.**" We will follow the same steps labelling each section "**video**," "**audio**," and "**text**."

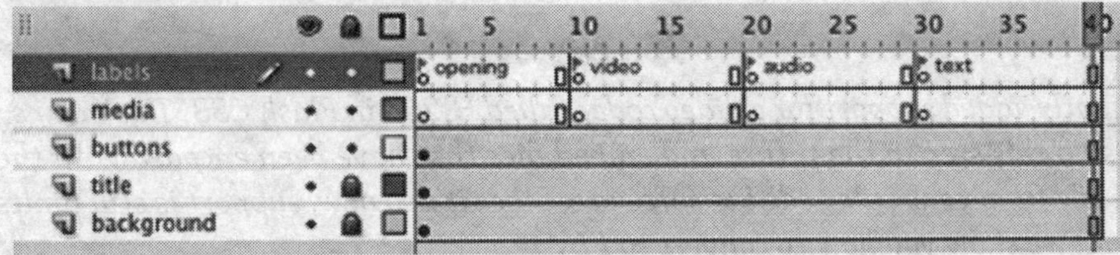

Your timeline should look like the one above. You can now lock your **labels** layer as we will not be using it again.

Adding a video player to your project

Drag your playhead to the video section of your project, and click on the keyframe that is on the **media** layer. You are going to put your video on this keyframe.

From the **window** menu, click on **components**. This will open up the **components window** pane.

(Picture shows additional components installed) ⇨

Components are pre-built items that can be used in your Flash project without a lot of knowledge of code or the technical aspects of Flash. The components found in this window are made available to you from Adobe, but you can install additional components from third-party vendors or Web sites.

One of the most popular components is the **FLVPlayback** component. This is a very basic video player that allows you to play Flash video (.FLV) files. This is overwhelmingly the most popular video format on the Web.

Drag the **FLVPlayback** component to the stage and position it where you want it. Your timeline should now show a solid keyframe in the **"media"** layer under frame 10.

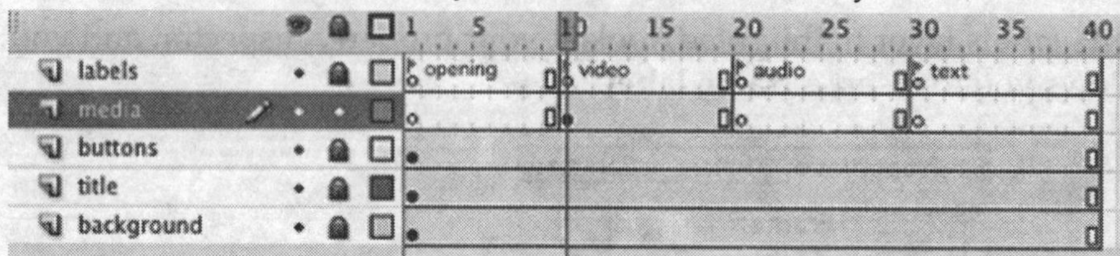

This means that you have content (the FLV player) on this keyframe.

Converting your video to FLV

Included in the Adobe Flash package is a program called "**Adobe Flash CS3 Video Encoder.**" (With Flash 8 this folder will be called "Macromedia Flash 8 Video Encoder") This simple program encodes most video types to **.FLV** or Flash Video.

Note....

Adobe recently added support for a video codec called H.264 in Flash CS3. This means you will probably skip this step in the future and embed files that have been encoded with the H.264 codec directly from your video editing software. Since it's so new, support is still limited, so in this tutorial we show you how to convert to FLV.)

Launch the program.

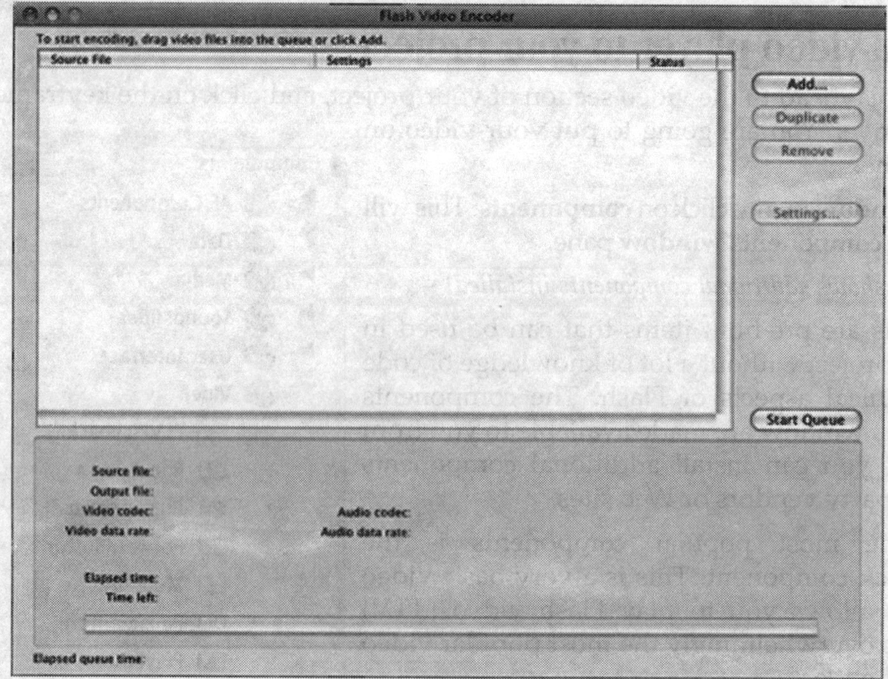

There are several ways to add videos to this program. By far the simplest method is to drag videos to the main source area. You can also click the **"ADD"** button and select the video file.

Next, click the "settings" button. While the settings vary depending on the situation, here are some recommended settings for general performance:

Codec: On2 VP6

Deinterlace: Checked if the footage is shot on non-HD or non-progressive.

Frame Rate: Same as source

Quality: High if a short video, Medium if longer

KeyFrame: Automatic

Audio: Encode between 96 to 128kbps

You can also use the Crop and Resize options to trim the length of the video you want to encode or to crop into the sides. The Resize option is especially important as you should always encode your video for the same size as the output, however resizing your video in the encoding process will add considerable encoding time per video (three to five times as long as the video itself).

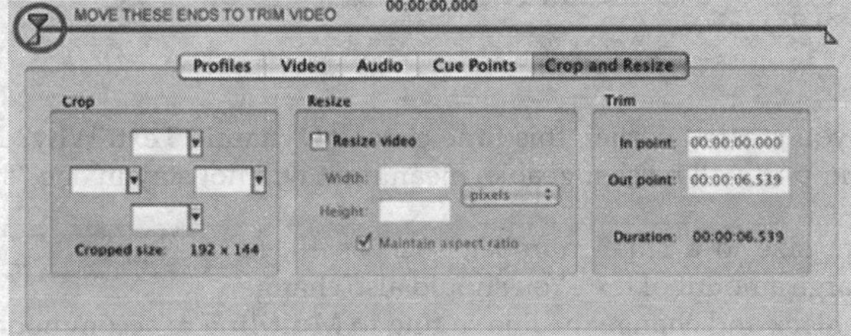

(Note this window appears differently in Flash 8. The same settings are available in the older version, however.)

To begin encoding, click Start Queue in the main window. You can batch encode several videos, but the video encoder will only do one at a time.

Setting the Video path in Flash

Once you have encoded your .FLV file, go into Flash and set the source path so that the FLV player knows which video to play. Set the source path by clicking on the FLV Player in your Flash project, and then clicking "Parameters" in the property inspector. (In Flash 8, open the **Component Inspector** window open to find these settings. The Component Inspector can be found under the **Window** menu.)

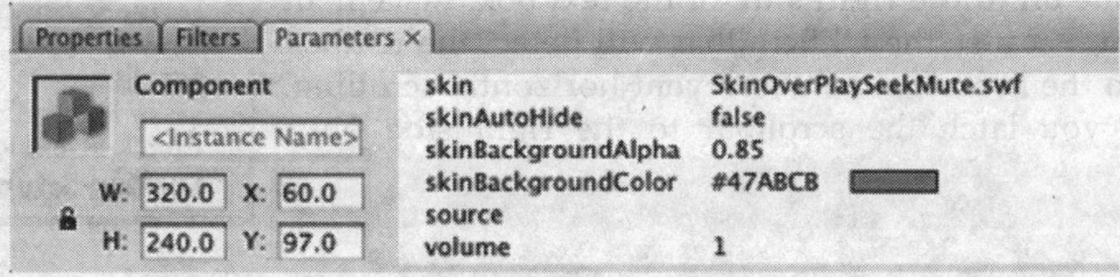

You will notice there are several features you can modify in the FLV Player, including the skin (scrubber) and the colour. One option says "**contentPath**", this is where you set the FLV file you just created.

Adding text to the text section

Drag your red playhead to the text section of your timeline. Click on the text tool in your tool pallet.

You will notice that your property inspector will change, giving you various text options.

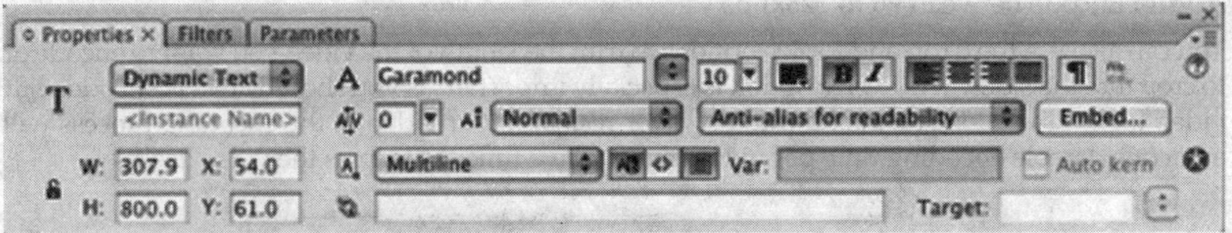

Unlike the titles you created earlier, this time choose **Dynamic Text.** Why? Because the text you are about to import will be changeable, meaning it will not stay in one "static" position.

Change your font size to a small number, such as 10, to accommodate a large amount of text. You should also change the text colour to black and change the line setting to **Multiline** to accommodate multiple line breaks.

Other options include the **Ab** button, which enables your text to be selectable, the <> angle bracket button, which means your text will render HTML, and the square button, which applies a background to your text.

Draw a text box on your stage and paste in some sample text from the tutorial file **sample. txt**.

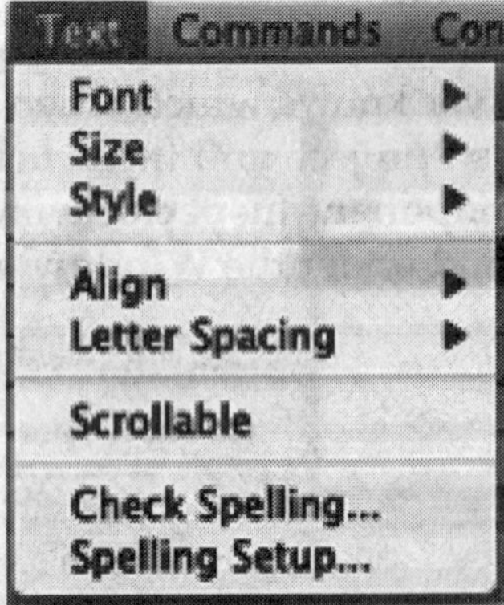

You might have noticed that there is too much text for the text box you have. In order to shrink your text box, you will have to turn on the **Scrollable** option found under the **Text** menu.

Since your text is **scrollable,** we need to add a scroll bar. Simply grab the **UI Scrollbar** component from your components window pane **on to the right side** of the text box. Placement is important, because the UI Scrollbar will detect the textbox and latch to the nearest side. To prevent horizontal scrolling, make sure you latch the scrollbar to the right side only.

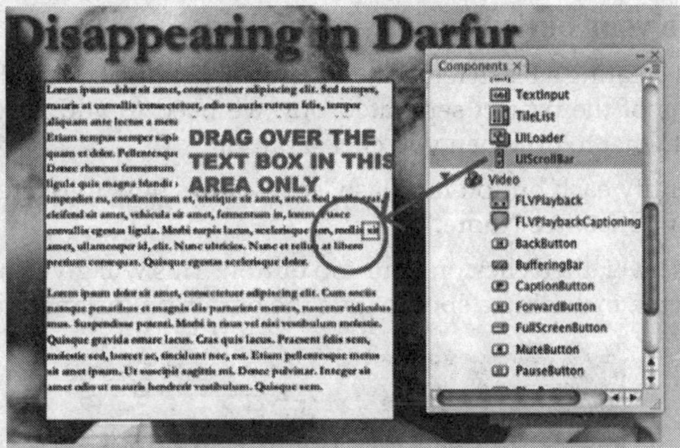

The scrollbar won't be functional in the authoring environment. You will have an opportunity to test it out once we create button actions in the next section.

Working with dynamic text: Dynamic text works a lot differently than static text. Flash converts static text into "outlines," or graphical images, so you don't have to worry about fonts. But dynamic text is more like real Web text, so you must embed the fonts.

After selecting a font, click the embed button in your property inspector and choose the glyphs you want to embed.

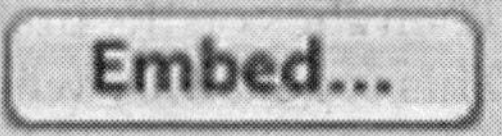

(The embed button will appear in the property inspector when clicking on a text box.)

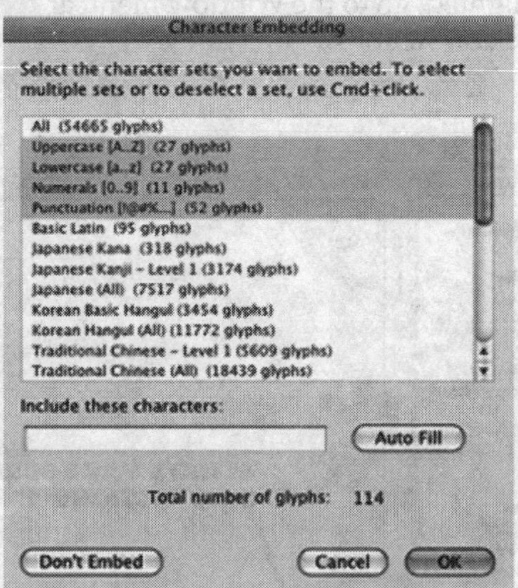

Hold the **shift** key to select multiple glyphs. For virtually all English text, you will only need four sets: Uppercase, Lowercase, Numerals and Punctuation. Flash allows you to select individual glyphs so that if you're only using certain characters, you don't have to embed everything, taking up memory on a visitor's computer.

Adding "Actions" to your buttons using ActionScript

This is the last part of creating a Flash template before publishing it. Now that we have buttons, and different sections of the project separated out, we need to add **"actions"** to give Flash information telling it what to do when you click a button.

First, we need to identify each button for Flash, so it knows how to reference it. This is called giving each button an "**Instance Name.**"

Unlock your buttons layer, then click on your top button. This will give you a set of options on your property inspector, including a spot to give the button an instance name.

Name your button "**video_btn**" (all lowercase) with an underscore. Name the next button "**photo_btn**" and the last button **"text_btn"**.

To add code, first create a new layer in your project and title it "**actions**".

Then click on the first keyframe of the first frame in your project. This is generally where you will always put your ActionScript, so that it is loaded immediately when your project loads. ➔

While this keyframe is highlighted, go to the Window menu at the top of the screen and click on Actions.

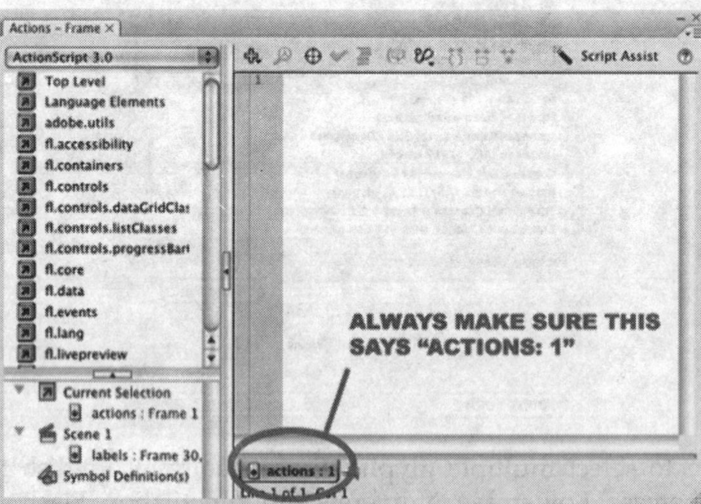

The actions window has a small tab at the bottom that tells you where you are putting your ActionScript. It will display the name of the layer and the frame number. If it says anything different, then you are placing your actions in the wrong spot. The actions window will also stay open even if you click on the stage behind it. **Be careful:** if you click on a layer other than the actions layer, the actions window will change where you are writing ActionScript. Always check to be sure you're writing ActionScript on the actions layer.

This part requires a little bit of programming with code. While at first sight it might look like Greek, there is one basic set of code that we will show you that can be used for virtually any Flash project involving buttons. This is one of the most basic and fundamental pieces of code in Flash.

```
//------- FOR FLASH 8 (ACTIONSCRIPT 2.0)-----------
stop();
video_btn.onRelease = function()
{ gotoAndStop("video");
}
audio_btn.onRelease = function(){
gotoAndStop("audio");
}
text_btn.onRelease = function(){
gotoAndStop("text");
}
//------- FOR FLASH CS3 (ACTIONSCRIPT 3.0) -----------
stop();

function video(myevent:MouseEvent):void {
gotoAndStop("video");
}

function audio(myevent:MouseEvent):void {
gotoAndStop("audio");
}

function txt(myevent:MouseEvent):void {
gotoAndStop("text");
}

video_btn.addEventListener(MouseEvent.CLICK, video);
audio_btn.addEventListener(MouseEvent.CLICK, audio);
text_btn.addEventListener(MouseEvent.CLICK, txt);
//--------------------------------------------------
```

Type the exact ActionScript above into your actions window. Just to make things more difficult, you must precisely match the capitalisation and case (uppercase, lowercase, etc.).

Notice that some of the words turn blue as you type.

This means those words are recognised by Flash. The black words are ones we just made up to name things. If you are naming a function and the word turns blue, then you should use a different name because that word is reserved by Flash.

Now test your movie by press CTRL + Enter (command + return on a Mac) and watch your project come to life! If you get errors, that means you might have typed something wrong. Carefully check the syntax and spelling to the above script. Even the slightest mistake will throw it off!

Corel Draw

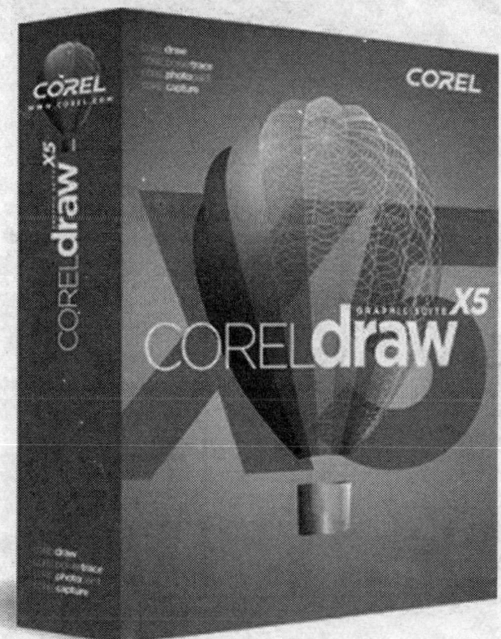

The Basics of CorelDRAW

Welcome to CorelDRAW for Tactile Graphics. CorelDRAW is a comprehensive vector-based drawing and graphic-design program for the graphics professional. It is also used by many tactile graphics illustrators throughout the U.S. and Canada to create graphics to be output on microcapsule paper, Tiger embosser, and other special production methods.

In this presentation, you will become familiar with the basic terminology and concepts of CorelDRAW as well as tactile graphics, and learn to use the tools provided by CorelDRAW to create tactile graphics.

CorelDRAW version X5 is used in this presentation. Similar features might be available in previous releases but may not be fully applicable.

CorelDRAW Workspace

Standard & Property Toolbars

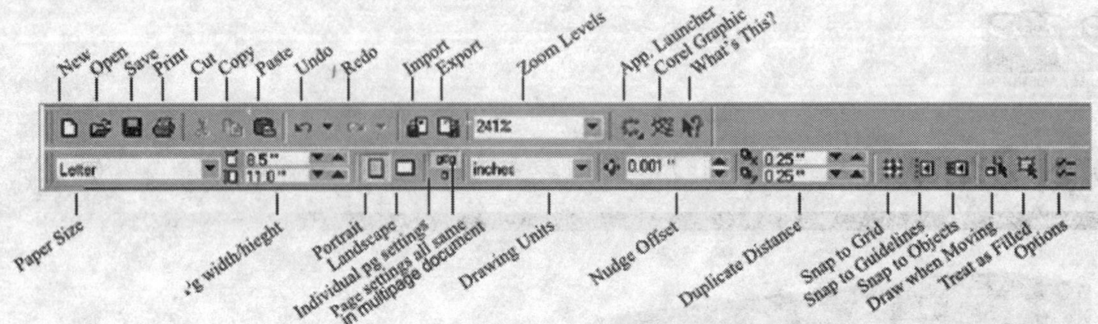

Toolbox & Fly-out Menus

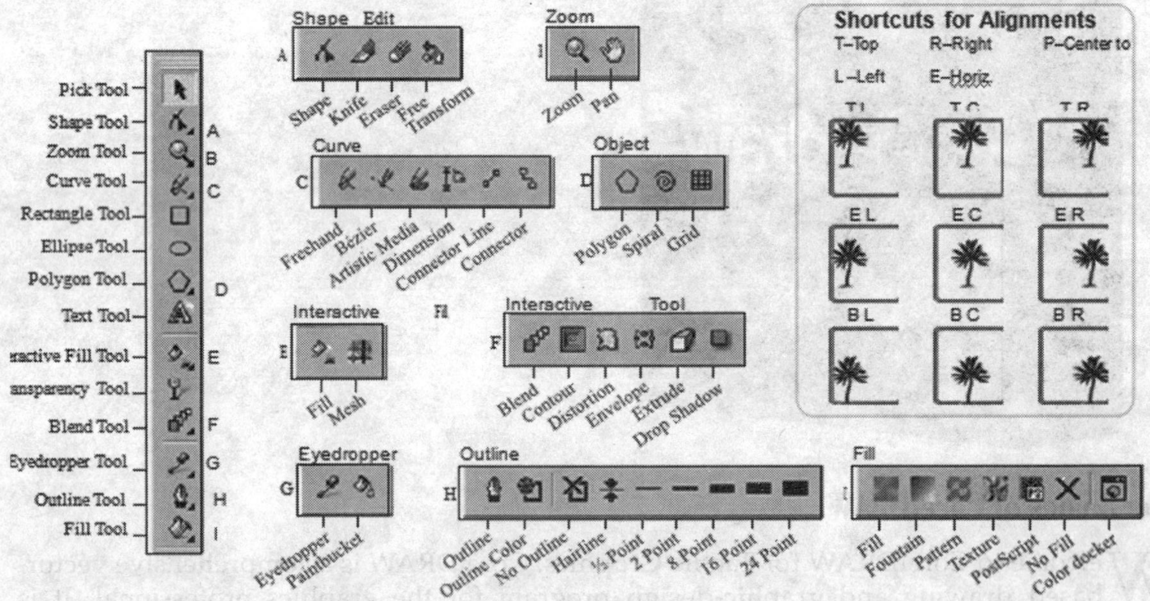

Setting Up Your Workspace

Steps to Follow

- ❑ Launch CorelDRAW by double-clicking on the CorelDRAW icon on your Windows desktop.
- ❑ If the CorelDRAW Welcome Screen appears, uncheck the box Show this Welcome Screen at Start Up and click on the New Graphic Icon.

- Your new document should be completely blank. Select the Text Tool and choose Arial from the drop down font list in CorelDRAW 12. The default font for CorelDRAW X3 or X4 is Arial.
- The Text Attributes Windows will appear. Make sure Artistic Text is checked. Click on OK. Your new default font will now be Arial. You can repeat this process to choose another font size as your default
- Select the **Text Tool** and choose **200** from the drop down font size list.
- The Text Attributes Windows will appear. Make sure **Artistic Text** is checked. Click on **OK**. Your new default font size will now be 200 points. 100 points is the same as 1 inch.

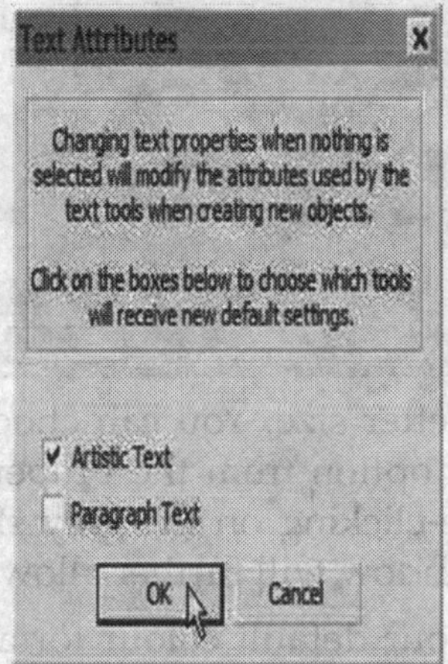

- The Default CMYK colour palette is useless for most imprinting processes. Right mouse click on your colour palette and select **Palette** and **Close** to close the Corel default CMYK palette.
- The Pantone Matching System Corel 8 colour palette is the best choice for spot colours and most imprinting processes. It is the only spot colour palette in CorelDRAW 12 that contains Transparent White.

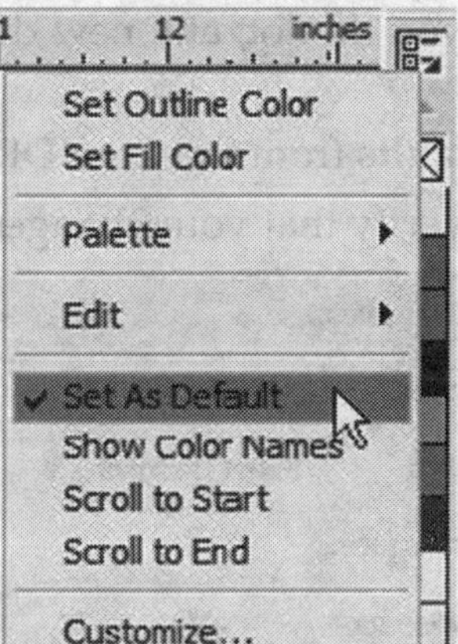

The Pantone Matching System Solid Coated colour palette is located under **Colour Palettes** in the **Windows** menu.

- ❑ Right mouse-click on the very top of the colour palette and select **Set as Default**. This will insure that the selected palette is the default colour palette in all CorelDRAW functions that have colour selection options.

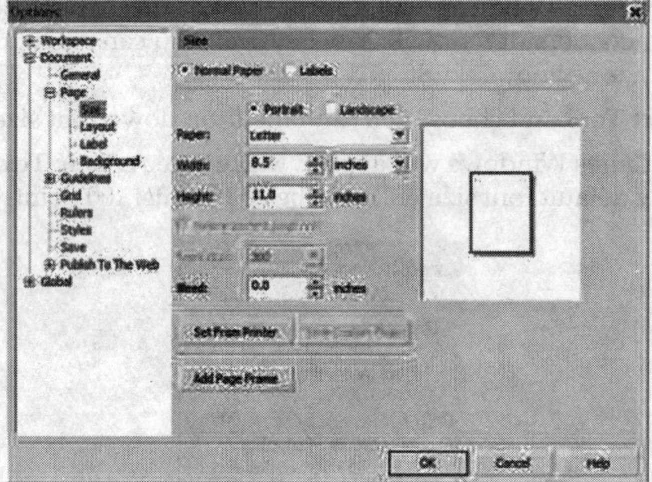

- ❑ Your default page size is letter size. You can choose a different page size and page orientation by selecting an option from the Property Bar. You can further customise your workspace by double-clicking on the grey shadow that is to the right of your work page. The Options window will further allow you to customise your workspace.
- ❑ You will want to change your default colour for all of the object tools including the Bezier Tool, Rectangle Tool, Ellipse Tool, Basic Shapes Tool to Pantone Process Black CV (5th colour from the top of the Pantone Matching System Corel 8 Palette). With nothing selected in your document select the tool and right mouse-click on the colour to change the default outline colour to **Process Black CV** for each tool. Left mouse-click on the colour to change the default fill colour for the Text tool.
- ❑ After making the changes to your workspace, you must save your settings as defaults for any new documents. If you do not, any new document will retain the CorelDRAW defaults.
- ❑ Select **Save Settings as Defaults** from the CorelDRAW **Tools** menu.
- ❑ Create a new document to verify that your changes have been saved.

In Coreldraw, application commands are accessible through the menu bar, toolbars, property bar, dockers, and toolbox. The property bar and dockers provide access to commands that relate to the active tool or current task. The property bar, dockers, toolbars, and toolbox can be opened, closed, and moved around your screen at any time.

- Toolbars consist of buttons that are shortcuts to menu commands, e.g. open or save a document, copy, cut, paste, redo, undo, etc.

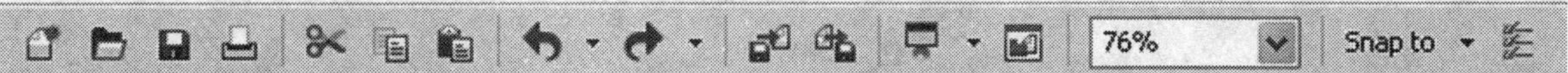

- Property bar displays controls that are commonly used with the active tool or for the task you're performing. The content of property bar changes depending on the tool or task.

- Dockers display the same types of controls as a dialog box, e.g. command buttons, options, and listed boxes. Dockers can be either floating (undocked), or attached (docked) to either side of the application window.

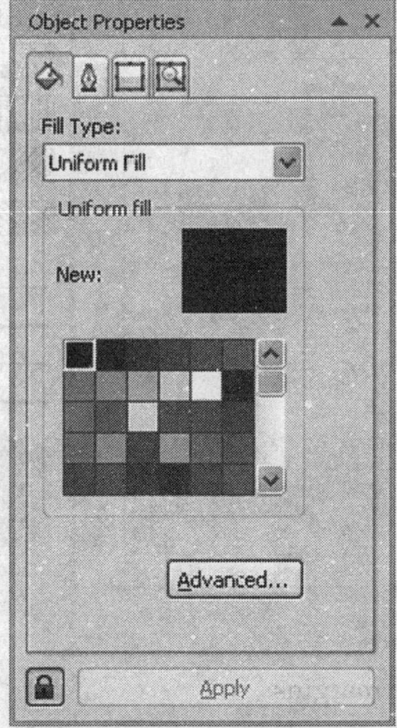

- Status bar displays information about selected objects, e.g. colour, fill type, outline, etc.

- Toolbox contains tools for drawing and editing graphics. Some are visible by default, others are grouped in flyouts.

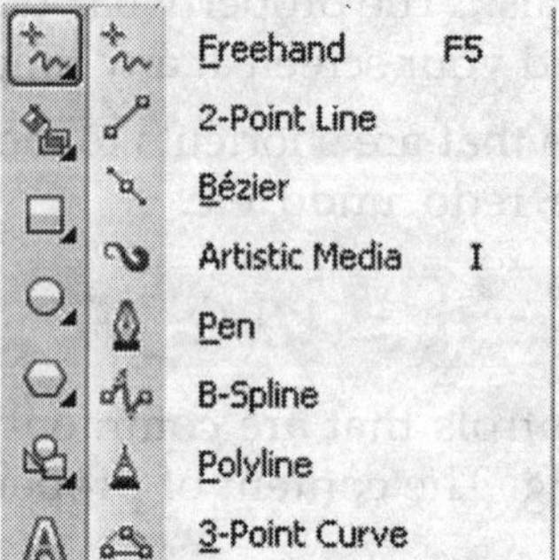

Working with a Template

A tactile graphic template contains tactile graphic components to assist in tactile drawing.

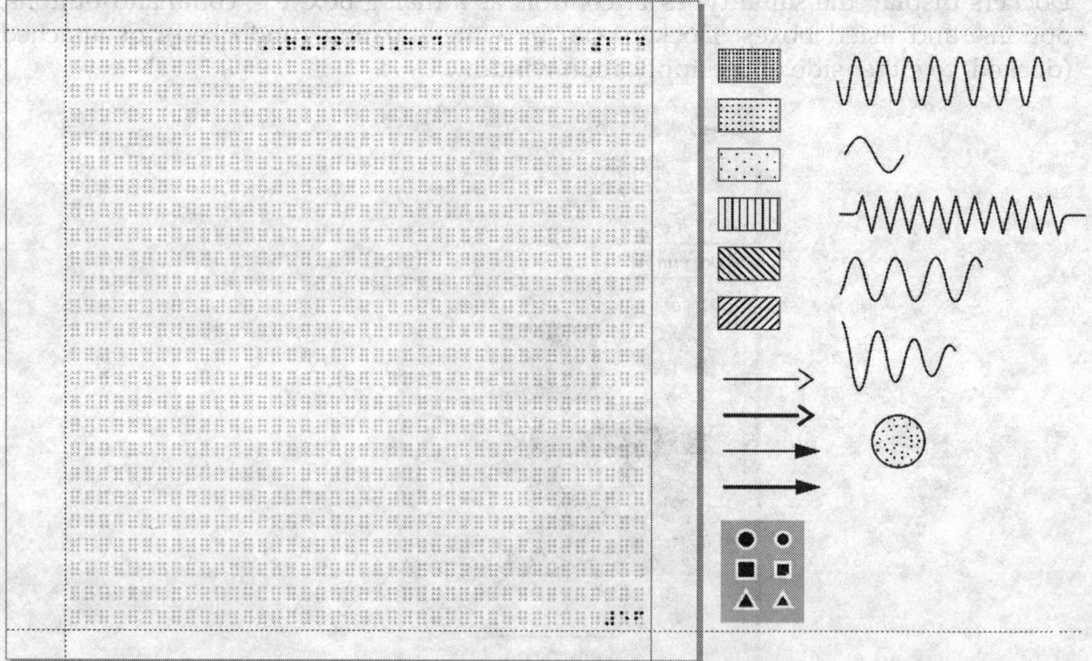

- Page size: 11.5 by 11 inches
- Guidelines indicate page margins
- 40 by 25 braille cells background matches embossed braille for easy planning
- Placement of running head and page numbers
- Commonly used textures, lines, curves, arrows, and points
- Customization of CorelDRAW workspace for tactile drawing

Turn off spell checking and QuickCorrect function

- ❑ Option > Workspace > Text > Spelling
- ❑ Option > Workspace > Text > QuickCorrect o Character formatting
- ❑ Font: braille or swell braille
- ❑ Size: 24 pt

Paragraph formatting

- ❑ Line spacing: 110%

The Shape Tool

The shape tool is one of the most frequently used tools in CorelDRAW. Its function depends on the type of object being reshaped. Shape tool is the standard tool for manipulating nodes.

Types of line segments

A segment is a line of two nodes. There are two types of segment:

- ❑ Line: Straight segment. Line nodes have no control handles.
- ❑ Curve: Nodes have control handles for adjustment.

A line can be converted to a curve without noticeable change in appearance, but it displays control handles that you can move to change the segment's shape.

Types of nodes

Nodes are the points at each end of a line or curve segment. There are three types of nodes:

- ❑ Cusp: Sharp transition. Control handles are independent of one another.
- ❑ Smooth: Smooth transition. Control handles move together but extend independently.
- ❑ Symmetrical: A smooth transition with symmetrical and opposite control handles.

Editing curve by manipulating nodes

- ❑ Select and move nodes
- ❑ Add and delete nodes
- ❑ Break curve and join two nodes
- ❑ Extend curve to close and close curve

- ❑ Stretch or scale, skew or rotate, and align nodes

Drawing and editing objects

- ❑ Transformations: position, rotate, scale, size, skew
- ❑ Shaping: weld, trim, intersect, simplify, front minus back, back minus front, boundary

Tips and Tricks

- ❑ Welcome Screen and Quick Start Window provides options for setting new document and helpful resources.
- ❑ Tooltips provide information about the icons and buttons found in the program. To view a tooltip, position the pointer over an icon, button, or application control.
- ❑ Hints docker provides instant information about the tools in the toolbox.
- ❑ Text toolbar contains commands for formatting and aligning text.
- ❑ Colour palette: Left-click a colour swatch to choose a fill colour. Right-click one to choose an outline colour.
- ❑ Select Tool
  - Rectangular or freehand mode
  - Select multiple objects by holding down Shift key
  - Ctrl – constrain
  - Shift – from center

Useful shortcuts

o + – duplicate

o Z – zoom

o F4 – zoom to all objects

o Shift + F4 – zoom to page

o Shift + F2 – zoom to selected object

Let's discuss some of the important things of CorelDraw:

Selecting, Positioning and Aligning Objects

- ❑ Double click the Pick tool to select all objects on the Page at once.
- ❑ Hold the "Alt" key down when dragging a box around an object. The object will be selected as soon as the box surrounds a portion of the object.
- ❑ Hold the "Alt" key down to select an object behind another object. Hold the "Alt" and "Shift" keys down to select multiple objects. Grab the "X" to reposition the selected objects.
- ❑ Hold down the "Control" key to constrain an object horizontally or vertically when repositioning.

- Without reselecting the pick tool, it is possible to manipulate an object's shape or position using any of the basic drawing tools including the Freehand Pen Tool, Rectangle Tool and the Ellipse Tool.
- Hold down the "Shift" key to resize an object from the centre.
- Hold down the "Ctrl" key to select an object inside a group.
- Select two objects. On your keyboard press "C" for centre alignment, "B" for bottom alignment, "T" for top alignment, "L" for left alignment and "R" for right alignment. The first object selected will automatically align to the second object selected.

Creating, Duplicating and Importing Objects

- Double click the Rectangle tool to create a rectangle of the size of the page and behind all other objects on the page. Hold down the "Shift" key when creating a rectangle, ellipse or polygon to create the shape from the centre out - hold the "Shift" and "Control" key at the same time to constrain the object to a circle or square.
- Duplicate an object (Control D). Once the duplicated object is repositioned, the duplicate command will use the new position to place the next duplicate (Smart Duplication).
- Select an object with your left mouse button, drag the object and select the right mouse button to create a copy.
- When importing a file, hold down your "Space Bar" to disable the placement feature and directly import the file.

Modifying Objects and Colours

- Right mouse click on any object or text and select "Properties" to modify the attributes of the object or text (fill, outline, size).
- Right mouse click on an object or text, hold the right mouse button down and drag the object over the top of another object. When the bombsight appears, release the mouse button. You can now copy Fills, Outlines or Properties from one object to another. You can also use this feature to PowerClip an object inside another object.
- Right mouse click on an object, depress the right mouse button and the "Shift" key to drag and drop fill colours from one object to another.
- Right mouse click on an object, depress the right mouse button and the "Alt" key to drag and drop outline colours from one object to another.
- Double click the colour palette to change the outline colour of an object. Single click to change the fill colour.
- Select two objects. Select the "Weld", "Trim" or "Intersect" icon on your property bar. The first object selected will weld to, trim through or intersect the second object selected.
- Right mouse click on an object. Select "Lock" to lock an object's position. Right click again to Unlock.

- ❑ Hold the "Shift" key down and double-click on a colour in the colour palette, the colour name will appear. Select another colour by Pantone Name or Number and the cursor will jump to that colour on the palette.
- ❑ Hover your cursor over a colour on the colour palette, depress the left mouse button and all of the shades of that colour will appear as a fly-out, select the desired shade from the fly-out to colour your image.

Manipulating Text

- ❑ Select a text object with the Shape Tool. Two arrows will appear. Select the left arrow to change the spacing between lines (leading).
- ❑ Select the right arrow to change the spacing between letters (kerning). Select the white box next to a letter to reposition the letters with the arrow keys or change the colour of an individual letter from the colour palette. Hold down the "Shift" key to select multiple letters. Hold down the left mouse button on a selected box to drag the letter(s) into a new position. Hold down the "Control" key to constrain the letter(s) horizontally or vertically while repositioning.
- ❑ Right mouse click on a text object, hold the right mouse button down and drag the text over the top of another text object.
- ❑ When the bombsight appears, release the mouse button. You can now copy the text properties from one object to another.

Displaying Roll-Ups, Dialogs or Views

- ❑ Hold the cursor over the Outline Tool and double click to display the Pen roll-up.
- ❑ Hold the cursor over the Fill Tool and double click to display the Special Fill roll-up.
- ❑ Hold the cursor over the Zoom Tool and double click to display the View Manager dialog box.
- ❑ Hold the cursor over the Shape Tool and double click to display the Node Edit roll-up.
- ❑ To see the printable area while working on a drawing, click on View | Printable Area.
- ❑ Double click the shadow on the right border of your work page to open the Page Setup dialog box.
- ❑ To toggle between the current view and "Wireframe View" select "Shift, Tab, F9".
- ❑ Double click on the title bar of any CorelDRAW toolbar to return the bar to its home position.

Node Editing

- ❑ CorelDRAW X4 has a Curve Smoothness slider bar for reducing nodes. Using the Shape Tool, drag a box around the excess nodes. The Curve Smoothness slider bar will appear at the far right of your Property Bar (it contains a "0" and an equalizer icon). Select the slider bar and move the slider to the right to reduce the nodes in the image. If the image starts to distort, simply move the slider bar back to the left.
- ❑ Double click on a line in an object to select the Shape Tool for node editing (make sure the object or text is converted to curves first). Click the right mouse button on a line to display the node editing options for that object or text.

- ❑ Double-click on a node with the shape tool to delete a node.
- ❑ Double-click on a line with the shape tool to add a node.

Rulers, Guidelines, Views or ToolBars

- ❑ Double click on a ruler to display the Grid and Ruler setup dialog box.
- ❑ Select a guideline and click "Delete" to delete the line. To select multiple guidelines, hold down the "Shift" key.
- ❑ Hold down your "Shift" key to drag a ruler out into your drawing area with your left mouse button. Hold down the "Shift" key and double click the ruler to reset the ruler to the original position.
- ❑ If a Toolbar is accidentally removed, simply right mouse click on any open gray space on the Toolbox, Property Bar or Standard Tool Bar. Place a check next to the name of the tool that has disappeared. It is possible to drag any floating tool bar to a docked location anywhere on the perimeter of your workspace.
- ❑ If your CorelDRAW workspace becomes corrupted or you lose a tool bar, start CorelDRAW while holding down the F8 key to restore CorelDRAW to the default workspace.

Contouring

- ❑ Select the Interactive Contour tool (fourth flyout from the bottom on your Tool Box). After selecting the tool, drag a contour line from the lower left corner of your object. Contour attributes such as steps, offsets and styles (inside, outside, to centre) can be adjusted from the Property Bar.
- ❑ CorelDRAW allows contoured text to be edited. After contouring the text, select the original text and click on "Control, Shift, T" to edit the text. The new text value will have the same contour.
- ❑ The "Convert Outline to Object" feature will convert outline strokes to contour lines. Place an outline stroke around an object, select "Convert Outline to Object". The stroke will be converted to a contour line automatically.
- ❑ Enter the wireframe view by entering "Shift, Tab, F9". The contour is a line on either side of the original object. Select both new objects and click on the "Trim" command on the property bar to remove the inside contour line.

Scanning and Tracing

- ❑ Scan directly into CorelDRAW by selecting "Acquire Image" from the File menu. Select your source device and click "Acquire" to activate the TWAIN software included with your scanner.
- ❑ After scanning an image or opening a bitmap file, right click on the image and select "Outline Trace" to convert the bitmap to vectored line artwork. Corel Power TRACE will open automatically. After tracing the image, the vectored image will be placed directly on top of the original bitmap. Select the wireframe view (Shift, Tab, F9) to compare the two images. The vectored image can now be ungrouped and edited.

Note....

The quality of your trace result is determined by the quality of your original image. The traced image will never look better than the original source artwork. SmartVector Pro will produce a vastly superior traced image as compared to Corel PowerTRACE.

Pre-flighting Overview

Preflighting

Preflighting is the process of preparing your design for output. There are different preflighting steps for nearly every production process. In general, you will be inspecting your design to resolve any problems with the artwork that may hinder the successful output of the file. This process is the nuts and bolts of art production. Pre-flighting skills are gained through knowledge and experience. If you know what to look for, you will be able to prevent problems in the future and resolve problems if they come up. The following section will give you pre-flighting guidelines for specific production processes.

Preflighting Checklist

The following is a list of simple questions that must be addressed before final production occurs on a design.

1. Does the design have sufficient quality to produce the desired results for the specific production process?
2. Is the design properly sized for the specific production process?
3. Has the design been properly coloured for the specific production process?
4. Does the design require colour correction for the specific production process?
5. Does the design have the proper outline properties for the specific production process?
6. Is the type in the design suitable and readable for the specific production process?
7. Are there a specific design or production concerns for your production process that need to be addressed before production?

General Quality Factors (Q&A)

Q.1. Does the production process require vector art or is a bitmap appropriate?

Ans. Each production process has different requirements. Some processes such as vinyl cutting, CAD cutting, routing and rotary engraving are only suitable for vector artwork. Some processes such as sublimation printing, direct to garment printing and large format digital printing will work with either bitmap or vector artwork. The artwork requirements must match the specific requirements of the production process.

Q.2. If the production process requires vector art, is the source artwork of sufficient quality to produce a quality imprint?

Ans. Poor quality vector artwork will produce poor quality results. The production process will only amplify any imperfections in the vector artwork. You may need to clean up the artwork using the editing tools of CorelDRAW or outsource the clean up with an art service such as Affinity Express.

Q.3. If the production process works with bitmap artwork, is the artwork of sufficient resolution to produce a quality imprint?

Ans. Low resolution bitmaps will always produce a low quality imprint. If you do not have sufficient resolution in the original bitmap, an image enhancement program can help adding extra pixels to the artwork to increase the overall print quality. A 72 dpi web graphic is going to produce poor results, but a 300 dpi image could be more than doubled in size using an image enhancement program. The absolute size of the image is just as important as the resolution. Larger and Higher resolution images will give you more digital information to work with in terms of resizing.

300 dpi Bitmap

150 dpi Bitmap

72dpi bitmap

The outward appearance of an image has very little to do with the readiness of the image for a specific production process. The only way to assess the ultimate readiness of an image is to examine the individual elements in the design. Wireframe view is a useful view for seeing how objects sit on top of each other. Also the CorelDRAW Object Manager docker will allow you to isolate and examine individual elements in a design.

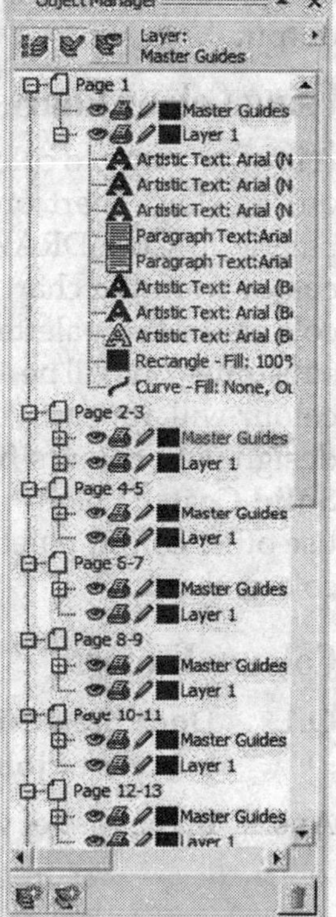

Size Factors

Q.1. Is the design properly sized for the specific job or substrate?

Ans. Each product has a specific imprintable area.

Q.2. Does the design have the proper bleeds for the specific production process?

Ans. Some processes will require a bleed. A bleed is a slight enlargement of the image that will prevent any substrate colour from leaking through in the event that the image is cut out. A bleed would normally be required for a button layout or a decal. You must be familiar with your process in order to compensate for a bleed.

Colour Correction

Q.1. Does the design require colour correction for a specific production process?

Ans. The colours that you see on your monitor do not represent the colours that will be output. The only way to see the true colours of any artwork is to print it. There are colour calibration techniques that will allow you to calibrate your monitor to more accurately display printed colours. Please consult your hardware vender for more information on colour calibration. Colour correction is the process of adjusting colours in the design for specific printers, medias or inks. There are several strategies for colour correction depending upon your production process or artwork.

Colour Profiling

One popular colour correction strategy is colour profiling. Some printers support ICC Colour Profiles that will adjust the colour space for an image for a specific printer, ink and substrate. Please refer to the manual to determine if your device supports colour profiles. Colour profiles should be provided from your ink, media or printer supplier.

Manually Correcting Colours

Another colour correction strategy is to manually adjust the colour values in your image using the tools in an image editing software. CorelDRAW X4 and Corel PhotoPaint both contain a **Colour Adjustment Lab** feature that will allow you to interactively adjust colours in a bitmap image. Remember that the design will never look the same on your screen as it will when it is output.

Using Colour Charts and Palettes

A low tech way to colour correct a vector image is to print out a colour chart on your device for a specific colour palette in CorelDRAW. You can then select the desired colour from the chart and recolour your image with the colours in the palette. After printing the chart on your substrate you will be able to see exactly how each Pantone colour will appear on that substrate. Simply colour your design with colours from the **Pantone Matching System Solid Coated** colour palette in CorelDRAW. You can also use other colour palettes to match colours from a printed colour chart.

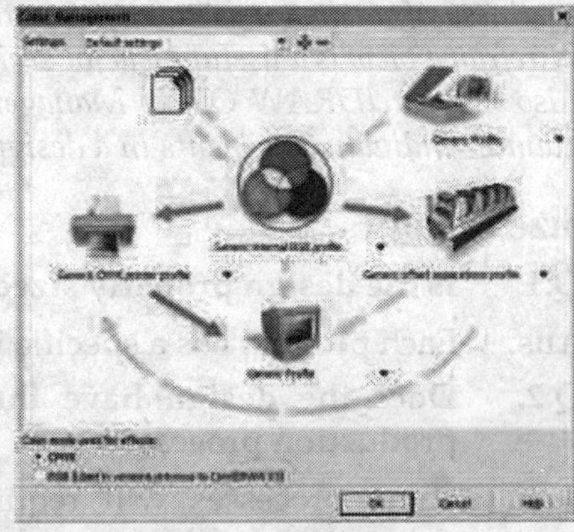

Colours Factors

Q.1. Does the design have the specified number of colours required for the production process or job when using vector art?

Ans. In the case of vector art, the design must be coloured with the correct number of colours for the specific job. You can use the **Colour Styles** function under the **Windows** menu in **CorelDRAW** to view and edit colours in a design.

Q.2. Has the design been coloured with the correct colour palette for the production process when using vector art?

Ans. The design must be coloured with the correct colour palette for the specific production process. If you are attempting to match Pantone spot colours, you must use a Pantone Matching System colour palette. You can use the **Colour Styles** function under the **Windows** menu in **CorelDRAW** to view and edit colours in a design. A low tech way to colour correct a vector image is to print out a colour chart on your device for a specific colour palette in CorelDRAW. You can then select the desired colour from the chart and recolour your image with the colours in the palette. After printing the chart on your substrate you will be able to see exactly how each Pantone colour will appear on that substrate.

Type Factors

Q.1. Are the proper fonts being displayed in the design, or has there been a font substitution?

Ans. Take a close look at the design to make sure the fonts you want are displayed in the design. If you opened up the design on a computer that did not have the fonts installed, CorelDRAW would have prompted you to substitute a different font. You can close the document, close CorelDRAW, install the correct font in Windows and then re-open the document and change the font. CorelDRAW must be restarted in order to display any newly installed fonts.

Q.2. Does the type appear large enough for your production process?

Ans. Small text will not work well in some production processes such as embroidery, appliqué and cutting processes. You always have the option of selecting individual text objects and resizing them. Hold down your **Shift** key to resize a line of text from the centre out by dragging with the Pick tool.

Q.3. Can the type be clearly read?

Ans. Some fonts are difficult to read, especially at small sizes. Carefully look at the design to determine if the final output will be readable. You also need to consider the distance in which the final output will be viewed from. You may need to change a font style or size to insure that the type will be readable at the correct distance. Script text will always look better in title case (first letter capitalized).

Q.4. Is the space between individual characters (kerning) or lines (leading) properly set?

Ans. Provide the text has not been enveloped, you can change the character or line spacing. Select the text with the **Shape** tool. If you see an envelope, must remove the envelope before changing the character spacing. If you see the up or down arrows, you can adjust the character spacing by moving the arrow on the right side. You can adjust the line space by selecting the arrow to the left side. You can also individually change character spacing by selecting one or more of the little rectangles that appear. Hold down your **Shift** key to select more than one character. You can remove an **Envelope** by selecting **Clear Transformations** from the **Arrange** menu in CorelDRAW. You can then change the character spacing and re-apply the text envelope.

Note....

CorelDraw Interface is similar to Adobe CS Softwares, therefore most of the parts are not introduced here, as you knew already.

Math Type

Math Type & Equation Editor

Now available in Word 2010, a powerful tool in DTP for Mathematical Operations. Let's begin from Setting Our Editor.

Setting Font Styles in Equation Editor

Setting font styles & sizes in Equation Editor is a simple process. Follow these steps:

- ❑ Open Equation Editor.
- ❑ In the **Style** menu, click **Define**.
- ❑ Set the styles to the desired font by using the drop-down lists. The styles Text, Function, Variable, Matrix-Vector, and Number may be set to whatever font you want. Normally these 5 styles are the same as each other, and the same as what you're using in Word.

CAUTION: These 3 styles must always be set to Symbol font: L.C. Greek, U.C. Greek, and Symbol. Failure to do this will cause unpredictable results.

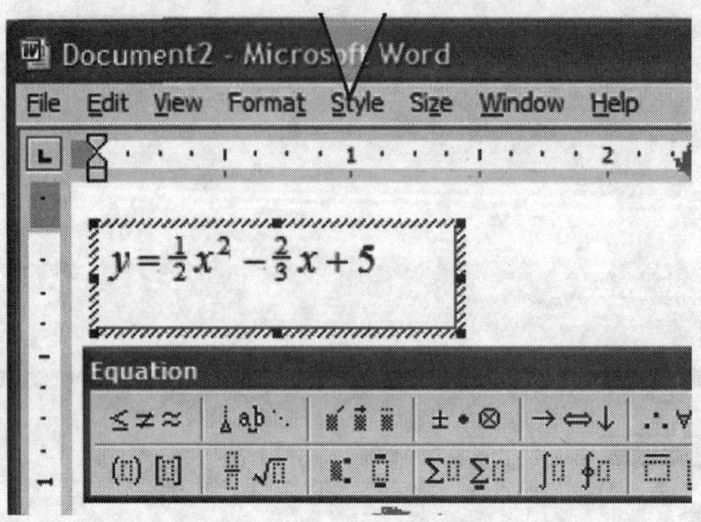

Setting Font Sizes inEquation Editor

- Open Equation Editor.
- In the **Size** menu, click **Define**.
- Set the Full size to the same size as your text in Word. Use "pt" to denote points.

Suggestion: Set the Full size in points, and the other sizes in percent. That way when you change the full size setting, you don't need to change the others. They will retain the proper proportion. Use these percentage values as a guide; revise as desired:

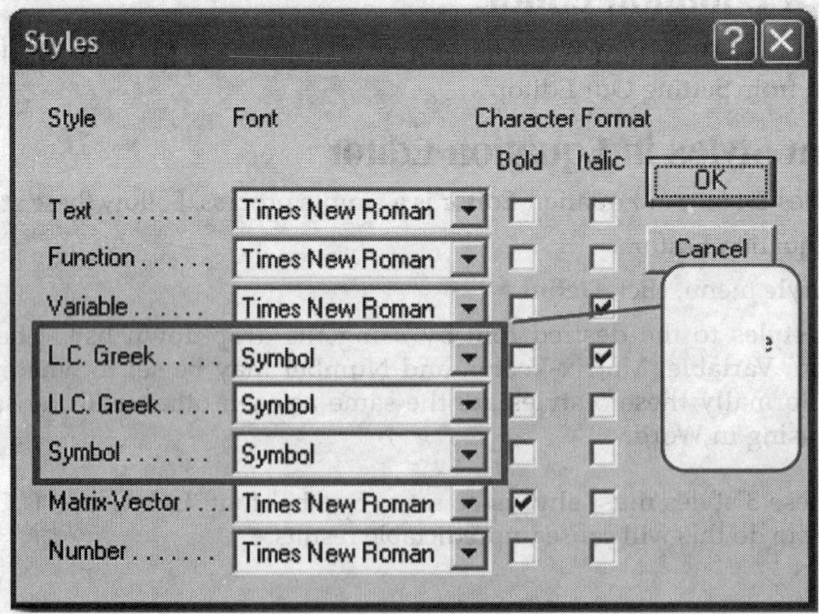

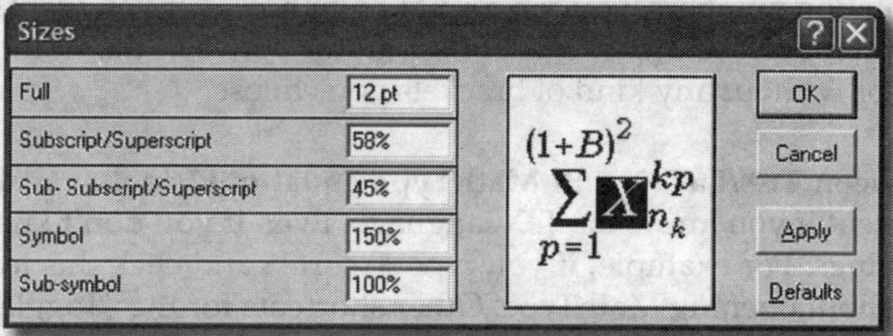

The Math Type Toolbar (in Word)

The MathType toolbar contains 10 icons, or 11 if you're using Windows 7 or Mac with Word 2010. The descriptions below should help you decide when to use each of the icons.

Note....

If you are using Office 2007 or 2010, these items are included in the MathType tab on Word'sRibbon. Some are also included on the Ribbon in PowerPoint 2007.

If you are using Office 2007 , there is one icon: Insert Eqn

If your toolbar looks like the one above, notice there are four Greek letter Sigmas. Each of these will open MathType and allow you to insert an equation into your document. The difference between them is in the placement of the equation and its relationship to the surrounding.

Σ – "Insert Inline Equation" – Inserts an equation inline with your text. An inline equation becomes part of your paragraph, and moves with the text when you add or delete text. This is an example of an inline equation – $a^2 + b^2 = c^2$

Σ – "Insert Display Equation" – Inserts an equation below the current line of text, like this one:

$$(x, y) = \left(\frac{x_1 + x_2}{2}, \frac{y_1 + y_2}{2}\right)$$

When MathType inserts a display equation, it centers the equation on the line, and places the cursoron the line below the equation, so that when you close MathType, you're ready to continue typing. Σ and Σ – "Insert Numbered Display Equation" – Acts exactly like the previous icon, except places anquation number either at the left or right margin, depending on which of the two icons you select.

Here is a "Right-Numbered Display Equation":

$$y = \tfrac{3}{2}\sin\left(x - \tfrac{2\pi}{3}\right) + 2$$

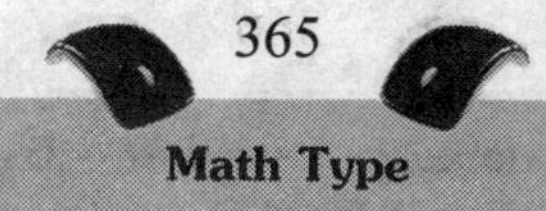

When inserting equation numbers, you can format them however you want – with or without section or chapter numbers, with any kind of separator between the numbers (e.g., 1.1, 1-1, 1_1,etc.), and with or without any kind of brackets you choose.

TEX **"Toggle between TeX/LaTeX and MathType equations"** (not available on the Mac) – This is a huge shortcut if you know the TeX language. Even if you don't know TeX, it's pretty simple for many things. For example, if you type $\sqrt2$ and click this icon, you'll get 2 in your document without opening MathType. Other shortcuts for the "Toggle TeX" button:

\frac{numerator}{denominator} produces a fraction

\sqrt{radicand} gives a square root, and \sqrt{index}{radicand} gives an *nth* root

For Greek letters, type the backslash followed by the name of the letter.

\alpha = , \omega = , \pi = , etc.

Be sure to enclose the expression in $ signs, e.g., $\frac{\pi}{4}$

The next four icons on the MathType toolbar all have to do with equation numbers. Note that these are not *problem* numbers, as in a test or quiz. They are *equation* numbers like you may see in a textbook or in a journal article when the author needs to refer to a particular equation number in the text of the article. There are very few times when a primary or secondary school math teacher would need to number equations.

(1) – **"Insert Equation Number"** – Inserts an equation number at the current position of the cursor. This icon is most often used to add an equation number to a display equation that's already in your document.

(1) – **"Insert Equation Reference"** – Inserts a reference in the text of the document, and links the reference to a particular equation number.

1.1 2.1 – **"Insert Chapter/Section Break"** – Chapter and section numbers are not required when you're numbering your MathType equations, but if you do use them, you'll need to change the chapter or section number when you move to the next chapter or section.

(1) – **"Update Equation Numbers"** – This icon isn't needed very often, because when you add an equation prior to an existing numbered equation, the equation numbers and references that follow the new equation are automatically updated, as I described above. When you remove an equation though, the numbers aren't updated. (They *may* update when you save or print the document, depending on how you have your Word options set up.) Selecting this icon will update the equation numbers immediately.

The last icon on the MathType toolbar doesn't have anything to do with inserting equations or equation numbers; this icon affects the entire document.

– **"Export to MathPage"** – This will transform the entire Word document into a nice-looking web page.

To the right of "Export to MathPage" is the "Browse by" window. You can choose to browse by equations, equation numbers, or chapter/section breaks. This is similar to the way you can click an icon in Word and go to the next page.

Equations Equation Browse – Clicking the right arrow will take you to either the next equation in the document, and the left arrow will take you to the previous equation.

Setting MathType Fonts & Sizes (the Style and Size menus)

You most likely want your equations to match the text in your document, PowerPoint presentation, orweb page, so that you need to know how to change the fonts & font sizes in MathType.

You'll see several style names listed on the MathType Style menu, but the one you'll use most often is called "Math". Actually, Math isn't a style of its own; it's a combination of other styles.

MathType is smart enough, for example, to know that when you're typing $\sin(2x)$, you probably want the variable and the lower-case Greek letter to be italicized, but not the function name or the number. Thus, MathType switches between Function, Variable, Greek-Symbol, and Number styles as appropriate. ("Number" isn't a style you see on the menu, but it is a separate style of its own.) To set all this up, select "Define", at the bottom of the menu.

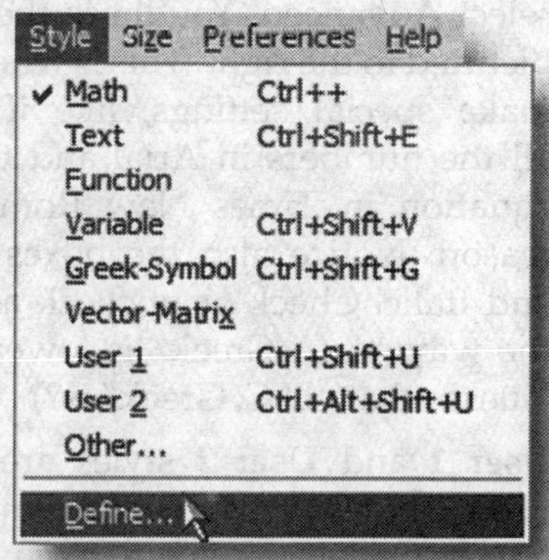

When you select Define, you'll see another "dialog box". (A "dialog box", or simply "dialog", is a window like the one shown to the right where you can select options and settings.)

In the Define Styles dialog, you'll see a couple of "radio buttons" labelled Simple and Advanced. We'll go over each of these. "Simple" is the one you'll use most often.

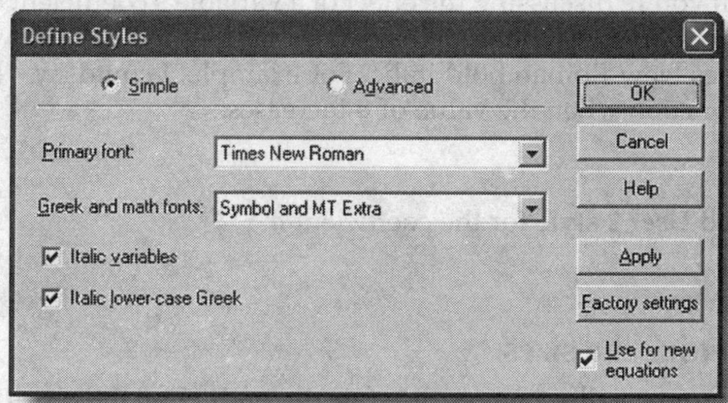

In the selection labelled "Primary font", the font you choose will be the font MathType will use for text, function names, variables, vector and matrix names, and numbers. Normally you'll want all of these to be the same font, but we'll see in a minute how to make them different. You'll probably want the Primary font to be the same font you're using in your document. MathType doesn't know what font you're using in your document, so it's important to set it here.

The selection labeled "Greek and math fonts" isn't normally changed. You'll see you have only two options there anyway – "Symbol and MT Extra" and "Euclid Symbol and Euclid Extra". You likely won't see much difference between these two choices, so leave it set as you are earlier.

At the lower right of this dialog is a final checkbox, labeled "Use for new equations". This is checked by default, and if you leave it checked, all subsequent equations you create will use these same font settings until you change them again. If you're just wanting the next equation to have a certain speciallook, but want the rest of the equations to look like the equations before the one you're working on, *uncheck* this box.

After everything's set the way you want it, click OK and the dialog closes. Now click on Style/Define again, and this time select Advanced. You'll see the dialog that's pictured to the right. This is where you would make special settings, like if you wanted all the numbers in Arial and the rest of the equation in Times New Roman, for some reason. Notice also the boxes labeled Bold and Italic. Check or uncheck as desired. (By the way, "L.C. Greek" is lower- case Greek. Guess what "U.C. Greek" is?)

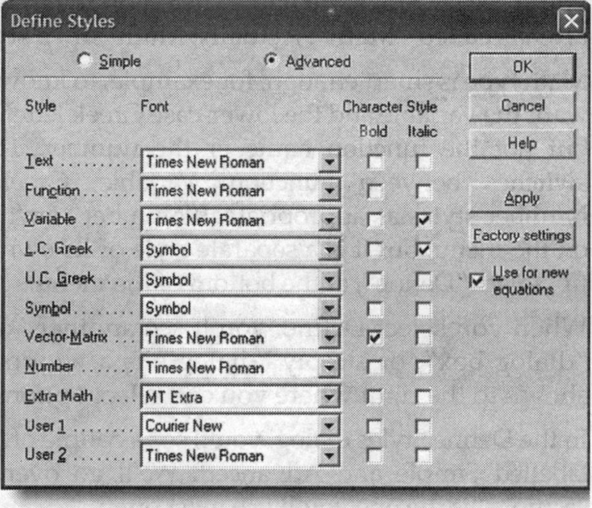

User 1 and **User 2** styles are not *normally* used, but when you need them, they're quite handy. One example where you may want to use a "User" style is if you're discussing the effect of a variable's coefficient on a graph (or you want the student to do so), so you choose to have the variables in Times New Roman italic, but the coefficient in Times New Roman bold italic. For example, I couldsay, "Describe the effect on the graph of the function when the value of ***a*** increases:

$$\boldsymbol{y = ax^2 + b + c}$$

In this example, I used **User 2** style for the coefficient ***a***.

$y = ax2 \ + bx + c$.

The Size Menu – setting the sizes

Just like MathType automatically changes the style depending on the types of items contained in your equation, it also changes sizes. For most of your equations, you'll just leave the size specification set to "Full". When you type an exponent, MathType knows you want it to be smaller than the base, so its witches to "Subscript" size. Likewise, if you're teaching sequences and series, and want to enter a summation template, MathType knows to create the Sigma symbol larger than the surrounding variables and numbers, so it switches to "Symbol" size. Even though this switching is automatic, you still have control over what sizes MathType uses when it selects these special sizes. To specify these sizes, select "Define" at the bottom of the Size menu. The "Define Sizes" dialog is quite different from the Define Styles dialog. One of the major differences is the presence of a "preview window". The preview window doesn't show you the actual equation you may be working on, but it does give you an indication of what exactly will change if you change the setting that's highlighted to the left of the preview window. For example, in the picture above, the only thing that will change in that sample equation when I change the "Full" size setting (notice the "12" is highlighted) is the *X*.

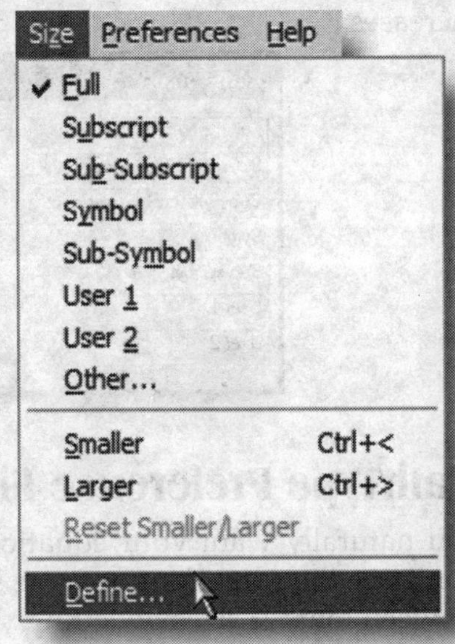

In MathType, the size setting called "Full" is the setting that you want to be identical to the text size in your document. If you're typing a test, and you're using 11-pt type size, make sure the MathType "Full" size is set to 11-pt.

Notice the rest of the sizes (except "Smaller/Larger Increment") are specified as a percent. Percent of *what*? These are percentages of the "Full" size. The beauty of leaving these set as percentages is that once you set them, you never have to change them! If you change the Full size from 10-pt (like you may use in a quiz) to 32-pt (like you may use in PowerPoint or on an overhead transparency), you don't have to change the other sizes because they're still proportionally correct. If you *want* to set these other sizes as point sizes, you have that option, but chances are you won't want to. (Notice there's a User 1 and User 2 size. Use these similarly to the way you'd use a User 1 or User 2 style.)

So, what's a "Smaller/Larger Increment"? Notice back up on the MathType Size menu (pictured at the bottom of the previous page), two items near the bottom are labelled "Smaller" and "Larger". If you want to make an item or items in your equation smaller or larger than the surrounding items in the equation, you can select them, and repeatedly select Smaller or Larger from the Size menu until you get the size you want. How much smaller or larger MathType makes them is determined by the "Smaller/Larger Increment" on the Define Sizes dialog.

BEWARE – It's generally not a good idea to highlight an entire equation and select Smaller or Larger, because the results will almost certainly **not** be what you wanted! (see below) If you want to increase or decrease the size of an entire equation, the best way to do it is by changing the Full size specification. You may want to deselect the "Use for new equations" checkbox.

Notice that the 18-pt expression is proportionally correct, but the 10-pt equation that was converted to18-pt by repetitively clicking "larger" on the size menu has an exponent that is too large. That's because both the base and the exponent are increased by 1-pt each time you click on "larger". say, "Describe the effect on the graph of the function when the value of ***a*** increases:

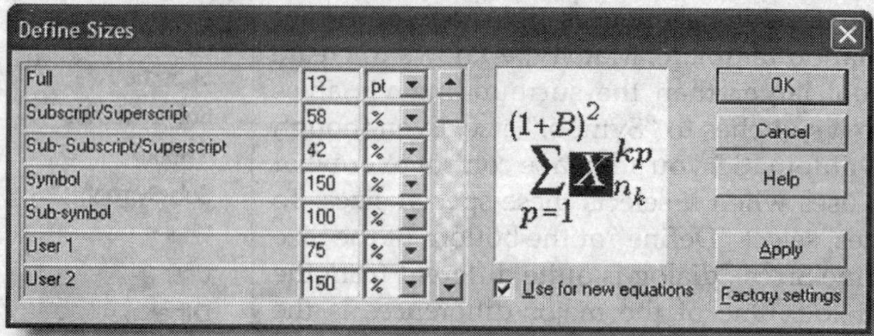

MathType Preference Files

You naturally want your equations to match the text of your document but you probably don't use the same font or same size font. MathType gives you a convenient way to change between fonts & sizes by letting you save these settings into a "preference file". Let's say you want to create your 7th Grade Math tests in 12-pt Times New Roman font, but you want to use 10-pt Arial for your 8th Grade Pre-AP Algebra tests.

The first thing to do is to save "12-pt Times New Roman" as a "Preference File". Those are the default settings when you install MathType, so chances are, that's what's set now. To save it, click on Preferences in the MathType menu bar. Now point to Equation Preferences, and another menu expands. In this menu, click on "Save to File…" In the next dialog, you'll get a chance to name the preference file. Since it's only a file like any other file, you can name it like any other file.

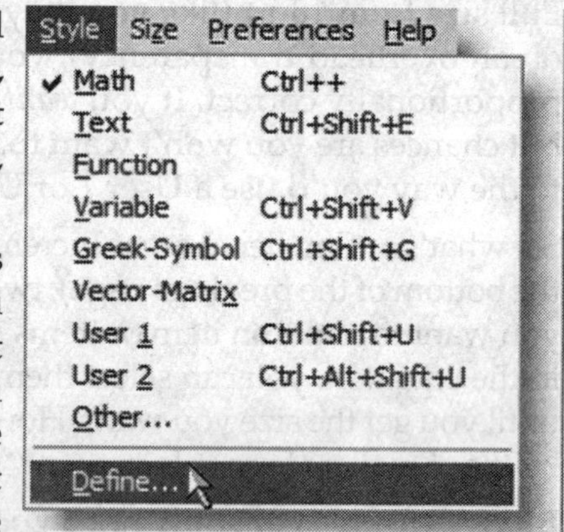

Notice how the others are named though. They are named with the name and size of the font. That's a good idea, because it helps you know what to expect when you select that particular preference file. After you type in a file name, click Save.

Now that we have a preference file saved for 12-pt Times New Roman, change your style to Arial. (Remember, you do this in the Style menu by selecting the Define option at the bottom of the menu. Also recall that it's easier if you select the "Simple" option.) Now change the "Full" size setting to 10. (This is in the Size menu, under Define.) Don't change any of the other sizes. Now save the preference file and name it "Arial-10", or another name of your choosing. (You don't need to type in "eqp" after the file name; MathType will add that for you after you click Save.)

So, what's saved in a preference file? We've already seen two of the three categories of data that are saved in a preference file, but there is one more – spacing. Let's say you're looking at your superscripted numbers and variables, and you think the exponent needs to be a little closer to the base, and the numerator in your fractions is a little too close to the fraction bar. By exploring the menus, you stumble across something in the Format menu labeled "Define

Spacing". In this menu, you discover how to change your superscripts and fractions to look more like the examples below:

You change ,

$$x^2 \xrightarrow{\text{to}} x^2 \text{ and } \frac{\sqrt{2}}{2} \xrightarrow{\text{to}} \frac{\sqrt{2}}{2}.$$

Any adjustments you make in the Define Spacing dialog are also saved to the preference file.

Creating a blank grid for student graphing

One of the most common questions we get is "Does MathType make graphs?" I always give a "qualified" answer to that question – No, MathType won't graph a function, but you can make a blank grid for you to do the graphing.

(This will be done using Equation Editor. If you are using MathType, the steps are similar.)

a. In a Microsoft Word (the procedure may be adapted for other software), open Equation Editor From the Insert menu, and select Object. From the list, choose "Microsoft Equation", and click OK.

b. On the Matrix templates palette, select Variable-size matrix or table.

You can look at the "Status Bar" – the very bottom of the Word or MathType window – to see what it is you're pointing to:

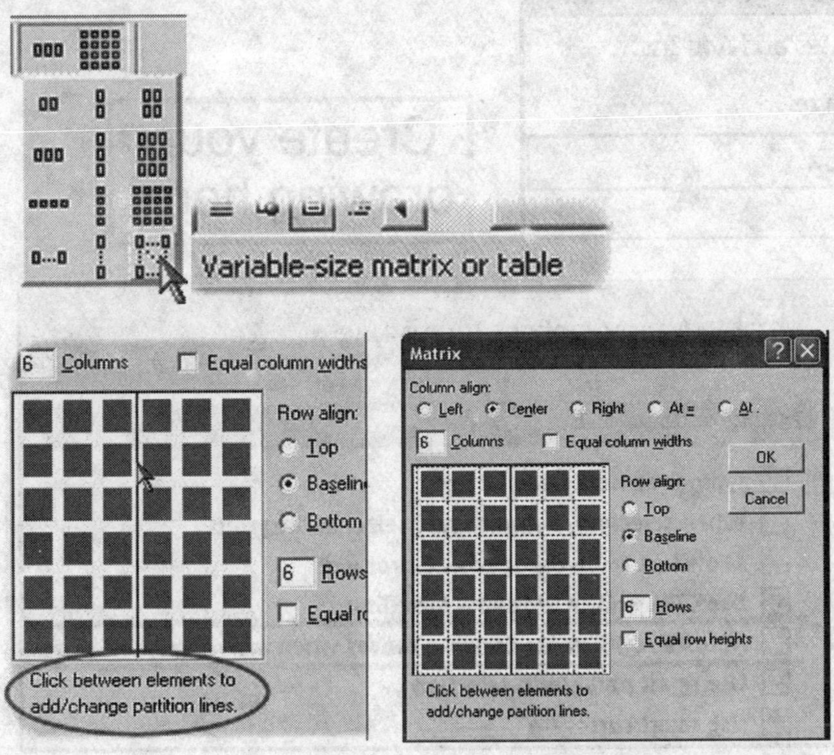

Changing Word defaults for menus & drawings (Windows)

A couple of aggravating features of Word 2002 and later (i.e., Office XP and later) are related to the Word menus and creating drawings with the drawing toolbar.

- ❑ The default is for Word's menus (pre-Word 2007) to show only basic commands after you first install Office. As you work, the menus adjust to show only the items you've used most recently. If You wait a couple of seconds the full menu appears, If you don'twant to wait, you can click the double chevron at the bottom of the menu.
- ❑ To change this behavior to always show the full menus, click on Tools > Customize. On the Options tab, check the box next to "Always show full menus".
- ❑ The default for using the "AutoShapes" on the Drawing toolbar is for Word to create a "Drawing Canvas", into which you'll insert your drawings. If you don't want the Drawing Canvas, you can change the default.
- ❑ *Except for Word 2007/2010*, click on **Tools > Options**, and click on the **General** tab. Near the bottom of the tab, ***uncheck*** the box labeled "Automatically create drawing canvas when inserting AutoShapes".
- ❑ *For Word 2007/2010*, click on the Office Button if in Word 2007, or the File tab if in Word 2010, then click Word Options. Click on Advanced, and the 5th option from the top is "Automatically create drawing canvas when inserting AutoShapes". Uncheck this and click OK.

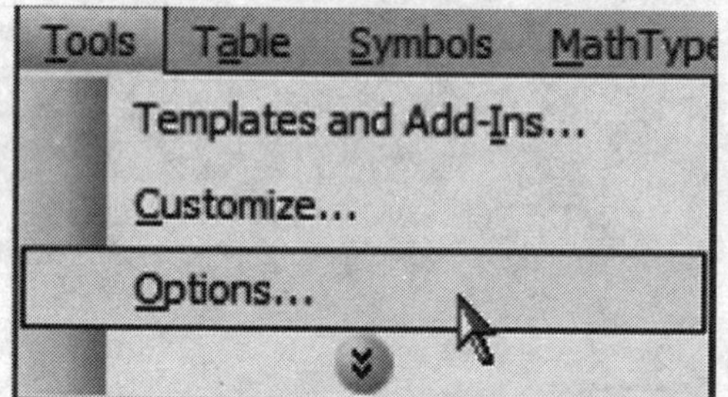

Create your drawing here.

Advanced options for working with Word.

Editing options

- Typing replaces selected text
- When selecting, automatically select entire word
- Allow text to be dragged and dropped
- Use CTRL + Click to follow hyperlink
- Automatically create drawing canvas when inserting AutoShapes
- Use smart paragraph selection
- Use smart cursoring

Nudging and MathType Customizable Toolbars

Nudging is a technique that can be accomplished in both Equation Editor and MathType, and isvery useful in achieving perfect positioning for your equations.

- ❑ For example, let's say you'd like more space between an integral symbol and the limits of integration. We'll add more space by nudging the limits to the right.
- ❑ Select the upper limit. The most common method to select items is to drag the mouse across the item. For small items though, such as limits, subscripts, etc., it's easier to use the Shift and arrow keys. With the cursor to either the left or right of the item you want to select, hold down the Shift key as you press the either the left or right arrow key, as appropriate. Release the Shift key after you've completed the selection.
- ❑ Hold down the Ctrl key. Use the arrows on the key board to move the selected item(s) in the desired direction.

$$\int_0^\infty f(x)dx \qquad \int_{\;0}^{\;\infty} f(x)dx$$

before nudging **after nudging**

Note that not all printers will print the limits as tightly-spaced as the ones in the "before" example.

You may have to experiment with nudging a bit in order to find the proper amount. If you're using MathType, you can save the newly-nudged expression or equation to the tool bar. That way you don't have to nudge it every time you use it.

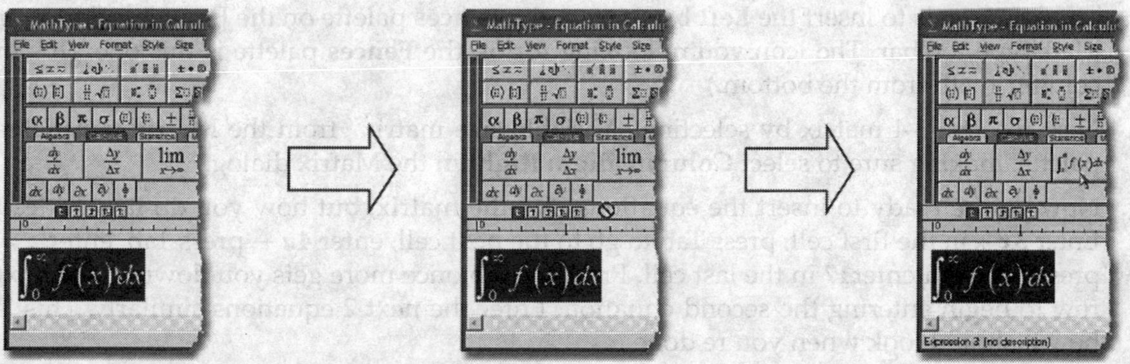

Aligning items within an equation

There are all sorts of things to align within an equation – the subtraction shown beneath a dividend in a long division problem, equations in a system of equations, items in a pictogram, responses in amultiple-choice question, etc. We will look at two of these: systems and multiple-choice. Note: Even if you don't teach the level of math requiring systems of equations, and even if you never create multiple-choice tests, the techniques learned here will still be useful to you.

Systems of equations and inequalities

a. There is no right or wrong way to "align" the equations in a system; it's basically a matter of choice, and a matter of what your students can read the best. (For simplicity, we won't specifically mention systems of inequalities, but these exact steps will work for those as well.) Here are 4 different scenarios:

$$\begin{cases}5x-3y=6\\2x+7y=2\end{cases}\qquad\begin{cases}3x+4y+\ \ z=17\\2x+3y+2z=15\\\ \ x+\ y\qquad=\ 4\end{cases}\qquad\begin{cases}x\qquad\quad=3\\2x+\ y\quad=3\\3x+2y+z=3\end{cases}\qquad\begin{cases}x=3\\2x+y=3\\3x+2y+z=3\end{cases}$$

1 2 3 4

b. Systems 2 and 3 above present the greatest challenge, so let's deal with system 2.

c. In this system, we want to align the variables, the operation symbols (+, , or =), and the sums so that they are vertically aligned with similar elements in the previous equation, and right-justified within each column (for example, z & $2z$ and 15 & 4 in system 2 above).

d. There are many ways to align a system, but let's just cut to the chase and say that using a matrix isthe best way to do it. So with that established, what size? The obvious number of rows is a number equal to the number of equations. There are several choices for the number of columns, but the best balance between utility and ease of use is a number of columns equal to the number of equations *plus one*. So our matrix for system 2 above will be a 3 4.

e. The first step is to insert the **Left brace** from the **Fences** palette on the Equation Editor or MathType toolbar. The icon you're looking for on the **Fences** palette is this one: (It's in column 1, 4th from the bottom.)

f. Next insert a 3 4 matrix by selecting "Variable-size matrix" from the **Matrix templates** palette, making sure to select **Column align: Right** in the Matrix dialog.

g. Now you're ready to insert the equations into the matrix, but how you do it is critical! Enter **3*x*** + in the first cell, press Tab to go to the next cell, enter **4*y*** +, press Tab, enter *z* =, press Tab, and enter**17** in the last cell. Pressing Tab once more gets you down to the next row to begin entering the second equation. Enter the next 2 equations similarly. This is how it should look when you're done

h. After you settle on a value (my personal opinion is that 25% looks best), either click in your document to close the Equation Editor window and go back to Word, or if you're using MathType, simply close the MathType window (click the in the upper right-hand corner, or the "stoplight" if you're using a Mac).

i. ***In MathType***, you have two attractive options you don't have in Equation Editor:

- You can save the matrix spacing to a preference file. This is a good idea, because you won't want to use this tight matrix column spacing in a "regular" matrix, and this will give you an easy way to change back to your "systems of equations" settings. A MathType preference file holds information on fonts, sizes, and spacing.

To save the preference file, go to the **Prefrences** Menu, scroll down to Equation Preferences, then choose Save to File. You can name the file anything you want, but here are some suggestions: **Systems** (if you always use the same font and size for your tests & quizzes); **Systems-TNR**, **Systems-A**, etc. (for tests written in Times New Roman, Arial, etc. font); **Systems-A-10**, **Systems-A-12**, etc. (for tests written in Arial 10pt, Arial 12pt, etc.). You get the picture.

- You can save a blank template for a 2-equation system, one for a 3-equation system, etc., to your MathType toolbar. The easiest way to do this is to delete everything out of the cells of the matrix in the system you just created, then highlight everything and drag it up to the toolbar:

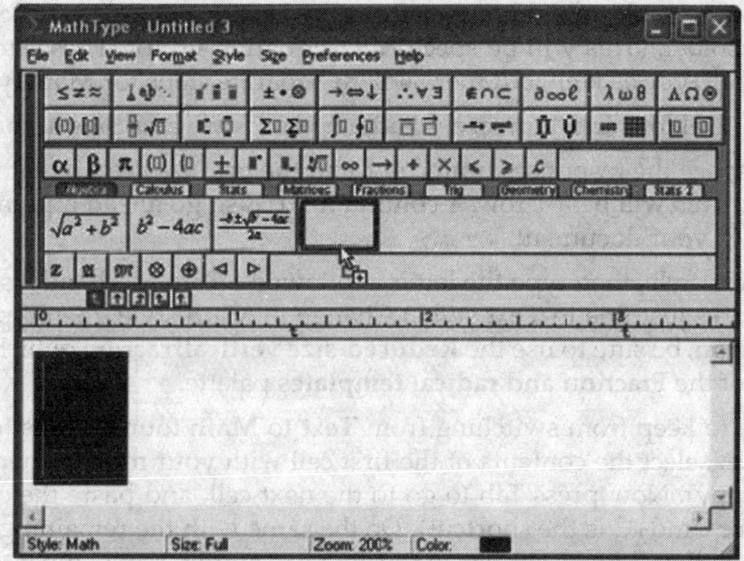

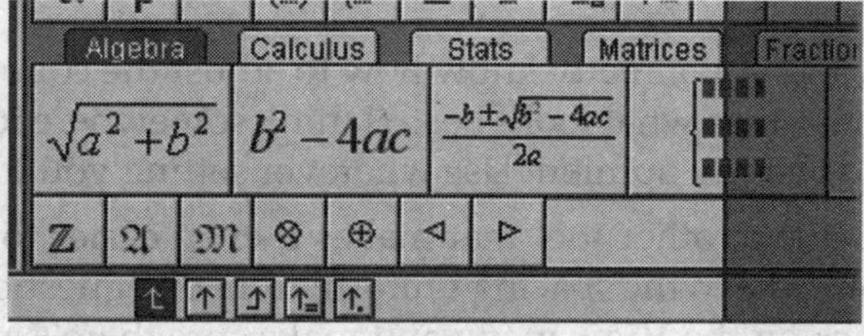

Multiple-choice responses

a. There are many ways to type multiple choice responses for a test or quiz. You may create each choice as a separate equation (remember, we use the word "equation" to denote anything created with Equation Editor or MathType, regardless of whether or not it contains an equals symbol), or you could include all the responses in a single equation and arrange them in various ways. Two common ways to arrange the responses are to place them all on the same line of text or to put two responses on one line and two on another line. We'll deal with the first option here.

b. For this example, we'll create the responses for this question:

1. Find the quotient: $1\frac{2}{3} \div 1\frac{1}{2}$

a. $2\frac{3}{5}$ b. $2\frac{1}{2}$ c. $1\frac{1}{9}$ d. 2

c. One option would be to type the question and all the responses as a single equation, but we'll type the question text in Word and the division expression and responses in Equation Editor or MathType. We'll type all 4 responses as one object.

d. Assuming you've already typed the question, let's work on the responses. Open Equation Editor as you normally would, either from the **Insert** menu or by clicking the icon on your Word toolbar. (This will be specifically Equation Editor. These steps will work, of course, in MathType as well, but there will be separate steps for MathType later.)

e. We're using Arial font and 11pt size, so adjust your **Style** and **Size** accordingly.

f. We want to space the responses uniformly, and the best way to do that is to use a matrix. This will be a 1-row, 4-column matrix, so go ahead and insert one of those in your document.

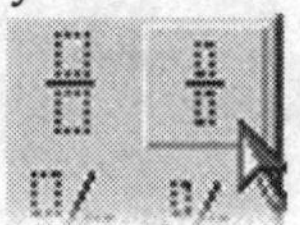

g. Change to **Text** style, then type the letter **a** followed by a period and a space. (Notice the space bar works just fine in **Text** style.) Change to **Math** style, then type $2\frac{3}{5}$. When you type the fraction, be sure to use the **Reduced-size verticalfraction**, which is the one in the upper-right of the **Fraction and radical templates** palette.

h. An easy way to keep from switching from **Text** to **Math** four times is to copy what you just typed (i.e. select the contents of the first cell with your mouse, then press Ctrl+C or Cmd+C to copy). Now press Tab to go to the next cell, and paste the contents into that cell (Ctrl+V or Cmd+C is the shortcut). Do the same with the remaining 2 cells, then edit the contents so that it looks similar to the above example. We'll adjust the spacing in the next step.

i. Since this is a matrix, and you already know how to adjust the column spacing in a matrix, go ahead and adjust it to see what looks best. (I think somewhere in the range of 300-400% looks best, but that's just my opinion. Use whatever setting you like.)

j. *In MathType*, you have another tool that makes it even easier to create multiple-choice responses, and easier to keep the spacing uniform from one question to the other. If you're using MathType, click on the **View** menu and make sure there's a checkmark by **Ruler.**

k. Notice above the ruler there are 5 arrows. These arrows represent 5 types of tabs that are available in MathType. From left to right, these are:

- ❑ *Left-justified tab.* This is the one selected in the screenshot below, and is the default. When you use a left-justified tab, the left edge of the text will be aligned at the tab.
- ❑ *Center-justified tab.* The center of the text is aligned at the tab stop.
- ❑ *Right-justified tab.* The right edge of the text is aligned at the tab stop.

- ❑ *Relational tab*. Use this tab only with more than one line of characters within your equation. This will align equations or inequalities at any relational operator, such as ≠, ≥, ≡, ∝, and of course =. (Basically, it will align on the equals, greater than, or less than signs from the keyboard, plus anything on the **Relational symbols** palette.)
- ❑ *Decimal tab*. Use this one also for more than one line of characters. This is for aligning a column of numbers, regardless of whether or not a decimal point is present.

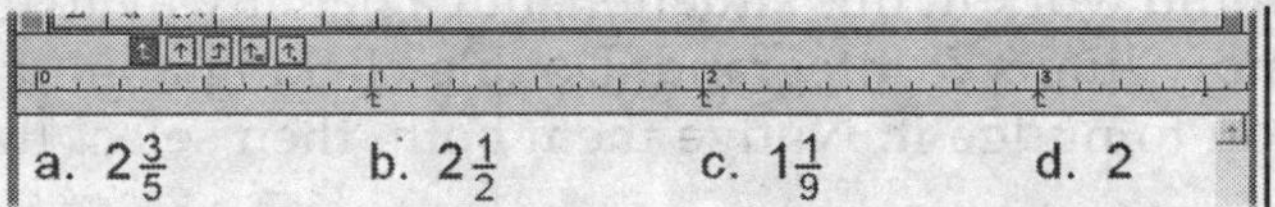

l. To set a tab stop, simply select the type of tab you want to use and click on the ruler below the number or tick-mark where you want the tab to be. **Caution:** Each template slot has its own set of tabs, so if you are inside a numerator slot (for example), and set a tab at the 1" mark, that tab will not be set outside the fraction! In the example above, make sure your "insertion point" (i.e., cursor) is outside the fraction before you set the tab. You won't run into this problem if you set your tabs prior to typing the MathType equation, but you won't always know where you want the tabs set before you start typing. Just be aware of this feature of tabs.

m. For our example, since we're using tabs to align the multiple-choice responses, we don't need our **14 matrix**. You *can* use the matrix if you want, of course, but you wouldn't use both a matrix *and* tabs.

n. One final point on tabs. You already know what the Tab key's for when you're typing in MathType; it's to move from one template slot to another, or to move out of the template. To moveto the next tab stop, you need to press the **Ctrl+Tab** key stroke combination.

Saving to MathType toolbar

Naturally you don't want to have to go through the process of creating this for each question. You *could* copy the responses from one question and paste them into another, then edit the responses, but there's an easier way. Using the example above, delete each response and in its place, insert a 1x1 matrix. Without the matrix, the insertion point (i.e., cursor) will appear after the "d.", then to type the "a" response, you'd have to click the mouse in that position. Having the 1x1 matrix in place before you save it to the toolbar gives the insertion point a place to land when you click on the item to use it next time. See the graphic below:

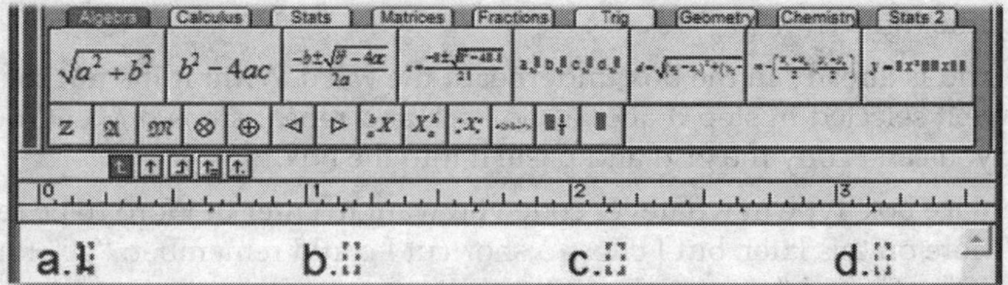

The 1x1 matrix is also handy for other purposes, such as the generic quadratic formula and the generic 2nd degree polynomial you see on the Algebra toolbar. It's a good idea to save the 1x1

matrix to the toolbar for easy access in future situations such as this. You see it saved above on the small Algebra toolbar.

The 1x1 matrix is also useful, but not really needed, for situations where you want to retain something you've nudged, but you want to remove the contents from the template slot. Take for example the definite integral we saw earlier in the handout. If you save the integral with nudged limits to the toolbar but delete the limits first, the nudging is removed. The 1x1 matrix would work in this situation, but a better way to do it is to insert an integral symbol with empty limits & integrand. Double-clicking a limit will select the limit slot itself, allowing you to nudge it. Nudge them both, then select the integral and drag to the toolbar.

Using Word's AutoCorrect Feature

Some things you create with Equation Editor or MathType are repetitive – the grid discussed earlier, for example. If you're creating a worksheet on graphing linear functions, you'll quite likely have 10 or 20 of these, so it's very useful to be able to insert a grid with just a few keystrokes – and without even opening up MathType!

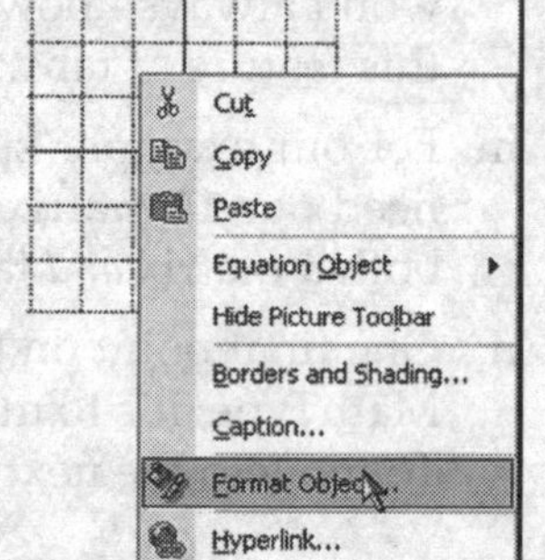

a. For the purpose of this mini-tutorial, we'll use the grid created earlier. Insert the 6-by-6 grid into your document.

b. If it doesn't appear to be perfectly square, you can make it square by clicking on it with your **right** mouse button (Mac, Ctrl+click), then selecting **Format Object** from the menu. If **Format Object** doesn't appear on the right-click menu, select **Object** from Word's **Format** menu. (In Word 2007, if **Format Object** isn't be in the right-click menu, click on the **Drawing Tools > Format** tab in the Ribbon, then adjust the size in the **Size** group.)

c. Adjust the height and width to the same number – whatever you want them to be. ***Make sure the Lock aspect ratio box is unchecked!***

d. Regardless of whether you re-sized your grid or not, make sure it's still selected (as the one is to the right). If it's not selected, click once on it with your left mouse button.

e. With the grid selected, choose **AutoCorrect Options** from Word's **Tools** menu. If you're using a version of Word ***earlier than Word2002*** – the one that comes with Office XP – it will just say **AutoCorrect**. If you're using **Word 2007**, click the **Office Button**, then click **Word Options**. Click **Proofing** on the left, and the **AutoCorrect Options** button will appear on the right.

f. Note the grid is already in the box underneath the word **With:** If it's **not** there, then you didn't have it selected in step d above. Go back and repeat steps d & e. (You must do it this way; you can't copy the grid and paste it into the box.)

g. In the **Replace** box, type in whatever code you want to enter in Word to be replaced with the grid. More on this later, but I chose a shortcut I could remember: "gr" for "grid", "6" meaning "6-by-6", and "a", meaning it has axes.

h. Click **Add**, then click **OK**.

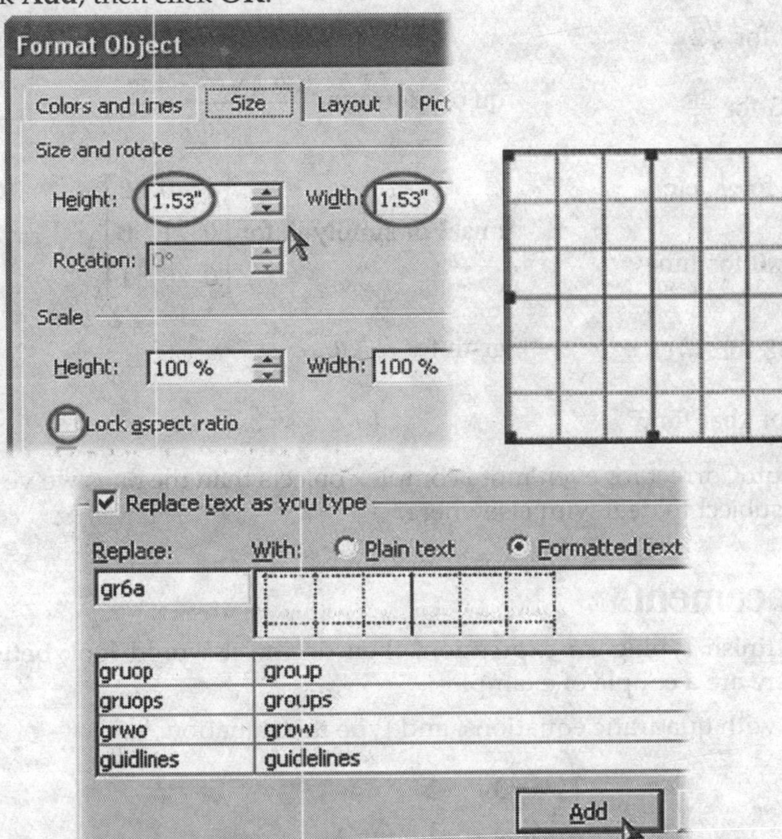

i. Now that you're back in your document, delete the grid and try your AutoCorrect entry. Type **gr6a** (or whatever code you entered), followed by the spacebar. Your code should be replaced with a grid.

Here are some notes about what we just did:

- I had you hit the spacebar after the code, but there's nothing magical about the spacebar. The important thing is that you tell Word that you're through typing that word, and in this case, our word was **gr6a**. Think about what normally "terminates" a word – a space character, any punctuation character, a Tab, a new line, or even a mathematical operator (such as < or =). In fact, any of these things will replace your code with your grid (or whatever you entered into the AutoCorrect box).
- The code I chose – **gr6a** – may seem a little cryptic to you, and you may not think you can remember that one. That's fine; choose whatever code you'll remember, but be careful! You don't want to choose a word that will likely appear in any document. The words "grid" or "graph", for example, appear often, so you don't want to choose these. I'm 100% sure the code I chose will never come up in any document ever – unless I want a 6-by-6 grid.

- ❑ What other uses for AutoCorrect can you think of ? I can think of several:

sq2 for $\sqrt{2}$

2p/3 for $\frac{2\pi}{3}$ qu or qform for $\dfrac{-b\pm\sqrt{b^2-4ac}}{2a}$

1/8 for $\frac{1}{8}$, etc.

imat3 or simply i3 for $\begin{bmatrix}1 & 0 & 0\\0 & 1 & 0\\0 & 0 & 1\end{bmatrix}$

limx0 for $\lim\limits_{x\to 0}$

u238 for ${}^{238}_{92}\mathrm{U}$ gr-th for θ, etc.

xb or xbar for $\overline{x}$

- ❑ You can use AutoCorrect for even more complex objects than the ones we've used, but that's really a subject to deal with elsewhere.

Template Replacement

Sometimes you may finish typing an expression, then decide it would look better with a different template. Here are a couple of examples:

- ❑ You're working with quadratic equations, and type this equation:

$$y=\frac{1}{2}x^2+\frac{3}{2}x+\frac{2}{3}$$

You realize the equation would look better with smaller fractions. Rather than re-type it all, you should use ***template replacement***. Here are the steps for template replacement:

a. Select the first fraction

$$y=\frac{1}{2}x^2+\frac{3}{2}x+\frac{2}{3}$$

b. While holding down the Ctrl key on the keyboard (use the Alt key for Equation Editor or on the Mac for either Equation Editor or MathType), select the **Reduced-size fraction** template from the **Fraction and radical templates** palette, as shown in figure, ➔

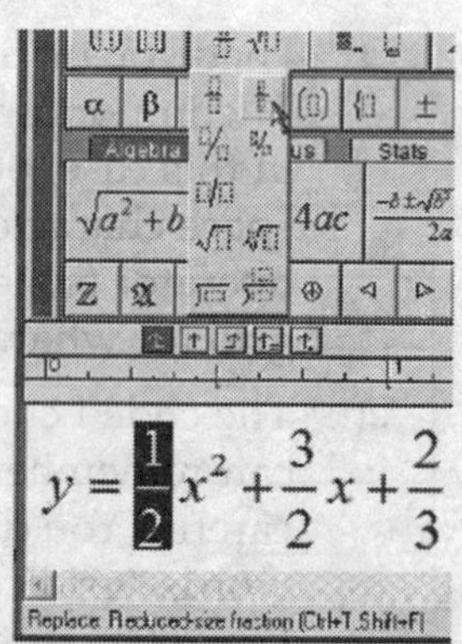

c. Repeat for the remaining 2 fractions

$$y=\tfrac{1}{2}x^2+\tfrac{3}{2}x+\tfrac{2}{3}$$

- ❑ You create an integral, and realize you should have specified an expanding integral:

$$\int \frac{1}{1+x^2} dx = \tan^{-1} x + c$$

You remember reading somewhere that if you hold down the **Shift** key while you select an integral template, it creates an expanding integral symbol. (This works in Equation Editor as well.) You also remember that holding down the **Ctrl** key (Alt key in situations listed above) allows you to replace one template with another.

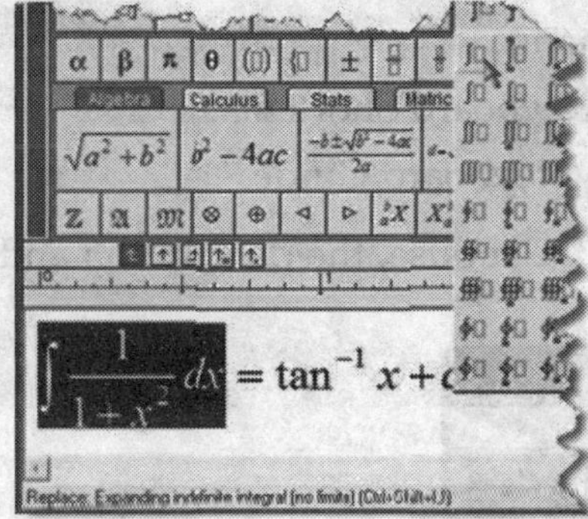

Holding down both the **Ctrl** and **Shift** keys lets you replace the integral with an expanding integral.

NOTE: For template replacement, it's important to select the entire template, but only the template (and the template contents) you wish to replace. See screen shot. Notice that only the integral and its corresponding integrand are selected.

Keyboard Shortcuts

The keyboard shortcuts built-in to MathType are listed in the Help file. You'll find, that most of the shortcuts are so intuitive that you can learn them quickly though, and be able to use the software even more efficiently to create professional-looking documents.

Many of the shortcuts used in MathType are "standard" shortcuts – such as CTRL+S for save, CTRL+C for copy, CTRL+V for paste, etc. (On the Mac, most of the time you can substitute the COMMAND key for the Windows CTRL key.) Listed here are some of the most commonly-used keyboard shortcuts:

Text mode	SHIFT+CTRL+E
Math mode	SHIFT+CTRL+=
Greek letters	CTRL+G, followed by corresponding letter of the alphabet (a for α, etc.)
Expanding parentheses	CTRL+9
Full-sized fraction	CTRL+F
Radical (square root)	CTRL+R

Superscript (exponent)	CTRL+H ("h" for "high"; COMMAND+E on the Mac)
Subscript	CTRL+L (" l " for "low")
Thin space	CTRL+SPACE
Insert equation in	CTRL+ALT+Q
Edit equation in Word	ALT+O (select the equation first)

For more keyboard shortcuts, you can refer to

- "Customize Keyboard" in the MathType Preferences menu
- The MathType Help file under "MathType Reference/Keyboard Shortcuts."
- The Equation Editor Help file: "Reference Information/Keyboard Guide."

Also note that in MathType, when you point to an item with the mouse, the description and keyboard shortcut are displayed in the Status Bar:

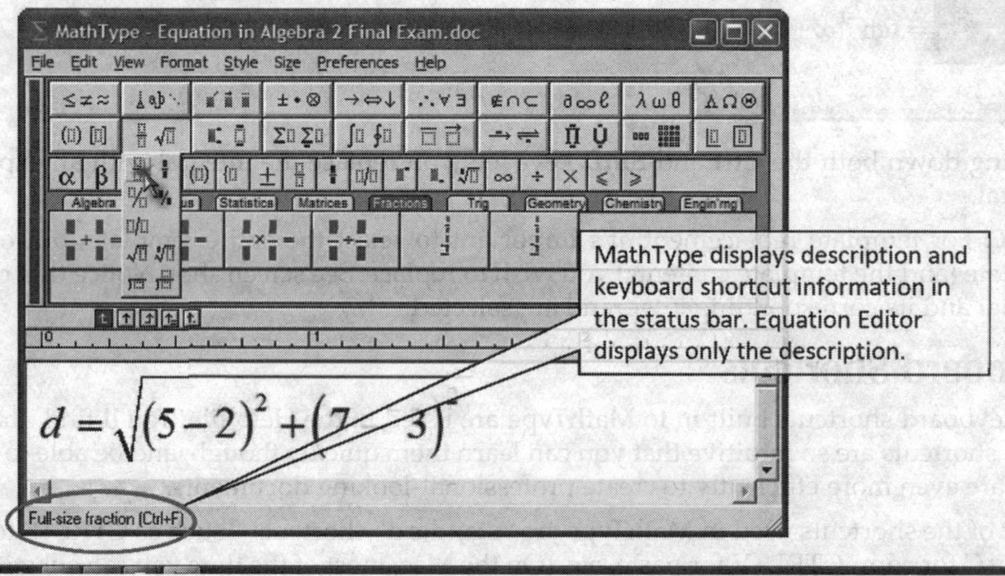

Note....

Most of the Features of Math Type have been included in word 2010.

QuarkXpress 9

QuarkXPress (often referred to as Quark) is a computer application for creating and editing complex page layouts in a WYSIWYG (What You See Is What You Get) environment. It runs on Mac OS X and Windows. It was first released by Quark, Inc. in 1987 and is still owned and published by them.

The most recent version, QuarkXPress 9, allows publishing in English ("International and U.S) and 36 other languages, including Arabic, Chinese, Japanese, Portuguese, German, Korean, Russian, French, and Spanish.

QuarkXPress is used by individual designers and large publishing houses to produce a variety of layouts, from single-page flyers to the multi-media projects required for magazines, newspapers, catalogs, and the like. QuarkXPress once dominated the market for page layout software with over 95% market share among professional users. While one publisher estimates that share has fallen to below 25% and Adobe InDesign is now the market leader, QuarkXPress still has significant marketshare. There are open source competitors in the page layout space, the most notable of which is Scribus.

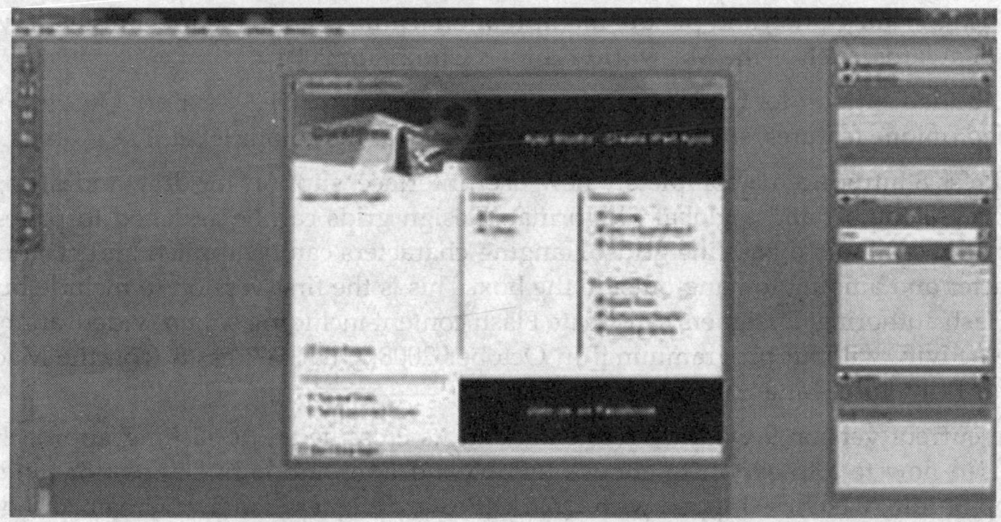

In addition to the basic functionality of font, alignment, spacing, and colour, the package also provides its users with professional typesetting options like kerning, curving text along a line, and ligatures.

A QuarkXPress document contains text and graphics boxes. The boxes can be reshaped, layered, and given varying levels of transparency and text alignment (run-around). Both box positioning and graphic or text positioning is allowed within a box with an accuracy of one-thousandth of an inch.

Colour control allows the full-use of printing-press standard Pantone or Hex chrome inks, along with a variety of other colour-space options. Draft output can be printed on conventional desktop printers. Process colour (CMYK) separation films can be produced for printing-presses. QuarkXPress also offers the ability for composite work-flows, both with PostScript and PDF output.

QuarkXPress offers layout synchronization, multiple undo/redo functionality, XML and web page (HTML/XHTML) features, and support for direct PDF import and output. Documents can be verified (pre-flight) before printing. This high-level print preview automatically identifies conflicts and other printing problems. Since then Adobe has implemented a similar feature in InDesign CS4.

Composition zones feature makes it the only desktop application with multi-user capabilities by allowing multiple users to edit different zones on the same page. Composition Zones pushes collaboration a step further than just simultaneous text/picture (as possible with Quark CopyDesk since 1991), as it allows layout and graphic elements to be edited outside the layout application.

User-defined rules, output specs and layout specs can be used for intelligent templates and enable resource sharing (for example, server-based style sheet definitions).

Version 6.5, released at the end of 2004, added enhanced support for the Photoshop format (PSD). The PSD integration and picture manipulation features led to QuarkXPress receiving a number of awards, such as the Macworld Editor's Choice for 2004.

Version 7 added support for OpenType, Unicode, JDF and also PDF/X-export. QuarkXPress 7 also added unique features, such as native transparency at the colour level.

QuarkXPress 8 introduced a completely new user interface, support for drag and drop, PDF 1.7 import, AI Import and a global file format. Design grids can be assigned to pages and boxes to allow unlimited baseline grids. Hanging characters can be applied and customized by character and amount to hang outside the box. This is the first version to include built-in Adobe Flash authoring. Designers can create Flash content including sound, video, animation and interactivity without programming. In October 2008, QuarkXPress 8 won the MacUser Award for Print Publishing Software of the Year.

With the current version 9 QuarkXPress extended its crossmedia publishing approach and can be used now to also export to eBooks (ePub3 and Blio) and native apps (for the iPad). With App Studio, which is shipped with QuarkXPress, designers can even create and design their own apps.[8] Additionally QuarkXPress 9 offers cascading styles (stylesheets based on text content), callouts (anchored objects that flow with the text based on position rules), create complex ad editable Bézier paths using a wizard (ShapeMaker), bullets and numbers (with import & export from/to Microsoft Word) and more.

The Mac version of QuarkXPress 9 is for Intel processors only, making QuarkXPress 8.5.1 the last choice for PPC-based Macs.

We are not including any tutorial for the Quark Xpress, because the interface is similar to the Adobe InDesign. There are some other issues with the content, if you however want to learn more about QuarkXpress, use their training courses. You may visit these links:

www.planetquark.com

www.quark.com

QuarkXpress have a very interactive style of tutoring student. See more about QuarkEd on their Official Website.

CD Script

The book comes with a CD containing 15 Video Tutorials for better understanding of some useful applications discussed in the book. For convenience of the reader we divide the videos section wise, such as Photoshop, InDesign, Illustrator.

Photoshop:

1. **Colour Setting in Photoshop:** This video tutorial familiarizes you with colour setting in Photoshop. The tutorial shows the methods of colour setting, such as how to make custom changes to Working Spaces, Colour Management Policies, Missing Profiles, etc., step-by-step.
2. **Introduction to Layer Masks:** This tutorial will show you how to work with layer masks in Photoshop. Different steps, such as unlocking the layer, applying masks, changing foreground and background colour, etc., are discussed in detail in this video tutorial.
3. **Merge and Combine Two Photos:** This video tutorial guides you on how to merge and combine two photographs in one document in Photoshop. The tutorial discuses different techniques involved in the process of merging two photos is a Photoshop document in detail.
4. **Change Hair Colour:** This video tutorial will show how to change hair colours of a person in Photoshop using different techniques. Various steps like creating a new layer, adding new colours, adjusting hue/saturation, etc., are discussed step-by-step.
5. **Change lip Colour:** In this video tutorial you will see how to change lip colour of a person using various techniques in Photoshop. Every step is discussed in detail.
6. Change Eye Colour: This video will teach you how to use Photoshop's techniques to change the eye colour of a person. You will get step-by-step instructions for every action.

InDesign:

1. **Exploring the Interface (1):** This video tutorial familiarises you with InDesign interface and shows you how various panels and menus look, and how keyboard shortcuts work in InDesign. The video also familiarises you with various keyboard shortcuts and teaches you how to customise keyboard shortcuts.
2. **Exploring the Interface (2):** This tutorial elaborates InDesign Interface in detail and shows you how a document appears in InDesign environment and how to create a new document using all the default settings in InDesign.
3. **Working with Documents (1):** This video tutorial guides you on how to work with documents in InDesign. The tutorial covers features like creating templates for documents that we can use many times and shows you how to create, open and save a template, and how to create a new document, save a document and open an inDesign document that is already saved in your PC.
4. **Working with Documents (2):** This video tutorial covers how to open an InDesign CS5 document in InDesign CS4 or other versions. The video also includes some of the features like Background Tasks Indicator and shows you how to export a document in PDF or any other format.

Illustrator:

1. **Welcome Screen:** This video tutorial familiarises you with the welcome screen you see when you first open Adobe Illustrator, and shows you what you can do with this welcome window.
2. **Shape Tool:** This video tutorial demonstrates how to create basic shapes in Illustrator and shows how to change those shapes using shortcut keys. Various ways of creating different shapes like rectangle, square, circle, hexagon, etc., are discussed in detail.
3. **Shape Builder Tool:** This video tutorial discusses Shape Builder Tool in detail and shows how amazing shapes can be created using shape builder tool along with other tools, such geometric shapes and others.
4. **Stroke and Fill Colours:** This video will demonstrate the differences between a shape's fill and a shape's stroke and show how to change colours on each one.
5. **Staking Order and Outlines:** This video tutorial shows how to change staking order of an object, and also shows how to just show the outlines of an object in Illustrator.

MS Publisher:

1. **Know it:** This video will guide you on how to create publications such as name badges, business card, brochures, menus, etc., using MS publisher 2010.
2. Printing and Publishing: This video will show you several different ways of printing and publishing a document created in MS Publisher.

Comprehensive Computer Learning

Windows 8

Windows 8

What You Need to Know About Windows 8

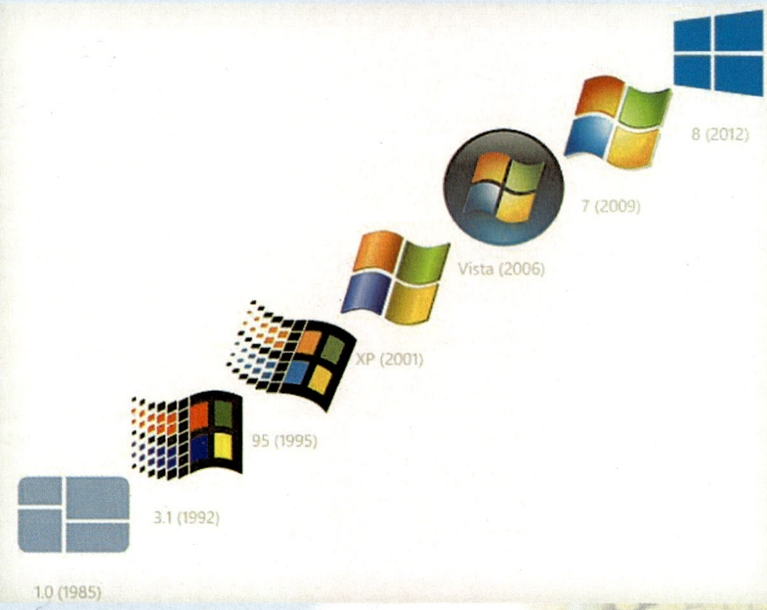

Back in 1991, Microsoft released their first version of Windows, a mouse-driven graphical user interface that revolutionised the way we use computers, both at home and at workplace.

Now, in 2012, they hope to stage a new revolution with Windows 8, perhaps Microsoft's most daring release yet. Featuring an unusual **Tile-Based Start Screen** that's optimized for touchscreen devices, Windows 8 will be available on new computers, laptops, ultrabooks, hybrid tablets and even a new range of Microsoft-branded, iPad-style tablet called **Microsoft Surface** and mobile phones also.

Whichever device you end up running Windows 8 on, you'll need to know a few things. First, how are you going to get the data from your current operating System to the new one? Second, you'll probably be wondering where the famous Microsoft desktop has gone. Finally, you might be wondering just what is going on? Why did Microsoft discard the Start menu?

Upgrading from Windows XP or Windows Vista or Windows 7

If you're upgrading, and you're already using Windows Vista or Windows 7, the new version of Windows offers an Upgrade option. This enables you to manage the transfer of data with little or no trouble – Windows 8 will effectively upgrade the existing OS without damaging your data – although you should backup your vital files anyway, just in case.

If you're upgrading from Windows XP, the process is a little different. Windows 8 cannot upgrade Windows XP in the same way in which it can Windows Vista and 7, in which case you will need to use a more detailed and drawn out process for saving your data and migrating it to the new operating system.

Where's the Desktop Gone?

So you've installed Windows 8. At least, you thought you installed Windows, but what you see doesn't look at all familiar.

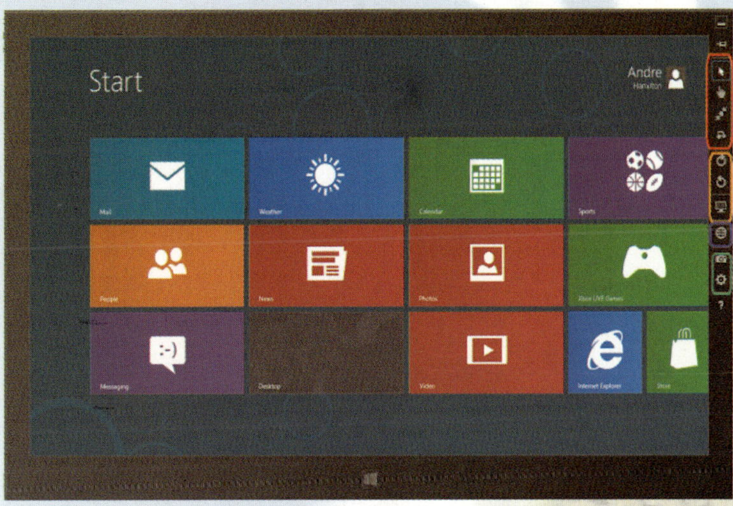

One of the most striking developments in the new version of Windows is the way in which the desktop – the area hosting the Start button, taskbar and icons in previous releases – has been demoted in favour of a new Start screen, Complete with tiles that can be clicked or tapped (depending on your hardware) to launch apps and adjust settings.

Have no fear, however – the old Desktop is still available. Indeed, it can be reached by tapping one of the tiles. While viewing the Desktop feels and looks like classic Windows, note that there is no Start button – all tasks related to this feature will need to be performed via the Start screen or by setting up some shortcuts on the Desktop.

Windows 8 Devices

There are many types of computer hardware capable of running Windows 8. First and foremost is the standard desktop computer. If your PC is capable of running Windows Vista, chances are it will run Windows 8. There are even some older computers stuck on Windows XP that can run Windows 8 effectively!

Similarly, existing laptop computers and ultrabooks will also be able to run Windows 8 – thanks to useful touchpad gesture apps, Windows 8 might actually be better for smaller systems than Vista or Windows 7 were. Despite this, Windows 8 is really intended for new devices. The reason for this is simple: the change in focus for the Start screen means that fingers are recommended, if not required. As a result new PCs shipping with Windows 8 will come with touchscreens and/or mice with gesture recognition tools, new Mac OS X-style touchpads will become available and laptops will almost all become hybrid devices, with pivoting touchscreen displays.

Microsoft aren't entirely playing nice with their traditional partners, the hardware makers – they've announced the release of a new tablet, Microsoft Surface, which will come in two flavours.

That's a big step for a company that doesn't usually make hardware. Windows 8 is designed to work on devices powered by a low-power ARM processor (found in typical Android and Apple tablets) as well as typical Intel x86 based processors (which is what most desktop, laptops and ultrabooks today use). Surface is seen as a competitor to Android and iOS tablets, and Windows 8's app store and tile–based interface are a big part of that.

With this in mind, there will be no shortage of suitable computers and tablets to run the new operating system! It should also be noted that a Windows 8 device powered by an ARM processor will be unable to run legacy Windows software, such as games and older versions of Microsoft Office. That software is Intel-only.

The Windows 8 User Interface

The major difference between Windows 8 and previous releases – the tile-based UI – means that you will need to spend a bit of time getting used to the Start screen. No longer will you need to click a Start button and browse the Programs list, or use the search function – at least not the way you're used to. Instead you will need to find a new way in which to perform tasks that have become ingrained, hard wired into your brain.

Understanding Metro

Probably the best route to understanding how to use Windows 8 is to forget that you're using Windows at all. There are various ways in which you can interact with the system, but few of them require you to click and drag, open properties or make any adjustments to the layout of the Start screen (although this is possible). Gaining familiarity with the tiles and the navigation is important, as is being aware of the **"charms"** – a hidden array of menu items. You'll need to move your mouse pointer to (or tap) the top or bottom right of your Windows 8 display to reveal the **Charm Bar**. If you are using a device with a keyboard, pressing WIN+C will also open the Charm Bar.

Appearing on the right-hand side of the screen, the Charm Bar provides other features and functions:

- **Search** – like the Windows 7 Start menu, simply type to find what you're looking for. When an app is open, Search will focus on that software rather than the computer itself. For a full computer search, use the tool from the Start screen. Note also that you can commence a search from the Start screen by simply typing – the Search tool will open as a result. Also note that Search can be used to find Desktop-based Windows items.
- **Share** – apps with sharing permissions can be used to share information such as links. Note that this cannot be used in desktop mode, only via the Metro browser.
- **Start** – this is yet another option to open the Start screen, along with the menu in the lower-left corner, or by pressing the Windows key on a hardware keyboard.
- **Devices** – settings for peripherals such as second/external monitors can be adjusted.
- **Settings** – Audio, Brightness, Wi-Fi, Power, Notifications and Language are all accessed from here. The **More PC Settings** link will enable you to access more options in the control panel. The Settings option will display settings for individual apps while they are active.

These options are displayed **Metro-style**. On the left side of your display, the date, time and battery and wireless networking information will also be displayed.

Note that many apps (native and third party) will have their own context menus. These menus can be accessed by right-clicking with the mouse.

Launch and Install Apps, Multitasking

One of the strengths of Windows 8's tile-based user interface is that the applications that are installed can be easily accessed. Another is that adding new apps is a case of tapping the Store tile and finding what you need to use. Multitasking remains a key element of Windows, although in the new-look Windows you'll notice that things have changed somewhat.

Meanwhile, any *legacy software* – applications and utilities designed initially for older versions of Windows – can be installed via the Desktop.

Launching Apps

You'll be stuck running applications in Windows 8 without knowing where your favourite applications can be loaded from. To find your applications, open the **Charm Bar** and click or tap **Search**. This will display the search pane on the right with the Apps list taking up most of the screen to the left of this. You'll be able to scroll left and right through the Apps list, while the search function will help you to quickly find the app you're looking for. You'll be able to open an app by tapping or left clicking.

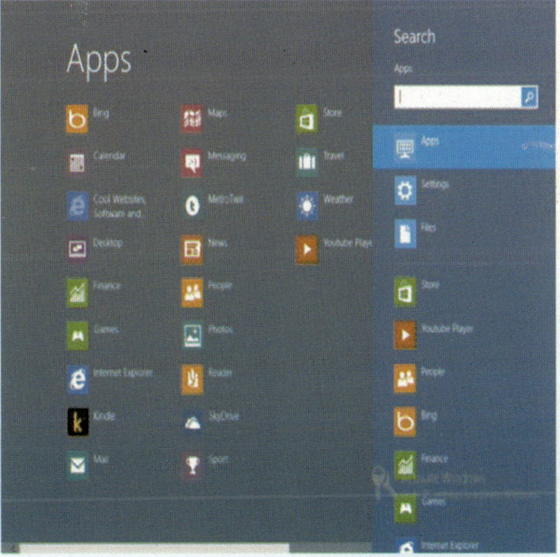

The Apps List can also be opened from the Start screen by right-clicking or long-tapping and selecting **All Apps**.

Switching Between Applications

As ever, switching between running apps is possible by holding **ALT+TAB** on your keyboard. This will display the task switcher window in the center of the screen, enabling you to select the open app you wish to use. You might also use the **WIN+TAB** keyboard combination, which displays a list of open apps to switch between.

If you're not using a mouse and keyboard – that is, you're using a tablet or other touchscreen computer – you'll find that switching between application is done by swiping left across the display in order to find the app you wish to use. Tapping the top left corner of the display is also an alternative. A quicker way is often to head back to the Apps List and select the desired application again.

Closing Apps

One of the difficulties of Windows 8 is that the method used for closing apps isn't obvious. It is very effective, however. To close an app you will need to use your finger (or mouse pointer) to drag the app down, and discard it. This is done by placing your finger at the top of the display where you should see a small hand icon appear; drag your finger from the top edge of the display to the bottom, where the app will shrink and fade away! The same action can be performed with a mouse.

If you run into problems, you can call on the redesigned Task Manager to get you out of trouble. This will open in Desktop mode, however, but can be used to quickly close unresponsive apps. Note that it isn't optimised for fingers!